Searching Out Loud: Giving Voice to Independent Investigations

Searching Out Loud

Giving Voice to Independent Investigations

A Digital Media and Information Literacy Curriculum for Reporters, Researchers, and Legal Professionals

COMPLETE WORKS

Copyright © 2019 Marc Solomon

All rights reserved. No part of this book may be reproduced in any form or by any electronic or mechanical means, including information storage and retrieval systems, without permission in written form from the publisher, except for reviewers, who may quote brief passages in a review.

ISBN (978-1-7332554-0-0) print version
ISBN (978-1-7332554-1-7) e-book version

Some characters and events in this book are fictitious. Any similarity to real persons, living or dead, is coincidental and not intended by the author.

Promotion of the books, tools, applications, and creative works of...
  Romantic Deception by Dr. Sally Caldwell and Darlene E. Adams
  Finding Birthdays and Related Persons in One Step by Stephen P. Morse
  SurfWax search engine by Tom Holt
  Gigablast search engine by Matt Wells
  L-Soft and LISTSERV® trademark by L-Soft International, Inc.
  SearchEngineLand by ThirdDoorMedia.com
  WorldCat image and trademark by OCLC.org
  BRB Public Records by BRB Publications, LLC

Reprinted by permission.

Book Design by Davin Pasek and Emma Koramshahi of Paradise Copies
All photographs by the author unless otherwise credited.

Printed and bound in USA
First Printing September 2019

Published by The Society of Useful Information
4 French Street
Hadley, MA 01035

Visit www.searchingoutloud.org

*For Patty, who taught me the root of all source knowledge:
Enduring gratitude*

"I was gratified to be able to answer promptly, and I did. I said I didn't know."

— **Mark Twain**

"The most courageous act is still to think for yourself. Aloud."

— **Coco Chanel**

"No provider or user of an interactive computer service shall be treated as the publisher or speaker of any information provided by another information content provider."

— **Communications Decency Act, Section 230**

SEARCHING OUT LOUD
GIVING VOICE TO INDEPENDENT INVESTIGATIONS

VOLUME I

INTRODUCTION i:1
- Searches I:1
- Investigations I:2
- When Searches Meet Investigations I:3
- We've Been Had I:5
- Information By Itself .... Hangs Itself I:6
- Form: It All Seems Geek to Me I:7
- Perception: Source Fluency I:8
- Substance: Lies, Damn Lies, and Factoids I:9
- Promises and Guarantees I:10
- The Web as Process for Learning I:12
- The Challenge of Using the Web for Research I:14
- Reducing Our Internet Capabilities I:15
- Focusing on Reasonable Outcomes I:16

UNIT ONE: How to Project Manage Virtual Investigations 1:1
- SECTION 1.0: How to Project Manage Virtual Investigations 1:1
  - The Knowledge Continuum 1:1
  - Knowledge Provision and Usage 1:2
  - Unit One Learning Objectives 1:3
  - If Time Equals Money Then Internet Time Equals...? 1:6
  - Unit One Benefits 1:7
- SECTION 1:1 Search Project Management 1:8
  - Pursuing Search Targets With Discipline 1:9
  - Selective Documentation and Failsafes 1:10
  - Action-based Questions 1:11
  - Rooting out the Sincerity of Self-interest 1:18
  - The Probable Risks of Being Certain 1:20
- SECTION 1.2: Search Logs 1:21
  - Definition: Search Log 1:21
- SECTION 1.3: Blindspots – The Gateways to Knowledge Awareness 1:29
  - The Black Hole of Blindspots 1:29
  - Blank Stares and Blank Pages 1:31
  - Dead Ringers for Blindspots 1:36
  - The Johari Window 1:38
  - Knowledge Awareness Cases 1:39
  - Blindspots Unique to Investigators 1:43
- SECTION 1.4: Becoming Knowledge-ABLED 1:45
  - Growing Eyes in the Back of Our Heads 1:48
  - Growing Antennas on Top of Our Heads 1:49
  - Characteristics of Computers: Overview of Online Answering Devices ... 1:51
  - Search Engines as Answering Devices 1:52
  - What's a Fair Question? 1:54
  - The Icebreaker 1:54
  - Interviewing the Computer (or, Message to the ""Hard Drive in Our Head") ... 1:59
  - Outputs – What Do Search Engines Do? 1:61
  - If Search Engines 'Thought' Like Researchers 1:67
  - Failsafes – When We've Reached the End of the Line 1:69
  - Search Engines and Databases 1:73
  - UNIT ONE: Wrapping
  - How to Project Manage Virtual Investigations 1:76

UNIT TWO: Using Search in Virtual Investigations 2:1
SECTION 2.0: Using Search in Virtual Investigations 2:1
Investigative Search 2:1
- Unit Two Learning Objectives 2:2
- Unit Two Benefits 2:4
- SECTION 2:1 Query Formation — How to Arrange, Express, Generalize, and Specify Research
  - Questions 2:5
  - Refinement Steps 2:7
  - Boolean Operators 2:14
  - Syntax 2:17
- SECTION 2.2: Semantics — What are the Best Terms for Conducting Research? 2:30
  - Expressing Our Intent with Semantics 2:30
- SECTION 2.3: Tool Selection — What are the Different Search Tools Available to Us? 2:39
  - Depends on the Question 2:39
  - Tool Selection – Refinement Tools 2:40
  - Tool Selection – Search Engines 2:41
  - Types of Search Engines 2:43
  - What are Clustering Engines? 2:43
  - What are Natural Language Processing (NLP) Engines? 2:48
  - What are Visualization Engines? 2:52
  - What are Metasearch Engines? 2:57
  - Other Kinds of Search Methods 2:61
  - What are Privacy Search Engines? 2:66
  - Turning the Tracking Tables 2:68
  - Custom Search Applications 2:72
  - Step-by-Step: Creating a Custom Search Engine 2:76
- SECTION 2.4: Subject Directories — Searching Beyond Search Engines 2:83
  - Subject Directories as Information Lakes 2:84
  - The Many Forms of Subject Directories 2:84
  - Why Directories Still Matter 2:85
  - Working from Strength: 'Pearl Culturing' With Directories 2:93
  - Summarizing Subject Directories 2:96
  - UNIT TWO Wrapping:
  - How to Search for Information 2:104

UNIT THREE: How to Source Information that Instructs 3:1
SECTION 3.0: How to Source Information that Instructs 3:1
- Discovery at the Source 3:1
- Source Knowledge as a Research Skill 3:1
- Unit Three Learning Objectives 3:2
- Unit Three Benefits 3:4
- SECTION 3.1: Information Types — How Do We Think About Information? 3:6
  - Introducing Information Types 3:6
  - Putting Point of Entry into Practice 3:9
  - Teaching the Engine How to Search Us 3:13
  - Resources 3:15
  - Putting Resources into Practice 3:17
  - Format 3:22
  - Putting Format into Practice 3:23
- SECTION 3.2: Source Fluency — How Should We Think About Documentation? 3:25
  - Learning Objectives: Source Fluency Pay-offs 3:25
  - The Harsh Glare of Fixations 3:28
  - Site Selection: The Concept of Ponds, Lakes, and Oceans 3:28
  - Getting From an Ocean to a Pond 3:30
  - Site Selection Factors: Knowledge and Ignorance 3:33
  - Site Selection Factors: Time and Expense 3:37
  - Estimating Our Time Commitments 3:38
  - Site Selection Factors: Location, Location, Location 3:46
  - Site Selection Factors: Simple Questions, Convoluted Answers 3:48

SECTION 3.3: Quality Control — How Do We Assess the Knowledge-ABLED Side of Websites? 3:51
    We Are the Only Regulators! 3:51
    The Three Levels of Quality Control 3:53
    Quality and Quantity Controls 3:54
    Ultimate Control Over Quality Controls 3:57
    Level I Quantity Controls: Results List Analysis 3:59
    True Life Crime: Fact and Fiction 3:59
    Surveillance 3:61
    Level II Quality Controls: Site Analysis 3:62
    Link Analysis 3:64
    Transparency and Site Ownership 3:65
    Topic-Specific Searches 3:67
    Level II Quantity Controls: Search Metrics 3:69
    Level III Quality Controls: Page Scanning 3:71
SECTION 3.4: Managing Project Resources — How Should We Think About Research Costs 3:74
    What's Public? 3:74
    People Finders 3:77
    Pursuing Executives 3:78
    The Visible and Invisible Web 3:82
    Deep Web Gateways: Getting From Oceans to Lakes 3:84
    Revisiting Source Fluency 3:88
    Discerning Source Self-Interest 3:91
    The Cost of Free Tools 3:93
    UNIT THREE: Wrapping
    How to Source Information That Instructs 3:97

VOLUME II

UNIT FOUR: Focusing on Information Context 4:1
    SECTION 4.0: Focusing on Information Context 4:1
        Taken into Context 4:1
        Stumbling into Context 4:1
        Unit Four Learning Objectives 4:2
        Unit Four Benefits 4:5
    SECTION 4.1: Individual-based Information 4:7
        Personal Motivation 4:7
        Introducing Provider Conjugation Frameworks 4:8
        The Three Type of Information Exchanges 4:11
        Containers of Information Exchanges within Groups 4:12
        Provider Conjugation: Individual and Group Motivation Vectors 4:14
        Individual: Second Person 4:16
        Individual: Third Person 4:17
        Group Behavior in Provider Conjugation 4:19
        Group: First Party 4:20
        Group: Second Party 4:23
        Group: Third Party 4:26
        Credibility as Social Dynamic 4:33
        Sourcing Credible References 4:35
        Lateral Thinking as a Credibility Check 4:35
        Analyzing Context: The Vectors of Integrity 4:38
        Integrity Vectors 4:41
        The Verdict on Vectors 4:46
    SECTION 4.2: The Value of Social Information 4:47
        Using PCF to Render Radar Screens 4:48
        Authenticity, Credibility, Conflicts of Interest 4:49
        Working Under the Radar 4:52

SECTION 4.3: Search to Converse 4:58
    Networking: How to Socialize What We Learn 4:58
    SOCIAL NETS: From Soul Searching to Online Searching 4:59
    The Concept of Social Circles 4:60
    SOCIAL NETS: From Searching to Conversing 4:63
    Build It – and They Will Dump 4:69
    Search to Converse 4:74
    Determining Your Online Identity 4:77
    Social Bookmarking: Somebody Knows the Sites I've Seen 4:80
SECTION 4.4: Misinformation as an Information Source 4:87
    Misinformation – When Context Disappears 4:87
    The Limited Perspectives of Information Providers 4:87
    Overcome by Events (and Misinformants) 4:96
    Scoring Systems that Rate Themselves 4:104
    The Dubious Freedom of Anonymous Speech 4:107
    UNIT Four: Wrapping
    Focusing on Information Context 4:107

UNIT FIVE: How to Present What We Learn in Teachable Ways **5:1**
  SECTION 5.0: How to Present What We Learn in Teachable Ways 5:1
    The Performance of Investigation 5:1
    Unit Five Learning Objectives 5:2
    Seeing the World Through the Perspectives We Research 5:3
    Unit Five Benefits 5:6
  SECTION 5.1: Quantifying Knowledge 5:8
    The Biggest Picture 5:8
    Scoring Formulas 5:9
    Managing the Project 5:10
    Setting up the Model 5:11
    When Clients Come Knock-Kneed 5:13
    Universe of Client 5:14
    Parting the Clouds of Judgment 5:16
    Hidden Assets 5:19
    Looking for Trouble in all the Right Places 5:20
    Media Performance Benchmarking 5:22
    The View from Below 5:25
    Institutional Credibility 5:26
    Determining Institutional Credibility 5:27
    Methodology 5:29
    Universal Laws of Self Interest 5:31
    The Value of Curatorship 5:33
    The Market for Curators 5:35
  SECTION 5.2: Information Bartering 5:40
    Conversational Icebreakers – Breaking the Case Open 5:40
    The Pulse-taking Virtues of Research Blogs 5:43
    The Cathartic Blogger 5:47
    Blogs as Calling Cards 5:49
    Pulling Selective Content Towards Us Through RSS 5:49
  SECTION 5.3: Message Delivery 5:57
    Confirmable Facts, Educated Guesses 5:57
    The Powerlessness of Numbers 5:58
    Prognostications 5:63
    Research Projects as Insurance Policies 5:64
    From Homework to Billable Work 5:66
    Reasonable Certainty and Honest Doubts 5:67

SECTION 5.4: Project Presentation ... 5:69
    Marking the Distance ... 5:70
    Integrating the Pieces, Packaging Your Presentation ... 5:70
    Planning the Presentation ... 5:72
    The Ability to Influence ... 5:73
    UNIT FIVE: Wrapping
    Focusing on Presentation ... 5:80

UNIT SIX: The Knowledge-ABLED Cookbook ... 6:1
SECTION 6.0: The Knowledge-ABLED Cookbook -- A Working Case Study ... 6:1
    Stirring Things Up ... 6:1
    Unit Six Learning Objectives ... 6:2
    Unit Six Benefits ... 6:6
SECTION 6.1: Knowledge-ABLED Case Study ... 6:7
    The Entrepreneur Transitioning from Commercial Clients to Nonprofits ... 6:7
SECTION 6.2: The Diagnosis – Change for the Better ... 6:8
    Initial Intake: Coming to Terms with Internet Confusion ... 6:8
    Building Credibility Through Reporting Requirements ... 6:11
    Self Evaluation Through Blindspots ... 6:13
SECTION 6.3: The Search — Learning How to Swim in the Deep End ... 6:16
    The Information Lake: Assessing Market Studies ... 6:17
    If at First We Don't Succeed ... 6:20
    Using Term Expansion to Segment Markets ... 6:20
    Information Packaging – It's All in the Delivery ... 6:23
    Connecting People to Groups ... 6:28
    Using Lakes to Vet Sources ... 6:32
    The Information Pond Where the Fish Bite Back ... 6:35
    Feed Reader Functions and Benefits ... 6:37
SECTION 6.4: The Engagement – Searching for Conversing ... 6:46
    Letting the Market Speak for Itself ... 6:46
    How Site Selection Opens the Door to New Business ... 6:51
    Provider Conjugation Frameworks ... 6:53

EPILOGUE: Searching Out Loud in Unreasonable Times ... 7:1
Giving Voice to Searching Out Loud ... 7:1
    A Shared Understanding of Facts ... 7:2
    Elements of Substance ... 7:4
    Re-imagining the News as Non-fiction Stories ... 7:6
    Independent Thinking (in these dependent times) ... 7:6
    A Run on News Feeds ... 7:7
    The Media That Chooses Us ... 7:7
    Beating the Competition to the Narrative ... 7:9
    The New Kings of Content ... 7:9
    Don't Mind Me — I Was Only Streaming ... 7:10
    Lingering Trust Issues ... 7:11
    The Less Popular Public Imagination ... 7:12
    Publishers' Remorse ... 7:13
    Up in the Crowd ... 7:15
    Privacy and the Public Mind ... 7:16
    Click Bait and Run ... 7:19
    Fake It Until You Make It ... 7:20
    The Reality of Perception ... 7:21
    Negativity Defenses ... 7:22
    It's All Sunking In ... 7:23
    The Freedom to Explore the Investigation ... 7:24

- Knowledge-ABLED to do List...7:26
  - 1) Track Your Pre and Post Knowledge Abilities...7:27
  - 2) There is No Right or Left or Center When It Comes to Affinity Bias..............7:29
  - 3) Resist the Social Media Circus...7:33
  - 4) Use Google (Manual Edition)..7:34
  - 5) Practice Source Fluency by Exposing Your Sources....................................7:36
  - 6) Save the Passion for the Hunt – not the Hunted......................................7:37
  - 7) Rinse and Repeat..7:39
  - 8) Publish the Map – Don't Bury the Treasure...7:40
  - 9) Net Neutrality is the New Objectivity...7:43
  - 10) Making-You-Act in the Made-You-Look-Economy...7:45
  - One for the Roadmap..7:47
  - Final Use Case...7:50

CURRICULUM GUIDE...c:1
- Knowledge-ABLED Curriculum and Book Structure..c:1
- UNIT ONE: How to Turn Information into Knowledge
- *Preparing:* How to Project Manage Virtual Investigations...............................c:1
- UNIT TWO: How to Search for Information That Informs
- *Seeking:* Using Search in Virtual Investigations.......................................c:3
- UNIT THREE: How to Source Information That Instructs
- *Sourcing:* How to Evaluate Information Quality...c:6
- UNIT FOUR: *Sense-making:*
- Focusing on Information Context..c:9
- UNIT FIVE: How to Present What We Learn in Teachable Ways
- *Presenting:* How to Connect What You Learn to Useful Outcomes.........................c:12
- UNIT SIX: The Knowledge-ABLED Cook Book *Using Information:*
- A Recipe for Success...c:15

INTRODUCTION: Searching Out Loud Giving Voice to Independent Investigations

Searches

No one likes to search.

Everyone likes to find — especially when we find evidence that reaffirms our conclusions and validates our hunches.

That works out fine if we're trying to determine what model of which version to park in our shopping carts or determining which pizzeria prepares the tastiest toppings within proximity to our locations and price points.

Finding search results that comport to our own purchase criteria and shopping cycles might support our preferences for quality, expedience, and even personal fulfillment. However, those same calculations might prejudice or even misguide our ability process to uphold, protect, and honor the people and institutions we have agreed to serve and represent.

It is this wider notion of community purpose and civic engagement that is entrusted to the reader, not the social media platform or search engine claiming to find results for us, regardless of our searching abilities.

Search is more than a command box, virtual confession booth, or answers mediated by machines. It is the foundation for the independence of thought required to fulfill our civic duties. This book is about posing our natural curiosities to a world of preformed and often artificial responses. It is a search that we form on our own that answers to this larger socially-minded concern.

A search that comes to us is surely predisposed to the very same biases and assumptions that limit our effectiveness as citizen-users of an Internet-based investigation. The Knowledge-ABLED approach is one that combines this wider social concern in the pursuit of impartiality, empiricism, and integrity. These aims are not considered, supported, or factored into the commercial objectives of big search: Those companies who benefit directly from grabbing hold of the steering wheel that interprets, navigates, and brokers our use of the web.

The evidence-gathering of these intended search objectives purges those assumptions, biases, and conceits of near-certain conclusions. There is simply no other path to decisions reached by elevated perspectives, open minds, and the unknowable destinations of a Knowledge-ABLED investigation.

INVESTIGATIONS

In the late summer of 2018, the American popular imagination was transfixed on the momentousness of one national decision. It was the confirmation vote for Brett Kavanaugh to the U.S. Supreme Court.

Beyond Justice Kavanaugh's fate, this was a vote that would determine the direction of the one government above the fray. The branch shielded from the pressures of election campaigns and accountability of election cycles. This was the institution that remained faithful to the rule of law, a guarantee of an *independent* judiciary.

On the Senate floor there were no such principles on display or built into the backroom deliberations of its members. Neither party had the stomach, grace, or latitude to dignify the merit of the other side's concerns. Ninety-eight of one hundred votes were cast along party lines. Those breaking ranks synchronized their dissenting votes to not be the deciding ones. Not a shred of integrity was evident on the Senate floor. After all the motions, no one had budged, except in acknowledging the need to beef-up Senate security in the wake of anonymous threats from outside the chamber.

Amid the accusations, and bombast, we onlookers observed one additional basis for agreement between the opposing parties:

> This was no way to conduct a confirmation hearing.

Far from a consensus, the only sliver of movement in this intractable mess was the move for an independent investigation. A fact-finding mission by a non-political actor might break the logjam by providing a more guarded forum for witnesses to come forward, for investigators to consider the emerging patterns, and for an overheated country to step back from the intensity of such a politically charged outcome. In effect it wasn't our faith in the political process or our institutions that was going to move us from splintering factions to a binding decision. It was the findings of an outside arm of the government whose job was to steer clear of the same preformed conclusions depended on by one hundred U.S. Senators.

This was our best hope as a country to preserve an independent jury.

© CSPAN: Supreme Court Nominee Brett Kavanaugh and Senator Dianne Feinstein, Confirmation Hearing, Day 3, Part 6

WHEN SEARCHES MEET INVESTIGATIONS

Searches meet investigations and out comes the info.

Information:

    1. It's a renewable resource.

    2. It's the lifeblood of a knowledge economy.

When we determine its worth, we surmise...

- There's too much of it.
- Too little of it means very much.

This begs a followup question: What makes information less abstract and more meaningful? When we ascribe a will to it, we learn that it "wants to be free." But what do we want out of the deal? Certainly something more aspirational than free information. We want information that informs. Now the conversation turns to knowledge:

    1. It's power.

    2. It's the economic heart of our material abundance.

Measure the world in units of knowledge and...

- No one suffers from an abundance of it.
- If anything there's a scarcity of it.

What would it take to close that deficit?

What's the most popular one-word definition of knowledge? It's power. And we appreciate that before we even know what to do with our knowledge.

But here's the rub.

Information wants to be free and knowledge doesn't aspire to anything. Power closes down dissent and debate. Knowledge is an open book. It's a quality that many of us covet more than any capture-worthy material or ideal we could ever hope to possess. So here's the question: How do we get from *free* to *power*? They're not polar opposites but they're not exactly complementary. Or are they?

Searching Out Loud: Giving Voice to Independent Investigations | Marc Solomon

This book is about how to take a surplus and narrow a deficit. In our case the abundance is in the volume of available information. The scarcity is an understanding of what to do with it.

The difference between collecting online information and putting it to use starts with a better understanding of how it operates — how it behaves once activated by our thirst for knowledge, and yes, our lust for power.

What's information behavior? It sounds like something we observe in a lab facility as part of an advanced degree program — too complex for mere mortals like us to grasp! Information behavior sounds like we'd need to pass through security and a web of high-ranking advisers in order to understand it, reason with it, and ultimately act on it.

What we'll do is break information down so that it is understandable to us investigators (its pursuers). No matter how advanced or plain and simple our understanding of the actual information happens to be, that means unpacking our pursuits according to:

1. **Substance:** The content and purpose of the information.
2. **Form:** What shape the information is created in and/or packaged and distributed.
3. **Perception:** How the content is received by the folks relevant to our investigation both in the way it's delivered and the degree of certainty it conveys through its form and substance.

That's right. Useful information boils down to form, substance, and perception — not rocket science or brain surgery. It's one thing to conclude that what we see and hear influences what we think and say. It's quite another to see how our own influence is determined by how others come to process, understand, and act on the information that finds them.

We'll get back to substance, form, and perception in a moment. But first let's agree on why this matters.

It matters because of what we do with the info. What we do with the info is what matters. Not the info blowing a solo. There's a duet we do with commerce. That's the long trail of transactions that record what we buy and sell. Then there are the deeper less chartered areas of human affairs that are non-denominational and largely off-limits to screens, and by extension machines. This is where a search engine under the controls of a capable researcher can prove out an hypothesis, break open a case, or throw long-settled arguments into doubt through new ways of looking at established evidence. Yes, this stuff truly matters.

Information is not always static. Often it too takes actions through behaviors that may still sounds abstract to our ears. This abstraction is about to get real. This book introduces practical approaches for effectively managing online information. This is news for those of us who were never shown how to judge its quality or blend it into our fact-finding or conclusions. This book is for those of us who weren't taught how to integrate our findings into the recommendations we make when we share our investigations with peers, clients, and the wider communities we serve.

We've Been Had

In this book we will push some assertions that will challenge us and maybe even cause us to push back. Here are two basic premises that have yet to be challenged by students, peers, and clients alike:

1. Most folks like to be useful.

2. No one likes to be "used."

We don't need to boot up a computer to experience the sinking feeling that we have been "used by information." Anyone whose sure-thing stock pick nosedives knows what it's like to be played – even when it's never clear who: (1) the other players are, nor, (2) who the actual culprit is who swindled us in the first place.

However, being on the Internet puts us squarely in the path of an information monsoon that knows no seasonal boundaries. To the novice just asking a question of a search engine can lead to an isolation-fed confusion. As a stranger the same question and our alienation with the machine could become an invitation to share with another person, maybe even strike up a common interest: "Yeah, I'm feeling used too!"

Used by information on the Internet means we have entered the vortex of Internet time. Ask a simple question? Get a convoluted answer! Even if we don't know much about the topic we're searching, the search engine knows even less about the extent of our knowledge! The result is that we are prone to fritter away our time...

- Trying to find answers to questions, and
- Trying to find meaning in useless details

Can't digest a gazillion search results at a time? The Internet can swallow our entire day and we can still end up starved for information. How can we force it to respect our time? How can we turn the tables from shopping options to questions answered? How can we nudge our investigation forward towards a set of choices offered in the evidence we turn up, not the ads visited upon us?

This book includes a series of approaches that will prevent us from falling into the black information hole of the Internet. These frameworks will defend us against the perils of exposure to "too much information." That way this surplus becomes a good thing. Not just an idle abstraction.

It's our own knowledge deficits that spark our curiosity to ask questions. How and where we ask them makes all the difference between drowning in a swollen tide of information and paddling to a shore of understanding.

Best of all unlike these impending floods, the book's frameworks are stable and will work for us regardless of the latest changes to the: (1) topics we're tracking, or, (2) the technologies we're using to track them.

INFORMATION BY ITSELF ... HANGS ITSELF

© Fraser Mummery: Noose from The Sex and Death Gallery

It's true that knowing what, how, and where to ask questions of computers is critical to using the Internet effectively. But even more fundamental than these skills is the need to come to grips with the very meaning of what information is.

Information to most of us is an abstraction. **(McCreary, 2008)**[1]

Not only is there too much of it. It bores us to tears with its cryptic, detached nature. Until we lose our shirt in the market, or our identity is stolen, it's hard to define our information-seeking requirements. How do we qualify accuracy? Validate assumptions? Learn from past mistakes? Enlist new methods to stay ahead of yesterday's news? On a personal level most information is not of interest to us.

But what people do with it is a fascination. We don't care what information is called. We care what it does. That's when we're not engulfed but engaged.

Maybe our company is tempted to cut the one cost that we can't – our position. Perhaps we are trying to find a clinical trial of a new medical procedure for a loved one with a quickly-advancing illness. What about finding a way to meet with someone whose expertise or powerful position precludes our reaching out to them? In all these instances, there is a clear risk and tangible reward for knowing upfront the underlying purpose of our investigation.

The risk is that the novelty of our in-boxes distracts us from our pursuits. The reward is that we're not collecting idle facts but piecing them into an explanation, a decision, a plan of action. That's how we know we've steered clear of the vortex. We know what actions we can take once we find what we're seeking.

So now it's back to the hunt. Why are we the ones, it seems, that are being hunted?

FORM: IT ALL SOUNDS GEEK TO ME

That's because most public discussions about using information focus solely on form – how fast is our network? How legible is our screen? How secure is our credit card information? How light, fast, and cool is our latest smartest phone for staying connected to the web 24/7?

Don't get me wrong. Without technology there'd be a lot less information to manage. The latest gizmos, graphics, and cyber-safeguards have their place. But keeping up with technology is not a job that non-techies are either qualified or interested in tracking – particularly when tomorrow's marvels leapfrog over today's advancements at breakneck speed.

On the other hand, learning how to handle the raw, unfiltered flow of information that technology unleashes is a skill that doesn't grow obsolete with the next generation of the latest version. Managing information is a lifelong pursuit. The goals, objectives, and methods for achieving them will be just as valid ten or twenty years from now as they were before the advent of the web or after the next killer app.

The more expertise we have, the more these approaches help to keep us current and informed about our field. Best of all, information management levels the playing field. We are just as qualified to become a capable information manager as the savviest techie – no matter how intermittent our hot spot, wide our screen, or deep our local drive.

Independent of our own needs, there are inherent systemic forces that shape the kinds of information available to us:

1. An environmentalist studies the influence of climate change on displacement of large human populations.
2. An economist examines the interplay of market forces and government policies.
3. A marketer considers the consumer behaviors that belie the latest spending trends.
4. A lobbyist compares the voting patterns of Congressional members with the opinions and sensitivities held by their constituents.

Each mission involves trade-offs, interpretations, case histories, and ultimately the roles and responsibilities that come with decision-making. That said, there are immutable laws and principles governing the supply and demand for information – regardless of the stakes and the turf covered in each pursuit.

Some information flows are cyclical. Other sightings are ad hoc as a need arises or an alarm sounds. Many eventful understandings are reached in the shadows and through handshakes. Other transactions are explicit. They don't transpire without documentation. All of these *form* factors conspire to make information useful or a hindrance. These informational forms instruct: (1) the way researchers conduct their investigations, (2) the way marketers survey consumers, and certainly (3) the way the leaders we elect try to influence public debate of their policies.

Searching Out Loud: Giving Voice to Independent Investigations | Marc Solomon

An information-savvy researcher needs to know how information is produced. More than that, we have to determine how it travels between message senders and receivers. That's how information behaves, or more to the point – how it changes people's reactions as it reaches them. If we're going to put information to work for us, we need to understand the events, conditions, and observable impacts of online information on our search targets. These are the behaviors of the people and groups that find themselves in differing circumstances, awareness levels, and most of all, how they act on their awareness of those circumstances.

PERPCEPTION: Source Fluency

© Pixabay.com

This book begins with a foundation for understanding what kinds of information are out there. Once we reduce information down to the basics, we'll better know what will ultimately work for us. Work literally means putting useful information to good use.

Those basics are reduced to some simple frameworks for understanding the motives of information givers. That's not simply what the search engine reassembles for us but what publishers *get* in return for making their content available to us.

The skill we will learn in **Unit Three** is source fluency. Being fluent in a language enables us to engage directly with native speakers. So too, becoming source-fluent means finding the right tool and how its proper use makes information work better for us. Better still, we won't be at the mercy of any one source. This is always useful in the fluid and evolving world of digital resources where publishers are looking for revenue models more frantically than we may be looking for search targets. Fluency increases our flexibility to call on information providers that may be pivotal for one search, or become time-honored sources, or fade from view altogether.

SUBSTANCE: Lies, Damn Lies, and Factoids

What are some effective procedural steps for getting the right information? Usually it's the stuff that increases in value once it connects to our own prior knowledge and experience.

Think about it. A piece of information is rarely of interest by itself. These are factoids. They may invoke amusement, curiosity, but not necessarily a call for action. That's called collecting more factoids! It's when we combine information with what we already know that it becomes part of the plan we're drafting, an outcome we're forecasting, a decision we're weighing, a turn of events in our favor.

Given that we have limited time and lots of questions, how do we meet deadlines while sidestepping the obstacles that distract, confuse, or overlook the information mission we're on?

The gateway into online information is the search engine. We will determine through search engine selection what is the best fit for the job-at-hand. Maybe refresh our knowledge on an area we're familiar with? Perhaps we'll land specific details on a case we're working? Like any productive interview, an exchange between us and the search engine requires some preparation on our part.

Preparation for what, exactly?

1. **Absolutes:** Are we attacking the specifics of facts and details? What are the possibilities for precision?
2. **Generalities:** Are we being introduced to a new topic? How broadly or narrowly do we define our topic?
3. **Comfort levels:** Most importantly, how comfortable must we be in order to logoff with the confidence that we can communicate our newfound knowledge? Do we need a few bullets and talking points? Is it our style to whack through the weeds until we're comfortable engaging the experts, witnesses, and members of the communities we seek?

Key to our preparations is a fundamental question: How do search engines work — specifically, how do I get them to work for me? In order to capture those pertinent answers, we need to understand the range of entry points, formats, and points of view presented on the web. These are known as the **Information Types** we'll consider later in **Unit Three**.

Unit Two will introduce us to **Query Formation**. This includes techniques for refining our search questions using operators, syntax, semantics, and unique IDs. Taken together these practices will help us to...

- Build a consistent, repeatable approach to managing Internet research projects
- Construct queries that produce specific answers or patterns that address our broader issues and concerns

Before we take action, we should reflect on...

- Why we are doing this research,
- Where we might find what we are looking for,
- What the outcome may be,
- How will we go about completing our search, and
- When will we get to it?

The answers to these basic questions will enable us to create a successful search strategy.

PROMISES AND GUARANTEES

© Lars Plougman: Ask.com anti-Google campaign on the London tube

In this book we will unpack the basic ingredients that go into getting our questions answered by a network of computers. The databases of facts, figures, opinions, and imagery which they contain. This method carries with it the following six solemn promises to you, the reader and researcher. Every investigation surfaces its own unique set of requirements and conditions. That said, we offer several unconditional guarantees for how we'll learn together in these pages:

1. **Out-of-pocket costs:** There will be no additional outlays to you. All sources discussed here are either free or premium content available through browser cookies (details collected in the registration process), tax supported sites such as local public libraries, and nonprofit and university websites.

2. **Memory retention:** There will be no memorizing of websites – an impossible task for even the most memory retentive super searcher. We will not need to memorize specific sites or remember exact locations where information is stored and accessed. Because we will not be using rote memory to store things, we will become more nimble about solving the diverse and unique problems that defy prediction or a set approach in solving.

3. **Reality check:** The research pursuits we showcase reflect the routine examples of actual problem-solvers. Our information seekers are not modeled on hypothetical but actual problems drawn from thousands of conferrals with hundreds of clients in my teaching and consulting practice. The practical side of reality-based lessons is that the solutions *plug in* to our daily work-based routines. Beginning in **Unit One** we'll be applying search project management practices to add value to the research efforts of our employer, client base, and/or project team. This makes us more valued as a contributor and more billable as a project consultant.

4. **Tolerance of ambiguity:** A clear commitment does not guarantee any greater clarity in our search results. Ambiguous results require patience and focus. In **Unit Two** we'll explore the refinements we can use to better connect our intentions with the results of our searches.

5. **The virtue of simplicity:** Technology *will* get in our way. There's no dancing around it. We can have the latest upgrades, access to everything, and all the bandwidth in the world. We will still experience moments of loss, anguish, and inexplicable outcomes to the most carefully laid search plans. We will be patient with ourselves. But also remember that technology is there to serve us. It's easy to reverse roles when troubleshooting why an application doesn't function or a page doesn't load. Ultimately it will be better if we step back, breathe deeply, and simplify our search plan. Don't play the blame game. The source of "user errors" is far from obvious for us users.

6. **Dexterity in problem-solving:** There is no single solution to any one search problem. We won't fixate on definitive answers. We won't get attached to any one source or way of doing searches. That source will be discontinued. The method that hit the mark the last time out may hit the same wall over and over the next time. Dexterity and improvisation will serve us over time far better than rote memory and scripted instructions. Because we will become more nimble, we'll not need to subscribe to password-protected information sources. In short we'll save money as well as time.

Here is one last promise or maybe more like a course sanity recommendation. Don't get hung up on the results. Try a little of this and that. See what works. It's not all going to make perfect sense or provide unequivocal responses every step of the way – even after we've had the time needed to absorb all the lessons and draw our own conclusions.

So if you haven't already done so, breathe deeply, let it out, and give yourself permission to not get it all at once. Let it seep in as only time can allow.

The Challenge of Using the Web for Research

Most subject experts approach problem-solving in a methodical way so that the solution gives an authority or client the knowledge they need to take appropriate action.

Now let's turn that question on knowledge-ABILITIES: The capacity we have to put information to good use.

Who would we hire if the problem at-hand was about conducting research on the web? How would we frame this assignment? What goals would we set so that the experts could produce conclusions that inform our future actions?

For ten years I worked in the expert-for-hire industry – otherwise known as the management consulting business. Our clients came to us because they believed their internal operations were faulty. Our consultants recommended improvements to their systems by...

- Seeking out the chief-in-charge (authority),
- Changing the rules applied to its workings (process), and,
- Revising the incentives and penalties connected to the success and failure of the overall operation (performance).

The web throws these rules and structures out the window to the chagrin of many sane, rational minds. There are no central authorities, governing bodies, or regulatory agencies responsible for our protection. Were you expecting safeguards against spammers and scammers? What if those hucksters pay our web service providers in dollars and not spam? That's the cost of free information writ into our virtual identities.

The watchwords are no longer *buyers beware*. Even the most unsuspecting recipient doesn't end up with snake oil in their shopping carts or acquire undesired friends without their consent. Avoiding the pitfalls of hucksters, viruses, and other forms of personal violation is largely an exercise in self-regulation.

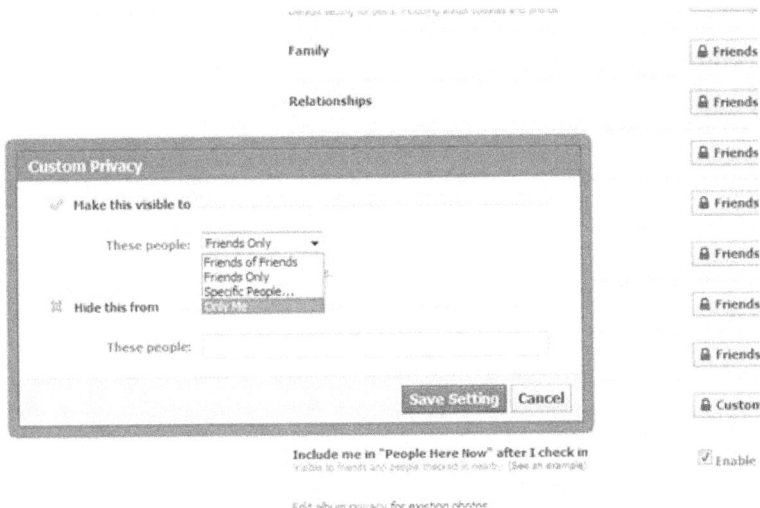

Focusing on Reasonable Outcomes

So how do we penetrate the system called the web to understand the patterns and disciplines that will help us take fullest advantage? Here are the five tenets of reasonable inside the lawless, unrelenting, unsecured vapors of the web:

Faith is the greatest temptation

Stay the Course is only a good idea if we're sure we're *on course*. Loyalty may be a noble trait for standing by close friends and family members. But standing by questionable practices or inaccurate data won't score us points for our steadfastness. Single-mindedness works when we're on a life-and-death mission to find a missing child. But sound investigations do not rest on faith in a pre-determined outcome. It's a healthy disinterest that gets to the heart of the matter. Research in pursuit of a fixed object is dependent on selective evidence. Few have ever hired a "dependent investigator" and perhaps even fewer have ever believed their findings. Pretending we're in control even when we're not renders us both mistake-prone and dense, i.e. failing to learn from them.

Thou shalt not distort, delay, or sequester information

You can drive a system crazy by muddying its information streams. You can make a system work better with surprising ease if you give it more accurate, timely and complete information. We will weigh this factor when we address quality control issues in assessing search results, websites, and even individual pages in **Unit Three**.

Experts do not invite clarity

An honest message giver should not be blamed as the bearer of unwelcome news. Sometimes, however, the message delivered by experts focuses more on their expertise than what it means for your next move. You will have to penetrate their jargons, integrate what they tell you, recognize what they can honestly see through their particular lenses, and discard the distortions that come from the narrowness and incompleteness of their lenses. Remember, sorting all this out is our expertise, not theirs.

The devil is in the over-simplification of details

There is much riding on the desire for closure. There is a constant temptation to simplify the presentation of the evidence you find. Yes, a certain level of order and predictability exists in the world. Some generalizations are useful in ordered circumstances. But this tendency to favor resolution can blind us to the very situations we are called in to investigate.

There's something within the human mind that is attracted to...

- Straight lines and not curves,
- Whole numbers and not fractions,
- Uniformity and not diversity, and
- Bedrock certainties for solving elusive, confounding mysteries.

We confuse purpose and objective

The web encourages the common and distracting tendency we have to define a problem not by the system's actual behavior, but by the lack of resolution it offers. We find it hard to divest of prior commitments that may have outlived their use: We tune out novel approaches and wholesale changes. We mistake symptoms and causes. We obscure the difference between words and deeds, between real experience and imagined metaphor:

> *"The candidate is locked in a war of words, fighting for their political life."*

We can't surge forward with certainty in a world of no surprises. But we can expect surprises, learn, and even profit from them. We can't impose our will upon a system. We can listen to what the system tells us, and discover how its properties, and our values, can work together to bring forth something much better than could ever be produced by our will alone.

Like any computer-based network, the Internet has the ability to match precise outcomes, flag imprecise ones, and calculate. Search engines have learned to synthetically stitch word patterns together in a way that discourages intuition. Websites do not synthesize the selective intelligence we would otherwise expect from the expert for hire. The Internet does not factor in our...

> *"Full humanity – our rationality, our ability to sort out truth from falsehood, our intuition, our compassion, our vision, and our morality."* **(Jucker, 2014)**[2]

It is with a firmer understanding of what the web cannot reasonably provide that we use it to achieve an outcome that only we as knowledge-seekers can deliver.

Marc Solomon
Summer, 2019

---

[1] Lew McCreary, "What Was Privacy?" Harvard Business Review, October, 2008

[2] Rolf Jucker, "Do We Know What We Are Doing? Reflections on Learning, Knowledge, Economics, Community and Sustainability," Cambridge Scholars Publishing, 2014

UNIT ONE:
HOW TO PROJECT MANAGE VIRTUAL INVESTIGATIONS

THE KNOWLEDGE CONTINUUM

The entry point for our discussion in turning information into knowledge is a framework called the Knowledge Continuum. This concept attempts to take virtual learning and break it into a more structured and predictable model for measuring where we are in the progress of our investigations. By this we do not imply a path from novice to master researcher or subject expert. The continuum is simply a path forward in understanding how the tools and methods we learn fit into the larger pattern of managing and delivering successful research projects.

Think of the continuum as a linear construct for how we find our true Knowledge-ABLED bearings.

How Inert Information Becomes Useful Knowledge

Access to information is often confused with understanding its inherent connection to our motivation for finding it. An endless supply of sites to surf sounds like an invitation to expand our horizons. But the bitter irony is that repeat visits to an unrelenting loop of dubious websites can be more damaging to our research than never having gone digital in the first place. The immense volume of information available detracts from its usefulness by concealing the answers we seek. Of course we're answer-crazed. We don't know...

- How to look,
- What to look for,
- Where to look, and,
- When to quit.

Here's where we're so used to settling for less, we're conditioned to accept uselessness – an inert state of information that does nothing towards enhancing our appreciation of the knowledge we're pursuing:

1. **How to look:** For starters we must acknowledge that the web as a research medium is no more self-supporting than the notion we're paying our way through the simple joy of learning. In the past, publishers charged subscribers for accessing their information products. Today those fees have shifted from content owners to aggregators in the form of search media giants like Google. Google's reward for enabling the distribution of free content is to flip the cost of producing it onto advertisers. This is the business model we must abide – a world where the product is our usage data, not our research. To succeed, we will need to turn the tables on the search media. That way we can leverage their technology for the sake of finding answers, not settling for the stock answers delivered to search consumers.

2. **What to look for:** Irrelevant results are not benign. They distract us from the real work we need to do with the qualified sources that can help us stay on track. Fraudulent claims do real harm. We are still compromised even if we can see through the masquerade. Unlike the volumes we access, our time and attention is not inexhaustible. We lose focus. We have little to justify in our investments, let alone the value recovered or created in the service of our project teams or clients. For us value is conferred by our research – not the aggregators or the advertisers. That means establishing a way to integrate the inputs of others that helps us make decisions, take actions, and reach conclusions.

3. **Where to look:** Even in its most basic form, the simple acquisition of facts and figures is only the first step towards determining their ultimate usefulness. Information alone means nothing if one does not possess the skills required to refine, package, and ultimately profit from it. Part of that resourcefulness is a reliance on our own frequented sites and networks. More important is our ability to understand how information behaves as the basis for knowing where to intercept or trap it. A tool or framework like the Knowledge Continuum brings our own project goals and sense-making patterns to the problem at-hand.

4. **When to quit:** Logging off with confidence means the completion of a thorough investigation. It also means testing grounded assertions, not rehashing foregone conclusions. That's a premise that lives inside every questions we ask, issue we open, and problem we resolve.

KNOWLEDGE PROVISION AND USAGE

The model below shows the search process progression, from acquiring raw data through converting that data to information, then knowledge, and finally the material we need to make a recommendation or decision on behalf of our clients and communities.

FIGURE 1.1: The Knowledge Continuum

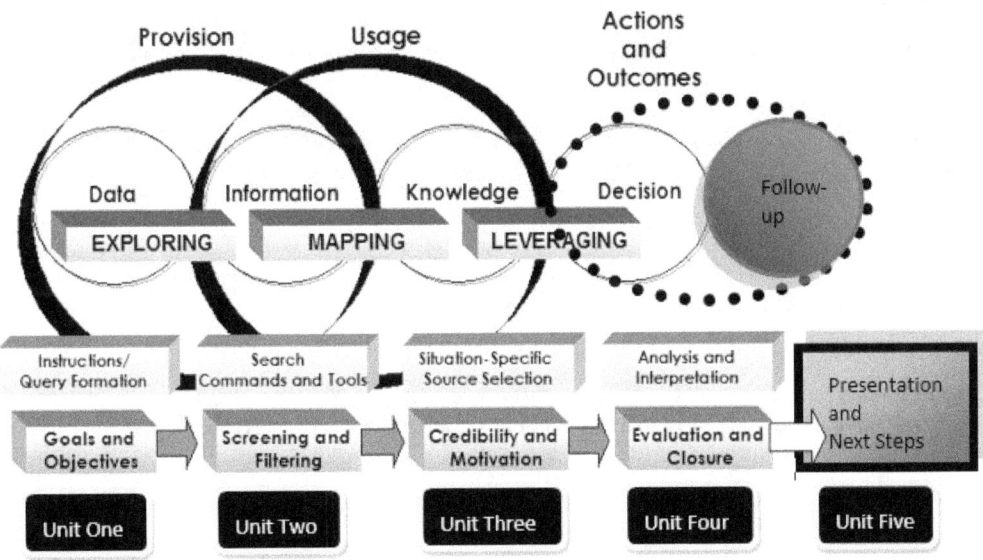

This book will feature a number of frameworks that will put into shapes, orders, and patterns the kinds of thinking used to rationalize our research projects. The first framework is one that illustrates the main goals and supporting topics for each of the five units. We'll reflect back on this continuum as we progress through the materials addressing each of these knowledge-enabling sequences:

- ■ **UNIT ONE:** In research projects think of the data stage as the evidence-gathering process. We anchor our discovery process to firm objectives and graspable goals.

- ■ **UNIT TWO:** Information is the initial questioning and subsequent refining of the evidence worth assessing. We achieve this through a deliberate and thoughtful filtering process that carries out our original intent in **Unit One**.

- ■ **UNIT THREE:** The third knowledge stage centers on context or how the evidence fits together to: (a) explain the actions of others or, (b) helps us to act on our own behalf. Here we connect the search refinements and tweaks from **Unit Two** to the reasons why our digital sources share what they know and how they arrive at those understandings.

- ■ **UNIT FOUR:** The analytical stage is where we stand back from our collection of evidence and the self-interest of our sources for providing it. **Unit Four** introduces the final arbiter – how the findings of the first three units inform the decisions and priorities of the colleagues, clients, and communities we'll communicate with in **Unit Five**.

- ■ **UNIT FIVE:** This is the packaging and presentation of the research based on the best of our Knowledge-ABILITIES. Our findings can be channeled in one of two directions: (1) building on the conclusions and recommendations in the form of a client report or business plan, and/or (2) how we present our research selves on the web through content curatorship, social media, and subject expertise.

- ■ **UNIT SIX:** Searching Out Loud's final unit features the business use case for applying the knowledge-ABLED curriculum through its frameworks and practices.

UNIT ONE LEARNING OBJECTIVES

By the time we cycle through the continuum, our newly acquired knowledge of web-based research will benefit us in our role as...

1. Inquisitive student,
2. Tenacious investigator,
3. Independent consultant, or
4. Insatiable learner in-between careers

All of us are looking to raise our research games or enter new markets and job opportunities.

That sounds like a pretty wide range of aptitudes and work situations, so you might be thinking:

> *I search the web every day at optimal speeds, the latest versions, and my favorite gadgets configured to my liking. What am I missing here? What else does this book address that I don't have?*

Yes, we're well-connected (from acquainted to hardwired) with the web. How well, however, does the web connect with us? Here are a few basic indications that our search skills could use a tune-up:

1. Does it still feel time-consuming and uneasy searching the web even when we know the needed information is there?
2. Are we getting dead-ends when we try to make social media connections, including a shortage of credible referrals and business leads?
3. Are our intentions co-opted by the search provider? How do we turn off their algorithms to preserve our independence?
4. Have we gotten interesting search results but are uncertain how to apply them? Are we unsure about how to follow up on our search results?

Being a skilled Internet researcher affords us the following benefits for us and our clients:

FIGURE 1.2: Unit One Benefits for Consultants, Researchers, and Career Changers

ROLE	VALUE PROPOSITION	SUPPORTING SKILLS
Independent Consultant	Establish objective and subjective value of the information disseminated to clients	Gather information more efficiently and effectively for your clients (Know where to look, how to look and what to look for)
		Outperform your competitors by producing your reports more quickly and cost-efficiently
		Gain a competitive advantage by acquiring a reputation as a fast, thorough, accurate, and competitively-priced professional investigator
		Accept more new work faster by scaling your practice to accommodate multiple clients with diverse cases

Researcher	Uncover overlooked sources, un-bury facts, and piece together explanations	Find 'invisible' databases that aren't indexed in the major search engines
		Test the waters by identifying neighbors, witnesses, past business associates, communities of interest, and other pieces of a suspect's social circle
		Quantify impact of omissions, undisclosed affiliations and nondisclosure of facts
		Generate effective sorting methods and pattern matching for verifying or refuting the evidence in question
		Help to prove or shatter theories sorely lacking in skilled researchers to test them
Career-changer	Advanced Internet skills open doors closed to more conventional job seekers	Skirt the distractions that obscure the information job holders need to maintain current positions, secure better ones, or stand out in a competitive job market

Unit One Destination: Where Do We Begin?

Many would-be investigators are confused by the Internet. They are not discouraged by a lack of incentive to perform good research. They are not terribly concerned about a scarcity of information or a lack of resources for conducting their work. But we do tend to doubt our own resourcefulness: Is this the best way to find what I need?

The restless parade of new sites, technologies, and gadgets for receiving them only adds to the uncertainty: Will the research I did before our last meeting stand up when we revisit this before the next one?

Before we stare down that blank page, we need to ask what any reasonable client would ask before they google us in advance: (1) to form their own conclusions about us; and (2) base an expectation of what we'll charge them.

> **Definition: Search Target**
> Who or what we're researching – a person, group, event, issue, location, etc.

IF TIME EQUALS MONEY THEN INTERNET TIME EQUALS...?

Too often we value our scarcity of time and information when a project is costing us 'real money.' Because the barriers are as low to Internet access as they are to asking a waiter for a glass of ice water, we assume that: (1) everybody has the same basic know-how and access to the same tools and sources; and (2) we really don't need to optimize our screen time since we're so rarely offline.

How is a researcher to respond if the cost question focuses solely on access? If it's a password to a predigested dossier about someone's personal finances, there's little point in either: (a) turning professional, or, (b) turning to professionals.

But someone who's a Knowledge-ABLED investigator doesn't sell her passwords or hawk her access credentials. Someone with actual source fluency can deftly move beyond the *givens:* The occupational hazards of conducting virtual research. Here are those assumptions:

- ■ A disregard for permanence in the virtual reality of the web – anything can change at any time
- ■ An unrelenting momentum to migrate paper-based documentation into electronic form
- ■ A preoccupation of marketers, government officials, and social engineers to log, connect, and even influence our virtual activities through our individual digital profiles **(Bennet, 2012)**[1]

For instance, knowing which specific states place which public records online is a full-time task for any army of lobbyists – not just our lone researcher. The stealth aspect for farming research out to surrogate investigators has its security merits as well. But the most valuable asset held by the most gifted researcher is not flexibility, resourcefulness, or anonymity. It's the distance and experience to size-up their search targets in abstract ways that people understand far better than algorithms. Attributes such as trust, reputation, and relatedness to what the client seeks is the way to flip the cost equation on its head:

How much is not hiring the right researcher going to cost me?

More of us use screens to search and investigate in self-guided attempts to educate ourselves. We're not frozen in our tracks. But there's an ever growing need to apply what we learn – to go beyond search results to justifiable and useful outcomes.

But how can we be certain we have what we need? That's where we're hung out to dry. That's when we become overwhelmed. A Knowledge-ABLED investigator captures and accesses information for the purpose of putting it to work: to know, and to act.

> *Definition: Knowledge-ABLED*
>
> *Knowledge-ABLED opens the web up to us in understandable terms and in manageable chunks. Ultimately becoming Knowledge-ABLED is not about revving the most search engines, memorizing the top websites, or even taking the most shortcuts. It's more basic than that. It's about putting what we learn to work no matter how different our own interests, passions and mental wiring are from the geekiest corners of the web.*

There is a roadmap or planning framework for reaching the promise of becoming Knowledge-ABLED. It's called SPM ("Search Project Management").

Unit One Benefits

By the end of this unit you will understand and apply...

- Learn SPM – A step-by-step process that helps us take control of Internet searches
- Set up goals, milestones, and resource limits for finding and applying pertinent information to our research projects
- Build information radars that reveal where our search targets are spending their time and attention and where they're distracted or unaware (blindspots)
- Identify the culprits that steal time from our web-based investigations so we can bypass them when they next arise
- Figure in the time and expense we save by applying sound site selection practices
- Calculate the value accrued in billing for our research services

Searching Out Loud

SECTION 1:1 | Search Project Management —
How to Write the Roadmap for the Non-Linear Web

Roadmaps get us from point A to B, presumably in the straightest, most expedient way. Apply this as-the-crow flies logic to a web investigation and that roadmap is a tangle of digressions. It can't be folded back up into the glove compartment. Yet that's precisely what the researcher must resist. It's the temptation to substitute the machine-based interpretation of what our terms imply to search engines:

1. Do I need a basic definition?
2. Am I looking for a probable cause?
3. Am I trying to rule out some less probable suspects?

Web search is good for steering us towards the cheapest checkout in our shopping cart. Looking for validation? Social media is the express lane for delivering us into the arms of agreement. Without the search map, these road trips have been prepared well ahead of our own specific itineraries — sort of a GPS ("global positioning system") of sense-making.

Effective Internet Researching means having a plan in place before we start a search. And it observes a rule of the learning road that's paved over by the commercial interventions in our searches: The web is not linear. There is no beginning, middle, and end. No two people enter at the same place or time with the same experience, constraints, personal narrative, or sense of how pages, videos, documents, or animations apply to them. For the Knowledge-ABLED, use of the web is not a manufactured outcome designed by advertisers. It's a unique, non-linear passage from asking questions to making informed decisions.

Our first unit addresses Search Project Management. SPM is based on the simple and often overlooked reality that being the virtual costs us. Okay, maybe not in connect charges or even subscription fees, but still. Just the sheer investment of time we spend in searching is sizable, often with little to show for it.

Let's start with what we do know. Every search produces a range of questions across the project time line of any investigation:

1. First glance — What kinds of information are out there?
2. Rear view — How can what I'm looking for justify my actions?
3. Moving forward — How can what I share actually shape the decisions looming before us?

While there is certainly a major time commitment to conducting extensive digital research projects, there's also this challenge: They come with time limits.

What's the result? We're on deadline and we need to break new ground without repeating ourselves.

SPM contains the discipline and focus that transcends technological change. In **Unit One** we apply SPM principles to recurring research assignments by setting out our information goals. To do this we will begin by…

- ■ **Defining** what separates useful from inert information in our information pursuits
- ■ **Deciding** on the appropriate research approach to mission-specific projects
- ■ **Managing** our search projects effectively so that the time and effort we invest merits the quality of our results

While most investigations incur their share of some bumps and forks in the road, an SPM will ensure our roadmap keeps to our original intentions. We remain the driver – not the technology that's been primed to treat us like passengers.

> *Definition: Search Project Management (SPM):*
>
> *A five-step approach for documenting trial and error patterns that emerge from mapping cause (searcher intention) to effect (search results).*

Unless we are looking for a fact-based question, few search missions boil down to one search. Most are a sequence of searches so that a search session is really a series of mini-searches. Each one is a response to a synthetic interpretation of our information-seeking requirements. Often the feedback we get is not the response we're looking for. We hit a wall, blaming our inability to talk with computers, or the stupid search engine, or both.

PURSUING SEARCH TARGETS WITH DISCIPLINE

How do I find answers that address my original intentions?

One of the best ways to keep a search *on the rails* and in-line with our original objectives is to step our mission through the five SPM procedures:

> *A search what? A search fog … oh, he said search log?*

But before we take our investigation offline, it helps to rethink just how sensible our hunches are in the first place. Sometimes our initial expectation might be reasonable. But the session goes nowhere because we can't make the search results address our intentions.

Other times, our expectations could be out of whack but we're willing to put up with 'no answer' for an answer. This is the swift and anonymous second opinion that confirms there's nothing out there. Either way, it's important to see search as a puzzle-solving process. It is not the last word or final destination where the user experience is defined as a sales opportunity or a product purchase.

The search engine companies and their advertisers profit from our reaching them. So they may consider search to be an end in itself. Knowledge-ABLED means never having to accept search results or the pages that search engines send us to at face value.

Search Project Management is a framework for figuring out what we want from our digital research session before we're in one. It's not as simple as picking a topic that interests us or selecting a search engine we feel comfortable using. The goal is to do what few search consumers (and surprisingly few researchers) confront before they begin a project: (1) what they want out of it, and (2) why!

SELECTIVE DOCUMENTATION AND FAILSAFES

Those two overlooked questions hold the key to where, how, and what we search. They also inform how we present our findings to others with a stake in the outcome. As we'll learn in **Unit Five**, one compelling way to kick off a client presentation is to compare actual results with our original expectations: The what's *out there* as past experience suggests.

On the other hand, SPM is not about recording every single nuance and wrinkle in the search results (or responding adjustments). Besides gaining insight, the most visible benefit of SPM is to save us time. We don't record every stop along the way to recreate our search expedition or recount conversations with our machines. We want to save our documentation for the client. The research is part of our consulting practices or service delivery – not the SPM form itself.

That said, it's useful in the course of a first SPM foray to record at least one success and one failure. A success reinforces the positive surprise stirred by connections we make as we review the evidence we're gathering. A failure is akin to chasing our tails. We're repeating a lesson already learned or veering from our SPM roadmap.

Road Test

Let's say we try to get a specialty-specific list of top-rated physicians. But the lists we get lack objective assessments or professional histories. We're not sold on the way these doctors landed here. It's useful to document this as a failsafe. The failsafe is something we find out once and are forced to repeat despite numerous attempts to fulfill our original objective.

Conversely, it's equally helpful to note our astonishment when uncovering details about surprise findings. Don't conceal the discoveries. Changing our calculations, refactoring unforeseen scenarios, shifting our thinking, ... these adjustments are on full display along with our capacities for using the web to do research.

Either way SPM is an action-based form for creating and executing searches designed to improve our searching. SPM also documents these productive outcomes to our clients, colleagues, and even the folks we're investigating.

In this book we'll experience one-way search tickets punched to the nearest abyss.This is the paperless equivalent of diving into a dumpster and never escaping. There are certain classical mistakes guaranteed to lead us spiraling out of control and hurdling into nowhere.

These dead-ends predate data networks and user interfaces. They've been around as long as there have been cases to investigate with evidence to uncover and identities to protect. That's the unproductive outcomes posed when purpose is mistaken for objective. Confusing the two is a time-honored tradition for leaders trying to create division between their adversaries (more on that later). In our case, it might be a client holding back on key information or even their core motive for hiring us.

> **Definition: Failsafe**
>
> *Information we encounter repeatedly no matter how we alter or differentiate our searches. Failsafes are useful as markers for gauging the awareness levels and search experiences of undiscerning investigators.*

ACTION-BASED QUESTIONS

What do we mean by asking action-based questions? How do they inform the SPM process?

Action-based puts the emphasis on the research process. These are the mechanics of asking questions and seeking answers. Each SPM step is foundational to the follow-up stage: *Now that I know this, I can act on that.*

As we've suggested, SPM is a step-by-step procedure that enables investigators to take control of Internet searches by...

- Building a consistent, repeatable approach to managing digital research projects, and
- Constructing queries that yield productive outcomes

Figure 1.3 lays the foundation for building a problem-solving structure into our undisciplined searches. A full explanation for each step and how they build on the SPM foundation follows. Also, bear in mind that this sequence will repeat later when we introduce the search log. That's the form that we'll apply to some real-life scenarios later in the unit. We'll review each SPM step and piece them together as we cycle from inception to completion of our research requirements. In addition to their sequential flow, we'll consider the questions prompted by each ensuring SPM stage.

Here is a construction of those steps organized by the questions they inspire. First and foremost are the *whys:* The primary motivations for the research project.

FIGURE 1.3: Search Project Management Steps and Questions

Step: Task	Questions Answered
1) Defining the search purpose; the root motivation for why we're undertaking this work	Why?
2) Define the supporting objectives – Set our own and our clients' expectations, anticipate potential risks, and access limitations	What?
3) Formulating queries, selecting search tools, and considering refinement techniques	How?
4) Setting search boundaries: Duration, failsafes, and burden of proof for the search phase of our research project	When?
5) Determining follow-up for direct engagement with search targets	Who?

Purpose: What is the motivation (Why am I doing this?)

Why ask why?

Simple.

We won't be able to find related evidence and details that would otherwise benefit our clients, communities, or causes. Think we're lost when we're trying to make a positive Google ID of Joe Smith or Mary Jones? Think again. We're actually worse off than lost.

We don't know which foot to place in front of what SPM step if we don't know why our client wants the information they're requesting. In GPS terms, we're not even emitting a basic signal between us and the destination or resolution the client seeks. Failing to ask the purpose of a project is the suspension of belief — the belief that we know how to proceed.

We can be coy about confronting a client with their motives. We're putting them on the hot spot by pressing the point. But is it more important that we factor in our comfort zones first? Or is it more important for the client to see how without motive, we'll may lose direction and the project will suffer? Our hesitation is only adding to the guesswork. You be the judge on that one.

Step 1: - *Why* is the key to our success

Why are we so intent on needing what we're seeking? Why does the client need this information? Why will knowing what we find out change events for the better?

It all starts with the question of motive. Why do we need to do the research? Are we pinpointing a fact, surveying a broad topic, seeking a source to interview, corroborating a premise?

Why must the client have the research? What actions must the client suspend until she has it? What is her intended purpose? Is she...

- Settling a dispute,
- Playing hardball in a contract negotiation,
- Sorting out a tangled affair that's rife with conflicting evidence (and conflict of interest), or
- Figuring out the market price of an asset they covet – or possess?

Surely it's not simply for the comfort of knowing!

Then why is *why* the key to our success? That's easy. Why can certain professionals charge what they charge? Often this is exorbitantly for high profile clientele. Other service providers need to charge *the going rate* for their services. Think of something exclusive and extravagant that's also commonplace and often showy and garish like a Hollywood divorce battle.

Why do the hired guns get hired at the rates they can charge? Is it because there are no other lawyers in the world?

Hardly.

It's because the legal team knows how much their services are worth to the client. A legal loss are the damages the client must pay the winning party and to their own legal team. In the first and final analysis, the client pays what the service is worth. The value of the service reflects the price of that outcome.

Who let in that big, hairy gorilla in the room? It's that gnawing sense that few like to question. Why? The shadowy presence of motivation reveals our otherwise concealed desires and intentions. We're compromised. We're found out. We're the emperors of our own nudist colonies. The finding is that we are perceived by others as venal and self-serving.

Why undercuts all other concerns because it gets to the root cause of the investigation – our motivations and by extension the outcomes they justify. In the digital world, motive often takes the form of someone's willingness to share what they know, or experience, or merely sense on the web. Why would someone be motivated to publish information on the web? Is it to clarify, mislead, question, or conclude? It is the equivalent to the realm of the detective inside all of us who asks: *"What motivates someone to call on me in the first place?"*

Objectives: What are the expectations (How do they support the purpose?)

Step 2: - *What* is the stated objective of the investigation (the expectation; the outcome)

Next come the *whats*. Are the underlying objectives designed to support the overriding purpose? Is there a conflict between the two? Specifically, what competing interests may arise between our target's professional duties and personal obligations? Is there a parting of the ways between words and deeds?

Then there is the outcome to consider. What are the likely implications if we succeed or fail in our research goal? What would an ideal answer look like? Anticipating the outcome helps to confirm hopes, dash them altogether, or square wishful expectations with reality.

Objectives serve at the pleasure of purpose. They hint at the motivation but do not divulge the purpose, sometimes knowingly, sometimes not. Like a skillful prosecutor, an effective investigator keeps the opposition on the defensive by prodding them with isolated questions that hint at contradictions, disputes, and holes in the evidence. But those flaws are not threaded together.

During cross-examination our prosecutor connects the objective dots to support of his closing arguments. Only then is the underlying purpose of the questioning made known.

In terms of the wider community, purpose is revealed only when a rival or potential conflict-of-interest is exposed. It may come from a parallel investigation. It may come from a competing one.

Remember, in determining objectives that there are many *hows* and a lot fewer *whats*. And there is no *how* without sorting through the agreed-upon objectives (including the project's own milestones, its terms and conditions). The investigator is guided by the question: What is it I'm trying to prove? That's before we can follow-up: How do I achieve this level of proof?

What are we trying to accomplish here? Get up to speed on a topic? Get up-to-date on a familiar one? Confirm a fact? Exonerate an innocent person? Cast doubt on a widely-held perception? Assess the adoption of a new public policy? Re-examine its impact on public attitudes?

When Purpose and Objective Don't See Eye-to-Eye

Clients will often substitute objectives for purpose because they either they don't want to reveal their intentions or they may not know them in the first place. They may also wish to be discrete so that the researcher discovers information that is not influenced by an *agenda:* Any pre-determined conclusions or biases.

Another reason has nothing to do with being evasive or detached. It might simply be that the client hasn't thought through the question. This is no longer the underlying question: W*hy* the investigation goes forward. The horse has left the barn. This begs the follow-up: What is the scope of what we're investigating?

Here again, perhaps we haven't thought this through all the way. We haven't defined the direction in our race to move forward. Author Olivia Parr-Rud compares the rate at which people talk to the way they think and it's no contest – we think much faster:

> "The human mind stores information for rapid processing of information, not for explanation. The mind stores knowledge to get things done, not to tell others why." **(Parr-Rudd, 2009)**[2]

According to Parr-Rud, pressing clients on why they think a certain way or desire specific outcomes not only puts them in a defensive position.It impedes an exchange of ideas necessary for successful troubleshooting and problem-solving. Parr-Rud contends that *why* questions should be used sparingly until we can win our clients' trust with the *how* part of our search projects. This holds true in our client relationships and in our SPM process. Then we can re-approach the more delicate question of why:

> "Asking 'what was the purpose of your decision or action' is a gentle way to ask why without appearing to question the rationale of the expert."

What are the likely implications? The Bias of Assertions

The *what* behind our search is not only about supporting objectives. It's about our expectations going in. Whether our hunches prove correct, they'll certainly influence where we'll press our case. Hunches are also implicated in our capacity to agonize over details. What's the depth of our assertion? It's how far down we're willing to dig before redirecting our focus, or cutting our losses.

FIGURE 1.4: Great Search Expectations

Objective	Hunch
I want to find companies that are in hiring mode.	I think most of them will be in healthcare services.
I want to find websites that advertise their professional investigations services.	I sincerely doubt that they're going to mention cost or even a range of prices that they charge for their services.
I want to find someone with direct experience at a company I'm targeting with no vested interest in the outcome.	I can screen former employees on a social networking site so my expectations are on solid ground.

It is relatively easy to determine the purpose and objectives of the search. Defining one's expectations can be more difficult. An effective investigation lives within the reasonable assumption that searches produce outcomes. These outcomes will contain known and unknown information. Being able to separate the two through...

- Public evidence (open web), and
- Private (offline or encrypted) disclosure

... is a simple, instructive way to track our SPMs.

There's no substitute for experience. Working a legal system and its disclosure practices in Iowa may not translate in Wyoming. Learning the ropes may mean a strong ability to transfer that learning across state boundaries. Others are not quick studies and lack the dexterity to break the problem down to a few SPM basics.

Once we apply them, the answers respond to the results of our research. It's no longer our hunches calling the shots, where the investigation will lead. This makes it easier to set our expectations as well as the client's sense of what we can deliver. This will be more apparent when we communicate our findings in **Unit Five** – *even if those expectations get knocked down a notch.*

Procedures: How and where we find answers? (What tools support our search?)

Step 3: - *How* speaks to the actual tools and methods. We'll use *how* to pry an answer from an information source. It could be an eyewitness or a specialized database.

The procedural basis of SPM centers on two cliché-ridden discoveries:

1. How to find specific answers (needles in haystacks), or
2. Analyze and decipher the patterns formed by an ocean of search results (tip of the iceberg).

What kind of search tools do we use? What query formation or browsing are applied to instrument these two types of answers?

Icebergs and needles represent the range of our prospects for finding fact-based clear-cut answers (haystack model). *How* is the question for how those expectations need to shift when digging for softer information of more conceptual, open-ended answers (iceberg analogy).

With SPM we'll be able to better track, and thus, save on the amount of time it takes to get direct answers to fact-based questions. SPM also brings closure on more abstract issues colored by human judgments and values.

The two primary ways to set expectations (or dash them) is to consider our questions as opinion or fact-based. Facts by nature are hit-and-miss propositions. Some things are black and white. Either we find a criminal history lurking below the identity of a potential suspect – or we don't. Opinions are less definitive and more plentiful. Do we look for opinions first before attempting to substantiate them? Which approach will be the best test of our independence and due diligence? Better not to get too comfortable with the *one* correct approach, lest we start looking for needles on the tips of icebergs.

The *where* part of *how* can cut two ways. It really belongs as an objective if it's about getting to a particular outcome. For instance, where do we want our conclusions to lead? Is this about reaching our goals once we satisfy our requirements? If it's process-related, there are virtual and physical location-based questions that light our way:

1. Where do the events in question take place?
2. Where have we already looked for information (and who put it there?)
3. Where is the best collection of what we're looking for likely to be?
4. Where do our search targets live (physically) and hang-out (virtually?)

Boundaries: When to stop? (How will these decisions impact the outcome?)

Step 4: - Pondering *when* means knowing the buzzer has sounded. When is it time to quit, or perhaps regroup and start fresh from the new knowledge we gained in step 3?

Have you ever felt like you knew less after a search than if you'd never done one? You're not alone. Don't get even. Declare victory from the jaws of stalemate by designing failsafes.

What are failsafes again? Indicators we define before starting a search that let us know when we've hit a wall or dead end and need to regroup or stop. The following two questions are what every researcher who runs on the clock must ask themselves out of the gate:

1. When will I know when to stop searching – the bullseyes and failsafes?
2. When would it make sense to pay for information?

It is important to determine how much time we'll spend on this search and when we'll stop. Before we start, set *boundaries:* A pre-determined outcome that foretells the finish line. A stoppage point may be that we're relearning something we already know. Perhaps there's a limited budget and the only results we get require access fees or pass codes.

One other common failsafe is the confidence that comes with a decisive conclusion supported by a credible resource and the authenticity of vested participants. That's when we'll know this credibility is conferred onto our work. It stands apart, without us.

In terms of an event in question, we might also ask...

- When did the event being researched take place?
- When did it conclude (and how definitive the conclusion?)
- Where might it reappear or revive in a slightly different form or context?

<u>Follow-up: Who do I want to approach about my discoveries? (Who can validate outcomes?)</u>

<u>Step 5</u>: - *Who* means it's time to start a new stage of the investigation. One possibility: We transition from querying databases to social networking, and finally to some actual *real-time* interviews.

When is it time to follow-up (the social dimension?) That *when* is typically answered by a *whom?* We'll know a thing or two upfront about that resource. So too, this person will be familiar with what we're researching. Perhaps that applies to our findings too, if that's a card we're willing to play.

As we progress further into the investigation, the who can assume some new identities:

1. Broadly speaking, with whom have we already consulted? Who in their circles could help us?
2. Who in our social circles connects us with these resources?

Two critical who questions loom, however we approach new informants:

1. In whose best interest would it be for this information be made known?
2. In whose best interest would it be for them to remain discrete?

ROOTING OUT THE SINCERITY OF SELF-INTEREST

We've now defined and unpacked the five steps of the SPM profess. Let's try the model on for ourselves before we apply it to our search targets.

Can I ask you a personal question?

How do you feel about landing a job?

Is that really even a personal question? What could be more motivational than supporting ourselves and feeding our families? No one would dispute that a person looking for work is honoring an economic necessity as well as a universal calling. Unemployment is not an option for most. However, the way we try to land the *right* job is all about options – overwhelming in number to many of us, regardless of circumstances.

How do we reduce the time it takes to get our collective feet *in the door?* We sell ourselves where we can make the most difference. We align what we do well with what we enjoy and where those opportunities lie. We cultivate social networks around prospective employers. These are sharable objectives, regardless of the goals they serve.

Does every motive answer to self-interest? Not necessarily.

Helping the less fortunate is no less sincere a motivation than panning for gold. Generosity and altruism are virtues. But they require objectives to serve our better instincts. How about digging past the stated mission to the actual execution and results it achieves? How about our ability to evaluate how well charitable organizations live up to their stated missions?

It's not always clear what distinguishes a charitable act from a selfish one. There are many motivations inspired by *enlightened self-interest:* Where the actions taken on one's own behalf are designed to help the larger community as well – (the proverbial 'win-win' situation). A shared risk and a mutual respect are examples of this common motivation. It can be concrete like forming a private corporation with the intention to create market value and split the profits. It could be an abstraction, like the protection of a constitutional right.

In either case, there is a clear intention to serve both personal interests and the needs of the community. Such goals are less susceptible to clashing objectives or conflicts of interest because these values are held in common by individuals and institutions. The key question is how open we can be with our motivations without compromising the purposes they serve.

THE PROBABLE RISKS OF BEING CERTAIN

No matter how timely the launching or noble the intention, investigations can be ruined as easily as they can smash the wrongdoing they're formed to expose. For instance, one way to sabotage an investigation in its early stages is to be certain of its outcome. Certainty is especially hazardous when creating an absolute goal around a shaky premise: One that invites a broad, unquestioning, and open-ended commitment.

The size of the investment will overwhelm the original premise or rationale for supporting it. Researchers are especially prone to investigating these kinds of conflicts when their clients are uncompromising in their requirements:

> "Find the perpetrator at any cost!"
>
> "Don't call me again until you have complete certainty."

Such airtight conclusions put pressure on researchers to *doctor* their results or limit their exposure to opposing views or competing explanations. This means selecting only the evidence that supports a pre-established outcome. Once the investigator crosses that line they are no longer a researcher but an advocate for the client. They *cherry pick* from a limited number of inputs and personal opinions, refusing to address the wider body of evidence.

For example, the former Canadian Ambassador to the United States refers to a series of public statements in the run up to the Iraq War. To the Canadians, the declarative nature of WMD ("weapons of mass destruction") belied a campaign masquerading as an investigation. Each assertion of stockpiled weapons ended with an exclamation point. The Ambassador's conclusions were reached with equally emphatic question marks.

Investigators are also often asked to sort out the fact from fiction. But in reality fact and fiction may not be so neatly contained or exclusive. Many actions are based on facts that all disputing parties can agree on but which result in conflicting interpretations about those bedeviling *whys*. Remember them? They're crouching behind the motives for actions, taken with these self-selecting and often static sets of facts.

A professional researcher will avoid the trap of posing as an independent investigator when their investment in the case is anything but independent. This requires the clear separation of motives and objectives. For example, solving a case is a motivation. It is a yearning for justice. It's also a genuine need for closure to conflicts and painful events that resist simple narratives or tidy resolution. Finding an expert witness is not a motivation. It is an objective that serves at the pleasure of the overriding purpose.

SECTION 1.2 | Search Logs
Driving Instructions for the Roadmap

Excepting the next power outage, we process search results just as readily as we fix our hair or check the time. We'll learn from our successes and shrug off repeated time-wasting with a systematic approach for creating and documenting our queries. Search logs are an easy and effective way to do this.

Search logs help us to structure our digital research assignments the same way we would want to control the scheduling, expense, and quality of our projects. That rings true whether we're tracking a clinical trial, a political scandal, finding a job, or screening a candidate.

The search log recommended is comprised of two major sections. The first section asks five questions about the search itself: why, where, what, how, and when. The second section will be covered later in **Unit One**. It helps us analyze the results of our search:

- Did we stop at an appropriate time?
- Did we document the gains, avoid repeat mistakes, and craft the follow-up plan?
- Did we create a plausible bridge from searching to conversing, engaging our search targets offline?

Creating a search log narrative involves three capture points:

1. **Inputs** — Drawing upon inputs from first or second-hand experience, depending on the type of search we're conducting
2. **Outputs** — Documenting our search log details, including source inventory, useful results, failsafes and follow-up actions
3. **SPM Steps** — Navigating the Search Project Management cycle to capture inputs and outputs through the narrative format shown in Figure 1.5.

The search log is intended to connect tools, and queries with the evidence they generate. We'll focus on search tools and query formation choices in **Unit Two**.

> **Definition: Search Log**
>
> Search logs are a systematic method for documenting our successes and failures according to the scope of our research, our project priorities, and the basic motivations driving our investigation. Using the Search Log method enables you to reuse successful strategies and avoid failed ones.

Here is our first stab at SPM through a systematic search log capture:

FIGURE 1.5: Search Log Template

SPM step	Rationale	Conclusion
Why: Purpose	Reason for the research	We want to research the web more effectively.
What: Objectives and Expectations	Objectives are the supporting evidence Expectations anticipate available resources and likely constraints	We want to review and compare different search engines and databases.
How: Tools and Methods	Task and goal-based procedures	Word selection and search commands are critical for evidence gathering.
When: Duration and Failsafes	Time commitment to search and noted failures to redirect project	We want to spend less time searching and more time analyzing, i.e. a failsafe occurs as set results lead to product ads.
Who: Offline follow-up	Who is a direct contact that will advance the goals of my project	We will increase our confidence in the answers we find and the resolution we seek once we're interacting directly with our search targets.

Putting Our Cards on the Table

Peter Morville

Search logs help us to stay true to our original intentions and keep our head in the discovery game. Besides keeping us focused and methodical the search logs help to steer us away from what Information Architect Peter Morville calls the disease of familiarity: The universal information trap of forgetting what it like to be an outsider. The outsider is the newcomer, the stranger to the shop jargon and insider lingo. Shop talk helps as linguistic shorthand, but often at the expense of clarity, inclusive language, and the stated aims of the search log.[3]

Morville refers to the craft of designing useful websites or improving their usability. But this reminder applies to our craft too as researchers. We waste our efforts in stale, circular reasoning. Chasing our tails is the end-result. We're looking for renewed ways of cycling through stock answers with a fresh approach that yields new, expansive means to problem-solving. Time for our search logs to hit the road.

Search Log: Travel Arrangements

In this scenario, we are traveling to a remote area of the United States where a family member has resettled. Due to a grave illness, that person is now in long-term palliative care. We need to book our travel so that we can be a caregiver. Our goal is to spend quality time with our family during this period of hardship, reflection, and ultimately transition.

When I give this assignment, I become the class *straw man*. I ask my students to send me to a nursing home in Southeastern Colorado to visit the ailing relative. It's up to the class to dissect the situational specifics.

FIGURE 1.6: SPM Travel Form

SPM step	Rationale
Purpose	Console the grieving, personal loss
Objective / Expectation	Instruction: "Cheap, easy transport." Includes destinations, dates, prices, connections...
Tools / Methods	Central travel site that pulls together reservation systems of most major carriers; on-time percentages and airport flight delays
Duration / Failsafes	Instruction: "10 minutes then stop." Includes layovers, rent-a-car, flight delays, far away airports, mid-day from hub city, no red eyes, turboprops...
Follow-up	Door-to-door pick-ups, frequent flier points, parking fees, house-sitters...

Let's unpack those travel plans before we pack our bags:

- **Purpose:** The sophistication of their questions and the reassurance of my answers are not important. What matters is that they see parallels between the managing search projects and successful resolutions to their research requirements. For example, by the time the purpose of my trip is clear, they have also figured out...

    * How frugal a traveler I am,
    * How rural Southeastern Colorado can be, and
    * What little regard I hold for the puddle jumpers that skid across these desert skies.

- **Objective / Expectation:** Because flying is a common social experience it's easy to imagine a full range of outcomes: Uneventful, problem-free trips versus being stranded in some big hub city terminal. That hit or miss proposition fires our imaginations with contingencies:

    * Expanding the range of airports,
    * Date flexibility,
    * The number of connections, and
    * Other trade-offs that will impact traveling options.

- **Tools / Methods:** The upshot is not whether my students know to check a website devoted to booking travel arrangements. It's not critical whether they put the right airport into the appropriate box. What does matter is that they can break the questioning process down in the same way as an expert searcher.

- **Duration / Failsafes:** Such a containable mission makes it easier to anticipate the minefields of air travel without first stepping on them. For example, an expectation of air sickness rules out small planes. Renting a car to avoid a rough landing may be the correct resolution. Perhaps negotiating country roads far from any interstate highway proves just as stressful? From an SPM perspective, that's the kind of on-the-spot training that makes for a more informed client interview the next time around.

Search Log: Nursing Home Facilities

In this next scenario, we move from fact-based air fares to a less precise and more abstract problem. What are the next steps for the ailing relative? In this case, our SPM log homes in on an opinion-based search to find the right elder care facility for a family member.

This is where the exact match of the *timely answer* must surrender its relevance to the trial-and-error of discovery. Students are led through the practical but dynamic mission to evaluate care-giving services in the ailing relative's community. The conclusion and the initial premise should be unified in the search log. That is, the search expedition should come full circle from a wish (wanting the best care for the ailing relative) to a plan that fulfills this desire.

FIGURE 1.7: SPM Caregiver Planning Form

SPM step	Rationale
Purpose	Support an elderly or ailing person's quality-of-life
	Amenities that can best service them
Objective / Expectation	Local resources including service evaluations, ratings, referrals
	Paperwork should be clear and straightforward, enabling a smooth hand-off between facilities
Duration / Failsafes	Create a short list of the top 5 < 30 minutes
	Long-term coverage is an example of extraneous information that bypasses original purpose and supporting objectives
	There is no substitute for an in-person inspection
Follow-up	Experts and advocates that have firsthand experience in the community as well as referrals from other families that have placed loved ones in elder care facilities

Now let's view the caregiver agenda through the SPM prism:

- **Purpose:** End-of-life care is one of those trying and tender milestones. We confront questions and doubts that seldom arise in life until age and disease force us to face big, philosophical questions. Although the research we do doesn't address these eternal mysteries it can often provide a source of bonding between families separated by time, distance, and the buried feelings that surface in these difficult moments.

- **Objective / Expectation:** 'Amenities' sounds vague only because it includes a full deck of care-giving requirements that are not nearly as clear and concrete as in our travel plans. For example, when we look at elder care, we're including...

    * The need for alternative care providers,
    * Religious / spiritual support,
    * Emergency transportation,
    * The ambiance of the rooms and grounds, and
    * The character of the staff.

    Maybe we need to keep other options on the table – home healthcare, visiting nurse services?

- **Tools / Methods:** The point of the laundry list is that opinion-driven research is resistant to a simple checklist with a finite range of outcomes. It helps to lose the mantle of *instant-expert,* rather than trying to anticipate every conceivable option. Start looking for inputs from social media pages, discussion boards, search directories, and mailing lists. This approach is useful when we're not prepared to face the world but we'd like to learn the cues and recurring questions that come up in these organized settings.

- **Duration / Failsafes:** We'll lose the folly of figuring everything out in advance once we develop the confidence to engage folks directly. It will become clear just how little of that final determination of where to place our loved one is based on static facts. That includes any statistic, paper record, ranking formula, or search-based advertising documented in our virtual work.

That said, there are failsafes that keep us on-task to endure the uncertainties stressful situations:

FIGURE 1.8: SPM Guidance for Failsafes

Failsafe	SPM Guidance	Search Syntax
Avoid paid searches.	You don't need ads – you need advocates. In **Unit Two** we will see how to screen our search results to avoid .com domains	–intitle:eldercare site:org
Be location sensitive.	In **Unit Two** we will address semantics as a tool for arranging and selecting search terms	–intext:(elderly OR aging OR eldercare) "(southwestern OR southwest OR Cortez) (CO OR Colorado)"
Match people to situations.	Make sure that the treatments you seek for a person in need have a legitimate track record and address specific objectives	-intitle:alzheimers alternative (inurl:directory OR inurl:index OR inurl:resource) intext:(~treatment OR ~medication)

In **Unit Two,** we'll start filtering our results with the help of helpful search syntax and operators for processing our intentions into what search engines understand.

Search Log: Crime Scene Evidence

The availability of digital mapping and GPS data has dramatically changed how surveillance is conducted. It's not just about getting top security clearance or spying privileges. With the advent of satellite and aerial imagery, any searcher can step across the police barricades and aim their spotlights at all points of interest within the crime scene vicinity.

FIGURE 1.9: SPM Surveillance Form

SPM step	Rationale
Purpose	Gather physical criminal evidence without appearing at the crime scene
Objective / Expectation	A list of informed questions for all relevant case actors, including suspects, victims, and law enforcement
Tools / Methods	Use surveillance mapping to establish or corroborate: driving routes, business hours of local retailers, bushes, receptacles (places to hide evidence), number of stories in buildings, proximity to cell towers, local precincts, parking areas Include aggregate data for the community in question such as crime census statistics Combine surveillance research with meteorological records of the time and date in question
Duration / Failsafes	Crossing the line from the case record to personal speculation
Follow-up	Confront all relevant case actors to verify any questionable inaccuracies between case records and crime scene evidence

Here's how our surveillance plan plays out through SPM:

- **Purpose:** Mapping sites enable us to connect dates and places to names and events. What makes them so compelling as a search tool is that they deliver two most critical benefits: (1) incontrovertible fact-based evidence, and (2) not tipping off any actors while gathering evidence.

- **Objective / Expectation:** Aerial surveillance enables us to place any street corner in most of the industrialized world under a microscope. How we poke or prod at the landmarks, retailers, and traffic patterns will tell us much about possible escape routes, ballistics, and even the role of natural and artificial light in determining what was evident to the actors and eyewitnesses. While it's no substitute for on-the-scene ballistics or forensics expertise, it does serve our fundamental need to generate a list of informed follow-up questions.

- **Tools / Methods:** There are many particulars that spark the drive for learning how to plug in and navigate web-based mapping tools. First in line is the investigator's passion for uncovering the physical realities of geographic regions:

* Access to hospitals,
* Major roadways,
* Cell towers, and
* Actual street corner and city blocks (size of buildings, angles of light, retail activity, etc.)

Maps are also useful for gauging distances and time estimates for sequencing of related events in both urban and rural settings.

- ■ **Duration / Failsafes:** The most important input for knowing when to take our research offline is when you pass from correct assumptions to unfounded speculation. For example, it's one thing to ground our research in eyewitness testimony. When was the suspect last seen? It's another to presume the deed was an inside job because the victim was slow to bring charges or the culprit made equal haste in their getaway. These are presumptions. No amount of map-reading will scale to mind-reading once our findings become case records.

- ■ **Follow-up:** An aerial view of a crime scene is a great way to reconstruct a criminal incident. But it is no substitute for direct questioning. It's a slippery slope once or ascribing motivations to strangers whose affinities and behaviors underpin the known orchestrations of that day and the unresolved outcomes.

FIGURE 1.10: CSI Through a Google Earth Lens

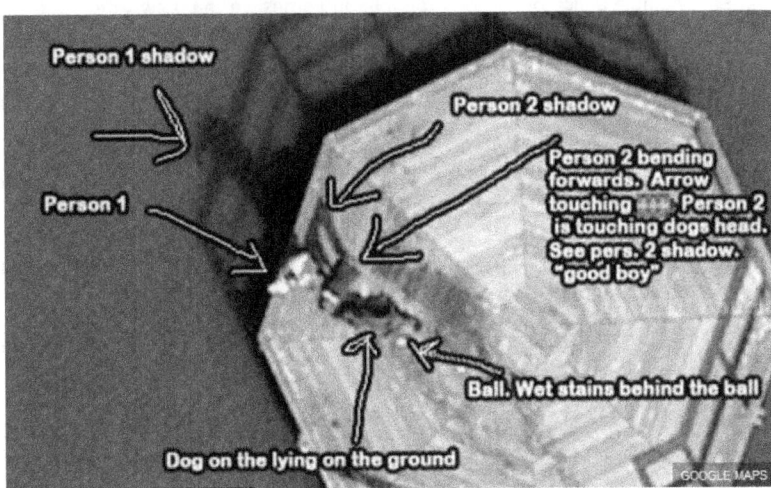

The undisputed truth or a hotbed for conspiracies? Here viral speculations of a gruesome murder were debunked by the duller reality of a boardwalk tanning occasion for a reclining dog and its two humans.[4]

SECTION 1.3 | Blindspots – The Gateways to Knowledge Awareness

"There are known things; there are things we know we know. We also know there are known unknowns; that is to say we know there are some things we do not know. But there are also unknown unknowns – the ones we don't know we don't know."
– **Donald Rumsfeld (2010)**[5]

In literary circles, they go by the term 'tragic flaws.' They are considered either sins of omission or commission in the army and government intelligence communities. In the churches and temples, they're on a first name basis. Sins will do fine.

In any of these contexts they are referring to that part of the world we are not wired into. This is an inherent liability that both shields and obstructs us from the larger truths others see, but we ourselves cannot.

In this section we will explore our own natural tendencies to look past or ignore the warnings that indicate our incomplete and compromised view of the larger world through our limited frame of reference or personal radar. We will then reverse perspectives. Instead of looking inwardly at our own blindspots, we will apply the same frameworks to the individuals and groups we investigate as researchers.

We turn the microscope into a telescope and aim it at our human search targets. What are some of the same signals that tip us off to the larger truths? What are the reliable indicators of the probable outcomes we can draw from our outsider perspective as a virtual investigator?

THE BLACK HOLE OF BLINDSPOTS

"I am an unreliable witness of my own existence."
– **Russell Brand**

Russell Brand

As we said earlier, knowing why we care is at the root of our core motivation and will keep us sharp long past when the casual pursuer is overwhelmed by an abundance of search options. Even with this incentive, there is a bigger risk in need of removal. It is the personal blindspot that we all carry into that black Internet hole. It is the 'unknown-unknowns' or what we don't know we don't know.

Without knowing how to uncover our blindspots, we are at the mercy of Internet noise or what David Snowden likes to call "microscopic arbitrary garbage." We are especially prone when we take our blindspots with us on a cruise across the information ocean!

It is important to recognize what we know *and* what we don't, both to devise an effective search strategy and to structure our search project management process. Sounds odd, doesn't it? When was the last time we were encouraged to become an expert at what we don't know?

What we know is information and knowledge that is consciously and readily available to us. And that we can control and consciously change.

What we don't know includes information that we...

- Assume is out there but don't recall and need to supplement with research
- Cannot look for either because we don't know we know it (intuition) or aren't aware we don't (blindspots)
- Understand falls outside our knowledge acquired through education and life experience

Coming to grips with 'knowing what we don't know' will enable us to...

- Anticipate what we're likely to find (or not) with our investigation
- Know when to collaborate with an expert that can lend understanding to cryptic meanings, obscure material, and ambiguous intentions
- Recognize we're in over our depth, back out, and rekindle our interest through a more suitable introduction to new and unfamiliar topics

The following Figure 1.10 is a framework for considering how we gather and maintain a core base of knowledge. Some of it is drawn from external awareness, common to us as participants in public forums. Some of it we gather on our own. This framework also maps how we assemble this knowledge (1) consciously through education and research, and (2) reflexively through our intuitions.

Facebook overdose © mkhmarketing

Finally it displays the inexplicable – that area of ignorance due to our own lack of knowledge, interest, and/or awareness. This void of awareness is universal in scope, a source of vulnerability in all of us, and a critical aspect of testing the orientations and limitations of those we investigate.

BLANK STARES AND BLANK PAGES

> *"Almost every man wastes part of his life in attempts to display qualities which he does not possess."*
> – Samuel Johnson

At first it might sound counter-intuitive: How can obtaining *more* knowledge be less useful to us? How can knowing *less* be a benefit – even a source of wisdom? It's not always clear how to fill them, once we get down to all those unused neurons in our brain.

First of all there are an avalanche of facts and figures we'll never digest no matter how immersed we are in them. Then there are the ones we captured once but somehow escaped through a fog of amnesia.

On the other end of what we retain is the thorny question of 'where do I know the least?' Even if our blindspots are visible to us, is it worth the exploration? Do we start now when we may never attain a level of mastery needed to not only grasp but apply this knowledge? This is not unusual territory for researchers. Every day we are plagued by such nagging doubts: What do we know that we don't know? What are the unknowns we're not even aware of – those darkest of blindsides.

FIGURE 1.11: Blindside Doubts

Anxiety	Source
Lack of exposure	Others I know are smart at something I've never studied
Surplus of secrecy	That area is off-limits to me
Ability to grasp	I know I'm weak in X area...

So what exactly are the benefits of knowing what we don't know?

If ignorance is bliss, is it better to feign understanding and move the investigation back to our areas of strength? The more educated our guessing here, the likelier we can return to surer footing, our areas of expertise:

1. We can hire out to compensate for our own shortcomings.

2. We can more clearly see the strengths and weaknesses of our search targets to reach decisions, solve cases, and bring closure to the investigation.

3. Knowing where to invest our time and attention means separating the *nice-to-knows* from the *need-to-knows*, discarding the non-essentials.

This is a humbling journey for the most learned and modest of researchers. Flying blind down a black hole with the intent of gathering evidence on our own ignorance is not for the faint of heart. Think of every subject we took in school with the expressed intent of getting it over with? And those are the courses we at least *knew* about: Here's the chapter about that part of us:

> "... Little did he know" – we can fill in the blanks ourselves."

What about all those lessons that were lost on us before they were even taught? Before we start stumbling around for the light switch, let's start on more familiar footing, shall we?

Knowing What We Know

Awareness	What you know
Public	Common experience
Private	Personal assets

Knowing what we know boils down two ways:

- What is common knowledge (what we sense in our public dealings) and,
- What we ourselves are expert in – in effect our own core knowledge beyond what we perceive as above the common level of a shared public understanding.

Knowing What We Don't Know

... and look for	What you don't know
Education	
Research	

One of the side benefits of being well-versed in a certain discipline is finding out what related areas we're not so worldly in. We taught ourselves how to use open source code to build an application that tells digital fortunes: *"Oh and by the way, I have no idea how to market this app!"*

For our purposes, we choose education and research (or self-education) to expand what we know and the relatedness of these new areas in our chosen study to our core knowledge base.

About that chosen study: What is it about our core knowledge that attracted us to learn more? Is it the kind of people that share in this expertise? Is it a higher attainment to serve a larger good? Is it the personal security or professional satisfaction that we feel from our achievement in this chosen field or core strength we have?

I'm asking you for your motives here. Without those, what's the point of knowing, right?

Not Knowing What We Know

... and don't look for	What you don't know
Intuition	
Blindspots	

Searching Out Loud: Giving Voice to Independent Investigations | Marc Solomon

That sounds like more double-speak, doesn't it?

How could we know and *not know* at the same time? It's counter-intuitive to know and not know the same thing at the same time.

Actually intuition is very much in play here. Much of our subconscious self exists through faith, unconditional reflexes, and our second nature. These are behaviors that can transcend conventional logic, our immediate surroundings, or even the roles we're expected to play.

These reflexes can be biochemical such as our brain's ability to regulate blood pressure. They could be as intuitive and sensual as our sense of humor or aesthetics. They could even be hunches in our gut: That instinctive sense of trust or suspicion that we'll sense in our first impressions around people we hardly know.

Parr –Rud refers to this form of shadow knowledge as 'unconscious competence.' The particular skill is so innate that it proves resistant to explanation. For instance, Jerry Grote, a former ballplayer and starting catcher with the New York Mets, had suited up in his athletic gear literally thousands of times. But being able to repeat the act by rote doesn't mean we can find the reason for the way we do things. Grote could not explain while fully alert the actions he could perform figuratively in his sleep. His expertise stifled his ability to share it.

Inexplicable Guts

As individuals, our assumptions and hunches may or may not be held up to the scrutiny of others. The gut intuitions ingrained in the muscle memory of a natural golfer like Tiger Woods were once exposed globally on a regular basis. But what about the assumptions of a con artist like Bernie Madoff?

Madoff's notions went unchallenged. They went largely unexposed for many years. Only when his own family members blew the whistle on Madoff's Ponzi scheme was an explanation even pieced together. The shadow knowledge was exposed. The get-rich scheme was so transparent to authorities that Madoff's testimony was hardly necessary. Unconscious competence can cut both ways – and not just in celebrated cases.

Have you ever been taught by a brilliant professor who knows their subjects inside-out? Ironically, their subject knowledge is no guarantee that they can teach us to be competent in their chosen field.

Being a good teacher requires a profound sense of knowing what it is like not to know the subject being taught. Domain experts who forget this or never struggled with the subject matter are not always equipped to teach others what comes so naturally *to them*.

'I Wish We Knew What We Know'

On a group level, this plays out a little differently. It sounds lamentable when we hear a leader or observer describe a group as *wishing we knew what we know.* That said, they are not bemoaning the regulation of body fluids, a strong sense of smell, or a particular fondness of a certain period in post-Modernist architecture.

A corporate executive lamenting that scalable desire is addressing how smaller groups within their organization are either unable or unwilling to share information. The inability to pool organizational knowledge is called *siloing* – a condition not limited to for-profit companies but also quite common in government circles and even non-profits chartered to education for the public good. The buck might stop at the top. But the info gets squelched by the minions below. Consider it birth of an upper management blindspot that crescendos in some future boardroom shakeup.

The hoarding scenario is more pronounced when it places more than shareholders at risk. Think of failures in U.S. intelligence agencies to link-up their resources for preventing terrorist threats. The prospect of surrendering knowledge was the more immediate threat to the non-cooperating agencies – until it's too late.

Not Knowing What We Don't Know

	What you don't know
... and don't know you don't know	
Clueless	

If not knowing what we know sounds contradictory, the next quandary of not knowing what we don't know sounds ... well ... redundant? Equally vexing. You either know something or you don't, right?

No, actually.

There's a world of difference between not knowing and not knowing what we don't know. One implies an answer key that comes with instructions and a path to understanding. The other doesn't come with a map, a shape, a translation, or even a sense of direction.

It's the falling tree that no one hears in the forest. It's the secret code that we can't decipher, or even garble We don't pick up its signal. These are our blindspots. They are detachable events that occur outside our own oblivion. Sometimes, an exception triggers and the alarm bells sound. Sometimes, we're fortunate enough to have them pointed out to us. But that doesn't mean we can now purge those blindspots from our personal radars.

It does however improve our chances for at least knowing to barter, buy, or petition for those who can compensate for our deficiencies. Perhaps it means letting a trusted adviser step in to manage them.

What are some common types of blindspots?

The most common types land off our personal radars. These are a kind of involuntary ignorance. Gullibility is a blindspot – the unfounded faith in people that exploit our trust. Another stems from being too personally vested in a process or outcome to see the situation with a clear-headed perspective:

- Why didn't I get the job?
- How come I'm clueless when the math lesson goes beyond arithmetic?

Here's one surefire blindspot test: Try our best and find out we don't qualify or size-up in a way that keeps us on the team or in the group. Take the best there is and then subtract our best effort. Here our blindspots are laid bare for all to see. At least to those that don't share the same blindspots!

Authentic Ignorance

Another form of blindspot is not innate but a simple dismissal or disinterest in a body of knowledge. We Americans are famous for learning only one language. It's not because we're incapable but because we practice a passive ignorance of the world's other dialects. It doesn't have to be well-established language to be ignored.

For example, I never learned how to text effectively on the keyboard of a pre-smart phone cellphone. I drew a line at just how many forms of electronic communications I was willing to master. Adding to that barrier were the many news items breathlessly intoned by the media that bore no relevance to my own set of interests:

Who won for...? Who died in the finale? Text me. I still wouldn't know.

Not all blindspots are created equal, rooted in selfish impulses, or a form of anti-social behavior. A parent will rush to protect a child. This is only natural. In fact, most of us would consider a detached assessment of one's son or daughter to be almost unnatural, if not uncaring. A less personal example is the goal of creating a color blind society by rectifying prior wrongs against minority groups. Seeing past our ethnic and racial differences is a desirable social goal. Holding to that view may influence our ability to blame or absolve individuals based on their minority status or social standing.

Personal Radars

These in-front-of-our-nose blindspots are conscious efforts we make to surround ourselves with meaningful people, ideas, and forums. Related views and opinions are exchanged. Each one of us has a watch list of potential opportunities and dangers that we try to anticipate. Each one of us has a to-do list of priorities and pastimes that indulge our sense of importance and our love of learning. Think of these lists as our own frames of reference, knowledge awareness filters, or personal radars.

We all got 'em.

We are deceived by our own self-centeredness to the extent we confuse our own radars with what others should care about. It's vanity to preen for the cameras. But it's also arrogance to impose our own bearings as the basis for where others should be focusing their attentions.

As former news anchor and media critic, Linda Ellerbee once said, every time the camera turns in on one subject, it is drawing our attention away from other another. We too are culpable when we suppress the meanings and importance of the topics and people that fall *off* our own personal radars. The more blinded we are, the more we convince ourselves that these things don't matter. The more a former crisis fades, the more pronounced our troubles become when it resurfaces: Some other context, someone else's radar.

The most important thing to remember about personal radars is not that they cause us to act selfishly, or compulsively, or that we're all by nature self-serving. It's that they do afford us researchers the chance to know our subjects and what motivates them. Even more importantly, it helps *us* to know *their own* blindspots.

That doesn't mean we know perfect strangers better than they know themselves. But it does give us the upper-hand in reconstructing events we can only assess as: (1) observers, (2) in hindsight, and (3) from afar. As participants this is the elevated perspective that few of us possess in retracing accounts of our own actions.

The Payoff from Blindspots

As we noted in our humbling discoveries, blindspots are the unknown-unknowns to us that are known to others. Now let's consider the inverse: What if we're 'the others' in that scenario?

Researchers connect the relevant details in the cases they investigate precisely to situations a blindspot would conceal. Astute examiners are sensitive to the lapses in judgment and compromises in the truthfulness of suspects, victims, and witnesses alike. That means focusing on the radar screens of the people we investigate. Those details that escape their notice because our search targets are either: (1) unaware, (2) confused and not *getting it*, or (3) pleading ignorance as a personal preference: They willfully don't wish to know.

Put another way: What is it on the personal radar of our search targets? What is it about their blindspots that distort their account of what happened during the events in question?

Distortion cuts a wide berth. Alterations can range from conscious to unconditional responses. Did key details slip their mind? Did they overlook the obvious? Did they bury an important fact because it made them out to be less sympathetic, perhaps more crafty in the way they testified?

Few answers are bullet-proof or unassailable in most trials. Even fewer conclusions rest on solid ground. Testimonies often conflict. Sequences fall out-of-step. But this is clear: The certainty we as researchers have over our investigation is based on:

1. A clear grasp of what lands on that person's radar, and
2. What falls below it.

Our search targets may be susceptible to blindspots. But through their personal radars, we can see competing versions, vested interests, and a larger perspective.

Dead Ringers for Blindspots

How do we know when we're seeing blindspots? Certainly the allure of certainty and absolutes are magnets for them. They encourage a singularity of purpose that dispels all doubts.

Ever hear someone talk about how they're going to get rich by the time they're [fill in the age]? Ever hear someone declare how they're going to achieve anything, really, no matter *what*?

Linda Ellerbee

For the investigator, it's not the achievement, but the *what* that matters in that declaration. That's where the blindspots are flying under the radar, beyond the grasp of the person we're investigating.

Institutional Blindspots

Blindspots cloud our personal judgments and our impersonal ones too. In professional circles, the consensus-building of groups and committees can compromise our decisions and our reasoning for arriving at them. The bilateral nature of groups suggests a natural dilution of the individual rationales driving those determinations.

Are we crossing the line? Are we exposed to potential litigation for committing violations of existing rules and laws? Or is it the mere *appearance* of impropriety? Either way, all but the most self-contained leaders or insular of groups think this one through. That's to say they race ahead to the finish line, then indulge in the great group ritual of second-guessing. The speculation flows whether a decision is unanimous or a prevailing argument carries the day.

FIGURE 1.12: Common Exposures to Risk

Exposure	Example
Ramifications	What will all the other groups think and say in reaction to what we did?
Negligence	Do we leave ourselves open to claims we ignored the rights and concerns of the other groups?
Concealment	Are there selective facts and events we're withholding that may convince our adversaries we're committing a cover-up?
Extortion	Can we be blackmailed for deciding this? By whom and on what grounds?
Hypocrisy	Do we pass the smell test: Advancing our own fortunes at the expense of a greater good?

Gathering Around Group Think

This form of collective scrutinizing is hashed out in countless closed door meetings. And then the press release goes out. Perhaps we'll catch a break from a distracted world if our group's idea of exposure is of the legal vantage. But consider this if we happen to notice and we're the investigator bringing *them* to justice.

Follow the money are the three most common words in the investigators' toolkit. *Following the blindspots* is a complementary method for piecing together the way teams and committees route their client's financial assets and their own. Risk aversion and vision void are two examples for how groups are governed by their blindspots in their decision-making:

- **Risk Aversion** – Group think favors conservatism. This is not a conservative political ideology per se. Risk aversion is politically neutral. Rather, it's an established rationale to discourage alternative thinking and perpetuate the status quo: It's easier to find reasons to do nothing, than be blamed for stirring things up.
- **Vision Void** – Forward-thinking decisions ride on prior history. Groups unwilling to own up to new realities or past mistakes are prone to vision void. This is what Peter Morville refers to as sunk cost: Making decisions for the sake of justifying past choices that may not be such obvious choices on their own merits.[6]

THE JOHARI WINDOW

We see what piques someone's interests in their photo-sharing, texting sessions, and Facebook pages. But if the web has found its voice through social media, where can we find its ears? There are equal opportunities for attentive snoops to pick up on signals not evident to less astute listeners.

One inspired answer comes from Information Theorist Barbara Flood. Flood's take theory is that privacy is based on the belief that *big* trust can only be conferred in *small* situations:

> *Families are tied together by information about members. Friendships exchange personal information and cede a certain amount of privacy. The larger the social aggregate, however, the less the individual is willing to sacrifice privacy and the more the individual needs to retain privacy in order to maintain a sense of self.*[7]

Political figures surrender this right the moment they announce their candidacies for public office. Hey, what about the rest of us?

What we decide to put out there on the web bears only passing reference to the stage-managed profile we would have our web snoops first come to know about us. *(Remember, that's assuming the 'total stranger' investigating us is completely positive we've been accurately identified).*

Of course, agents of control like my social media profile is a world of perception removed from what my user log reveals about how I use my computer. These are the awards, achievements, and even endorsements that we display in our virtual display cases. But there is a probability even greater than our digital behavior: Our blindspots are on full display. They are not password protected. There for the taking.

Ms. Flood's framework for describing the blind zone is a framework called **the Johari Window**. Like the Knowledge Awareness framework, this construct diagrams how blindspots are hidden away from the beholders and visible to others.

There is also the additional element of what is unknown to us and others. Perhaps this enigma lies in the shadows of empirical truth. It exists in spirit and faith, transcending conjecture and evidence gathering. Aspirationally speaking, unknown-unknowns are the subconscious side of our capacities for knowledge-seeking, no matter how tangible or slippery that awareness may be.

FIGURE 1.13: The Johari Window Framework

	Known to Self	Not Known to Self
Known to Others	Open	Blindspot
Not Known to Others	Hidden	Unknown

The goal of any effective researcher is to focus on the blind self. The blind self contains our limitations and their unintended consequences: The impact *my* actions have on *us* beyond our own awareness. It is the world of former colleagues, spouses, and witnesses on the scenes of past wreckages. These are the booby prizes that don't find their way to the trophy case.

Our delusions, suppressions, misguided faith, willful ignorance, and past admissions of guilt are now open to question, if not actual publication. As our own blindspots suggest, we would be well served to test our own vulnerabilities before we cast our investigative nets out to others.

So how do we address the blindspots of others in an ethical way? Especially when we are being asked to investigate what are often complicated and emotionally charged situations? Let's look at a few such scenarios for applying both the knowledge awareness and Johari Window framework, and see what we come up with.

Knowledge Awareness Cases

Known-Knowns: Simple Contexts

Simple contexts are seductive to investigators and clients alike because they are set apart by their consistency and clear cause-and-effect relationships. Correct answers are reducible to one. It is self-evident, undisputed, and requires little need for persuasion or supporting argument. In this realm of 'known-knowns,' decisions are unquestioned because all parties arrive at a common understanding.[8]

Here, conditions don't change. Decisions are automatic. Future plans rest on past successes. Complacency sets in. The willingness to reconsider or adjust to the unexpected requires a wake-up call or *shock* to an insular *system*. In severe cases, any correction is a shocking development. Any change is an unwelcome one.

In their heart of hearts this is the desired outcome that institutional clients covet. In practice, the allure of a neat, clean resolution is great wish fulfillment – and deplorable research. This longing for simplicity and closure are temptations that truth-seekers of all persuasions are well served to resist.

Any of us wandering into the realm of unknown information should try to soften the ingrained thinking that takes root and often festers in simple contexts.

Investigating Known-Knowns

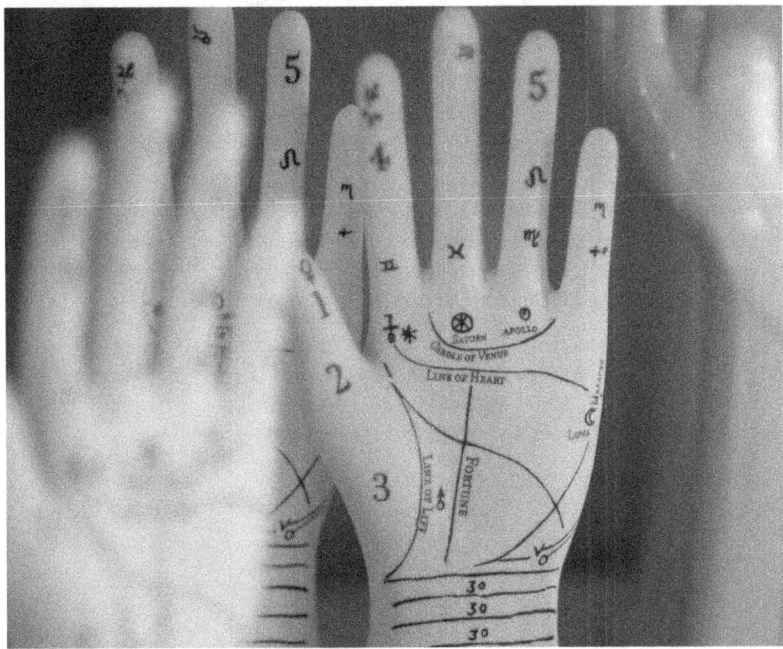

© Dave Fayram: What we know

The investigator is often brought in after the initial surprise has subsided. No one knows what the next steps should be. The time is ripe for outside help.

Investigators can use the certainty of simple contexts to prepare their clients for heeding the warning that's been sounded. Yes, an emergency has been averted. The alarm bell's been silenced. But the days of living free of outside interference are waning.

The client will need to be more mindful, if not welcoming, of these potential outcomes. More importantly, it is essential that they're made aware of these looming realities. They persist whether the client decides to engage, ignore, or revisit them.

Certainly the long resistance to change in the American automotive tradition is a text book case of known-knowns. How does the financial bailout of Detroit in 2009 factor into the dynamics of known-knowns? First and foremost: No matter how much federal assistance resolved the immediate crisis, only dramatic and fundamental shifts by the industry itself could ultimately trigger the rescue it was seeking.

Known-Unknowns: Complicated Contexts

A much likelier scenario for the virtual investigator is to frequent the domain of complicated contexts. Here no single right response fits the problem at-hand. This is not always so evident to clients who are more susceptible to big pains than large perspectives.

That's because they still see a clear and direct connection between the simplicity of the problem's cause and the impact it has on their business and/or piece of mind. These are what complexity consultants David Snowden and Mary Boone term the 'known unknowns.' The problem is known. The cure is not.

The challenge here for investigators is to overwhelm the unknowns by piecing together the optimal number of knowns. That's when multiple answers can evolve a variety of sensible approaches.

Searching Out Loud: Giving Voice to Independent Investigations | Marc Solomon

Investigating Known-Unknowns

How can web-based research help fuse awareness of a problem with consensus on solutions that defy easy, one-note answers? For one thing, a trained Internet researcher can categorize and distill the best *outside thinking*. These are internal problems that find their way into the public domain as case studies, white papers, and journal articles.

A focused array of alternative approaches is more comprehensive than exhaustive. A disciplined researcher resists the temptation of *piling on* information. Investigators exert a level of discipline and brevity that our untrained peers resist. In fact, the reasoning behind our selection process is perhaps more important to our projects than the actual use cases. It's this focus on a few core examples where SPM can shine as an internal check for us. It can shine equally as an outside validation for our clients.

Any search tool can return a set of documents arranged in some inscrutable order by their search formula. No Internet site, and few people, can deliver a well-reasoned answer or response to a complex problem. This means factoring in the quality, origin, and even context of the information providers. Only through these quality controls can the researcher hope to inform a responsible and well-documented set of conclusions and recommendations.

One of the challenges is that we have a tendency to disclaim unknowns. We don't want to deal with them. If an error occurs during a flight and the plane lands safely, our interest wanes. Why would we try to connect this to other indications that the error was a near miss of a catastrophic nature? It's much easier to dismiss it as an isolated or chance event. It takes a Cassandra, a pariah, until that day of reckoning. It takes someone with an imaginative and questioning nature.

Certainly someone who's likelier to count on human error more than human cooperation, no?

Unknown-Knowns: Complex Contexts

© Eric Raynor: Known unto God

Complex contexts such as unknown-knowns introduce an additional wrinkle to known-unknowns. No clear relationship exists between causes and effects. A complicated context could mean that the engine is knocking and the next stop on the way is the right repair guy.

But in a complex scenario, there's a knocking, thud, whirr, and pop-bang rattling under the hood when I drive. The pop-bang is more of a bang-pop when I hand the wheel over to you. In other words, there is no single correct answer, no matter how much evidence we gather. Snowden and Boone regard this as the most common scenario for most contemporary business problems. Here's an example, starting with what is known.

Fact:

Some publicly-traded company announces sub-par quarterly earnings.

Question:

1. Is this because one of their financial executives is under indictment for *cooking the books* from a prior quarter?
2. Is it because the governments in countries where their overseas manufacturing is done are suddenly unstable?
3. Is it because a rival beat them to the punch in a segment of their business pegged for high growth?

The answer could be all, none, or some of the above.

It is impossible to predict the ultimate outcome of these overlapping factors in the realm of unknown-knowns. The unpredictable nature of complex contexts requires the investigation to be exhaustive. And maybe even a bit courageous. We must create research models that enable their clients to build on, or adjust to, conditions outside of their control or mind's eye.

Investigating Unknown-Knowns

Mary E. Boone

David J. Snowden

It is a point not lost on companies that have benefited from such models that many of their best market opportunities are posed by the behavior of peoples' virtual behaviors. YouTube, for example, found its video streaming technology enabling a new channel of political discourse. It responded by sponsoring a series of campaign debates, thus responding to a market demand that their technology helped inspire.

Unlike with 'known-unknowns,' there is no hypothetical way to rationalize a risky behavior. The more a white collar criminal commits financial fraud, the likelier he will become a repeat offender. By their nature, 'unknown-knowns' defy consistency, or any kind of cyclical patterns. For that reason, the researcher needs to expand the realm of the possible before any kind of probabilistic logic can be applied to research templates like SPM.

For instance, a scenario like a popular website crashing can't be limited to a limited range of likely culprits. It could be an inside job. It might be an externality. Heck, it could be something as unintended as a regional blackout devoid of all malicious intent. Expansive analysis must apply to the risk mitigation involved in unknown-knowns.

In **Unit Five** we will consider a framework called **the Biggest Picture.** *This is a research model investigators can use to help their clients in assessing and responding to complex contexts.*

Unknown-Unknowns: Chaotic Contexts

Chaos is the ultimate response to any semblance of control over chaotic contexts. As Snowden and Boone remark:

> "... [N]o manageable patterns exist – only turbulence. The events of September 11, 2001 fall into this category."

There is no role for detachment or research when all follow-up actions are colored by the same calamitous events. The first and only priority is the re-establishment of the pre-existing order.

Investigating Unknown-Unknowns

From a digital research perspective, we need to understand what that pre-existing order really means on the web. Any hope we have for structuring the way the web authorizes or performs, rides on our ability to map its vast and chaotic nature. How humans come to find and understand information is one thing. How machines process it ahead of that understanding is a lesson for the next section.

For the Knowledge-ABLED, grappling with blindspots means focusing away from how we collect information (which changes from person-to-person) to how we act on information. This is an exercise that invites a much more predictable and standard set of outcomes than discovering or collecting information ever will.

BLINDSPOTS UNIQUE TO INVESTIGATORS

No discussion on the role of blindspots in solving investigations is complete without considering the dead zones. Once in the heat of the chase, these pose risks to the most gifted of researchers.

Even if we're in for untidy details, defiant witnesses, and competing opinions, we still want to nail it. The passion for solving cases fuels our determination to hear all sides, to turn each new discovery on every angle.

That said, there lives a set of temptations that can skirt under our reliable skepticism without our vigilance. Here are three such biases to guard against:

1. **Anchoring** – When considering a decision, our minds are unduly influenced by the first information we find. Initial impressions influence subsequent judgments and it's difficult to restart an investigation with a fresh eye.
2. **Confirmation** – Through selective search and perception, we subconsciously seek data that supports our existing point of view and avoid contradictory evidence. We measure progress in a case by our proximity to closure – even when the evidence says otherwise.
3. **Memorability** – We are unduly influenced by recent or dramatic events. We need to let them take their due course if we hope to put them in perspective, or weave them into the fabric of our evidence-supporting arguments.

FIGURE 1.14: Knowledge Awareness Case Summaries

Level	Awareness	Blindspot	Opportunity
Known Knowns: Simple Contexts	Patterns in the form of trends, habits, cycles that are likely to continue	No room for novelty, variation, or chance occurrences; complacencies range from detachment to fatalistic gloom	Self-fulfilling prophesies; plausible revelations that upset existing order; element of surprise tips odds in favor of instigator
Known Unknowns: Complicated Contexts	Likely events that defy easy prediction	Don't know the when or the where of next bombshell; masking uncertainties in the form of computer models	Go out on a limb with a forecast of the inevitable; introduce checkpoints to hedge bets; sniff out motives of influencers
Unknown Knowns: Complex Contexts	Remotely believable possibilities based on murky or conflicting signals	Underestimating dormant forces or adverse effects of latent-turned-explosive interactions of multiple factors, activated by 'perfect storm' conditions	Range of plausible outcomes from looming crises to sporadic interruptions of status quo
Unknown Unknowns: Chaotic Contexts	Black swan events with no prior history, pattern, warning, or mitigation plan	Unmeasured responses such as immediate retaliation for surprise attacks; refusal to confront or adjust to the unexpected or inconceivable	Prioritizing concrete steps to re-establish order, authority, social norms

SECTION 1.4 | Driving to the Outcomes —
Becoming Knowledge-ABLED

At the beginning of this section we talked about a surplus of information and a deficit of knowledge. We talked about how with strong virtual investigation skills that we could balance these two extremes. The welcome result is that this glut of information actually meets or supplies our demands for knowledge.

We talked about how knowledge wasn't based on accumulating more facts, opinions, and answering past questions. It was about having a clear command of what actions to consider or take based on the evidence we gather: In short, becoming Knowledge-ABLED.

We also played out the stresses of delivering complicated news to clients with a singular purpose: Seeking resolutions. That is the clearest backdrop for understanding the forks in the investigation road. These are the diverging paths documented in our SPMs. This is what happens to all researchers regardless of skill level or the nature of our work. All we can know at the outset is that the road forks without warning, somewhere between departing on an exploration and arriving at a conclusion.

Perhaps the clearest way to assess the state of one's Knowledge-ABILITIES is to begin at the end. The end here means a virtual 'dead end' of frustration, causing us to doubt our problem-solving abilities. Here are seven show-stoppers that derail our quest for resolution. Unchecked, they can even foil our own natural curiosities.

1) Being sold something – Maybe there's a purchase in our future? Perhaps we're not buying the product or the proposition? But we're going to spend down a perishable resource when we're on our screens, no matter why we're there. That's the time we spend. We once measured our virtual sessions by the time invested to logoff. The assumption was that we'd come away with a greater clarity than before we logged in. As the century has evolved, we have ceased to measure time in this way. The digital age and the clock on our devices have become one in the same.

CONCLUSION: There is no greater distraction to web-based research than online shopping. Acting as a capable investigator means working around this fact of digital life. As we'll see in **Unit Two**, having an advanced command of a Knowledge-ENABLED approach of query formation will actually disable much of the marketing apparatus that shadows our search projects. So will disabling the cookies in our browsers used to pedal the ads.

2) Convoluted answer – The second reason our searches go down in flames is not because we're distracted by clickbait and limited time offers. It's because of the resulting dispersion. The answers are muddled, contradictory, or incoherent, no matter how focused our questions. The old saying that we can prove anything with statistics is now getting a run for its money. Most opinion-based searches lead to the documented proof or counterclaim of just about any charged or divisive subject under the sun. And that's when we can even make sense of arguments we don't clearly grasp or support. This isn't a failsafe per se, but a hedge against the researcher frustrations that sow doubt in our grasp of conflicting accounts.

CONCLUSION: The more abstract, theoretical or conditional our question, the likelier we'll be weeding through a jumble of loosely connected websites, leading to our next encounter with futility that says...

Oscar Wilde

3) *No answer* is sometimes *the answer.* To paraphrase Oscar Wilde, failsafes are the names we give to dignify our search mistakes. The key lesson here is not that mistakes are a must to avoid. It's the repeating of them where the futility sets in.

CONCLUSIONS: One of the clear benefits of documenting our searches through SPM is to demonstrate a checklist-like method of an accountable body of evidence. The other direct benefit is to create a working stop list of accrued failsafes that will serve us again and again.

4) Lists, not ratings – Another popular temptation is to limit our searches to the first results pages. In this scenario we get lists of pre-approved sources, products, events, or even people whose quality and credentials have been screened and fabricated to fit on that single results page.

CONCLUSION: Experts and rankings aside, few lists sync with our own assessments and the way we're conducting our investigations.

5) Everyone's a Jane or John Doe – Perhaps there is no greater or more common test for our solution-seeking abilities than discerning whether the person we're googling is the same individual we're investigating. Many of us would rather go down to the precinct and make a positive ID in a police lineup than sit behind the privacy of our laptops and data mine thousands of search results. Does the client pay us to plow through a towering pile of false positives? Or do they assume that we know how to move beyond those shared names of mistaken identities?

CONCLUSION: Later in **Unit Two,** we will introduce query formation techniques that will set us on the right path and narrow the odds in our favor for making positive IDs.

6) Clueless keywords – As our investment in digital skill-building increases, so may our expectations around what kinds of results will follow. Part of this shift in outlook can include more conclusive proof. SPM supports fact verification to substantiate theories and produce a more qualified range of client options to consider. Increasing, the quality of these outputs is not about spending extra time and money searching more sources. We don't typically get rewarded by the size of the data sets we're reviewing.

CONCLUSION: It's about improving our inputs on the front-end. It's our own well-informed judgments about search terms, filtering, and expressing our subtle intentions in ways a machine processes. It's the Knowledge-ABLED who do the understanding, perform the analysis, and deliver the expression of this. Relying on a few common keywords ain't gonna cut it any more than a single first pass of synthetically selected text snippets.

7) Less than final words – Love of search is not a pre-requisite to get better search results. We don't all thrill to the touch of some new search engine! Searching is not the goal of this book nor is it assumed to be a goal for most readers. But we do all share a common need to raise our collective research games. This means nurturing a relentless pursuit of information providers. Researchers need a firm command not only of names and dates but of publishing motives and frames of reference. These are the personal radar screens of the people and organizations that provide our source materials.

Opinions are not unassailable. Even factual answers have their own set of human fingerprints: Which facts? Who selected them first? Just because they're often invoked, do they still resonate with the more obscure details in the fact base?

CONCLUSION: Don't validate them until we know who's done the same when vetting our own searches.

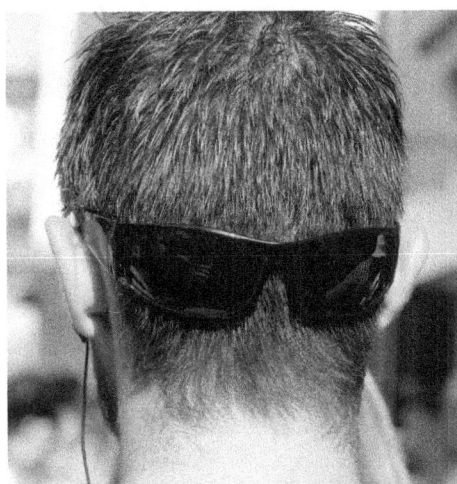

© FunkyDooby: You need eyes in the back of your head

GROWING EYES IN THE BACK OF OUR HEADS

Another key aspect for becoming Knowledge-ABLED is about connecting the motivations of the people and groups we're targeting to their blindspots. P.I.s ("Private investigators") refer to the *smell test:* Their gut read of the case they're working.

And if it doesn't quite seem right, the P.I. sniffs around.

Topping the list? Those would be the passions that fuel ambition, love, sacrifice, and loyalty. These are all compromises to the larger truth the investigator is seeking. All are hotbeds for blindspots.

From a radar perspective, these dominate the screens of the major actors in our case. Consumed by passion, they fixate on these desires to the exclusion of the more peripheral and practical concerns.

These preoccupations form the pressure points for the informed P.I. An off-hand remark is casually stated as fact. The suspicion turns out to be true and triggers further doubts about what was said under oath. But there's an element of truth at work here whether we're watching a grade B TV cop drama or testing our suspicions on the web:

1. Where are the potential conflicts between deeds and actions?
2. What key details is our suspect most likely to let slip once under scrutiny?
3. In appearing to be open and forthcoming, what are some unsolicited responses that reveal more than our suspect wants us to know?
4. We've seen the re-runs but how does this process play out as a digital research scenario?

Growing Antennas on Top of Our Heads

What is true when we gather background information on individuals? They might be...

- A person of interest in a criminal investigation, or
- A minor celebrity in a field we're trying to break into.

Either way, what separates a flat rundown from a more rounded profile? What isolates a static list of facts from a Knowledge-ABLED presentation we'll be delivering at the end of **Unit Five**? It's not a restatement of known facts. It's one that connections them in ways that suggest possible outcomes and potential next steps.

Elsa Lanchester in Universal's Bride of Frankenstein, 1935

Many of us are familiar with the phrase *It Takes a Village* that was popularized as a bestseller written by then First Lady Hillary Rodham Clinton.

Actually, the same could be said for the kind of profile we're trying to build. It takes a village to raise a child so they can stand on their own. So too, it takes a village to bring down a criminal. The communal aspect is not voiced as a gossip contest or war of words. It stems from the reputation that precedes our search target.

Conversely, it's worth approaching an exemplary leader or champion of a cause we share. This is not because they sing their own praises. It's based on our gathering feedback from the communities they support. Hopefully, we'll buy some credibility too. Tapping non-vested persons and parties is a persuasive way to vouch for a word-of-mouth reputation.

Is a full-blown investigation warranted if the question is limited to the paper trails blazed by one person? It doesn't take a research genius to order public records with a breached social security number. On the other hand, the kind of reporting we're talking about rarely rests solely with one round of public records, or one person's legal history.

A well-constructed profile usually casts a more expansive net around our search target. We include the perspectives gathered about the person's home. Put on our realtor and human resources hats for that one. We assess both personal and professional associations. We consider co-workers, particularly ex-employees that are at greater ease to discuss the inside dealings of former firms.

We even go through the entire resume. Time to fill in some well-placed guesses about job offers, employment gaps, and who they've reached out to. That kind of choreography steps to the unplanned setbacks, turbulent transitions, and disruptions to one's career path. The inspiration behind post facto explanations for filling perceived holes in the resume.

Recruiters and headhunters take note.

© www.shopcatalog.com

The main point to take away from this small screen version is what traditional P.I.s refer to as *legwork*. Don't outsource the rationales our conclusions rests on to search engines and databases. Technology is not the goal. It is the processor in a two-step brokering cycle:

1. Search
2. Converse

It is the search phase that informs the direct discussions with the people we engage. In **Unit Four,** we'll review the conversational aspects of our digital pursuits. We'll come full circle in **Unit Five** when that dialog extends to the results we share and present to our clients.

Growing eyes in the backs of our heads means we're ready to reverse direction with the same confidence as moving forward. That means answering to the self-reported evidence of our targets. That means deciphering their blindspots as well. First, however, we must have a little sit down with that artificial intelligence agent plugged into our own virtual interactions.

Characteristics of Computers:
Overview of Online Answering Devices

People once talked to themselves in public.

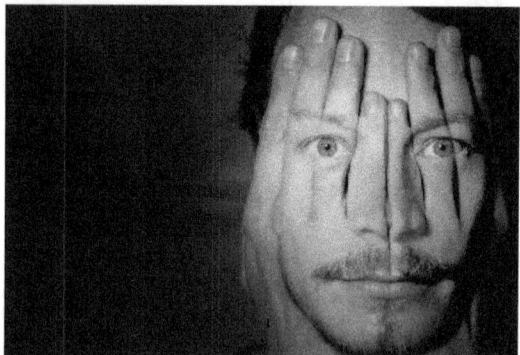

© George Hodan: The face of the man in the hands

Hard to believe. Before the advent of cell phones it was not uncommon to walk down some big city streets. Besides the cabs, buses, and planes overhead, we'd find ourselves hearing the innermost thoughts of total strangers. This was no police sting. We had not the slightest interest either in eavesdropping, or the thoughts themselves.

Nowadays so many of our thoughts (verbalized or otherwise) are triggered by non-human interactions. Look into the storefronts of any Starbucks. It's just us and our machines. What would it sound like if a log of those exchanges could be recorded?

- Great, my in-box is clear!
- Did my cover letter get flagged or snagged in the spam filters of these applicant pools?
- I set up all these news feeds and there's no news?
- Why am I being asked to load the latest version of something I just downloaded?

What if our laptops came with us to couples therapy? What if we propped our feet up on an upholstered IPod instead of an analyst's couch? What would we tell the therapist we have a hard time trying to explain? Is it clarifying or even expressing to our flashing screens, blinking tool bars, and bleeping keypads that we need to get a life? These are difficult conversations. That's for another book.

In this area of study, we don't need more gadgets, more horsepower, or even better programming skills. We just need to know our machines well enough to trick them into telling us what *we need to know*. The trick is realizing that the folks who do the programming have little or no incentive to do this. It's up to us investigators to service our own needs in the service of our clients' wants.

It's up to us as researchers to make information useful for others. Anything less is self-referential and void of learning.

SEARCH ENGINES AS ANSWERING DEVICES

© Mahmoud Hassan: Scam

Search the Internet and answers are rare. You don't get a response. You get a result:

1. Sometimes what search engines give us is so off-the-mark, we forget what problems inspired us to ask in the first place.
2. Often there are too many results. They can't be reduced to a simple yes or no or even a straight-forward best or worst we can expect.

To the Knowledge-ABLED, this abundance of information overload is not a black hole but a golden opportunity.

So here's a novel idea. Let's forgive search engines for being poor interpreters of our wishes. Let's assume they can't read our minds and that's probably a good thing. Let's forget about how many new search engines we won't have the time to try today and that many more pages will be uploaded tomorrow.

Instead, let's learn a few essential lessons that will be worth repeating next week and next year. Let's see the fundamental limits of the Internet and lean on search technology for the often overlooked benefits it reliably provides us. Let's not accept search engines as the final word on any question but as an invitation to continue a discussion we can steer in our favor.

Even more fundamentally, let's look at the behaviors of the humans who keep and pass on the answers we seek. Let's figure out what motivates them to publish or squelch the information we seek. Finally, let's stop writing a blank check to the Internet search bank. That's all the time in our worlds we blow on unproductive search results.

Just because search engines rev without our credit information doesn't mean the investment of our diverted attention is without a cost. By conversing with a search tool, we can arrive at conclusions as rapidly as our blank search page swells with set results – and pocket the difference with our own clients and colleagues.

UNIT ONE: How to Project Manage Virtual Investigations | Page 1:53

The web fosters the illusion that, given enough technology, it is both possible and desirable to know anything about everything. In **Unit Two,** we take on some obvious sticking points (poor information quality, too much of it, etc.) But there are more insidious dangers. They are not so much concealed as they're so obvious as to overlook them.

We just returned from seven potential dead-ends that hold the power to hijack our investigations. Now let's consider the premise that makes us prone to slip down these rabbit holes. These are the presumptions we fall back on when we invest too much faith in technology, and not enough in our own critical thinking.

Here are four:

> 1. **Access:** Anyone with a password can navigate a database.
>
> 2. **Knee-jerk:** Acting on information requires an instant response.
>
> 3. **Infopolitik:** Everyone likes to learn; not everyone likes to share.
>
> 4. **Sacred cows:** Messengers take precedence over their message.

Each of these miscalculations will be on display as we introduce new tools and approaches for best managing our search projects. The SPM form is a worksheet for recording our searches. The cycle for delivering our research is documented through the **Knowledge Continuum**. As we saw at the beginning of **Unit One** and will span this book, the continuum encompasses our Knowledge-ABLED skills as virtual investigators.

© The New York Times

Searching Out Loud: Giving Voice to Independent Investigations | Marc Solomon

What's a Fair Question?

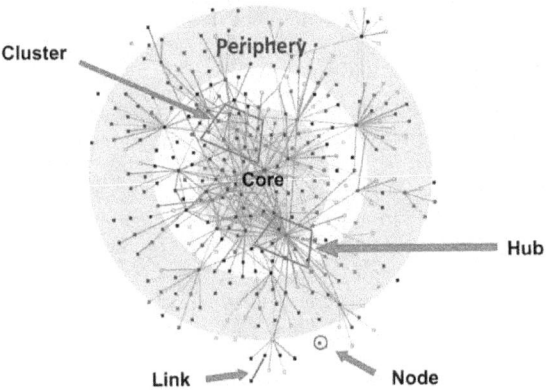

Network Terms Source: Monitor Institute

What's a fair question? Now there's a search project in itself!

- Do you prefer red or white?
- Do I work near where you live?
- Do you have a famous cousin?
- Do I have an advanced degree? Is it in library science?

We might be up for interrogating a suspect. But are we up for interviewing a computer? Are we prepared to tackle the question of how search engines *think*? What do we think the differences are between conversing naturally with people and artificially with computers?

Now that the web is baked into our daily routines, we converse with technology like we talk to ourselves. This may have seemed like muttering under our breath more than getting our point across. But our independence is compromised the more search mimics our behaviors and browser cookies record our click patterns. We become beholden to social and search media companies for prodding us to check-in on our networks. There's a reason that commercial search media are in the business of selling keywords – *not key questions*. And that reason is both our most consuming frustration and greatest opportunity as investigators.

The Icebreaker

How can we revisit this discussion so that computers are no longer notorious time sinks or magical wish grantors? They are simply tools whose effectiveness rests on how we use them, not how they might ever use us.

The ice-breaker here is prompted by our research needs. How do we ask the right question? Probe the right pathway? Drop the correct name? Interviews with computers are more productive if conducted on the computer's terms. This means using the tools and expressions that trigger useful information for our investigation. Not asking questions in plain English, or worse, letting the algorithm decide the answer before our questions have formed.

UNIT ONE: How to Project Manage Virtual Investigations | Page 1:55

That means caring about how Internet search engines process their response to us:

1. Do our terms appear together?

2. Are they prominently placed?

3. Do they appear together in the same categorical reference (a.k.a. database field)?

Will these terms even appear when the page retrieves? You mean they might not be there?

Did we introduce our search terms to each other before we introduced them to the search tool? Did we say we wanted 'crime' "AND" 'Boston' "AND" 'police corruption' as a phrase? Or did we mean "OR" 'police' "OR" 'corruption?'

FIGURE 1.15: The Language of Boolean Logic

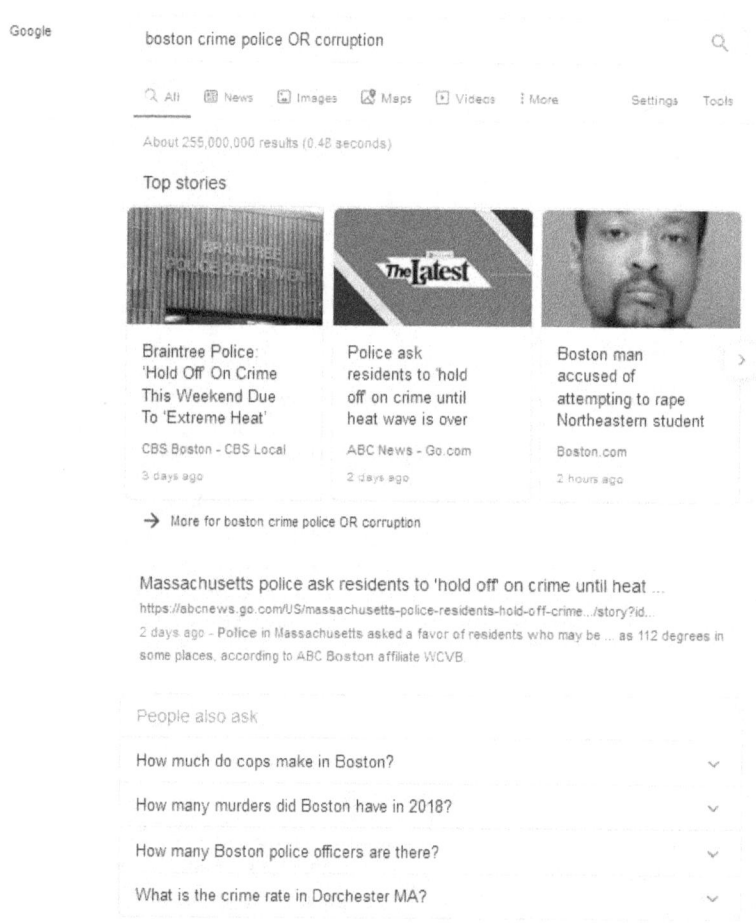

We're telling Google we insist on 'Boston' and 'crime' but don't care whether the third term is 'police' or 'corruption.' Note which of the latter two terms is the more popular choice. Another subtext: An alleged rapist comes to define Boston crime stories even though the search was not intended for news sites or the crime beat of the latest news cycles.

Searching Out Loud: Giving Voice to Independent Investigations | Marc Solomon

Then there's the question of how the answer is presented once the results have been assembled. This is the part of the conversation where the differences between search tools are most pronounced.

It's also the point in the discussion where the search engine company collects a heady fee from the would-be answers that appear at the top of our search results.

But just how good a match is this commercial match to our initial curiosity? If we're only planning on spending our Christmas bonus, this is a one-way conversation that needs cutting-off. Where are the matching words positioned? How about the types of sites that are carrying them?

Finally how much input to do we have over how those results get presented? Can we sort them? Can we search within this search? Do categories suggest alternative paths? Are there additional filters and searchable groups to focus on a more engaging back-and-forth with our answering devices?

Some Organic Thoughts about Artificial Intelligence

Let's start closer to home before we get under the hood of a search engine or kick the tires of a database worth interrogating. Let's focus on the kind of week we're having on our screens. Let's relate digital research to any of the countless interactions we have every day with technology.

Continuing on the last example, let's ask Google to define police corruption in the city of Boston:

FIGURE 1.16: The Failure of Search Algorithms

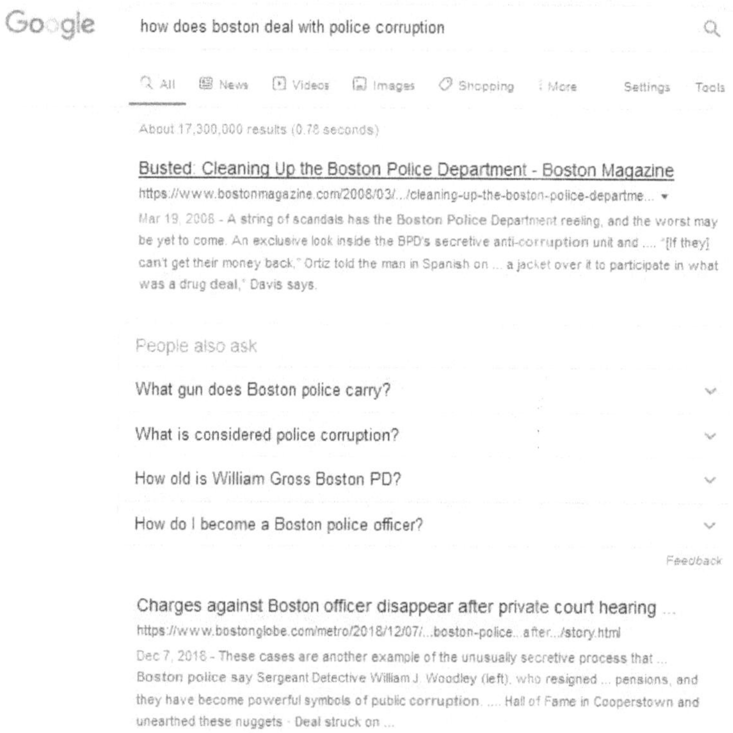

[Google search screenshot for "how does boston deal with police corruption" showing results including "Busted: Cleaning Up the Boston Police Department - Boston Magazine" and "Charges against Boston officer disappear after private court hearing," along with a "People also ask" section containing: What gun does Boston police carry? What is considered police corruption? How old is William Gross Boston PD? How do I become a Boston police officer?]

We're asking Google to address the interrelationship of two topics. Google gives us isolated examples but no broader historical context. In this case it cannot generalize the cross-referencing of Boston and its handling of cops who act outside the law.

It's appropriate to look into our machines and draw some lines between their wonders and their limitations. We draw them clearly when we ask too much of them. It's then we find ourselves discovering fresh insights with skills we are just now starting to master, or ever knew we had.

Here are some flash points for stopping some earnest research missions in their tracks:

FIGURE 1.17: Conversation Stoppers

Conversation Stopper	Limitation	Example
Devices cannot create	If there was a book of Genesis according to the gospels of technology, it is this: They don't have a single inspired thought that wasn't recorded from some other origin. The moment this essential truth ends we may bond better with little green men from Mars and big yellow women from Venus.	In our example Google points towards Wikipedia in order to reference a common definition for police corruption. It's speechless when asked to filter one aspect of law enforcement through the lens of a specific locality.
Devices cannot analyze	Processing power is no substitute for human judgment. The computer only executes. We can take a programmer at their word – not at the programs they write.	Google may know what sites we've visited and perhaps our purchasing habits. But it cannot extrapolate our depth of experience or the distinction between what's obvious/common versus what's novel/unfamiliar.
Devices cannot deliberate or confer	There's no higher intelligence on the other end; just a dumb and very picky program that needs to be interrogated in a precise manner – the average spell-checker notwithstanding.	We cannot question the system and it cannot answer us back: We can only survey its index of records, and it can only cross-reference fields of data within each record.
Devices cannot forget and they cannot fail	Where would we be without the archiving capacity of computers? Who would hold our place? Keep accurate records that define these actual places? An insatiable appetite for storing memories. Not a single thought in their heads, loops, and drives. Yet.	Engineers view failure in a very different regard from the people who use their devices. An error is introduced when the device fails to heed the programmer's instructions – not the layperson's intentions.

Interviewing the Computer
(or, Message to the Hard Drive in Our Heads)

Except for the geeks who tinker under the hood, most of us use search engines to serve some other purpose. They are not a destination unto themselves.

Becoming Knowledge-ABLED means practicing the act of searching for the purpose of conversing. Sometimes our ultimate goal is to talk with computers who can tell people apart. Other times, we're trying to engage the actual people who can make a difference in our specific goals and investigations. As we'll see in **Unit Two**, the success of our interactions with search tools and subject directories is defined by our confidence for going *offline* and into that deposition, job interview, or client meeting.

To do this, we need to see how a search engine thinks. Namely, how it translates our intention based on words and phrases. Part of that expectation is an understanding of how search engines interpret (and routinely flub) the human intentions embedded in search queries.

We begin with our main purpose: To create a self-sustaining and even profitable research practice. Here are three loaded questions on our SPM agenda:

1. How can search engines increase our value to a client or an employer?
2. How can we work around their shortcomings and avoid being tripped up by the marketing aims of their masters?
3. What would the computer learn if it interviewed you?

Question #3 is question commonly referred to computer forensics professionals. They're the dumpster divers who can tell where we've been even after we purge our virtual sessions. They're the ones who can determine how firewalls are compromised and our identities are lifted.

But what if we were less interested in hacking into personal records and more interested in the personal habits for how we find and store information? What can our computer reveal about how we use it?

This is not meant to put you on the spot. Don't be intimidated. Computers may seem inscrutable. But once we understand how they figure us, it can become a lot easier to...

- Converse with them,
- Put them on the spot as if they'll squirm, and
- Get them to tell us what we need to investigate.

In short, how we can have technology broker our intentions as well as it collects information.

To get started we need to be aware of where search engines and databases excel, and where they fail. We then see how their pros and cons compare to some of the typical problem-solving skills we apply in our own research. Fortunately for us there's not much overlap. No matter how slick the interface, rapid the processing, or customized the response, there's plenty of human work to go around.

Eli Pariser

Characteristics of Search Engines

Search engines are the basic way we interface or *talk* with technology. We have a need for knowledge. They link to an inventory or *over supply* of information. But search engines are more than pointers or placeholders. They are ports of entry into the Internet's ocean of information. How that port looks to each one of us on that initial results page will have a profound influence on where we go and what we learn in our investigations.

The fact that each search result page varies is a reflection of our individual usage patterns. It's not about extra processing power. It's not about the speed with which search engines update their indexes.

That means there is no 'standard Google.' No two people positing the same two keywords will see the same outcome. Every Google result page is tailored to your Google. There is no longer an *our Google* and we're no likely to see its return than my ability to peer in on *your Google*. Every account is an opportunity to apportion that person's interests and attentions to an awaiting legion of attention chasers. Their mission is a simple one: To be the answer to a question formed with the assistance of ... you guessed it – the search engine! No one search engine is...

- An information source (they are conduits – not destinations)
- The final word for rounding up the sources available to us on the web
- An answer machine that responds to the specifics of our own deadlines and knowledge

They store our search habits but that doesn't mean they understand our motives, goal orientation, or, what we'll do with the information we're referencing. What they do with us as information containers is no great mystery. Our habits, preferences, and choices are the products they sell on a scale made possible by free and universal access.

Yet by and large, what we do as researchers is not for sale by search engines. Google sells words to advertisers – not queries to investigators. They have no stake in own unique assets and the effort we invest in our learning and research skills for leveraging them.

OUTPUTS – WHAT DO SEARCH ENGINES DO?

Search engines are the unofficial greeters of us unannounced web visitors. We are *announced* when we make repeated visits to the same sites. Browser *cookies* recall our past purchases, passwords, and other demographic information that we share at the registration phase. For all the sites we've yet to visit, there are search engines. And we're no strangers to search screens.

Search engines stock their own enormous databases of web sites. Each database is compiled by an automated *bot* or crawler that seeks them out and indexes them. More precisely, a small sampling of them. The indexer or crawler scans for URL links on web pages and goes back to index those links.

Also, note, we are not searching the Internet. We're searching the pages and websites the engine has already categorized and stored. Also, consider there the lag time between the crawl stage, indexing, query, and page loads of our search results. Changes to these moving pieces may scramble repeat attempts to replicate the same set of results. Keep in mind: We're often visiting updated pages that don't match the content displayed in our search results.

Finally, the crawler eliminates noise words or stop words. These are terms used too frequently to index effectively such as "the, a, an, and, or, these, those ..." and so on. The only way to protect those terms is to surround them with quotation marks: More on that later in **Unit Two.**

FIGURE 1.18: Anatomy of a Query

Step	Description
Processing	Crawl metadata and limited snapshot of each page
Retrieval	Match words, multi-words and complex queries.
Relevance	Sort documents by matched terms, frequencies, locations
Format	Present results page and lay-out results format

Here is a more detailed accounting of what search engines do:

Spidering or Crawling – Search engines search the web for new web pages, index words and/or links on those pages, and match the indexed words with the URL of the page on which they appear. An example of this would be a *cache result* or last recording by the search index or a *spider crawl*.

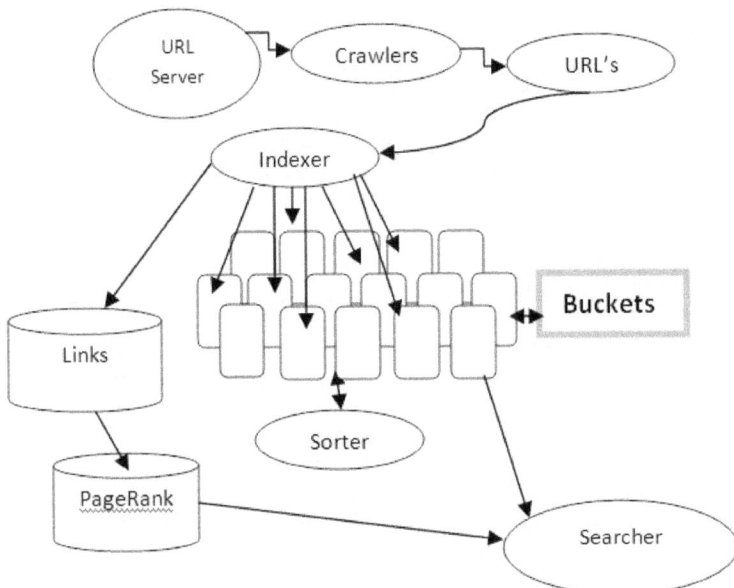

© SEO Malaysia Digital Marketing Agency

Searching the Index – This is what the searcher interrogates. Not the actual pages as they appear when we land on them. These are ranked according to different relevancy factors, software codes (a.k.a. algorithms) that analyze the location and frequency of the user's search terms against matching pages.

This is the distinction that truly separates the way search engines interpret what we see and eventually act on. This is what Google refers to as *PageRank*. It's the attribute most often identified with Google's competitive advantage when it was still a single market company.

Presentation Layer – This is what we can manipulate by our interrogations of the search results. These customized interfaces contain features, operators, and query functions that generate presentation of results to the searcher. Examples of this include the outputs produced by the engine such as the fields or columns we can sort in order of our own viewing priorities.

Content Groupings – Search engines create options for searching content-specific collections such as blogs, wikis, catalogs, videos, etc. They are typically separated in the search interface by tabs or dropdown menus. Here are those four steps again referenced with examples from building an inventory of pages to assembling the results list:

FIGURE 1.19: Search Outputs

Step	Description	Example
Spidering (a.k.a. crawling)	Searching the Web for new Web pages, indexing or crawling words and/or links on those pages, and matching the indexed words with the URL where they appear.	Cache result is a record of the crawl
Searching the index	The index is what we actually search. What we actually see is brokered by algorithms that analyze the location and frequency of the user's search terms against databases of prioritized server pages, documents, and images.	Google Page Rank determines ordering of search results
Presentation layer	Customized interface containing features, operators, and query functions that generate presentation of results to the searcher.	Display and sorting of search results (by relevance, by date, etc.)
Content groupings	Separation of information sources for searching specific types of content.	Exclusive collections for photos, videos, blogs, wikis, etc.

Mechanics – How Do Search Engines Work?

So it can dance, sing, and tell stories – just not its own story. How does the search engine perform these whimsical feats?

- **Processing:** First the tool must process the contents of the index and pore through the essential bits. For search engines this typically means field names, metadata, letter casing, and additional identifiers such as language or lexical properties, (i.e. part of speech).

- **Retrieval:** Then the tool matches what's been processed to the keywords, multiple terms, and phrases contained in the query.

- **Relevancy:** The relevancy gauge is sometimes referred to as the secret sauce.[9] The ordering of relevant hits is what determines which sites or pages will be considered based on the sorting of results by matched terms, frequencies, proximities between words, and their prominence.

- **Format:** The final packaging or format stage presents the results page and the various layout options for review.

Here's the breakdown on the ingredients that factor into relevance:

FIGURE 1.20: Defining Relevancy

STEP	DESCRIPTION
Prominence	Sort the matching items so that most common matches appear first
Proximity	Sort matches by order they are entered
Recurrences	Sort by term popularity
Stature	Sort by appearance in metadata fields

What We Delegate to Search Engines

As we've established, search engines *get* the hard details and miss the soft ones. Relevance is hard to define and situation-specific. In fact, the very term *relevance* is losing 'relevance.' That's the degree of faith we place in algorithms to interpret our intentions. On the other hand, we're not so confident in our own innate sense of what's attention-worthy. We used to gauge importance and decipher context based on a limited number of news sources. The gravity of our decisions and consequences of our actions, channeled through the microphones, airwaves, and news presses of traditional broadcast media.

Today, the conversation is no longer one way from providers to recipients. There is one notable exception: When it comes to interpreting search requests, there is one direct path to the all-interpretive search engine. There is no second-guessing these calculated approximations for what we need to know and do. The unassailable response on our need-to-know basis is on a dropdown of definitions, a sequence of pages, or a series of suggestions posed by the Search Media. And we trust them to do so.

Search engines are all over names and places. They can decipher absolute values like flight departure times and election results. They can anticipate what we will do with hard facts. They sort picnic tables by price. They list pizzerias by the mileage from our phones or homes. With the onset of social media, what's begun to be factored in is softer information consisting of relative properties: Human values, opinions, the priorities they impact, and the behaviors they influence.

What hasn't changed is this. Most search engines will cut us little slack in the goal interpretation game if we're not a potential consumer of a good or service. We need to be both the middle man *and* the end-user in advocating for our information needs. To get there, we must cut the Internet marketer out of the mix. The commercial interest that is only interested in our spending capacity – not our passion to learn!

What Search Engines Cannot Do

Perhaps it's not about the limitations of computer code. It might not be about the programming of search software. Maybe it's all about us. In other words, how do we recognize the assumptions that sabotage our search?

Search engines are famous for getting us halfway to an answer or solutions and then leaving us high and dry in the middle of the information ocean. There are many scenarios where the most promising searches bring us to an unrelated topic, vague conclusion, or brick wall with little recourse for avoiding a ponderous and unproductive outcome.

We need to do one of two things when we reach this moment:

1. Cut our losses.
2. Redirect our focus.

It's important to know when to play which card. Not every research question can be addressed virtually. The sooner our hunches line-up with what's actually out there, the less time we'll spend spinning our wheels. The more we remain true to our overall objectives.

Why are such detours the rule of the search road rather than the exception?

Most of us use search engines to serve some other purpose other than research. They are not a destination by themselves. In this book, we'll practice the act of searching for the purpose of conversing. Our ultimate goal is not to mix it up with an artificial intelligence that catalogs human behavior but with actual people: The experts, eyewitnesses, and stakeholders who can make a difference in our own ongoing investigations and professional goals.

The key to getting offline with confidence is a successful interaction with the search tool.

How Search Engines 'Think' and Where They Get Their Thinking

One fundamental disconnect exists between using search engines to do research and to make money by building and maintaining search engines. None. Zero. Zilch. There are no connections whatsoever

Does Google profit from our use of its advanced search features?

Not in the slightest!

Was Yahoo any happier in the days we appreciated their deeper indexing and higher threshold of search terms? Probably not nearly as pleased as letting both Microsoft and Google license functional and ad-based operations of Yahoo! Search beginning in 2010.

Another non-starter of search mysteries is the nature of Google's business model. It's no different for web-based media companies than traditional TV, radio and newspapers. Google sells ads. To a large extent, we non-advertising researchers are the beneficiaries of this business model. We're not complaining about not paying Google directly for use of its search engine. Perhaps therein lies the ultimate irony of Google's success: The heaviest users are not even paying customers.

FIGURE 1.21: How Search Engines Think

STEP	DESCRIPTION
Spidering	Search the web for new web pages, index words and/or links on those pages, and match the indexed words with the URL of the page on which they appear
Search index/database of web site listings	What the searcher interrogates; ranked according to different relevancy factors. These factors are software codes ("algorithms") that analyze the location and frequency of the user's search terms against this list of matching websites
Interrogation /retrieval process for searchers	Customized interface containing features, operators and query functions that generate presentation of results to the searcher

This process is littered with bumps and loose-ends. Here we witness the resulting gaps between how search works and how it works *for us:*

FIGURE 1.22: How People Want Them to Think

STEP	DESCRIPTION
No dead-ends	Display only fruitful paths – suppress black holes like paying for phone numbers and addresses
No false hits	Weed out pattern matches with no plausible context, (i.e. runner finishing times on endless list of charity road races)
'Why' I got what I got ...	KWIC: Keyword in context
Built-in spell-checkers and thesaurus	Quality check for entry errors and term expansion
Related concepts for enhanced filtering	Concepts associated to the original query ranked by category and strength of their association

IF SEARCH ENGINES THOUGHT LIKE RESEARCHERS

Here's the fuller description of the above table from the following premise:

What if Google one day tried to make a search business around supporting researchers? If we were to contract the coding wiz and say: "Build me a search engine that does what I want it to do." Here are a few features that might appear on our wish list:

- **No dead-ends: Display only fruitful paths** – Don't show me a blank page or millions of results. Organize the results so that they point in several directions any of which I can understand without having to go in the wrong direction.

- **No false hits: Weed out pattern matches** – Don't weigh a page with super-rich detail the same as a sparser source with fewer terms. Certain sites get pulled on the simple premise that they attract more keyword matches because of their density of detail.

- **Why I got what I got: KWIC ("Keyword in context")** – Give me the terms I use in a sentence the same way we would require this as a contestant in a spelling bee. The difference here is that we're not trying to spell out words but their meanings in relation to our goals and supporting objectives.

- **Built-in spell-checker and thesaurus: Quality check for entry errors and term expansion** – The *read my mind* element to Google has a lot more to do with correcting common misspellings than it does with anticipating our thoughts. Here's where a listing of like-minded terms can help us to isolate our true intentions from false hits. True intentions are what information we need to support the actions we're considering. False hits are keywords that match our queries but not our intentions.

- **Related concepts for enhanced filtering: Topics associated with query results** – They are presented as related categories and ranked by the strength of their association to our search terms. Ideally a related concept is not only topically in sync but helps us to isolate information providers from the information they are providing. Another key distinction often lost in search results: Who's the actor in an event we're tracking? What steps they are taking, and who is on the receiving end of those actions?

Rolling the Search Dice

One of the hardest aspects of web research to overcome is the temptation to *feel lucky*. This is the appeal of letting the search engine define the best response to our curiosity-free questions. The inducement is particularly strong when we're certain of one thing: We only want the facts. By this we mean that a straightforward question will likely generate *the top* result such as the home page for a well-known company or a fan site for a popular celebrity.

Getting off the beaten path doesn't always ensure that we can keep our bearings, let alone journey forward in a direct, predictable and repeatable way. This is the rule and not the exception for anyone who's ever tried to connect a person or company to a specific set of actions. Even when we expect the unexpected, the path one cuts is rarely as the crow flies.

Here are some of the familiar detours that hijack our search intentions and lead us astray from the original research objectives and project requirements:

1. **Limited Indexing:** Commercial search engines are rewarded for indexing individual sites – not all the pages contained within them. For instance, Google will typically index about the first 100 kilobytes of an individual site before moving onto a new web address. Other indexes may carry more detail. This small data sample might constitute a drive-by snapshot if a website was considered an individual home. It ignores the individual rooms, garage and all the furnishings apparent to an actual visitor.

2. **Term Limits:** Another trade-off for the swelling number of web pages is not only the limited depth of their index but the number of words permissible in a search statement. A 'term limit' in a search statement is not about restricting the number of times a politician may run for elected office. It's the threshold of words that can be used within a given search. Ten, twenty, or thirty plus term limits sound like plenty of room to work in. But consider how many search tools reject truncation or word-stemming? That's the ability to introduce variants to root words. Typically this is expressed through asterisks such as controvers* as a wildcard for 'controversy' or 'controversial.'

3. **Sorting Problems:** Search engine limitations are not restricted only to search statements. The search results that materialize are constrained by an inability to sort results according to any single useful organizing principle (i.e., by date, alphabet, domain type, popularity, etc.) The only factor that determines ranking is the highly disputed and forever evolving notion of relevance. We are at the mercy of the search engine for defining what exactly relevance means: unless we invoke the query formation tools in **Unit Two** so stay tuned.

Google, the Heinz of Search Ketchup, is worth a closer look in assessing how search company business objectives can trip up our research aims:

1. **Speed:** There is some sleight-of-hand going on that search firms use to keep their engines humming and the traffic flowing that can compromise our research. For instance, Google set the pace back in 1998 with near instantaneous search results. In order to achieve that engineering feat Google decided early on that they weren't going to *boil the ocean.* They chose to skim it by only crawling a sliver of the content available on each and every page it indexes, hence limited indexing.

2. **Simplicity:** Another brilliant stroke had nothing to do with the processing speed at all but with the bold, clear interface that kept the search results uncluttered. While it gave users a sense of openness and clarity, it also oversimplified the results screen.

3. **Definitive Results:** Search results could only be distinguished by how high they ranked – not by the pattern or grouping they belonged to. We'll see in **Unit Two** how faceted search enables a better refining of search results. This holds true even when the results are a less clean and simple.

4. **Visibility:** Finally, as we mentioned earlier in this section there are many vital resources that defy indexing. They glance right off the Google radar. For example, the homepages of major federal and state government sites may appear. But their principle resources such as contact listings and databases do not. We'll address this again when we introduce the *Invisible Web* in **Unit Three**.

Here's how those programming decisions play out in brief:

FIGURE 1.23: Google Search Trade-offs for Researchers

Objective	Trade-off
Speed	Thin layer of sites are actually indexed
Simplicity	Clean interface sacrifices relevance of our own project requirements that can't be expressed in selected threshold of keywords
Definitive Results	"Search within search" allows search results to be more conversational – responses provoke follow-up questions that lead to chance discoveries
Visibility	Many topic-sensitive databases and project-relevant directories never land on Google's radar

FAILSAFES – WHEN WE'VE REACHED THE END OF THE LINE

How do we manage? If the business models of search engine companies have no stake in our success as researchers, what are the workarounds? How do we support our own investigations within their existing infrastructures and revenue goals? Let's dust ourselves off for a minute and re-introduce a term we first considered in the Search Project Management section. This is a **failsafe**.

For our purposes, failsafes tell us what our search terms can do for us when we've come to the end of the line. We accept the results as-is or scrap our terms and start fresh. This is not always easy, especially when we've invested big chunks of time in ponderous links and fruitless pages.

A failsafe is not the mark of failure. Oftentimes no answer is the best available answer.

Remember, our ability to inventory a checklist of tools, practices, and sources are not standard operating procedure. It gives our investigations an air of validity and completeness that can't be attained through keyword associations or a casual browsing of subject directories.

Yogi Berra once said that when you come to a fork in the road, take it. We may well reach that fork several times on the same road. Still, here are some strategies for dealing with potential failsafes:

1. **Completeness:** For starters no self-respecting investigator would call search an ends in itself. There is no finality or closure in search unless our game is search engine optimization and we justify the purchase of keywords and phrases of online advertisers. The search ocean is the first plunge. But the follow-up work is about zeroing in and sharpening our aim. Try this from the remote confines of an Internet search and we're taking isolated stabs in the dark.

2. **Credibility:** Secondly, the cases they solve are the badges investigators wear with the greatest distinction. Investigators take pride in the skepticism they maintain about the facts, opinions, and shreds of evidence that cross their desk. Such scrutiny can't exist from the heights we're scaling or in the heaps of search hits we're attracting.

3. **Refinement:** Our use for search engines is not to make sense of all this or even to hit one exposed nail on its tiny head. It's to narrow the possibilities to a plausible range of outcomes and then to start testing our assumptions. We will proceed: First by sites, then by pages, then by our confidence – to go forward with a recommendation, a decision, or a credible greeting to those with the knowledge we seek.

4. **Analytical:** Yes, it's true that analysis is still a job for mortal humans. That said, the web and its many recordable movements are fodder for technologists and technophobes alike to compare prevailing and deviant patterns. The web can now tell us in graphic detail just how *shared* common knowledge really is. As researchers, we can assess how familiar this all sounds to the players in our investigation. How do they see their roles? What assets can they use to advance their own priorities? That question opens many doors entered through a search tool.

5. **Personal:** The abstraction of testing theories recedes into the background when we're searching specific individuals. Does he have a criminal history? Has she filed more than once for bankruptcy? One potential advantage to researchers is that a search engine answers direct questions with a tangible yes or no. The larger benefit is that the researcher is not limited to *point blank* search requests. Instead of one personal history, our scope expands to include their communities and associations – their influences and impacts. This is where we call in our chips. This is where we start engaging our search targets as actual people we're looking to know and learn from directly.

Here's a summary table that nails our opportunities through failsafes:

FIGURE 1.24: Working Within Search Engine Limitations

Objective	Supporting tasks
Completeness	Include visible and invisible web to dig for critical details and uncover overlooked connections and opinions
Credibility	Trace site ownership, traffic patterns and visitor profiles
Analytical	Expose motivations and priorities of people and organizations relevant to our investigation
Personal	Leverage social networks to engage the people we research to progress from searching to actual conversing

Hidden Minefields

The boundaries of search engines are not just part of what we see in search results pages. Their limitations follow us down into the sites they crawl. These are the added 'minefields' swept in with our search requests. We are all susceptible to minefields as search tools are powerless to prevent us from wasting our efforts. This is the garbage that masquerades as relevance because one or more keywords in our query match the search index record of the site in question.

Here's how that plays out in practice and what remedial steps are available to us:

1. **Landing Pages** – Search results lists and many of the pages they index are littered with links to shopping sites and link farms. While commerce certainly has its digital place, I'll lay this sizable bet: We don't plan on bringing our credit card on our next research assignment unless we want to outsource our sleuthing skills. A familiar drop-off point is for a search result to deposit us in the middle of a product catalog or some other sales-related location. These are called landing pages and they are designed by merchandisers to match our keywords against the inventories they are trying to move.

    SOLUTION: *The best way to re-orient ourselves is to lop off the extended site address and trace back to the site root or homepage.*

2. **Poor Word Affiliation** – Frequently we will see our keywords highlighted in distant proximity to one another; in other words they bear little relation to one another.

    SOLUTION: *A simple way to boost their affiliation is to apply quotes to anchor multiple keywords we would expect to see as phrases on a page.*

3. **Broken Links** – Links are severed when an indexed or cached record appears in our search results but has been deleted or taken offline since the index was last refreshed.

    SOLUTION: *If the publisher of those materials is important to our case we can track down the site ownership through the cached record and quality control tools that we will consider later in the course.*

4. **Actions and Actors** – Search engines never went to grammar school. They can look at words in isolation. They can do a spell check and match of the frequencies and proximities of keywords. But matching is not the same thing as meaning. Search engines can't tell objects from subjects or nouns from verbs. It's one thing to key in the name of our case of a potential suspect. It's another to consider what the police have done with the evidence, or what charges the District Attorney considers bringing to trial.

   SOLUTION: *We'll talk later in **Unit Two** about the role semantics can play in helping us to distinguish actors from actions in the way we form our queries.*

5. **Time Frames** – Search engines are notoriously poor at documenting publication dates. Some of this blame lies with the uncertain definition of when publishing actually occurs since one posting or story can have multiple publication dates.

   SOLUTION: *Discussion boards and blog postings are two web-based publishing conventions that clarify the business of 'when.' These entries have a clear and certain date stamp on each dispatch.*

6. **False Perfection** – One of the dead ends we often arrive at is the disappointment there is no definitive or most *perfect* document that answers all our questions. Rather, the Knowledge-ABLED investigator assimilates and synthesizes all relevant documents according to the broader social context:

   * For marketers, these *big idea* indicators include market climate, perception levels and campaign awareness.

   * For researchers. it might be around who are the authorities or first to grasp or gain credit for the importance of a particular trend or idea.

   * For investigators, it tends to focus on the flow of how details become known about the case they're working: Who knew what – and when.

   SOLUTION*: In **Unit Five** we'll build these analytical reports using a Knowledge-ABLED framework called ***The Biggest Picture***.

Search Engines and Databases

What are the differences between search engines and databases?

Aren't they one in the same on the web?

Why does this even matter?

The question is both more critical to our success and more difficult to resolve than it may sound. On their own, search engines contain vast databases of the pages, links, and metadata that they index. Also the term 'database' is broadly defined. It refers to many interconnecting dimensions of the digitized world. From shopping catalogs to the shipping manifestos, this is the coding logic that distributes the merchandise or instructs the flight reservation systems used to transport ourselves around the planet.

Databases handle virtual traffic too. That means websites, the folks who visit them, what they do through their click patterns: The last place (known as the 'referring link') that got them there.

For our research purposes, a database is not about iconic shopping carts or moving the flow of goods and services. Databases serve two important lessons for demonstrating the value of our search projects to our colleagues and clients:

> 1. The **Ocean, Lake and Pond** Framework that we'll consider in **Unit Two**
>
> 2. The Invisible or **Deep Web** that we'll explore in **Unit Four**

The databases we're focusing on are as off-limits to search engines as is our own direct entry. These are the complex systems at the operational nerve centers that store our financial trades, payments, and account records. These databases are maintained by governments, enforcement agencies, educators, and open source communities. They contain small, concentrated collections of public records:

> 1. This could be related to local tax records based on real estate assessments.
>
> 2. It could be the licensing history of a professional or contractor we may consider hiring.
>
> 3. It could even be assessments made between service providers who are required to file their performance records with a federal or state authority, e.g. hospitals, banks, airlines, etc.

One prevailing notion runs through databases whether their ultimate purpose is to serve the public or a group bounded by a common interest. Database owners and stewards have no incentive in making their records available to the likes of Google. There are other technical limitations in the way search engines index databases that we'll address in **Unit Two**.

Characteristics of Databases

So databases on the web hold research opportunities beyond search. Seizing them signifies a lot about our resourcefulness as Knowledge-ABLED practitioners. So before we get started we need to consider: What are some rules of the road for accessing and searching databases?

Here is a set of limitations and possibilities to consider when we're working our way through them – one resource at a time:

1) Databases cannot...

Tell us how to read people.

The person that we profile from afar may have little or no relation the individual we meet in person. First meetings don't always give us always accurate reads. They'll prove even less reliable if our assessment is limited to the size of our database.

But they can...

Tell us where to read about them.

The context that forms a person's overall virtual identity goes beyond public records, blogging posts, Facebook pages, or the communities they take part in. But each of these pieces offers a glimpse into the views we hold and the roles we play. Taken together, they afford a more rounded view of our achievements and failures than any single resume, fact sheet, or first encounters could reveal about our own personal pathways.

2) Databases cannot...

Prioritize our best opportunities.

© Healthy Aging Network: Personalized and Customized Health

Sometimes, we get caught up in the thrill of the chase. We find some intriguing factoids from some promising sources and there lies the temptation. The collection phase went so well, it wrote the analysis by itself. And now we've got our marching orders. Think again. If our clients only wanted the facts, they'd be running the investigation themselves.

But they can...

Show us how trends are being set.

What we can do is tabulate those collection numbers into a scoring system of our design. We can funnel the factoids from our search results into a set of metrics. These indicators connect external events and market data to our client or firm's internal capabilities and development efforts. We can see how others do it if we're not sure yet about which dots to connect. For example, Google Trends monitors the passing fashions and crazes based on the search patterns in public Internet usage. It also tracks the volume of media coverage generated on the same topics. More on this in **Unit Three**.

3) Databases cannot...

Answer fuzzy questions in absolute terms.

The operative term here is 'fuzzy.' We're lured into our own assumptions. This includes what we accept as fact or truth to be universal in its agreement and understanding. Test some common assumptions on the web and we're bound to find contrarian opinions and competing explanations on issues we considered long settled.

But they can...

Reveal the relationships between our search targets.

Most of us accept the cross-referencing superiority of machines to our own fallible missteps for connecting people and groups to places, events, and the timing for it. There is no instinctive judgment better served than a multi-concept search if we have a theory or suspicion that needs supporting:

> "Hopi Indian" Tibetan ~culture

This statement combines one phrase, keyword, and search operator to find correlations between these two prolific, indigenous civilizations. It is not the kind of definitive answer demanded by a quantifiable conclusion: How alike are these two traditions from opposite parts of the world? But it does offer an immediate payback for using similar rituals and customs to test the strength of this suggested association.

Hopi Angel, Hopi girl, c1905, Edward S. Curtis, photographer

UNIT ONE: Wrapping
How to Project Manage Virtual Investigations

Now we're ready to project manage what no one bothers to track – let alone master: The common, repeatable, and often elusive process of purposeful, virtual investigations. In the next unit, we'll connect our new understandings around how search technologies work with the less abstract business of answering our clients' questions and concerns. We'll continue to build on the frameworks and models introduced in **Unit One** with the hands-on examples to come. These use cases will help us apply search project management steps to our interrogation of search engines. That process is called query formation and it's the headlining subject of **Unit Two**.

[1] James Bennet, "The New Price of American Politics," The Atlantic, October 2012
[2] Olivia Parr-Rud, "Business Intelligence Success Factors: Tools for Aligning Your Business in the Global Economy," 2009
[3] Peter Morville, "Ambient Findability – What We Find Changes Who We Become," O'Reilly Media, September 2005
[4] Claudia Cuskelly, "Google Maps Street View users spot dead body on pier - but image is not what it seems," Daily Express, October 11, 2017
[5] Donald Rumsfeld, "Known and Unknown," Sentinel Trade, 2010
[6] ibid, Morville
[7] Barbara Flood, "ASIS Mid-year Preview Meeting," The Emotionality of Privacy, 1997
[8] Mary E. Boone and David J. Snowden, "A Leader's Framework for Decision Making," Harvard Business Review, November, 2007
[9] That secret became even more guarded once Google introduced personalized search results in 2012.

UNIT TWO:

USING SEARCH IN VIRTUAL INVESTIGATIONS

Investigative Search

We all know what it's like to be searched. Our hands are thrown in the air. We're not blowing off steam. We're following an order that we're in too deep to question. What about when we're in control. We're the ones doing the searching. Or are we?

Unit Two tosses out the driver's ed instruction manual, gets behind the wheel, and takes established interests and new skills out for a test drive. **Unit Two** applies how search engines support our aims. The priority is finding the best available tool for the job at hand. Having looked under the search engine hood in **Unit One**, here are the driver's seat issues we'll address in this unit. First, concerns the nature of investigations:

1. Are we trying to nail down definitive facts or weigh differing opinions?

2. How likely does documentation exist that supports our knowledge-seeking objectives?

3. What will that cost in terms of time and effort? When is it better to forego search completely?

Next are the questions about the search tools that respond to these questions:

1. What are the different search engines available to me?

2. Which is most appropriate to the questions that we'll be asking in our investigations?

3. Why is using the correct tool so vital to finding qualified facts or useful answers?

4. What are some of the important trade-offs between common types of search engines?

Our discussion will focus on the conversation. This exchange is not between you and me. It's between us and the searches we perform to open new doors, stay informed, or keep ahead of the projects we're managing before and after the exchange concludes. Let's start with our offline project goal. Who are we trying to engage...

- The hiring manager as we attempt to join her fraud detection unit?
- The forensics experts with whom we're trading insights?
- The persons or groups of interest in an ongoing investigation?

Our goal is not to lean on screens for the sake of never leaving. It's to put questions to the search engine on the terms it understands. This prepares us for the deeper, richer interviews with the people whose experience and ideas first sparked our interest.

As we rev our search engines in **Unit Two**, it's worth remembering: There are no stupid questions – only convoluted answers and too many search results!

Our mission in **Unit Two** leads us to this pivotal question: What is the best tool for the job? That's our ultimate aim ... whether our objectives are to learn about a new topic for the first time, refresh our knowledge in familiar places, or obtaining specific details on a case we're working.

UNIT TWO LEARNING OBJECTIVES

No search tool review is complete without considering often more effective alternatives. This is true especially when our newness to a topic overwhelms our ability to navigate it. Research navigation has come to mean using familiar keywords and a compromising reliance on the commercial motives of search media to deliver pay-per-click search results. One common example of this are the site owners who pay Google for their top positioning based on the terms we search. Later in **Unit Three**, we will expand our alternatives to consider results that don't show up on Google search – paid for or not. Here we'll introduce the off-radar merits of the Deep or Invisible Web.

> *Definition: Research Navigation*
>
> *Research Navigation refers to the rapid and sometimes superficial way that we use web-based search to understand novel ideas and unfamiliar concepts. This understanding is limited to static sets of information such as definitions, dates, and people associated with these topics. It does not extend to a working knowledge of the subject, or relating it to the needs and priorities that inspired this research.*

As in **Unit One**, we will learn some helpful frameworks for determining how to approach and breakdown common research problems into manageable tasks. We will start by picking up on **Information Types**. This is a concept we'll explore more fully in **Unit Three** when we integrate our search findings into a useful form. Part of determining the right search tool for the right job is anticipating one of two common pathways:

1. **Fact-based questions** – Where we narrow down the search results to a finite set of precise or fixed outcomes

2. **Opinion-based questions** – Where we broaden our horizons to increase our knowledge of areas that invite multiple interpretations and defy absolute answers

Considering these pathways before we search steers us toward effective **Query Formation**. Query formation is the most effective way for breaking the virtual ice. We ask our most pressing questions of the most appropriate tool in the clearest and focused way.

The second important construct in this section will be the concept of **Oceans, Lakes and Ponds**. The metaphor of these figurative water bodies are key to consider how big the information buckets we're searching might be. Oceans, Lakes, and Ponds refer to the size of the database, collection, or index we're searching. The number of available pages, records, and documents can have a profound effect on the caliber of our answers.

> **Definition: Oceans, Lakes, and Ponds**
>
> The OLP framework ("Oceans, Lakes, and Ponds") is a framework for understanding how search results are influenced by the volume of available pages, documents, and/or records in searchable indexes. We rarely, if ever, know the size or scope of the databases we search. Yet their size has a profound impact on the nature and quality of the results we can expect to find.

Unit Two Destination: Search Analysis

We first encountered the *Knowledge Continuum* in the previous unit. We explored how to formulate our queries and manage them using a search log. In **Unit Two** we will look at a variety of ways to conduct research investigations through web-based search. This will involve the selection of sites, the choice of appropriate tools, and query formation in order to...

- Talk to computers so that the responses invite follow-up,
- Advance our research aims, and
- Communicate these interactions to our stakeholders.

The chief objective here: Enhancing our ability to refine raw information into useful knowledge.

Unit Two targets the most effective practices for connecting search results to (1) investigation particulars, (2) analytical backing, and (3), our own established information-seeking behaviors. They include:

1. Understanding the inherent constraints present in query formation
2. Observing the expansion and contraction properties of fact and concept-based search methods
3. Practicing these methods in both searching as well as in browse-mode of directory-based resources

We will consider a variety of problem-solving scenarios where we assess the trade-offs between search engines and subject directories. Each example will integrate query formation and tool selection. The purpose is to...

- Determine when it is appropriate to use one or the other, and
- Craft a search strategy that recognizes the respective strengths and shortcomings of both.

Is each outcome conclusive or definitive? Hardly! Revising a search strategy based on the usable remnants of a failed prior attempt is equally important for increasing our confidence as researchers. That we can prevail over unclear or conflicting search results. This confidence will be demonstrated by our ability to...

- Recognize the consequence of overly precise or vague terms
- Call out the assumptions that sabotage our search
- Demonstrate how search automation can actually lengthen the discovery process by making incorrect assumptions about our real intentions (and our clients' motives for hiring us)

Unit Two Benefits

By the end of this unit you will understand and apply...

1) **Query Formation:** Recognize appropriate search commands and word selection options for leveraging Internet resources

   - Work with numerous syntactical operators to gain an understanding of advanced search commands
   - Draw on search operators, unique IDs, and pointers to either generalize or specify around the topics or targets in question

2) **Semantics:** Understand and manage the factor of word choice to express our research objectives and information-seeking intentions

   - Apply fact- and opinion-based search guidelines and constraints to construct queries that yield productive outcomes
   - Use appropriate semantics to arrange and express effective queries

3) **Tool Selection:** Differentiate and select the right digital search and discovery tools, including:

   - Visualization, cluster and NLP ("Natural Language Processing") engines
   - Build your own search engines such as the Google CSE ("Custom Search Engine") application

4) **Subject Directories:** Determine the best starting point for the task at-hand

   - Determining when a subject directory is a superior information reference to a search engine
   - Modifying our search strategy to fit the constraints of direct source and directory structures

SECTION 2.1 | Query Formation —
How to Arrange, Express, Generalize,
and Specify Research Questions

In our return to the Knowledge Continuum, we can understand query formation as the exploration phase. The mapping phase continues with the refinement elements. These are a blending of the search tools and their search commands.

Why do we care?

Our investigation needs to speak directly to the next stage actions and outcomes of the cases we research. We are not only fulfilling expectations, but shifting them in a convincing way. Our findings will not always be conclusive. Our recommendations may not remove all doubt. Our research methods, however, must be unassailable. **Unit Two** addresses the *how* of the *what* we came to know in **Unit One** as search logs. And at the top of that how list is the need to (1) close the distance between the enormity of the recorded universe, and (2) the selected bits that find their way into our **Unit Five** presentations.

We want to screen impossibly large sets of search results so that we can drill-down or filter out the background noise. That's the distraction of ad-sponsored sites, link farms, and even information boxes designed to generate a self-contained side bar to crowd out the less ornamental results — optics be damned.

In **Unit Two** we translate the goals and objectives of our search logs and personal radars from raw, unfiltered data to refined information. Those refinements are worthy of our attention and potentially our clients' or colleagues' attention later on in the project.

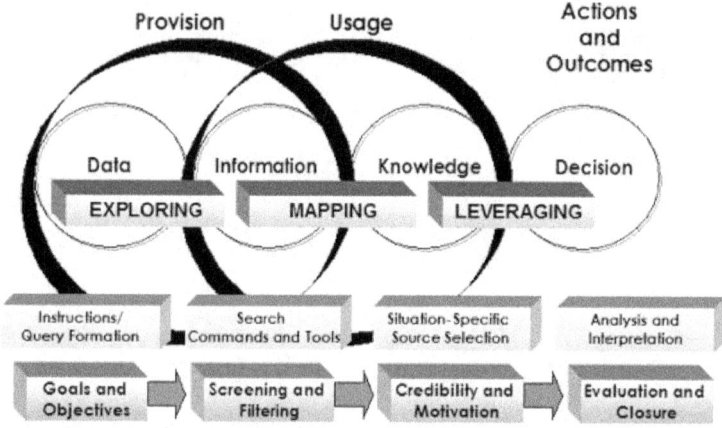

We have determined what pool we are going to look in. We know whether or not we are doing a fact- or opinion-based search. Next we'll apply the operators, syntax, and semantics that search engines often use to make sense of humans. This will help us focus on getting fewer and better results from our searches.

Query formation is the convergence of three information filtering methods:

> **1. Syntax:** How to arrange
>
> **2. Semantics:** How to express
>
> **3. Points and unique IDs:** How to generalize and specify

Syntax, semantics, and operators are all refinement tools. We use them in order to create better filtering and more incisive findings. The syntax and operators we review are specific to Google. But this syntax is transferable to many of the search engines we are about to cover. One way you can track this? Record the syntax and semantics used in your search log.

Constructing Effective Searches

Now we consider the mechanics of producing a capable question on the computer's terms. Yes, we're entering another dimension. A dimension not only of sight, sound, and mind but of pattern-matching and connection-making. *You've* just crossed over into the *Twilight Zone of Research*. We will come to know it in more clinical terms as *Query Formation*.

In one sense, the web is idiot-proof. But using it well is not always obvious or easy. The nature of the questions we ask determines where and how we ask them. Are we just spinning our wheels when we use a few top-of-mind associations? Is it foolish to ask away through the great *information yonder,* assembled by the seeming universal human need to document and publish?

This section is intended to provide an overview of how to construct queries that address a wide range of information-seeking objectives. Furthermore, it is intended to focus on the significance of high quality search results as a motivating factor for constructing the effective questions that generate them.

Constructing the Query

What are the right questions to ask? How should they be refined from the results we get?

How do the results shape one's conclusions? How should they be packaged and presented to other vested parties such as colleagues, business partners, prospects, and clients?

Before constructing our query, we need to deconstruct the thinking that goes into it. Let's break those three elements down to meaningful choices and sequential steps:

> **1) Semantics** – When constructing a query, try to arrange the search terms and phrases sensibly:
>
> - **Word selection** – Consider words and phrases that defy ambiguity and uncertainty. They define the context in which they're used.
>
> - **Grammar** – Align actions with outcomes through predicates and objects. Unlike most, don't limit your queries on topics to *things* when *verbs* are there to set us straight.
>
> - **Relatedness** – Pick words that enjoy widespread usage but are familiar tags or labels for defining or grouping important topics.

2) Syntax – When constructing a query, select the syntactic operators that will match the term to the category most closely matching our requirements:

- **Prominence** – How important the term is to the theme or topic addressed, e.g. title, lead paragraph, hyperlink, folder name, etc.
- **Location** – Refers to physical location or virtual one, e.g. the URL or domain where the site, page or document is stored.
- **Affiliation** – Connects sites and pages through a strength of association that directly influences search result rankings, e.g. Google's PageRank formula (also called link analysis).

3) Operators – When constructing a query, select the search operators that will determine the conditions to help us succeed:

- **Unconditional** – A binary conclusion, (e.g. Yes, No)
- **Conditional** – An open-ended outcome, (e.g. Either, Or, If)
- **Proximity** – The nearness or distance between two or more search terms
- **Term Expansion** – Broadening the range of your root term to include variants, stemming, and synonyms

REFINEMENT STEPS

What do these meaningful choices look like at the time we're weighing them?

Each set of search results is not only a roll of the dice or a stab in the dark. It's an interpretation of what the web offers us in continuing the exchange. It's the discussion that begins every time we form a query. There are three basic reasons for scripting or sequencing these refinement steps:

1) Better quality results and fewer of them

2) Reduce click-thrus to worthless sites

3) Match our query formation to the size of the potential results pool

The size of our results list is the single biggest factor in how far we can filter down to the essential details (as the *Ocean, Lakes, and Ponds* framework will attest!) The following Figure 2.1 is a conversational roadmap between us and the *call-and-response* routine we perform with the search engine or subject directory.

FIGURE 2.1: Stepping Through a Search

Query Step	Refinement Tool	Refinement Method
First pass: Here's a wild guess ...	Feeling lucky?	Too many hits or uncertainty to begin click-thrus to sites
Second pass: Sometimes it's called ...	**Operators:**	AND, OR, NOT (SEE Figure 2.2)
	Term Expansion	Synonyms, Variants
	Proximity	Word Range, Field Range
Third pass: Sometimes it's related to ...	**Semantics:**	
	Content Providers include ...	Authors, Experts, Sources
	It has its own category	Directories, Source Groupings
Fourth pass: It's likeliest to appear ...	**Syntax:**	
	Site Domains	.com OR .org OR .edu, etc.
	Titles	Intitle:
	Language	English only?
Fifth pass: It's still appearing since ...	**Pointers and IDs:**	
	Page Content	Dense word pack
	Unique IDs	Attributions, Codes
	Administration	Advertising, Visitors, Links, Updates, Ownership, etc.

Now it's time to break down these refinement tools into an evaluation of what they do and how they help us. That means where they take us as we travel from the exploration to the mapping stages of the knowledge continuum.

Operators

First we address Operators. Operators have a few identities. They're the symbols on the top line of your keyboard. Like in a *hot key* or a *macro*, some programmer designated negative signs, asterisks and tildes to perform important, repetitive tasks. Another kind of operator are the Boolean twins commonly known as *Tweedle Dee* and *Tweedle Dumb:* OR and AND. Knowing when to use which, especially in tandem, can tip search outcomes in our favor.

Operators also include:

- Quotation marks to surround a phrase in order to protect multiple word search terms and enforce word order
- The tilde (~) as a term expansion device

The negation sign (-) rules out wasteful outcomes or *noisy* hits such as -release. It screens out press releases from an information provider where we're looking for credibility. For instance, "-www.walmart.com" filters out self-reporting: It includes mentions of 'Wal-Mart' by others *besides Wal-Mart.*

As Figure 2.2 suggests, operators are both compelling for their simplicity and ability to narrow intentions:

FIGURE 2.2: Search Operators

Symbol	Function	Example
+	Explicit inclusion	+oranges +apples
-	Negation – explicit exclusion	-bananas –release
"	Phrase Containment	"eye to eye"
*	Word wildcard – not stemming!	"eye * eye"
OR	Explicit inclusive	apples OR oranges
~	Synonyms and term expansion	~fruit
"*	Explicit inclusion – any term preceding our search target	"* mountain, GA"

Letting the Search Breathe

One of the simple and splendid services provided by search operators is their ability to enforce our *deal-breakers:* Those terms that are mandatory. They must be present for our search to work. The unique benefit of operators is that we can afford to be more flexible with the non-essential words that surround the critical terms. We call this the practice of allowing the search *to breathe*. We let the search algorithm pull in related terms we would otherwise overlook.

There are two primary *breather* operators in the way Google processes search requests: Asterisks (or wildcards) and tildes (or term expanders).

Wildcards

Wildcards are a great way to exert control over a search outcome. We're not just insisting on the presence of specific terms in a simple keyword query. We're saying that we want those terms – on our terms! That means we still want them if they're part of a phrase. That means we want them to appear in a certain order. We can be fussy. Sometimes it's well worth our fuss.

For example, we might care a lot about the choice and ordering of certain words. But we might not care at all about the more common words like prepositions or conjunctives that get between those words. The asterisk or wildcard allows different variations on the ways the phrase may be expressed. This allows for all different outcomes to occur while preserving the essential details we need to surface in our search results. Think of asterisks as interchangeable place-holders in-between the essential keywords that qualify the query.

Another use of wildcards is to factor in numerous propositions and pronoun combinations. Again, whether the term is "in" or "within" is meaningless. What matters is we capture the unique terms that *must appear* and are anchored within a phrase by interchangeable terms. We see this in applying two placeholders to generate the many wordplays on the notorious Bernard Madoff:

> "Madoff ** money""

Within this expression, we can capture: "Madoff with the money" or "Madoff took the money" or "Madoff with your money." Each variation works within the search operation. We can also use wildcards to invert the order in which the terms appear. Once again, it's not the ordering of terms that matters. It's their presence within a subject clause and predicate that counts:

> "Ponzi * (is | was) ** Madoff" | "Madoff (is | was) * ponzi"

Inverting the two terms means we can capture the same intention whether *Ponzi* or *Madoff* is serving as the subject or object of the command statement, (a.k.a. query).

Defining Senior Moments

Another saving grace for wildcards is to use them as word substitutes for half-forgotten phrases. This came up recently when I wanted to google a former colleague and could only recollect that he lived in...

"[S]omething Mountain, Georgia."

This can be expressed simply as:

> * Mountain GA"

The answer came back free of embarrassment or confusion:

> "Stone Mountain, GA"

Even when our recollections are not blurred, the placeholder role of wildcards can pay-off when we're trying to track or tally numbers of organizations by location. Let's try this: We're interested in well-resourced non-profits that focus on the environment at the Federal level:

> "* Foundation" environmental 703

In this example, 703 is the area code of Alexandria, VA, home to most of trade and advocacy groups that lobby the U.S. Congress.

Finally, placeholders can fill-in the specifics on a fact-related query posed to a natural language search engine:

> "There are * types of hawks"

If we're looking for an exact number we can negate the guesswork by eliminating an approximation:

> "There are * types of hawks" -many

> **Definition: Wildcards**
>
> *The asterisk or wildcard is a search operator that acts as a placeholder for commonly used words such as articles (a, the, an) as well as prepositions (for, of, in) and upholds the keyword matches in common phrases despite their variations in form.*

There are limits to where we can play wildcards. For instance, we can't mix wildcards and exact match phrases (also known as *verbatims*). Search engines will not understand the request *restaurant** to mean any variant on the dining experience. *More on that in* **Unit Six**. One substitute we can try is to use the tilde (~). This expresses the same request as *~restaurant* and yields both synonyms and variants. However this surrenders all control to Google in defining a set of related restaurant terms. In my experience, Google is more useful for being *queried* than *questioned*.

Term Expansion

Term expansion means asking the search engine to think outside the search box. In effect, we're asking for more than a literal keyword match. We're interested in them more as concepts than exact matches. For instance, we may express our interest in time and dates with the word 'events.' But we're just as okay with 'calendar' or 'schedule' to express the same idea. The 'tilde' or *squiggly* is a term expansion tool that includes word variants and synonyms with our keyword. For example:

surgery	→ surgical; removal
treatment	→ treating; cure

The other factor here is that many common search engines, including Google, limit the number of search terms that will be processed per query. Thus the tilde is a handy tool for economizing on the number of keywords without sacrificing the relevant terms germane to your search.

Wildcards and term expanders are especially important because search terms are more powerful as phrases than as separate terms. Just as scientists are watchful of false positives in their lab experiments, the Knowledge-ABLED researcher must weed out the equivalent in search investigations. That's the random chance of a keyword match without regard for proximity, prominence, or relatedness.

The more terms which appear together in a particular order, the more precise our search results. The problems with phrases is that they are often inflexible and don't allow for reversible ordering of the same terms. For example, including *prostate* as the object or subject of a 'surgery' or 'treatment' ensures that the search engine indexes both instances.

Over-expansion

It's important not to overdo our reliance on term expansion. Be careful when applying it to words with multiple meanings because it will actually create more confusion than clarity. Expressing the term *~report*, for instance, may be designed to call up 'reports' and 'studies' along with important 'papers.' However, Google may read too far into our intentions by also delivering 'reporters,' 'reportings,' and even 'sightings.'

A more helpful way to invoke term expansion is to limit it to terms with many word variants and few, if any, other meanings. *~Controversy* will yield 'controversies' and 'controversial' as well as 'trouble' but at least the results are a suitable match for our intentions.

Wikipedia is a great information pond to fish in for synonymous and relatable terms. Considering lake-sized resources like the Open Source Directory will give the directory classification for finding like terms. There's the overlooked utility of the Google 'define' feature that helps to broaden or narrow a search term based on referencing its definition as we'll see in Section 2.3. Surfwax is another excellent tool that both broadens and narrows search scopes.

Unfamiliar Territories

Term expansion is your rescue mission. It is your Saint Bernard. It is your fearless companion that will run to your aid every time your search expedition ends up lost in the woods. There is no flashlight, firewood, or even breadcrumbs. Term expansion is about making lemonade from those proverbial lemons: "If at first you don't succeed, try shortstop." You will call upon your trusty term expansion friends when you hit a wall. In the search trade that's called *zero hits* or just plain failure. We may get no answer for an answer on our first pass of search results. With term expansion, we can still be reasonably certain there is an answer out there.

Patience is advised when it comes to identifying people. My P.I. students want to nail the perpetrator and focus on the name of one person to the exclusion of their public identity and social affiliations. My input? Resist this temptation!

Don't go all out for one person. Include the groups they would join. Widen the focus to their family, neighborhood, colleagues, and personal networks. That's how we find the folks they hang with. Not only do people know people but they also tend to connect in more meaningful ways than a database or Facebook page could ever reveal. There is no pre-packaged dossier we can buy over the web with a credit card that adds the level of authenticity and completeness we can build through direct networking.

Putting It All Together

Below we demonstrate the wildcard operator (*) and the term expansion tool (~) within a nesting or parenthetical expression:

> "(cancer OR ~surgery OR ~treatment) * prostate" OR "prostate (cancer OR ~surgery OR ~treatment)" -malpractice

I know. It's a mouthful. Let's break it down in the following seven-step refinement sequence. The hit counts on the right illustrate how Boolean operators can zero-in on our search targets:

FIGURE 2.3: Winnowing Down With Search Operators

Search command	Search intent	Hit Counts	Count Reduction
cancer	The 'kitchen sink' (no qualifying search operators)	240,000,000	—-
cancer treatment	Implicit "AND" between "cancer" and "treatment"	30,400,000	87.33%
"cancer (treatment OR surgery)"	Combination of "OR" and "AND" so that search understands "cancer treatment" OR "cancer surgery" (also known as *word algebra*)	18,600,000	93.25%
"cancer treatment"	Quotations protect the precise match of the word choice and ordering (apply to phrases, including people searches that pair first and surnames)	17,700,000	93.63%
"cancer (treatment OR surgery)" ~alternative	Introduction of term expansion: "alternative" to include variants and synonyms	5,150,000	97.86%
"cancer treatment OR surgery " ~alternative -litigation	Introduction of negation command: no mentions of "malpractice"	5,140,000	97.86%
~ alternative "cancer (treatment OR surgery)" – litigation ~scam	Inclusion of both "malpractice" AND "litigation" as required terms AND addition of "scam" and all affiliated variants and meanings	3,060	99.99%

BOOLEAN OPERATORS

Boolean operators stand out as the most common reference point for using search statements to produce meaningful outcomes. They are the traffic signals on the superhighway of Internet searches. AND, OR, and NOT are the green, red, and yellow of signaling the appropriate actions to take for processing queries. These three critical traffic signals or search commands produce the following outputs:

FIGURE 2.4: Boolean Search Outcomes

Operator	Symbol	Relationship	Meaning
AND	+	exclusive implicit	every term is present
OR	OR	inclusive implicit	any term is present
NOT	–	exclusive explicit	single term must not appear
AND / OR	"(VVV OR WWW) AND (YYY OR ZZZ)"	Inclusive explicit	one or more terms can combine with one or more others

When to use AND

The AND statement is a given. It will assume the AND operator between each text-string if we don't instruct the search engine on what to do with our words and phrases. This means that unless you tell it otherwise, a white space between any words or numbers in our query will be treated as a necessary piece of our question. It must be present in each result returned to us.

When to use OR

The OR statement keeps two or more options open for us as we juggle the possibilities of what our search will yield. It could be this OR that. Remember to keep your OR statements capitalized or Google will mistake your operator for a noise word and ignore it completely.

When to use them together

Interestingly, the best use of AND / OR is not when they operate to the other's exclusion but together in a complementary way. Remember your high school algebra? You've done your best not to? I understand. But the same concept of cross multipliers works in Boolean logic too. We call this practice 'Word Algebra.' For example, let's say you're interested in concepts more than exact phrases where a few of the keywords are interchangeable. We could express our interest in drafting a marketing plan for our fledgling business:

> "(business OR marketing) (plan OR plans OR planning)" nonprofits

That way, we are leaving open the possibility of business or market plans or planning – any of these outcomes is valid. That's how we're combining the otherwise opposing forces of AND / OR in a precise and expansive way. We will be returning to word algebra in later examples.

When to use negation

The NOT or negation symbol is the bluntest of filters. It removes all instances of the term that precedes it, regardless of its meaning, or how meaningful the term is in the instance cited.

The negation operator excludes false positives, sometimes at the expense of useful search results. A false positive is an irrelevant term that's dragged into our search results because of an unrelated association. For example, if we're interested in birds but not places named after them, we might try this:

> *canary –islands*

Yes, we've eliminated the Canary Islands. But at what cost to our investigation? What if we're interested in the canaries that migrate to the Canary Islands. And we can't care less about the shopping and the windsurfing?

Perhaps the birdwatcher in us will reach out to canaries instead. If it's too early in our search to offer specifics, let's consider the plural form. We can skillfully remove most of the sports connotations if we're interested in *dolphins* as-in the *mammals* and not the football team:

> *Dolphins –football –players –game –coach*

How about negating words like season? How about team? It's your call but words that carry multiple meanings carry a high rate of ambiguity. They can easily cut both ways when it comes to eliminating them from your query with the negation operator.

Here's another point worth mentioning: We cannot negate phrases but only one term at a time. For instance, in the following example...

> *Dolphins –"national football league"*

The minus sign only removes the first word –'national.' 'Football' and 'league' escape scot-free. Another common misconception is that upper and lower case letters matter to search engines. Most are case insensitive. Just because the football team is capitalized and the animal is not, means nothing to search engines. Case sensitivity requires that we place the term in quotes. Even if it's a single word.

> **TIP:**
> *We can use the negation operator (-) with the site command to eliminate shopping sites from our searches. For example, we can request no merchandise appears from certain high traffic commercial sites in your search results like this: -site:amazon OR -site:barnes*

One terrific use of negation is to rid our results of those supplied by a first party. First parties are the organizations whose interests are served by ranking highest, regardless of our intentionality. As we'll see in the Source Conjugation section of **Unit Four**, eliminating specific messengers is an effective tool for safeguarding the credibility of our findings. This is particularly useful when an organization acts in its own best interest, ahead of: (1) the abstraction of the greater good, or (2) our own tangible interests!

In the following example, an information technology manager works with a software product developed by Microsoft called "SharePoint." However, past experience with Microsoft has taught the manager that this software vendor is not the best source for developing solutions around his current predicament:

> *intitle:Sharepoint ~problem "how to" OR ~fix -inurl:Microsoft*

Here the minus sign is used to steer clear of any problem-solving advice dispensed by the product owner. The information provider's own expertise and priorities are engaged in selling – not necessarily in supporting what they sell. We will revisit this use of negation when we address the practice of link analysis as a quality control for assessing provider motives.

Negation is a great way to reduce the marketing noise in our searches. For instance, I tried "how to stitch" -sew and had no associated advertising trail me to the search results page.[1] Then I tried it without the negation and received *Online Sewing Classes* as a sponsored link.

Search operators in action

Now let's put these new understandings about Boolean operators to work in the example we introduced earlier in [Figure 2.3: Winnowing Down with Search Operators]. First, let's step back and look at the entire search statement:

> 1) cancer
> 2) cancer treatment
> 3) "cancer treatment"
> 4) "cancer (treatment OR surgery)"
> 5) "cancer (treatment OR surgery)" ~alternative
> 6) "cancer treatment OR surgery " ~alternative -litigation
> 7) "cancer treatment OR surgery " ~alternative -litigation ~scam

The quotation marks enforce the word pattern within their boundaries. The parenthesis holds two sets of word combinations for which any two words can form a search term, (i.e. 'cancer treatment' or 'cancer surgery').

The OR statement keeps two or more options open for you as you juggle the possible search results. It could be this OR that. Remember to keep your OR statements capitalized. Most search engines will ignore it as a noise word. The parentheses have no effect on the search results. They are a visual aid – a prompt to remind us of the algebraic possibilities in using AND / OR together.

The tilde is a term expansion device. It connects a single term to other synonyms and variants. Notice that a second instance appears in the last statement because we don't want to be sold surefire cancer cure-alls, snake oil, or both.

Finally, the minus sign is intended to eliminate any mention of the term that precedes it. Let's close those doors before they open. If we're more interested in a medical cure than in the legal entanglements of doctors, we put any talk of malpractice suits to rest with one keyboard symbol: [-litigation].

Overcoming False Positives

As we saw before, when we tried to chase down of dolphins and canaries, false positives happen frequently to you and me. They are keyword matches with the wrong meaning. We are prone to false positives whenever our keywords are capable of ambiguous outcomes.

Searching Out Loud: Giving Voice to Independent Investigations | Marc Solomon

For instance, we enter the words...

> bank California flood

This combination produces many more disconnections than related terms and outcomes, including...

> *"Bank of California floods mailboxes with checking account offers"*
>
> *"Banks of California River breached in flood."*

The best way to avoid ambiguities like these is to include...

- Phrases in quotes
- Multiple terms, and
- Unique identifiers

SYNTAX

The next element of query formation is syntax. Syntax is a simple and powerful way to reduce the noise and increase the signal in your search results. Think of syntax as a way of telling the search engine it doesn't have to race to the moon and back, trying to find all matches that might matter. Instead it can relax and just focus on a selective slice of its index. We forget this because the search results appear so quickly regardless of whether we're selective or not. We'll remember syntax though when our refinement spells the difference between slogging through the muck of meaningless links and working them to a manageable number.

Curiously, order is not usually a factor when including syntax and operators. It only becomes an issue when we're sequencing a particular phrase or compound phrase. We saw this exhibited in [When to use AND/OR together] when introducing *Word Algebra*:

> *"(VP OR president OR c*o OR director OR chief) * (hired OR selected OR announced OR named OR fired)*

In this example, any combination of job description is teamed with a consequential action associated with senior management.

> *TIP:*
>
> *Notice in the above example that "VP" is capitalized along with the "OR" operator. In practice the only characters that are case-sensitive are the operators (AND, OR, and NOT). None of the search terms themselves are case sensitive, even when they are contained in quotes.*

Syntactical Operators

Syntax will help us focus on getting fewer and better results from your search. Although the syntax and operators we review are specific to Google, we will find that this syntax is transferable to many of the search engines we'll cover in this unit.

What follows are some common examples of effective syntaxes and when to call on them.

Inurl:

What

Inurl restricts your search terms to the Internet address in question. Inurl presents a wider outcome than the more restrictive site: or intitle: commands as URLs can be much longer in nature than the simple root directory or server hosting a particular page.

When

The inurl: syntax is especially useful for including a whole range of outcomes within a web address that may hold the key to searching in a lake or subject directory. It works best with other syntax limiting thematic searches in commonly used strings like *dir* for directory or *lib* for library.

How

> inurl:about

This includes single search term that must appear in site address.

Why

The inurl: syntax is useful for including a whole range of outcomes within a web address that may hold the key to searching in a lake or subject directory. Inurl: works best with other syntax limiting thematic searches in commonly used strings like *dir* or directory or *lib* for library.

The syntax inurl helps to dramatically reduce our hit counts to a manageable number. We refer to this query formation method as *getting from an ocean to a pond* through the use of multiple inclusive OR operators. This approximates the way that key web resources are described:

> *inurl:directory OR inurl:lib OR inurl:library OR inurl:index OR inurl:database*

> **TIP:**
> *Consider other jargon-specific shorthand for words that categorize the bodies of knowledge containing our topics. Also, we're not limited to our own vocabularies. When creating inurl syntax, let's be on the lookout for popular slang or shorthand to describe commonly requested reference information: www.acronymfinder.com | www.webopedia.com | whatis.techtarget.com | www.netlingo.com. We can combine fragments of terms like pedia, lingo, acronym, whatis, finder, intro, FAQ, or beginner and include them in a long OR statement.*

Allinurl:

What

Similarly, if one has to query for more than one word in the URL or address of a web pages, then allinurl: can be used. It replaces inurl: to get the list of pages containing all those words in its web address.

When

For example, using inurl:tech inurl:support is the same as querying allinurl:tech support...

> *inurl:tech inurl:support*
> *allinurl:tech support*

On the other hand, the syntax allinurl: retrieves only pages containing the term *tech* in the url and the word *support* anywhere on the page. While the first several URL results may include *support*, we will fail to exclude all its appearances regardless of where it's being used. Also note this is a verbatim response, meaning exact matches only, i.e. *technical* and *support* will not be returned.

How

> *allinurl:tech support*

Allinurl includes all query terms in site address – no other syntax can be used.

The allinurl: syntax retrieves only pages containing the terms tech and support. This is a verbatim response, meaning exact matches only, i.e. *technology* and *assistance* will not be returned.

Why

Allinurl validates all search strings and should be invoked only with a high degree of confidence that all terms are both present and prominent to the page in question.

Allinanchor:

What

An anchor is known to web designers and software programmers as the point or origin or arrival for the connections they create between websites, pages, and cross-references within the same document.

When

An anchor is a tag for marking either the source or destination of a hyperlink. They are frequently the most effective syntactical filters since hyperlinks contain explicit coding language. Inanchor: describes why and where the user is being taken from one web page to the next.

How

Here's some advice that search engine analyst Mark Sprague shares with copy editors and site designers:

> *"The phrases 'click here,' 'learn more,' 'sign up,' 'contact us,' and 'about' appear on every website on the planet. I know what it means, you know, but the search engine assigns no relevancy value to this text. Sometimes real estate constraints dictate that you use these as is, but if you have some flexibility, try to place some context around these labels. For example:*

> "Click here for Product X demo"
> "Learn more about QR Codes"
> "Sign up for a free Newsletter"? [2]

Why

Why is this relevant for researchers?

The same strategy Mr. Sprague is suggesting for advertisers can be tapped by researchers. His 'click here' approach helps us focus on specific images or calls to action with the allinanchor syntax:

> *allinanchor:investigation crime degree program*

It includes all query terms as tags that describe the sending or receiving of hyperlinks embedded in web pages. No other syntax can be used.

The allinanchor: syntax retrieves only pages containing all the terms: 'Investigation,' 'crime,' 'degree,' and 'program.' This is an effective way to capture the language that web marketers use to suggest we click on the links they create. That means the coder must be clear about the destination they're leading us to (and the resulting benefit) if they want to refer us to an agreeable place.

Here's a second example of anchors that come to terms with an emerging sustainable tourism business segment in the travel industry:

> *"(social OR socially)(responsible OR responsibility)" (inanchor:ecotravel OR inanchor:ecotourism) (inurl:dir OR inurl:directory OR inurl:list)*

It's not anything definitive. That's not the goal when we're just trying to make sense of a fledgling or nascent market like this one.

Site:

What

Site is the top level domain. That means no matter how long or convoluted the URL becomes, it still upholds the root directory or site it originates from:

> *site:edu (publications OR newsletters)*

This restricts to all academic sites with the terms 'publication' or 'newsletters' on their pages.

Why

The site: syntax restricts Google to query for certain keywords in a particular site or domain. For example: detectives site:pimagazine.com (without quotes) will look for the keyword 'detectives' in those pages present in all the links of the domain 'pimagazine.com.' There should not be any space between 'site:' and the domain name.

Define:

What

Define is a simple way to do word look-ups or generate a definition for a term in question. But remember, we're limited to one word at a time. There is no 'alldefine: syntax' for multiple terms. One way around this is to skip the define: syntax altogether and simply express the phrase with the expression '[blank] means.'

> *define:taxonomy*

This summons definitions contained in leading dictionary and glossary sources to offer multiple meaning and connotations of the word or phrases in question.

Why

The Define: syntax fetches a dictionary listing to define your search term. "Subject taxonomy means" OR "subject taxonomy stands for" retrieves pages that match your phrase. In effect, we're dispensing with syntax to achieve the same goal.

Intitle:

What

The intitle: syntax helps Google restrict the search results to pages containing that word in the title:

> *intitle: login password (without quotes)*

Intitle: will return links to those pages that has the word 'login' in their title, and the word 'password' anywhere in the page.

> *intitle:login (password OR passwd)*

The syntax intitle:login returns pages with login in the title (or header) of the page and the term password or 'passwd' contained on the same pages.

> *intitle:login (password OR passwd)*

This restricts key word mentions to the title field of an indexed web page to insure a more prominent role or meaning for the term in question.

Why

The intitle: syntax filters out all mentions of the keyword accept when it's featured in the title of the topic or article it's addressing. This is usually not a substitute for a byline when invoking an author field to screen for subject experts and journalists.

Allintitle:

What

Similarly, 'allintitle:' can be used instead of 'intitle' if one has to query for more than one word in the page header or article title:

> *allintitle:login password*

For example, using allintitle is same as querying...

> *intitle:login intitle:password*
>
> *allintitle:login password*

This includes all key terms in the title field of an indexed web page. It excludes the use of any other syntax and inclusionary OR operator.

Why

The allintitle: syntax filters out all mentions of key terms accept when they're applied together within the title of the topic or article they're describing. Using this and any 'all' syntax nullifies the use of additional filters and operators. The exclusionary 'AND' operator is implied for every term used in an 'ALL' filter.

Cache:

What

The cache: syntax that once displayed the version of the web page that the search engine has *cached* or indexed.

> *cache:hp.com*

The cache syntax view has been discontinued. The cache result can still be accessed in Google or Bing by clicking the green down arrow to the right of the site's URL. Why does this matter? The search engine is referencing its own index when it processes our query – not the current HP ("Hewlett-Packard") site.

Additionally, the query cache:hp will list every web page within the Google index that includes the term 'hp' in the address of that webpage (just like the inurl syntax). If we include other words in the query, Google will highlight those words within the cached document.

> *cache:mit.edu alumni*

For example, cache:mit.edu alumni will show the cached content with the word 'alumni' highlighted. Cache retrieves fully indexed record or pages cached in the search engine's index along with your search terms highlighted. The highlighting is not typically included unless cache records are requested.

Why

The cache: syntax displays the most recent version of the site root or web page we're referencing. If we don't specify the root or page, the search engine will return a list of all sites indexed that contain the query term. Including the site root, web page, and any additional terms will produce the latest version of that record with the additional terms highlighted in the cached record.

The cache: syntax is also helpful to researchers that need to recover pages since taken offline by their publishers. A cached record highlights our key terms on the page we're referencing. This is also instructive for understanding where are terms are appearing or *why we get what we got.*

Related:

What

The *related:* syntax will list web pages that are similar to a specified web page:

> related:bittman

For instance, related:bittman will show pages related to food writer Mark Bittman, and a range of topics reflected in the body of his work.

Note that using related: with specific sites it is necessary to express the entire link – not just a fragment. That means specifying the URL of the exact article, or at least including the domain name. Invoking a popular website without specifying the particular page is useless.

> related:nytimes

For example, related:nytimes fetches millions of useless hits while [related:nytimes.com] returns a handful of media organizations within the New York Times industry or peer group.

> related:www.nytimes.com/2008/01/27/weekinreview/27bittman.html

This includes either full web address (URL) or domain name to list other references with either a common theme or content grouping such as a common industry or subject interest.

Why

The *related:* syntax correlates specific domain names and/or articles to other similar information sources. *Related:* must be used in conjunction with the correct article address or site root such as nytimes.com to be effective.

Link:

What

The link: syntax will list web pages that have links to the specified web page.

> link:www.theparisreview.org

Link:www.theparisreview.org will list web pages that have links pointing to the Paris Review website homepage.

Note that this functionality is severely constrained in Google. We cannot combine a link: search with a regular keyword. Because of its AdSense advertising service, Google tries to discourage the use of SEO methods that could distort their search results (gaming their system) to inflate the number of links and thus a higher ranking.

Why

The *link:* syntax generates a list of all sites that anchor or connect to the web page or site domain in question. The usefulness of this filtering method is limited on Google due to Google's popularity and the efforts of information providers and resellers to boost the rankings of their web properties.

One effective work-around is to use a rival like Bing to understand both the referring links and the types of key terms that all referring sites hold in common.

Site:

What

Site is the top level domain. That means no matter how long or convoluted the URL becomes, it still upholds the root directory or site it originates from. The site: syntax restricts Google to query for certain keywords in a particular site:

> detectives site:pimagazine.com

Site: will look for the keyword 'detectives' in those pages present in all the links of the domain 'pimagazine.com.' There should not be any space between 'site:' and the domain name.

> site:edu (publications OR newsletters)

Site:edu restricts to all academic sites with the terms 'publication' or 'newsletters' on their pages.

> site:pimagazine.com detectives

This includes all mentions indexed by the search tool of the term 'detectives' on pages that share the same site domain.

Why

The *site:* syntax tells you how often our search targets are mentioned by the information source that's mentioning them. It can be used more broadly to include all sites that share a common domain name like *.gov, .org,* or *.mil* for military. This is helpful for generating lists of related sources that cover germane topics or deliver information in a prescribed format such as a map or subject directory or newsletter.

Define:

What

Define is a simple way to do word look-ups or generate a definition for a term in question. But remember, we're limited to one word at a time. There is no alldefine: syntax for multiple terms. One way around this is to skip the Define: syntax altogether and simply invoke the "[word] means" in the query:

> "head injury means"
> define:taxonomy

Put another way define:taxonomy fetches a dictionary listing to define our search term:

> "subject taxonomy means" OR "subject taxonomy stands for"

Define: retrieves pages that match our phrase, in effect dispensing with syntax to achieve the same goal...

> define:taxonomy

The define: syntax fetches a series of dictionary, Wikipedia, and glossary references that define our keywords, and sometimes term phrases that extend across multiple connotations.

Why

The Define: syntax is a word lookup tool that gives us some working definitions for the term in question. It is more likely that all but the most unique terms will result in competing, often unrelated definitions of the same word.

Intext:

What

The intext: syntax searches for keywords. It ignores links or URLs and page titles.

> intext:exploits intext:ransomware intext:preparedness

For example, intext:exploits will return only links to those web pages that has the search keyword 'exploits,' 'ransomware,' and 'preparedness' in its web page. The term is used in the content or body of the page – not as part of the coding or administration of the site itself.

Why

We need intext to make sure that our search terms appear in the context of our research. For example, if we were to search the term 'HTML' without syntax, your query would pick up all hidden or otherwise computer-to-computer processing and presenting of HTML-based web pages.

> *html*

On the other hand, intext:html will return pages that actually discuss the use or presence of the HTML programming language with a human reader or user in mind – a big difference!

> *intext:html*

Intext: retrieves words that appear in the body text of web pages rather than in metadata fields or as extraneous terms in the headers footers, and advertisements placed on the page. The intext: syntax limits key terms to text-based references.

Filetype:

What

The filetype: syntax restricts Google search for files on Internet with particular extensions such as '.doc,' '.pdf' or '.ppt.' Filetype is helpful when we can anticipate the format of the content we're looking for. Looking for a statistic instead of a street address? For spreadsheets, we might consider...

> *(filetype:xls OR filetype:xlsx) (chart OR graph) texas counties crime*
> *filetype:doc site:gov confidential*

This returns all Microsoft Word documents on a server registered to a government entity on pages where the term 'confidential' appears. The filetype: syntax restricts our searches to formats used in common software applications like spreadsheets, presentations, and word processing documents.

What about files that are saved to a different file format?

We can combine keywords with the format we expect to find them in. In fact, the filetype command gives more power to your keywords by ensuring the format – if not the context – they are used in.

> *"landscape architecture" filetype:pdf*

For instance, landscape architecture filetype:pdf returns all PDF documents containing the phrase "landscape architecture" within Google's index.

Why

What if we want to turn up something of a sensitive or classified nature?

> *filetype:doc site:gov confidential*

The statement filetype:doc site:gov confidential will look for files with the '.doc' or '.docx' extension in all government domains – that's the '.gov' extension. Finally, they must also contain the term 'confidential' either in the pages or in the '.doc' file. In other words, the result will contain the links to all confidential Microsoft Word document files on indexed government sites.

We can also mix filetype with other syntaxes. If we want examples of organizational charts presented in Microsoft Excel on an academic server, the example would be...

> *intitle:gantt filetype:xls site:edu*

Phonebook:

What

The phonebook: option was discontinued by Google in November 2010 for unspecified reasons. Most likely, it raised privacy concerns at a more sensitized time in the evolution of personal identity. It once shifted the part of the Google index we were searching in from the Google Web search to a specialized search in phone directories only:

> *phonebook:Lisa CA*

For instance, phonebook:Lisa CA listed all phone numbers registered to persons with 'Lisa' in their names and located in 'California (CA).' This was helpful when we are trying to narrow down our target range with partial names. Perhaps we knew the area of a state the person lives in but not the town? One could approximate by sprinkling a few area codes that cover the region of the state where they reside.

> *phonebook:mary hopkins ca 213 OR 310*

Phonebook: restricted all contact listings of surnames used together with first initials and first names along with two letter state abbreviation and area code. The results may have included local exchanges instead of area codes if the state code is not included.

As a substitute, we can also dispense with this command altogether and combine other syntax with selective keywords such as...

> *inurl:phonebook OR "phone book" site:Harvard.edu –mgh*

Why

Using the web as a phone directory for individuals can be perplexing and resistant to simple unaided searches.

When looking for organizations or institutional contacts, sometimes it makes sense to focus on what the group publishes on its website rather than in any phonebook. The query above involves the inurl: syntax or "phone book" as a key phrase from Harvard University servers that don't include references to its medical school at Massachusetts General Hospital ('MGH').

Mixing Syntaxes

Combining two and more different syntaxes can be an efficient way to increase your signal-to-noise ratio on your search results, skipping from an ocean to a pond full of results in one painless step. One common mix is to include a combination of intitle:, inurl:, and site:

> *intitle:new inurl:lib site:edu*

This query fetches recently posted materials by libraries that slant academic (typically for colleges and higher education collections).

Here are combinations that work well together:

FIGURE 2.5: Productive Examples for Combining Syntaxes

Combination	Syntax	Purpose
Websites and page titles	inurl: and intitle:	Filters by prominent mentions of keywords along with category the page is grouped in
Page titles and site domains	intitle: and site:	Refines by prominent mentions of keywords and types of site that publish them
Websites and site domains	site: and inurl:	Groups by site types and their categorical listings

What doesn't work?

Sometimes a syntax that works in one search engine is called something else in another. Other times, it doesn't exist at all. Sometimes a syntax that works in one part of a search engine's content grouping or collection doesn't work in another part of its index. It can be frustrating. Certainly the amount of factors make it difficult to provide an accurate list of what works where and when without our checking in first with the specific tool and collection.

Here are several common limitations and some workarounds for getting where we need to be:

FIGURE 2.6: Overcoming Some Common Pitfalls of Syntax

Command / Objective	Limitation	Solution
Location – Trace events and information providers to specific geolocational origins	Confusion results from whether location refers to information provider or event being described	Use semantics that indicate centricity of target city such as ["* based"] or ["(located OR headquartered) in"]
The ALL option – Enforce a common filter for multiple search term s	All option eliminates use of keywords, multiple syntaxes, or selective and conditional OR statements	Limit ALL syntax to a large but fixed source – [allinurl:ibm pc support] will isolate all customer service pages published under IBM.com
Date ranges – Consider chronological sequence between events and when they were first published	Doubts persist on whether the date refers to actual events (such as presentation or publication date) versus when the materials are uploaded to a web server (such as the time stamp affixed to uploaded files)	Focus on RSS-enabled content sources like blogs, tweets, and most social media sources where the presentation and transaction date are one in the same
Link analysis – Find out the popularity and origin of target websites	Google obscures the number and source of referring links to protect their rankings formula	Work-around Google's secrecy by enlisting other large search indices for the same job

SECTION 2.2 | Semantics —
What are the Best Terms for Conducting Research?

Basically it all boils down to words – a few choice words.

We first focused on syntax in our introduction to Query Formation. Syntax is about how to reduce the noise in our searches by limiting the appearance of our terms to specific fields and search commands.

Once we know how to write an effective search command, it's time to address what we're commanding. Syntax is about arranging questions by applying the right codes and shortcuts. Semantics is about bringing out those parts of our research that we wish to emphasize. Semantics addresses how we express search statements in the terms we choose.

The most common form of semantics is to include a series of complementary terms that reinforce the associations we are trying to draw. The first example is an invitation into the structural complexities of immense multinational conglomerates. Not a bad strategy if we're getting lost on one of their many homepages.

Another common approach is to form positive IDs around multiple people with the same name. We validate those identities by including details of their environs and other contact details like employer, job title and other professional associations.

EXPRESSING OUR INTENT WITH SEMANTICS

What are the right word choices? How can our search statements tip the results in our favor?

First, try to force your words together as phrases by connecting them through parentheses. Use terms that have a limited and focused number of references, even if they are commonly used. For instance, the phrase "heavy at times" could in theory be used to describe a melodramatic play or a fork lift inside a warehouse. But it doesn't take a news junkie to know that the most popular reference centers on the intensity of precipitation in a weather forecast.

Verbatims

Another way to work with semantics is to leverage the common connotations of verbatim phrases such as those that appear in the fine legal print on the footers of pages. In their book Google Hacks, Rael Dornfest, Paul Bausch, and Tara Calishain offer up the verbatim phrase:

> "copyright * the new york times"[3]

Capturing the linguistic branding of popular news sources is a surefire way of finding references to those sources scattered on countless websites over time. If we throw in some syntax, we can isolate the news source from the source as story – references by others to its own reporting:

> site:nytimes.com -site:nyt.com "copyright * the new york times"

Proximities

Proximity is another way to apply semantics to search formation. It's a common refinement tool in paid subscription services like LexisNexis and Factiva but not in Google or Bing. The advantage of a proximity command is that we can name a range of words or a grammatical format like a paragraph.

Then we tell the search that these two terms should meet somewhere between the first and last sentence of that paragraph. Unlike with Google commands, two or more terms need not appear consecutively or as a parenthetical phrase.

Recurrences

Multiple mentions of our search target suggest the content we pull actually addresses our primary concern as a main topic, not a passing interest. Repeating our terms one or several times is an effective way to *weigh* the results in our favor. Especially when there are too many of them to consider.

For instance, what happens when we mention our term repeatedly instead of once? Investigation fetches different results than if we mention the same term to the maximum number Google permits. Semantics enable us to capture contributing sites that share our same obsession.

Reinforcers

Semantics demonstrate the need to forge commonalities by including multiple terms that reinforce the context and strengthen the relationship between our primary and secondary search targets. One effective use is to include a series of complementary terms that reinforce the associations we're trying to draw. Below, the term *Target* is literally a term when we're looking at the rivalries among leading retailers:

> *macy's target kohls tjmaxx ~competition inurl:finance.yahoo*

Events are another useful collection point for selecting word choices that serve to isolate specific occasions. An added bonus is to weigh the intensity or volume of coverage generated by perennial events from year-to-year or the participation or presence of select sponsors, participants, and/or groups that have a stake in the staging of such events:

> *Frequency + Venues + Campaigns*

Perhaps the connection is internal to the workings of a specific corporate target:

> *Organizations + Rivals + Partners + Subdivisions*

From a professional angle, turning people into productive search targets is a semantic exercise. One useful strategy is to map a potential range of job titles to a specific employer and/or skill or credential associated with the position in question. The case below includes both titles, companies, and the specific product we wish them to have in their job experience. The formula here is:

Phrases + Credentials + Titles that is translated as...

> *SharePoint "(knowledge OR project) (leader OR manager OR executive OR coordinator) (at OR from) Microsoft"*

This detailed expression contains several potentially relevant job titles and a preposition connecting them to the employer. Interesting how long-winded verbatims can dramatically cut down the number of hits!

Semantics in People Search

Another common strategy is to form positive IDs around multiple people with the same name by including details of their environs and other contact details like employer, job title and other professional associations. From a more personal angle, people as search targets can be most effectively identified by geographic proximity to their primary residence. Semantically, this means including a pool of possible zip and/or area codes within a broader regional context such as a town or city:

> *"Marc Solomon" (617 OR 978 OR 508 OR 781) Boston*

Keep in mind that the numeric codes don't guarantee the context they're used in. For instance, they may signify the clauses in a local regulation or times turned in at a local road race or charity event. Text-intensive web-pages are magnets for false positives. Especially when there are no filters to control the placement or context of irrelevant keywords.

Unique Identifiers

One productive use of search engines is to ask for things by name.

Remember how your mom always told you to ask broad questions when you talked to strangers for the first time? That was not a chapter from your mom book on etiquette? Here me out on this one...

Maybe they weren't interested in what we were? Maybe being too direct or specific would put the person on the spot, or worse, come across as little professor know-it-alls. Well, the invitation's back on the table to unleash our inner poindexter with our search interrogations. Cut to the chase. Blurt it out. Don't sweat the category or the history or the breeding. There are no bruised egos to handle – just our own frustrations:

- Don't ask about jets, ask about 757s.
- Don't search on interiors, insist on wall-coverings.
- Don't request low-cost hardware prices when you can search all retail locations where competing big box stores are engaging in a price war.

If we don't get right to the factual point, our search results will reflect the wishes of the marketers who purchase these search terms. It will bear little resemblance to our motives for asking.

Unique identifiers pack a strong semantic punch in helping to short circuit the pains taken to pin down the specific item we're trying to identify. In the example below, legal code is combined with information sources and electronic file formats to generate the required documentation in litigation support, for lawyers as well as laypersons.

Consider the classifications structures used in rulebooks or entries in a catalog. Each code, formula, and stock number functions as a keyhole into the particular item that solves our puzzles.

FIGURE 2.7: Some Common Unique IDs

- Date of birth
- Driver's license numbers
- Geo-specific locations and addresses
- Glossary terms
- Government programs
- Industry-specific jargon
- Passport numbers
- Peoples' names
- Social Security numbers
- Shipment tracking numbers

When Fussiness is Preferable to Fuzziness

The surefire way to nail our search prey is to think like a search engine. Basically this means identifying terms and expressions that can be codified into numbers or text strings that are exclusive to the domain we're searching. For instance, no one would ever assume that searching on the name of a famous person will limit our outcomes to biographically-based results, no matter how unique or big the name may be.

However, we are much likelier to filter out other individuals sharing the same name if we were to include a middle initial, job title, or birth date. Below are some other examples of some common identifiers that many search engines warm to immediately for their specific connection to some common stores of knowledge such as flight schedules, trading indexes, or stock inventories:

FIGURE 2.8: Applying Unique IDs to Familiar Situations

UNIQUE ID	CONTEXT
Ticker symbols	Corporate financials
Birth dates	Biographies
Phone numbers	Personal addresses
Zip Codes	Realty listings
Product models	Performance reviews

Pointers

We see how unique IDs are a short-cut method designed to expedite our searches. A pointer is another discerning tool that serves the same purpose. Pointers are exclusive terms that match the task to the semantics. For instance, the word *about* in the context of a website is a pointer because it only leads to one place: An explanation of what the sponsoring organization stands for. As a keyword, 'about' remains a preposition with too many uses to enforce the exclusivity needed for a sufficient high confidence level.

Instead of codes and numbers, pointers are unique identifiers in the form of words and phrases. Unlike most wording they are resistant to multiple meanings and interpretations. What makes a phrase a pointer? It can only mean the thing we intend it to mean. Pointers can also act as cultivators of like expressions or comparable items.

For example, we can invoke the phrase: "compared to *" to summon up similar items:

> *Organizations + Rivals + Partners + Subdivisions*

Additionally, terms like *varieties* or *kinds* or *types* are ways to close the open-end of the fact base in question:

> "There are * kinds of handguns"

These are all isolated examples of common pointers that are evident in the site maps and web addresses (a.k.a. URLs) that are entry points for many common search targets:

FIGURE 2.9: Some Common Pointers

Phrases	Keywords
"about us"	Digest
"bill of materials"	Directory
"community sites"	FAQS
"how to"	Links
"index of"	List
"last modified"	Problem
"official"	Resources
"process flow"	Support
"specialty directories"	Thread
"top sites"	Troubleshooting
"what's new"	Compatibility
"site index"	Glossary

FIGURE 2.10: Reinforcers for Common Search Targets

Target	Query	Example
Organizations	Rivals + Partners + Subdivisions	Samsung Apple HTC
Events	Frequency + Venues + Campaigns	Olympics 2020 Tokyo NBC
People	Phrases + Credentials + Titles	VP OR "head of" OR President OR CEO "time with * family"
Codes and formulas	Standards + Laws + Requirements	emissions "state of California" filetype:pdf

FIGURE 2.11: Seeking Specifics

Task / Problem	Resolution Method
Need to pin down a fact or two	Unique IDs and pointers
Confirming public awareness levels ranging from social issues to specific case-related details	Hit count analysis
Short list of pre-determined ranking criteria (most, best, least, cheapest, safest...)	Syntax combined with link analysis
Tracking movements for key search targets	Set-up RSS reader for routing and filtering changes to web pages, event status, etc.

FIGURE 2.12: Exploring Generalities

Task / Problem	Resolution Method
Most current information on a familiar subject	Set-up RSS reader for routing and filtering topical news
Unusual or unfamiliar subjects	Use a subject directory hosted by humans
Foremost authorities on said topic	Include link analysis to measure influence and literature search to assess publication history and track record as a 3rd party opinion-maker
Doing exhaustive research	Include multiple sources and points of view – particularly those that don't agree – more than one kind of engine and directory for these please

Relevance

Relevance is the secret sauce of most commercial search engines because relevance determines the natural pecking order in the Internet keyword animal kingdom: Who ranks highest in a set of returning search results. The reason for the secrecy is simple. Should word ever leak about how relevancy is determined, then all those coveted positions would be skewed by artificially inflated word counts, embedded links and hidden meta tags. This would call the search results into question.

This would also displace an increasingly important revenue stream for search engines. These are the placement fees they can charge advertisers to appear alongside the *most relevant* search results. *We'll discuss search engine optimization as a research tool in* **Unit Three**. In the pre dial-up days, relevance was loosely defined as a combination of...

- Adjacency (the ordering or sequence of search terms),
- Proximity (how closely they appeared together),
- Prominence (how close to the top or beginning of a record or article they appear), and
- Recurrences (how frequently they appear).

Individual Words

Before Google, most search engines supported stemming. This means that variations on a root word would be included as part of the search term. For instance, the term controvers* would stem to include controversy, controversies, controversial, etc. but would not include any variants existing before the asterisk such as controvertible. Google takes the word form we use literally at your word. 'Apple' does not scale to *apples*. 'Talk' will not apply to *talking*.

Repetition

Multiple mentions of our search target suggest that the content we pull actually addresses our main topic, not a passing interest. Repeating our terms several times is a surefire way to *weigh* the results in our favor. Especially when there are too many for human consideration.

Verbatims

Verbatims are exact mentions of your keyword requests. That means what it means. Plurals are not substituted for singular expressions. All word choices are strictly interpreted by the search engine. The tool for applying verbatims is quotation marks. Any keywords placed within quotes are treated as verbatim expressions, including the order they're expressed.

Verbatims are excellent tools for preserving terms that may be otherwise indecipherable but important to act on. For example, we can extract a line from a suspicious email and append the term 'virus' to your search. The outcome may well lead to hoax and scam-related sites that instruct you on what to do, should such a message be opened on your computer.

> *TIP:*
>
> *Verbatims are an effective way to override the search engine when we need to include noise words that are otherwise excluded in your search results. For example if we're looking for musical group 'the Who' rather than the term 'Who,' we really need to embrace verbatims as the tool for enforcing your intentions. This rule also applies to other more common phrases: Namely any person's first and surnames when mentioned together as a phrase.*

Proximity

Proximity is a refinement tool that is available from paid subscription services like LexisNexis and Factiva but not commonly provided on most public search sites. Proximity commands declare a range of words or grammatical conventions, say a paragraph, in which to connect two terms that may not appear consecutively or as a parenthetical phrase.

Actions and Outcomes

Remember that grammar school teacher in the back of our heads that tells us not to name the same thing the exact name more than once in the same paragraph? Well the same whip is cracked when we say a sentence out loud where the subject does not agree with the predicate. Search engines are not burdened by bad grammar.

The problem is that they crank out search results where there's often little or no connection between...

- Our search targets (actors), and what they do (actions),
- Who they're doing it to, teaming with, or what they're achieving (outcomes).

Quite simply, the most common gap between how search works and how we wish it could comes from the technology's inability to make semantic sense of keywords. For instance, a complex search on Gigablast (drug abuse among ADHD) resulted in emphasizing drugs that address the diagnosis than the misdirected use of medication by those diagnosed with ADHD. A subtle distinction for the itinerant user. But perhaps, not a trivial distinction for someone on these medications.

The inability of search engines to understand context is just another way of saying that humans have not taught machines how to master particles of speech. The only way to guarantee subjects and predicates is to entrust them within the safety of quotation marks. Even then, a stray comma or period can make this a dicey proposition.

I tell my students to reserve the power of verbatims while tossing in an asterisk or two. This allows for context and the likelihood of some minor variations within a phrase. Especially indefinite articles, and pronouns. These are common words that are not important to the context. Here's one example:

"(drug OR substance) (overdose OR abuse)" OR "(overdose OR overdosing OR overdosed) ** (meds OR medication)" "(prescribed OR ordered OR written) by * (doctor OR physician OR doctors)"

The results are not always ... shall we say crisp and definitive? They don't always capture the intent of our search request but they do help generate related topics. They also help us to sidestep ads for treatment centers and books addressing the Opioid Crisis. But be prepared for inversions and reversals. The results are not respectful of our semantics: The ordering of nouns, verbs, and modifiers we want to describe the actions and outcomes we're pursuing.

Another way to look at the dilemma of actions and outcomes is through the absurd reversal of the tail wagging the dog. This confusion around cause and effect is so prevalent in search that we've long accepted this predicament as a fact of bogus search results. The idea that an actor is taking an action in the quest to:(1) achieve a goal or (2) avoid a risk is a basic tenet of any analytic foundation. Problem is, our befuddled, overmatched search engine can't decide whether 'conviction' is a desirable character trait or a guilty verdict in a jury trial.

SECTION 2.3 | Tool Selection —
What are the Different Search Tools Available to Us?

Now that we've learned about query formation, it's time to ply some of those practices through actual search engines. Additionally, now that we're introducing syntax, semantics, and pointers, we're also refocusing on how to read search results. The call-and-response nature of search informs our choices about where to search in the first place. Before we began **Unit Two**, Google was likely the default in your browser. It remains our *go-to* for settling many scores, including most prevalent word choices through the popularity of keywords. However, there are many case-based instances where our investigations are better served through other search engines.

DEPENDS ON THE QUESTION

For example, we'll require a date range option if we're searching the cause and effect of sequential events. If we're trying to capture the metadata that determines the indexing of your own website, then a search engine called Gigablast is more helpful to you than Google, Bing, or some once renowned portal now in demise.

Tool Tracking

How do I track of which tool to use?

Search features will come and source collections will go but the part that will only grow with education and practice is your own skill for determining writing good queries, reading the results, and, refining your strategy so that we reconcile what our clients *want* to know with our assessment of what they *need* to know. A growing sense of tool selection isn't limited to case work: Even passing interests and idle curiosities can turn into useful outcomes with the right search engine.

Tool Context

Which one is most appropriate to the question I'm asking?

Are we looking for facts and figures? Or are we searching for concepts and meanings? Looking for the cheapest flight or the closest pizzeria are fact-based questions that require precise answers. There is no mystery as to the details or how the answer will be acted on. More esoteric concerns like who the best doctor is for a particular ailment or why a certain local company is considered a bad employer require digging. In the digital world, that digging requires some foreknowledge of what we'll be digging in.

Tool Purpose

Why is using the correct search tool important for finding the most qualified facts or most useful answers? Generally speaking, a search engine is a commercial medium. Originally, search vendors were rewarded by advertisers for two things: (1) Capturing the largest set of search results, and (2) making sure that a potential customer sees the advertisers search results before anyone else's. With the advent of smart phones, the reward footprint expanded to include the tracking device capacity of mobile search. For instance, now Google sells both your physical location and your mental framework.

Assuming researchers have a different outcome than ad dollars in mind, we may be better off digging elsewhere. Perhaps we'll seek and find our own reward in a more controlled setting that may not even be indexed by a commercial search engine. In fact it may not even be a search we do. Depending on how responsive the information provider is to our case, we'll browse subject directories to answer questions we never even thought of asking. This is that's not possible today or tomorrow in any search engine.

TOOL SELECTION — REFINEMENT TOOLS

We've been looking at how search engines operate and how that can support or contradict the way we want them to work. The next step is to fill in the gap between their limitations and our potentials. Bridging this difference is critical for acting on the information we're about to receive...

- We have reviewed choices for presenting those intentions (query formation) and have walked through the two fundamental approaches for achieving successful search outcomes.

- We presented several tools to guide our research effort, including the seven procedural steps for creating Search Logs or self-guided instructions for increasing the completeness (breadth) as well as aboutness (relevance) of our searches.

Where is this all leading?

In **Unit Two,** we added three powerful methods to the fundamental techniques introduced in **Unit One**: syntax, semantics, and pointers. Now we come to the engines available for applying these practices. Tool selection involves determining whether or not to use a search engine or a subject directory, along with various refinement tools that can expedite the search process.

Tool Retracing

How do we cut a navigable path? Without haste, prejudice, or overlooking important clues, how do we pick up the scent of relevance? How do we detect the shortest distance between the facts we need to connect? How do we slice through heaps of websites and databases to forge a path that only we could blaze but which others can soon follow?

In **Unit Two** we apply the lessons of query formation to screen, filter, and increase the precision, clarity, conclusiveness, and ultimately persuasiveness of our search results.

We will build on the foundations of information quality and search engine proficiency presented in **Units One** and **Two** respectively. The Refinement Tools section is designed to enhance our tool selection savvy with a new set of skills that are transferable within any search environment. They are valid within any domain of electronically stored information within our grasp. The following four goals summarize the refinement skills that complement our new knowledge for how search works — and how it fails:

1. To sensibly arrange search terms and phrases (semantics)

2. To express search operators and field constraints (syntax)

3. To shield yourself from bogus and distracting information designed to waste your time and curiosity (screening), and

4. To sort and classify potentially relevant search results according to your primary objectives (filtering)

Tool Selection – Search Engines

Kicking the Tires: Search Engine Attributes and Evaluation

Here are a couple of different indicators that tell you about the engine in question and when is the best time to apply which search tool:

1. How many pages are indexed
2. When pages get indexed
3. When results are sponsored
4. What are the defaults of the engine's search operators, and
5. Refinement Tools (i.e., link analysis, meta-tags, delimits, clustering categories, or correlating phrases)

Understanding search engines attributes will help your evaluation process as we plan our search strategy. The table below details some common search engine features that are useful for screening search results.

FIGURE 2.13: Summary criteria for evaluating search engines

Operators	Indexing	Commands	Outputs
Boolean Logic	Indexing of Search Sites (layers within search sites)	Field constraints – Limits	Display (subject directories)
Nesting	Indexing of Search Terms (Exalead)	Field constraints – Syntax	Sorting (subject directories)
Negative Operators	Lost pages	Full word wildcarding (in phrases)	Tagging
Stop Words	Cache Mining	Search defaults	Keyword highlighting: "why this?" KWIC
Proximity	AltaVista?	Non-combining Filters	Spell check

FIGURE 2.14: Summary criteria for evaluating search features

Below is a comprehensive table of search features that have evolved (or in some cases vanished) since the inception of the World Wide Web:

What it's called	What it does	Why should we care
Boolean logic	AND, OR, NOT	Traditional, time-honored search statements
Cache mining	Frozen snapshots of websites and directories	Archival searches to validate disputes or corrections on dated materials or decommissioned sites
Case sensitivity	Exact matches of the specified case — capitalized or lower case lettering	Turning off this function makes your cases inclusive: There is no distinction between lower-case and capital letters
Character +Word Limits	Query cut-offs	We need good words to represent you
Clustering	Query-relevant words and phrases	'Search within a search' creates a machine index that may provide you a few pearls
Date insensitivity	Page updates versus publication updates	Search engines tell time according to their crawler schedules — not the publication dates of the article we're requesting
Field constraints: Limits	File types, language, geographic regions, etc.	'Slash commands' or delimiters for reducing bloated searches
Field constraints: Syntax	Body, title, referring and contained URLs	'Field commands' [FIELDNAME Term] for defining the use of your search terms (varies widely by tool)
Keyword highlighting — why this?	Search terms do not appear in your search results	Search terms may not appear on page retrieved — check cache and meta tags
Indexing of search sites	Number of pages and frequency of refresh	Deepness of what gets crawled — important for intext searches
404 errors	Lost pages	Can't connect to URL on search results page — try cached result
Mutually exclusive filters	Syntaxes that can't be combined	Can't combined [LINK] and [URL] fields — to prevent SEO tinkering with PageRank
Nesting	Parentheses	Remember algebra? Good way to combine and separate terms and filtering formulas (SEE Page 2.14)

Operators: Negative	Eliminates false positives	Remove irrelevance at the source
Operators: Stop Words	Indefinite articles are ignored, except within a phrase	Must place 'and,' 'the,' 'an,' or 'a' for them to count
Outputs: Display	Set results size and metadata extracts	Limited or no choice in commercial web search
Outputs: Sorting	Output choices limited to relevance or date	Limited or no choice in commercial web search
Proximity	Build multiple phrase combinations	Common subscription database search option — available only as a work-around Google hack
Search: Defaults	AND operation by default	Search industry's response to irrelevance — overcome with OR
Search: Phrases	Quotes	Use quotes to bind important noun phrases and parenthetical expressions
Search — Spell Check	"Did you mean?"	Wonderful survey tool
Tagging	Display meta tags in results list	Some engines provide this — good for *pearl culturing* (SEE Page 2.95)

TYPES OF SEARCH ENGINES

We'll be kicking the tires on seven search engines types, including (1) clustering (or facets), (2) Natural language processing ("NLP"), (3) Visualization, (4) Metasearch, (5) Suggestion search, a.k.a. type ahead, (6) Privacy, and Custom search engine ("CSE").

WHAT ARE CLUSTERING ENGINES?

Clustering is a two-stepper. First, it does a search within a search, then presents some potential areas of follow-up explanation. Engineering-wise, this means that it looks at all the sites in its index. Next, it analyzes the top ranking sites. Finally, it creates an index of the key concepts covered within the most relevant search results.

Generally speaking, a clustering engine skims the ocean like say a Google or Bing search. Skimming here means looking at a limited number of pages and then only indexing the metadata or first 100 kilobytes of content. Then a clustering engine performs a second step. It's a type of a search within a search of what it deems to be the most relevant results within the first search. It then presents these refined results in the form of clusters or bucketed results that are labeled by specific subjects or content sources.

Clustering engines can compensate for some of the traditional weaknesses of Google such as distinguishing between nouns and verbs (or actions and actors), word limits, and serendipitous searching. For the Knowledge-ABLED, a clustering engine can help us get up-to-speed on an unfamiliar topic when we're not sure exactly what we're looking for.

Clustering engines are also crossover candidates from ocean into lake based searches. They are similar to machine-enabled directories that classify or group similar concepts. The ability to compartmentalize search outcomes can help you to organize loosely-defined or voluminous set results *on-the-fly* with no familiarity of what we're stepping into.

Clustering engines are most valuable for the groups or facets that appear usually in the left navigation panel of the search results page. Without needing to dig very far, this foretells what's promising from what's pointless. It is much more efficient for researchers to peruse groupings of results than fill in the missing contextual details or click through to individual pages.

FIGURE 2.15: 9-11 Report Part One – Example Through Faceted Search Engine

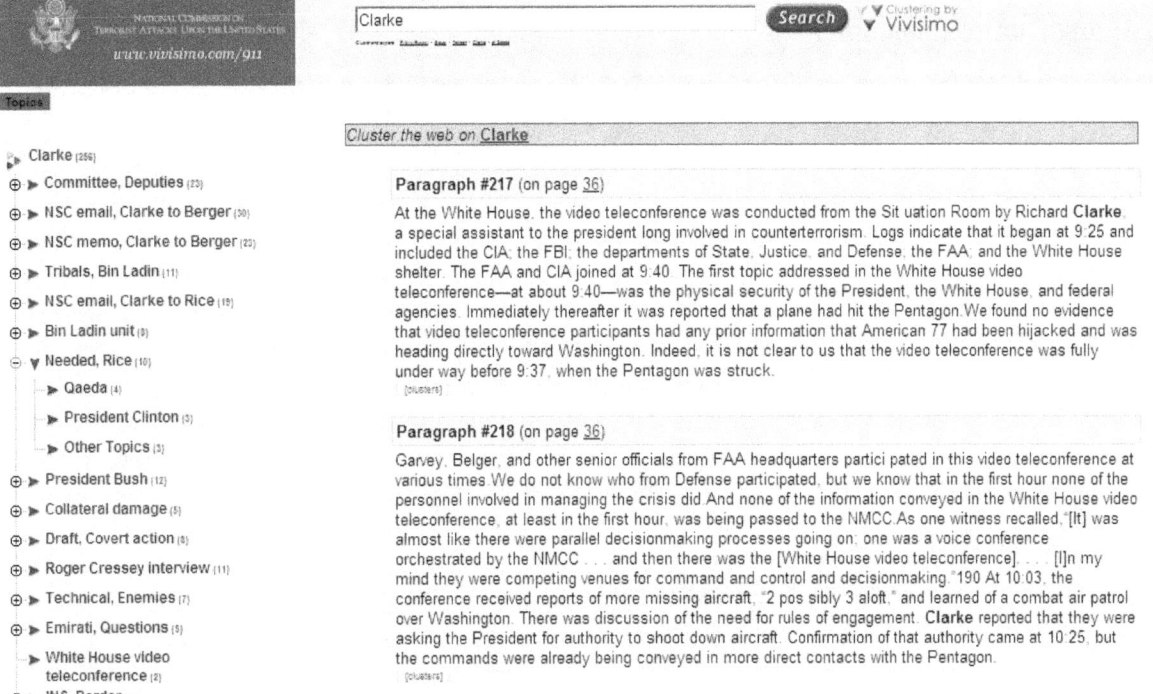

Sometimes these clusters will group according to information providers regardless of websites, or even according to the actions ascribed to an information giver. For instance, from the 9-11 report in Figure 2.15, we see that Richard Clarke *needed* then 'National Security Adviser Condoleeza Rice.' This is a difficult feat for most search engines to perform. We saw this earlier in the limitations of attempting to isolate actors from actions and subjects from predicates.

Serendipitous Search

Clustering engines are the best approach when: (1) we're not sure where we're going, and (2) we need to know where we'll end up ASAP. Results are clustered or grouped automatically into categories. This is what search engine geeks call auto-categorization. We'll see the same concept again when we talk of the differences between machine and human-enabled subject directories. The truth is that some of these artificially-derived classifications are meaningful to your search request. Some are completely bogus and require some major tweaking.

Even when the cluster misfires and presents bogus results, it's easier to identify trivial results than digging through endless pages of non-clustered outputs. Another advantage is that the buckets lower the importance of the ranking or what ends up closest to the top of the search results. This means that your search objective – the individual context – determines what is displayed: The labels that bucket the information hold the ultimate relevancy, not the link sponsors or rankings formula.

Clustering engines are a rich source of term expansion. We can aim our terms at the affiliated categories or facets they generate. This is subscribing to the *look what the cat dragged in* school of term expansion. It's not what we expected. But after the first few attempts we're not going to be as choosy. Yes, we missed the mark. In the process, we learn we don't need to be a sharpshooter to land our prey. We can at least remain in the hunt.

Clustering Our Investigations

At its best, clustering or facet-based search tools do what no other general search tool can even approach: Tell nouns from verbs. This is pivotal to understanding context. Who is the actor, what is the action, and ultimately what's in the outcome.

Let's take some fairly common lines of investigative questioning around criminal activities:

1. "Who knew what and when?"
2. "Where's the smoking gun?"
3. "Why did they place themselves above the law?"

On question three, it's hard to imagine a query formation that can capture these supporting questions with mere keywords...

> *"Which affiliates may have conspired with the suspects in question and what were their motives? Were they in agreement or coerced?"*

These concerns may be significant to the success of an investigation. This requirement is marginal at best to the geeks who calibrate search tools to one or two keywords. Fortunately, with clustering we can attach a name to an action or a place to an outcome. People are connected to events not because they both appear in random sections of a document. It's due to actual participation in those dealings.

Speaking of outcomes, let's revisit that 9-11 investigation and using name associations to pursue investigative leads.

FIGURE 2.16: 9-11 Report Part Two – Uncovering a Lead through Faceted Search

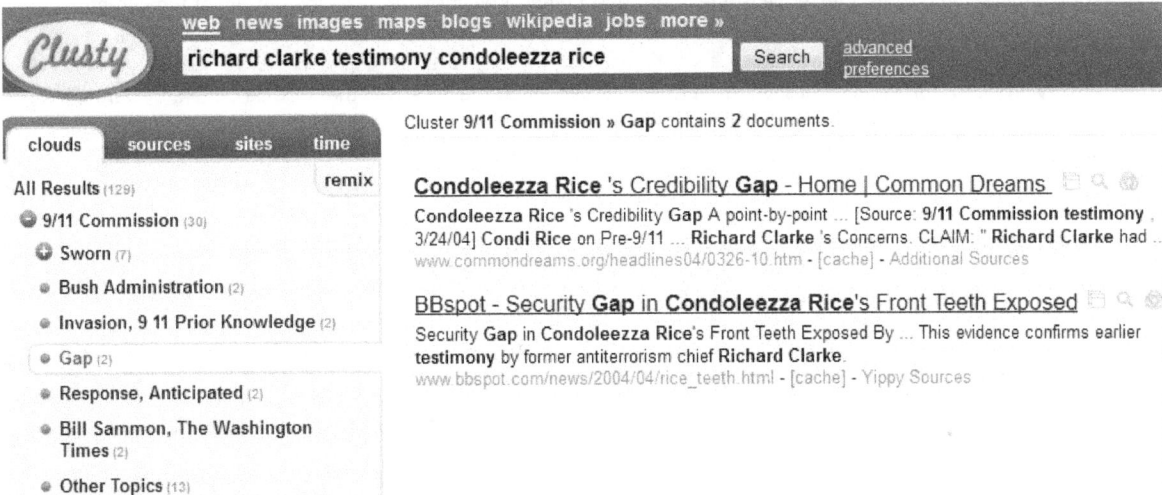

Making connections' like in the above example of Clusty (rebranded as Yippi in 2010) is not limited to detail-rich reports and transcripts. There's also the practical matter of eyeballing the quality of search results quickly so that we can tweak our queries to capture subtleties and passing references we might have lost in the Google Ocean.

FIGURE 2.17: 9-11 Report, 2019 Edition

Now consider the same detail-laden excavation used in a mobile version of the 2019 Mueller Report, nearly two decades later:

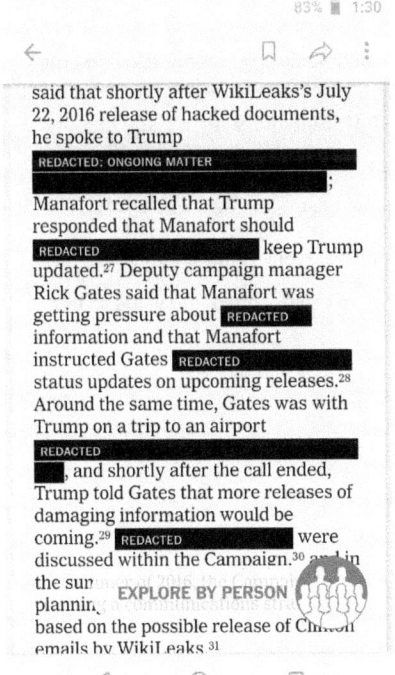

No degree of design sophistication can substitute for providing a large enough interface to support the discovery process.[4]

Many folks waste lots of hours scrolling through a bottomless number of search results. The practice adds new meaning to the expression *diminishing returns*. Clustering is one of our best defenses against sinking to the bottom of the pile-on.

Out of Our Depth

We're especially prone to fruitless searches when we're not certain about the depths of that Google Ocean. By depth, I don't mean the number of results. I mean the frustration that comes with needing to click through to sites to even sense their potential usefulness. That's another advantages of facets or cluster searching.

Talking with your smart phone works when you know what you want to...

> *"Make me a reservation at a cheap Italian restaurant near where I live for three at 7 on Saturday."*

Cluster engines rock precisely when we *don't* know what we're looking for.

The keyword for this is *serendipitous*. The phrase for describing this feature is 'discovery search.' You'll find in any interviews with suspects, witnesses, victims, and clients this perennial quality of serendipity:

1. The stuff they volunteer (the answers they give to questions we don't think to ask) are meaningful in a way that rises above our best efforts to be good interviewers.

2. We may try to cover all the bases. But there will always be an unturned stone. We won't even know we're tripping over it unless our information sources alert us to them.

That's the basic idea of clustering. They break down complex and obtuse subjects into more manageable buckets. Sometimes it's a bucket of videos. Sometimes it's a bottomless pile of press releases. But at least you know what you're stepping over. Or *into,* if you're so inclined.

Summarizing Clustering Engines

In sum, clustering engines are useful when we're at the early or exploratory stages of unfamiliar and new topics. They provide the backdrop of related subjects and groups affiliated with our search targets.

A good clustering tool is almost conversational. It begins with some keywords that can be tweaked and refined around the emerging themes revealed in each cluster or grouping. In fact, we can switch gears more quickly here than in a conventional results screen by drilling down or clicking directly on the sub-grouping contained within the larger group.

Clustering engines...

- Present groupings of search results arranged by common threads like news topics, sources, or locations.
- Let us see at a glance how close our search results align with our information-seeking requirements.
- Save us from the time sink of needing to visit questionable sites to determine their context and value to us.

What are Natural Language Processing (NLP) Engines?

Are they clueless or insightful? Is this a one-stop answer for cumulative curiosities or a one way ticket to oblivion?

Natural language search engines invite you into a world where friendly computers patiently answer all the questions we're too proud to saddle with our fellow humans. Their goal is to deliver a granular response that focuses on the particulars of your question. It's not about the engine's pattern matching of keywords to the sites it indexes.

Fortunately or regrettably (depending on your trust in technology), it's the search solutions that are the humbled ones in this exchange. The desire to have software that interprets our information-seeking goals and behaviors is an earnest and even practical desire. On the left-side, we see a carefully constructed, well-disciplined, and frankly, fairly standard kind of business research question.

To the right, we see an interpretation by a corporation librarian to interpret the same information request:

Plain English (Policy Analyst)	Advanced Boolean (Corporate Librarian)
"All documents (and content) discussing, referencing, or relating to company guidelines or internal approval for placement of tobacco products, logos, or signage, in television programs (network or cable), where the documents expressly refer to the programs being watched by children."	(guide! OR strateg! OR approval) AND (place! OR promot! OR logos OR sign! OR merchandise) AND (TV OR T.V. OR televise! OR cable OR network) AND ((watch! OR view!) W/5 (child! OR teen! OR juvenile OR kid! OR adolescent!))

The thinking is that the intent can be interpreted by the software programmer before the hand-off between the information requester and the researcher ever takes place. In reality, the technology has a long way to go. Below is an example of a typical reference question. However, from the 'Related questions' in the left navigation, we see that the engineering lags behind the desire for guidance:

FIGURE 2.18: Approximating a Pattern through Natural Language search

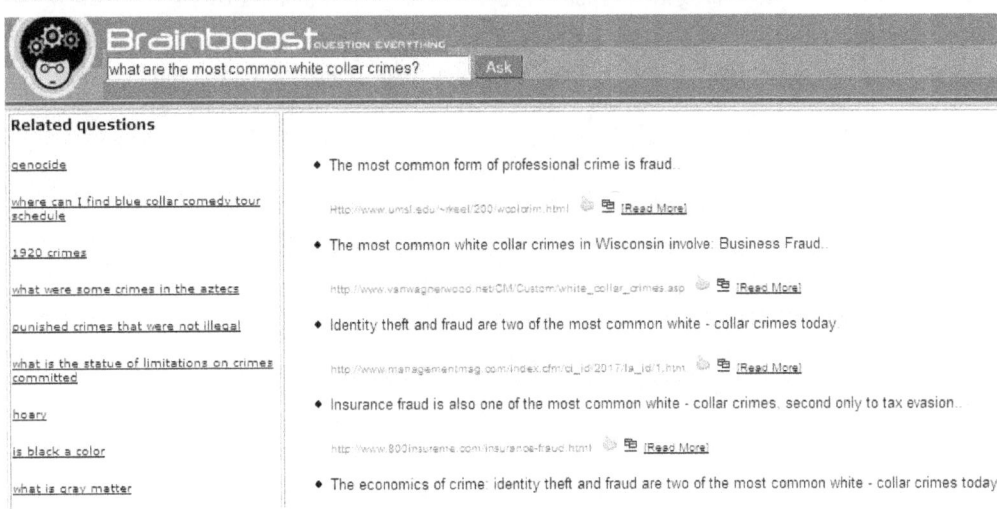

How does technology handle all the squishy approximations that enter a straight-forward question to humans?

There are certain situations in which natural language tools can improve search outcomes. It helps to maintain a strong affiliation between causes and effects. A strong relationship between ranges of conditions and expected results will boost relevancy. One example involves hiring a forensic specialist in the area of cybercrime. Natural language processing or 'NLP' is designed to understand the way we ask questions of humans. Generally, we'll have more relevant interactions if we focus on hard, tangible, fact-based questions.

Soft Questions, Mushy Answers

Softer, more opinion-based questions tend to confuse NLP engines: "What field should I enter in order to find steady work?" is a nonstarter.

A search tool cannot know your skills, professional assets, and career ambitions. Not yet. On the other hand, if we place the onus on the market as search target, we may get a more accurate response.

For instance, if we ask which professions have the greatest growth potential, we'll probably fare better. In a similar vain, my PI class considered the most common areas for white collar crimes. This target also led to useful outcomes concerning medical fraud and malpractice claims.

Natural language engines are marketed as one-stop answers for our persistent and fleeting curiosities. Some of these mysteries are perennial leftovers from our grammar school studies:

> "Why is the sky blue?" or "When did World War II begin?"

Answers, not Documents

Another interesting outgrowth of natural language is that search engines are developed to generate answers to questions. This is a dramatically different set of requirements both in how the NLP engines are programmed and in how we use these tools in our investigations.

NLP finds answers to *plain English* questions instead of keyword matches. Advanced NLP technology processes the most relevant pages and extracts short and concise answers. The less advanced version leads to pages that tackle potentially relevant topics. But they fall short of attempting to customize a direct answer. The second, more modest approach might actually work in our favor. The qualifier? We're looking for an approximation or a range of potential answers.

NLP engines break down units like web pages and documents even further. It's individual lists, paragraphs, or even sentences can be responses to queries. The results are intended to be more directly related to our questions than a set of records. Otherwise, we get the *discardables:* Documents containing passing references to our search target that we're better off passing over. NLP engines can help us out in situations that generate plain question answer patterns. This means they are common questions offering a predictable range of acceptable answers. They are also useful if we can lose the expectation that they are answer machines or Jeannies in wish-fulfilling bottles. We exist merely to *unscrew the knowledge cap.*

Instead of expecting the correct answer, think of them as gauges for better understanding the right question to ask. For instance, taking a figurative question and hoping for a literal outcome is an open invitation to a failsafe:

> *"From where does the Dali Lama draw his inspiration?"*

On the other hand, we make better headway asking where the Dali Lama was educated or what spiritual works he cites – literal, not figurative questions.

More vexing and complex matters like the divinity of Buddhist belief overwhelm NLP technology. Interesting conceptual questions of a more concrete nature can generate some relevant pages, if not an informed response: "What causes income disparity" is the kind of multi-dimensional social issue where NLP lends some credible light on a weighty and esoteric topic.

Curious Responses to Natural Questions

One of the more useful examples of NLP engines is QueryCat. QueryCat limits the pages it crawls to FAQs ("frequently asked questions"). These appear in sections of websites dedicated to common questions, recurring uncertainties, or clarifications around points of interest and concern. FAQs are great for sniffing out points of ignorance – those doubts and suspicions that survive in cultural misunderstandings and old wives tales.

QueryCat is built on much sounder footing than most other two NLP entrants. The entire database is answer-based by default. Anytime you're working from an index of FAQs. It consists entirely of FAQs so every record is the answer to a question that's already been anticipated in the responses it stores. Other offerings are flimsier, delivering less consistent results.

Of course some of those questions run right off the ranch and the limitations can be pretty obvious. But the answers are formed by higher quality source data. This is a concept we'll revisit when we address the OLP framework ("Oceans, Lakes and Ponds") in **Unit Three**.

Hits and Misses

Back to the present: What happens when we compare our quest for the meaning of life with our **Unit Two** mission? To define different kinds of search engines and describe what they do?

These kinds of big picture questions are both specific and obtuse and designed to throw NLP search engines out of whack. Some are better at handling curve ball questions. Others are too literal, too binary, too much like it was designed more by a software engineer than by a content curator or linguist.

We may also try NLP to narrow down a definitive but ambiguously formed question like...

> *"What are the most common white collar crimes?"*

NLP sites like Ask.com hope that we'll settle for one of their preselected responses:

> *"How long does it take to be a private investigator?"*

The pre-canned responses range from incomplete to pathetic. We click on the first choice:

> *"What are the responsibilities of a forensic scientist?"*

The answer...

> "[p]retty much looking for who killed someone"

I kid you not.

Another favorite produced by one of my students was...

> How old is old

My hairline is receding just thinking about how clueless the NLP creations are in trying to decipher the implied nuances comparing *old* to 'old.' I'm guessing that when the machine crashes from overheating, we'll be sharing a laugh and not scratching our heads.

Queries by the Paragraph

Another approach is to cut and paste a sentence or two from a writing we find revealing or provocative and then see what the technology does with it. I tried this with Ask.com by inserting the following paragraph:

> *Another strong trait that plays out in markets is loss aversion. "In people's minds, losses loom larger than gains," said Sanders. "People just don't like losing money. The only thing they dislike more are money managers who lose it for them." In effect, Sanders argued, sellers fearful of losing money will wind up undercutting the price of their assets. "The sellers are paying the buyers to rid themselves of the stress of ownership that they can no longer endure."*

Believe it or not, the results were actually more accurate chewing on that large stash of words than if I had simplified the problem statement in plain prose:

> *Why makes people freak out the most about money?*

The tool obsesses on the *freak* colloquialism and overlooks the psychological dimension completely. Any meanings between the anxieties we face as our assets drain are completely absent in the NLP results. When it comes to NLP, perhaps more is better? (*More* here means pasting paragraphs, not formulating queries).

A more clear-cut choice like entering a person's name doesn't mean answers that are any more germane or specific. Doing a people search in NLP is a little bit like asking Google for the most lucrative fields to enter for investigators. It simply was never built to wrap boundaries and bidirectional conditions around multi-step instructions:

"Find me X so I can go figure out Y because Z is too abstract right now."

Summarizing NLP Engines

In sum, NLP engines are good with repeated questions and enduring curiosities. They are not there yet in terms of more original or figurative questions. This is so whether they're philosophically bent or just plain abstract in nature. Look for an NLP tool that's honest with you when a straight-forward answer is not at-hand. This will save time on fact-based searches and opinion searches, In short, when causes and effects are less clear to an evolving technology than to a flawed human being.

NLP engines...

- Find answers to 'plain English' questions vs. keyword matches
- Process most relevant pages and extract short and concise answers to your questions
- Are not intended as a page redirect, and no pay per click campaigns are engaged as of this writing
- Are honest when a straight-forward answer is not at hand: Better with facts than opinion-guided searches, but worth a try on cause-and-effect concepts

What are Visualization Engines?

Visualization engines display search results as thematic maps. When we type in a search phrase, the program creates a map where topics (keywords) and Web sites are laid out based on relevance. Some visualization tools create images based on the scale of interest in the terms we use. One example is Stockcloud whose responses comport to the volume of news coverage generated by publicly traded companies.

Visualization tools try to take some of the mental effort out of deciphering search results by using graphical cues to signify the patterns they contain.

Visualization tools map the interconnectedness between our search targets and the circles they travel in. This kind of visual mapping involves the circuitry of social networking and is a technique for summarizing the interconnections. It includes:

1. Graphical links and line thickness
2. Bubbles and clouds
3. Degrees of separation, or
4. Use of color, symbols, images and dimension (e.g., the cascading effect)

The Lay of the (Virtual) Land

Visualization engines display search results as thematic maps. When we type in a search phrase, the program creates a map where topics (keywords). Websites are displayed by relevance. Some visualization tools create images based on the scale of interest in the terms we use. Others show the connections between your search terms, the sites your query attracts, and even the relationship between information providers: A story airing first on one site gets picked up on another.

Visualization engines display search results as thematic maps, connecting your keywords to both the supply and demand side of topically-generated interest. For example, a popular keyword will appear larger in size than a more obscure one inside a tag cloud. Tag clouds are typically keywords listed alphabetically and then represented by how often they are tagged or referenced. The literal size of the words is connected to the number of users that tag it.

Visualization is a compelling way to happen on surprise discoveries. The semantic mapping clues the researcher into possible leads or search terms not considered. The presentation allows us to visualize or see a connection/possible lead that wasn't apparent when sifting through seemingly disparate links.

But the layout has a practical side too. Many of my students find that the layout lends itself to better focusing a search than the unaided alternative: Scrolling through endless lists of links, not knowing until a site visit whether it's worthy of one.

Test Drives

One common reference is a tag cloud whose labels sizes expand and contract based on their popularity. Since then we've seen tools that generate the tag clouds we'd like to see.

Wordle creates visual maps that could be applied to a community of practice wiki, set of job postings, a political speech, or any other transactional undertaking worthy of tracking or comparison. The tool will generate a tag cloud for any RSS feed we throw at it. We can then re-stage the representation as a widget in our blog, Facebook page, or other social media of choice.

FIGURE 2.19: Using Word Recurrence to Visualize the Prominence of Key Concepts

Wordle generates tag clouds and displays keywords based on their frequency of use from the page in its index.

Kartoo was another visualization tool. Like Stockcloud, Kartoo showed the interrelationships between your search terms, the topics they map to, and the most relevant sources for covering them. One of its unsung benefits was revealing an important Knowledge-ABLED pattern: The often vexing and back-channel ways that information travels.

Mousing over a source revealed how it connected the stories being tracked to the sites carrying them. Kartoo provided common elements that glued those stories to the originating sources. That's certainly a handy detail to have. It's hard to present the sequential logic of who published what and when. It's even harder to weave a narrative over a jumble of details that defy a chronological pattern. Kartoo was the literal interpretation for *connecting the dots*.

Kartoo processed that same two-step relevancy processor that we saw in the clustering tool. Then it displayed search terms as connection points between information sources, referencing common words and phrases between sources. For instance, an original story picked up in other places would display primary and secondary sources (and the paths between them).

As we saw in Wordle, we can use visualization engines to uncover unlikely connections that might otherwise get lost in the details of text-based search results. In Kartoo we could divulge our target and include potentially compromising terms into the mix:

> *Shamshak PI online ~crime*

The results below showed the *usual suspects.* These were the professional affiliations and alliances courted by the investigator in question. In Figure 2.20, we also notice a whole set of unexpected strangers who crash the party among the mix of regular party guests.

FIGURE 2.20: Using Metasearch to Show how Sources Connect to Search Terms

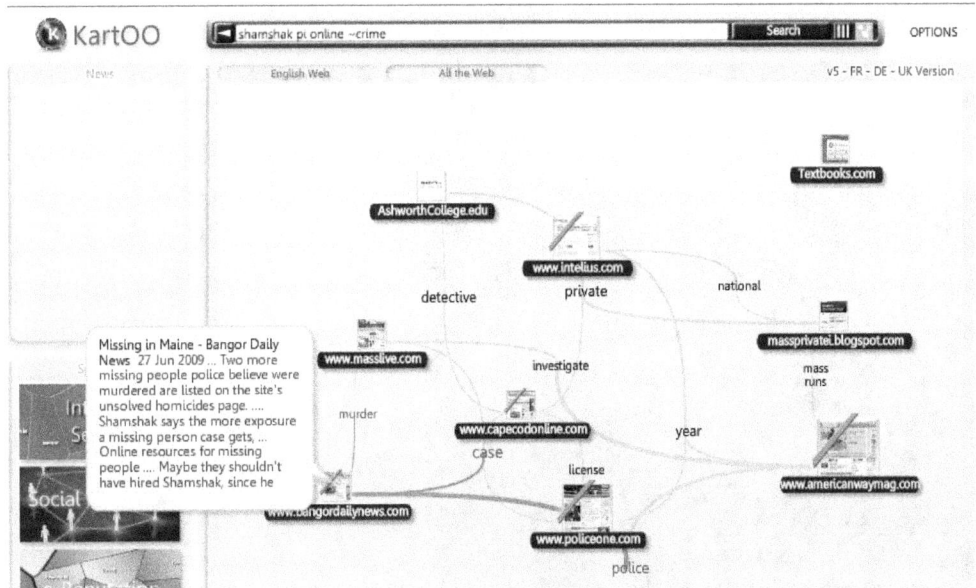

What drew me to the now defunct Kartoo was the connect-the-dot connections so lacking in the NLP engines. More than snapshots, SPAM filters, and even the arrows between the pages displayed, I liked the terms that bridged the concepts together. You'd find that it's rare the keywords we use end up in these bridges. That's a credit to how well Kartoo's builders interpreted user intent.

Maps and Mashups

Of course visualization is not limited to the abstract world of hit counts or associated links in order of relationship strength. Sometimes it's about a tangible reality of the physical world. Yes, we're talking about maps that depict oceans, lakes, ponds and highways that are not metaphors but natural creations.

Mapping or GPS sites and applications silenced the once longstanding joke that men don't ask for directions. From a research perspective, they show us the geophysical environment. They place it within the context of a crime scene or connection between a departure and an arrival point. Other mapping sites also track the reporting of events within a locality or region, ranging from police blotters to school closings.

This kind of illustration is called a 'mashup' because it displays a data received from one or more information providers. It then overlays that on a known interface, classification system, or the navigational tool we know as a *map*. Mashups are what we use to understand real estate values from neighborhood to neighborhood. Just click through the appraised values or last sales price commanded by the properties on our block. But they can just as easily display the number of cell towers in a given area, incidence of disease, reportings of a virus, or even criminal behavior by reporting patterns.

FIGURE 2.21: Aggregating Search Results Via Location Coordinates

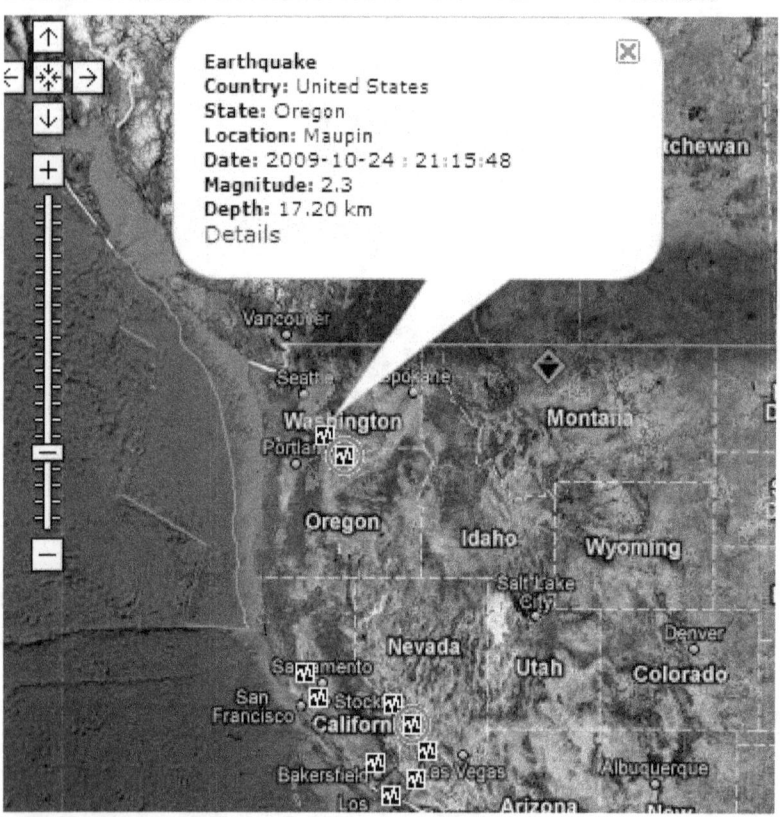

Here's an example of a mashup called an alert map that depicts real-time disasters and emergencies across the U.S.

We turn to mapping sites to plan our driving routes. But they can help us role play the options mulled by a criminal in considering an escape route. That idea can be extended across many cases for comparing the circumstantial evidence to the testimony gathered from police reports and legal depositions.

But using maps as visualization tools is more fundamental than plotting out probable getaways. They can place a crime scene under the magnifying glass of buildings, architectural features, and even the atmospheric conditions at the time of the incident. They can offer up shadows, ricochets, shrubs (for stowing weapons), and nearest hospitals. Add the time of day and season and we can deduce the angle of the light, visibility, and even the traffic patterns and noise levels.

The mother ship of all GPS is Google Earth. Google Earth was launched in the mid-2000s. At first, it ran parallel to a web connection but appeared as its own interface. Google Earth was terrific for...

- Testing theories,
- Gleaning the physical, irrefutable details of the time and place in question, and
- A convincing way to de-construct the events following the perpetration of externally committed criminal actions.

Another emergent use of visualization is in hand held devices so that the graphical properties of the physical world can be rendered through a two-dimensional screen. Augmented reality extends the role of metadata from mapping programs, social networking pages, and plain old advertising. The destination is to layer or append these details to the street scenes, landmarks, and even people we encounter. How do we define that encounter? Typically it's come to mean the display in the viewfinders of smart phones and computer screens. Superimposing such details could make it more likely we'll cavort with our phones than through them. (Pogue, 2012)[5]

Summarizing Visualization Engines

In sum, visualization engines are graphical tools that generate charts, icons, and images that symbolize the flow, nature, and direction shaped by patterns in information reporting and usage.

Visualization engines...

- Render as real or concrete an abstraction like the number of keyword tags or frequency of common search terms.
- Effectively depict time series analysis and relationships between keywords and events through sequential change logs and reporting patterns.
- Are strong when trying to recreate the geophysical and meteorological conditions, i.e. crime scene investigations.
- Are not limited to individual crimes. They're useful for uncovering patterns of reported crimes based on the type of crime over specific time frames and localities.

WHAT ARE METASEARCH ENGINES?

Metasearch is harder to explain than other kinds of search engines. Metadata are the defining elements in any database that indexes text or web pages. Metadata is what we experienced in our introduction to syntax such as title, source, author, description, and date stamps.

Metasearch is about indexing selective portions of a web page by some common properties:

1. Address or location of the host site

2. Meta tags describing the content

3. Time stamps indicating when the page was last indexed, etc.

To some degree, this describes all search engines. As we saw in **Unit One**, they crawl web pages or indexes compiled by other search engines. They all have their own formulas and scoring systems to determine the ranking and presentation of their databases. So what's remarkable about metasearch? And why does it warrant its own category? Metasearch engines are not unique for what they do but for how they do it: Present information on a finer, granular level than as a list of web pages, documents, or files.

In the case of a tool like Surfwax, metasearch can function like a microscope. It can disseminate densely-worded materials like testimonies and legal exhibits to extract particular entities like people, locations, and the organizations they represent.

Click on the actual person and we can see where they appear within these thickets of details. On the other hand, metasearch can provide a macro lens on the wider sweep of multiple engines on a single search page. Dogpile is one of many such examples.

However, while one statement may pull numerous search results, there is a metasearch trade-off. We'll need to concede the precision and control offered by the syntax and search operators of individual engines. The benefits may be worth the costs if we're in the earlier investigation stages. We can always refine once we know the volume of results we're triggering.

Test Drives

Surfwax can narrow in on the pressing details related to our project work. That's an important factor when we want to drill down on the specifics. This means moving beyond the media rehash of what repeatedly comes up in more traditional searches. Pouring repeatedly through the same details does nothing to further our understanding of…

- Our search targets,
- Their social circles,
- The motives across the wider circle, or
- Priorities that fill the personal radar screens we considered in **Unit One**'s introduction to blindspots.

A metasearch tool can explode the details of individuals and their actions. Surfwax is one-stop way to get from too many results to the crux of the matter.

UNIT TWO: Using Search in Virtual Investigations | Page 2:58

FIGURE 2.22: Parsing the Details of Legal Testimony with Metasearch Results

Surfwax combs the finer details of what gets reported in exposes, investigations, and voluminous reports that are difficult to paw through but might reveal some vital and overlooked particulars about your case.

Searching Out Loud: Giving Voice to Independent Investigations | Marc Solomon

Not all sizes fit all

One note of caution on metasearch: Even though they're built to consolidate the results of multiple search engines, that doesn't mean they carry the same functionality with those results. For instance, we might be fond of using the tilde or term expansion operator in Google to approximate other terms similar to our keyword. But that operator is only supported when we work through Google. It disappears in metasearch, even though the metasearch runs off the Google index.

That's not always the case. Some operators such as quotes, Boolean logic, negation, or asterisks as wildcards are common to *all* search engines. Others are different depending on the engine. Syntax can also change depending on the tool. It can drive one batty trying to keep it all straight! The truth is that when we find something that works, that's what we'll return to again and again.

One of the many virtues of the social tagging tools we'll learn about in **Unit Three** is that we can capture our metasearch successes by tagging them in memorable ways. That's especially compelling in metasearch when we're already on the slippery slope of learning not only to search, but how to search the search engines too.

We can save our productive queries to an account in a tagging tool and pattern off that success.

This granularity is present when we broaden our search terms to include the metatags used by relevant websites to describe their content. Gigablast is another metasearch tool worth tracking. It shows a top level of ancillary details that may contain the secret word which gets us through the door. Gigablast calls these Gigabits: A series of phrases and words related (but not invoked directly) by the searcher.

In Gigablast, you can impose the same categorical boundaries you would expect to see in a subject directory. The categorical details are included within the site's own unique index. Another neat feature is that Gigablast enables us to include phrases within metadata fields.

FIGURE 2.23: Applying Categorical Distinctions through Metasearch Results

In the example above we see the expression "best of the best" belongs to the title of any page that also mentions 'experts.'

An open source metasearch engine called Carrot² displays each data source in a separate tab and then creates a custom visual of the search results. The interface highlights the specific category we focus on by displaying the frequencies of our search terms in the dot pattern below the circle of related topics. In this case, the reference is to 'audio interviews' of eyewitnesses to UFO sightings.

FIGURE 2.24: Applying Graphical Cues to Meta Searches

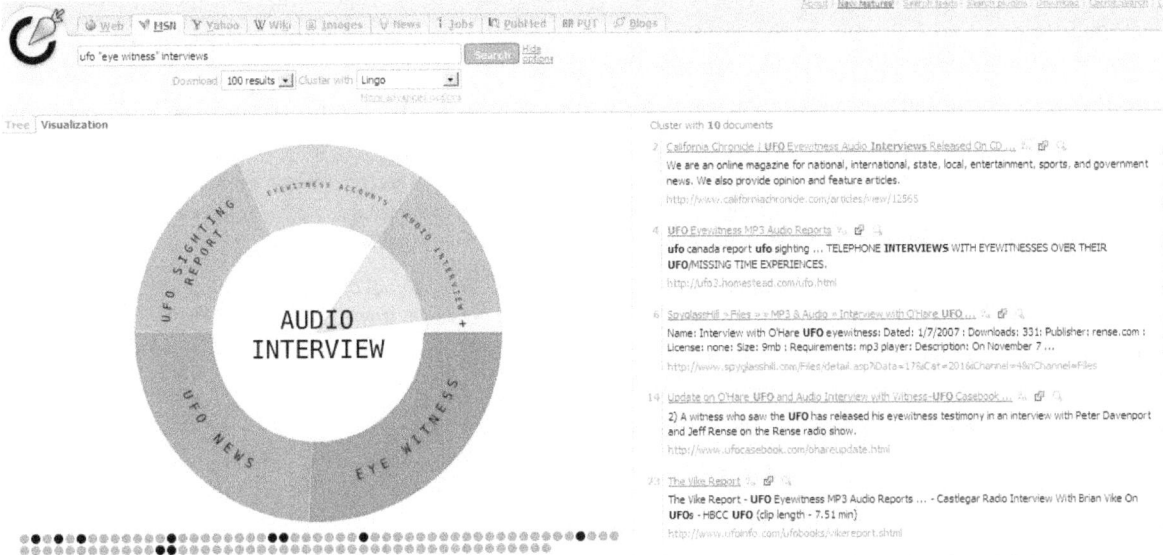

The complexity of text-based search results is simplified through alternative interfaces like this one from Carrot².

Summarizing Meta Search Engines

Meta search cuts two ways. It can both amplify and narrow the scale of your searches. In expansion mode, it can provide a one-stop delivery of multiple search results. Metasearch helps us make connections or possibilities that may not have been apparent when sifting through seemingly disparate text links. The ability to pull-out key details in detail-laden environments underscores their virtues in a number of ways:

1. Metasearch engines are especially powerful as text-based microscopes. They provide granularity and specific details at the document level. This enables us to analyze wordy, exhaustively detailed accounts of criminal activities and legal transcripts.

2. One particularly useful tool in this capacity is Surfwax because it breaks results down on a page-by-page basis.

3. A listing of the site's focus words enables us to see the people and subjects raised in the index of each ensuing article or record.

4. It can also be used to zoom in on the particulars of isolated pages and articles, indexing the appearance of individual events, organizations, and actors in proceedings that require careful attention and tracking of dates and participants.

OTHER KINDS OF SEARCH METHODS

Before we conclude our search engine review, it's important to talk about ways that all search engines are becoming better at matching our intent to the results they produce. These changes to the way search results are ranked, grouped, displayed give us new ways to flex our Knowledge-ABILITIES. They give investigators new opportunities for filtering, analyzing, and act on search outputs.

Suggestion Search

Suggestion search is based on a simple and effective premise that searches are better understood by example. In Suggestion search, queries are formulated from the past experience of others (past searches). We're not taking a stab at what we believe to be out there (our own untested theories).

The obvious benefit to this approach is that that success on finding the words we need to steer by can happen in our first attempt. Not the repeated trial-and-error that typifies so many of our own serendipitous searches or *fishing expeditions*. These are the occasions where we're sure we need to search but are less certain what we're pursuing.

Suggestion search may be the way to go even when we have a clear idea of an end goal or destination. But the concept is abstract. We can't conjure up the correct keywords, or the right terms are proving elusive. (Ferrara, 2009[6])

FIGURE 2.25: Some Earlier Forms of Google Type Ahead Capabilities

Here we see dynamic results that vary from character-to-character in a screen capture from 2009. The results sizes guided us in how popular a term is and how evolved or detailed it was as its own topic or subject category.

What about when the goal is concrete and our meaning is precise? These are called 'known item' searches that are mostly fact-based look-ups of contact details such as products, phone numbers, common categories, etc.

The suggestion list needs to be well-tended by our search site if we're looking for a specific detail like a title or author. Why? What are we to make of this omission when the book we want doesn't appear in the suggestion list? Probably that it wasn't available. That all changed in September 2010 when 'suggestion' went instantaneous. Google Instant showed suggested queries as we typed. Every stroke sparked a new response. The Instant piece of Google receded with time. The functionality did not.

Not a Gentle Suggestion

Google marketed this as a time savings to users. This assumes that most searches would rather pattern off the top-of-mind association of most searches. Who wants to waste time teeing up the quintessential query when Google will sell you an answer off the rack? The problem is that the answer might be more responsive to Google's idea of resolution than the researcher's.

At a recent trade gathering of local techies, a forty-something social media marketer was addressing the virtues of Google Analytics to the conference gallery. He mentioned how his pet store merchandiser/client delivered him a handful of variations on the naming of some hot-selling accessory for dogs. But then he ran the keyword combos through Google Ads (formerly Google AdWords) and the verdict was unanimous: There is only one commonly accepted way that customers use to search for this item. That's right — one way to the keyword bidding auction or the highway of web marketing road kill. In effect, Google was selling us two bills of service on suggestion search:

1. The prompt to keep the user *on track*
2. The marketing ultimatum to keep link sponsors buying *off-the-rack*

The larger story here is that a new class of media brokers is all too willing to confuse the business model of a software giant for the marketplace itself. The fact that this single expression for doggie collars, leashes, or dinner bells is reducible to one expression says as much about the media buyers as it does about the search media. Each term in succession describes one thought planted in front of the next. That's the extemporaneous stamina of Google as mind-reader. There are no original search terms under the Google Sun.

It's one thing to "organize the world's information and make it universally accessible." It's quite another thing to appropriate the language for doing so as an auction-based sweepstakes where Google has trademarked all the consonants, vowels, and punctuation symbols. Every keypad stroke prompts a type-ahead. Our minds may be shooting blanks but our stares have been paved over by the power of Google suggestion.

I'm not suggesting this power is sinister any more than I'm suggesting that Google is acting as our scalable, benevolent, reference librarian in the cloud. Google is acting in its own corporate interest when it channels our curiosities into manageable chunks of its revenue model. The fact that the service is so compelling and the model is so persuasive means that Google's evisceration of the ad business sounds like the sour grapes of a dead fruit tree. Yet this hasn't seeded the grounds for anti-trust litigation. Remember that browser-bundled PC empire of Microsoft that the Clinton Administration prosecuted in the late nineties? It seems an eternity since the suggestion horse left the Google Barn in 2010.

A decade later, any potential anti-trust action brought against Google is still *down the road* and as likely to hit the market as the latest Google instruction guide. Really, can you imagine an instruction manual of all the new features, discontinued functions, and decision path pointing us straight: Are all these updates worth our while? By the time we'd decide, Google would be onto the next release.

"The perfect search engine," says co-founder and former Google CEO Larry Page, "Would understand exactly what you mean and give back exactly what you want." Page might be casting a perfectly earnest engineering posture. Or cynicism may compel him to see the non-paying Google public as a customer that doesn't know what it wants *(other than for an intermediary to broker their virtual needs in a clean, visually unassuming interface)*.

My money is on an enduring love of search science. That's as far as Larry's sincerity needs to travel for my purposes. I'll know that Larry shares my enthusiasm when he figures out a way to pad revenues from servicing the needs of researchers.

Test Drives

What if we put in a common name like *Johnson* into Amazon.com? We might get back a link to baby shampoo as much as the name of a recording artist? The nice touch here is the where-to-search dropdown. The ancillary nature of the index reinforces which *pond* within the Amazon *ocean* or catalog where 'Johnson' plays out:

FIGURE 2.26: Some Earlier Forms of Amazon Type Ahead Capabilities

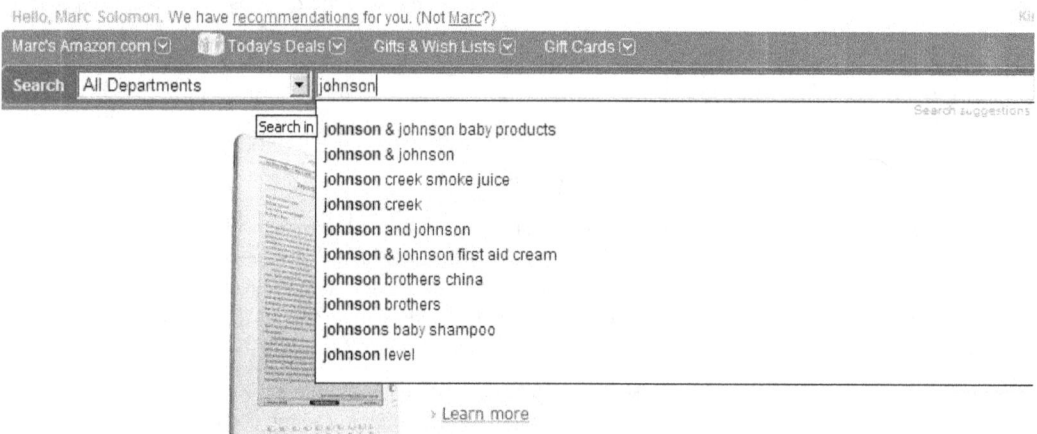

Speed of thought response rates lets us survey the index at the same time we're searching it.

Perhaps the biggest benefit of all is that suggestion search encourages longer queries based on established phrases that led to past successes. For instance, instead of simply searching on a broad topic like 'literature,' the suggestion box introduces us to *term expansion:* A host of related but far more targeted ways of narrowing down the topic – even from a half-formed variant like 'liter' (SEE Figure 2.27):

FIGURE 2.27: Sensitivity at the Speed of Thought

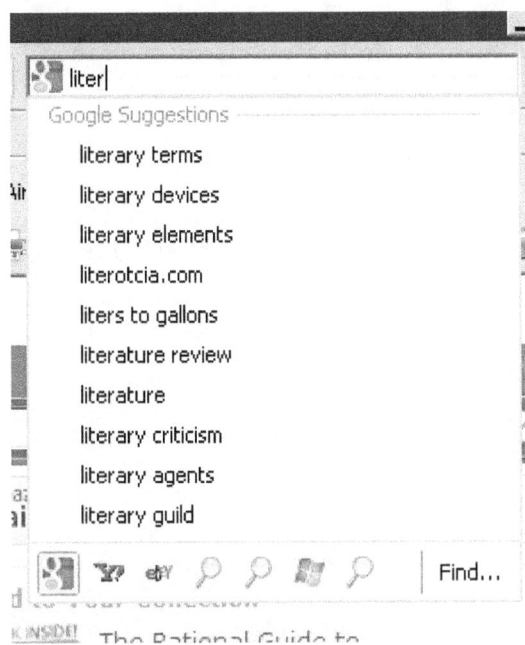

Suggestion search is not word-by-word but literally letter-by-letter.

Sentiment search

In my professional estimation, the leading cause of long walks off short search piers is a direct but elusive info-quest. I speak not of panning for gold but dishing for dirt.

After all, the impulse being served here sits at the table of avoidance. And that dining guest we're trying to scratch off the guest list goes by the name of 'surprise.' We do not wish for surprise to be seated at our tables. If they arrive despite our best efforts we need to be sure we can respond to the dining conversation that the element of surprise may throw our way.

Enter Sentiment search.

Sentiment search is the term used to describe search engines programmed to understand the social context of our search targets. For instance, it's one thing to know the hit counts for popular keywords. It's another to know how precise facts like phone numbers can lead to a trail of electronic droppings containing a person of interest.

But what if you're not just interested in links to friends and affiliations but the strength of those relationships? What if you're not only drawn to a subject based on a passing reference, but want the bigger picture that shapes a company's reputation? A leader's stature within their own profession?

A well-tuned sentiment search not only works as filtering tool to determine who's connecting to whom. It actually tells you who is the best known and what are they *best known for*. It's within that larger social dimension they provide a meaningful perspective on the footprint cast by our search targets.

Test Drives

This perspective-gathering is not limited to individuals. In fact, it's even more powerful for researching organizations and assessing their exposure to potential rewards and risks. One way to do this is to measure the impact of social, environmental and legal actions on a company's brand or reputation. Sentiment search helps public relations firms and corporate risk professionals to assess their potential liabilities. It also helps prioritize their resources for managing them.

Perhaps the most compelling use of sentiment search is when particular threats and opportunities can be quantified. The higher the number, the more elevated the impact. This is a major benefit to analysts who must plow through the murky, subjective and piece-meal nature of external risk assessments. Policy, media and business analysts must transform diffuse and pattern-resistant opinions into a single, defendable position. All the better if it's based on reducible, easy-to-interpret numbers.

A tool called Newsift provided this form of validation during its relatively short run in 2009.[7] In the test drive, we enter a single four letter word — *corn*:

1. We find out that corn is not a place – imagine that, no Corn, IA zip code to be had!
2. We also scoop up a 'Cornelius' and a 'Cornwall' in the first and last name mappings and there are no business topics.
3. Think of Suggestion search. But in Newsift, the suggestions land in particular buckets.
4. Then we eye the themes tab and pause to slurp on the corn syrup oozing from the media pile-on for HFCS ("high fructose corn syrup").
5. Now our contextual moorings are anchored to the correlated clusters of people, organizations, places, and related themes.

Remember cluster engines? They're essential to the success of any search tool designed to score opinions (as opposed to finding facts). But what about those scoring formulas?

Remember, analysts need to defend their positions. They need to justify their conclusions. It certainly helps that an impartial technology comes to their aid with a number that approximates an organization's exposure level. Let's return to the thrill of the chase and our *big corn hunter*.

One-in-five articles mentioning HFCS is controversial. (Note the 21% of the media pie carved out to be negative coverage). A quick inventory of the body counts show slackening demand for the product, lawsuits looming on the horizon and bent out-of-shape nutritionists planting doubtful stories like "Are grape jelly and chocolate milk bad for kids' brains?" In the movie version, this is where the camera pans to the left and right of newspapers falling on doorsteps. Calendar pages become unhinged like the crackling fortunes of corn empires near and far.

FIGURE 2.28: The Categorical Distinctions Mined from HFCS News Articles

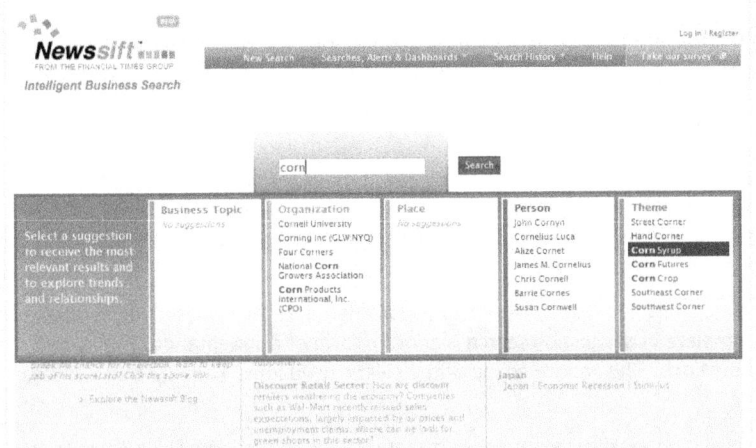

In the now defunct Newsift, we could tap into a simple narrative with little forethought or background knowledge on moving and complex search targets – especially the ones we didn't know we were looking for ... before we searched.

WHAT ARE PRIVACY SEARCH ENGINES?

Popping the Filter Bubble

Privacy engines are a reaction to the misuse of personal data by third-parties like Microsoft and Alphabet, Google's holding company since 2015. From a research perspective, a search that doesn't know us sounds like a warm embrace. This ensures repeatability of search log queries and set results. The recent proliferation of login-neutral search sites breathes new life into the quandary on how to carve up the ballooning index of tweets, images, and webpages. Basically, they answer to an evolving need we have for letting in (or at least previewing) our information providers while locking down our digital trails: What we search on and where it takes us.

What's to Lose By Regaining Our Privacy?

Many of these privacy engines outsource their indexing to Big Search (primarily Google and Bing). But as we've seen in **Unit One**, there's a vast distinction between crawling pages and presenting search results. Big search results ranks results by locality or in-result pointers. For instance, when Google leverages its other apps in support of completing your task loop on Google Maps, or an instruction video on YouTube.[8]

Duck Duck Go is the biggest mallard in a small search pond that only promises to expand. That growth is fueled by a public's growing unease with social and search media data collection. And the collection effort involves the shadowing, profiling, and reselling of our digital selves by unregulated and omnipresent search and social media interests. It's insult to injury when forces hostile to those interests, global citizens, and their governments can hack into these accounts.

A Credible Weakness

From the user perspective, the browser-based filtering is modest. There's a dropdown that parses results by nationality, timestamps, and smut factors (screening for adult content). There's also an attempt to augment results pages with instant answers extracted by information providers. But there's nothing rivaling Big Search engineering efforts to program answers to popular questions.

Duck Duck Go offers placeholder capabilities, encouraging users to save their display preferences through site registration. A curious invitation considering how creating a personal account defeats the primary motivation for using privacy engines. You will see paid sponsoring links of related catalog item on your products, even if you're just using Duck Duck Go to window shop. To be sure, there is a dedicated products tab in addition to 'web,' 'videos', 'news,' etc.

Privacy engines don't know you like Google or Bing know you. Some users may feel alienated, some liberated, depending on your own expectations. The disabling of auto-complete or suggestion search is another form of disorientation. The *People also ask* dropdown with cascades of common questions? The annotated bio of the celebrity du jour? They are free and clear of the privacy search experience.

As search expert and research blogger, Tara Calishain notes, they're not based on actual user queries. Why would a search engine focused on privacy do that? Rather than expose the cumulative curiosities of its users or the interests of its advertisers, privacy engines keep our queries in confidence. Instead, they rely on a generic blend of authoritative sources, from dictionary sites to Wikipedia. To be clear: It's a limited range of search-mediated suggestions.

How Do They Succeed If We're Not the Product?

Like their social media brethren, Google and Bing operate on the assumption of creating compelling apps, opaque algorithms, and uninhibited regime of untrackable, targeted ads – from panty hose to hate speech. The privacy engines lean on a familiar revenue mix of partnerships, affiliate links from online shopping, and contextual ads. The latter are not driven by personal usage but more generically through the topics we're searching.

FIGURE 2.29: Startpage.com Advanced Search Mimics Google Syntax and Semantics

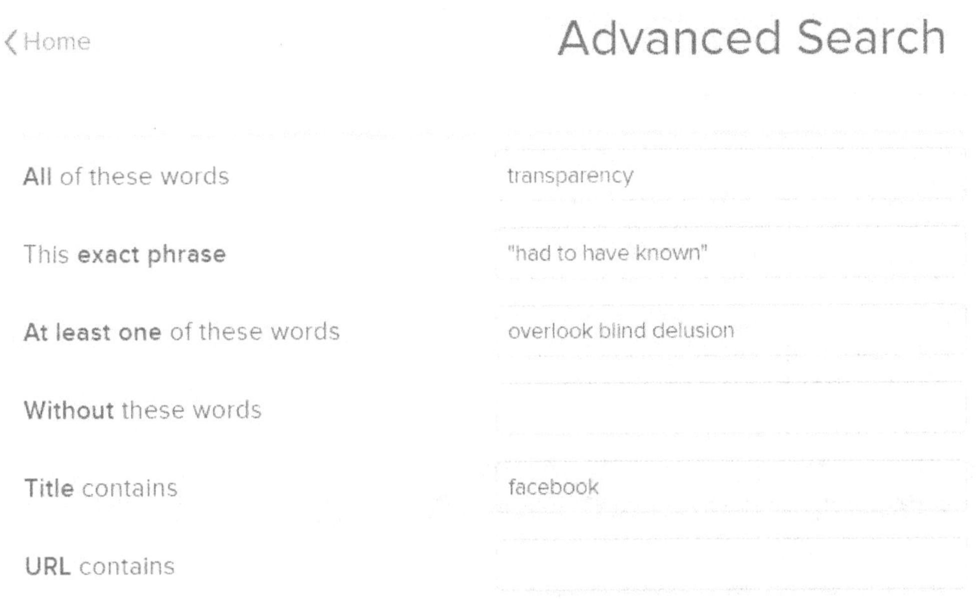

Advanced Search

⟨ Home

All of these words	transparency
This **exact phrase**	"had to have known"
At least one of these words	overlook blind delusion
Without these words	
Title contains	facebook
URL contains	

The Startpage Advanced Search options are a more guided way of building our query formations than expressing them as a single statement inside a search box.

Startpage.com preserves much of the syntax we considered earlier in **Unit Two** with its advanced settings. The following menu settings generate the following statement pictured above in Figure 2.33:

> *"Had to have known""title:facebook" + transparency (overlook OR blind OR delusion)*

TURNING THE TRACKING TABLES

Startpage's Anonymous View is a productive way to preview potentially malicious sites without being exposed to malware. Previewing also shields us from the less predatorial but equally insidious nature of the tracking codes embedded in the pages we visit. This is the tracking code that identifies us through 'browser fingerprinting' and 'device fingerprinting.' Just to be clear: What we're calling adware is not the same as the more respectable 'web analytics.' Analytics are a marketing function, often served by a single department inside companies subscribing to tagging services and/or applying analytics to their own customers and site visitors. It's when a site you visit or a purchase you've made triggers additional promotions for your repeat business when differences between malware and web analytics begin to blur.

FIGURE 2.30: Site Previews Under the Cover of Startpage.com

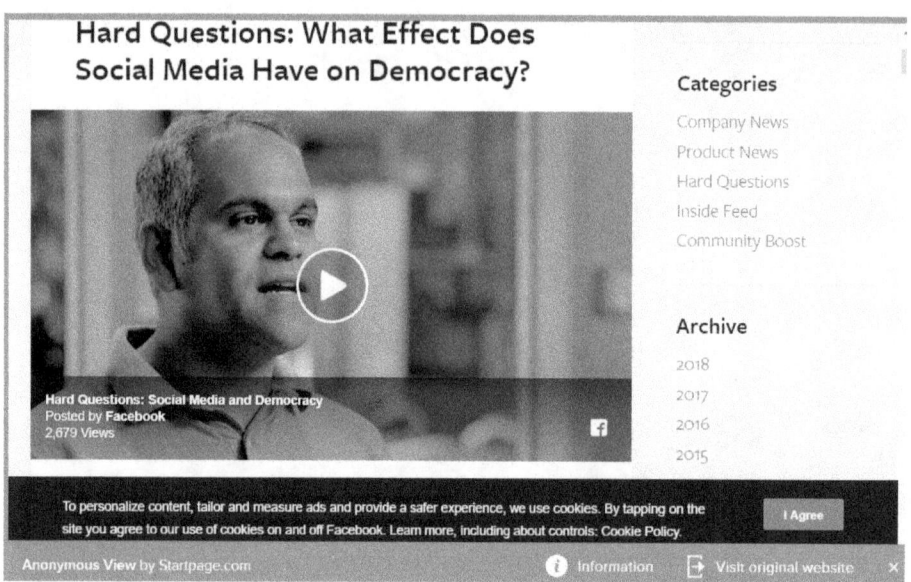

The Startpage Anonymous View lets users experience sites without exposing personal details such as surrendering an IP address.

It would be easy enough to disable the javascript that runs the site cookies in most advanced browser settings. However, this can often break many of the commercial sites we need to access in our research. 'Anonymous View' protects our identities without compromising our use of the sites trying to track us. This protection comes with two trade-offs: (1) page loads are slightly slower while the program untracks us, and (2) it's not foolproof. Some sites break anyway.

Leaving the Premises

One common myth of privacy engines is that your privacy is maintained once you leave their protection. Not true! We're tangled in the browser cookies and behavioral tracking we're trying to avoid once we click through the results page. There are notable exceptions. At this writing, Startpage.com uses a proxy server that maintains user anonymity when serving up pages too.

Swisscows encourages call-and-response query formation by including a facet-search design. Unlike a cluster search or a tag cloud, each related term forms an extended AND statement by steering the searcher in a suggestive direction.[9]

FIGURE 2.31: Word Maps as Search Facets

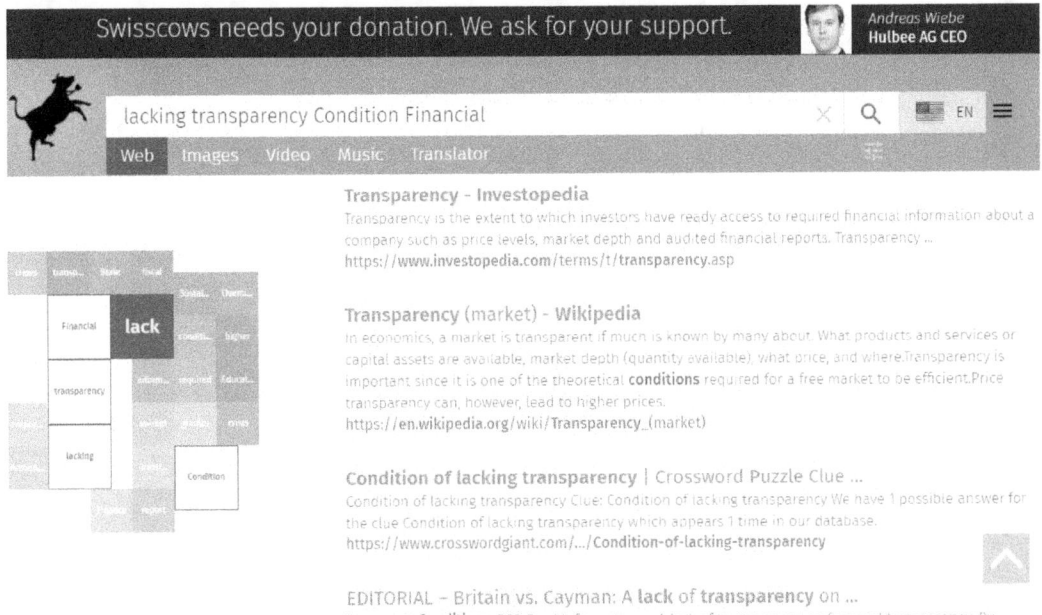

Swisscows generates a lexicon profile of the prevalent language found in a composite of the highest ranking search results. Clicking on these select terms adds them to the query.

Searx has the deepest toolkit and presents a wide assortment of both display and programming options. This latter capacity takes a page from the custom search engines we'll explore in the next search type we explore in **Unit Two.** Another handy virtue is that Searx is the one privacy engine that borrows the capabilities of meta search engines we evidenced in Meta Search with Gigablast and Surfwax. In fact, you can select from a ballooning list of search engines in the system defaults and configure them as your own unique blend: A throwback to what we we'll see with pioneering curation efforts like Rollyo.

FIGURE 2.32: Configuration Listing of Available Search Engines in Searx

Allow	Engine name	Shortcut	Selected language	SafeSearch	Time range	Avg. time	Max time
●	archive is	ai	not supported	not supported	not supported	0.4	7.0
●	asksteem	as	not supported	not supported	not supported	N/A	2.0
	wikipedia	wp	supported	not supported	not supported	0.187	2.0
	bing	bi	supported	not supported	not supported	0.319	2.0
	currency	cc	not supported	not supported	not supported	0.007	2.0
●	ddg definitions	ddd	supported	not supported	not supported	0.195	2.0
●	erowid	ew	not supported	not supported	not supported	N/A	2.0
	wikidata	wd	supported	not supported	not supported	0.681	3.0
●	duckduckgo	ddg	supported	not supported	supported	0.779	2.0
●	etymonline	et	not supported	not supported	not supported	0.723	2.0
●	faroo	fa	not supported	not supported	not supported	N/A	2.0
●	findx	fx	not supported	not supported	not supported	N/A	2.0
●	gigablast	gb	not supported	supported	not supported	N/A	3.0
	google	go	supported	not supported	supported	0.557	2.0

This inventory of search and directory indexes can be cobbled together to produce your own unique blend via the Searx open source community.

Leaving the Back Door Ajar

Not everyone's convinced that privacy engines are as airtight as they would have us believe. The temptation to share user histories is a well-trodden road to backdoor profiteering. Search engines derive limited benefit for serving users they can't track. Both Duck Duck Go and Searx display queries in your browser search histories. Note that Startpage does not below:

This means that anyone with browser access can access your search history. The unguarded back door tests the claims of these search engines that users leave no data trails in their privacy search travels. Unlike the ability to opt-out of being tracked, we're all free to delete our search histories. Manually.

A rival search engine to Duck Duck Go remarks that...

> "Privacy by design means that the most private settings are enabled by default. This extra step makes privacy inconvenient, and the product less user friendly."

It also means that Google and Microsoft offer browsers that contain those undeleted search histories -- even when the search is performed *in private*.[10] Despite their limitations and inconsistencies, privacy search engines are a first step the Knowledge-ABLED can take for reclaiming our personal data, repeatability and impartiality of our search logs, and even our negotiating power as consumers:

> "Reducing your digital footprint limits the ways that companies with your data profiles can use this data against you. It may feel like a convenience that Google can show you ads about things you're interested in. However, it also uses its data to let businesses charge you more, if you appear to be someone willing or able to spend more."[11]

FIGURE 2.33: The Search Histories That Expire (and Those That Live on)

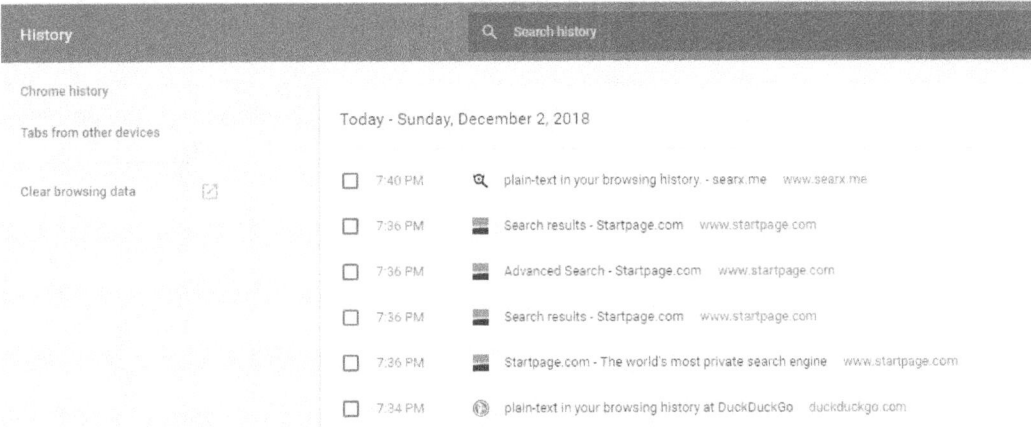

As we can see, the Startpage queries only divulge the site pages we visit. The Duck Duck Go and Searx entries also reveal the actual queries.

CUSTOM SEARCH APPLICATIONS

Regardless of the interface or the rankings formulas, the most important factor to distinguish one search from another is the single question: What is it pointing at? What's the size of its index? Who's included in it? We've already seen how dramatically results can turn on this single question. With custom search, that same factor lands in our own laps:

What kind of search would we build if we could decide what sources to feed it?

Feeding the Engine

One traditional form of custom or specialty search is to make sure that we're only searching a pre-selected group of sources. On premium sources this is a staple, a given. Paying for subscription services is akin to deciding which sources we want searched.

Configuring web-based sources is a lot more challenging. Not just because there are so many. Subscription-based sources don't typically end up aggregated by search engines. So most search results lack any kind of consistency for sorting the origin of the content.

Yes, they can tell you websites and they can cache specific web pages. But how often is the website the information source? As any librarian or newshound can tell you, the connection between where we see something and who produced it is often tentative, hard to trace. Even in the case of well-resourced news organizations, a fair number of stories filed come from wire services – not from staff reporters.

The way that search engines handle this is to partition content by the traditional formats used to trap this information. For instance, Google can apportion all leading U.S. universities simply by compiling a list of prominent .edu addresses and then bundle this list as a searchable *lake* or 'University Search.' The same can be done for popular media formats, discussions, or blog entries. Each information type is recognized by the format it's written for.

Searches within Searches

Other so-called specialty search tools only index sites specific to the task at-hand. Do we want a single point of contact for most airline schedules? Kayak.com might be your next ticket.

Kayak is an example of a search within a search. The site indexes a large number of travel, lodging, and airline sites to sort the best selections. The common organizing principles revolve around price, distance, and stops. The slider bars to the left allow the user to create a range of prices or a window of travel times that constrain or expand the search based on the first pass of search results.

FIGURE 2.34: Kayak Reflects the Dynamics of Booking Travel ... and Travel Pricing Factors

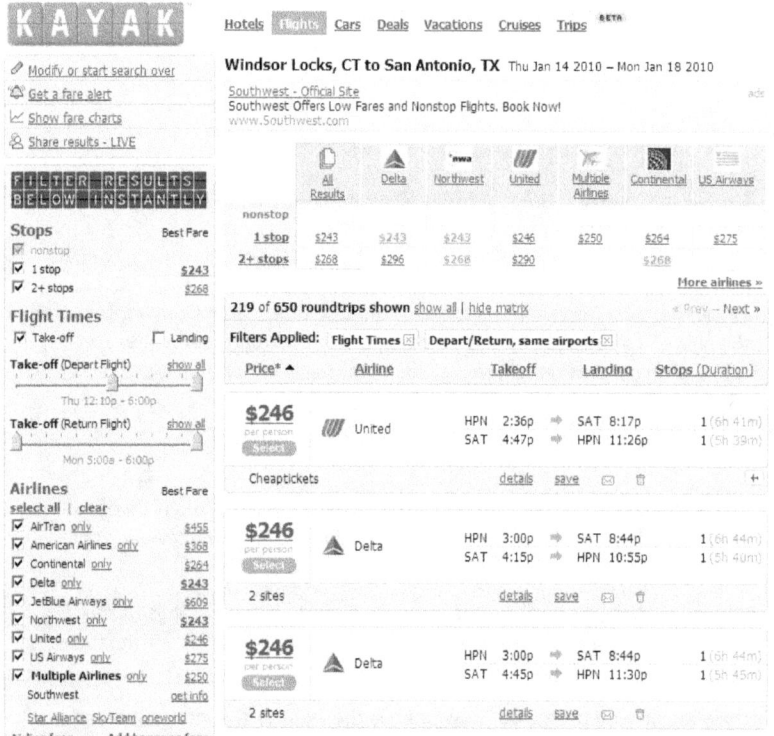

Kayak gathers only flight schedules published by major airlines and then buckets the key decision drivers of most travelers, including price, flight duration, and number of layovers.

Do we want to roll major job sites into one interface? **Indeed.com** has some great guided navigation paths provided in its clustering capabilities. It also does a much better job of presenting open positions and job descriptions than the sites where these positions are originally posted in a more two-dimensional cross-referencing dynamic such as Monster, CareerBuilder, and even Craigslist.

FIGURE 2.35: Indeed Does for Job Salaries What Kayak did for Travel Pricing

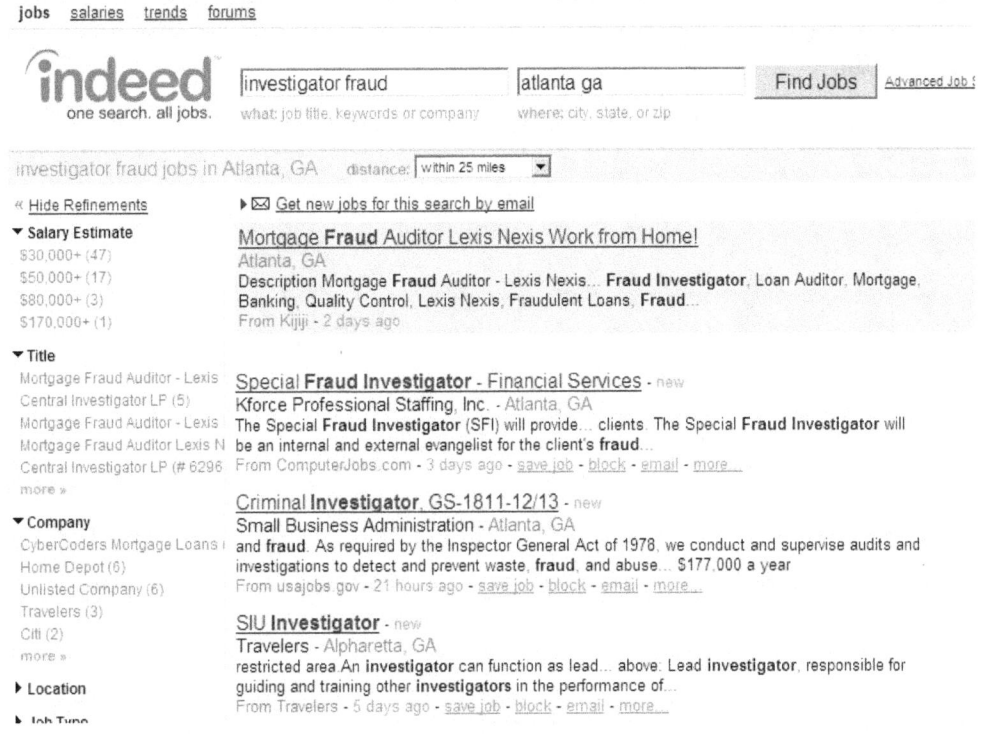

Indeed not only builds a clever index but anticipates the common job-seeking questions that dominate most job searches such as employers, titles, locations, and salary bands.

In the mid-2000s, search tools began to get the social networking bug. Besides indexing individual blogs and tagging sites in their search results, some search vendors invited curatorship. Some even encouraged user-visitors to build their own search solutions by organizing favorite sites by a binding theme.

Until 2012 Rollyo enabled visitors to group sources by key areas of interest for discriminating web searchers. Topics included alternative medicine, home repair, skeptics, and yes, private investigations.

FIGURE 2.36: Rollyo (Short for "Roll-Your-Own") Supported Web Curatorship

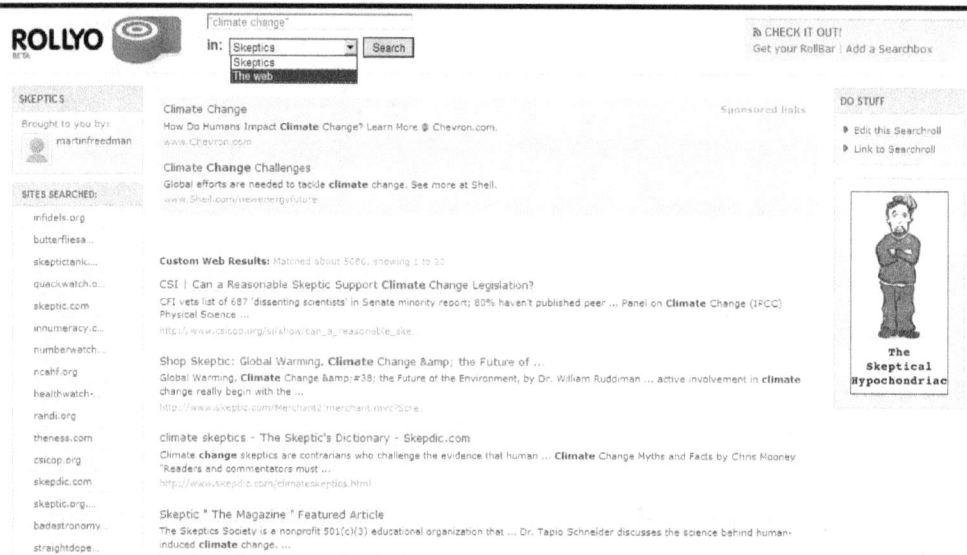

Unlike the other examples Rollyo invited us to use pre-configured source groupings or to build our own. The composite of 'Skeptics' sites are listed down the left-hand column.

Test Drives

Our custom search test drive is demonstrated with the Google CSE ("Custom Search Engine"). Google invites the opportunity to deploy its search technology in pursuit of our own source preferences and research assignments. If we want to google them, the syntax is:

```
inurl:cse inurl:coop site:google.com
```

We finish off the request with the particular flavor of search, say forensics, investigation, maps, or crime. We'll find the Google searches that have been customized to those topics.

Let's put some of those search tips to the test. First what happens when we overlay a search engine with a series of pre-defined sources? Our example here is an application written for Google to go out and fish in a pond full of culinary and recipe sites.

Before we wade into the specialty search waters let's do a little prepping with a custom engine appropriately titled 'Cookin' with Google.'[12] Here we're invited to toss whatever leftovers in your fridge we wish to make more inviting by sharing a pot, pan or casserole dish together. Select several ingredients and then specify the type of cuisine we would like to prepare. We will return to food preparation as a metaphor for query building in our **Unit Six** search cookbook case study.

While we're gathering ideas, consider:

- How many ingredients is the right number?
- Should we be entering food items in their singular and/or plural forms? What happens to your results if we target "potato tomato egg" from the expression "potatoes, tomatoes, eggs?"
- What happens when we provide a cooking related action word like caramelize or blacken?
- What happens when we have the diet-based version of a failsafe – say a food allergy or aversion to grease?

Try to eliminate outcomes we want to avoid by using the exclusion operator with *fried* or *boiled*. What happens when we specify *low or no fat* – does Google catch your drift?

Our Own Special Blend

Culinary directories sites, foodie sites, and recipe indexes are obvious enough for customizing a search request. What about when the sources are not so obvious or more specific than fulfilling a general and well-documented interest like cooking?

The custom Google engine can be pointed in the direction of whatever collection we build based on our own project requirements. The Google CSE enables us to literally perform a search within a search where it can trap useful sites by limiting the search to specific site domains or URL terms. The first thing we notice is that we're given the option of determining whether our sources are exclusive to our CSE, or should include all of Google.

STEP-BY-STEP: CREATING A CUSTOM SEARCH ENGINE

Below is the forensic evidence of what's inside my fridge. Cookin' with Google has a focused group of sources so that we're *cooking with gas*, not *throwing the kitchen sink* at our provisions.

FIGURE 2.37: Cookin' with Google as CSE Recipe (and for Clearing out the Fridge)

Cookin' With Google is a good working example of a custom search engine (CSE).

Next, under the ads we see ten possible refinements, including specific keywords that highlight subtopics and the sources that address them. We also see that keywords are highlighted in the title or text fields as well as URL links to the recipes cited.

It's one thing to assemble some ingredients in Google before we toss them from the fridge. What if we want to carve up our own slice of the web with our own recipe of sources? The sites to search box below is where we stack the addresses where we want Google to focus.

Step 1 – Setup the custom search engine

First, let's pick a unique theme and then build a query that's up to the task in step 1. We'll create a search topic called "Research Blogs" and then contribute sources to this topic:

FIGURE 2.38: Configuration Template for Google's Custom Search Engine

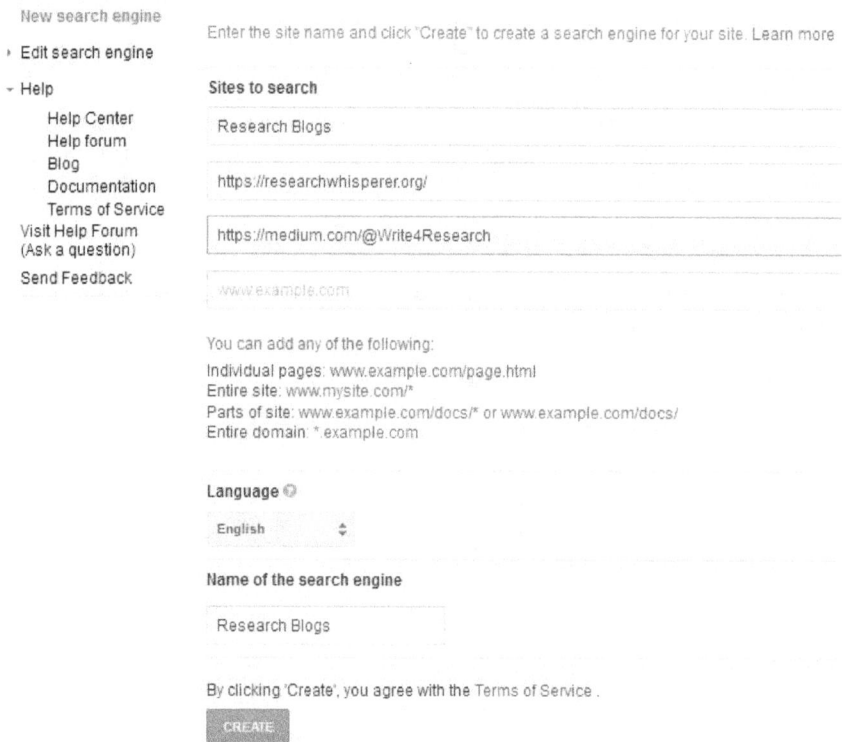

The Google CSE ("custom search engine") has been a stable and effective add-on for DIY website search hosting since 2006. Fingers crossed, it will continue as a flexible demonstration across a broad range of digital investigations and research scenarios.

Step 2 – Adding keywords

Next we want to guide the search over to prevailing themes, recurring narratives, and/or any language that validates the kind of findings and contexts we're trying to pull from. Note that we can create refinements around search topics by building queries that accentuate the unique properties of the sources we select.

FIGURE 2.39: Determining Search Engine Keywords

New search engine				
Edit search engine	**Basics**	Ads	Admin	Advanced
Media Groupings	Provide basic details and preferences for your search engine. Learn more			
Setup	**Search engine name**			
Look and feel	Media Groupings			
Search features				
Statistics and Logs	**Search engine description**			
Help	Web-based media used to collect and analyze mainstream news and opinion			
Visit Help Forum				
(Ask a question)	**Search engine keywords**			
Send Feedback	crime OR investigation OR litigation OR law OR trial OR police OR suspected OR evidence OR alleg			
	Edition Nonprofit, ads optional.			Get code
	Search engine ID 001548590360358651906:gkqhagh5uls			Copy to clipboard

The search engine keywords located below the search engine description contain the thematic terms we expect to emerge in our search topics.

Step 3 – Adding sources

Next we need to pick other source groupings to complement our search topics.

As we see with the assortment below, this is a useful way to center on our own fields of expertise. In addition to staying on top of our field it helps us understand how that subject is addressed by different source groupings. Newspaper sites versus press releases, trade media, or influential bloggers for example.

- Wire Services
- upi.com/*
- reuters.com/*
- ap.org/*
- businesswire.com/*
- prnewswire.com/*

FIGURE 2.40: Adding Sites to Custom Search

Adding sites could be specific to individual pages or all pages within a given site root such as the homepage of a popular news portal:

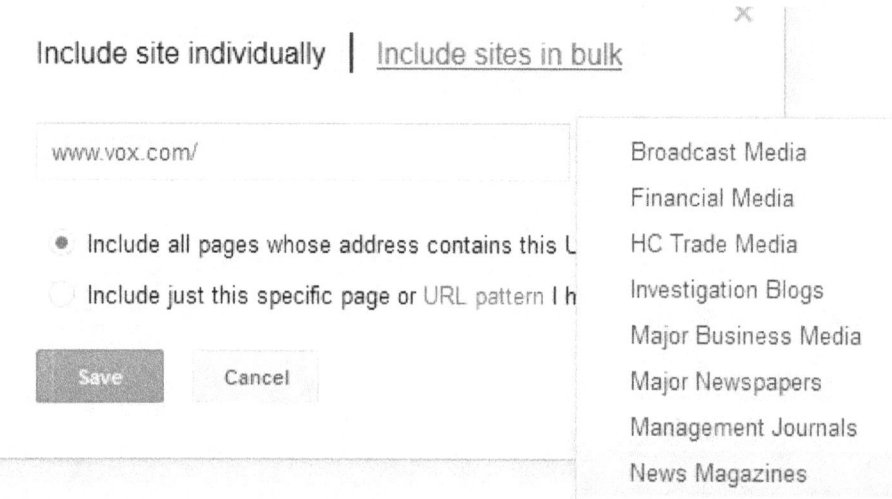

You can add the main web URL in the default settings above. You can search on sub-domains by placing a forward slash and asterisk after each new site to pick up on any changes to pages within that sub-section of the main site domain.

Step 4 – Reviewing the Output

It's now time to assess and tweak each of our custom searches (displayed here as media groupings).

FIGURE 2.41: WYSIWYG Search Engine Editing

digital literacy

All   Major Business Media   Management Journals   HC Trade Media   News Magazines
Major Newspapers

About 331 results (0.20 seconds)

Six social-media skills every leader needs | McKinsey
https://www.mckinseyquarterly.com/PDFDownload.aspx?ar=3056

Organizational social-media **literacy** is fast becoming a source of competitive advantage. Learn, through the lens of **executives** at General Electric, how you and your ... of management and organizations, with its emphasis on linear **processes** and ... of **literacy** is General Electric, where one of us is **responsible** for leadership ...
Labeled Management ...

Why Financial **Literacy** Programs Require Long-term Follow-up
https://knowledge.wharton.upenn.edu/.../why-financial-literacy-programs- require-long-term-follow-up/

Apr 28, 2015 ... New Wharton research shows that financial **literacy** programs are ... Ideally, **researchers** would set up two or more identical groups, offer ... "Those [types of **studies**] are hard, they are expensive and they take a long time," Mitchell observes. ... hours on the **computer** instead of waiting 80 years," Mitchell says.
Labeled Management ...

Measuring what matters in nonprofits | McKinsey
www.mckinseyquarterly.com/article-page.aspx?ar=1053&L2...

Every nonprofit **organization** should measure its progress in fulfilling its mission. ... Most nonprofit groups track their performance by **metrics** such as dollars raised , ... Statistical **studies**, updated periodically, have clearly shown that Jump$tart ... The study got around the problem of defining the term "**responsible** citizens" by ...
Labeled Management ...

Study | Blockchain for Social Impact: Moving Beyond the Hype
https://www.gsb.stanford.edu/.../study-blockchain-impact-moving-beyond- hype.pdf

File Format: PDF/Adobe Acrobat
the hundreds of **test** cases, pilots, and experiments that are using .... (See **case study** on page ... A blockchain is a digital, secure, public record book of transactions .... technologies also require internet connections and **digital literacy** for .... publish **case studies** and results, so that best **practices** can be ..... all the **processes**.
Labeled Management ...

Here's the output of the 'Management Journals' refinement. Note the keyword phrases associated with it are bolded as well as the keywords used in the query.

We can further refine our outputs in the advanced settings. Here we can determine sorting and ranking criteria as well as outputs for reviewing the metadata of our search records. These are the unseen tags that the engine uses to determine relevancy and display criteria.

FIGURE 2.42 Advanced Custom Search Settings

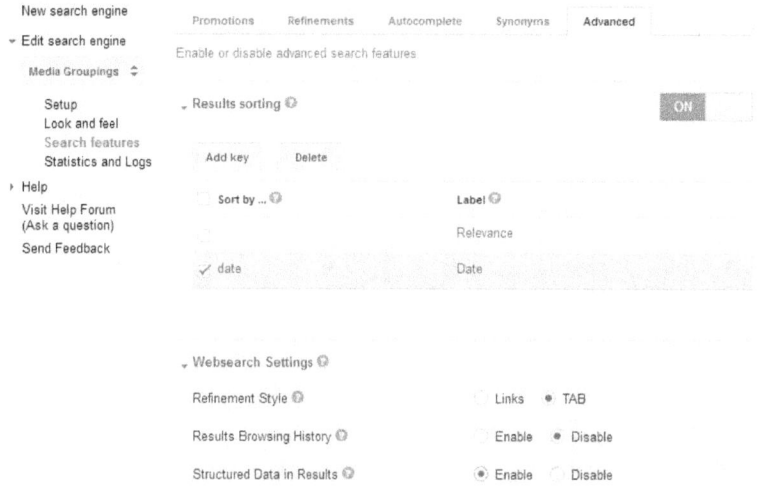

Below is an example of the metadata properties enabled through the "Structured Data in Results" option in the Site Features tab.

FIGURE 2.43: The Metasearch in Custom Search

Note the social media tagging that accompanies an otherwise formatted news aarticle from a mainstream financial news organization (Forbes Magazine).

Step 5 – Publishing your CSE

Finally, it's time to host your custom search engine.

Generate the HTML code so that your CSE can be hosted on any social media site that grants these design privileges. Blogspot is the example used below:

FIGURE 2.44 Hosting CSE Results on your Blog Page

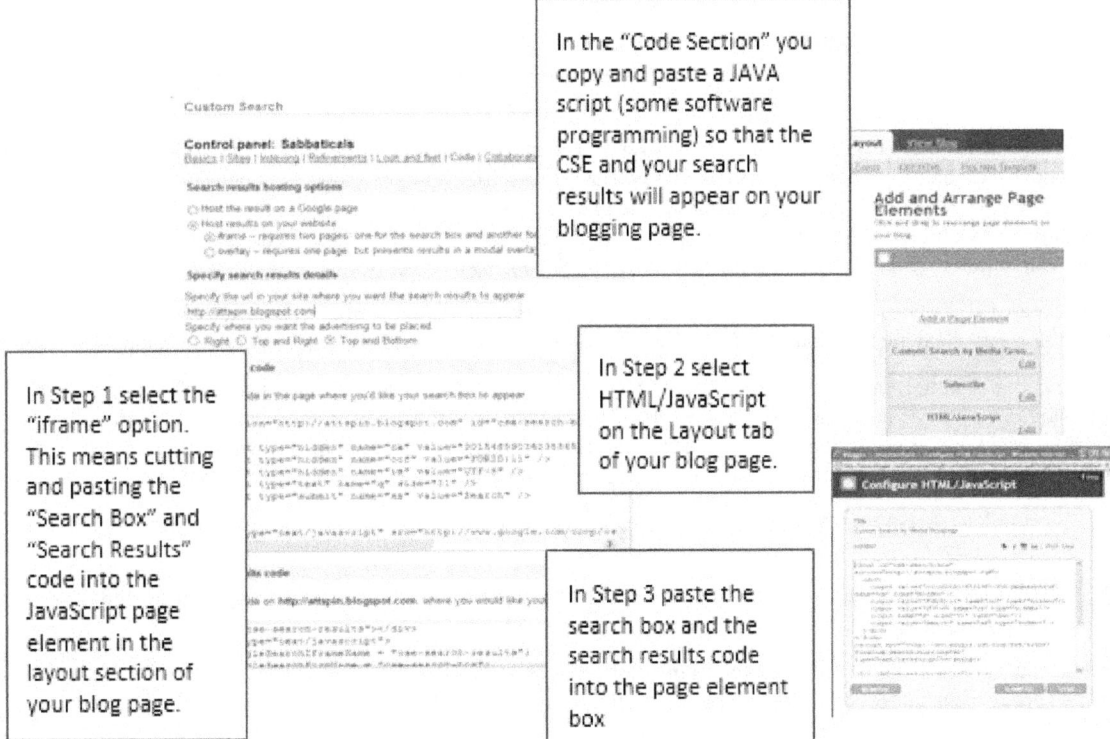

It's easy to redeploy our CSE on other pages to augment our own social media presence.

SECTION 2.4 | Subject Directories — Searching Beyond Search Engines

We've all seen the brave questioner step to the microphone. Maybe they want to bring attention to the issue they're about to raise. Maybe they want to impress the panel they're addressing by injecting their own new take on an old issue. Maybe they just plain want an answer? No matter the motive, we've all heard the adage:

> *"There are no bad questions."*

No one wants to be accused of ridiculing curiosity or not respecting the modes of inquiry we seek for a more educated and open society. But it's possible to defend the path to knowledge and still allow that there are some misinformed questions out there.

Misinformed questions often fail to anticipate how well suited an offline question is to a digitized answer. For example, fact-based questions that can be contained to a pre-defined set of records, like an airline schedule. A gift catalog can generate a customized outcome. Maybe, it's specific to garments size and floral patterns. Perhaps it's the time to make a connection between travel destinations. Such questions should produce exacting answers. A bias towards action yields instructions the questioner can rely on to produce specific outcomes whether it's booking a trip or buying a dress on their device of choice.

Such formulated and specific responses can be counted on not only for their action-producing outcomes but for the relative speed of their arrival. Searching a database of standard stock items can and should elicit rapid, *speed-of-thought* responses.

However, this kind of pattern-matching is more challenging when searching databases that consist mainly of words, not numbers. No matter how advanced a search technology, it's slower going in the world of ideas. A world of abstraction. A world of interpretive judgments, i.e. opinions). Chances are remote we can create point blank answers around opinion-based questions. We're acting on a misinformed assumption about the time commitment to complete the following:

1. How long do we estimate it will take to research the number of hospitals that offer surgical procedures within a certain city?
2. Now how long will it take to establish who is the best surgeon? Can the question even be answered without direct experience?

One way to apply the best-tool-for-the-best-job to the particulars of web research is to consider whether we are best off fishing in an *ocean* of web pages or a *lake* of subject directories. In this model, the ocean is represented by a commercial search engine such as Google, Yahoo, or Bing. These services compete to effectively crawl or index the most web pages. They were initially rewarded for delivering the most visitors to the sites advertised through their search result listings. Nowadays, proximity is no longer measured by the number of words between search terms but the distance between a device owner and the advertiser's ability to influence their purchases right through to the drive-up window.

Even if our goal is to find correct answers, not rankings, a search engine may be our best bet. Especially if we have a specific answer in mind. Search may not cut it, however, if we're looking for a range rather than a definitive outcome. In that case, a directory may well have fewer but higher quality pages. These results will complete more answers as our investigation unfolds.

Enter the information lake or subject directories.

SUBJECT DIRECTORIES AS INFORMATION LAKES

Often a cry for information help is just another variation on drowning in too many search results. This is not any just form of confusion. Here, we are dwelling at or close to the surface of an information ocean. What can we do to keep this search project afloat? How do we reshape a misinformed question?

A subject directory is a resource that specializes in linking to other web sites and categorizing those links. Web directories often allow site owners to submit their site for inclusion. Human editors review submissions and often reclassify sites based on a more formal classification system or taxonomy.

Another way to compare selecting a subject directory or a search engine goes straight to the question of site selection. That's right. What kinds of waters do we wish to fish in? The metaphor we use to capture this is the OLP framework or *Oceans, Lakes, and Ponds*. OLP refers to how deep a reserve of content we're wading into during any particular stage of web-based research.

As we mentioned earlier, **DMOZ** (or the Open Directory Project) was the largest human-assisted subject directory. Launched three years ahead of Wikipedia, DMOZ reached slightly more than three million web pages. This is epic in size for a purely human mental labor. It also came to pale in comparison to Google's own automated subject directory entree of 64.7 million pages, a staggering sum for a topical index at the time.[13]

Google and Yahoo's own former web directories relied on DMOZ as foundations for classifying the sites sourced by their own crawlers. For this reason, DMOZ remains an historic knowledge resource. It was the first known go-to source for mapping the web. It was the first electronic reference to validate the *aboutness* of any known topic, how it's classified, and even contextualized in terms of rankings and related affiliations.

THE MANY FORMS OF SUBJECT DIRECTORIES

Subject directories are referred to in many forms, including:

- Searchable indexes
- Integrated search indexes
- Specialized meta engines
- Specialized subject directories

But regardless of the nomenclature, all subject directories classify a grouping of links, lists, sites or records according to a central organizing principle. Sometimes they're exhaustive and aim to be the systems of record for an entire industry (http://www.martindale.com). Sometimes it's pay-to-play and only members have access to use them (http://www.familyreunion.com). Sometimes they're portals into more specialized resources (http://www.usa.gov). No matter what the resources we're referencing, it helps to keep an open mind about what constitutes a subject directory, i.e. they're not all slang dictionaries, physician review sites, or wikipedias.

Sometimes it's a collection of links with a common bond. Maybe a directory of listservs or discussion boards arranged by topic. Other times, it's a grouping of experts organized around their field of expertise. Either way, we're far closer to acting on our research because we're browsing a directory to draw from a fact base tethered to the topics in question.

WHY DIRECTORIES STILL MATTER

There are two different ways to control information quality on the web at the source level. The first is from the use of search engines. The second is from the use of subject directories. Why subject directories? Perhaps the ultimate term expansion tool is to pull our fishing poles out of the ocean and cast them in a lake.

Not sure how large is big? How colorful the colors? How safe the safety record? How cornered or crowded the market? In terms of scale, that's the directory option.

Unlike search engines, subject directories already have a structure formed around the topics we're investigating. This structure is established around the boundaries that contain the topic. Then there's (1) the bridging, (2) the relatedness, (3) the branded anchoring, and (4) the channels in and out designed to keep the content fresh, the site unique, and the records accurate. Sometimes, this means the site can monitor changes through its own indexing technology. Updates are automated. Other times, the communication originates with the community that uses the resource as we see below in Figure 2.45:

FIGURE 2.45: Reference-worthy Search Results in ipl2 (Internet Public Library)

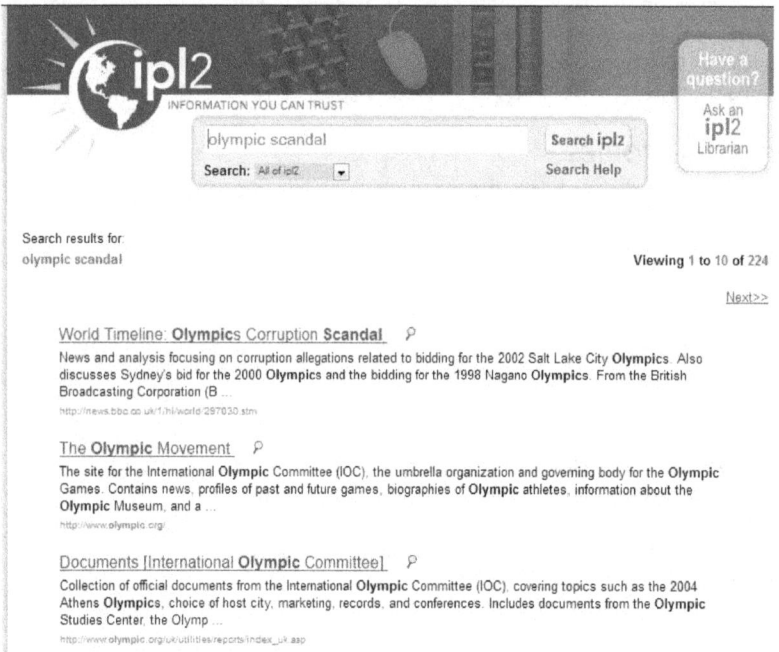

The IPL suggest a site form is a throwback to the days where a formal vetting process determined the value of specific resources – not the number of sites linking to the resource. However advertising formulas like Google's Page Rank don't obviate the need for brokers. Here the IPL narrows the gap between the information surplus of the web and the knowledge deficits of us researchers. [14]

There are two types of subject directories:

1. **Human Filtered**: This occurs when a person develops the boundaries for a particular topic area. Think Wikipedia, the web's closest approximation to a monastic order.

2. **Machine Enabled**: This occurs when the same classification imposed by the human is imposed by the directory, usually with similar type of indexing capabilities we would expect from a search tool.

Let's talk about the trade-offs inherent in each and how the Knowledge-ABLED can accentuate the strengths of each.

The Importance of Being Human

By definition, human-filtered sites are less numerous and date-sensitive than automated directories. But that extra TLC ("tender loving care") has some distinct advantages. The labors of subject experts and librarians provide an important quality check for filtering out misleading or possibly fraudulent sites. Instead of millions of results, a human-made lake can be measured in the thousands, increasing the odds that we will connect, if not with the ideal site, at least with (1) the right category, (2) a more nuanced exploration, and (3) free of commercial search intrusions.

Subject directories can be harder to navigate than the billions of pages indexed by the leading search engines. What do fewer records mean exactly? The payback is less immediate. The gratification is delayed. It's in the second pass or *drill-down* into human directories where the virtues of information pruning, and peer review start to pay-off.

Human-filtered directories like Wikipedia are also pre-qualified source referrals regardless of the mission at-hand. Those referrals take us from the *searching* to the *conversing* stage of primary intelligence. Here, we actually engage the people we have been researching. Not as background knowledge. But to start filling in the foreground —the key questions in our case!

Stay tuned for a more formal introduction to Search to Converse ("STC") in **Unit Three**.

It's not likely that such a list will be residing in a Google map of our home town, say, if we're trying to come up with a listing of PI firms or investigation agencies. However there's a good chance that the more prolific outfits would have an entry in DMOZ. As we've learned, DMOZ predated Wikipedia and operates on a similar principle – an open source directory created by community volunteers that compiles sources around a common index.

Consider the following factors as we weigh our subject directory options:

FIGURE 2.46: Examples of Human-mediated Subject Directories

Directory Type	Examples
Subject categories:	**Infomine** (http://infomine.ucr.edu): 'Librarian-built" archive of research-based directories, databases, journals, and listservs **Internet Public Library** (http://www.ipl.org) Wrote the book on how to vet public sites that work in the public interest, including such factors as credibility, legality, authority, scope, design and function
Academic disciplines:	**Academic Info** (www.academicinfo.net): Subject guides organized by classroom syllabus
General and working definitions:	**Wikipedia** (http://en.wikipedia.org/wiki/Main_Page) largest reference site on the web where volunteers submit, edit, and cross-reference non-original topic-based articles
Listings and registries	**American Society of Association Executives** (http://asaebuyersguide.com) maintains a buyer's guide of associations, agencies and professional finders among its 22,000 members
Specialized directories	**About.com** (www.about.com) consists of guides who cover diverse topics with an accent on consumer goods and services[15]

In each of these examples, human intervention reduces the noise to signal ratio that we muddle through in keyword-prompted searches. In each case, there is a domain leader to connect their own expertise with a favorable use of the resources they're touting.

The Practicality of Building to Scale

Sounds like a research plan? You're now sold on the idea that librarians have their way with the Internet?

In this hermetic pipe dream, no subject is worth documenting unless a Wikipedia entry already exists. This static view of a moving world is further compromised by the math: That even the world's largest encyclopedia pales in comparison to the volume and scale of a machine-enabled reference like Google. The sobering truth is that without a robust index, there can be no bone to pick with subject expert editors or content-vetting librarians.

Let's say we're interested in researching medical outcomes. We're about to help a loved one find the best health care provider for that particular treatment. However, we also know that most hospitals are hard-pressed to share their rates of success regardless of the medical condition or procedure being considered. Our search in Wikipedia ends with few openings. There are no entries under medical or patient outcomes.

However, if we use the same angle in a specialty subject index like PubMed, we get a list of related subjects from which to further pursue our course of action, including sub-specialties, clinical trials, and all things medical short of the faith-healers, and malpractice lawyers. This is not a one-shot, bullseye approach to problem-solving. But a machine-enabled directory is likelier to focus our efforts better than either a human-based one or a search engine:

FIGURE 2.47: Examples of Machine-generated Subject Directories

The pre built classification structure of the Yahoo directory shows a diverse but robust set of options for pursuing follow-up exploration of an otherwise new or alien topic. (The Directory was discontinued at the end of 2014)

Strength in Numbers

Compared to the scale of a lake constructed by humans, the web crawlers of the automated indexes will win every time. That's not comparing subject directories to search engines. That's contrasting human to machine-enabled directories. Human-curated listings are still a small drip in the overall search bucket for Big Search.

Think of machine-enabled directories as man-made lakes. An order is imposed. A reserve is held. Even though the local climate and atmospheric conditions don't support it, a group of engineers have organized a single container that can now grow without human intervention or vetting.

UNIT TWO: Using Search in Virtual Investigations | Page 2:89

Also take notice that both of these services include the open directory listings of DMOZ for structuring their directory-based results even though the types of content they index can vary greatly?

Don't believe me? Try this a metasearch mashup tool that shows you just how divergent the results can be:

FIGURE 2.48: Comparative Results of Side-by-side Search Engines (circa 2010)

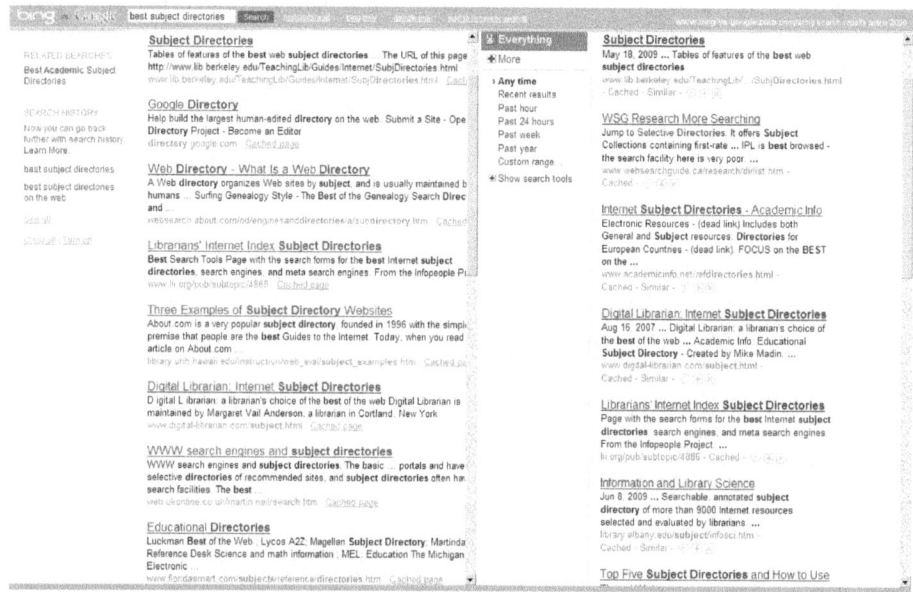

Comparative Results of Side-by-side Search Engines (circa 2019)

This comparison of outputs between Bing and Google shows just how non-definitive any single tool is for sourcing the research corners of the web – especially when the subjective notion of what's best comes into play as it does here. Note: How overrun with sponsored links Google has become over the past decade.

Understanding subject directories attributes will also help your evaluation process as you plan your search strategy.

FIGURE 2.49: Browsing Public Lists to Cull Experts

CataList collects listservs or the public discussion boards that predate the Web 2.0 or rise of social media. Note that the collection can be viewed by location and popularity. Otherwise a directory search by keyword is the only other point of entry offered.

Yes, it's true. Directories are structured. Does that mean search engines are not? It's true that directories are smaller in size and more discriminating about what they index. But that says little about what's useful and what's distraction.

The best directories are easy to navigate for experts and novices alike. They are also seen as credible source references, even if they're not the originators of the content they distribute. In fact, if we look at the rules governing Wikipedia, we see that editors are expressly forbidden from presenting original research. It all needs to have been published elsewhere before Wikipedia references the work in question.

The topical boundaries of a subject directory can exert higher standards than in search results in other ways. For instance, many subject directories consist of peer reviewed material that's vetted prior to its publication. Librarian reference sites like Infomine and the Internet Public Library are cross-referenced and fact-checked to a quality level that far exceeds any search result. As we see in Figure 2.50, the underlying metadata is both exhaustive and searchable in its own right.

FIGURE 2.50: Advanced Search Reflects the Categories Found in Subject Directories

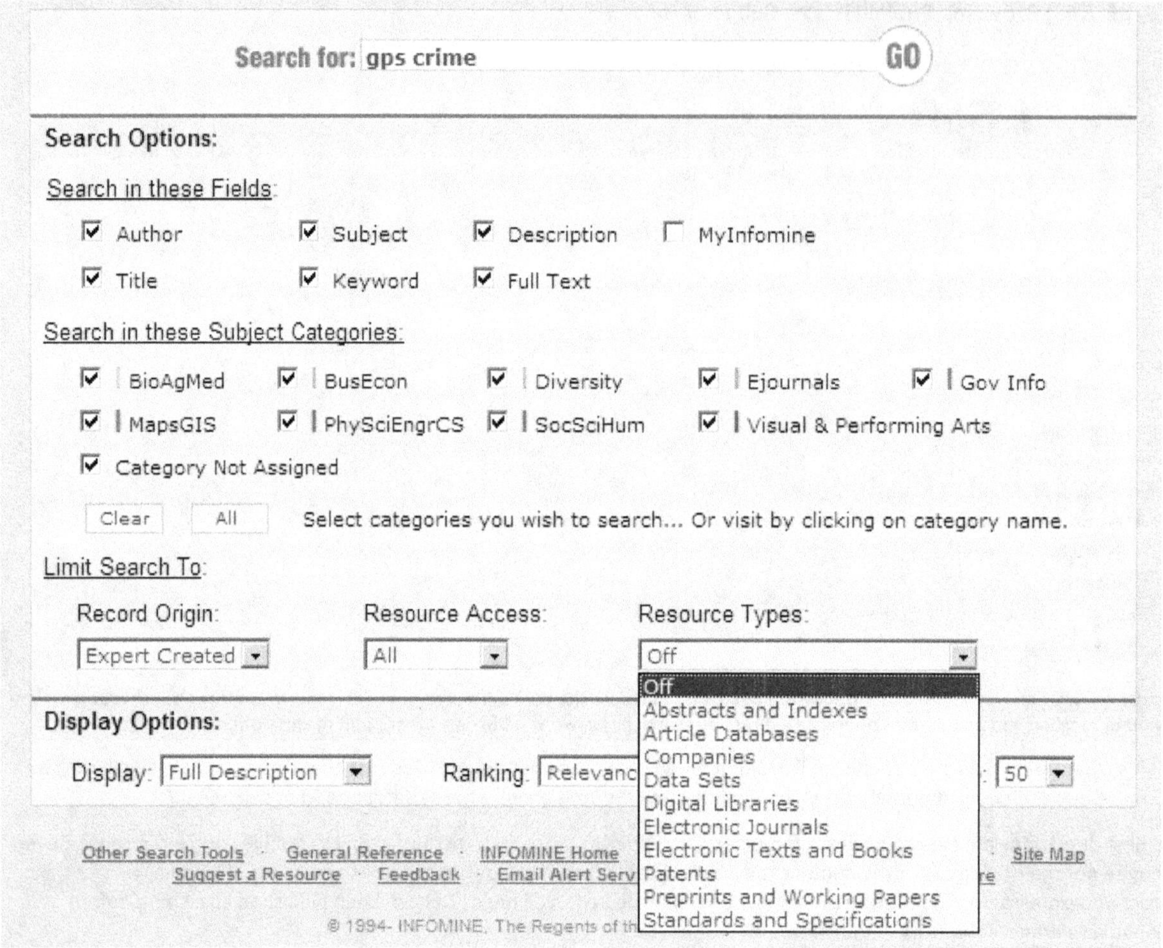

The advanced search screen on Infomine gives us the ability to cross-reference sources, subjects, document fields, and even the source groupings we see in the dropdown menu called Resource Types.

Not all winning directories need to be run by librarians. Many domain experts build and run directories aimed at helping non-professionals to broker an introduction. These directories help novices to navigate the ins and outs of services and disciplines they may turn to before seeking direct advice from an insider. There are many popular examples of this in evidence and some of which we may already know. **Findlaw.com** is a great diagnostic tool for laypeople involved in legal research. **WebMD** offers the same treatment for medical conditions. For those of us who require an escape from reality, there's a directory for that too. In the entertainment world, the **IMDB** or Internet Movie Database indexes every leading actor and stagehand to be listed in the closing credits of most film, broadcast TV, and streaming productions.

In the following example, we use both a human and machine-enabled approach to finding categories relevant to malpractice. In the DMOZ example, we see distinctively different social, business, and legal contexts for the term *investigation* including categories that address expert witnesses, the security industry, and current investigations and scandals.

FIGURE 2.51: Static Versus Fluid References in Subject Categories

Search: investigation

Open Directory Categories (1-25 of 7)

1. Business: Business Services: Fire and Security: Security: Investigation *(210 matches)*
2. News: Current Events: Investigations and Scandals
3. Regional: Europe: United Kingdom: Business and Economy: Industries: Security: Investigation *(46)*
4. Society: Paranormal: Organizations *(17)*
5. Society: Relationships: Cyber Relationships: Cyberinfidelity Investigations
6. World: Français: Commerce et économie: Services aux entreprises: Investigation *(36)*
7. Society: Law: Services: Expert Witnesses: Accident Reconstruction *(28)*

[investigation] [New Search] Advanced Search Help on Search

DMOZ distinguishes timeless or static references from more fluid or event-driven sites that track the same subject.

We see far more categories from the same PI query in the Yahoo example. In fact, we see surveillance equipment, insurance, privacy law, Scientology, and state-specific PI or 'private investigation' services. The location is a key organizing principle that's built into the directory index. We can also assume that these links are more current than the human-enabled links and that they are commercially motivated.

FIGURE 2.52: Provider List Generation from Subject Categories

The Yahoo Directory was not only helpful for getting a handle on a topic but for rounding up lists of organizations or providers of the goods or services in question.

In its day, the Yahoo directory read like a substitute business listings service that never made it to the local Yellow Pages. Remember those? For instance, if you included "(private OR professional) investigator" in the Yahoo directory search...

You get what appears to be mostly unfiltered agency listings (n=587). If you add 'Florida,' you get 130. 'Massachusetts?' Eighty-six hits.

Those numbers are consistent with what we should expect when transitioning from oceans (search engines) to lakes (subject directories). Think of the latter as latching onto a page, site, or listing that either (1) a librarian (manual classification) or (2) programmer (automated classification) has already appropriated a place it calls home or within a hierarchy of related topics.

Exhaustive? No. Overwhelming? Absolutely.

But at least the orientation is more focused in a lake. The relatedness or *aboutness* of your topic, as Peter Morville likes to say, is easier to piece together. Not all directories are conduits like search engines. Some are actual destinations. Can you think of a few?

Working from Strength: 'Pearl-culturing' With Directories

It helps to *get a feel* for what's out there. But in many professions, there are exacting standards used to determine specific outcomes and decisions. How can we exert the same level of control on the public web that we could in an industry specific database or specialty collection?

Chief among our Knowledge-ABLED incentives is the need to view the web. More than another information source, the web is our virtual ally in solving common business problems and even in marketing our own professional assets. Enter pearl culturing to our growing set of problem-solving tools. As we've seen, one of the advantages of browsing a directory is that we are not *trawling the ocean* with Internet searches but actually fishing in a lake (and a fairly well stocked one at that). The practical outcome is that the rich indexing of a directory allows us to expand our search to terms. These terms are true to our project objectives, summoned from our own limited exposure to unfamiliar subjects.

Pearl culturing is a term coined by Mary Ellen Bates, a pre-eminent business researcher to describe the ability to build on our limited knowledge of unfamiliar domains. Pearl culturing gets around the frustration that comes with head-scratching search results the first time out. Instead, we use our initial searches to mine for more productive search terms.

Mary Ellen Bates

Pearl culturing is in many respects the opposite of the *feeling lucky* impulse we indulge when we expect a few keywords to fill us in on our search targets. We begin with keywords and then enlist affiliated terms that reinforce our intentions. They pry open some related subject otherwise passed over. The goal with pearl culturing is not to expect bullseyes each time out. It's not a leisurely browsing of intriguing but historically out-of-step directories. It's to strike a balance between extensive indexing and domain specific search terms.

Below, we return to our quest on medical outcomes. Only this time we're planting our question in the fertile bed of the **PubMed**[16] index:

FIGURE 2.53: Looking up classification terms in a subject index

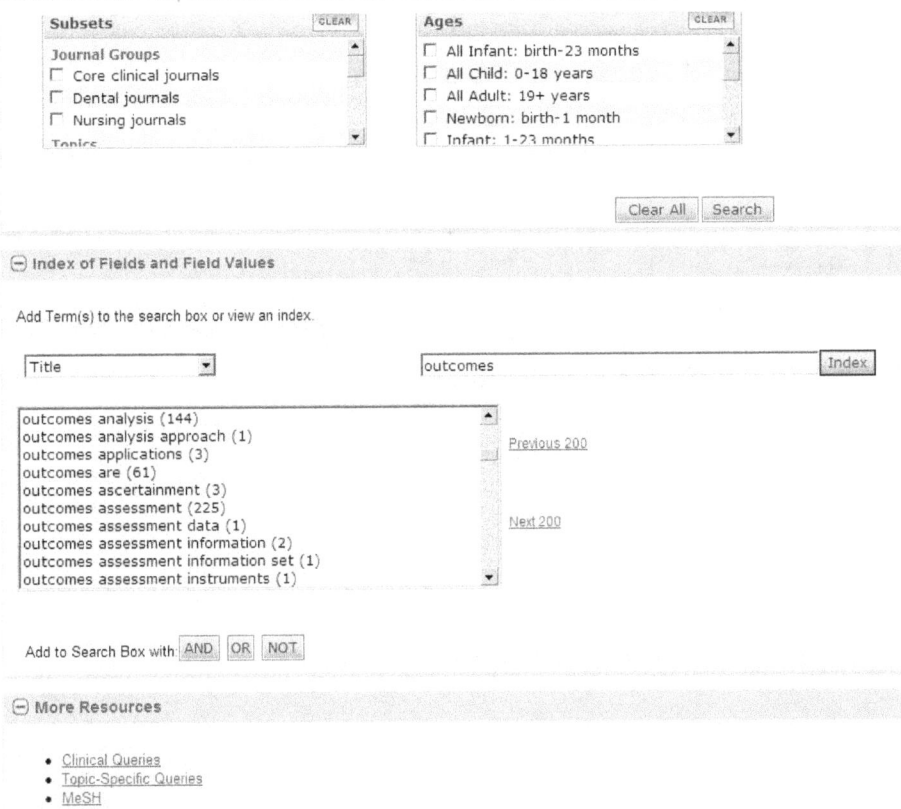

Next, we run a search with *outcomes assessment* in the title:

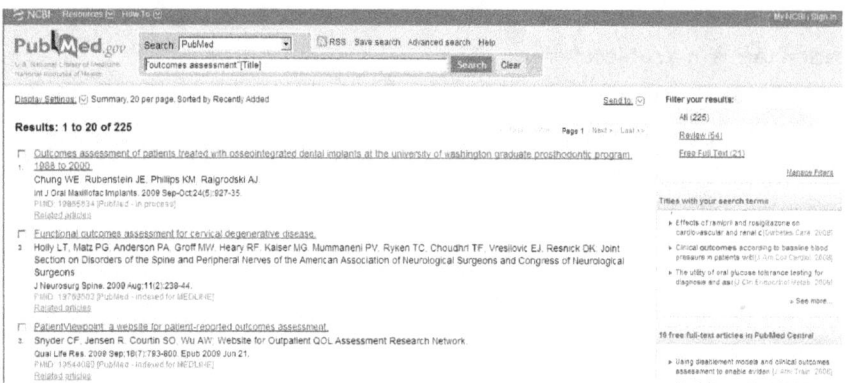

Then we click through on the terms associated with one of the articles in question. Presto! It's a gold mine of query strings and classifications that we can now apply in a *larger ocean*, a.k.a. corpus.

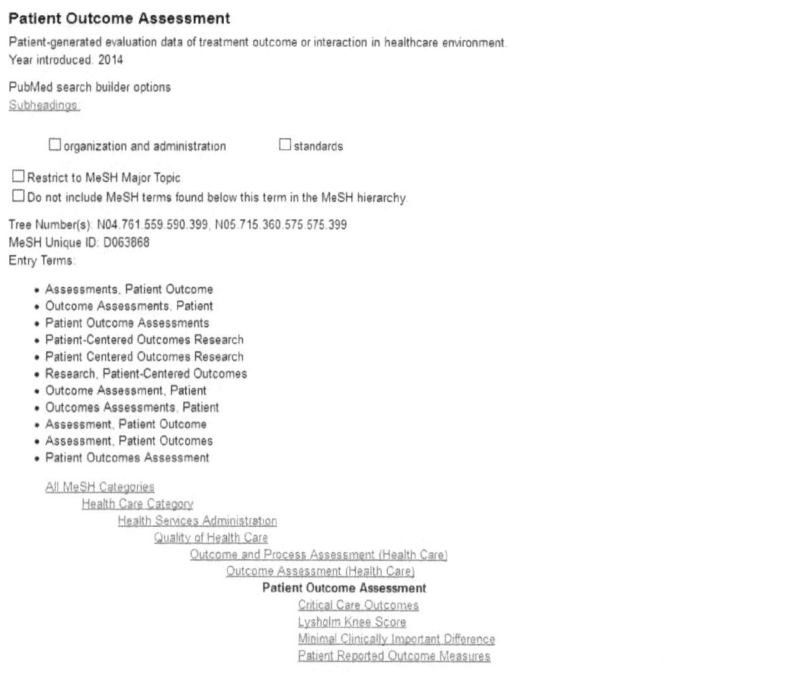

At the bottom of this abstract the MeSH terms or what librarians call 'descriptors' serve the same purpose as the topic classifications in DMOZ or the Yahoo Directory. The most promising terms can be cycled into subsequent searches to improve specificity and comprehensiveness, a.k.a. pearl culturing searches to improve specificity and comprehensiveness, a.k.a. pearl culturing.

FIGURE 2.54: Using Pearl Culturing to Locate Virtual Communities on Targeted Topics

Search results

DHS-PCMH-ADVISORY-COUNCIL@LISTSERV.DPW.STATE.PA.US
DHS- Patient Centered Medical Home Advisory Council *(62 subscribers)*

1 list matched your search string.

Learn more about: Announcement Lists • Discussion Groups • Email Marketing

LISTSERV is a registered trademark licensed to L-Soft International, Inc.
CataList is a service mark of L-Soft International, Inc.

Last update: 12 Dec 2018 04:00 -0500 (54,851 lists, 1,286 sites)
® L-Soft International, Inc. 2018

A search of the CataList Listserv directory from Figure 2.50 yields a community focused on the prior topic targeted in PubMed (Patient-centered Outcomes).

SUMMARIZING SUBJECT DIRECTORIES

Subject directories are typically database of titles, citations, or websites organized by category – similar to the subject categories organized in a traditional library-based card catalog.

Subject directories are...

- Either organized, evaluated and cataloged by humans or compiled automatically by machine indexers otherwise known as crawlers or spiders
- Broken down dimensions of a subject according to facets or related topics
- Designed for browsing, not searching, due to size and quality
- Likely to include summary descriptions of links so we know the subjects they cover without needing to crack them open first

Subject directories are most useful when we don't know what we are looking for but we *would know it if we saw it.* This kind of situation is likely to arise around...

- General or popular topics
- Product information
- Histories and time-lines
- Finding correct related phrases and jargon
- Portals to second person/party communications (contact information, communities of interest, key officials, and enforcement agencies)

Engines Versus Directories

It's been a long, exhaustive Searching Out Loud unit on using search and subject directories. But we're not quite done with either. Let's revisit the question of when to consider which tool in our research.

The distinct differences between the engine versus directory trade-off are highlighted in precision (fact) versus abstract (opinion) searches:

1. Is it best to search a small group of sources or a large one?
2. If we have a relatively small target, say an individual who is interviewing you for a job, what can we expect to find out about their preferences in candidates?
3. What if we have a highly fixed one like a travel itinerary between two destinations? How discriminating can we be in voicing our own preferences?
4. On the contrary, what if our target is expansive? What if it's resistant to easy keyword definitions? Is it better to trawl an ocean of web pages or be more selective in our tool selection?

Perhaps the best way to determine the right course is to take our first *screen test*. This is an analysis we may already perform in our routine searches where the first page of search results either: (a) gives us the answer or, (b) sets us on the right course, meaning we're in a range of potentially productive jumping off points.

FIGURE 2.55: Comparing Search Indexes to Subject Listings

ENGINES	DIRECTORIES
Words about Specific Nouns	Words about Subject Headings
Layouts and floor plans and lighting	Interior decorating
"Philip Roth" (1.2 million hits)	Authors **Philip Roth** (12 relevant categories)

FIGURE 2.56: When to Search it Down and When to Look it Up

ENGINES & DIRECTORIES
Strengths & Weaknesses

Search Engine	Subject Directory
One Song	Lyric Collections
What's Unique	What's in Common
High Precision	High Recall
Low Recall	Low Precision
Too Many Hits	Too Few Hits

When to Do What

We've introduced different frameworks for posing questions to machines, including:

- OLP (Oceans, Lakes, and Ponds)
- Fact versus opinion questions
- Search engines versus subject directories
- Source fluency (coming in the next unit)

Each of these models address this basic question: When to use what.

We already have an instinct for this with an emphasis on people searches or specific kinds of legal documents. We'll gain that same level of confidence in softer, more conceptual searches as we start to apply query formation techniques to these new kinds of search tools.

To many of my students, it makes little sense to favor subject directories over search engines. Search engines they argue are faster and expansive. Directories are limited in scope.

I ask them to re-frame this impression around an unproductive failed search. How can we expand on their failed search terms? One alternative is to let the search *breath*: It's focused enough to be on topic but extensive enough to be comprehensive.

When we're in a lake, there might be millions of entries (compared to billions in Google, Bing, Yahoo search, etc.) That means a much lower probability that the numbers will support the kind of refinements we've been considering in **Unit Two**.

Specifics and Generalities

Another way to think of the difference between search and subject directories is to weigh specifics against generalities. If we want a precise answer to a fact-based question like "where's my UPS delivery" we can plug unique IDs into Google (your UPS tracking number) and out comes the travel itinerary of our package.

That's specific.

Subject directories handle softer questions around approximations, general awareness, subjective assessments of topics and opinion-related issues. Remember, they are more selective environments than search engine sites. This means a more structured (and much smaller) data set can anticipate the ambiguities and interconnections that form in fuzzier, less definable concept-based searches.

Here are some working definitions in thinking through the trade-offs of and generalities and specifics on virtual investigations:

1. **Generalities:** First, screen tests show that reference or topic questions are best answered in a selective environment. Here a more structured and smaller data set can anticipate the ambiguities and interconnections present in opinion or concept-based searches.

2. **Specifics:** On the other hand, the more exacting work of fact-based searches not only requires but forcefully demands we pull from the most sources possible. This is true especially in PI work. Investigation of obscure facts is a common requirement when we're pursuing the personal assets and biographical details of everyday people. They don't stand out in public. But we still need public domain sources to reveal the key details where their backgrounds are relevant to the investigation.

What are the general strengths and weaknesses of each tool? How do we fit our oversized goals into the reasonable box of likely outcomes? We must adjust our expectations accordingly.

Think search engines when the priority is to find out what's unique about a certain person, event, or organization. Let's say there's one case we're chasing down and it's got to be about the circumstances surrounding *that case only*. Consider a directory when we're looking for the shared properties that two or more cases have in common, say for instance a series of Amber Alerts or reports of missing persons within the same jurisdiction.

Factoring OLP into Our Queries

It's an overlooked and important distinction that the query formation rules of oceans don't apply when we're in a lake. That means no syntax or operators – even quotation marks. We can test this below by comparing...

> [professional investigation training]
>
> ["professional investigation" training]

FIGURE 2.57: Formulating Queries for Searching a Lake (circa 2010)

YAHOO! SEARCH — Web | Images | Video | Local | **Directory** | more »
[professional investigation training]   [Search] Advanced Search

Directory Results

« Complete Directory Results

RELATED DIRECTORY CATEGORIES

1. Law Enforcement > **Training**
2. Extreme Temperatures > Cold
3. Investigative Services > Background Verification
4. Investigative Services > Distance Learning **Training**
5. American Psychological Association (APA) > Divisions
6. B2B > Computers > Security and Encryption
7. B2B > Forensic Accident Reconstruction
8. B2B > Geographic Information Systems (GIS)
9. B2B > Investigative Services
10. B2B > Security Services
11. B2B Reliability Engineering > Consulting
12. B2B Teaching and Learning Aids > Health and Fitness
13. Chemical and Biological Weapons > Nerve Gas
14. Chemical and Biological Weapons > Ricin
15. Computer Services > Forensics

Yahoo! My Yahoo! Mail

YAHOO! SEARCH — Web | Images | Video | Local | **Directory** | more »
["professional investigation" training]   [Search] Advanced Search

Directory Results

« Complete Directory Results

RELATED DIRECTORY CATEGORIES

1. Crime > Arson
2. Canada > British Columbia > Greater Vancouver > Vancouver > B2B > Indoor Air Quality
3. United Kingdom > England > Lancashire > Blackburn > Investigative Services
4. Wisconsin > Waunakee > B2B > Scientific

Related Regional Categories for **"professional investigation" training**

["professional investigation" training]   [Search]

Copyright © 2009 Yahoo! All rights reserved. Privacy / Legal - Submit Your Site

FIGURE 2.58: Formulating Queries for Searching a Lake (circa 2019)

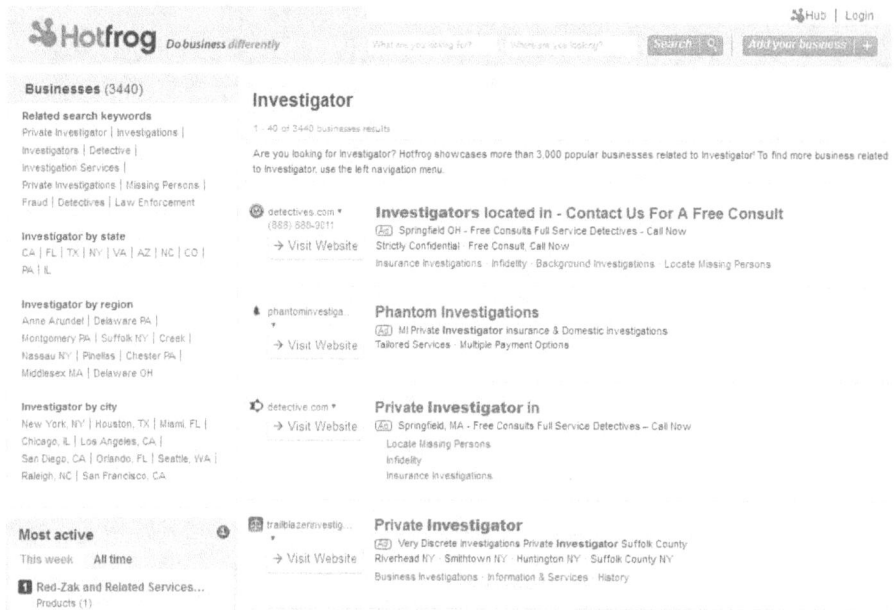

Here are the stark distinctions in our results sets between keywords in a search index and categorical browses through a subject directory. Note that we can only use a single keyword in the Yahoo Directory substitute. This indicates a thinning of subject directory indexes over time.

It's pretty dramatic, huh?

Also we can better leverage the strength of the directory index by clicking on *more* in order to expand on related categories and potentially fruitful associations. This card can't be played in a large search index. The result is a potential time savings by sourcing the categorical boundaries – not the original keywords.

Some pathways will be productive, most won't. But at least we'll know right off the bat without having to drill down on the hundreds of links buried below each heading.

Overlay of Engines and Directories

What happens when the engines versus directories argument is a false choice? What happens when a hybrid appears that takes on the virtues of both?

For an example of topic searches, we turn to a search engine that presents results in directory format. Exalead allows you to divide your questions up into both keywords and topics. This is an excellent way to benefit from the precision of exact word matches and the relevance of those matches coming from appropriate categories. It is also a productive way to...

- Make sure that the term we invoke is used within the right context, or
- Test the overlapping of two terms that would otherwise go unconnected in a more conventional search.

What do we mean by right context?

Say for instance we are interested in 'the Hurricanes' and not *hurricanes*. Our interest is rooted in college football and not weather forecasting. The advantage of a directory structure is that we have a better orientation to navigate the results. They don't simply come from a single occurrence of one website but often from a source collection that lends more depth and clarity to your question – a critical part of any topic search.

The advantage of fact-based searches is that we know what we're looking for. An exact keyword match is both unique and specific enough to pave the way towards the matter we are trying to determine.

Fact-based questions should spare you the hassle of scrolling down a results page.

FIGURE 2.59: Using Ontologies to Relate Multi-dimensional Contexts

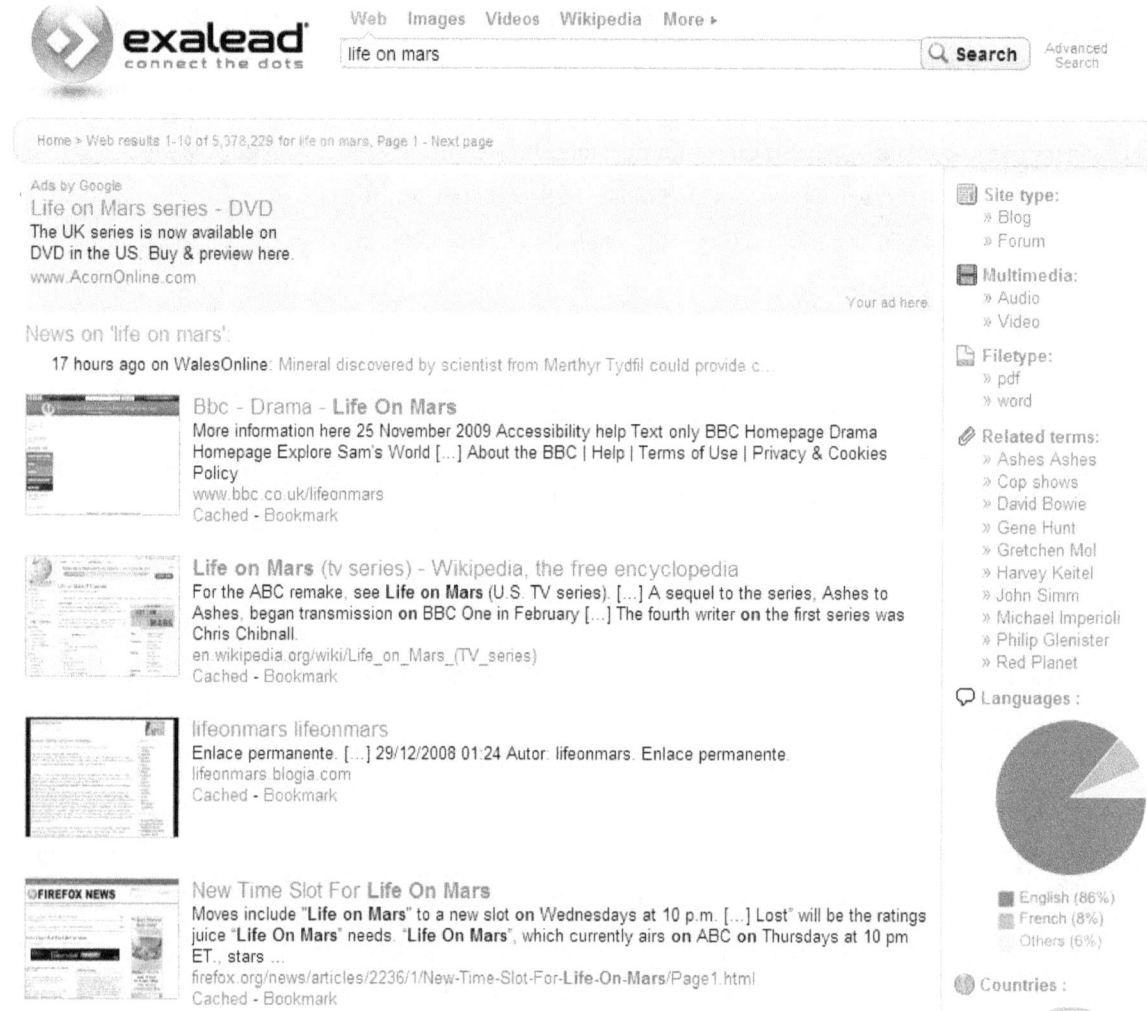

One exception to a search index with strong categorical mappings is a resource called Exalead. It's a search engine that behaves like a subject directory – sort of like Clusty but with a deeper set of ontologies. Ontologies are categories that explain their relatedness to each other.

UNIT TWO: Wrapping How to Search for Information

We've approached the matter of managing projects and teeing up our searches. Now we're about to turn our attention from the search bar to the results list. That's the matter of evaluating the quality of the source material that flows up to the front of our search page. Mastering the finer points of query formation in **Unit Two** gives us a lot more control over the types of results we want to see. We can adjust the volume and nature of the returning hits that are of use to us or to our clients. As we'll see in **Unit Four**, this intent takes on the added dimension of how others perceive information specific to their own interests: We'll make educated guesses about what different communities are aware of or concerned about — even when undiscerning folks are exposed to non-delineated content from unvetted information providers.

[1] This is referred to as the SEM trail ("*search engine marketing*" or PPC — "pay per click advertising").
[2] Mark Sprague, "Best Practices for Copywriters," https://marksprague.wordpress.com/enterprise-seo-2/content-seo-for-copy-writers/
[3] Rael Dornfest, Paul Bausch, Tara Calishain, "Google Hacks: Tips & Tools for Finding and Using the World's Information," O'Reilly Publishing, 2006
[4] The Mueller Report, Published by the U.S. Department of Justice, The New York Times, April 18, 2019
[5] David Pogue, "Google Glass and the Future of Technology," The New York Times, September 13, 2012
[6] John Ferrara, "Using your Users' Taxonomy," Enterprise Search Summit, 2009
[7] "Goodbye Newsift, We Hardly Knew You," February 23, 2010 https://blogs.the451group.com/information_management/2010/02/23/goodbye-newssift-we-hardly-knew-you/
[8] Tara Calishain, Researchbuzz, "Startpage.com Has a New Look," November 27, 2018
[9] Dan Price, "Avoid Google and Bing: Seven Alternative Search Engines That Value Privacy," July 9, 2018
[10] Search Encrypt, DuckDuckGo Doesn't Hide or Encrypt Your Search History," October 16, 2018
[11] Search Encrypt, "Private Search Engines – A Complete Guide," October 15, 2018"
[12] Marziah Karch, "Joke and Game Google Search Engine Mods," Lifewire, December 1, 2018
[13] Please note that Google's subject directory was discontinued in 2011. Yahoo directory met its demise in 2014. In 2017, DMOZ was shuttered by AOL. An archive of its classification structure and mappings lives on.
[14] The IPL suspended operations in 2015.
[15] In May, 2017 About.com was rebranded as Dotdash.com.
[16] PubMed is the search application for MEDLINE, a database maintained by the U.S. National Library of Medicine (NLM) at the National Institutes of Health (NIH).

UNIT THREE:

How to Source Information

That Instructs

Discovery at the Source

Source knowledge can be useful. Knowing who publishes what information and when can be a handy way to nail a popular reference question. The problem with source information is that it's limited to sources! The key is to understanding how the word gets around – why do individuals and groups want to play the role of publisher when the lead story is called: "What we know *(and want the rest of us to find out)."*

Unit Three focuses on our capacity to see the forest from the trees. This is how we analyze the emerging patterns from search results. This is how we connect the dots in social networks, group sources together, and decipher the prevailing themes, priorities, and popular notions that transcend any single website, news organization, or information provider.

Scientists describe these skills as fluid intelligence. These are the smarts that find meaning in confusion and solve problems, independent of what we knew prior to addressing them. Fluid is not reciting facts, skills people normally associate with brain power. **(Cascio, 2009[1])** In web investigations this ability is called **Source Fluency**. Source fluency is the set of Knowledge-ABLED skills we'll use to analyze, interpret, and attract the sources that inform our research objectives.

Information Types, Quality Control, and Source Fluency

1. Information Types: First we'll focus on the delivery of search results. We'll learn how to channel an overload of details into the four basic ways that search results are pre-packaged in advance of our knowledge or knowing what to do with them. Breaking our results down by information types is the way we begin to impose our own order on the unstructured nature of unmediated search results.

2. Quality Control: Secondly, we'll apply a quality control formula that reduces the time it takes to go from searching to addressing our investigations. That means knowing where to invest our attention. The better we can document the quality of our sources, the more credible we become as analysts and investigators. To do this we'll consider three quality control levels for assessing results sets, websites, and individual pages:

> **1. Big Picture** – The equivalent of skimming the ocean so that the surface level details lead us to what's worth deepening our commitment.
>
> **2. Street Level** – We liken street level to one or several measured jumps into the information lake so that we can round up the best sites for the task at-hand.
>
> **3. Micro Level** – This is where the potential pay-off merits diving into the details at the source level.

3. Source Fluency: The nature and scope of our research questions changes with the wind. The sourcing of answers on the information ocean changes with the tide. How do we manage that level of uncertainty? It's not just answers. We need consistency and accountability from credible sources.

We must apply sound sourcing methods no matter who's demanding the answers or who's supplying the source materials. Source fluency enables us to bend, shape and mold the size and breadth of the web around the specific requirements for the mission at hand. Fluency is defined not as one but a series of techniques to analyze, interpret, and attract the sources we need to fulfill our search project objectives.

4. Managing Project Resources: Optimizing our research assets means knowing the extent of the commitment we're about to make. How recoverable will those costs be? Where can we side-step the time sinks that sandbag the most dedicated researcher? These sourcing issues all factor into cost.

Key to costing out a project is testing the eye-of-the-beholder: How much our clients value the work we provide them. Will that justify any out-of-pocket expenses and the extent of our due diligence efforts? Such cost/benefit calculations focus on...

- Determining when to use what source, including fee-based information and the deep web
- Sizing up free versus fee – When it makes sense to use premium content and where to find it for minimal cost, and
- Using content groupings and specialty collections to narrow in on specifics or expand on topics

UNIT THREE LEARNING OBJECTIVES

Let's take a glance back at the foundational settings from **Unit Two** that we'll be using as building blocks in **Unit Three**:

1. We explored how search engines can be fine-tuned to trap the particulars of fact-based investigations and increase the relevancy of opinion or concept-based searches.
2. We reviewed different filtering methods to help search technologies to interpret our intentions.
3. We presented several ways to anticipate the presentation of search results so that we can short-circuit the discovery process. That means presenting a complete analysis without needing to open individual pages to clarify *the why* in what we pull.

Unit Three Destination: Source Fluency

We can't possibly know everything. That's no less true for knowing who to go to. Committing an inventory of leading references and go-to experts on any subject is too daunting even for the most experienced reference librarians. Our goal is not to become librarians but to develop a critical Knowledge-ABLED skill we've just introduced above. **Source Fluency** ensures that we're looking in the right place. Even when we're a first-time visitor to unfamiliar topics. Source fluency has the open expectations of the beginner's mind. But it structures the discovery process according to (1) how search works, (2) the focus-bearing nature of investigations, and (3) the constraints of project deadlines.

Part of that discipline is a quality control process. It not only reduces the search noise that clutters our screens but also helps us to attract, analyze, and interpret the sources we need to fulfill our project objectives. We'll develop those quality controls on three levels: (1) Search sets, (2) Websites, and (3) Individual pages (but only the ones worth opening!)

UNIT THREE: How to Source Information That Instructs

In **Unit Three** we begin the interpretation process. Mainly, what do the results tell us about...

- The naturally selected sources (the ones we don't specify), and
- The ones we should call upon that would otherwise go unheeded in the investigation.

Unit Three focuses on acquiring source fluency and learning how to leverage those sources to improve the quality of the digital information we source. The unit starts by confronting the essential form of how information is delivered to us and the questions it inspires:

1. Where is it located?
2. What is it called?
3. When was it done?
4. Who did it?
5. Why do I care?
6. How do I find it again?

Unit Three is also devoted to unlocking the secrets, pitfalls, and potentials of searching topic-focused Internet databases. Building on our **Unit Two** understanding of search engines (oceans) and subject directories (lakes), we'll dive into the information pond. The pond provides more narrow and targeted specialty databases to uncover scarce and often overlooked information. OLP ("oceans, lakes, and ponds") is the primary method for determining when to pursue what size database in our web-based investigation.

In **Unit Three,** we take the refinements we explored through query formation and turn to the substance of what our searches turn up. We're not taking the search engine's word on what's news to us, or what's vital to our investigation. Sourcing information that instructs means our searches are informing our research objectives. An algorithm is no substitute for our own powers of sense-making: Our critical assessment of *why we got what we got* from our queries and how well this supports our goals for conducting them.

Effective information sourcing focuses on five Knowledge-ABLED practices for collecting and vetting web-based information providers:

1. **Information Types** – Understanding search results according to the form they're stored in as the first step in determining how well they suit our purpose and objectives.
2. **Source Fluency** – Knowing where to look for information without knowing what it is called.
3. **Site Selection** – Deciding how large a collection is appropriate for the questions we're posing.
4. **Quality Controls** – How to qualify our search results in the aggregate (by results sets instead of individual sites or pages).
5. **Managing Project Resources** – Costing out our projects so that our budgets can meet our delivery ambitions.

Unit Three Benefits

Upon completion of this unit, we should be able to understand and apply...

Information Types:

- How do we break large chaotic sets of data down into manageable chunks of information that can be pieced together to inform our investigations?
  This job is routinely performed for us by search engines designed to reward a pre-selected, self-interested, and opaque set of information sources.

- How do we reduce those informants to the simple calculation of what's in it for them?
  Only then can the merit of the information we're vetting rise above skepticism to qualify: (1) as evidence worth introducing to the investigations we conduct, and (2) the communities we serve.

Source Fluency:

- How to source?
  Use appropriate techniques to analyze, interpret, and attract the sources you need to fulfill search objectives.

- How far to drill down?
  Fluency helps us determine how far down to dig before reaching out to others, generalizing answers, and drawing conclusions.

- How referenceable are the sources?
  Deploy specialized search tools to gauge the web presence of target sources.

Site Selection:

- How precise an answer do we need?
  Pursue sources likely to produce definitive answers or cast an authoritative stature.

- How relatable or connected is one source to the next? How does grouping our sources justifying our source choices?
  Use the explanatory power of source groups to support client recommendations.

- How original is the news we're getting?
  Understand how providers package their information so we can integrate it into our client presentations.

Quality Control:

- *How do we access and evaluate sets, sites, and pages?*
  Review editorial checks to qualify information providers.

- *How can we be vested in the sources we select?*
  Use specific assessment criteria to qualify Internet resources and quantify our confidence in them.

- *How do we analyze large data sets in a consistent and expedient way?*
  Present a complete rendering of search results without needing to open individual pages.

Managing Project Resources:

- *When do we turn to fee-based sources?*
  Recognize where the likely boundary lies between public and proprietary information.

- *When do we go below radar for sources not indexed by commercial search media?*
  Know and apply the rules for uncovering overlooked information.

- *How do we trace the actual source?*
  Differentiate source inventory from news origination.

- *How do we understand the commercial incentives of our information providers?*
  Differentiate deliberate from serendipitous discoveries.

Definition: Source Fluency

Source fluency builds on source knowledge without becoming overly dependent on any one source. This is a core Knowledge-ABLED skill. Because of the web's dynamic and fluid nature, it's essential to pursue information sources with dexterity while remaining grounded in our research goals.

Searching Out Loud

SECTION 3:1 | Information Types —
How Do We Think About Information?

When designing a digital search strategy, it is important that we understand the range of available information on the Internet. What we are looking for varies greatly by situation, subject, time to discover, and urgency to know. However, *how we look* is critical, no matter what we're seeking. That's where the four information types kick in.

Back in **Unit One** we were introduced to two frameworks for conducting Internet research:

- ■ **Search Project Management Forms:** Search logs systemically capture our search objectives in support of the project's underlying purpose. They provide a sequence-based structure for recording the approaches we take, the investigative tools we use, and the lessons drawn from our results.

- ■ **Knowledge Awareness and Johari Window Frameworks**: Model for developing what and how our search targets see and interpret the world. These constructs are designed to solidify the often sketchy and ill-defined process of developing a person's frame of reference. They map to our awareness levels – specifically where we are most attentive and oblivious, a.k.a. our Knowledge-ABLED sides and our blindspots.

INTRODUCING INFORMATION TYPES

Information Types are another handy framework for transitioning search results into case evidence. In a world of complexity and shades of gray, information types suggest some welcome absolutes. Think of information types as our simple on/off switch. It's either black or white without sacrificing the subtleties of meaning, there for our powers of interpretation.

Where the **Search Log** is about documenting the discovery process, information types prepare us for a set of conditions we anticipate in the collection phase. Information types help us to organize our search results like no search engine can. That's because (1) it tracks the state that we find the information in, (2) its relatedness to our original intent, and (3) the purpose it serves for being provided in the first place.

Information types give us a vocabulary for anchoring our investigation in research terms that are well understood by researchers and most domain experts we're seeking to engage. Certainly they're a referenceable and transparent way to retrace the pathway that leads us to those experts. This is always a useful ice-breaker when we're trying to size-up how willing or capable someone is of leading us to that next step of discovery: The *why* aspect in our search project logs.

Finally, information types are a reliable and repeatable way to build on source knowledge without becoming overly dependent on any one source – the defining measure of source fluency.

The Damp Basement of Fruitless Searches

Remember the last time your spouse sent you down to the cellar to search? Only this time the search results included some kitchen utensil or dining room decoration? Wasn't there hiding in the corner? Maybe the search requester was right. It wasn't their fuzzy directions. It was that the search target here fell outside our abilities to recall, or even imagine.

Does this conjure up fruitless searches in storage areas that surrender shadows and mildew. But none of the mystery? If the thought of opening box-after-barren-box stresses you out, consider this: Imagine how most Internet users feel on an open-ended search of a conceptual and sketchy subject? It's not willful ignorance or even poor search etiquette where honest doubt succumbs to a stiff learning curve. We leave the water-logged search basement empty-handed.

The purpose of information types is to offer some solid and predictable outlines. Information types inform what the Knowledge-ABLED should expect to find before we ever formulate a query, select a tool, or manage a search project.

For example, are you document-centric? Think of your field of choice. Professions all adhere to their own scientific, medical, academic, regulatory, or legal reporting formats. A document-centric view is sound preparation to impose a task-based rigor on the discipline of integrating search results with professional objectives.

Defining Information Types

Information types encompass four categories commonly found in the most virtual investigations:

1. **Entry Point** – How our search begins.
2. **Resources** – The kinds of information sources that may turn up.
3. **Point of View** – The subjective opinion of the information provider and motivations for making those views public.
4. **Format** – How the information is archived or in what storage location.

How can we categorize and organize some common forms of information so they suggest next steps. These forms can help us predict what we will find in our searches, and further on within the sites worth our visiting.

Each of the four categories will include...

- Between 3-4 subsets,
- Shown as pairs of opposite characteristics, which
- Play a role in assessing our project results.

The reason for the opposites is to create a range of outcomes or scale of possibilities. By opposites, we're not talking about the clashing of ideas or talking over each other in this age of hyper-partisanship. That comes in **Unit Four's** Vectors of Integrity. Rather, the opposing relationships in information types aren't political or psychological but specific to digital technology The range of these relationships traverse the many elements that impact our web-based investigations. Let's break this down into more concrete definitions and useful examples.

Entry Points

Where do we come in? Stage left? Perhaps before the last teardrop falls?

Navigating the web is not exactly an easy-on, easy off proposition. The road map can take us in one or several directions, or all of the above. We need to consider our point of entry in order to establish some gravity and orientation. What discussion are we eavesdropping on? When was the information first published? Just how public is this information to the communities it was designed to reach?

We also start with entry points because the questions we form and the search engines where we relate those curiosities are all familiar on-ramps for digital research. But it's more than search. We could be following a trail of blog posts. We could be browsing through a series of tags or bookmarks or Tumblr pages or Reddit articles. We could stumble on a site that speaks directly to our issues. Yet we can still be clueless about who, when, and why the information was ever published.

FIGURE 3.1: Listing out Points of Entry

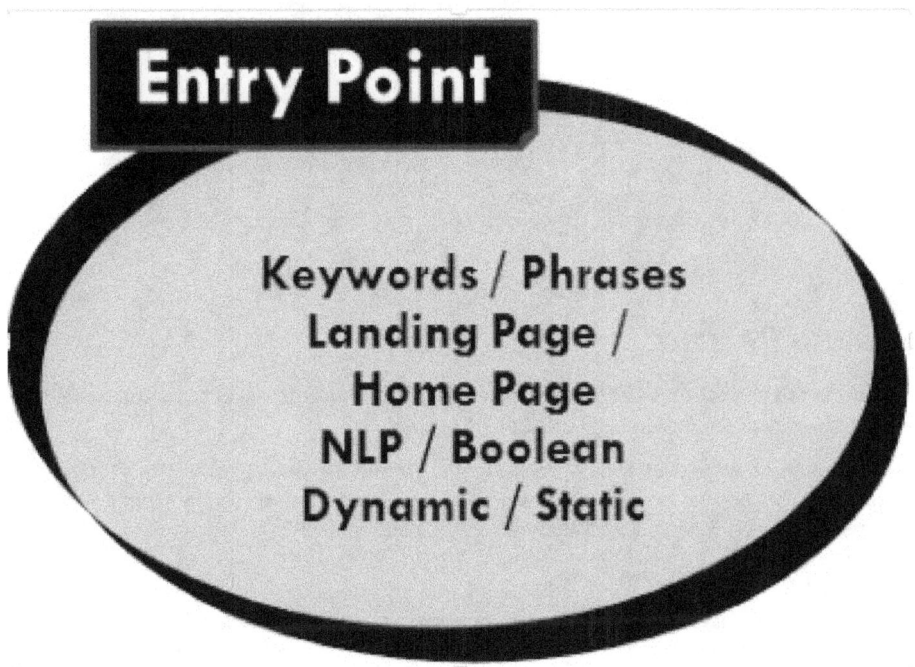

Entry points consist of:

- ■ **How we start out** – Are we relying on keywords only? Do we include phrases as search terms? Do we some of the advanced commands we introduced in **Unit Two**?

- ■ **Where we end up** – Are we being taken to a landing page, or the site root, or homepage listed in our search results?

- ■ **What search tool we use** – Do we trust a search engine to interpret our questions in plain English (Natural Language) or more traditional search commands (Boolean logic)?

FIGURE 3.2: Entry-based Information Types

Category	Information Types	Resource	Examples
Entry Point:	Keywords / Phrases	Keywords: Bag of words Phrases: Multiple consecutive word groupings surrounded by quotation marks	Lighting, floor plans, kitchens "interior design"
	Landing page / Home page	Landing page: Page extension creating to match query Home page: Root URL site	Froogle results Domain type is cut off
	NLP / Boolean	NLP: plain English questions Boolean: and, or, not statements	"What causes income gaps to widen?" Income and (disparity or inequity), not "class warfare"
	Dynamic / Static	Dynamic: Blogs Static: Site map	Page change alerts FAQs

PUTTING ENTRY POINTS INTO PRACTICE

Now let's put the theory into practice. Let's talk about the last time we expected clarity and hit a wall of confusion instead. What happens if we start out with high hopes of pay dirt and end up spinning our wheels?

By *spinning,* we're not talking about something ambiguous or half-promising that doesn't pan out. We're talking a total wipe-out with no recourse (and no resource). So how do we face down this wall of bricks? What are some common pitfalls or well-trod dead-ends that can be overcome by redirecting our searches down a more productive path?

First, let's unpack some of these familiar potholes in our search path:

1. **Disorientation** – This is the queasy factor. That knotting of our neck muscles when our searches are been kidnapped, blindfolded, and dropped under a bridge before sunrise. Most times, this is due to the co-opting of our intentions by link farms. These sites are the trolls lurking under that bridge. They exist for no other reason than to be landed on. Sometimes we land in a dust pile of confusion because a merchandiser has created a landing page customized to our location, click pattern, registration details, or designed to deliver audiences to inventories they're trying to move.

    CURE: Track our location back to the home page or root URL. Then we'll have a few breadcrumbs between the site owner and the hole we're climbing out from.

2. **Ambiguous Terms** – The leading cause of ambiguity is too few terms and too many nouns. Searches devoid of actions can compromise the outcomes we're testing or hypothesizing. That's a real problem because subjects and objects can't be clarified without predicates:

> "Google only returns exact matches for search terms ... so conjugating verbs, nouns, adjectives and adverbs catches a wider net of terms that people might search by." (**Stocking, Matsa, 2017[2]**)

That rings as true in our ears as it does in the search bar. Information scientists call this 'disambiguation' – the process of matching word choice to user intention.

CURE: Disambiguation is a big word but our task is simple: Include actions that clarify the things we're looking for. This is the same problem as connecting causes and effects in web searches. We can't distinguish actors from their actions unless we apply the correct query formation. For instance, instead of searching on individual suspects in a criminal case, expressing this in **Word Algebra** terms:

"(accused OR alleged) * (wrongdoing OR criminal)"

3. **404 Errors** – These are the hard stops and the dead-ends. 404s are the universal *lights out* sign that greets our untimely arrivals at defunct or malfunctioning sites. This is particularly vexing when we're retracing a path that we crossed days earlier, only to have the page pulled out from under our recent visits.

CURE: The easiest workaround is to recall the cache result. This is the most recent page record recorded by the search engine prior to changes on the live server or production environment. These disruptions are especially common on news sites. News stories may have a short shelf life, regardless of reader interest or longevity of the item being covered.

> **Definition: Cache**
> *Cache results (pronounced "cash") is the imprint made by the crawler or search engine indexer. Cache results are the pages crawled and ultimately captured and processed by the search vendor. Cache results form the actual database that the search engine references before rendering the results page.*

4. **Over-precision** – One way to price ourselves out of a productive search outcome is to become so consumed by our topics that they rob us of alternative ways for describing them. One student was fixated on the false claims of household cleaning products that he continually referred to 'deception in advertising' to the exclusion of its many variations. In these cases, we're not just looking for term expansion but topic headings that stretch our own categorical boundaries.

CURE: This is where subject directories are so powerful. They can generalize about specifics. They can overcome over-precision by augmenting the intention of the search without adding unnecessary details and unrelated tangents.

5. **Definitive Ranking** – There are two types of searchers: Those that make lists and everybody else. List-makers have a tendency to rely on rankings for prioritizing or comparing their *apples and oranges*. This is particularly common when needing to evaluate or recommend a product or even a problem-solving approach. As authoritative list is a common search goal because of the credibility it confers. The problem is that the more abstract the comparison or novel the topic, the likelier that the list-maker must act as their own de facto authority. It follows that source confidence comes first before determining the trust levels appropriate for web-based authorities and experts. Sourcing professional databases such as LinkedIn is one way to create better transparency between search rankings and subject experts.

CURE: The easiest way to swing the list-making momentum in our favor is to run searches peppered with the names of known competitors or choice ranges for handling the matter at-hand.

6. **Time Frames** – As a greater portion of our daily lives are spent on screens, the gap between when things happen in the physical and virtual world continues to narrow. Even so, it's not possible to reconcile traditional time series conventions like publication date and such anomalies as when that same article is time-stamped by the web server now containing the same file.

CURE: One of the major steps forward in terms of cataloging web content has been the emergence of blogs and social media for standardizing chronological sequence. The most trivial post on my Facebook wall comes with the time and day it was posted. This is a huge improvement over trying to approximate a date range in a publishing cycle by using 'months' and 'years' as key terms.

Definition: Disambiguation

Disambiguation is the process of matching word choice to user intention. This capability is especially challenging for search engines when users enter single search terms or incomplete information. GPS has emerged as a demonstrable way to contextualize user intentionality by the location from which they launch their searches, i.e. 'path' is not a metaphor for knowledge discovery but the physical address they're trying to locate on their phones.

FIGURE 3.3: Disorientation on the Web

Pitfall	Challenge	Solution
Disorientation	Landing pages challenge our bearings: why did we land here?	Navigation to home page
Ambiguous terms	Context is not evident without further detail, e.g. "Convictions" – is this a number or a depth?	Quotes to anchor phrases, e.g. "how to sew"
404 error	Broken link based on discontinued sites or network interruptions	Use cache results that generate screen captures
Over-precision	We fixate on one hard fact or search target and generate zero "0" or limited search results	Unique IDs: From airline flights to UPC codes and tracking numbers
Definitive rankings	Exhaustive list in orderly ranking of all members worthy of mention	Inclusive groupings that expand on overlooked members or questions the status of others
Timeframes	The web is notorious for warping the chronological sequence of time and events	Focus on web media with a consistent time stamp such as social media postings

Before we move onto resources we should also consider some familiar pitfalls that we have little or no control over – mainly the inherent shortcomings of search technology.

Faults and Breakdowns

Let's plan our escape now that we've flipped on the lights in the chamber of search horrors. First we'll need to reconstruct how we got to this compromised state in the first place. Let's revisit some false assumptions we may carry in our search habits that sabotage our intentions as well as our outcomes.

Before we point the finger at ourselves for these roadblocks, we'll confront the source of our frustration. Let's take a hard look at what the most seasoned searcher cannot overcome: The inherent flaws and limitations of search tools. Here are some search engine detours. Two variations on query size form two such unwelcome points of entry:

1. **Indexing Size Counts** – Renowned web researcher and Google Hacker, Tara Calishain observes one of the overlooked but important limitations about search engines. Not only do they not index large portions of the web. They also skimp on the pages that they do crawl.

   Google has a particularly small cache (or file size) when it comes to indexing html pages or PDFs. That means that words not found on the surface of spidered websites are not retrieved in our search results. File sizes are no longer conform to rule standards which stood at 100K per HTML page in 2015.[3] This point was refuted with little fanfare or corroboration two years later.[4] Either way, if we anticipate searches that attract lengthy pages like directory listings or full text articles, skip Google.

One way to apply page size as a quality control is to check for it before clicking through to the site. For instance, if the page size is just 5-10K it may well be too small any index to find the details we're seeking. Some search tools like Bing are better, not only at increasing the page size but at displaying the depth of the page within its domain. This tells you how buried a page is from the site that spawns it, giving you a sense of a page's depth, or the overall site dimensions.

2. **Character Limits** — One trap door is recognizing how many terms we can use when we throw down the search dice. It's tempting to let Google intercept our thoughts when it shoots us suggestive phrases in mid-stream. But that limits our choices to the ones already carved out for us by the word index. It also means we're following the herd. This may work for shopping around and assessing search trends but it compromises our ability as researchers to tease out the details of our investigations.

Unlike results lists, queries can't go on forever. Google is constantly expanding the threshold for how many characters its algorithm can chew on but more open-ended arrangements pose their own risks and limitations. For example, what happens if we cut and paste a sample sentence from a useful response we get into the search box? How about an entire paragraph? We must assume that Google with imply the exclusive AND Boolean operator between every single term it processes. That kind of long-windedness is guaranteed to form a choke-hold around any web page other than that containing the source page itself. The limit as of this writing is thirty-two words per query[5].

Other search tools encourage long-winded queries that catch the subtleties inherent with complex topics. For these entry points, it helps to capture an abstract or summary and see how well the same themes and categories hold up beyond simple keyword matches.

Teaching the Engine How to Search Us

Remember in **Unit One** when we talked about the inability of search engines to read our minds, let alone set our priorities and litmus tests? How do these shortcomings not defeat but actually liberate us from the confines of search technology?

For starters, the most brilliant query in the world won't produce a continuous parade of useful results. But it does keep our heads in the game. That's key to effectively rationalizing the response we get. In effect, reading *the minds* of search engines.

How does this work? More importantly, how do machine-made minds deviate from our own thinking?

Human logic is inferential. Ours is the mental domain of educated guesses and ballpark estimates. It is based on conditional, relative, or changing conditions. Search engine logic is well ... mechanical. It is binary. It can only be precise. It is 'yes' or 'no' but never both or conditional relative to an unknowable number of extenuating factors. The outcome is A or B. In fact it is a rather advanced machine that can conclude it has to be X or Y for Z to happen.

A human on the other hand can know that Z will happen regardless of X and Y based on familiarity, experience, intuition, or just plain commonsense.

Sounds Geek to Me

Establishing the right give and take with a search tool doesn't mean we have to become software programmers or native geek speakers. That said, interviews with computers are more productive if conducted on the computer's terms. This means using the tools and expressions that trigger useful information for our investigation. Not asking questions in plain English.

So what happens when our search results tell us one thing: The engine has no clue what we're looking for? One of the first prompts when we shoot blanks is to ask a series of inferential questions:

1. **Term Expansion** — The first level is of response is to widen your horizons with the following term expanders. C'mon, flex that instructor muscle within: Okay, sometimes it's called... what? What are some synonyms or like-minded terms? When was it last used in a sentence? Speak its name and listen for the response.

2. **Connections and Associations** — The next level is the connectors. These are the affiliations or relationships that are bonded to our search terms. Ready? Okay, it's related to ... what? What are the other topics, subjects and disciplines it touches? What's the strength of the association? Is it less abstract to think in terms of people? That's fine. Who writes about this? What are some common and reliable authors, experts and sources? As we saw in **Unit Two**, clustering engines offer some unexpected, but potentially useful outcomes.

3. **Results Lists** — The third level of coaxing in the education of a search engine is to look at the page characteristics of the content results: What's the size of our hit counts. (As we'll learn later on in **Unit Three**, it helps to know if we're fishing in an ocean, lake or pond). Do our terms appear in the titles or URLs or are they buried? What are the site domains? Are they commercial, foreign, non-profit, government or educational? We'll look at how to analyze results lists without needing to read a single result.

4. **Pages** — The final prompt is to dig into the details of the sites themselves. What are its unique properties? Is it original content or does it aggregate content from other sources? What is the nature and number of attributions or references to the site? How often is it updated and what's site traffic does it attract? Finally, we'll look at how to scan individual pages and sites to assess credibility and motivations. That's the quality of information based on the interests of those providing it.

RESOURCES

What do we mean when we refer to *resources*?

Resources refer to the value of the information we're accessing in terms of what it costs us in time, money, and quality. But those factors pail compared to their value to us as researchers, consultants, and investigators. What's our aim here? To demonstrate the pay-off to our colleagues and clients – that's at the root of our resourcefulness.

Perhaps the most important dynamic is not how dated an article is or how accessible. It's the line we can draw between external and internal. This is our perpetual status as an insider or outsider. It's a perspective that will serve us well as virtual investigators.

Those with membership credentials pass internal communications along whether they belong to is a company, school, church or peer group. External communications are *outward facing*. That's a marketing term that means how our group communicates with the outside world, especially group communications to non-members with a vested interest in how and what our group is doing. The marketing term for this group is *stakeholders*. Stakeholders span a broad cross-section of constituencies from customers to cousins, from parents to government regulators.

FIGURE 3.4: Listing out Types of Resources

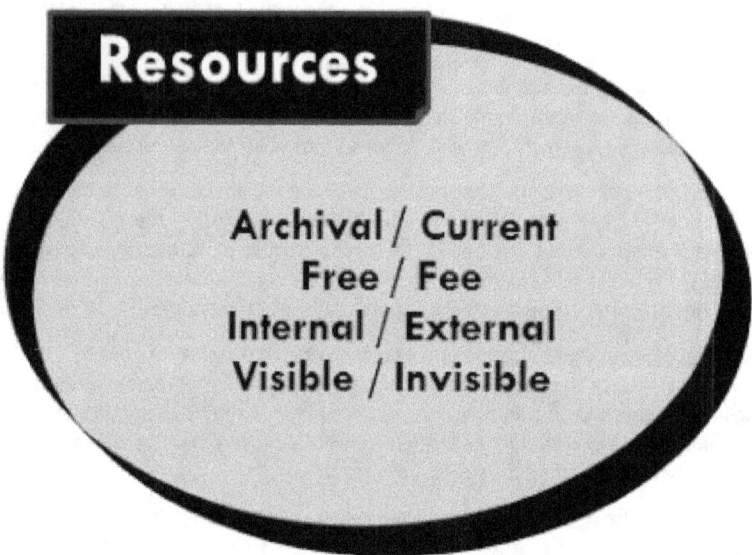

Resources are about…

- **What they cost us** – Do the benefits outweigh the risks? We question this in terms of (1) recovering those costs through client fees, or (2) finding free sources that tend to disappear when the novelty wears off of non-revenue-producing resources.
- **How far we need to dig for them** – What are the time commitments necessary for meaningful discovery? When do we pass the threshold for closing the due diligence loop on any number or nature of search targets?
- **Point of origin** – Where do our discoveries come from? How does this impact the conclusions we draw, the probabilities we consider, and the recommended actions we confer?

FIGURE 3.5: Resource-based Information Types

Resources:	
	External / Internal
	Archival / Current
	Free / Fee
	Visible / Invisible

Here's a fuller accounting of the resources factor:

1. **External versus internal** – This is the connection between those providers and us as the recipients. Did it come from our employer or a group we belong to? Did we hear about it as a third party, removed from any personal affiliation with the newsmakers or those reporting it? The external versus internal perspective is especially useful for assessing how information providers source their own research. In other words, an insider's view from an outsider perspective.

2. **Archival versus current** – Time-wise resources can be archival, meaning they are pages stored in their original published form, or current to reflect the most recent update.

3. **Free versus fee** – In terms of cost, resources come in two familiar flavors. Either they're (1) free, devoid of passwords and shopping cart metaphors, or (2) fee-based, meaning we pay as we go or surrender our card numbers to the subscription renewal cycle. What information is in the public domain and what is either unavailable or proprietary, requiring an access fee? This black and white question is not always an open and shut proposition.

4. **Visible versus invisible** – Visible and invisible refers to what shows up on our results page and what does not, no matter how hard we look or deep we dig. The search results landing *below the radar* of common search engines is also referred to as **the Deep Web**. The abyss that falls between us and the Google search index.

FIGURE 3.6: Resource-based Subject Categories

Category	Information Types	Resource	Examples
Resources:	Archival / Current	Archived: Wayback Machine	Yahoo '96
		Current: Yahoo	Most e-mailed articles
	Free / Fee	Free: ERIC	Lesson Plans
		Fee: Highbeam Research	Liberal Arts
	Authoritative / Dubious	Authoritative: Link analysis	Wall Street Journal
		Dubious: Conspiracy sites	"Urban Legend" profile
	External / Internal	External: Newsgroups	Listservs
		Internal: Communities of practice	Discussion boards
	Visible / Invisible	Visible: Google search engine	Sponsored links
		Invisible: Infomine subject directory	Spider checking a dynamic database

PUTTING RESOURCES INTO PRACTICE

Before we move on, here are a few more pointers on cost.

It's odd. But no standard has emerged to determine when we should expect to pay for information and when we shouldn't. The closest indication is the simple question of whether we still want yesterday's news a month from now. The chances are if we do, it must carry more meaning than simply trying to stay informed about today's events. And we will have to pony up for it.

Not all sites function this way. Many trade magazines for instance keep their past issues available long past the typical shelf-life of a general circulation source like a newspaper or news magazine. Another way we can sometimes retrieve archival content free of charge is to use the cache version of an article as it appears in the index of the search engine we are using.

Perhaps the *kingpin of cache* is a resource called the **Wayback Machine**. It's a site that takes literal screen-shots of popular web pages and lists them according to the date they were indexed. Think *Wayback* for investigating any fraudulent business that used a website to substantiate what later became a baseless claim.

Viewpoints

At first glance, the term of viewpoints does not sound like a concrete example for grounding our expectations. We've all seen how one issue can create countless opinions, holding as strongly to the same view dismissed completely by an opposing side. How solid is that when we're trying to gain our footing? How reliable is that even for trying to describe our experience to the clients and colleagues we're attempting to support or influence?

Viewpoints, viewpoints and more shades of opinion: Who doesn't hold one? Who feels sure they know the most important ones to pursue? It's slippery going out there.

The purpose of an information type is to provide a guard rail to grab onto for describing, repeating, or avoiding any future investigations we conduct virtually. What about viewpoints? The term itself invites more questions than any working definitions, boundaries, or common ground for understanding the results we're reviewing, the sites we visit, or the databases we search.

Points of view consider...

- **How definitive or certain we can be** – Are we dealing with incontrovertible facts or softer, shiftier shades of opinion?
- **How far we need to dig for them** – Do they float to the surface of Google in plain view? Do we head for the deeper web that lies below the search engine radar?
- **Point of origin** – When and where does the content that catches our eye come from? Is it the original source or a conduit, a pass-through?

FIGURE 3.7: Listing out Viewpoints as Information Types

Point of View:	
	Individual / Group
	Fact / Opinion
	Time-sensitive / Analytical
	Authoritative / Dubious

Here's a deeper dive into points of view:

1. **Individual versus group** – One of the most fundamental questions about the information we're screening is whether it represents one person's views or those of a group. That perspective is critical for determining the motives our sources hold for delivering the information now before us. Let's say for instance that we know a lot of folks have their hands in that process. What kind of group are we talking about? If the viewpoint is from an institutional perspective, is their core motive to maximize their profits, uphold the law, win a contest, or improve the communities they serve?

2. **Fact versus opinion** – How does fact and opinion play out on the web? If we're looking for exact dates, specific pricing, or precise wording our expectations should be for a rapid, *point blank* answer. Opinion-based assignments tend to run on and require more discipline to manage as search projects. A fact-based search with a hit or miss outcome works better on tight deadlines and finite sources. More conceptual search projects often feature both hits AND misses that defy brevity. We can get to our explanatory goals. But it's a conversation. Not an interrogation.

3. **Time-sensitive versus analytical** – Another dimension related to viewpoint is whether the information at hand is time-sensitive or analytical. What are our expectations around a cool, detached perspective when unplanned and sudden events occur? Should they be downgraded? Yes, perhaps so. At least until the preliminary reports are in, more likely after a full investigation is completed.

4. **Dubious versus authoritative** – The influence factor of resources can be hard to pin down. In the past, it was measured in circulation numbers for readers or TV households for viewers. Counts can still be generated for page views, file downloads, search rankings, subscribers (mostly unpaid), and dashboards of web analytics about our search behaviors. What's less certain are the beliefs that form in-between clicks. That's because the lines between content producers and consumers have blurred. So too is the once respectful distance between experts and laypersons has closed. The distinction between official news and unofficial speculation is also in doubt. We will address ways to restore some meaning to this important question when we focus on documenting credibility later in the Quality Control section of **Unit Three** and as we explore information context in **Unit Four**.

PUTTING VIEWPOINTS INTO PRACTICE

Category	Information Types	Resource	Examples
Point of View:	Institution / Individual	Institution: link:, related: Individual: Blogs	Corporate & educational sites Bloogz
	Commercial / Non-profit	Commercial: site.com Non-profit: site.org	Amazon (past purchases) Idealist.org
	Time-sensitive / Analytical	Time sensitive: news sites Analytical: in-depth investigations	Press release Christian Science Monitor
	Public / Proprietary	Public: Mandated disclosure Proprietary: Black market resale	Sex Offender Registry Personal bank statements
	Fact / Opinion	Fact: Times, places, specifics, absolutes Opinion: concepts, meanings, values, gray areas	Shipping schedules Caretaker strategy

Dubious Distinctions

By far the hardest definition to nail under Information Types is the slippery notion of information quality. The two extremes we present under Viewpoints is the degree of certainty we have in its quality. Are our resources authoritative or dubious? What's the determinant? One tangible way to think about quality is in legal terms. What will it cost the information provider in terms of their reputation and credibility if they get a story wrong? If it's a major publisher, the answer was once everything. Those costs have come down in a digital news climate. If it's an anonymous posting, a self-important blogger, or a source with a pre-set conclusion, the damage to one's credibility may be considerably less, even irrelevant to the desired outcome.

Facts, Opinions, and the Certainty of Outcomes

Before we move onto formats, here are a few more comments about facts versus opinions.

Fact-based searches are in a very real sense what people think of when they expect a certain outcome. A fixed objective requires a well-defined conclusion. It is a linear relationship between a stated cause and a clear effect. It is start-to-finish and the path is direct.

Fact-based questions fall into two categories: Transactional and informational. The transactional stuff can be summed up in one succinct keyword — shopping. However, the domain of facts extends beyond commercial transactions. There are archives of weather patterns. There are shipping manifestos that contain both immigrant populations and imported products. In fact, we could trace our ancestral routes through the slave trade when we return to a time that people and products were one in the same.

If there's a contract, a sale, a birth, or a milestone, most likely there are cyclical passages to mark...

- Its arrival,
- Gauge its reading, or
- Close the sales loop.

Feed a search engine a steady diet of digits and it will reveal patterns and cough-up the details. Better still, it will perform this tedious service with the same unfailing response regardless of the person asking or their motivations for doing so. To the human mind, this is the form of servitude machines were designed to assume in the Garden of Technological Eden. Unfailing reproductions of transactional trails and the paths they weave.

Informational questions are well within the reach of search technologies. In terms of milestones, what happens to us humans in our lifetimes is as finite as it is conclusive:

1. I went to this university and received that kind of degree.
2. You sat on that many boards and several involved working with the same management team that later hired you as the CEO of such-and-such.
3. She accesses hard-to-find audio files of her favorite songs through YouTube and searched Google yesterday for the easiest way to convert video streams to MP3 files.

In the above examples, there is little need to have personal contact or knowledge with these individuals in order to gather informational particulars. Personal histories all resonate from the addresses we've called home, to the scope of the networks we build in those communities. Even to the size of the debts we take out to finance those homes. Again, computers hold the memory cards so the informational stuff lies just below the transactional surface. The network effect of our movements and milestones tells us who we're likely to know, how we're likely to connect, and even how we size ourselves up vis-à-vis those comparable assets and peers in our social networks. That's the informational piece.

Then we wade into waters where no search engineer can approach from a position of strength. Soft, squishy, anecdotal experience. That's where opinion searches evolve from *concrete facts* to abstractions such as mental concepts, personal meanings, and non-financial values in our information-seeking information behaviors. Instead of needing a precise answer, we can start with a narrow objective and stem outward to include related associations and their implications. *(We'll see both approaches play out more fully when we explore the haystacks versus iceberg approach to sources later in this unit).*

Opinion searches fall into two camps: diagnostic and advisory. Both kinds of questions stretch the boundaries of information science because both types are complex in nature – for machines anyway. For instance, they require the resolution be based on a clear command of the actors and their actions.

The human brain is trained to handle this in our grammatical upbringings. We learn nouns and verbs. We can make tenses agree. We can tell a subject from a predicate and an object. There is little genius or novelty in bringing our sense-making to bear. It's what we humans do in processing information. We avoid repeating the same name for things when referring back to the same repeating *item*. We subtly avoid explicit meanings when an insinuation gives us the wiggle room to dismiss the threatened person as paranoid or too serious.

A diagnostic is information-gathering based on an eventual course of action formed from the findings gathered. An advisory is the recommended next steps: [We believe] this is the correct course of action based on the evidence gathered, the applicable options, and the probable outcomes.

Search on its own can't deliver on either count. But it can augment our ability to think more conceptually than computers. That's the essence of query formation. An informed view of syntax, semantics and operators may trick the search tool into doing our bidding for us. Ultimately, it's to help us ask better questions of the humans in our midst. That knowledge falls into levels of abstraction, experience, and understanding a synthetic intelligence is unlikely to touch in our lifetimes.

(c) Andrew Morris-Friedman

FORMAT

Finally, there's format. Format refers to the state we find the information in before we reassemble it to fit our own reporting structure or project goals.

Formats address...

- **Completeness** – Do we want the full artifact or just the excerpt from our point of entry?
- **Integration** – How much work is it to augment our reports with the content we capture from our web research? Does it come from a video? A flight reservation system? A spreadsheet? How do we embed these points of entry into our findings?
- **Structure** – How well-defined are the containers that hold the information we seek? Are there tags that describe and generalize the broader meaning or aboutness of the pages we're surfing? Is the passage in question an explosion of words that come crashing down on us because of a random keyword match?
- **Visibility** – How does structure play out based on what falls above or below the search engine radar? If we seek a highly structured outcome like a legal action or a shipping manifesto, is that our cue to google? Do we instead head straight for a specialty search or database resistant to search engine indexing?

FIGURE 3.8: Format-based Information Types

Format:	
	Structured and unstructured
	Metadata / Full record
	Indexed / Unstable
	Authoritative / Dubious

Here are the main factors in play when we consider format:

- **Structured versus unstructured** — At its core, format is about packaging. How is the information organized? When we access professionally managed collections, we can choose the detail level we wish to delve: Prefer an abstract or summary? Do we insist on the full article or record? This choice is sometimes extended to free sites, sometimes not. Often pages containing free articles will vanish in lieu of a financial incentive to keep the archive available.

- **Metadata versus full record —** Then there's the basic question of whether we are looking for a number, an index, a database entry, a spreadsheet, a summary, or a full-blown narrative. Metadata are tags applied by information architects, librarians, and vested users that organize web content by categories and expressions we can browse, dispensing with queries and search engines. The meta-tags will steer us in the direction of specific collections, be they lists of licensees, articles on topics, or even directories of relevant websites. Once we click through to the source, we usually find whether the full article is viewable and downloadable.

- **Indexed versus unstable —** Where did we start out? Are we on a site or in a database? It's static or indexed if the page we're on was indexed by a search engine. We can re-engage it through the back button. The footing is less certain inside a database. If the page disappears once we leave it, we've been escorted there by a dynamic link. Not so stable.

PUTTING FORMAT INTO PRACTICE

Category	Information Types	Resource	Examples
Formats:	Metadata / Full record	Metadata: Gigablast	Lesson Plans
		Full record: 9-11 Report	Vivisimo
	Visible / Invisible	Case study: intext:"case study" site:edu	The Wharton School of Business
		Database entry: Town real estate assessments	Land parcel, physician performance history, etc.
	Indexed / Unstable	Indexed: Reference sources	About.com topics
		Unstable: aspx or cgi database results	Flights and reservations

Metadata versus Full Records

It may seem counterintuitive to the unwavering truth-seeker in us researchers. But most times it's the building blocks that get us where we need to go, not the building itself. Most times, we don't require the complete text to reinforce a supporting argument. We just need the recipe that can recreate our path back to the full recording source.

No single best search result is any match for a reliable set of keywords that are placed in the sensitive entry points of titles, addresses, anchors, and formats. That's the distinction between a keyword match and metadata. The former are what floats to the top of our search results. The latter is more powerful because it taps the plumbing that flushes out the Internet sewage. It's the metadata plumbing that produces pre-assembled and unique results. It's these granular findings that are tasked to our project priorities, emerging themes, and even reporting formats.

Stable versus Unstable

Anyone who makes a flight reservation on a travel site knows that we're not dealing with a permanent record or even a re-creatable event – unless we book the flight. The page assembled that shows available seats according to our timeframes, travel points, and price ranges is not a page at all but a snapshot. A placeholder frozen in time for a matter of minutes. It's what a programmer refers to as *a call* to a database: An on-the-fly assemblage of inventory gleaned from all the empty seats on all the potential itineraries that conform to our travel arrangements.

Come back to the same page five minutes later and that arrangement is scrambled because the price may have spiked. Our seats have been taken! That's what's referred to as a dynamic web search or unstable search outcome. How do we know when we're in a search environment that is not repeatable? Look for the lookup program that's been scripted into the URL of the web page. PHP? or CGI? for example at the end of a text-string tells us that this is not a static page but a dynamic one. It will expire during the same session unless we commit to the reservation.

Local Drive versus Network Drive

There's one more domain to tackle before we finish with the formatting aspect of information types. Let's focus for a minute on our own private universes that existed before cloud computing. They went by the name of the 'C:' or *hard drive* of our own MACs and PCs. What would happen if a total stranger looked at the way we organize our files? Would they have a clue what goes where or how we label and store our files? Is there a naming convention that we follow which they can too?

Chances are that all of us may be slightly confused about overlapping document titles and files that contain both copies, competing versions, and unique content buried towards the back. A certain effort is made to enforce electronic hygiene on a shared network. How would we leave a network drive clean and tidy, the way we would our bathroom sink?

For starters, we would give reasonable descriptions of a folder or file's contents based on precedent and order as much as on the whims of its author. There may also be efforts to embed document properties with common data fields such as a document's description, associated tasks, intended audiences, shelf-life, and/or entities, locations, and time-based information captured inside the file.

The larger point is this: Basic level of quality control are hard enough to come by when we're trying to clean up after ourselves – let alone what it's like to keep a whole houseful of databases in order. Figuring out the naming convention is a first step towards understanding the organizing principles of folders and files created in advance of our accessing them. In some instances ... way in advance.

SECTION 3:2 | Source Fluency —
How Should We Think About Documentation?

Unit Three is devoted to unlocking the secrets, pitfalls and potentials of searching business and reference-focused Internet databases. The goal is to conduct sophisticated, time-effective searches with a minimum of preparation (and fees).

So far, we've looked at internet research by getting a feel for orientation. Where am I when I come to that search results page, site destination, or highly ranked information source ... that turns out not all where I need to be!

Our discussion now moves onto where and how we can figure out our document needs. Not just the right length, formatting, and supporting detail but moving onto the sources we gather: Determining the credentials, credibility and very nature of the informants we intend to target. These determinants form the basis of our *source fluency*. Without it, we drift into two familiar and unproductive states:

1. **Source overload** — When have we reached overload? When we're more concerned about chasing down sources than the actual pay-offs: Finding evidence that will sway an argument, prompt a decision, or crack open a lead in our investigation.

2. **Source inventory** — Does it make sense to memorize the *top websites* by topic? Does it make sense to build a new list every time we approach one? That's called a *source inventory* and I don't recommend it. Here's why. Sources are dynamic. Archives are not. Websites launch, die, atrophy and refresh in a continual cycle of change. How to analyze, interpret, and attract the sources we need to fill our search objectives does not change very often. It means adopting and tweaking a few basic approaches that wear well — even improve, with continual practice.

LEARNING OBJECTIVES: SOURCE FLUENCY PAY-OFFS

Source fluency has numerous benefits. We will see how the size of our search pools affects the kinds of answers we get. We'll screen the results to avoid wasting time on redundant, bogus, or misleading information sources. Again, let's circle back to the first two units in order to understand where **Unit Three** is taking us:

1. **Filtering and Refining** — Better still, we will be able to package our reports to clients so they understand the "noise level" operating around the signal we're delivering. This will help us to educate them around the idea that *access* enjoys only a tenuous connection to *usefulness*. Our Knowledge-ABILITIES are helping them to acquire the right pieces, fitting them together, and shaping potential actions and outcomes demonstrated in our findings.

2. **Incentives and Motivations** — We will begin to see all the relevant facts and viewpoints gleaned so far by applying the SPM framework that we first introduced in **Unit One**. These perspectives will be guided by reviewing the incentives that information providers receive for (1) sharing what they know, and/or (2) rewarding the agendas they advance.

3. **Conclusions and Recommendations** — Where is this all going? Up ahead, we'll bring together the search project management steps, the refinement methods, the screening techniques, and the perspective-taking required to verify and resolve conflicting details. This clarity will inform our recommendations and prioritize follow-up actions.

Based on our ability to perform these activities, our clients will be able to see how our informed use of Internet research tools and practices is bringing value, economy, and even closure to a complex and resource-hungry investigation.

Fluency as the Focus

One of the biggest challenges to using the web for research isn't just about finding credible sources or verifiable facts. It's something even more basic and elusive. That's staying on track. Is our fundamental goal to check-out by resolving the reason we first checked in? If so, we need to get a grip around the distracting and fleeting nature of the web as a research medium. The chaotic nature of the web puts great claims not only on our attention. It's our ability to deal with ambiguous, open-ended questions raised by conflicting opinions from fleeting and sometimes untraceable sources.

Researching on the web is navigating through a maze of confusion. There's no avoiding it. Having our intentions garbled or ignored by search tools is a common predicament we face in doing digital research. Below we will find examples where searches are diverted by technical glitches, shortcomings, or commercial sites more intent on responding to their own business interests than our research questions.

When Sources Undermine Answers

Here's a bland and obvious roadblock to web sourcing: Internet information sources are confounding. But what's causing all the confusion?

- There are too many to keep track.
- We need to source them as well as the information they present to really *get* where they're coming from.
- The free ones disappear without warning. The ones we pay for usually ask for our credit cards before they vanish.

We need to adapt to the moving target of internet sources to be secure in our source knowledge. But few of us see source knowledge as the one-stop answer to a definitive question. Most of us rely on sources to settle scores and make decisions. Typically it's not the layperson but professionals who *fixate* on specific sources. That means they tend to see the information source as the prime, if not sole determinant for their search.

Promoting highly-regarded sources at the expense of most qualified answers isn't limited to lawyers, academics or journalists. It's a temptation for many of us mystified answer seekers. Limited topic knowledge to source awareness simplifies the problem: If it wasn't *in the Times,* it couldn't have been very important.

The other problem with keeping an open mind to sources is that by focusing on the 'what' we can sometimes lose sight of the 'why' behind our searches. For instance, maybe last spring we were looking for reviews of barbecues. This holiday season, we want one membership in the bacon of the month club for a loved one on our shopping list. Will our sources be the same?

Probably not.

Will the way we arrive at decisions be similar? Yes, indeed. We don't partake in *mission bacon* with an empty grease pan for catching the useless scraps from *mission barbecues.* Source fluency means never having to work from scratch. It means not having to reinvent what's already worked. We're not boxed in by self-limiting sources or answers to unique questions, conflicting answers, and constantly changing search conditions.

A Hands-off Approach

What would happen if we let the problem decide sources rather than the reverse? What would the result be if we wanted to encourage certain kinds of information without being too exclusive or prejudicial? What would happen if we could discourage the *fire hose effect* of too many sources – especially those whose self-interest does nothing to advance our own?

Below are some surefire ways for bumping into higher quality search results, without knowing a single source or expert:

FIGURE 3.9: Using Syntax and Semantics to Find Experts

Search Statement	Explanation
site:org OR site:edu OR site:gov	Self-interest of these sites not directly affected by the profit motive in many .com sites
(professor OR teacher OR author) bibliography	Authority or expert figures teamed with pointer term designed to yield more vetted references
"(how OR ways) to" "(search OR research) ** (web OR internet)" link:edu OR org	Connecting actions to outcomes within a set of non-commercial sources

The Harsh Glare of Fixations

Yes, it's possible to focus too much. Especially when our concentration returns to the same obsessive target. It's fine that we're engrossed in the work we do. But when the center of our attention is reduced to the first ten hits on Google, we tend to miss the larger picture. Myopic behavior works for heart surgeons and diamond cutters. But that kind of thinking can't adjust to the bumps and swerves of digital searching. On the web, flexibility is a more prized asset than single-mindedness. A successful search strategy is not about finding a seven letter word that means hello in one dialect and goodbye in another. In the impure and fast-moving world of the web, precise answers can work for formulas and facts, not for interpretative or abstract ones.

Site Selection: The Concept of Ponds, Lakes, and Oceans

We've considered all kinds of search technology, what different search tools do, and how to get search engines to understand our research needs. But what exactly are we searching at? Now it's time to point our search in the direction of where we're searching. Enter information-sized oceans, lakes and ponds, a metaphor for sources: Specifically, the number of them that may turn up in our searches.

Oceans, Lakes, and Ponds (or OLP) refer to the size of the database, collection, or index we're searching. The most sophisticated search tool is only as smart as the caliber of sources it collects and indexes. Conversely, the crudest of tools can uncover the most revealing detail if the database is exhaustive and the searcher knows how to search it.

The OLP concept uses the analogy of bodies of water to describe the size and scope of potential search areas. Another way of describing an ocean is a database of websites. That's what a search engine collects and organizes prior to our searching it. A lake, on the other hand, consists of websites that contain databases. Many of these databases cannot be searched through a public search engine like Google. They require us to be *in the lake* before we can actually jump in.

Defining Bodies of Content

So how do we define *what's what*? After all, there are no *ocean sources* any more than there are *pond subscriptions* or *lake-sized websites*. How do we apply these abstractions to actual destinations in our searches?

More importantly, when do we call upon an *ocean* of sites indexed by a search engine? When do we summon the *lake* of sites reviewed and categorized by a subject directory such as Wikipedia? When do we dispense with generalized bodies of information altogether? That's when we head straight for much smaller *pond* collections (that are much better organized!)

The Ocean/Lake/Pond concept uses the analogy of bodies of water to describe the size and scope of potential search areas:

1. **Oceans:** Oceans are a database of websites. That's what a search engine collects and organizes prior to our searching it.
2. **Lakes:** A lake is a website that contains databases. Many of these databases cannot be searched through a public search engine like Google and requires us to *jump in the lake* before we can actually search or browse them.
3. **Ponds:** Ponds are the databases themselves. You can google their existence, but you cannot search them until you're in the pond itself.

FIGURE 3.10: The OLP Framework

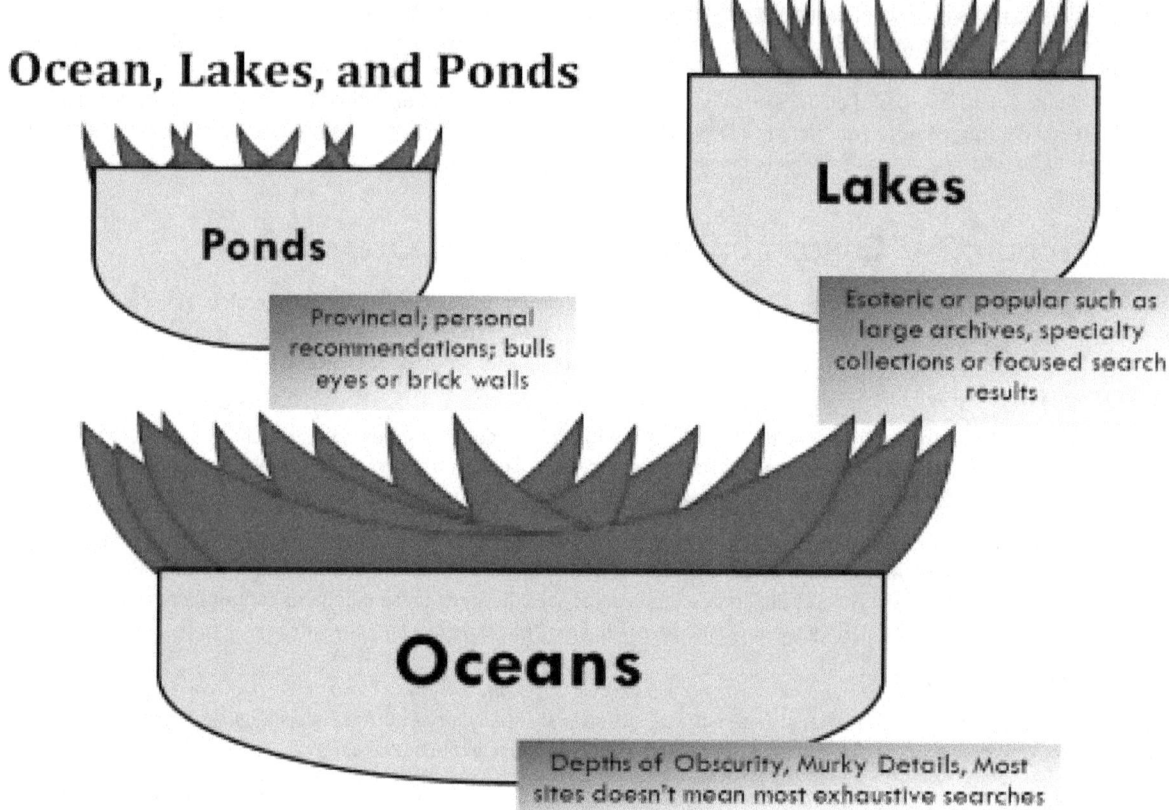

Working Samples

As we first experienced in **Unit Two**, Judy Hourihan's **Cookin' with Google** was a site that invited us to clean out our fridges. The answers were based on throwing a pot, pan, or casserole dish together. The questions consisted of selecting ingredients, then specifying the type of cuisine we wished to prepare. The customized *Cookin with Google* search demonstrated what it's like to search within your own personalized pond of information. This was a novel entry point for filtering content sources In a world that pre-dated social search.

A second example is **Worldcat**. Worldcat is an excellent human-filtered subject directory for producing peer-reviewed media and literature typically missed by the machine-enabled search engines and subject directories.

FIGURE 3.11: The Worldcat Subject Directory

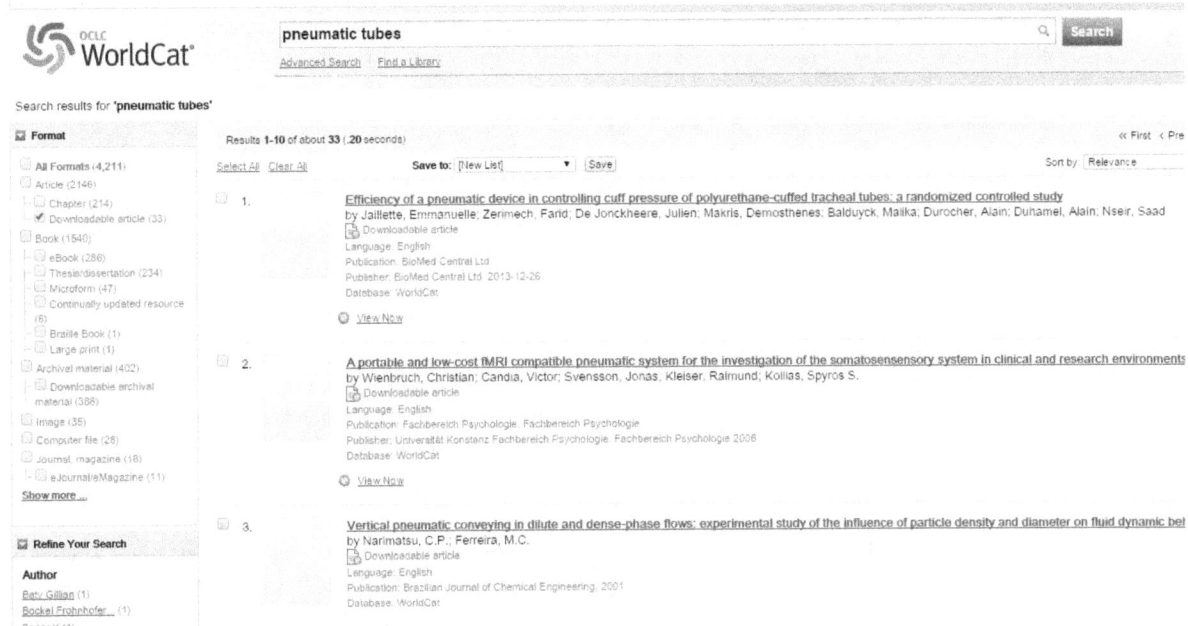

The Worldcat site will map tangible resources to the actual location (usually a university research library) where we can directly access the original source materials.

GETTING FROM AN OCEAN TO A POND

When semantics and syntax are working together ... well that's a beautiful thing. How do we get pulled into this magical mix? That's where we're zooming in on resources specific to our topic without sacrificing the comprehensiveness and detail we may need later on. When does our gratitude get tested? It's when the later on arrives. We know that information we're pursuing is *out there* – just not in the form we find it in.

As we'll learn this unit, there are large chunks of the web that land off the Google radar. In source fluency, we'll discover the Deep Web as an additional dimension to the ocean metaphor.[6] That's because the top search engines can only skim it. Plumbing the depths requires that we're fishing in a selective and *well-stocked* pond.

A pond refers to the countless databases that exist as gateways or starting points in Google but cannot be accessed directly without registering or at least accessing directly. A manageable number of similar sources are the essential difference between: (1) landing the big prey in a small pond, and (2) drowning in the open ocean, fishing for sites that never surface.

Here are some examples of how our **Unit Two** query formation tools figure into the sourcing process:

1. **Syntax** — This search features a long string of potential names for collections and archives referenced in the URL. Syntax enables us to gain access to databases whose contents evade the crawlers of common search engines like Google. Additional syntax further restricts the site domain to [.us site] – limiting the results to all state government-based web pages in the U.S.

UNIT THREE: How to Source Information That Instructs | Page 3:31

2. **Semantics** — Including the term 'sex offender registry' was not a random decision. This popular phrase touches on such policy issues as the public's right to know and the sensitive area of privacy and constitutional freedoms. Strong media focus on the topic serves to inflame these passions by driving search traffic to the sites covering related stories.

3. **Pointers** — The word 'searchable' is a unique term that aptly describes the kind of outcome we're looking for: A database we can search. If we used the term 'search' in isolation ... chaos ensues.

Putting OLP into Practice

"This site comes up in every search. My client knows all this stuff already."

"I keep getting a certain view of events that are anything but certain."

"I was very disappointed, as I consider myself to be resourceful and fairly decent at digging up information/dirt in the past."

Dear tired, questioning, information seekers: I hear you. It's high time to file your frustrations under a mental placeholder called *getting from an ocean to a pond*. It's all rehash if we keep drinking from the information fire hose. While search engines have become better at shaping our user experience, that is largely a commercial undertaking. There are no algorithms to help investigators *shop for ideas* or *buy arguments*.

The trick is hooking up to a hydrant where we control the nozzle. Sometimes that means using syntax that refines our results better. Sometimes it's to use a different type of search that filters the results into discrete groupings. Sometimes it's better to predefine a list of sites and just focus on a narrow group of sources. As we saw in **Unit Two**, that's an availing feature of a CSE or 'custom search engine.'

FIGURE 3.12: Getting from Oceans to Ponds

Google   searchable "sex offender registry" site:us inurl:dir OR inurl:lib OR inurl:archive OR inurl:ind

The Official Web Site for The State of New Jersey | Online Services
liberty.state.nj.us/nj/community/features/services/index.html
Get a Library Card Online · NJ Municipalities Search · NJ Mayors Directory Search · Online Traffic Ticket Information · NJ Sex Offender Registry Search · Offender

Government — Sibley Public Library
https://www.sibley.lib.ia.us/useful-websites/guide/iowa/iagovt
Code of Iowa: State laws searchable by keyword ... (The Iowa Code, Travel and Tourism, Legislature, the Court and Corrections system, Sex Offender Registry) ...

Olin Public Library
https://www.olin.lib.ia.us/@@search?SearchableText=&sort...search...
Search results. 363 items matching your search terms. ... Iowa Code, Travel and Tourism, Legislature, the Court and Corrections system, Sex Offender Registry).

[PDF] Pass Brittany's Law...
www.assembly.state.ny.us/member_files/131/20140814/index.pdf
Aug 14, 2014 - comprehensive legislation that would create a searchable online database of ... felony offenders, similar to the existing sex offender registry.

This ocean-to-pond expedition enlists the help of syntax, semantics, and pointers. Also note the total hit count falls below 3,000 for a target ("sex offender registry") that attracts over 800,000 pages.

Searching Out Loud: Giving Voice to Independent Investigations | Marc Solomon

The responsibility in running for the pond is that we really have to know what we want in advance of getting it. Investigative work has a long set of tasks that lend themselves to ponds. For instance, searching in a pond is implicit in every public records search. We will gladly surrender all the Google tricks we've learned because:

1. We're closing in on our target, and

2. It sure as well can't be found within Google.

Just as no one pretends to sourcing the water in a self-contained pond, so too, sane prospectors don't seek fortunes panning for gold in oceans. Are Massachusetts Doctors' malpractice records on Google? They're not. But we can use Google as a gateway to any number of public records sites where we get the real deal – primary evidence for our cases.

One well-established example for pond fishing is a patent search. Think of some common elements to dedicated resources like patents. Now think of some of the new syntax we've introduced. What happens when we include the following?

> *"searchable intitle:patents inurl:index (inurl:search OR inurl:dir OR inurl:directory OR inurl:database OR inurl:archive OR inurl:records)"*

In this example, the word *searchable* is a smart semantic choice since it exists exclusively to describe what we're trying to do. Use the word 'search' in isolation and it's like using the term 'environment' to describe global warming. (Good luck on finding the right 'search environment.') The other exclusions are that the term 'patents' exists in the title and 'index' describes the web page crawled by Google. Every other 'OR' is a rough attempt to land inside a pond that will help us find the granular bits we need to build our case.

Site Selection Factors

So which one is it going to be? Do we wait to book our tickets on an ocean liner like the next guy or do we attempt a soft canon ball off a rickety bridge into the creek? Can we hope to hit pay dirt (and not our shins and knuckles against some protruding rocks and branches?)

That process is called 'site selection.' Where do we cast our fishing lines for the prized catch? Factors that can affect which site (pond, lake or ocean) to start the expedition include the following:

1. Knowledge (expert) and ignorance (novice)

2. Facts and opinions

3. Time and expense

4. Simple questions, convoluted answers

Each pair of factors exists on a continuum. Determining where we are on each continuum is essential to developing a time- and cost-effective search strategy.

A search engine contains an ocean of information. It is far more useful to a researcher who knows what selective part is worth searching in than a novice with little exposure to the topic or actions under consideration. A subject directory is a 'lake.' It is far smaller in scale than a search engine in terms of its index and the information it contains is much better documented. Often, that's through the work of human classifiers. Not a *bot* or web-crawler in the case of Google.

In our ocean/lake/pond model, the pond is for diving while the ocean is for *skimming*. This is a commentary on both the depth of oceans as the cause of our drowning in information, casing the ocean surface by seldom looking beyond the first results page. Pond diving means that we have defined our information needs clearly enough to contain them – typically to one or several databases that would otherwise constitute drops in the information ocean.

In any search expedition there exists a tension between the guesses we make on the volume or supply of information at-hand and the answers we receive on the demands we place – namely on being able to act on the information we're given.

It's one thing to divide the overall supply into oceans, lakes and ponds. It's quite another to map these to our project requirements and our expectations for meeting those requirements. What site selection does is create a framework for determining where we need to be in terms of (1) our mastery of the topic, and (2) how far along we are in exploring it. We'll look at those plot points from four common site selection perspectives:

1. Knowledge and ignorance
2. Facts and opinions
3. Time and expense
4. Dates and locations

> **Definition: Site Selection**
> Site Selection applies the filtering process of the Ocean, Lake and Pond Framework to determine the most authoritative content sources for site and not search-based investigations.

SITE SELECTION FACTORS: KNOWLEDGE AND IGNORANCE

The black holes in Figure 3.13 suggest a couple of potential blindspots and failsafes for experts and novices alike. For the novice, the black hole occurs when they are besieged by deep, often arcane information about an unfamiliar subject. They are out of their depth when they encounter a foreign species: A specialty database that's organized according to criteria or classifications they can't follow or define for themselves. For them, perhaps a subject directory or Wikipedia entry would be a safer haven to begin their explorations.

On the other hand, an expert risks being subjected to introductory or commonly held knowledge that they've long since mastered. For them, a directory that limits the outcomes to scholarly works or academic journals may prove more productive. Better yet, a topic-specific database might contain the specific evidence or records they need to validate a hunch, test a theory, or confirm that they hold a unique piece of unpublished information.

FIGURE 3.13: Determining site selection through subject knowledge and ignorance

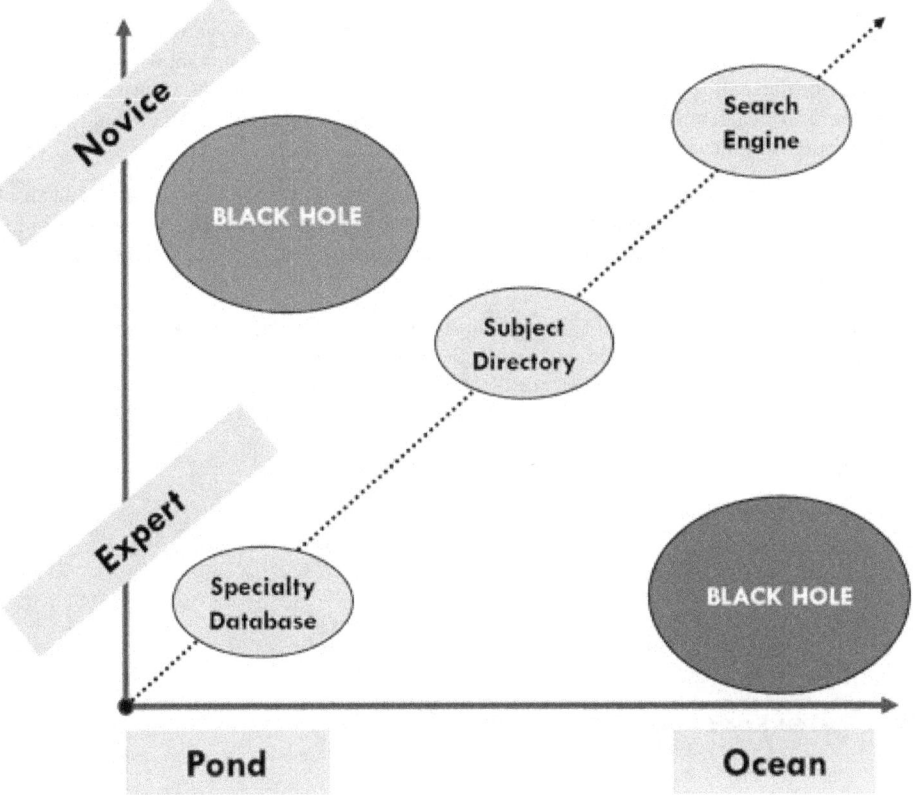

Site Selection Factors: Facts and Opinions

How do we fit our information-seeking goals (those facts and opinions) to the correct size of information sources we need to address them?

Oceans are the place to go for 'fact-based' reference information. Lakes tend to be better environments for delving into gray areas like subject-driven and opinion-based information. This is the province of topics and perspective-gathering. Ponds are dedicated to single topics. What we lose in the comprehensiveness of our results, we get back in relevance to the task at-hand. In our example, this might be the safety record of our car or the efficacy of a medication, given its side-effects, or interaction with other treatments.

It helps to wade into lakes when we're looking at unfamiliar subjects. If we know what we want, the ocean gives us more options. Ponds take them away but hold out the highest return on our research if...

- Our answers are fact-based, and
- We limit our focus to events and people through public records in the public domain.

We must be able to recognize and target the search area correctly to perform time- and cost-effective searches.

Most of us are not complete newcomers to the subjects we search. We're not typically world-renowned experts on them either. In Figure 3.14 we anchor to a set of facts (the lighter box on the Y Axis). Then expand our knowledge by filling in the most closely affiliated details (the darker box on the X Axis). We can straddle the line between the *known* and the *unknowns* we explored early in **Unit One**. The ideal strategy is grounded and expansive: *Grounded* in that it's rooted in some established facts or our familiarity with the subject.

Every investigator wants their fact-base to be *loaded and ready*. It contains numbers, locations, coordinates, and absolute values: The stark relief of times and distances calibrated to physical objects and mapped locations. But we also want to building from that strength. In other words, we expand our understanding by opening up to the complexities we invite in from the opinion side of our questions.

This is the analytical piece and from it enters human judgments, values, and perceptions. It is the less certain path. But remember this: It is less certain for all. The more insight and perspective we gain, the more credible our own opinion will become in helping to define the: (1) relative, (2) subjective, and (3) largely personal meanings that tug at the hearts of the folks we investigate.

FIGURE 3.14: Determining Site Selection through Facts and Opinions

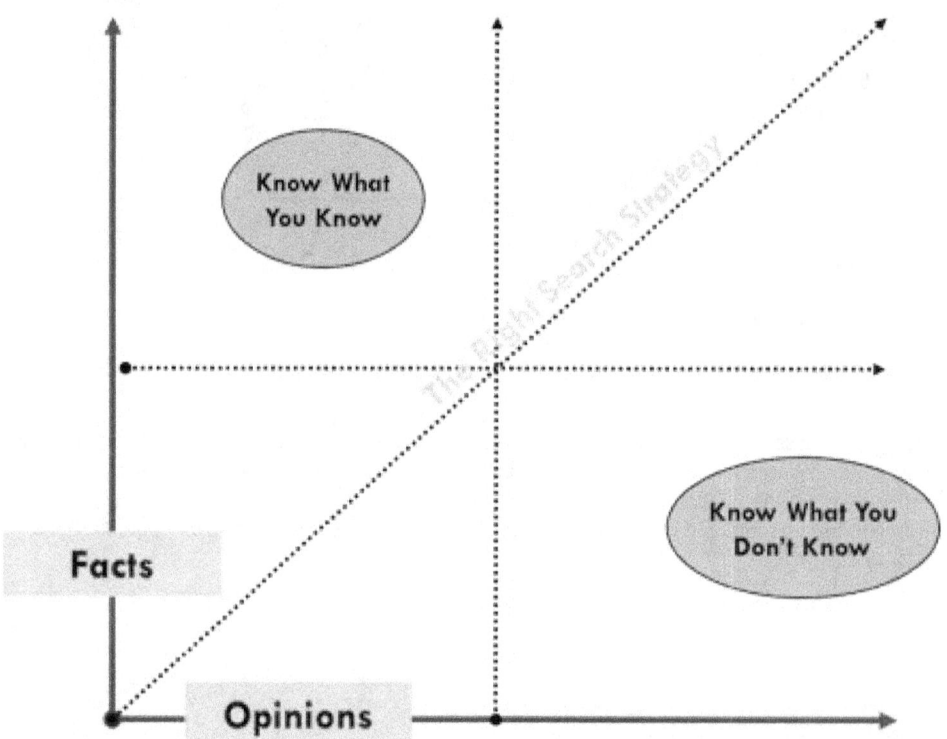

Haystacks and Icebergs

Here's an additional framework for understanding how facts and opinions play out in the way search engines process your query. The analogy of Haystacks and Icebergs helps to explain...

- How to select the right pool (ocean/lake/pond) in which to search
- Which tool to use for the type of search we want to perform

In this model, the haystack needles are the fact questions. The icebergs signify the opinion questions. Understanding how search engines interpret these different question types will help us to...

- Build better queries, and
- Receive results more aligned with our expectations and project requirements.

The needle in the haystack in Figure 3.15-3:16, top left, describes the exclusionary and exacting nature of fact-based questions. The priority here is to...

- Thread the needle,
- Strike the center of the bullseye, and
- Be vested in our use of source fluency.

Our confidence lies not only in the answers or where they came from but in the range of outcomes they suggest: We have a full accounting of the facts we need – whether they're...

- Unassailable or disputed, and
- On *our* side, or not.

FIGURE 3.15-3:16: Using Haystacks and Icebergs to Signify Precision and Recall — Two Opposing Web Investigation Methods

Haystacks
- Precision
- Facts and figures
- Specific details
- Implicit "AND"
- Unique IDs and pointers

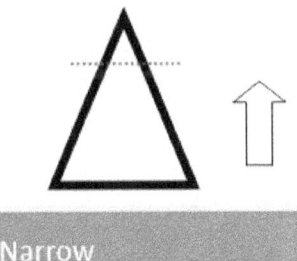

Icebergs
- Recall
- Concepts and meanings
- Generalities and categories
- Implicit "OR"
- Opinions and influences

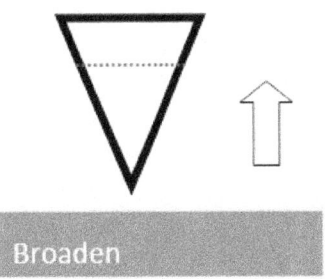

The lower figure in 3:15-3.16 displays the iceberg (tip and all). The iceberg exemplifies the expansive and less definitive nature of opinion-based searches.

Searching Out Loud: Giving Voice to Independent Investigations | Marc Solomon

To the machine logic of a search tool, an opinion search is about keeping options open and entertaining possibilities:

I know for sure it's X but it could also be Y and Z or either Y or Z.

Any level of uncertainty requires us to look more closely at: (1) competing versions of events, and (2) conflicting sources of opinion. To a search engine, this means an inclusionary outcome so long as that Boolean 'OR' command is present. The emphasis has turned from precision to recall: Being able to include as many potentially useful sources as possible.

SITE SELECTION FACTORS: TIME AND EXPENSE

In this book, we have begun to focus on how to be economizing with the amount of time we spend searching. We've begun to factor in the amount we spend on resources such as subscription-based information providers. We can now see the trade-offs between time and money. When it is justified to *call it quits* and consider offline pursuits of the answers we seek.

Most of us don't search for the sake of searching. We hunt for the thrill of closure, informing decisions, and settling scores – not for the pure *thrill of the chase*. If we reversed the query process and asked people about search engines, what might they say? Based on the widespread practice of unquestioning acceptance, I conclude most prefer their results not only fast and cheap. Ultimately, most would settle for free and instantaneous: The less need for interpretation, the better.

Just because most Internet access is either free or flat fee pricing, doesn't mean that fruitless searches don't carry their own costs. Generally speaking, research professionals are paid to find information quickly and budget their resources accordingly. The rest of us compensate for a lack of resources by hopping from site to site with often inconsistent and questionable results. Typically in a less efficient way. But a lack of resources doesn't necessarily mean a lack of resourcefulness. The trick is to yield productive outcomes with minimal effort. That's why we focused from the outset on documenting our SPM efforts with an emphasis on hitting walls, not home runs! So when do we play, when do we fold?

The upper right-hand quadrant in Figure 3.17 signifies searches that are too costly or time consuming. Generally this occurs when the researcher begins to sense their question cannot be answered by secondary or published sources. It requires firsthand or proprietary information to resolve.

FIGURE 3.17: Holding Down Costs and Time Sinks

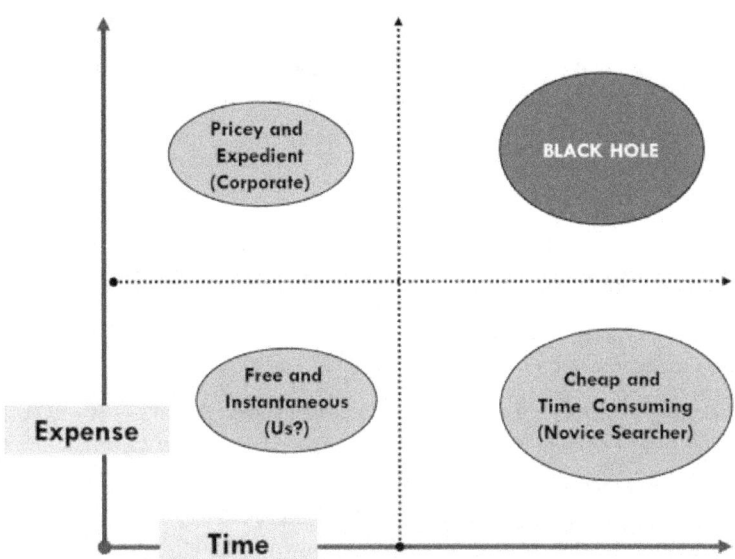

ESTIMATING OUR TIME COMMITMENTS

One way to begin measuring our effectiveness as researchers is to start timing how long it takes to get to *the bottom of things.* The path from ignorance to knowledge is rarely a straight line. Getting to the bottom implies not racing through *the middle* as-in running past...

- The unexpected, or
- Reasons for probing further.

In the search log that follows, we consider 5/10/15 minute intervals of search sessions. This diagnostic associates levels of awareness based on our time commitments. What happens when the same search is refined and repeated based on the addition of additional facts? New source knowledge as it materializes?

Consider the search log for a parking ticket dispute. Our motive is to avoid paying an unwarranted parking ticket. Our objective is proving the grounds for the ticket are baseless. Consider each milestone and whether the deepening time commitment is worth the effort:

1. **5 minutes:** Base level awareness of a common concern – *How to appeal a parking ticket in the neighborhood in question | Contact information for figureheads and bureaucrats*

2. **10 minutes:** Revisiting the issue from the violator's perspective – *Tips for fighting tickets that apply anywhere | Government sites that post parking regulations; individual motorists venting at un-posted rules; new crackdowns on illegal parking*

3. **15 minutes:** Corruption and suspicion in the administration of the process – *Hypocrisy in the papers | Corruption in the ranks, documented waiving of disputed tickets, etc.*

Site Selection Factors: Dates, Dates, Dates

Chronology – the art of plotting the sequential order of events – might as well be an ancient, outdated and lost science practiced by some dark, obscure research cult. We're sunk if we need to know what happened and when. Looking at a set of search results can be as edifying as trying to book a flight using a sun dial. Chronology is not spoken here.

Searching Out Loud: Giving Voice to Independent Investigations | Marc Solomon

It's hard to be sequential with a plain vanilla Google search. But we needn't let this limitation distract us from the end game: (1) A legal rationale for documenting the potential of wrongdoing, and (2) a timeline of questionable judgments that lead to legal trouble, even tragic consequences.

One suggestion is to shy away from the use of dates in general Google searches. There are ways to overcome the chronological shortcomings of most search engines that we'll get into when we begin focusing on important credibility factors like timeliness and ordering events in their true historic sequence. Not transactional dates like when a file gets uploaded to a site or when that site is rebranded by its host.

Getting in on the transactions

Another investigative instinct that serves us well in archival searches is to dig into the actual evidence, not to settle for media accounts of these same events. That's the stuff that's trivial at first, critical in hindsight, and completely disconnected from the crime until pieced together by the legal team. These are the logistics, event-planning, and operational details that are really on trial here. That's where the dates of filings and rulings trigger more accurate date ranges: Did this missed deadline, traffic infractions or court decision ever landed on the media's appointment calendar?

It's worth remembering that famous or infamous dates in history are search terms unto themselves: December 7th, 9/11, 2/23/03 for the Warwick Rhode Island night club fire use case that follows, etc.

In an investigation, the most significant aspect of dates is that they signify the sequential order of events in a criminal case. The problem on the web is that our timeline falls apart pretty quickly because general web search makes no distinction between when files are uploaded to a file server and when reality happens (events in the physical world).

However, as more reality moves to the web, that separation is becoming less clear. Even what constitutes 'an action' is changing. If a thought pops into a blogger's head and they share it without leaving their chair, is that reality? Maybe yes. Maybe not. But it's searchable all the same.

What we do know is the blog program runs on a markup language called XML. Unlike the HTML language that was with us in the web's formative stages, XML (and its offspring) embed the dates the files written to it are loaded automatically. That's why every blog entry is time-stamped. Sequential order has been restored as part of a publication calendar.

It's becoming easier to include dates in our searches when there is a direct connection between the time stamp on when a page is posted and the event it's depicting such as on news sites or blogs. Here are several examples for including date in our search:

FIGURE 3.18: Examples of Date Ranges in Web Searches circa Early 2000s

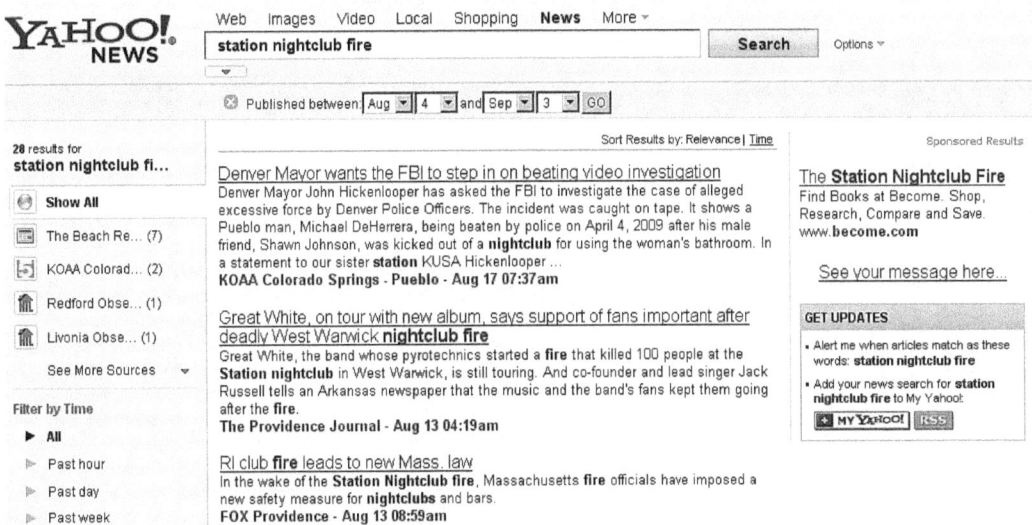

Note the date range option that pops up on Yahoo News searches. The same option does not suffice for general web searches or any collection where there is no linkage between an upload event and the chronology of an unfolding news story.

UNIT THREE: How to Source Information That Instructs | Page 3:41

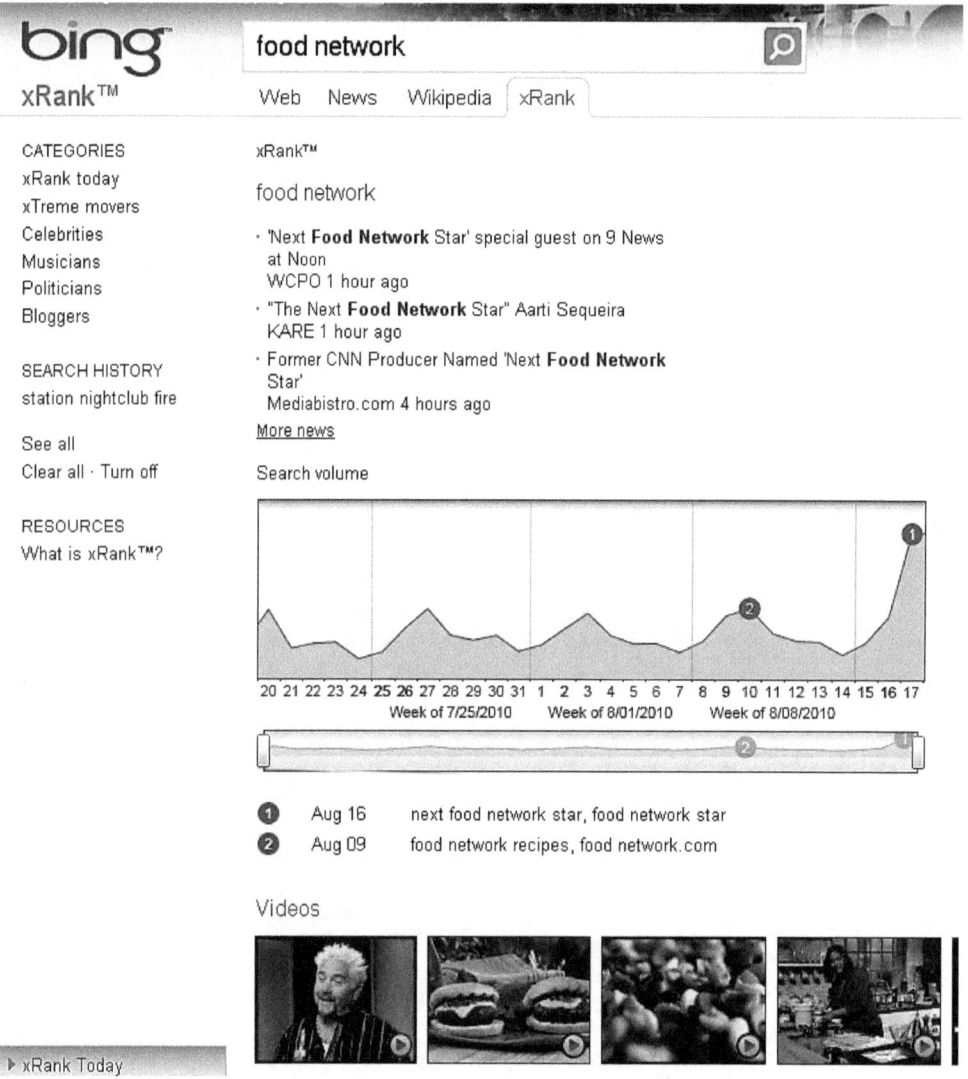

▶ xRank Today

Time sequence metrics are applied here to popularly searched news items. Spikes in news coverage can be correlated to dramatic events or calendar cycles.

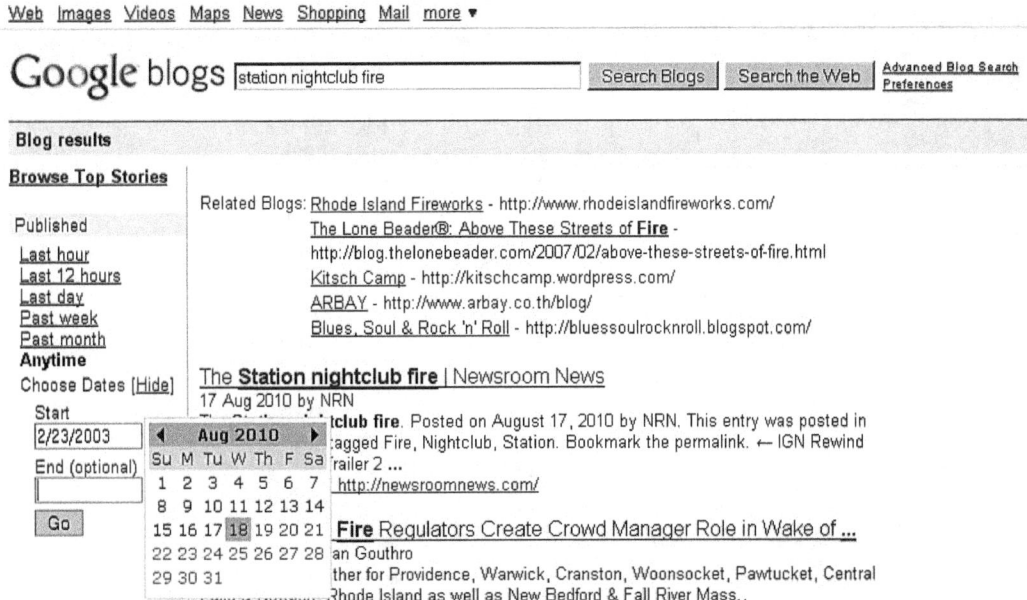

The time window option in Google blogs is a reminder that all XML-based content such as blogs, tweets, and RSS feeds are all ripe for timeframe searches. Google distanced itself from RSS with the 2013 discontinuation of Google Reader.[7]

Note that most of these date ranges are limited to a tight time window. An alternative is to gain access to fee-based subscription content through our local library or state library system. The best way to include meaningful date ranges is to search a commercial database like Infotrac and PowerSearch. They are free to search in my home state of Massachusetts:

> *https://libraries.state.ma.us*

Archival Searches

Time is not only money but also memory. Records are routinely obliterated from view. When the site that reported compromising behavior about a school teacher in our district is removed from the story index, where do we turn?

Going back in time? That would be the waybackmachine.com site that features cache results of select websites and their periodic updates. The main site address is:

> *http://web.archive.org*

UNIT THREE: How to Source Information That Instructs | Page 3:43

It's intriguing to see how static and text-based it all appears when you return to the web through the Wayback Machine.

FIGURE 3.19: Examples of notable web archives

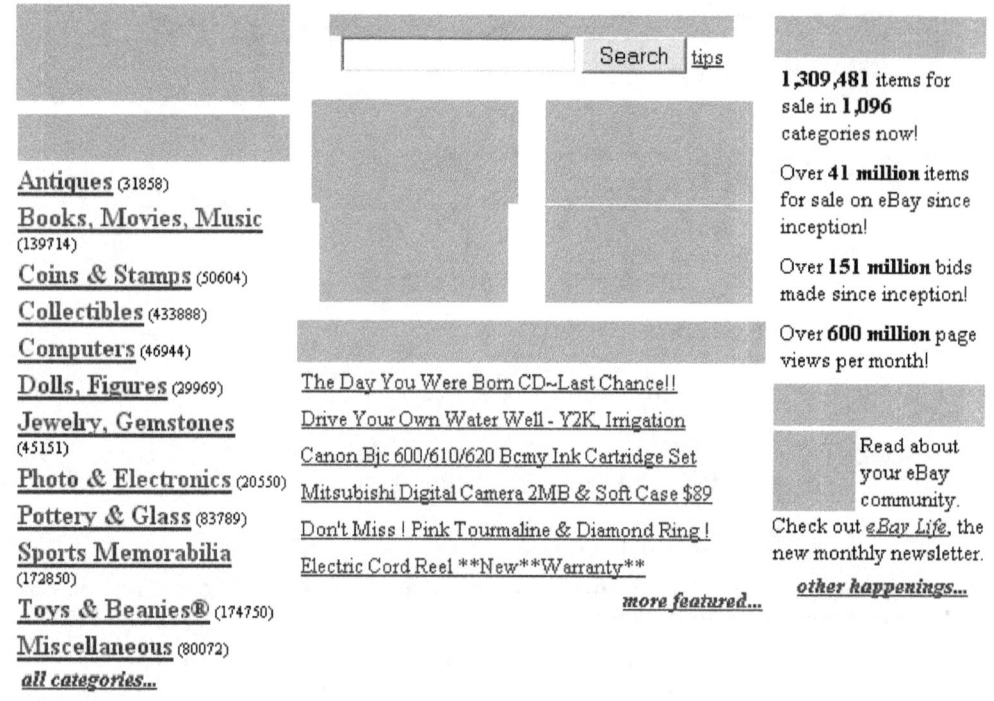

Ebay in October, 1998

Yahoo! Deutschland — CLICK HERE TO VISIT THE STARS LOS ANGELES — Weekly Picks

[Search] Options

Yellow Pages - People Search - City Maps -- News Headlines - Stock Quotes - Sports Scores

- Arts - - *Humanities, Photography, Architecture, ...*
- Business and Economy [Xtra!] - - *Directory, Investments, Classifieds, ...*
- Computers and Internet [Xtra!] - - *Internet, WWW, Software, Multimedia, ...*
- Education - - *Universities, K-12, Courses, ...*
- Entertainment [Xtra!] - - *TV, Movies, Music, Magazines, ...*
- Government - - *Politics [Xtra!], Agencies, Law, Military, ...*
- Health [Xtra!] - - *Medicine, Drugs, Diseases, Fitness, ...*
- News [Xtra!] - - *World [Xtra!], Daily, Current Events, ...*
- Recreation and Sports [Xtra!] - - *Sports, Games, Travel, Autos, Outdoors, ...*
- Reference - - *Libraries, Dictionaries, Phone Numbers, ...*
- Regional - - *Countries, Regions, U.S. States, ...*
- Science - - *CS, Biology, Astronomy, Engineering, ...*
- Social Science - - *Anthropology, Sociology, Economics, ...*
- Society and Culture - - *People, Environment, Religion, ...*

Yahoo! New York - Yahoo! Shop - Yahooligans!

Yahoo in in October, 1996

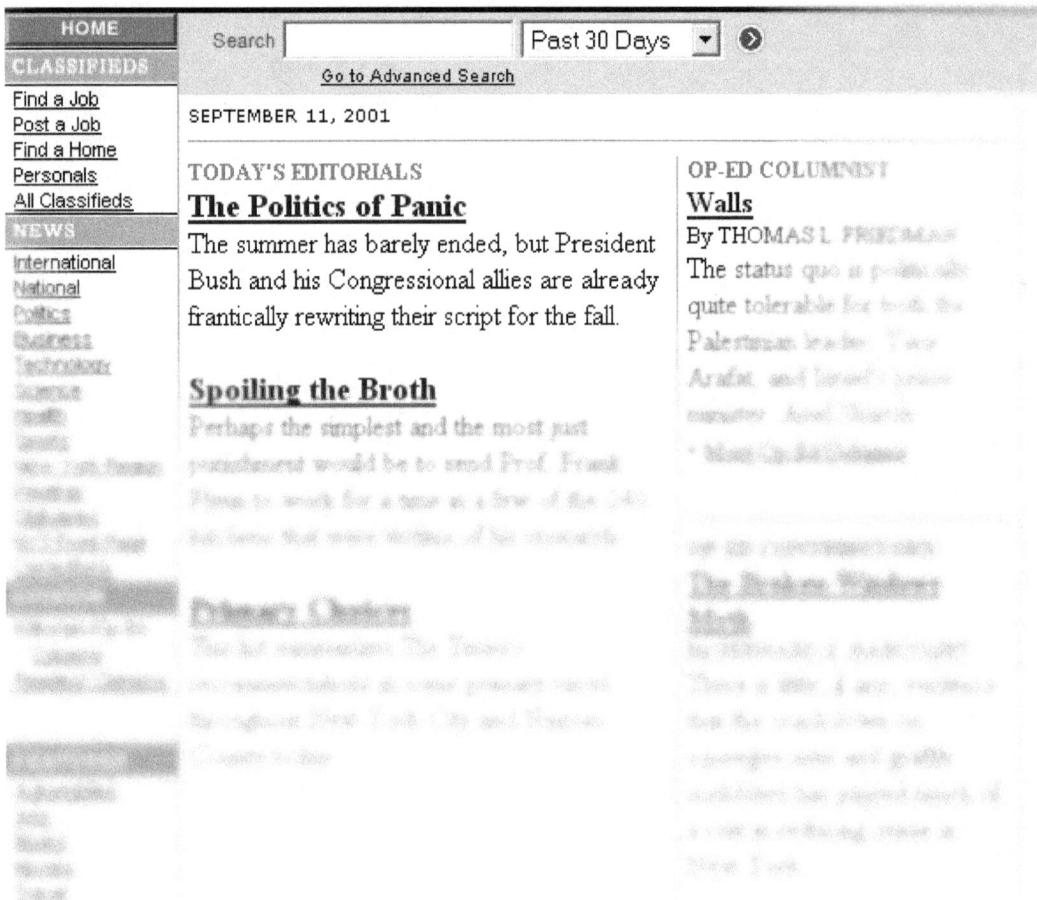

The New York Times Op-Ed section the morning of September 11, 2001

UNIT THREE: How to Source Information That Instructs | Page 3:46

This tool is also helpful for tracking down fraudulent claims or controversial stories that get pulled when new facts come to light. But remember: This is not the definitive archival trail on all Internet sites we may want to track down in our investigations.

SITE SELECTION FACTORS: LOCATION, LOCATION, LOCATION

In addition to date, another elusive and often missing piece in web investigations is the notion of physical place in the virtual universe. It's one thing to check in on what weather to expect before we leave for work. It's quite another to document the weather conditions at the scene and time of a criminal act was committed. For that we have **Wunderground:**

FIGURE 3.20: The Weather as Evidential Exhibit

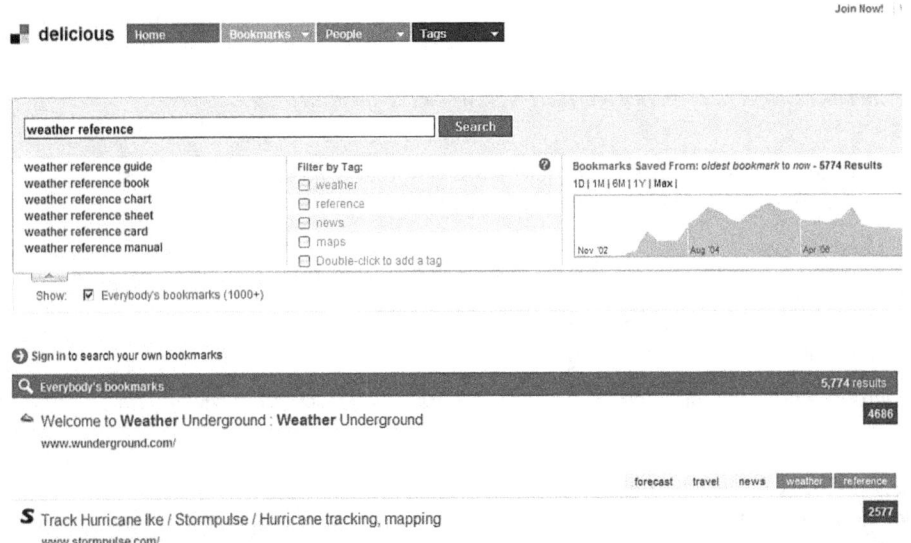

Here we use common labels from the once pre-eminent tagging engine called Delicious to identify sites endorsed by other Delicious members.

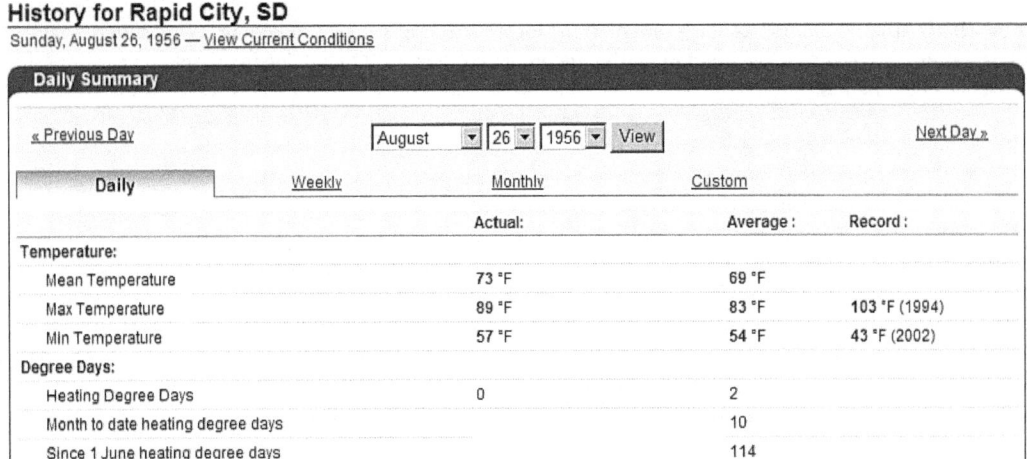

These are the spoils – micro details of a well-stocked pond like Wunderground!

Another example where location works is to search the geophysical proximity of bloggers to a potential crime scene in need of investigation. There's little mystery when it comes to mapping a local IP address to the actual residential locations of registered bloggers. While that may seem somewhat revealing, mapping search behaviors to our travel patterns has moved well past the invasive stages of profiling citizen users. *(More on big search and social media surveillance in **Unit Seven**).*

But what happens when we move beyond weather trivia and blogger tracking? Let's say we're looking to tweak our telescopic searches. Let's start with a routine example. What's a basic location question? Those have been reduced to simple GPS exercises:

> "Where are the pizzerias near my local skating rink?"

That's not where we're going here. What's a more complex one?

If we wanted to stump a natural search engine, we could determine whether it's worth attending our high school reunion with this:

> "Where do my unrequited loves live now? Are they married? How well have their marriages turned out?"

Either way, we end up nowhere in a hurry. Even in its most sinister forms of sophistication, no one expects web searches to lead us into the arms of confidantes or the beckoning doorsteps of informants.

From oceans and ponds to cities and streets

One way to factor in location is to return to the ocean to pond approach. To do this, we anchor ourselves in the LinkedIn directory, the leading social network of working professionals. Note the syntax that enables Google to focus on the one site. Then we add some semantics to approximate job title and expertise:

> "site:www.linkedin.com "(group OR organization)(leader OR manager OR executive)(at OR from OR "part of"") ("florida real estate law")

Certainly there's *some* relevancy here. We can tighten it up though by balancing the semantics we've done with the compound search terms. We let the search breathe a little more with a few selected keywords. The real killer is to match job titles and expertise to actual cities in Florida. So we try this:

> site:linkedin.com (realty OR "real estate") "(miami OR fort.*. OR tallahassee OR orlando OR tampa OR jacksonville OR st.*. OR west.*.) area" florida ~law ~investigations

The second time's the charm. The other important ingredient in the location example is that searching ponds with ocean-sized search tools enables us to bypass some of the boundaries we bump into when we're looking up people on Facebook, LinkedIn, and other social networking sites.

Site Selection Factors: Simple Questions, Convoluted Answers

The diagram below lays out the 'law of diminishing search returns.' This precept is an important project control check for making sure that we don't overstay our digital welcomes. Sometimes the best search strategy is to logoff, regroup, and fight another day. A respite from failsafes.

Generally speaking, the stiff-upper-lip approach is a non-starter for working through a research quandary. This describes a fixation on finding a particular person or fact without a backup plan: The benefit of an alternative outcome or substitute choice of search tools and strategies.

So, when should we quit? Generally speaking, it pays it reach for your second wind, if not second opinion, once we have the full regimen of search tools and resources under our belts. We've tried all our own tricks too within the scope of one hour. Ironically, the simpler the search, the more complex the outcome may prove to be. That's the typical dilemma of seeking a person with a fairly common first name and surname.

As anyone who ever tried to google the most popular high school chums will attest, asking a straightforward question can produce the most convoluted answers – if that search is unqualified or free of supporting identifiers.

FIGURE 3.21: The Law of Diminishing Search Returns

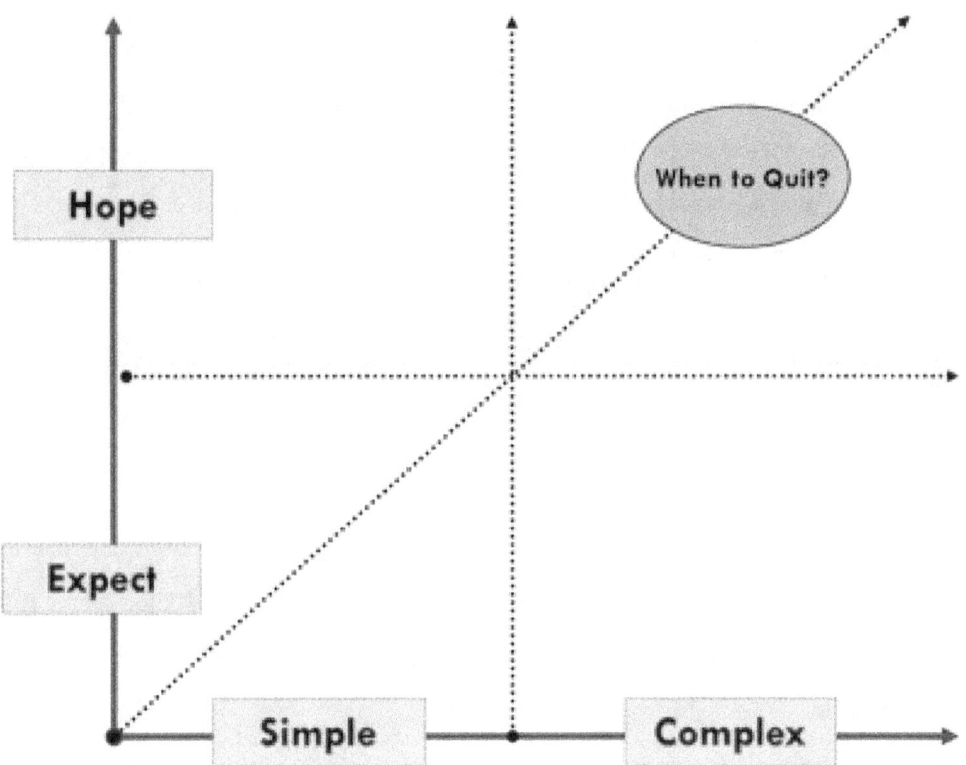

Facts v. Opinions

Let's break it down. Not by our objectives which here means finding the best sources. It's more basic than that. Our primary research goal is never about the size, number, or even quality of our sources. It's about getting our questions answered!

As we saw with the haystacks and icebergs model in figures 3.15-3.16, two dominant types of questions emerge: Fact-based questions and opinion-based questions. There's a good chance that our investigation includes elements of both.

We need to confirm or deny the recording of an event. We need to find out the road visibility on the date that a car accident occurred. But we also need to expand our questioning to include...

- Interpretations of what the recording means, or
- The eye witness testimony of the folks in proximity to the car wreck.

These factors are typical. Not only in terms of goal structure but in: (1) how they diverge in the types of questions they form, and (2) how this impacts both *how* and *where* we do the asking, a.k.a. site selection.

Here's that fact-based yes or no answer we must insist on:

We require the exact amount. We can't plan our day until we track the arrival of a parcel. Even when there are potentials for multiple conditions, we need to base our assumptions on a finite number of fixed conditions, i.e. reviewing case particulars like those that follow in Figures 3.22 and 23.

Opinion searches require *softer* answers that by definition are not *hard* facts. They evolve from concrete facts to abstractions such as concepts, meanings and non-financial values in our investigation. Instead of needing a precise answer, we start with a narrow objective and stem outward to include related associations and their implications.

The hard absolutes like weather conditions and prior driving record converge in our accident scenario. Then we move onto less certain variables like motives: Why the driver was in a hurry? Maybe their judgment was impaired in some other way: Poor signage, overgrown foliage, liabilities posed by the other drivers involved, etc.

Opinion-based searches are seeking subjective references for gathering perspectives on evidence that is by nature framed by experiences and associations – not definitive boundaries like times, dates, locations, or yes or no outcomes.

The best way to seek these less settled search targets is through a subject directory. A lake-sized directory attempts to show the multiple dimensions of a topic based on the diverse and sometimes clashing views of the people and organizations we are evaluating. With some sound sources and inferences, we can ascribe motives for their involvement or removal from our investigations.

FIGURE 3.22: Examples of Fact-based Questions (haystack model)

- **WHO:** Person, SSN
- **WHAT:** Company, Organization, Financial Index, Product Name, Facility, Weapon, Vehicle (Make, Model, Color, VIN, License Plate)
- **WHEN:** Date, Day, Holiday, Month, Year, Time, Time Period
- **WHERE**: Address, City, State, Country, Place (Region, Political, Geo-coordinates), Internet Address, Phone Number
- **HOW MUCH:** Currency, Measures
- **PATTERNS:** Rankings, Standards, SKUs ("stock keeping units"), Chemical Compounds, etc.

FIGURE 3.23: Examples of Opinion-based Questions (iceberg model)

- **CONCEPTS:** Unstructured Data, Good/Bad Actors, Spirituality
- **INFLUENCE:** Leadership, Role Models, Inspirations, Pastimes
- **TEMPERAMENT:** Principles, Tendencies, Character, Personality
- **PERCEPTION:** Awareness, Cultural Values, Socio-economic Status
- **SOCIAL NETWORK:** Affiliations, Events, Professional / Education Background

SECTION 3.3: | Quality Control —
How Do We Assess the Knowledge-ABLED Side of Websites?

In this section, we'll idle our search engines for a while to call attention to the review process for analyzing our results. As much as we can refine our results, tune our engines, and select from a wide variety of search tools, there is still a stack of stuff awaiting our inspection. That stack is bound to require more time than the hours in a day we have budgeted for searching out loud:

1. Anyone with a point to make can make one.
2. Anybody with an opening to post can circulate it for free – even if the opening is a fiction and it's only to test passing interest in it.
3. Any group with a shared interest can bond over it and invite others.

There are few risks or rules about using the web as you communications medium. From a research perspective, here's the bottom line: Most searchers can't process the pages they visit. The better you can document the quality of your sources, the more credible you become as an analyst and investigator.

We will consider the ingredients that go into determining the quality of our search results from a big picture perspective. That entails skimming results lists without needing to drill into individual pages. We will look from a street perspective which is to look at the ways to evaluate individual information providers. Finally, we will look from the microscopic level of quality control through page scanning: A technique used to evaluate individual pages and content providers.

WE ARE THE ONLY REGULATORS!

All investigators must remember that it is the responsibility of the information user – not the provider and not the search engine – to be accountable to the final arbiter of information quality (our research clients). Anyone can put up a web page about anything and give the First Amendment a run for its money!

Many pages are not kept up-to-date. Broken links are both a dead-end and giveaway that a site registration has lapsed. Equally bogus and more deceptive are expired site domains that have been resold to other controlling interests.

Regardless of ownership status, there is no government agency that handles web registrations. There is no central review board to determine the veracity, exactness, or reliability of statements, claims, or questions arising in or about web pages – especially allegations.

No quality controls mean that most sites are:

1. Not peer-reviewed or consumer vetted like a restaurant or a doctor
2. Less trustworthy than scholarly publications
3. Teeming with ads exploding with urgencies that underwrite and undermine our desire for commercial-free content

Does that mean we need to dismiss everything we see on screens? Does a lack of accountability mean the web is a questionable medium for conducting research? No. Not in the least.

What it does mean is the need for an approach that connects what's out there with meaningful standards to assess its legitimacy – namely *why* it's out there. To achieve this, we'll focus on three bottom line approaches for evaluating web content:

1. Through search engines (quantification of what's available)
2. Through subject directories (qualification of information providers), and
3. Through source conjugation (motivation for providing it).

But first, let's consider how shallow or deep we need to be in order to make these assessments. That means returning to our Oceans, Lakes, and Ponds framework in order to address the quality of what we're finding.

FIGURE 3.24: Key Issues Surrounding the Quality Control of Web Content

Quality Control
The only regulator is – Us!

Anyone can put up a Web page
About anything…and give the First Amendment a run for its money!

Many pages not kept up-to-date
Broken links are a dead-end/giveaway

No quality control
- Most sites not "peer-reviewed"
  - ✓ Less trustworthy than scholarly publications
- No selection guidelines for search engines
  - ✓ No commercial reward on "free information"

The Big Challenge:
Recognizing usefulness through qualification and quantification

There are three core ways (levels) to monitor search results.

The deeper the level, the higher our time commitment, as Figure 3.25 illustrates.

THE THREE LEVELS OF QUALITY CONTROL

The Bottom Line:

To realize that most searchers can't process the pages they visit. The better we can document the quality of our sources, the more effective we become as analysts and investigators.

FIGURE 3.25: The Three levels of Quality Control

Quality Control
Three levels of quality control
- Level 1 Big Picture
- Level 2 Street Level
- Level 3 Micro Level

Another way of looking at the three levels of quality control is to consider the following perspectives for focusing in on your research findings:

- **Level 1: Big Picture** – This is our first at-a-glance inkling of how close or distant we are from our Knowledge-ABLED destination. Our clues are in the form of titles, addresses and keywords. Since this is the entry level for casual surfers we need to pay particular attention to the *road most traveled*. It's one thing to learn all the tricks in the query formation toolbox. It's quite another to compare our superior SPM skills to the view of the web that our clients see. That cursory understanding is what floats to the top of the level one surface.

- **Level 2: Street Level** – We have now picked a handful of sites that show the most promise but we still need to vet the orientation of the site. That requires we understand what they're known for, who knows them, and what they do to shape the events they cover. From a social media perspective the street level needn't be so formal: what's the experience of clicking through? That's where we link site ownership, content generation, and keyword marketing to the editorial agendas of the sites in question.

- **Level 3: Microscopic Level** – The final quality check before a quote, fact, or important piece of evidence surfaces in our report. This phase runs closest to the basic tenets of journalistic tradition. This means the fact-checking once part and parcel to working in the newsroom. A reporter might be influenced by the beats they work and the informants they keep. But they are not the final arbiters of what sees print or *makes air*. Stories are corroborated, circumstances are confirmed, the sequential ordering of events is tested, and sources are named prior to publication.

Figure 3.26 lays out the key quality controls for assessing web-based research in order of granularity: results, sites, and pages:

FIGURE 3.26: Quality Controls by Assessment Level

Assessment Level	SPM Stage	Quality Control
Level 1: Results lists for analyzing keyword matches and influence of suggestion search and SEO campaigns	Review of search engine results lists	New-to-known Signal-to-noise Schedules Timeliness (date ranges) Locality (geographic ranges)
Level 2: Analysis for grouping pages according to common site characteristics	Screening pages by site root, (e.g., all pages share a common pattern such as .edu for education sites; blog in the URL for blogging sites)	Site ownership Site traffic Link popularity Link analysis Keyword analytics
Level 3: Page scans according to the motivations for publishing content, a.k.a. editorial agendas	Opening individual sites to vet content providers page-by-page	Tonality Story selection Content providers (message posters, authors, publishers, aggregators, etc.) Litigation Cache results (publication histories)

QUALITY AND QUANTITY CONTROLS

How do we read a set of search results? How do you make sense of countless web pages when we're not sure there's any definitive answer to our queries?

It's time to switch on our pattern-matching apparatus. We're going to go scouting for a few tell-tale signs:

1. Do we see a string of pages from the same site root or parent site?

2. Is the domain what we'd expect?

For instance, do we see...

- Dotcoms light up our screens when our results have to do with purchases and financial transactions?

- Dot.orgs and dot.edus if our questions are of a non-profit nature?

Is our intention to find and compare the differing requirements of states, localities, or other countries? This becomes apparent when our response includes dot.gov and sites hosted abroad.

Another important factor is whether our results come from a trickle or a warehouse of search pages. For instance, highly visible retailers and marquee corporations may have their entire catalogs inventoried on websites that span thousands of pages. A blog or personal page suggests the other extreme – even though the page may be hosted by an immensely sprawling host such as Facebook or Twitter.

The surest way to connect our query to search results still requires us to open the page and check for the prominent or fleeting appearance of your keywords. Are they close to the top of the page or buried in the terms and conditions?

The easiest way to trace this is to click on the cache or version of the page indexed on the search engine database. There are likely to be competing versions between the cache edition and what we see today on the production site – especially on frequently updated pages sites like those generated by news and entertainment sites.

Our first encounter with quality control starts in the familiar surroundings of the search result page. Here we'll introduce some new terms and tools like **content weight** and **new-to-known**.

Level I Quality Controls: Results List Analysis

A search results page is a listing of web page contents that our browser displays, which provide sufficient information to peruse without needing to open individual links.

There's no getting around the search results page. For search engines this is a universal billboard for their advertisers. For most of us (and I mean most people who find no joy in the act of searching) the priority is to escape level one ASAP. This escape is premised on two vital outcomes:

1. They needn't go past the first page
2. There are results to click on in the first place

But we can be certain of one thing whether we're in it for the research or the shopping. The faster we process a search result page the less time we'll flounder from site to useless site. A skilled deciphering can spell the difference between re-emerging with the jewels from a forgotten shipwreck – or drowning in the attempt.

The Google Truth

For the rest of us (I guess that leaves you and me) there's this remaining challenge: Result lists can determine information quality more than any single page, site, or ad that appears on them. That's because the first results page that assembles from commonly used keywords to frequently asked questions is our baseline. It tells us exactly what a layperson's view of a response looks like.

You and I are too curious, skeptical, and restless to accept the answers given. We're not going to succumb to suggestion search either. But in our haste to dig deeper, it is essential to reference this baseline. Especially when we are reporting the distinction between general awareness and the uncommon knowledge we deliver to our clients.

The other important bellwether here is to frame our results page experience in two words: What's new?

New-to-known

It might be time to move on if the deepest revelation is the dull surprise that the same erroneous facts we checked a week ago are now parroted by the Twitterpedia link farm. On the other hand if we're less familiar with our fresh subject then it's likely we're going to see foreign terms and strangers dotting the surface details. It may take 3-5 search result pages before we even begin to see a pattern emerge. This comparison of *new-to-known* is a helpful gauge for determining just how much Level One review is necessary in our search projects.

Content weight

Content weight was another helpful diagnostic that was discontinued in 2011. It told us the size of the web pages Google indexes. Generally speaking, the smaller the size, the better the fit of our search terms to the pages we're referencing. That's because longer pages are likelier to produce bogus results.

Size matters in other ways too. When trawling the ocean it's important to remember that we are not plumbing the depths. We are skipping across the crests of the waves.

That might not sound like a major readjustment when we're *submerged* in millions of search results. However an in-depth focus on specific people and events begs for the complete story when we're focusing on our results – not Google's advertisers!

FIGURE 3.27: Page Size Indicates Content Weight

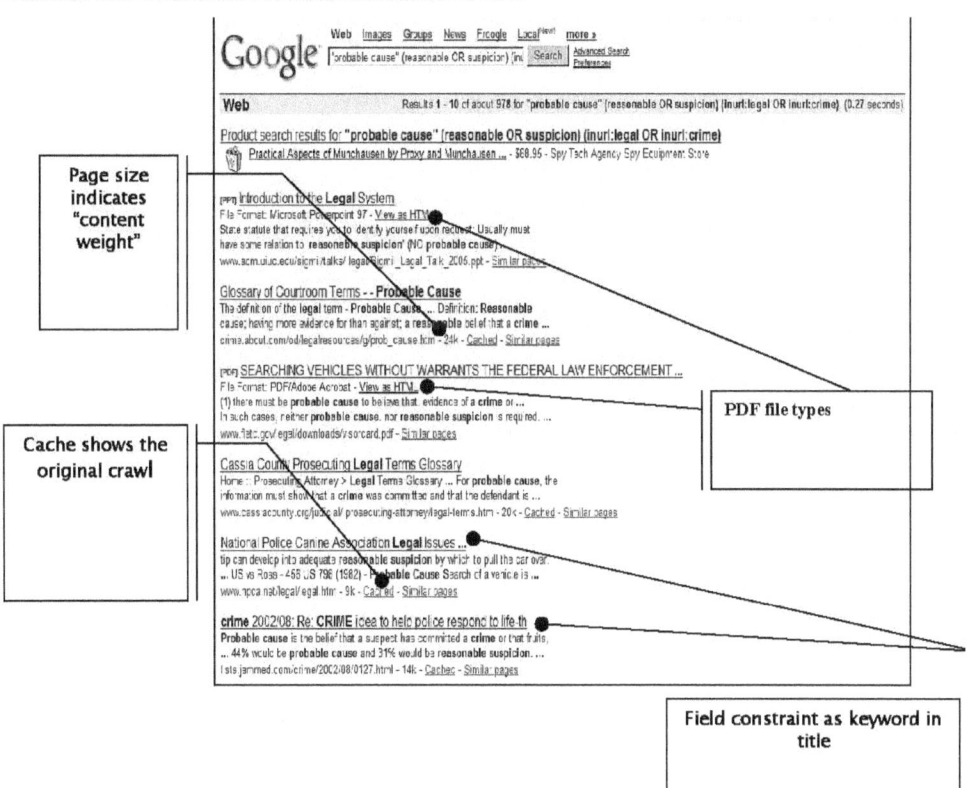

Cache Result

Cache results (pronounced "cash") is the imprint made by the crawler or search engine indexer. In an index as large as Google's it is a small imprint to be sure and it is rare to see a cache record exceed 100K per site. Even if that site runs not hundreds but thousands of pages just on its own! Cache is an important marker for establishing site revisions or wholesale changes such as when entire pages and/or sites are removed. It also best answers the question: "Why did I get what I got?." That's because we can see our keywords highlighted. This makes it easier to discern them in context and whether they're aligned with our learning objectives or *search intent*.

Site Root

Another useful tool to factor in is the concept we first addressed as an 'Entry Point' in the 'Information Type' section earlier in this unit. That's the notion of site roots in questioning whether the search engine is leading us to the main entrance or homepage of a website or to the side entrance. We'll be arriving unannounced if this is our first visit so we'll need to be expecting some disorientation. Even in above-board and well-documented sites.

File Format

One overlooked control factor in our favor is that we can contain your search results to file types whether they're stored as Microsoft Word Documents, Excel files, or PowerPoints, html pages, or PDFs. PDFs can be especially useful for web investigations because they hold a perception of higher credibility than a web page or even a Microsoft Word or PowerPoint presentation.

Why is that?

For starters, PDFs have long been the format of choice for editorial staff who wish to preserve the content and formatting of their written documentation in a read-only format. While it will become increasingly easier to convert PDFs to read/write formatting that sense of authorship and version control will remain a strong if not completely accurate property of PDF documentation.

This view is reinforced by the countless legal, regulatory, and academic papers that are saved as PDFs. If we're looking for government reports, public statistics, and other quantifiable evidence whether produced in a lab or a thesis study, chances are every table is preserved as a PDF. Something that appears "official" and peer-reviewed will often have the sheen of a PDF to set it apart from the more fluid formats used to post routine and daily changes to most websites.

ULTIMATE CONTROL OVER QUALITY CONTROLS

Okay, now. Let's put our terms up and post them where we can see 'em! It is reassuring to receive the stamp of our selected terms as top-of-mind appearances in the title fields of our search result pages. All search engines try to elevate the importance of our terms by literally pushing them to the top – not just of our lists but in the labels that describe the sites we attract.

As we saw in the 'Search Operators' discussion in the **Query Formation** section in **Unit Two**, it helps to be *general* in a *specific* way.

I know that sounds confusing but hear me out on this one!

One especially effective refinement strategy is to use the term expansion properties of the tilde with a word appearing in the title:

> *allintitle: ~strong ~opposition*

This query will produce variations on the strength of the resistance whether our items include your original or like-minded terms. In other words a common expression is placed in: (1) a powerful context, and (2) an expansive scaling of that strength.

In the following Figure 3.28, we summarize these Level I elements when analyzing results lists:

- URL
- Domain/protocol
- Root / Cache
- File Formats

FIGURE 3.28: Level I Quality Controls

Quality Control	Example / Comments
URL – is this a group-based or personal page?	[~ or %] or users or members; sponsor links – *Who is at the controls? These are some telltale signs.*
Domain/Protocol – is this appropriate to our intention?	com, net, gov, state.us, uk, etc. – *What does the domain registration say about the credibility of the registrant?*
Site Root – are we on the parent site?	Generating .php or .aspx pages mean that we've stumble in the side entrance – *The key is connecting the landing page to the site root or homepage.*
Cache Result – is there keyword highlighting?	Changes between current and indexed versions – *Cache is helpful for documenting editorial changes between the production site and its archive as well as confirming why 'we got what we got.'*
File Format – is this a read only version?	docx, pptx, xlsx, pdf, mp3, htm, etc... – *What does the file format say about the quality of the information it contains?*

Level I Quantity Controls: Results List Analysis

As the title of this section implies, there is more than one way to read a results page. True, the more conventional read is to assess whether it's worth the leap from our questions to the responding site and page destinations. But another approach is to make the results pages the final destination.

The ability to read or interpret hit counts is a key pattern recognition skill and screening tool. It can help us to see the larger patterns that emerge so often in opinion-based and conceptual searches. Social scientists, authors, and most certainly marketers need to assess the bigger picture cultural trends before they can strike a nerve or tap into the popular imagination.

There are some major advantages to maintaining quantity control:

- Calculating hit counts (the number of results matching our queries) mean we can create better questions faster without the interruption of opening pages and needing to review individual sites.
- Establishing search metrics helps us to determine the likelihood of finding exact matches such as identifying unique targets, including people, facts, and locations, or isolating specific details.
- Quantity control is also important in terms of softer or less tangible targets such as testing awareness levels or the popularity of search targets. Looking at set result patterns is essential not only for correcting and perfecting search statements but also for distinguishing normal from exceptional levels of attention paid to our search topics and the topics we are targeting.

In the case below, however, we will stay quite literal. We will apply quantity controls to discern what mayhem is *real life* and what's been inspired by pure fantasy. In this case we will attempt to distinguish the actual crimes from entertainments.

True Life Crime: Fact "and" Fiction

In the first instance we use syntax to go from an ocean to a pond. The contents of the pond are the bidding lots indexed on the auction site eBay. Here there are about 192,000 results containing an appearance of the term 'murder' But were real people involved more in commercial or criminal activity? Can we even assume reality when homicidal consequences hold so much sway over fans of horror films, pulp fiction, and whodunits?

Now the plot shifts. We add some semantics around escapism. Hark: The bottom drops out of our hit counts. We've reduced our result set to one-hundredth of its former size by focusing on non-fiction. We've eliminating movies, novels, games, comics, and murders committed by the pen and keyboard, not the weapons collected on the site of most crime scenes.

FIGURE 3.29: Level I Quantity Controls – Fiction and Reality

```
intitle:murder (manslaughter | homicide)
```

About 4,290,000 results (0.73 seconds)

In the first query, we're seeing 4.2 million hits for pages with murder in the title and the mentioning of either "manslaughter" or "homicide" on those same pages.

```
title:murder (manslaughter | homicide) -novel -TV -video -movie -drama -amazon
```

About 619,000 results (0.92 seconds)

How do we reduce the first result set by 85%? Remove murders told with the embellishments of fiction, that's how. Each negation operator eliminates another element of drama in the storytelling narrative. It's not only a text book case of information quality by subtraction. The massive hit reduction speaks to the realities of perception: What goes on between the readers' ears is likelier to populate a search index more readily than the evidence captured between the police barricades of a crime scene.

What does this tell us about human nature and how does this increase the quality of our investigation? Hands-down we've confirmed with numbers what we know in our hearts: Taking another person's life is a prolific part of our inner imaginings. It's a timeless way to tell stories, play out fantasies, and do some spectacular box office. From a Level One research perspective here are some other outcomes to ponder:

1. From four million down to six hundred thousand search results – what's a manageable basis to start the page level vetting process?
2. What do the page summaries for each hit say about *real life* events and how does that square with how people connect to them?
3. How does the fantasy aspect of the murder-mystery play into the escapist nature of dual personalities? Is that element a factor in the case of an individual we're investigating?

We can't read their minds but we can understand them better if say we don't know a gaming console from a roulette wheel and the gamer we're investigating seldom leaves their personal domain or what in pre-social media days the political columnist George Will referred to as the *electronic playground.*[8]

Meta Surveillance

Data mining is another way for applying quantity controls to web investigations. Data mining is the pattern recognition approach used in software programs that process enormous numbers of electronic records. The data miners are expected to detect the outliers or anomalies that diverge from the larger pattern. That's the rationale for using phone records to catch terrorists or to spy on persons of interest who would otherwise act under the cover of anonymity. Another is marketing. It's where advertisers and store merchants look for correlations from inputs like their ad spend and point-of-sale data to help influence what we buy based on our usage patterns.

Data mining is considered a best practice by companies who do business in the public arena. Their corporate relations and PR units routinely monitor newsgroups and neutralize incorrect information. These are rumor control functions that detect and understand rumors in their infancy and address them forthrightly on intranet sites:

1. Initiating early warning systems to detect possible sparks, (i.e. an upcoming labor negotiation).
2. Comparing the proportion of media coverage to differing crises.
3. What external forces should be part of your preparedness strategy? What reputation is worth protecting?
4. Scenarios for crisis management, including predetermined Q&A, approval procedures, crisis team contact information.
5. Best practice companies routinely monitor newsgroups and neutralize incorrect information – rumor control functions that detect and understand rumors in their infancy and address them forthrightly on intranet sites.

What innuendos creep into the questions posted to the crisis company spokesperson? How successfully is the crisis company in: (1) steering the discussion, and (2) responding positively to unfolding events? Is it being tarred and feathered by other vested, agenda-driven parties?

True Life Confidential: Data-mining for Medicinal Purposes

However, there's another emerging discipline around data-mining that's not related to espionage, retail marketing, or crisis communications. Those are the large data sets captured in the search logs of the digital giants (or what we came to know in 2012 as 'Big Data'). For them, what we ask has the potential to outweigh any conceivable service or product that can be sold over a web browser.

Google co-founder Sergey Brinn detailed the compelling nature of data mining search logs when he cited Google's two week jumpstart on the CDC ("Center for Disease Control") to confirm a flu epidemic. The evidence was based on a spike in the number of flu symptom-related keywords contained in Google searches done in areas where the outbreak was occurring. Google queries were a cheaper and more reliable data collection method than primary evidence-gathering such as checking drug store purchases of cold medications or tallying the number of flu diagnoses by local doctors.

In our case we never have to visit a doctor's office. We don't even have to open up another web page. Of course if we're getting the sniffles, it pays to proceed directly to Level Two Quality Controls.

Level II Quality Controls: Site Analysis

Up until now we've been using telescopes and field glasses just to grab a passing glance at the immensity and movement of the Web. We've now passed through Level I. We've used a set of quality and quantity controls and now we've cleared the Level I *Sniff Test*. That means we've reduced the noise and our signals are clear. Now we're clicking through on the hits we get.

We're also switching over from looking outward to inward. We're turning in our field glasses for the scrutiny of the microscope. We're descending to the entrance of Quality Control, Level II. Welcome to the world of website transparency: The way to maintain source quality at the site level.

Fit to Review

Traditional information literacy guidelines suggest that we verify the content we review. That's not only a tall order but an impractical task considering the dynamic and viral nature of non-vetted information. Remember how the only regulator is ultimately us? That's not just a bold statement about the web's potential to mislead investigators. It's also a cautionary reminder that suspicious accusations are often as untraceable as they are dubious.

A much more realistic goal is to determine what others say about our sources and who they are attempting to influence. We can sometimes estimate how well they are succeeding if we include quantity controls as well.

Rather than reading between every line, it's more productive to examine digitally-based evidence at the site — not at the quote, paragraph, or page level. It's possible to learn from second parties of fraudulent web sites. Another option is to scrutinize the publication history of works ascribed to specific authors. It's easier to hide in a discussion boards and social media site behind an alias or false identity. This shifts when content providers self-identify as authors because it is in their interest to maintain a consistency of brand. That's when we can begin to examine the biases and motivations of individuals that were formerly reserved for publishers and publications.

Aside from an editorial review, there are basic questions to be raised regardless of whether the provider is a soloist or group-based content provider:

1. How long has the site been running, how often does it refresh, and does that include follow-ups or corrections to priori art?
2. How much feedback and public commentary does it attract?
3. Is the information current? If so is it original or streamed from other sources?

Level II Acid Test

Contrary to the research traditions of print, a lack of objectivity on the web does not necessarily mean a source provides substandard information. To the contrary, a website at Level II may use unimpeachable data to the exclusion of less certain details that could raise more questions than answers. On the other hand, a preoccupation with inconclusive results may spark a rush to judgment when we need not be rushing or judging.

When analyzing content providers on the website level, it's critical to include the following Level II quality controls. The following quality control factors confer the intentions and partiality of content providers.

Accuracy

This is the former gold standard for what was once referred to as the journalistic objectivity of a free and independent press. The premise is based on the belief that a non-vested third party could present two sides of a dispute without becoming entangled in the debates they were reporting. That role as referee also included the ability to fact-check – specifically, to spot and sort through conflicts-of-interest between the debaters. A lot has changed in the news business since the advent of the web. *(A fuller assessment of the post social media impact on knowledge-ABLED practices is addressed in the* **Unit Seven Epilogue***).*

But this much is clear regardless of one's stance on corporate self-interest, declining news budgets, and partisan clashes over what facts to check (and even how to check them):

Altered or forged evidence is rampant.

The opportunity to re-key or invent wholesale versions of news stories is easy to devise as such fabrications as plagiarized term papers or doctored news photos with photo-shopped faces inserted or missing from the original source materials. Plagiarism tools like Copyscape are effective for testing questionable assertions. Ocean-to-pond approaches that include myth debunking sites like **Snopes** (a.k.a. Urban Legends) are also useful for this purpose.

Attributions

In the print world a credible source would demonstrate the merit of its analytical rigor and source transparency with academic conventions such as bibliographic details, footnotes, and glossaries. Those markers still apply to academic and scientific journals. But the *fine print* of web-based content has been replaced in large part by hyperlinks, Facebook Walls, friend's lists, and even sponsored ads.

Site Ownership

Site ownership is a simple, effective way to assess commercial and other outside influences. This usually boils down to self-preservation or how the site manages to stay in business:

- Does the site accept advertising?
- If so what's the attraction and does it result in advertisers holding sway over the editorial?
- Are they prone to making claims? If so are they continually supported by the same sources?

Site owners and sources are another hotbed and often overlapping area of concern for establishing the legitimacy of content providers:

- Are there connections between quotable experts and sites they are quoted on?
- Are there recurring claims about the roles and responsibilities of an organization under investigation?
- Does that suggest a concealed agenda that would weaken the case being brought by the content provider?

Feeds and Streams

As anyone who's ever vetted information at Level II knows, it's rare that any single website is limited to a single information source. Even premiere news sites find it hard to resist the ease and economy of repackaging wire services and blog posts when an original news piece costs more to produce. That reduces our quality control issue to these simple questions for any single site in question:

1. How much of this stuff is theirs?
2. Where else does it appear?
3. How much of it reflects the inputs of vested outsiders who post on the site?
4. What's streamed in from other sources? For instance, are there RSS feeds from other publishers? Are these feeds further shaped to fit a particular audience or market niche?

LINK ANALYSIS

So what's a web researcher to do if bibliographies are slowly going the way of the do-do bird? While not a replacement for more established attributions, link analysis is vital. Link analysis traces the origin of accepted facts and quoted passages. An authoritative lake-sized database like Wikipedia insists on its contributors bundling the links from where they base their entries. Link analysis serves the dual social function for addressing a site's visibility and the type of visitors it attracts through back links, related, and similar pages. It also includes site ownership details we'll consider shortly with such a quality control resource called Alexa.[9]

In Level I questions such as 'bias', 'incompleteness', or a 'commercial' focus, our skepticism suggests that search results pages are skewed in favor of search vendor self-interest.

That doesn't mean search engine companies are inherently sleazy any more than one is nobler or publicly beneficial. As a researcher, it helps to play them off against each other: In other words bypassing the inherent weaknesses of one in favor of the collective strengths of the whole. That's one benefit of the metasearch capabilities we introduced in the 'Metasearch Engine' discussion in **Unit Two**. We really get to see the huge discrepancies between the entrenched, mainstays of web search.

Why is that? Aren't they all pretty much the same?

Actually they're not. Not only do results vary. But they also differ in the way they deliver results.

Quite a bit, in fact.

For example, Google is highly restrictive about what it will divulge about linking practices for fear that search engine marketers will try to skew its PageRank formula in favor of the sites they own – READ: Gaming the system. Because of that vulnerability, other search engines tend to be more open about which pages link to the sites we're evaluating. Thus, easier to conduct a meaningful link analysis. This is an important assessment for determining what an information source says about itself and how that contrasts to what outside parties have to say.

What does this have to do with site evaluations or quality control?

Generally speaking, the less commercial a website appears the more credible it may seem. But the potential for bias remains in play even when motivations are unclear. That's where a rounded knowledge is our best defense against our wholesale acceptance of 'the whole story' from any single source. A deeper understanding means an appreciation for the degree of completeness from each content provider. Link analysis also means independently verifying the sprawl of validations and potential sponsorships generated by the overall web presence of the site in question.

Transparency and Site Ownership

Another approach for vetting websites is to focus on the ownership details of the site in question. **Alexa** is one example of a transparency tool that identifies mission through the site's 'About Us' statement, links, traffic patterns and site registration status. About Us statements are not only helpful for establishing a baseline awareness but can help distinguish the editorial tone, i.e. serious intent from humor.

Alexa ranks websites according to site visits, referring links, and connection speed. The site also connects a Whois lookup (site owner) as well as cache histories of the site over time (**Wayback Machine**). It also saves (or caches) our own search history and compiles that for creating a suggestion list of sites accrued by all site visitors who have entered the one in question.

In sum, Alexa provides a single reference tool for finding:

1. Site ownership

2. Reciprocal links that reference the site in question

3. Site popularity, including speed and site traffic (number of visitors)

4. Related sites in the form of other sites visited prior to this one

FIGURE 3.30: Level II Quality Controls – Alexa

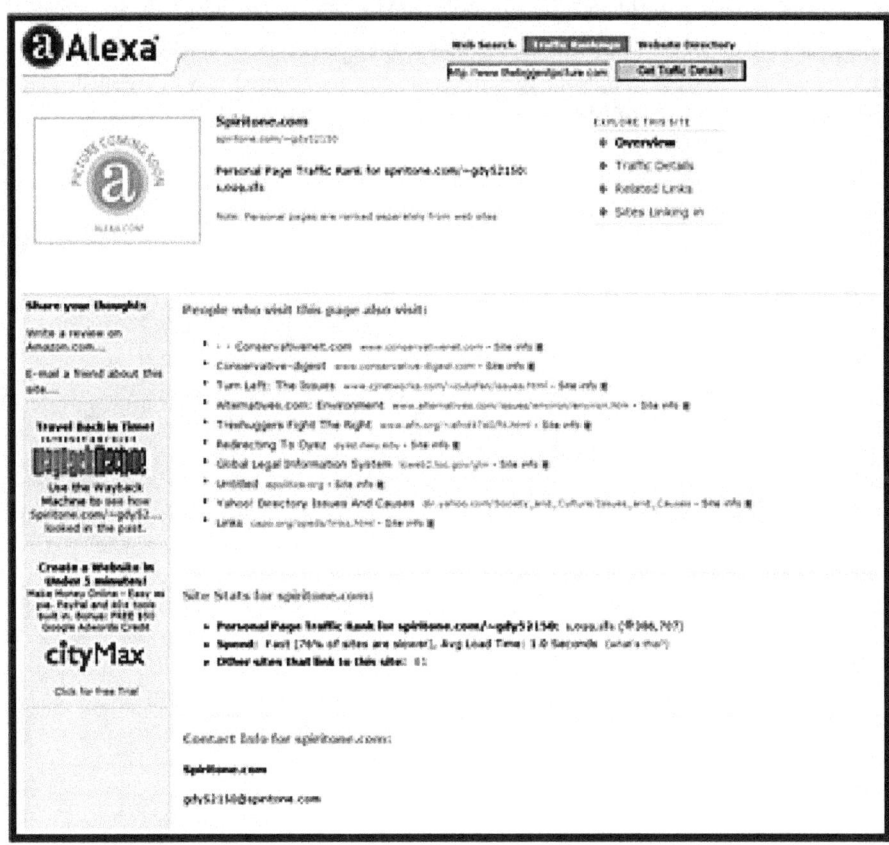

Topic-Specific Searches

Sometimes search engines try to atone for not knowing what we want by creating a boxed search – a set of results packaged according to a specific archive or collection. Some are exclusive. Some are common. Some are pretty generic. The nice thing about topic searches is that they let us bypass the ocean and start our search projects in the lake. That means all our topic-driven search results share a common property:

      1. Format (images, video, audio, maps)

      2. Time frame (news stories, blogs)

      3. Origin (wikis, educational / government sites)

Specialty collections can expedite our searches because topic-specific searches are predefined source groupings that create containable buckets of content. These groupings limit the outcome to subjects covered within that collection — for instance, recipes on cooking sites, or federal policies within a collection of government agencies and bureaus.

What are some additional factors that would determine our success or satisfaction by running a topic-specific search?

For starters, anyone who uses syntax in a broad Google search knows that those settings fall apart when the same query is run in Google Images or Google Videos. That speaks to the pivotal role that semantics and pointers play in the smaller and less structured collections of topic-specific searches. We can constrain our searches to the lake of telephone listings:

rphonebook:johnson 207

That means all the residential phone records for one of the more common surnames in the State of Maine.[10]

Another example is to take a simple term like 'investigator' and invoke it in Yahoo's lake of subject directories:

FIGURE 3.31: Level II Quality Controls –Topic-specific Searches

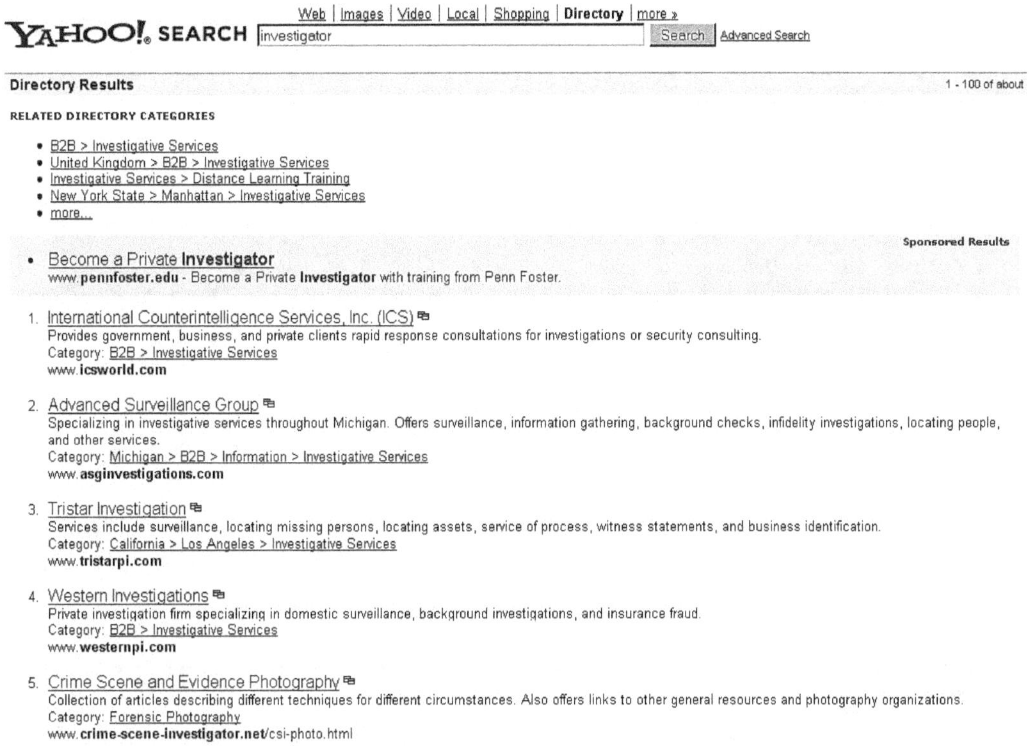

As we considered at the beginning of this section, so we remain the ultimate regulators. It's true. But there's still a place for government-sponsored quality control on the web. The most reliable quality check for source content remains the .gov domain for ensuring that the content of all DotGov sites is produced by the auspices of the U.S. Federal and State governments. We'll be re-introducing government-sponsored databases when we assess the Deep Web in the next section of **Unit Three**.

We're seeing two levels emerge here. The macro lens of related directory categories shows us the categorical buckets that our search term falls into. The micro view below is the routine set of search hits with one key distinction. The search rankings are not delivered through the advertising of keyword matches as with general web or ocean searches. Instead the rankings are determined by the strength of association between each website and its stature within the topic it's grouped in.

Finally, consider public records when reviewing Level II quality control options. Rather than subscription-supported, government information is tax supported and therefore needs to clear a much higher threshold on its accuracy and completeness than the lax standards governing private sources of information. This is not to suggest that governments always tell the truth or what we need to know. But it does mean that we still have a right to both. Something no one rightfully expects when searching cost-free information with an unlimited data plan.

FIGURE 3.32: Level II Quality Controls – Government Statistics

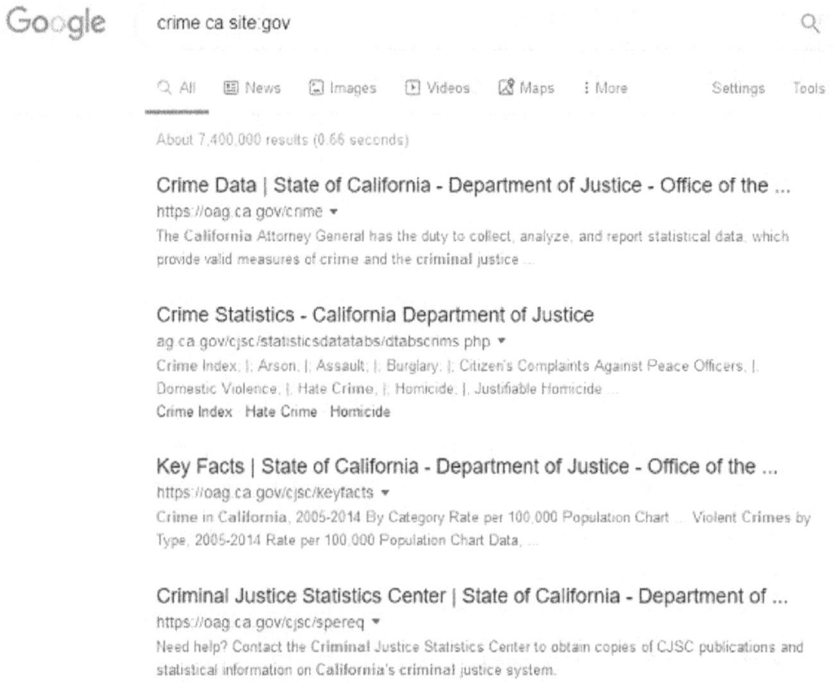

Google crime ca site:gov

Q All   News   Images   Videos   Maps   More   Settings Tools

About 7,400,000 results (0.66 seconds)

Crime Data | State of California - Department of Justice - Office of the ...
https://oag.ca.gov/crime
The California Attorney General has the duty to collect, analyze, and report statistical data, which provide valid measures of crime and the criminal justice ...

Crime Statistics - California Department of Justice
ag.ca.gov/cjsc/statisticsdatatabs/dtabscnms.php
Crime Index. |. Arson. |. Assault. |. Burglary. |. Citizen's Complaints Against Peace Officers. |. Domestic Violence. |. Hate Crime. |. Homicide. |. Justifiable Homicide ...
Crime Index   Hate Crime   Homicide

Key Facts | State of California - Department of Justice - Office of the ...
https://oag.ca.gov/cjsc/keyfacts
Crime in California, 2005-2014 By Category Rate per 100,000 Population Chart ... Violent Crimes by Type, 2005-2014 Rate per 100,000 Population Chart Data, ...

Criminal Justice Statistics Center | State of California - Department of ...
https://oag.ca.gov/cjsc/spereq
Need help? Contact the Criminal Justice Statistics Center to obtain copies of CJSC publications and statistical information on California's criminal justice system.

This is a selective ocean skimming that the site:gov syntax affords us as we pursue factual evidence for crime patterns both statewide and in unspecified California cities.

LEVEL II QUANTITY CONTROLS: SEARCH METRICS

So we choose our terms carefully and we try out a bunch of advanced tools to help refine our search results and we still produce thousands of sites that are probably more misses than hits. Does it really matter that our hit counts add up to 12,000 than 4 million? After all we're never going to open visit them all, let alone go beyond the first 1-2 screens to even guess whether it's worth continuing through on our expedition or whether it's time to regroup, right?

Well, believe it or not ... it does!

Quantifying hit counts allows us to exercise an overlooked evaluation tool that sits alongside quality control. Unlike site analysis or page scanning where one has to assess websites on a case-by-case basis, the high-level filtering afforded by quantity controls is critical to the success of our mission.

Ratio of Key Indicators

How do we manage the anticipated overload of search results from broadly-worded queries? The size of our search results can be just as important to your research as the content of any web page within those returns. Key ratios are important tests of hit counts that help investigators to...

- Budget their time
- Reformulate their queries
- Consider the popularity or visibility of particular issues and events

Key ratios are especially helpful for determining our proximity to an answer. This is when a realistic search goal means getting to the right person – not to the most relevant article or popular website. For finding people, key ratios...

- Determine the accuracy of hitting fact-based search targets such as specific individuals, event details, or groupings
- Rationalize the expense of follow-on work such as ordering individual background checks based upon the accuracy of the IDs provided

How many hits are too many hits? There are two ways to determine this. The *Sniff Test* measures how close we are to exact matches, such as making a positive ID on a particular person. The other way is a signal-to-noise ratio – a comparison of useful to useless results addressing the broader dimensions of topic or opinion-based searches.

Sniff Test

There is certainly one question that Google is not likely to answer any time soon. That's the reason for ballooning or declining hit counts. That's a test we can't rule out in the hot pursuit of the right individual, event, or topic we're targeting. Remember, it's the fact-based searches you are trying to prove or disprove. In the opinion searches, we are out to validate or invalidate where conclusions usually take longer to form. Hence, it's the tendency of higher counts to be less conclusive.

FIGURE 3.33: Hit Counts as Query Formation Indicators

Hit Counts	Modification
+50,000	Introduce syntax restrictions to limit your results to specific site addresses, page titles, or file formats
<50,000	Consider placing keywords in quotes
<10,000	Try expanding the number of search terms – introduce new keyword(s) to reinforce productive associations such as a group of relevant area codes to the person's residence and/or job titles and employment record

Now what are we getting back?

Are the results within our targeted area codes, state of residence, or even town or city? Can other nouns be added to the mix such as former employers, former colleges attended, mother's maiden name? What's the probability of a direct match? If not direct, what are the chances now that we've found some *homies* from the *hood*? Failing that, how about some potential colleagues within their social circles?

Signal-to-Noise Ratio

If we're looking more broadly at a topical search, the actual size of our counts matters less than the quality of the hits you're receiving in the first returns of your search results. What is the proportion of click-worthy sites (sites worth visiting) to dubious results? When sampling the first 30 records, first make sure they are unique pages. Single sites will often spawn multiple results. What should be our signal-to-noise ratio? Any result where at least half the results are click-worthy is a productive outcome.

FIGURE 3.34: Signal-to-Noise Metrics

Ratio	Click-worthy
33-50%	10-15 pages – above average
15-33%	5-10 pages – average
< 15%	Fewer than 5 pages – low

So in our first pass, how many of those first 30 records are worth a second look?

One way to separate signal from noise is to question their novelty. How many of these pages may tell us something useful we didn't already know? Another consideration is about the placement of our search terms. Do we see an abundance of highlighting in a majority of our page titles and summaries? Is this what we expected? Are we familiar with some of the recurring terms that are not highlighted?

LEVEL III QUALITY CONTROLS: PAGE SCANNING

So we've finally gotten to the light at the end of the bottom of the pile. We've tightened our control knobs. We've tweaked our site roots and content weights. We might not hold absolute mastery over every lever and metric. But we do know this. We're going in for the kill. Yes, we're convinced one search result or more are click worthy. We are now proceeding to Level III and there's no turning back. We are opening the links on our results lists.

Analyzing Page Scans

As we've seen in Levels I and II, we must monitor the query results for both quality and quantity. The tools and criteria vary depending on our site selection methods. Generally, the deeper we go, the greater our time commitment.

Now that we've landed on the actual page, what can we grasp immediately to know whether we're just passing through or here to stay? When making that determination, consider how much weight and credibility to give to individual information providers: Specifically, their motivations for sharing the details they select and opinions they provide.

FIGURE 3.35: Level III Quality Controls – Page Scans

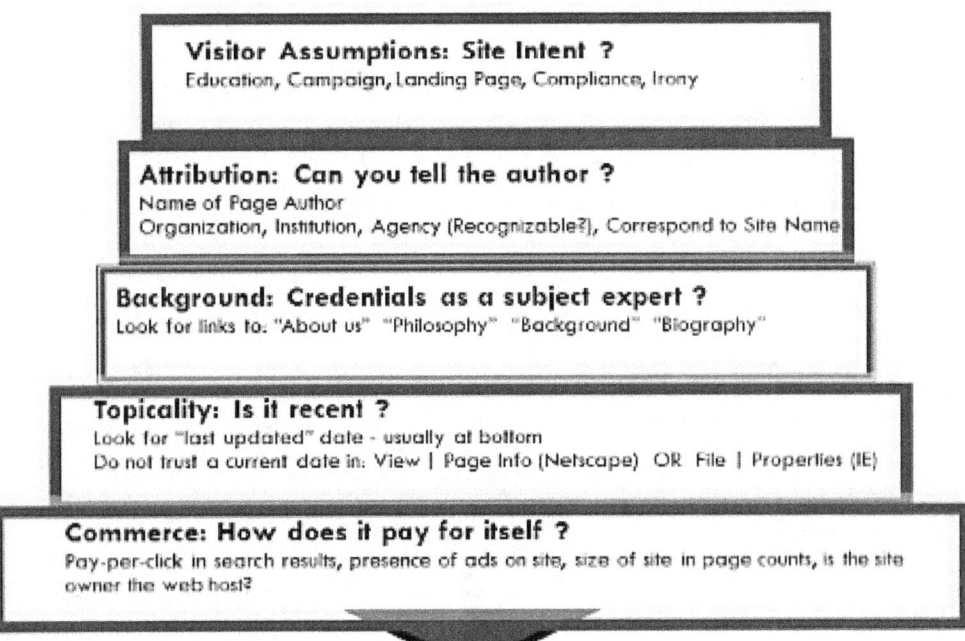

Visitor Assumptions

What is the site intent? Why is it there? What calls to action does it implore to you, the visitor: education, marketing campaign, public issues and policies, landing page (shopping), regulatory compliance, humor (irony)?

Attribution

Can we tell who the author is? This is easier concluded with individuals than groups. Be wary of individuals who hide behind the mantle of representing an entire organizational structure as a means to inflate their own stature.

One simple credibility builder is the posting of a physical address and alternative means to make direct contact with the information provider – not just the site administrator who may have no control or interest in the content of the site itself. What kinds of associations are formed by the sites that link back to this one? Do we recognize these other sources and are they credible? Are the links reciprocal or are they unbalanced – either more linking to or from this site? Are there typos and broken links? These administrative details call a site's credibility into immediate question – regardless of how high the quality of its content.

Background

Does the provider offer credentials as a subject expert?

From a broader perspective what separates this information provider from related sites? We begin with links to some commonly used site conventions:

'About us' | 'Philosophy' | 'Background' | 'Biography' (pointers)

Are there experts on the team? Does the site present an assembly of their talents and contributions as a collective whole? How well do individual credentials serve the organizational mission or a company's competitive edge and key differentiators?

Topicality

How recently posted is the content on the site? Is it delivered through third parties or does it originate from this one? Is original content offered through alternative delivery such as RSS feeds? Monitor changes on pages and frequency of changes (profusion) – good for blogs and social media pages.

Is a pay-per-click program present on the site such as Google's AdWords? Will the acceptance of advertising influence the views they express. Will all the ads presented work in the site owner's favor or against, or some of the ads clearly irrelevant to the topics they cover?

Look for 'last updated' date - usually at bottom. The 'last updated' script automatically resets the displayed date on a web page each time the html source document is modified in any way – even if that update is based on pure automation like the refresh of an RSS feed. People assign more credibility to sites showing they have been recently updated or reviewed. Do not trust a current date in:

View | Page Info (Firefox), Chrome, or File | Properties IE ("Internet Explorer").

The lights may be on. But no one's home.

Now that we've tunneled down from our search binoculars to our page-scanning microscopes, it's time to focus outward. From the *what* to the *where* factors are what influence the content we're assessing before it ever reaches the quality control stage.

SECTION 3.4: | Managing Project Resources —
How Should We Think About Research Costs?

Before "we had privacy from obscurity," says David Ardia, fellow at the Berkman Klein Center for Internet & Society, and the director and founder of the Digital Media Law Project:

> "Now, almost everything worth knowing about anyone is online." **(Milliard, 2010)**[11]

Has that assertion lost its revelatory shine? The distinction between *always being on* and have such status apply to one's virtual rather than social life is long past the transition period.

It's important to note that the public side of resources here is the traditional view of milestones and legal histories such as...

- Births / Vaccinations,
- Mortgages / Deeds,
- Marriages / Divorces, and
- Criminal trespasses.

It does not reflect the personal details found in our browser plug-ins, downloads, email records, streaming patterns, and all transactions forming a digital identity that's concealed from us by its creators. That is an aspect of web investigations left to computer forensics experts, the courts, consumer advocates, and the legalese buried in the user agreements of the social and search giants that sell our personal data.

We will cover the following cost-related components of project resources:

1. Public and private records
2. The visible and invisible web
3. Free or fee (subscription) services
4. Consistent guidelines for searching

WHAT'S PUBLIC?

There is a big distinction in the availability, abundance, and legal standing of personal and impersonal information. Personal information has been held traditionally in confidence by the party being described. However, all that is changing with the increase in electronic records, the ease of wireless communications, and loopholes that invite infringements of our privacy. More often, the invitation to acquire personal information is not waiting on legal rulings or even questionable judgment. It's simply a matter of price.

As I promised before we started along the knowledge continuum, all of our discussions rest on this assumption: There are no additional surcharges or subscription fees involved in accessing, analyzing, or presenting the resources tackled in this book. Where do we draw the line? With so many personal details for sale by credit bureaus and information brokers, what rules do we follow to determine...

- What's available to us at the asking price of cost free?
- Also, what would we expect to find if we did pay a premium?

On the second point, we should reasonably assume that our clients have some experience in paying out-of-pocket for public records. The limitations of what they found prompts them to go the additional step. They come to us. In such cases, how do we demonstrate...

- The value we add as domain experts?
- The costs we've either reduced or sidestepped for our customers in that effort?

Here's our working definition: When a site or a page is *above the radar*, some type of documentation exists. Let's go back to the quality control section we've just concluded. Let's consider the likelihood that some record or web-based artifact exists before we commit to its capture. How do we determine if...

- It's public, and
- It's in a useful form.

We'll refer to this boundary between public and private as 'the radar.'

Being *above radar* means:

1. The visible web (what lives in the indexes of search engines) and not the deep or invisible web (more on that later)
2. Contact and biographic details but not hacking into subscription databases or password protected account details, encrypted messages, GPS-based travel settings, browser histories, etc.
3. Public records available online but not courthouse proceedings available through a court-order

Defining the Radar

It's difficult to overstate the slippery nature of what passes between public and private on the web. It cuts both ways. More records go online every day while other repositories can be pulled offline without warning or fanfare. Funding sources dry up for government sites. Business models fail in commercial ventures. Pilot projects get pulled — often through lack of revenue potential more than lack of use or interest. Also, there is nothing static about the kinds of information we wish to post about ourselves. Partly that's because social networks can increase the ease and distribution of experiences shared virtually. The other reason is us. A breach or compromising episode with social media may chasten our embrace of it. Again, it cuts both ways.

Another tool for sharpening our digital radar screens is to think about project sources in terms of content groupings. Some are easier to access than others. Some are more evolving and fluid. Some may require us to pay an access fee, and there's no getting around it. These personal effects include:

1. Social networks
2. Medical and driving records
3. Births, marriages, deaths
4. Career / employment histories
5. Personal assets
6. Credit histories
7. Transactions[12]

Now let's plot these project source groupings on our radar screen. The center line that runs through the radar perimeter is the surface between what we may expect to be public (above) and private:

FIGURE 3.36: The Great and Sometimes Blurry Divide Between Above and Below Radar

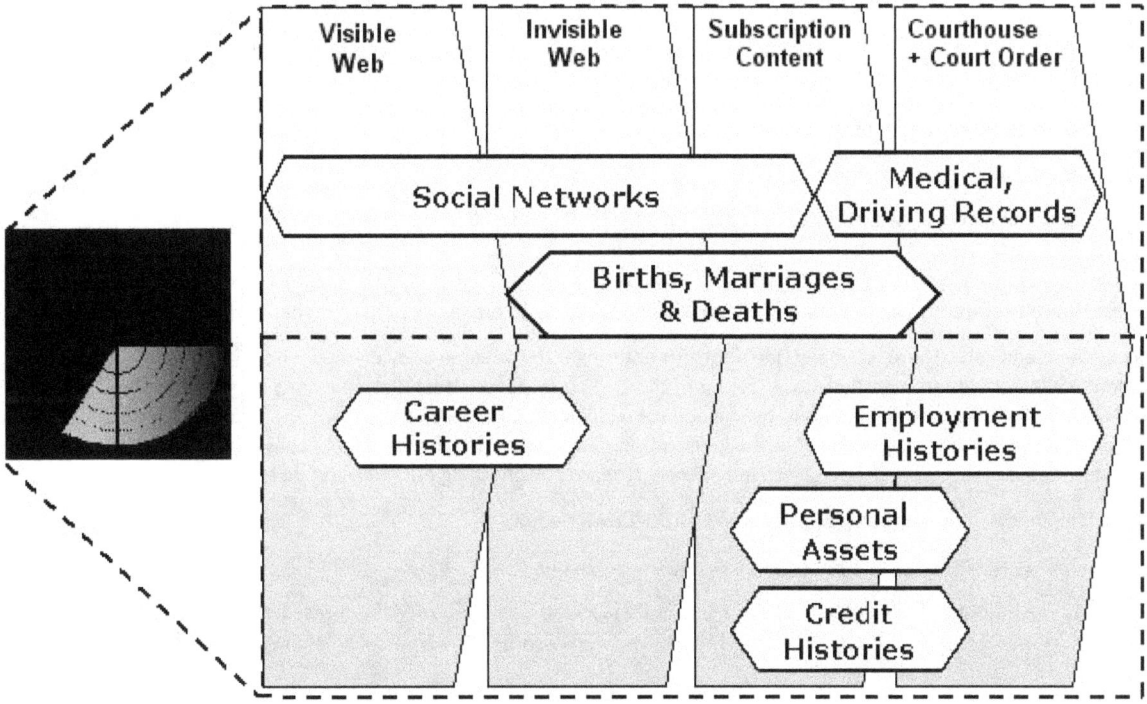

This diagram defines the above and below radar project sources through the availability of typically fee-based content in the pre-Smart phone era. Not surprisingly, the radar has and will continue to trend in the online direction of the visible web.

One way to put some of these concepts to the test is to enlist them in the number one investigative pursuit: Finding people — the world's oldest information profession.

People Finders

So we're back at the tail-end of those quality controls. Those are the indications we should float on the ocean surface or dive down for a deeper exploration. Nowhere is this method put to a greater test than deciding whether the John W. Doe we're looked for is *the* John W. Doe.

There's the temptation to let go of the search page for the confirming rush that a person we've spotted in the highlighted keyword summaries is *the* person we've been targeting. Bullseye! Despite all the noise and common surnames, home towns, and pastimes held by our search target and throngs of imposters, we've nailed it down. It's not just a click-through worth tagging. It's a piece to the larger picture we're puzzling through in our search logs.

All too often that click-through is a proprietary database. It's disheartening to spend money in advance for details that may be useless to an investigation. But it's no less discouraging to stop in the same tracks as novice searchers who reach the same place through a garden variety Google search.

When someone offers public records, most times they are providing the range of background material we can pull on non-celebrities. That's right. Ordinary folks like you and me, matched to...

- Vital data: birth, marriage, death
- Education and certifications
- Religion and ethnicity
- Addresses and next of kin
- Employment and professional affiliations
- Real property ownership and liens
- Credit and payment histories

That's the checklist.

As long as there's compromising information, there will be traffickers to broker it. So here's what I think.

Put away the credit card. There are many side doors for entering into the same body of knowledge. While it helps to document a bad debt, or an unsettled score, the more compelling evidence doesn't come from a database but from the firsthand experience of those connected to the person we're searching. In these cases, searching is no more a means to an end as the discovery of a bad debt or a youthful indiscretion. We're searching for the sake of conversing: To establish a dialog or more formally conduct what used to be called *primary research* by engaging our networks directly.

Here are two important lessons on free resources to track down people:

1. They're best used on the front-end to narrow down our choices and document false positives beforehand.

2. The amount of diligence we apply needs to be factored into the terms of our research services. Just because a resource is public doesn't mean that the knowledge for how to use it is broadly understood or shared.

As we've seen with subject directories and cluster engines, the best interfaces can generate that periphery around a crime. The social circle surrounding the case. It's especially useful when we pool together our leads first. Then we search them as individuals on search engines that are dedicated to personal identities.

Sites such as Pipl and 123people sprung up in the mid-2000s[13]. Then the field became overrun with fee-based personal record brokers. These days, the number of social media profiles far eclipses the reach of any third-party broker. It's big search and social media who hold the master key to our personal effects, cross-referencing them with our demographics, travel patterns, and virtual identities. The personal lives of Facebook members are within the prying eyes of the faceless.

PURSUING EXECUTIVES

> ""There's only one thing worse than being talked about, and that is not being talked about."
>
> – Oscar Wilde

Before social media began in earnest, there was a common rally cry for which individuals were fair game to target and track on the web. Celebrities weren't counted. (If they're not tracked, they're not *celebrated*). Business leaders on the other hand, are usually more comfortable having the limelight shine on their stock splits, shrewd acquisitions, and gravity-defying earnings. By and large, the corporate executives of publicly-traded companies remain ripe for picking. No undercover required for sourcing the personal backgrounds, perks, inner circles and sanctums of the upper echelon. It could be bonuses, stock options, real estate holdings, yachts, or Lear Jets. Space tourism to follow!

Personal property is an important validation tool for corporate researchers in fundraising operations. They support development officers needing to break the ice with well-heeled, potential donors. Real estate is one part of that pursuit. Many realty sites have popped up that approximate the housing and property values of exclusive neighborhoods where executives may own one or several upscale homes. Other personal assets may include private yachts, planes and other luxury transportation items that include some form of public registration.

Board affiliation sites track the executive's professional network beyond their own corporate borders. Donor status on political campaigns and alumni connections are other options for expanding the executive's networking profile.

Finally, there are numerous subscription-based sources for tracing corporate rumors and scandals to internally generated memorandums and email. But remember, however *premium* these sites claim to be, your fee pays admission to documents now combed over by anyone accessing the same password protected database. These sources while fee-based are by no means exclusive. Nor is their data always accurate and up-to-date.

Free Versus Fee – When to Use What

When is it better to use subscription or fee-based information sources than what is available free of charge via the web. We broached this idea earlier in this unit under Site Selection with the observation that conventional investigations tend to require chronological accuracy. That means a sequencing of discoveries that match the unfolding of the events they're based on. This is elusive on the web where sources disappear and time stamps can be misleading.

Another major improvement to our research is that we are instantly searching a well-stocked pond rather than an uncharted lake or ocean. That means sources are traceable. Credibility is resting on the good name of the publisher, at least when they're acting in the dual role of distributor. It's also fairly easy to discern the communities where the information we find has been circulating.

Speaking of circulation, what are some new frontiers that we can sway to our advantage as investigators? For starters, we can now put our fingers on the collective pulse of public opinion in ways that the best-financed polling operation could never have delivered through phone interviews or mall intercepts. Put another way, why is public awareness best addressed in a common web search? The answer lies in the radar devised in the following Google Trends interface:

FIGURE 3.37: The Powerful Pulse-taking Abilities of Google Trends

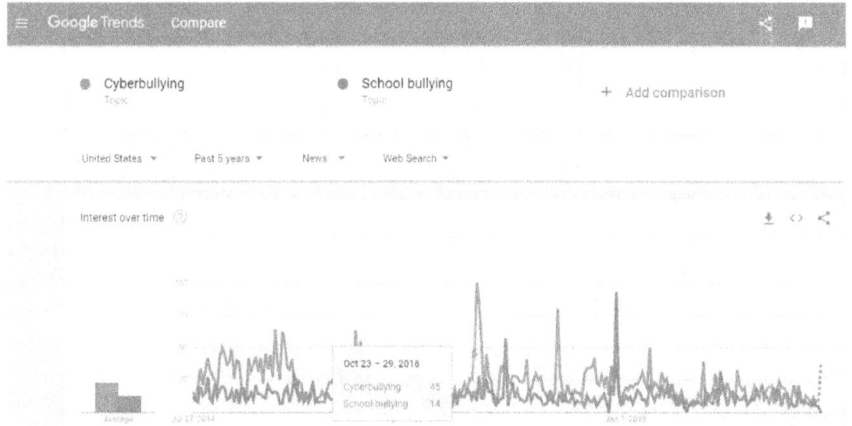

Here's a five year comparison between virtual and school yard bullying. Note the cyber-bullying spike in the home stretch of the 2016 election. These frequencies are restricted to queries.[14]

UNIT THREE: How to Source Information That Instructs | Page 3:80

FIGURE 3.38: Correlating a Topic to Catalyst Events

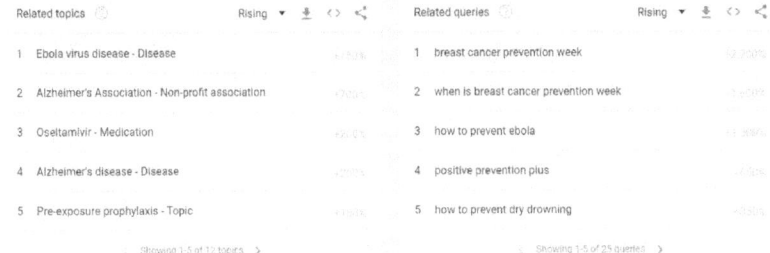

FIGURE 3.39: Comparing a Topic (Preventative Healthcare) to a Drug Type (Antibiotics)

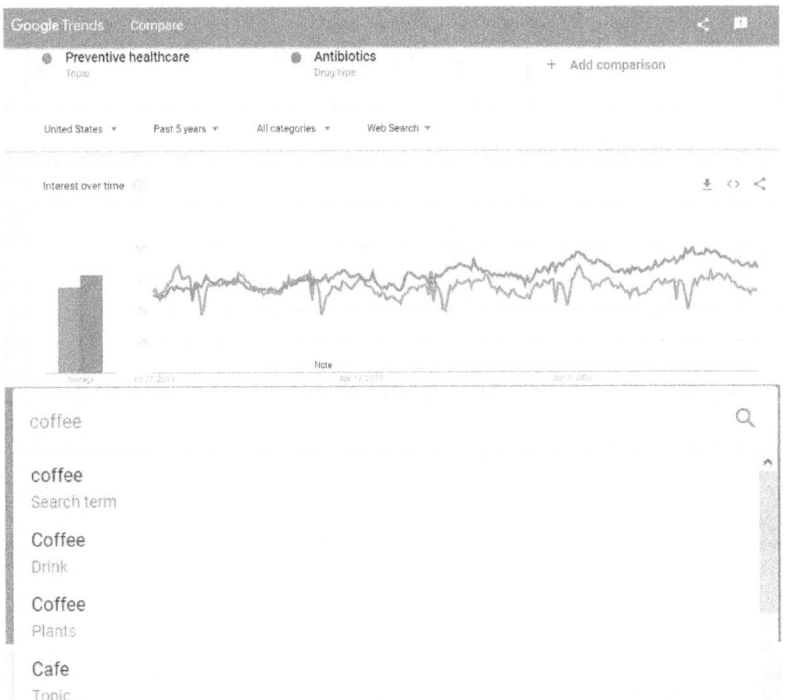

Above, a query on 'antibiotics' is identified by Google Trends as a medication. A selection table [LEFT] displays its classification codes in support of more accurate comparisons and contexts.

Searching Out Loud: Giving Voice to Independent Investigations | Marc Solomon

Another common challenge and opportunity for web investigators speaks to that gnawing question about fee-based public records. Are all public records available only through private vendors?

Absolutely not.

Resources from genealogists like Stephen P. Morse make it possible to confirm addresses and phone numbers otherwise commanding the surrender of our credit cards through brokers:

FIGURE 3.40: A Read-out from the Birthday Finder Application
(written by Stephen P. Morse)

	Name		Born	Address				Phone
1	MITCHELL	BANCHIK		161 73RD ST	NEW YORK	NY	10023	(212) 579-4656
2	MITCHELL	BANCHIK		161 73RD ST	NEW YORK	NY	10023	(212) 799-1734
3	MITCHELL	BANCHIK		161 73RD ST	NEW YORK	NY	10023	(212) 579-4656
4	MITCHELL	BANCHIK		161 73RD ST	NEW YORK	NY	10023	(212) 799-1734
5	MITCHELL	BANCHIK		300 76TH ST	NEW YORK	NY	10021	
6	MITCHELL	BANCHIK		161 73RD ST	NEW YORK	NY	10023	(212) 579-4656
7	MITCHELL	BANCHIK		161 73RD ST	NEW YORK	NY	10023	(212) 799-1734
8	MITCHELL	BANCHIK		161 73RD ST	NEW YORK	NY	10023	(212) 579-4656
9	MITCHELL	BANCHIK		161 73RD ST	NEW YORK	NY	10023	(212) 799-1734
10	MITCHELL	BANCHIK		300 76TH ST	NEW YORK	NY	10021	
11	MITCHELL	BANCHIK		161 73RD ST	NEW YORK	NY	10023	(212) 579-4656
12	MITCHELL	BANCHIK		161 73RD ST	NEW YORK	NY	10023	(212) 799-1734
13	MITCHELL	BANCHIK		161 73RD ST	NEW YORK	NY	10023	(212) 579-4656
14	MITCHELL	BANCHIK		161 73RD ST	NEW YORK	NY	10023	(212) 799-1734
15	MITCHELL	BANCHIK		300 76TH ST	NEW YORK	NY	10021	

15 matches found

These are public records gleaned from published directories and include wire line phone numbers and residential addresses. Mr. Morse has developed a mashup – a search interface that crawls different people finder databases on the web, allowing users to access those details for research purposes, a.k.a. free.

Perhaps the greatest opportunity for above radar people searches is to focus the bigger people finder picture on social networks. Again, the relative openness of the web enables a more complete picture – if not always a clear one. We'll need a positive ID before we can glean an individual's connection to these other aspects of a social identity: Communities, employers, professional affiliates and authored works.

Figure 3.41 details when it's more productive to use openly accessible or premium sources. As we can see, the more concrete the answers called for by your project, the likelier that definitive or subscription sources will be called on. Conversely, the more socially connected our research, the likelier we'll call on free sources that measure and reflect popular opinion or a broader public awareness.

FIGURE 3.41: The Checklist of What's Best Answered on a Free and Fee Basis

	Web (free)	Premium (fee)
Perception	X	
Public Records		X
Motivation	X	
Publication Archive		X
Legal Documents		X
Social Network	X	
Source Distribution		X

THE VISIBLE AND INVISIBLE WEB

Search engines perform an amazing service. They trawl the vast expanse of the virtual world, mapping for us an ocean full of information that can appear as incalculable and infinite as the universe itself. And they do it not in days or weeks but in milliseconds.

Yet if truth be told, this engineering feat is not the whole truth. It brings its own shortcuts and distortions. This includes lots of below-the-surface depth the never makes it into the search index. That's because there are many places that are either too detailed to document or off-limits to commercial search engines.

Period.

Remember that old adage that we humans only utilize a scant portion of our brain capacity? The same analogy might well serve the 3%-5% of the web which surfaces in Google[15]. Basically, there's a lot of *stuff* that search engines can't or won't search. These include:

    1. Dynamically generated pages (weather, news, job postings, market prices, travel schedules...)

    2. Web accessible or common theme databases that require information be typed in (laws, dictionaries, directory lists...)

    3. Sites that require password or logins to access

    4. Commercial resources with domain or IP limitations

    5. Intranets

If we consider the limited scope of what a search tool can index, it would be appropriate to refer to Google or Bing as the *visible* or *shallow* web. The recesses of the Internet resistant to being indexed are alternatively called the *invisible* or *the deep web*. Either way, the stuff below the surface might be a worthwhile place for an investigator to scope out.

Here's what we might find in the deeper recesses of the web:

1. It is narrower in scope with greater depth of documentation than more conventional sites.

2. OLP-wise, it's full of lakes. Over half its pages derive from databases, primarily from government-maintained archives like U.S. National Oceanic and Atmospheric Administration, NASA, the Patent and Trademark Office and the Securities and Exchange Commission's EDGAR search system.[16]

3. Not surprisingly, its content is highly relevant to domain and subject matter experts.

4. Fully 90% of its content is publicly accessible information — not subject to access fees or subscriptions.[17]

More than half its content resides in topic-specific databases. This is where researchers can use the deep web to drill down into the matching patterns formed by overlapping facts and document properties contained in database records. If this sounds like that Ocean-Lake-Pond routine again that's good. Just remember the deep web doesn't mean we're in too deep when it takes us to the correct pond for checking in on the specifics of our case.

In sum, remember to take the deep web plunge when...

- Standard search engines aren't working
- We need data or statistics (from one source addressing one topic)
- We need high quality or authoritative results
- Timeliness is overruled by the need to get our facts straight through validation and confirmation
- We either know the subject area well or have confidence we'll find what we're seeking
- We are looking for collections (images, sounds, manuscripts, birth/death records, etc.)

FIGURE 3.42 Why Two Internets? Defining the Deep Web

Searching the web =
  dragging a net across the ocean surface.

- Engines create indexes by crawling "surface" Web
- Discovery requires pages to be static and linked
- Can't retrieve searchable databases that only appears dynamically in responding

DEEP WEB GATEWAYS: GETTING FROM OCEANS TO LAKES

Throughout **Unit Three** we've considered some of the complicated syntax to get from a commercial search engine like Google (ocean) down to a searchable database (pond). It's in the pond where we can actually yield specific facts, historic records, and contact information we typically need in searching reference sources in support of virtual investigations.

In our OLP examples, we first prove the existence of an index or an archive on the shallow web. First, we come up with a list of searchable directories and indexes. Next, we use syntax or go to the site directly. We view the site map to confirm that databases, statistics, or other reference materials mentioned. Finally we fish. We use the site's internal search tool and do the trawling that only investigators, not algorithms can provide.

There is a more direct approach than relying on convoluted text strings and metadata fields. There are specialty search engines designed to capture more scholarly-inclined sources and archives. They offer publicly accessible databases in domains welcoming to researchers.

That said, a simple page design can conceal lots of potentially useful details. Remember our discussion about visualization engines in **Unit Two**? The results, though attractive, don't impart a sense of how much more is left to cover once we consume the visuals.

It's easier to tell a search engine by its advertising than by its *cover*, meaning design elements. The top level view of the deeper story can be misleading. That's the flip-side of the analogy: The lack of depth under the visualization scheme.

FIGURE 3.43: Getting from an Ocean to a Pond Through a Deep Web Search Engine

It's interesting to note that resources billing themselves as deep web searches are really metasearch engines. They don't index websites. They search the indexes. And like its source, only a scant amount of information is actually indexed. That's another reason that the Internet Ocean is a *shallow* one. Deep web sources like databases (Internet ponds) cannot be stored within these memory limits.

That's the most important takeaway from the humbling limits of search engines: They perform the illusion of searching the ocean when at best they are searching a few inches below the surface. If we want access to the sites that don't float to the Google surface, it's a deeper web where we can find much higher value information. The trade-off is that we know where we're going. We can't scale the deep web like we can search the ocean surface. By definition, we're searching pond-by-pond. It is exacting and often painstaking work. But well worth the effort when landing the gold nugget that closes the books on our case.

The dynamic nature of the web as a publishing platform is a more subtle but notable limitation of search engines. Searching the web can be like dragging a net across the ocean surface: Search engines create indexes by *skimming* the *surface* web. For a page to be discovered, it must be static and linked. We cannot retrieve searchable databases that only appear dynamically in responding to queries. Database records cannot be bookmarked or tagged. Remember: Each invisible web source is an index. That index become part of its cached record on the search engine site – even if a particular page or record is altered or removed.

Visualizing the Invisible

Contrary to self-serving motives, not everyone wants more traffic to their websites and social profiles. Sometimes sites are built to satisfy a legal or regulatory order. Sometimes a small group hosts discussions for a select group of participants. Sometimes a body of knowledge is indexed. It's stored by domain experts in the same way that scribes and archivists copied and preserved ancient texts. This goes on regardless of whatever the appeal may be to a wider audience. So we've cracked open the door of the deep web. We have these basic ideas about what it contains that the commercial search engines can't or won't index:

1. Thousands of specialized searchable databases that require us to enter information into their own search structure (laws, dictionaries, directory lists...)

2. Sites that require a password or login

3. Commercial resources with domain or IP limitations

FIGURE 3.44 Databases as Search Results on the Deep Web

The invisible web is a rich combination of databases, new or non-linked text files, other file types, etc. Many of these are accessible through a front-end or specially designed search programs. Here a deep web search like Complete Planet offers databases as search results. *This site has since been decommissioned.*

Searching Out Loud: Giving Voice to Independent Investigations | Marc Solomon

Premium Services

Premium or fee-based subscription services are an effective way to close the gap between the shortcomings of the free web or public domain and the objectives of your investigation.

Premium services date back to the 1970s when vendors such as LEXIS/NEXIS, Dow Jones News Retrieval, and DIALOG became online access providers to commercial publications, financial reports, and specialized government and scientific databases. These sources were sourced and searched almost exclusively by librarians and information professionals. Small wonder the documentation they contain is consistent and thorough in how it's gathered and classified.

These premium information services enable researchers to do the impossible on the web: Trace their findings to specific information providers. There is little doubt who the information provider is when an investigator takes direct testimony or interviews eyewitnesses. Collecting evidence off the web is a bigger challenge.

Many are not up to this challenge. They focus on the evidence-gathering to the exclusion of where they're getting it from. As we've seen, this carries is a potentially grave risk to any investigation given the unregulated state of the web's content suppliers.

In addition to the added trust of traceable sources, premium services are effective tools for connecting keywords to organized topics. Their structure makes it possible to sort information chronologically. That helps us verify a proper sequence of events in our investigations. Figure 3.45 contains some of the key distinctions in favor of using premium sources in our investigation.

FIGURE 3.45: Fee Services: Defining Added Benefits

Benefit	Feature
Concept of "added value"	Large archive
	Repeated access
	Complex concepts
Concept of source organization	Higher selectivity
	Better bundling
Syntax used in large subscription-based collections	More exacting, literal – 1-2 word queries are often useless
Sites	www.factiva.com
	www.highbeam.com
	infotrac.galegroup.com

So what are the trade-offs of using premium services? The downsides are pretty simple:

1. Because they are not published by the information providers.
2. They are not up-to-date.
3. They are not free.

Dated Information:

It's ironic. But in the days before the web premium services were disparaged as *secondary sources*. The inference is that secondary research is second-hand, old or dated. The premise here is that we can't rely on their data. There's nothing new about the tendency for history taking a backseat to immediacy. But it's also a timeless reality that background and context reveals everything about a campaign, market, or management practice. What worked? What was was scrapped? Which lessons bear repeating? Which decisions still haunt those who made them?

Exclusive Sources:

Going exclusively with premium services introduces another risk to our search projects. Think of subscription-based collections as the walled-in gardens of the information forest. They are seeded, weeded, and watered by professional groundskeepers (database catalogers and taxonomists). However, that control level only extends to a postage stamp-sized footprint of cultivated, higher quality information. The overwhelming world beyond its borders carries an entire set of actions and outcomes that will never grow within the delicate confines of a premium database.

REVISITING SOURCE FLUENCY

Earlier in this unit we introduced the concept of source fluency: The practice of building up our source knowledge as an independent researcher. In this final section of **Unit Three**, a reintroduction is in order as a project resource in its own right.

Knowledge is no longer books and periodicals: it is content and substance.

In the post-Web Wide World, a source is still a source. But *how* one finds the source is an open invitation to better and varied sources. In this new environment, *book smart* is supplanted by navigational whim. Route takes precedence over destination. A fixed set of sources is pure baggage. Collections are now the province of churches and museums – not Internet-based investigators.

Re-enter source fluency. As we've established source fluency is about knowing where to look for information without knowing what it is called. It means having the discipline and dexterity to determine both *how* and *where* to search.

Source fluency is the ability to know and develop where to look for information without needing to know what it is called its specific storage location. One commonly used and often ineffective process for cultivating fluency is bookmarking previously or potentially helpful sites for future recall. The problem with bookmarks is that they lose their utility over time. That's because they require us bookmarkers to recall the original reasons and places where we put them.

With source fluency, the emphasis is on the action we're trying to accomplish. Not the source, tool, or application that served us once and may yet again. This means that the resource will be there when we need it, regardless of the investigation, or our prior understanding of it.

Another important element of source fluency is that we can trace a topic to the best interest of the information provider on the subject. We're fluent in web sourcing without needing to know established authorities, back channels of gossip, or official keepers of records. That means we can reliably find credible and vested sources that cover subjects we'll need to familiarize and understand – if not master – in our research travels.

Information as a Verb

At first it may sound self-evident that source mastery boils down to how we assess them (quality controls) and where we going looking (site selection). But there is a temptation to hire the answer doctor. That's the source expert who never needs to ask an original question because they've committed every qualified information provider to memory. The myth of the answer doctor lives on even in this day and age of Twitter handles and instant analysts who fabricate their sites to look authoritative.

Here are a few ironclad tenets that come with the source fluency turf:

> 1. There is only one 'what' (the question we're addressing) but there are many 'hows' (sources).
>
> 2. Sources do not count unless you know how to pose the question.
>
> 3. The focus is not on the ever-shifting answers you need, but on fielding the right set of questions to find them.
>
> 4. Information devoid of its social, marketing and technical implications is meaningless.

So if source fluency is so superior to answer doctors, how do we put this new asset to work in our search projects?

Defining Credibility

Reputation colors information providers like shadows follow suspicions. One misleading headline and all subsequent reports are stained with a lurking suspicion that the news source has given a limited or self-selective base of facts around a breaking story. At least that was the role reputation played before the only barrier to conjecture and publication was the <send> key on our keyboards. Reputation still matters because gauging one is more elusive than ever.

To a generation raised on the web, the term 'credibility' may carry a different meaning. For instance, being credible may have less to do with being believed and more to do with ability to be influential because of their numerous connections or ample resources. It could also simply mean greater clout or personal stature:

> "I don't know what your face looks like. [W]e're twitter beefing now. [I]t's gonna raise my credibility as a rapper so yeah. [b]eef." **(Lynette, 2010)**[18]

At first, it may seem like a subtle distinction between taking someone seriously and taking someone at their word. But the differences and their consequences can be dramatic.

Let's say for instance that I'm a blogger who could use a few spare dollars. I allow Google to post what it deems to be relevant ads to my website. Well, this cuts in two opposing directions. On one hand, my blogging site might seem less credible because the ads may undermine the editorial style and substance of the blog. On the other hand, the site may appear more established and even a more authoritative source. That's because the Google ads lend institutional legitimacy to what is essentially a one-man band.

Regardless of how we define credibility, our common goal as researchers rests in one determination: What matters the most in the discussions inspired by our search targets? We can weigh what facts rise to the head of a debate. We can formulate how widespread those facts are distributed and how much agreement actually exists about them among the groups most likely to lead the charge or be impacted by the events in question. We can even pinpoint hypocrisies between what a well-known person says in settings of their choosing versus the actions they take. Actions taken assumes less guarded and often less favorable or riskier circumstances.

Later on in **Unit Four** we will introduce **Provider Source Conjugation**. This is a framework that helps us to see the social value of information. That means how we appear on the web and how this impacts how others perceive us. If we use the same framework on the people we search, we can also use it to assess source bias as well. That could mean distortions and character defamation, intended or unintentional – for instance, what facts get selected and which ones don't.

Discerning Source Self-Interest

The top of the source fluency list of priorities is getting to the question of self-preservation. That's right. Finding out why information providers share what we're sourcing. Motivation focuses on classifying sources in two ways:

> **1. Peer reviews** – Specifically the inherent strengths and weaknesses of provider types.
>
> **2. Packaging** – Understanding how providers bundle their content *before* we integrate it with our own findings to the client.

First let's address the question of provider peer groups.

What we've lost is not some track record or backlog of questionable decisions. It's the notion of a 'reliable source' for information. It's the separation between who's making the news and who's reporting it. Without that distinction it is difficult to isolate what others say about us from what we petition on our own behalf. And nowhere is this problem harder to contain than that critical group of observers from which all reputations are grounded, shaped, and most importantly ... believed:

> 1. Direct experience with the search target.
>
> 2. No vested interest in any status change to that target, (be it a lawsuit, a job offer, or a substantial and pending sale).

A profusion of newsmakers masquerading as information providers does little to clarify this question of self-interest. It's especially hard to find impartial judges who are firsthand witness to the character and reputation of the individuals and groups we're investigating.

Now, let's consider packaging.

The primary benefit of premium sources is that they eliminate the uncertainty of who the ultimate source is for the information we're receiving. It doesn't hurt that they also provide...

> - Better classifications
> - Chronological sorting, and
> - Mapping keywords to topics

We'll delver further into these benefits in the next section.

Think about all the searching we've done where we knew definitive authorities? Where we could even reference the underlying fact-base that supports our assertions? But because it's the web, there's no clear path from search results to the subject knowledge we've accrued through our experience.

It's frustrating at best to vet the specific interests or incentives behind any one provider. The web remains largely an unregulated resource of self-selecting information sources. In **Unit Four,** we'll explore new frameworks that can help make this expectation reasonable and objective possible.

The Hidden Value in Paying for Information

Premium services have a number of advantages over the public or free web. For starters when information is paid for that usually confers some immediate advantages over free web-based content:

1. **Editorial oversight** – Having actual humans minding the info store means we benefit from formal tagging structures called taxonomies. That guarantees we get something in a structured database that's so elusive on the web: The context of categorical boundaries. Categorization maps news articles to their topical value. Want more of the same? Just click on the topic that the piece falls under. How the information we're targeting is grouped by professional classifiers is a level of control commercial web searches can't offer because they have no commercial incentive to provide this.

2. **Legal boundaries** – The fact that a for-profit or peer-reviewed publication formally releases a series of articles on a periodic basis makes them an information publisher in the traditional sense. That means they are held up to the standards and safeguards inherent in the First Amendment, including constitutional protections against slander and other civil liberties. Proving the same on the unregulated web carries a much higher legal burden for would-be plaintiffs.

3. **Causes and effect** – Another overlooked benefit is the simple assertion that we have a confirmable source, and with that, the reasonable certainty of a specific audience they're intending to reach. Connecting that relationship as the backdrop to the articles we're assessing helps us to understand the unstated nature of news coverage: Mainly *why* certain stories are covered and how these stories are told. The other advantage of cause-and-effect is to exploit the chronology of publication dates. That makes it easier to source the sequential order of the events we're tracking. In a fee-based model, date ranges speak to publication dates, not crawler sessions for indexing web pages.

4. **Repeatable responses** – This sounds like a scientist who over thinks the problem of inconsistent search results. Actually, few findings are more compelling to an investigation (and the client we're working for) than their ability to repeat our research. That means coming up with the same evidence we're using to draw conclusions in our investigations. That level of validation is much easier to attain in a stable resource than the dynamic and slippery web.

Figures 3.46 and 3.47 serve as examples of those benefits and some situations where they're of highest value to our investigation.

FIGURE 3.46: Advantages of Premium or Fee-based Content

Advantage	Examples
Concept of "added value"	• Large archive • Repeated access • Complex concepts
Concept of source organization	• Higher selectivity • Better bundling
Syntax used in large subscription-based collections	• More exacting, literal • 1-2 word queries are often useless

Below, we see how a fee-based service retained by the University of Michigan classifies subjects according to keywords. This is similar to the kind of results we find with a robust subject directory. The primary difference here is that the results lead to abstracts or complete articles from magazines, journals, and newspapers.

FIGURE 3.47: Context Through the Categorical Boundaries of Fee-based Content

"missing children" investigation unsolved autis*   [Search] Advanced

Subject	—
missing persons	303
criminal investigations	268
kidnapping	190
unsolved crimes	149
murders & murder attempts	143
law enforcement	119
children & youth	117
investigations	110
murder	73
families & family life	65

Above we see our search target as both organizational and topic-based classifications. A further breakdown of those topics cross-references the main subject against a myriad of related themes that factor into it.

THE COST OF FREE TOOLS

So it's nice to know actual dates of articles grouped into understandable categories. It's also reassuring to know they were placed there with the care and discretion of a human editor. But let's get real, you say. Even if we did have a budget and a more flexible deadline, none of that matters. It won't change the fact that the action falls outside these subscription-based news archives. It's happening as we speak. And just because we don't know the source doesn't mean it's any less relevant to our investigation.

I'm not here to fall on my credibility sword over confusing or poorly-documented information sources. But it is important to know and identify the nature of the beast. And the monster in question is not out to conceal truth or hide criminals so much as act in its own self-interest.

As Andrei Hagiu and Bruno Jullien write in "*Why Are Web Sites So Confusing,*" there is a fundamental conflict between the needs of web investigators and web advertisers. **(Hagel, Julien, 2009)**[19] They argue that gateways like Google have little incentive to help us become more efficient searchers. Hagiu and Julien say that the revenues generated by pay-per-click ads push the more useful search results off the first results page. The effect is what the authors call 'search diversion.' That means steering users to products that yield the highest margins for search vendors.

This bias towards generating revenues ahead of insights is not limited to the ranking of web sites. Since 2011, it includes the 'search suggest' patterns that complete the half-formed queries now in all Google searches. That means that we're not only being guided in the direction of the sponsored ads but even the search terms that are bid up in the auctioning of keywords through the Google AdWords program.

Institutional Credibility

Personal credibility is a quality we assign to a trusted confidante. Someone who knows us well enough, communicates in ways we understand, and knows their way around the issues they advise us on. Institutional credibility is different. Like person-to-person counsel, believing what organizations tell us probably means we've been steered correctly by them in the past. But it also means something a lot less personal is taking place – even impersonal in matters of dispensing advice.

The reputations of advice-giving groups like stock brokerages and law practices hinge on how far removed they are from the counsel they keep. The closer their fortunes align with the professionals they advise, the likelier they place their own interests ahead of their clients. Having a direct interest in the connections they broker is sometimes called double-dipping because the adviser is compensated twice – both by the client and their own referral networks. It is also a clear conflict of interest.

Credibility before the Web

In pre-digital days of fee-based content, it didn't take a rigorous methodology to determine credibility. It meant that if the bastions of business media and research had an insight to share on their pages then their big wheel subscribers had an edge over non-subscribers: Those *yokels* who turned to the local paper but not the Wall Street Journal, for instance.

Figure 3.48 shows what a *food chain* of credible information providers might have looked like in the mid-nineties at the advent of the World Wide Web:

FIGURE 3.48: Traditional Publishers of Fee-based Content (and Their Former Spheres of Influence)

Who	What	Why	Cost
Investment Reports	Advice to investors and underwriting of future IPOs	1 hour lunch meetings with CEO, CFO	Fee
Major Business	Full 'take no prisoners' investigations, industry report cards	Large editorial staffs and readerships	Fee
Regional Business	Intimate reporting on changes in management, labor, infrastructure operations	Unfailing way to see intimate side of global competitors but local angle means having turf to protect	Free
Management Journals	Gurus, methods, and teachers	Business development tool for academics and management consultants	Free
Trade Publications	Distribution, sales, spending patterns, product evaluations, and launches	Trade sources geared towards managers have more credibility than those aimed at marketers. Put your faith in what customers experience, not what vendors promise	Fee
Newswires	Real-time updates with an emphasis on financial transactions	The most prolific intelligence sources and the least analytical	Free
Blogs and Newsletters	Real-time with analysis	Need for rapid opinion formation favors speculation over reliability	Free
Press Releases	Generated by the source it addresses	The antithesis of integrity. Self-serving by definition	Free

Nowadays there is little distinction between breaking news and analyzing what it all means. Instant analysis is a paradox of the 24/7 news cycle where a restless parade of events overwhelms the cyclical rituals once used for pattern-matching and perspective-gathering. So who is worth paying attention to? It was a simpler matter in the old days where information made no distinction between *fee* and *free*. Whoever drew the biggest audiences commanded the most authority. This is not that different from the social media definition of credibility: The more followers, the more worth following. Below is an illustration of that top-down framework in Figure 3.49 for assessing institutional credibility in bygone days.

FIGURE 3.49: The Pyramid of 20ᵗʰ Century Institutional Credibility

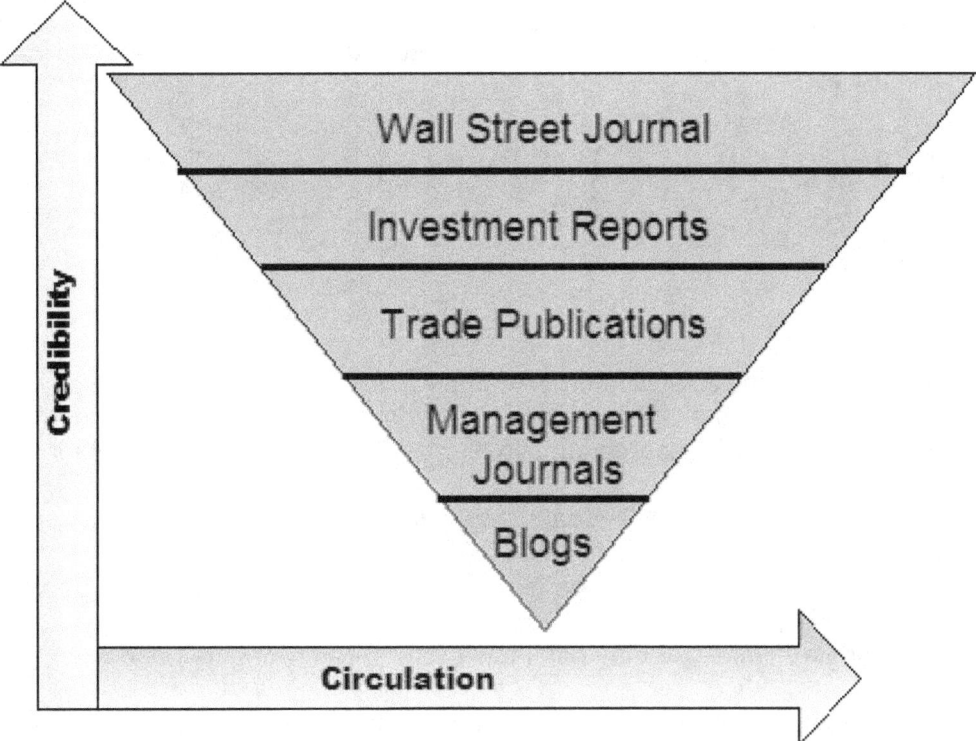

The wider the audience the higher an information provider's credibility as the above model from the fee-based era indicates That level of certainty has been obliterated by page ranks, reciprocal links, pay-per-click campaigns and the highly dubious business of quantifying influence in a web-based media environment.

UNIT THREE: Wrapping

How to Source Information That Instructs

Unit Three continued the discovery process modeled in the Knowledge Continuum. **Unit One** introduced the idea of organizing the discovery process through Search Planning Management. **Unit Two** centered on the vigorous tweaking needed to filter the noise from our search results. **Unit Three** focused on the frameworks used to address the motivations and priorities of providing web-based source content. We assessed the context, credibility, and cost factors associated with determining the merit of our references and quality of the information they produce. Once we understand how to plan, filter, and assess our research, we'll be poised to analyze and interpret our search results (**Unit Four**) into the core findings that we'll share with our clients (**Unit Five**).

[1] Jamais Cascio, "Get Smart," The Atlantic, July / August 2009
[2] Galen Stocking, Katerina Eva Matsa, "Using Google Trends data for research? Here are 6 questions to ask: First, what sort of research questions can Google data answer?" Medium, April 27, 2017)
[3] "What is the maximum size of an HTML file that Google will crawl through?" https://webmasters.stackexchange.com/questions/47233, April 12, 2013
[4] Barry Schwartz, "Google Crawl Limit Per Page Now Couple Hundred Megabytes," Search Engine Roundtable, August 3, 2017
[5] Patrick Stox, "20 of Google's limits you may not know exist," Search Engine Land, September 6, 2017
[6] The deep web is often confused for the dark web, a small subset that plays host to criminal activity, illegal transactions, and deviant behavior, i.e. sex trafficking, counterfeiting, pedaphilia, contract killing, etc.
[7] The Google Blog search application was discontinued in 2011.
[8] George Will,"Boredeom and the Cost of Constant Connection," Newsweek, August 14, 2010.
[9] This Amazon Alexa predates the robotic assistant by 20 years..
[10] Both the phonebook syntax and Google Videos were discontinued by Google in 2010 and 2011 respectively.
[11] Mike Milliard, "The World is Watching," The Boston Phoenix, September 23, 2010
[12] This is a pretty deep well and spans from purchase orders and phone logs to virtual sessions, payment patterns, and GPS coordinates (our physical whereabouts).
[13] 123people closed shop in 2014..
[14] A former version of the product compared keyword queries to press coverage of the same keyword-derived queries.
[15] J.J. Rosen, "The Internet You Can't Google," May 2, 2014, The Tennessean
[16] Jose Pagliery, "The Deep Web You Don't Know About," March 10, 2014, CNN Business
[17] Open Education Database, "The Ultimate Guide to the Invisible Web,"

https://oedb.org/ilibrarian/invisible-web/
[18] Tweet from Nikki Lynette, September 20, 2010
[19] Andrei Hagiu and Bruno Jullien, "Why Are Websites So Confusing," HBS Working Knowledge, October, 19, 2009

UNIT FOUR:
SENSE-MAKING THROUGH INFORMATION CONTEXT

Taken into Context

In the previous unit we began to look at search results in terms of quality and quantity. We also learned how to assess information suppliers through **Source Fluency** and **Quality Control**. These methods are designed to improve the quality of the information we source from the web.

However, if we rely on sourcing alone we're still missing an essential ingredient in the search mix. That's the critical question of social information or context– how all this quality information is perceived by others:

- Who's aware of it?
- How does it help or hinder one's own objectives?
- Where do our findings deviate from the awareness baseline: What a layperson would learn about the same search target (without the tools and methods we're tapping into here?)
- When are we likelier to be believed or seriously questioned by those impacted by our research?

It's no longer the information supply but the demand side of web content be we'll consider in **Unit Four**. Context is what we still need to address before we produce our reports and lock-in our recommendations. Context must be established before we can meet our clients and colleagues with full confidence in our findings and accounting for our conclusions.

STUMBLING INTO CONTEXT

It's a paradox that the term 'context' is most commonly mentioned when it is missing from the discourse or situation in question. No one is said to *discover* context. The implicit understanding of context is that it lies there for the taking — like the numbers on a mailbox.

How often have we heard that the words of public figures and officials have been taken *out of context?* Now compare that with the number of times where a political rival, reporter, or intermediary was said to have taken the quoted source in the proper context? It's no contest.

Misunderstandings attract attention. Agreements are implied. So we take them for granted. There's no need to report them. In fact, it's because proper contexts go unreported that we need to understand them better as investigators. We are not involved in these discussions and the implicit assumptions they inspire. Investigators by our very nature are outsiders. We're more active as observants. Our capacities as team players are tested by the groupthink that develops when a band of like-minded insiders skirt the law. The insider sidesteps or suppresses conflicts-of-interest that place their own gain ahead of the larger groups or social forces they served, typically in a leadership context.

We will address context in a number of ways in **Unit Four**. We'll begin by examining the credibility of a website and the motivation of the information provider. Later, we'll learn how to evaluate the information exchange of others over the Internet. Finally, we'll turn our attention to a growing and prevalent form of group-think: The proliferation of social networks residing on the web. From a demand perspective, our interest is not about how to market one's services to friends or connections through a social site. It's how to deftly observe and assess the behaviors and tendencies of search targets as members of these communities.

UNIT FOUR LEARNING OBJECTIVES

Let's take a glance back at the foundational settings from **Unit Three** that we'll be using as building blocks in **Unit Four**:

1. We established a set of quality controls to: (1) qualify, and (2) quantify the information we're sourcing from the initial search results, down to the site and page level of our sources.

2. We introduced source fluency as a way to attract quality information suppliers, even when targeting unfamiliar people and topics.

3. We considered how premium (or fee-based) information offers advantages to power users, a.k.a. investigators, insisting on the news origination and chronological sequencing often lacking in free public web sources.

4. We also addressed the 'Internet Radar' as a model for assessing the likely boundary lines between public and proprietary information – another key determinant in whether to opt for free or fee-based web content.

Unit Four builds on these foundations by focusing on the demand side of web content or the social dimension of digital information through...

- Group-based information – conflicts between personal loyalties, public credibility, and the need for group discipline
- Individual-based information – incentives to share and the inclination for belief through candor and authenticity
- Social networks and their impacts on both individuals and groups from the researchers' perspective

By mastering these skills, we will take our investigations to a deeper, more exhaustive level. We will look at the goals and motives of our search targets as both content producers and consumers. We will also see how these behaviors shift when we're investigating the same individual as a group member. What issues are addressed? Which ones are overlooked? We trace this back to the sincerity and goal orientation of individual versus group information providers.

Unit Four Destination: Evidence-gathering and Perspective-taking

Context is the one dimension from which information cannot be divided or filtered. By definition, context is the cross-referencing of two or more factors from which it forms. Maybe it's senders and receivers. Perhaps it's time and place. Remember all the dimensions we considered in compiling information types? Additional inputs like entry point, point of view, resources, and format all create the richer complexities that define the context. Context often does and should not exist in isolation, no matter how vehemently our accusers say we take them out of context.

In **Unit Four,** we will begin to apply situation appropriate tools and techniques to both traditional group-based and emerging individual-based information suppliers. We will be documenting the context, not only the content of the evidence we're citing. This requires that we create a framework for analyzing our search projects prior to presenting them in **Unit Five**. We will achieve this from the following perspectives:

1. **Persons of interest** – This is where our focus naturally shifts in criminal investigations, but also in business dealings where we're looking for contacts to influence or approve us and our clients as vendors

2. **Layperson** – The baseline for establishing awareness levels and common knowledge around the issues relevant to our project

3. **Third-parties** – Experts and experienced professionals with deep domain knowledge who have no vested interest in the outcome of our research efforts

Being able to process these frames of reference is the last critical piece between searching (query formation), sourcing (fluency), and delivery (final reporting). The perspective-taking framework aids our investigation in the following ways:

1. Enhances the perspectives of these other participants, without threatening the trust needed to embrace their full participation.

2. Explains the probable chain of events where scant documentation exists.

3. Analyzes the gap between words and deeds that explains the hypocritical behaviors we so often see between how we act as individuals and as group members.

4. Rationalizes the difference between public statements contained in sources like press releases, official records and policies versus personal disclosures that often run in conflict with on-the-record and contractual roles and responsibilities.

Definition: Context

The immediate circumstances that connect a single event to the broader meaning of motivations and perspectives of the actors in question.

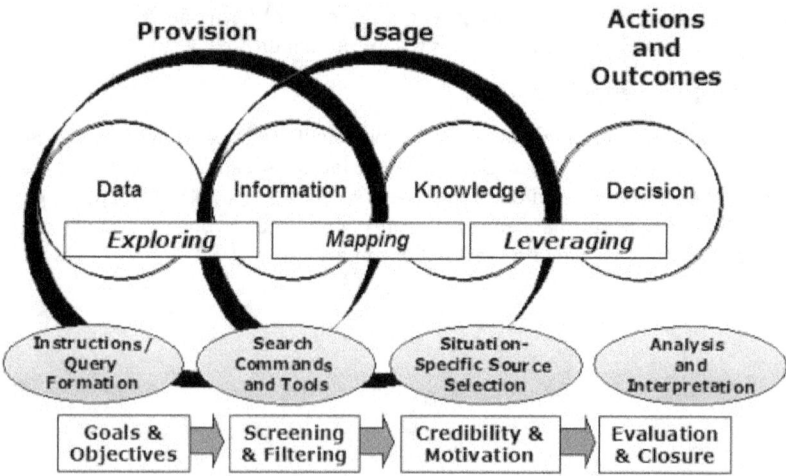

Along the Knowledge Continuum, we are now evaluating the credibility and determine the motivation that lies behind the information.

The demand side of the Knowledge Continuum is where we anticipate actions and outcomes. It's also where we conduct perspective-taking on what others will think or do once made aware of the information we gather – even the reports we're piecing together.

Unit Four bridges the 'what' to 'when' steps of the SPM process. That means that we're transitioning now from what are expectations are to when we'll pursue both missing and disputed details firsthand. In terms of sources and search results, what are some educated guesses about what we'll discover? In terms of *when,* that means when we'll engage our search targets directly – either virtually or in-person.

Our device for doing so is through the prismatic lens of provider conjugation. Provider conjugation builds on the source fluency methods we learned in the last unit by describing the context of the information we're evidencing as researchers. There are three basic ways we will come to define, view, interpret, and apply this framework to the analytical requirements of our investigations:

1. **Individual-based information** – incentives to share and the inclination for belief through candor and authenticity
2. **Group-based information** – conflicts between personal loyalties, public credibility, and the need for group discipline
3. **Social networks** – their impacts on both individuals and groups, from the researchers' perspective

Unit Four Benefits

Unit Four shows participants how to proceed from the collection to the analytical phase of their search projects. This is the sense-making stage that all investigations reach between the discovery process and delivering those findings, often with a set of recommendations and/or a plan for actions.

Upon completion of this unit, you should be able to find not only the facts and opinions we addressed in the last unit but the context of *how* and even *why* this evidence was reported. Here are those learning objectives we will master based on the three main sections within **Unit Four:**

Individual-based Information

- Recognize information providers' perspectives from the vantages of insiders and outsiders
- Distinguish between perceptions of private (informal) and public (formal) communications
- Recognize perception differences between firsthand and secondhand experiences and their impact on information providers and users
- Assess conflicts of interest, hidden agendas and predetermined limits on the range of encouraged or 'acceptable outcomes'

Group-based Information
- Recognize the institutional biases of third-hand information providers
- Group media sources by their business objectives and traditional cultural roles
- Recognize the ability of groupings of news media sources to shape public awareness and opinions around sensational crimes

Social Networks
- Assess and monitor the group behaviors and participation patterns formed in virtual communities
- Define the failsafes and terms of success on *people searches* and the grounds for closing such investigations
- Assess the differences between the way information is communicated informally through word-of-mouth and institutionally through groups

Search to Converse ("STC")
- When it makes sense to engage a search target directly and whether it's best to do that virtually or in-person
- Background research the people you're going to meet
  – Deploy specialized search tools to gauge their web presence and digital identities
- Build a stable of advisers and referral networks for finding experts and second opinions
- Pick a blogging theme that can used as a professional calling card (and showcase for our research)

Misinformation as an Information Source
- Apply the **Vectors of Integrity** to determine the credibility of information providers, and their own involvement in the issues they report
- Gauge the reputation of our search targets (it's not in the eye of the beholder!)

The Value of Social Information
- Test our knowledge through virtual networks
- Apply visualization tools to our networks
- Leverage social networking tools to raise our digital profile as an independent investigator
- Use alerts and notifications to stay on top of fluid and evolving situations

Searching Out Loud

SECTION 4:1 | Individual-based Information —
Personal Motivation

Why do people do what they do? Okay – for now that's above our pay grade. How about this: What are some common motives for sharing our views on social media pages, discussion boards, news articles, in blog postings, YouTube videos, etc.?

<u>Common Forms of Motivation for Message Senders</u>

- Justice
- Revenge
- Redemption
- Ego

Okay, so how well does the sending impulse sound to the ear of the recipients?

<u>Common Forms of Motivation for Receivers</u>

- Impartial
- Vested
- Action-based
- Comprehensive

It's funny. But when we look at the pay-offs, none of these emotional satisfactions include cash or material gain of any sort. It's also ironic that each one of these universally-held desires is in direct conflict with the other. A hard-nosed assessment is compromised by owning a direct stake in the outcome of that evaluation. A report predisposed to swift and certain actions is slowed down by the weight of due diligence and the need for broad-based input. The universal desire for an informed decision is not so easily satisfied. What seems reasonable as a single objective can become complicated or even at odds with other dual objectives:

1. How do we sort this out? How do we derive the context of our research findings?
2. Where does context meet up with our own conclusions and recommendations?
3. Do we show all our investigative cards? Do we hold them in reserve to appear less partial than we may be letting on?
4. Why is it essential that when we report our findings to clients and colleagues, that we also share a repeatable and simple model on which our assertions are based?

INTRODUCING PROVIDER CONJUGATION FRAMEWORKS

Provider conjugation is a lot like verb conjugation.

Remember when we took a foreign language in grammar school? We could always memorize the nouns. But we really couldn't speak in sentences until we learned how to conjugate the verbs. The same is true within the *to inform* aspect of information. *How* it travels from person-to-person and group-to-group is every bit as important to our understanding as the content of what's communicated.

Remember all those rhetorical battles pitting style against substance? The medium is the message and the power of the media? Conjugating providers is not only about communication styles. It's even more useful in trying to decipher what folks do with information once new information is added to one's existing knowledge and prior experience. It's not about a piece of information. It's about a piece of the action – the actions taken by ourselves and others when we're informed, and more to the point, *how* we are informed.

PCF is a model that combines the concept of individual and plural verb forms with the framework of degrees of separation. Taken together, source conjugation helps us to understand the distance between the information provider and their proximity to their information source. Are they one in the same? Did it happen to them directly – are they the news provider and news source? How does this both strengthen and compromise authority figures fond of quoting themselves, in the first person, in the third?

What if they're the intermediary? Say the reporter who receives the confession that solves the mystery? Does she go behind the perpetrator's back and spill the beans to the authorities? Was it an affront to the perpetrator? Is he part of a network where another members comes forward with information now relevant to a related and open investigation?

> **Definition: Provider Conjugation Frameworks ("PCFs")**
>
> A model that determines the degree of separation between information sources (or messages) and information providers (messengers). PCFs are also used to clarify what information recipients do with information once it becomes assimilated into existing knowledge and prior experience.

Transparency

Who-knew-what-and-when-did-they-know-it is a phrase made famous in the Watergate investigation of the early 1970s. Journalists have their inverted pyramids and attorneys have this familiar concept for framing the details of a public investigation. However, we can't fill-in the *who* and *when* particulars until we factor in transparency or the third-person element in source conjugation.

The notion of who knew what and when is not just about information sources and providers. If it was, there would be no calls for investigation. In an truly open source world, all cases would be closed.

Successful investigations rest on two bedrock notions:

1. Persons of good faith will come forward to steer the investigator in the right direction.

2. Criminal evidence lives on in the heads of those they confide in, no matter how careful the masterminds are in burying that body of knowledge.

There could be nothing written down, no recordings of any spoken evidence. Just winks, nods, and a feint grimace or facial tic. But a body of evidence is truly unrecoverable if there is no third-person. This is an observer, not an accomplice. The third-person is not directly involved in the planning, execution, or potential consequences of the plot in question. Looking for your person of good faith to come forward? Don't look in the first or second person of your source conjugations.

The Giant Listening Ear

Transparency is not limited to individuals. It's an important aspect in the source conjugation of groups too. Group communications by definition are not two-way but three way transactions that include first, second, and third parties: The message maker, provider, and its receivers.

How we're informed as members of groups is typically a more passive act than how we interact as individuals. That's because when we communicate in groups, we are either seeking an audience or forming one. It's even easier if the group has already assembled at a pre-arranged time. We attend the meeting in listen mode. We buy a ticket and find our seat. We flip on a switch. Presto! We're receiving the same signals as every audience member. And the communication is traveling our way in two forms: (1) the substance of the message itself, and (2) the social context shared by the message receivers.

This premise rests on the following inferences:

- How big our message receiving group is
- The common bonds, shared priorities, and rallying points that unify us
- Other events, people, and outcomes the group references in its reactions
- What kind of commitment the message sender seeks from us (our rapt attention for starters!)

Transparency in group communications is not limited to big media events. Sometimes the third wheel in a two-way dialog is not tuning into a regularly scheduled program or an updated web page. Sometimes that giant listening ear is not sitting in the studio audience but crouched in a van with headphones and a device for taping discussions they are privy to, but not present in.

For example, in a sting operation there are investigators that overhear evidence through wiretaps and eavesdropping. We are horrified when we as third-parties learn that an elected official is trying to trade public appointments for personal privilege. We're not aghast at the politician's hypocrisy but that his indiscretion was done with the knowledge he was under investigation – again the third leg of a two way communication.

Three Way Conversation

In fact, all public discourse is a three-way. When the celebrated TV interviewer interviews TV celebrities, it is the audience that creates the social value communicated by the newsmaker and intermediary. No matter how intimate the settings or revealing the subject, the prying eyes of the camera form a peep hole for the viewer. It may be fiction. It may be a fabrication. Either way, this a social exchange witnessed by countless people with no personal connection to either party. The role of celebrity enables us to relate to these otherwise strangers as members of groups – not directly as individual acquaintances but indirectly as observers, as fans, as audience members, as site visitors.

The more direct the connection between provider and subject, the greater the information provider's authenticity. *We believe that they believe what they believe.* Their authenticity is often conveyed in a stage whisper style. Authentic leaders can rally large crowds while commanding the intimacy of a much smaller group setting.

Authentic speakers introduce higher probabilities of tampering and distortion — especially when the provider's belief lies in their ability to influence, not in the actual facts selected or supporting details, if they're even offered. Unsupported evidence requires the close loyalties of recipients who pledge a faith-based allegiance to a higher truth, transcending the empirical inspection of facts on the ground.

I've never been a fan of three ways. Two way conversations are tough enough for me to keep track of. To be frank, sometimes talking privately with one's self can feel like a noisy and crowded room. Crack a window. It's stuffy in there!

The Three Tenses

Returning to our conjugation model, we remember that there are three types of conjugation:

I, you, and they, or first, second, and third person.

In PCF, this denotes the singular form for individuals and plural for groups. We express this as first, second, and third *person* for individuals. We refer to first, second, and third *parties* for groups. The source conjugation framework provides us perspective in (1) connecting information sources to their suppliers, and (2) how these providers behave as soloists and in groups.

Let's contrast persons and parties. First we'll map two opposing vectors which we'll chart more fully later in this section. We will connect *credibility* to third party information sources and *authenticity* to first person participation – someone on the *front lines* of public conflict (soldiers, medics, firefighters, law enforcement, campaign workers, etc.)

Who are the go-betweens? Who are the intermediaries between the first and third tenses? Those would be second person informants and confidantes. Second parties are not only recipients but sources in their own right for passing on their own assessments onto third parties. Think of the traditional relationship of newspaper reporters to readers, and expert witnesses to jurors. Second parties are always one step removed from the actions they assess and the potential outcomes they may trigger.

Ultimately, PCF ("Provider Conjugation Framework") is designed to help the Knowledge-ABLED on two fronts...

   1. As researchers: Understand the motivations of senders and receivers, and

   2. As investigators: Engage experts and decision-makers within our passionate interests, fields of choice, and chosen communities.

How Information Travels

In addition to senders and receivers, we need to deepen the conjugal model by laying the groundwork for the transfer: How is this information transferred or exchanged? Applying PCF to context triggers questions about the nature of the exchange:

   1. Are we communicating with one or many?

   2. Is it the intimacy of one trusted adviser?

3. Is it an announcement that we've crafted to hundreds of former colleagues that we've accepted an offer with a new employer?

4. Is it somewhere in the middle where we're reaching out to groups and selective members?

THE THREE TYPE OF INFORMATION EXCHANGES

In addition to the three PCF tenses, it is also important to factor in the nature of how providers choose to communicate. These are the kinds of information exchange that describes the relationship between senders and receivers. There are three information exchanges:

1. Source to listener (1:1) – first person/party (one-on-ones are both intimate and unstructured)

2. Source to small group (1:several) – second person/party

3. Source to large group (1:many) – third person/party

Who Belongs Where?

The source conjugation chart below defines individual and group information exchanges according to the role of the information giver. These examples parallel the information sources and recipients that are common to criminal investigations:

FIGURE 4.1: Provider Conjugation Framework ("PCF") for Assessing Personal Motives

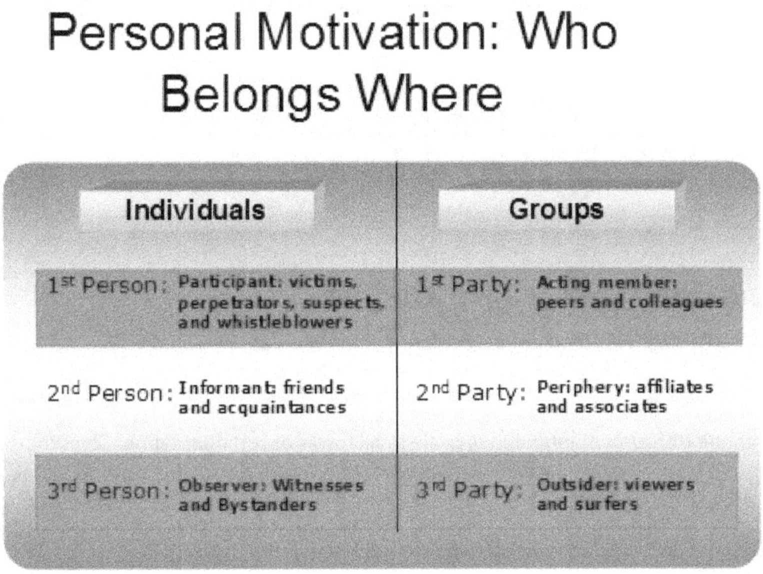

Personal Motivation: Who Belongs Where

Individuals	Groups
1st Person: Participant: victims, perpetrators, suspects, and whistleblowers	1st Party: Acting member: peers and colleagues
2nd Person: Informant: friends and acquaintances	2nd Party: Periphery: affiliates and associates
3rd Person: Observer: Witnesses and Bystanders	3rd Party: Outsider: viewers and surfers

In the diagram above we're seeing two levels emerge here: 1. Individuals – represent personal opinions and individual choices. This is the province of private matters, informal exchanges, and casual conversation. 2. Groups – represent group consensus, dissent and affiliation (label, brand, party affiliation, etc.).

Who Belongs Where – Applying the Framework

PCFs are perspective-gathering tools for understanding the context of information exchanges. Instead of focusing on the message, we look at the roles we're used to performing ourselves – or seeking out in others:

1. How would we use this framework to plot the roles and motivations of our search targets?
2. Where are there natural connections between informants and investigators? Where are there natural blockages?
3. What alternatives are available to the resourceful investigators?
4. How do the roles change from personal involvement at an individual level to playing a professional role at the group level?

FIGURE 4.2: PCF for Ascribing Roles and Responsibilities

Individuals		Groups	
1st Person:	Primary source: diaries and interviews	1st Party:	Vested authority: speeches and roundtables
2nd Person:	Voucher: cross-checking and verifications	2nd Party:	Reporter: articles and investigations
3rd Person:	Commentator: interpretation and conjecture	3rd Party:	Researcher: surveys and forecasts

CONTAINERS OF INFORMATION EXCHANGES WITHIN GROUPS

> "I know more than I can say. I say more than I can write down."
>
> — David Snowden, Founder, Cognitive Edge

These exchanges that we are placing within the PCF are not intended to scale to all forms of communication. Transcripts of most therapy sessions don't get uploaded to mytherapysessions.com. Most lawyer-client communications are privileged and are implicitly off limits to investigators, if they are documented at all. That said, we are including a broader representation of interactions than what will turn up in a web-based investigation. Our purpose is to make sense of the many digitized messages that lack context or a basis for...

- Assessing the motivations of senders, or
- How receivers process, frame, and potentially act on them.

Anyone who ever studied a second language in grammar school can recall how traditional conjugation methods address informal and formal second person verb tenses. In provider conjugation, this distinction is expressed as:

1. Internal (informal or casual) communication, and
2. External (formal or official) communication

Figure 4.3 shows the conduits or media for hosting and conveying these exchanges within two types of groups:

1. **Internal Groups:** Communities of personal contacts – This kind of communication is generally expressed through word-of-mouth or informally communicated through face-to-face communications. Not surprisingly, the explosive use of social media has redefined the boundaries of internal communities within a largely open, virtual setting.

2. **External Groups:** Communities of impersonal contacts – This kind of communication is conveyed through public forums or *the media* and is usually more formally stated. It is implicitly group-based and generally passes through multiple stakeholders before it is released to a wider audience of second and third parties.

FIGURE 4.3: Internal and External Communications

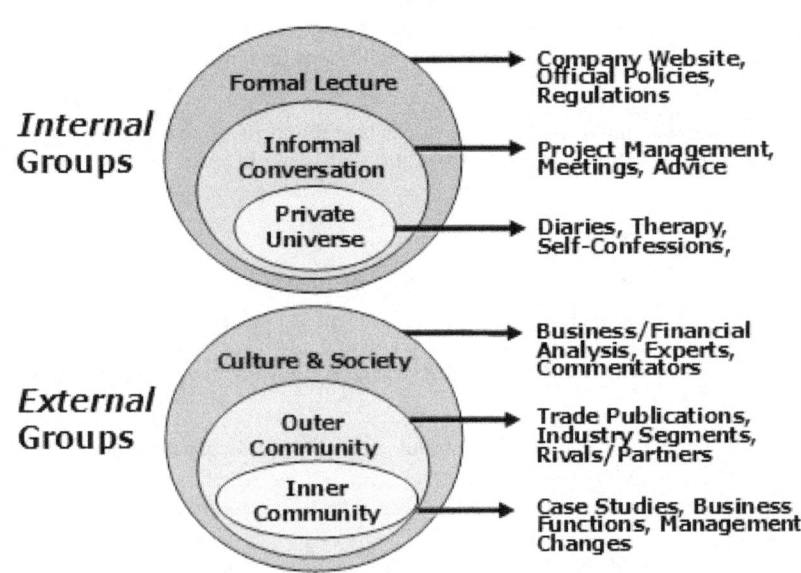

The Intermingling of Persons and Parties

Does that mean singular and plural are isolated from one another? Not in the slightest. Not only do individuals address groups. Groups dress down individuals. In delicate matters, we are prone to intimate exchanges with members of external groups. We look to trained counselors and professionals such as doctors, attorneys, and therapists. In those cases we may be preparing for a difficult conversation with a loved one or girding for a legal battle. Whatever the confrontation that lies ahead, our instincts for validation and detached feedback are often served by seeking advice. That trusted advisor belongs to a disinterested second party, not through the direct involvement of a vested second person.

Second Parties as Communication Vessels

Second parties often act as conduits between first and third parties. An office colleague could function as a second party. So can advisers like job coaches, stockbrokers, or the clergy. All require an additional layer of second party detachment in order to provide community leadership and the professional perspective and personal bond required in these roles. Third parties are creatures of the aggregate. That means large groupings of people who share an ordinary and passive bond as consumers (shoppers, demographics, fan clubs), and citizens (voters, taxpayers, volunteers, etc.).

PROVIDER CONJUGATION: INDIVIDUAL AND GROUP MOTIVATION VECTORS

The most accomplished web investigator never forgets how hard it is to truly nail a question that has many angles, nuances and shadings. But if we break our problems down to the PCF model, it's easier to see where the personal element figures into real world events, opportunities, and outcomes. We are several steps ahead of the targets we're investigating if we can speak to the context of our evidence-gathering. We won't have produced a better answer with a team behind us and an open-ended project calendar if we don't place our questions in the correct context. Neither will we lose any perspective from severing our reliance on social media where the personal touch is diminished by our in-network connections or distorted by the conforming pressures of virtual group behaviors (public shaming, compromising memes, etc.).

The next section introduces vectors for describing the perspectives of information providers. This includes the full conjugal range of first and second persons and parties. What powers of persuasion do these message senders summon within the range of their experience? How do they get their points across? Each conjugal provider is set to a standard scale of information attributes. Each attribute can be expressed as a vector that maps the motivations present when information is imparted from providers to receivers.

This helps us understand their incentives for making their messages known to us whether the carrier is an email, a blog post, a Facebook wall, a press release, or a journal entry. Motivation vectors of information exchange can also help us evaluate the nature of both individual and group exchanges.

Our analysis of these vectors includes the following dimensions:

- **Perspective** – Is this work self-referential or grounded in a more group-based agenda?
- **Documentation** – What is the likelihood these details have been (1) recorded, and (2) made accessible to us?
- **Verbiage** – What kinds of word choices (or semantics as we discussed in **Unit Two**) are unique to the situational specifics of the evidence in question?
- **Medium** – What is the transmission method likeliest to have distributed the evidence in question (book, database, web page, listserv, text message, public venue, etc.)

Individual: First Person

All messages begin to some extent in the mind of the individual before they're ever typed, edited, published, or disputed. There are no intermediaries or interpreters or critiques. All paths lead from first person whether or not that individual chooses to document and share their ideas. What form does this take? What's the incentive to do so? What does first person even sound or look like? The motivation vectors help guide our thinking here about the self-referential nature of first-person exchanges.

- **Perspective** (motive of information provider): "I am therefore I exist"
- **Documentation** (form of documentation): Last Wills and Testaments
- **Verbiage** (economy of detail): Prayers
- **Medium** (form of delivery): Safety deposit box; personal journal; voice-over
- **Temptation** (exclusive property or privilege of provider): Relationship status on Facebook

FIGURE 4.4: First Person Motivation Vector

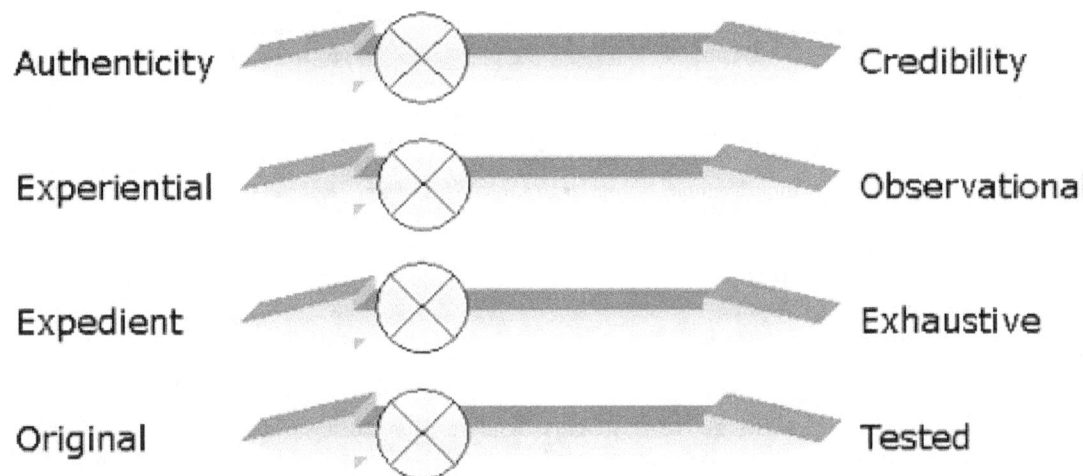

Vector two can apply to a writers' perspective. This means that all first person narratives are by definition the direct experience of the author when chronicling one's own accounts and viewpoints.

Vector Ranges

There is no audience so there is no need to persuade with the head or conceal from the heart. First person is the center of abject authenticity. There's no pretending or protecting or points to negotiate. The heart believes what it believes beyond any reasonable doubt. There are no justifications for its actions or the laws and policies that frame our professional conduct and organizational behavior. This is the gut talking and it is uninhibited by prying ears, competing explanations, and the hindsight used to rationalize the instinctive nature of its most intimate details.

First person accounts tend to run from due process and lose patience with the complexities that turn black and white situations into gray. First person narratives doesn't wait around to hear the other side of stories already concluded – hence the expedient nature of first person. Ironically, this is both the most compelling evidence for answering why people commit unspeakable acts in their own incriminating words.

Discussion Points

- Where are the blindspots of first person accounts on the web? How can we use source fluency to reduce them or be receptive to learning from them by sources we would otherwise spurn or ignore?
- Where would our information sources in our current investigations fall in the spectrum?
- Do they assume a personal or professional role and how does this potentially serve as well as compromise our own objectives in the case?

Individual: Second Person

There is a second person reckoning once a first-person message is intercepted by a receiver. Sometimes this is a passive role as a listener or a lurker. Sometimes a more active voice can mean interpreting and passing alone a filtered version of a first person story to the larger group. Sometimes the second person is not a go-between but a resource, responding directly to the comments and questions posed by the first person. From an Internet perspective, think of this interaction as an informal collaboration between individuals with a mutual concern and the direct experience they draw from to express this.

Layperson medical communities are a prime example. It's easier to compile list of well-regarded disease-related social networks based on firsthand referrals than to reach consensus about the websites best equipped to address which treatments to consider for the same illness. That's because second person trumps third party both in terms of sincerity and familiarity. Victims and their families telling their stories, trading advice, and coping with their afflictions by sharing first-hand experience through electronic word-of-mouth.

Vector Ranges

One way to look at second person discussions is whether we're prefer an open social media environment or a closed loop like email. The former is easier to capture, archive, and attracts more potential collaborators. The latter means we have a much clearer idea of who we're communicating with. In opting for email this choice is expressed well by a local colleague of mine named Sadie Van Buren who writes:

> *"I'm not so much looking to leverage the experience of people I don't know as desiring to make a connection with those I do."*

As researcher/observers in these forums we need to consider the chumminess factor. Are first and second persons offline friends and colleagues or are they strangers who meet virtually over a common interest? This vector shows how to interpret the notable differences between first- and second-person information exchanges.

- ■ **Perspective:** "We're on the same page"; crowdsourcing
- ■ **Documentation:** Memorandums; testimonial
- ■ **Verbiage:** Communities of practice; conference call
- ■ **Medium:** Email; group discussion boards
- ■ **Temptation:** Spilling a secret a first person has sworn to their safekeeping

FIGURE 4.5: Second Person Motivation Vector

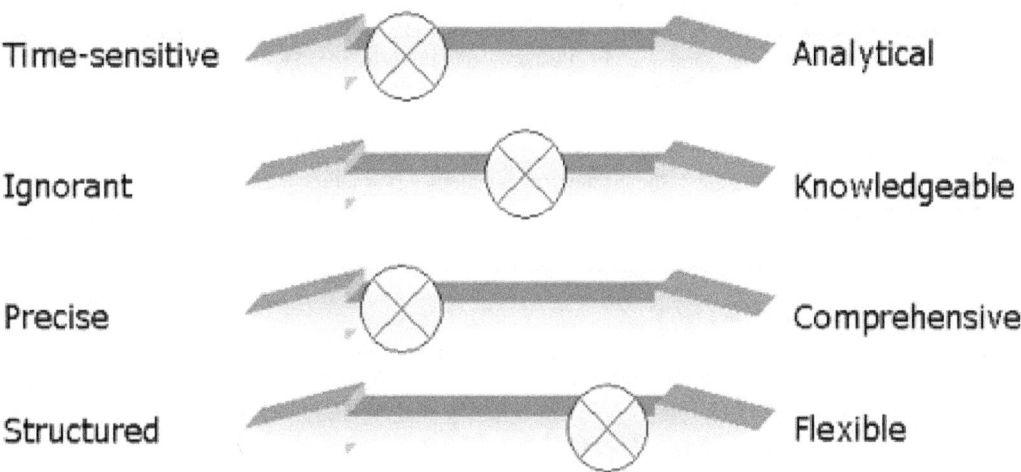

Second person, like first person, is fluid, freewheeling, and for the most part unfiltered. A sender's awareness of a confidante or small group of receivers will prompt self-censoring, particularly if they are seeking counsel.

<u>Discussion Points</u>

- In vector 2, first person knowledge seekers meet up with second person responders. Is the second person better equipped to offer comfort or expertise? That's a key consideration when determining whether such feedback may be used for coercive or educational purposes – think political lobbying.
- Vector 3 might be a status check or a debrief such as the exit interview given by a departing employee. A fifth vector might be presentational or formal communications versus conversational or more informal exchanges.
- What doubts and uncertainties can we expect in word-of-mouth exchanges? How do we apply PCF to meetings where two parties start on the same page and leave the same meeting with diverging or even clashing interpretations?
- If word-of-mouth is such a flexible medium, what does that say about the documentation (or accountability) of these exchanges? How well does social media capture the dynamic of a roundtable discussion? How about a call-in show between a regular listener and a panel of experts? The dynamic is beholden to the channel of that communication — just as much as the points raised by the caller or shared across our table of experts.

INDIVIDUAL: THIRD PERSON

Who's the third person? That would be us – assuming we don't know anyone we're investigating. The irony is that even if we do, we need to develop a third eye that sees the world from the lens of a third-person. This is someone who may take notice of the discussion but is disinterested in the first and second persons. They are not vested in any specific outcomes. They have no *skin in the game*. That makes them ideal for passing judgments because they can focus on the merits of an argument instead of the interpersonal dynamics that cloud the judgments of first and second persons. That's why this vector considers the elevated perspectives of detached observers.

That detachment includes a sensitivity towards sequence. In the case of first and second parties, that means identifying who speaks first and the dynamic it triggers. Does our first person continue to break the ice by introducing related topics and concerns? Does a second person steer the conversation in a completely new direction? The assertiveness of message senders and receivers is key to understanding their roles and influence in these exchanges. It's a dynamic less likely to escape the attention of a seasoned third person than someone directly involved in the discussion.

Vector Ranges

If third persons have a common bias, it's that they remain so. They prefer their independence to the commitment of active participation. We will see how this plays out in the insider and outsider roles assumed in the group behaviors of third parties. For now, we think of third parties as the clear-eyed stranger that we open up to on a long bus or flight, knowing that we will part company at the end of the trip in complete anonymity. It's the impersonal nature of third person affiliations that gives us the freedom to be astute judges of character, thorough researchers, and ultimately, effective investigators.

- ■ **Perspective:** 'Rules and procedures'
- ■ **Documentation:** Employee handbook; arbitration guidelines
- ■ **Verbiage:** The passenger in the middle seat (we're on the aisle of the same row)
- ■ **Medium:** 3-ring binder; jury box
- ■ **Temptation:** Crawl under a rock until the crowd clears out

FIGURE 4.6: Third Person Motivation Vector

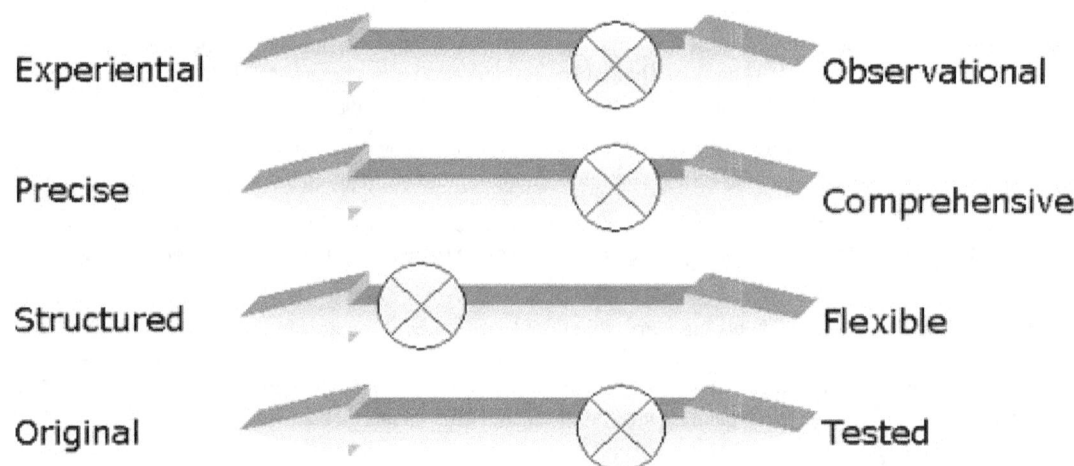

Third persons don't hang on the details of the first person's breathless accounts. Third persons may be drawn into conflicts at random as innocent bystanders. Their roles can also be more deliberate and clarifying when they function as the hypothetical 'every woman' or 'every man' meaning that they represent the approximated perception ranges of a grouping of people.

Discussion Points

- As vector 1 suggests, third persons insist on competing versions of the same story and can usually spot self-promotion and circular reasoning at the expense of a more balanced and evidence-based accounting.
- This skepticism suggests that vested opinions are vetted or tested against what the first or second person hopes to gain or influence in how and what they communicate to others.
- How does a third person perspective add to the endorsement or sanctioning of otherwise dubious ventures? How do we spot that an independent voice has been corrupted or co-opted by someone with a stake in the ground?
- What could it cost the information provider if such a credentialing backfired?

GROUP BEHAVIOR IN PROVIDER CONJUGATION

We all like to join groups. The most disagreeable curmudgeon takes solace and strength from being a card-waving member of the grumpy contrarian association. The reason we hear for this is that humans are 'social animals.' It's in our nature to bond with other tribal members. The less trumpeted reason is because being in a group can bring us power and influence that we could never wield as individuals.

As we just saw with individual conjugation, first persons have a tendency to pull third persons aside as control groups for confirming their own feelings and experiences. Then there's the validating power of third persons as proof these assertions are shared on a broader level. The punch line lands: "It's not just me!" That's a complex maneuver, no? It sounds like a variation on the Abbott and Costello baseball routine about 'who's on first?' ... 'I don't know who's on third!' ... and second base is not even on today's scorecard.

One of the great benefits to grouping individual behaviors is that it's easier to keep score. People band together because they all share the same priorities and viewpoints. There's no need to argue the point among members. This frees the group to make its case by marketing to individuals ("come join our crusade") or lobbying third parties:

> "We are correct so vote for us,"
>
> "Rule in our favor,'
>
> "Change this law," etc.

The simplicity of uniform agreements held by all of its members does have a downside for groups. It buries dissension and discourages internal debate. It objectifies opposing points of view as not only different but inferior and lacking merit. This belief denies the other party the legitimacy and respect needed to come to accommodations that consider both sides. As satirist Jon Stewart points out, the other side is not simply the opposing side, but the *enemy*. There can be no other view but the one held by group members. The collective denial of a first party is the same as the self-deception of a first person – just on a wider scale

Group: First Party

First parties are the collective form of self-interest. They are prone to overstepping their bounds when claiming to represent the interests of those falling outside the group. Political parties are prime examples, claiming that they are acting on behalf of much larger majorities than the actual numbers of the electorate that vote for their candidates.

The genesis of first parties is the universal human need to be part of something larger. Groups draw strength from a powerful desire to belong. Pressure to conform is almost irresistible – even when we're not members. Here's one example.

A hotel chain wants to save money on its cleaning operations so it hangs placards asking guests to reuse their towels to save energy and water. In the first attempt, the signs implore guests to join the crusade. Twelve percent go along. In the second attempt the hotel reasons that other guests are already doing this as a matter of habit. Over a third of the guests began doing so. The point here is that when made aware of them, we tend to stay in the boundaries of social norms – even when those definitions are designed to benefit the first parties who create them. Robert Ciardini calls it *social proof* – peer information, not peer pressure. **(Maney, 2009)**[1]

Vector Ranges

First parties are not all hellbent on conquering the world of public opinion or vanquishing the groups and policies that stand in their way. On a generic level, all organizational behavior falls under first party provider conjugation. There are protocols to follow whether we belong to an employer, a block association, or a mutual admiration society.

First parties are rife with conflicts of interest. First parties arouse suspicion whenever a mixed verdict is interpreted as a mandate to take actions that unites the party and supersedes the outcomes of any election. The larger the first party, the likelier that this is a domain where leaders and followers tend to congregate. A power structure emerges. Beliefs become systematized into codes. Representatives are elected to draft the rule-making that will be adopted by the larger body. Is this based on the consent of the members? What are the schisms that form around the rulings that follow? Is power-sharing part of the leadership role? How binding are these executive decisions? Does a void ensue between the rulers and the rank and file?

- **Perspective:** 'We lead – others follow'
- **Documentation:** Shredded
- **Verbiage:** Closed door meeting
- **Medium:** The White House lawn
- **Temptation:** Recruit outside analysts and experts for hire

FIGURE 4.7: First Party Motivation Vector

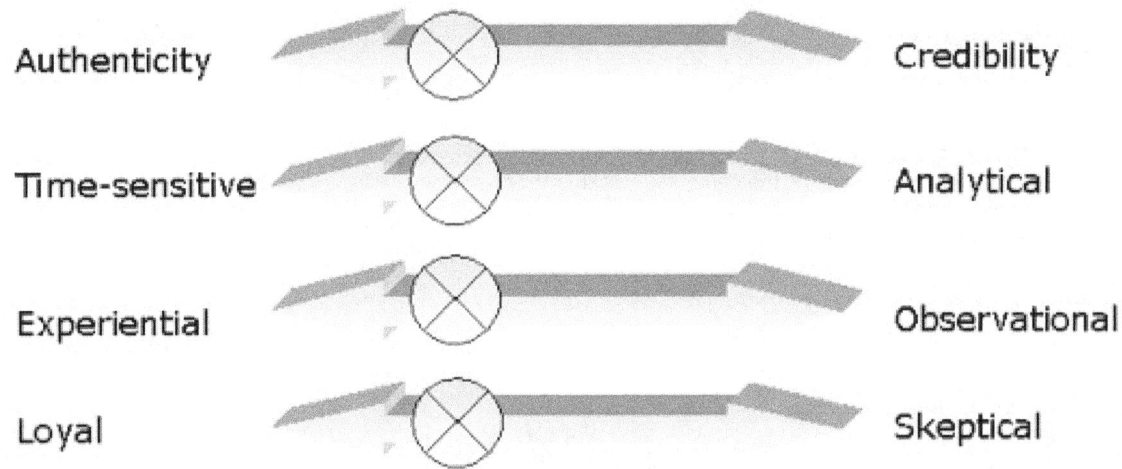

First parties share solidarity of belief that unifies them in their authenticity: (we believe that they believe what they communicate). This unity of the 'true believers' can also blind them to the views and beliefs of other groups as we see in vector 4.

FIGURE 4.8: Verbatim Query: First Persons Belong to Which First Party?

"we belong to a ****"

About 701,000 results (0.20 seconds)

We belong to a Yahoo group. When we read the messages with ...
Oct 19, 2010 ... A text box shows on the computer screen with the file name and the ... The owner of the group has two choices. One, the attachements can be ...
answers.yahoo.com/question/index?qid... - Cached

    Do you give your toddler a daily multivitamin? - Sep 27, 2010
    What hip-hop site do you belong to? - Aug 5, 2010
    More results from answers.yahoo.com »

Videos for "we belong to a ****"

  Tim Neave - We Belong To A Time
  51 sec - Feb 3, 2009
  Uploaded by nunnytv
  youtube.com

  laura zimmerman manager of clintonville ...
  7 min - Sep 27, 2010
  vidds.net

Answers.com - Why do **we belong to a diocese**
Uncategorized question: Why do **we belong to a diocese?** Can you answer this question? ... Why do **we belong to a diocese?** In: Uncategorized [Edit categories] ...
wiki.answers.com/Q/Why_do_we_belong_to_a_diocese - Cached

Virginia Bed and Breakfast, Staunton, VA, Shenandoah Valley B&B ...
We belong to a local Farm Co-op, supplying us with fresh locally-grown organic produce from May through October. The Blackfriars' Playhouse, at The American ...
www.stauntonbedandbreakfast.com/ - Cached - Similar

Joe Cocker & Jennifer Warnes – Up Where We Belong – Video ...
Jun 11, 2010 ... Monday morning; karigasniemi added Up Where **We Belong to a deleted playlist. Monday** morning; phantomviper, skynet2777, skeetey and 8 other ...
www.last.fm/music/.../_/Up+Where+We+Belong - Cached - Similar

Environmental Commitment - bioMérieux Corporate Webportal site
"**We belong to a community**" **is one** of bioMérieux's guiding principles. At each of our sites and subsidiaries throughout the world, our employees are joining ...
www.biomerieux.com/servlet/srt/bio/portail/dynPage?... - Cached - Similar

Mutual Admiration Society (song) - Wikipedia, the free encyclopedia
[edit] The song. Ubiquitous in the mid to latter 1950s, the song is famous for its catchy chorus: **We belong to a Mutual Admiration Society,**: My baby and me. ...
en.wikipedia.org/wiki/Mutual_Admiration_Society_(song) - Cached - Similar

Discussion Points

- In Figure 4.7's vector 1, we see that authenticity overwhelms credibility. However, first parties like to co-opt credibility so that they are perceived as less self-serving by third person and third parties. This is a familiar pattern of corruption when the first party squelches potentially dissenting views or uses information providers from groups of their own creation to elevate their priorities and share their views.

- Where would we witness this conflict-of-interest? Typically, it's when we connect the first party's financing a stake in the third party that unduly praises or advocates their views. These are in fact second, and not third parties since their interests are now entwined with their sponsors.

- The authenticity of first parties is rooted in the direct experiential stake they place in their organizations and activities. When viewing them as outsiders, where would we look for fissures or cracks in party unity? How could that widen the gap between the group mission and the actual tactics it practices to achieve its aims?

- First party expediency and control enable swift decisions. In a crisis, first parties take precedence over the consensus building reached through second-party deliberation and validation. For example, leading armies into combat is first party communications premised on the practicalities of survival. As noted in vector 2, decisiveness is the only option.

- Most importantly what's the smell test for first party corruption? When the leader or a select group from within use their privileged status for their own advancement at the expense of the membership. That is the world's oldest profession in the hypocrisy business: *Watch not what I say but what I do...*

GROUP: SECOND PARTY

Second party sources consist of the professional community of business partners, shareholders, regulators, customers, and rivals who all have one stake in your organization's success and at least two stakes in their own.

We're all familiar with the sensation of being blindsided. Few of us have the presence of mind to see how our blindsides figure into this. Instead, we lash out at the tattle-tale (grammar school), newsleaker (media and politics) or smell a rat who disavowed a code of silence (organized crime and old boys networks). Either way, we aim to shoot the messenger when the message they bear has escaped into the open, too late to suppress. Whether the act is a heroic defiance or a backstabbing betrayal is in the eye of (1) those directly implicated in the disclosure (first parties), and (2) the folks who hear about it third-hand via the web (third parties). Either way, their judgments are cast in the direction of second parties.

Vector Ranges

In the first vector, it's ambiguous whether second parties are behaving in a conspiratorial or collusive way or whether they are acting in a credible manner. A fairly good indication is to consider the impact on the second party for making public their opinions, i.e. a local newspaper publishing the details of falling housing prices will potentially undercut its real estate classifieds – thus elevating its credibility.

In terms of perspective-taking, second party credibility is related to how much direct influence first parties wield on them. It is often more effective to go 'off record' with second parties to gain a more personal or authentic view than the official record provides.

Second parties lie at the root of two very prevalent and universal human sensitivities – envy and resentment. Envy is a factor in the minds of onlookers when peers raise their public profiles (and the privileges and rewards that bestows). The responsorial chant echoed in the fickle nature of public opinion is to dress down or dismiss the unworthy – those undeserving of third party recognition. Resentments are stirred not necessarily when second parties deliver the good news that happens to the unworthy. It's when bad news happens to us.

- **Perspective:** Who's ahead; who's losing ground
- **Documentation:** Gossip rag
- **Verbiage:** Speculation; rumor for its own sake
- **Medium:** Paparazzi; supermarket checkout line
- **Temptation:** Compensate the first parties they expose in their reporting and bill the third parties who subscribe to the information they supply

FIGURE 4.9: Second Party Motivation Vector

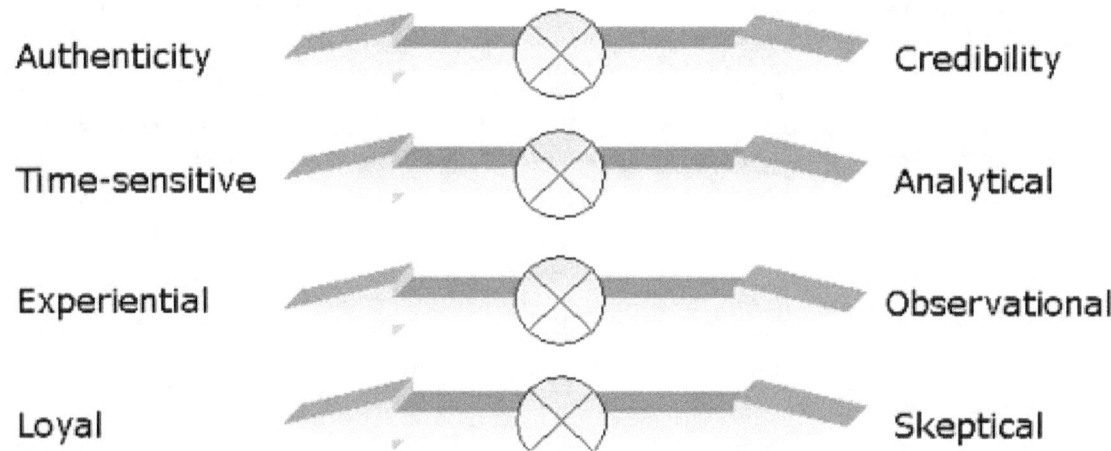

Second parties straddle the line between both ends of the motivation vectors. Too skeptical and they lose access to their first party networks. Too loyal and they may be tempted to protect their news sources from winding up as news. Too analytical and they miss their deadlines. Too authentic and their involvement supersedes the story they're covering.

UNIT FOUR: Sense-making Through Information Context | Page 4:24

FIGURE 4.10: Word Algebra Combined with Paradoxical Syntax: Talk about Mixed Signals!

Google   "(viewed | seen | perceived) as **** intitle:coward intitle:brave

Images for "(viewed | seen | perceived) as ...

 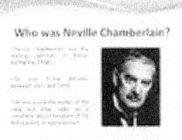  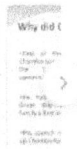

→ More images for "(viewed | seen | perceived) as **** intitle:coward intitle:brave   Report images

Was Chamberlain brave or a coward? - ppt video online ...
https://slideplayer.com/slide/3749964/
Oct 26, 2014
Learning objective – to examine the arguments for and against the policy of appeasement through cartoons I can ...

Reflecting on a Coward's brave email | The Daily Californian
https://www.dailycal.org/2013/11/22/reflecting-cowards-brave-email/ ▼
Nov 24, 2013 - I was studying on one of Dwinelle's uncomfortable benches on Wednesday when I heard a faded song from afar get louder and louder.

A coward's escape or a brave step? - Women Make Waves ...
womenmakewaves.com/cowards-escape-brave-step/
Mar 7, 2015 - One writer travelled around the world to get some clarity on an unhealthy relationship.

Searching Out Loud: Giving Voice to Independent Investigations | Marc Solomon

Discussion Points

- How do second party dynamics play out? Try this out for size:

    The messenger communicates through the second party channel to the entire group, not directly to the person directly impacted, i.e. by a layoff or passed over for a promotion. Know the scene where the shunned party points first to the newspaper and then to the first party messenger? "It's bad enough you're making the wrong decision. But you had to go behind my back for me to find this out?" That's the comprising light of second party dynamics.

- How do second parties approach first parties? Do they tip their hands or expect the same intimacy or check-in privileges as the inner circle within the organizations they're approaching? Here's one noninvasive way to pry:

    By keeping our profiles low and egos in check, we can learn much about whether second parties are behaving in a conspiratorial or collusive way or whether they are acting in a credible manner. In terms of perspective-taking, second party credibility is related to how much direct influence first parties wield on them. A fairly good indication for us is gauging the impact on the second party for making public their opinions, i.e. a media organization admits on its own website to potential conflict-of-interest between its news coverage of companies who advertise on its site.

GROUP: THIRD PARTY

"The single biggest predictor of hostility is third person plural – defined by existence of the oppositional group."

– Pennabaker, Chung, 2007[2]

Third parties have several conjugal identities. The most common to the vernacular are acknowledged experts and analysts who are entrusted to put their subscribers' interests above those of the first parties they evaluate (see Figure 4.11 below). In our motivation vector model, third parties are on the receiving end of what's filtered or processed through first and second parties. Third parties are the audiences, the juries, the focus group panels, and the viewers furiously punching their votes into their devices. Broadly speaking, third party equals *the public*. The message is an *official* one once it reaches that level of circulation.

For that reason, off-the-record comments that would be tolerated or ignored among peers have the potential to become moral scandals once they reach third party level. Even the mechanics of message creation may be standard practice between colleagues. But in the wider public sphere, ghostwriting and the falsification of authorship is fair game for litigation. **(Elliot, 2010)**[3]

It's more complicated to reach the third party when a first party communicates through a second party. Why? They want to win more votes, sell more products, or simply to gain greater advantage with or without the participation of the larger society.

Third parties are the faces in the crowd who cast their votes, respond to surveys, and don't get hung up on their fifteen minutes of fame. Instead they have fifteen minutes per day that they use to read or hear about the fame of celebrities they follow. Third parties are the audience that assembles to hear speeches or consume the latest fashions. The media keep their finger on the pulse of third parties to determine social trends and cultural dimensions of what's falling in and out of favor.

Vector Ranges

Third parties as commentators and analysts speak in the media on behalf of abstractions like *the market,* or *the consumer,* or a disenfranchised group playing the role of underdog in a public debate. Third parties are also a common way for understanding exposure: Both positive, as in receiving popular recognition for a deed or achievement, and negative, where a person's reputation can be irrevocably damaged.

Those swings of the exposure pendulum are based on this other identity of third parties as *them*. The more removed, the more impersonal, the less vested, and detached from the actual consequences to individuals.

One way to distinguish this split identity for third parties is to think of third party experts as favoring complexity because complications require their direct input. The opposite holds true for third party audiences who are predisposed to simplicity and clear-cut distinctions.

How so?

Think of the superficial stereotypes that fill the void of real experience, i.e. pro-border Americans who think that legal and illegal immigrants can be easily separated.

- **Perspective:** Why should you care
- **Documentation:** Wall Street Journal; New York Times, etc. (exception is op-ed)
- **Verbiage:** Pundits analyze relevance of day's events
- **Medium:** Top news stories; most emailed stories
- **Temptation:** Have surrogates and representatives fight on their behalf without the need for direct involvement

FIGURE 4.11: Third Party Motivation Vector

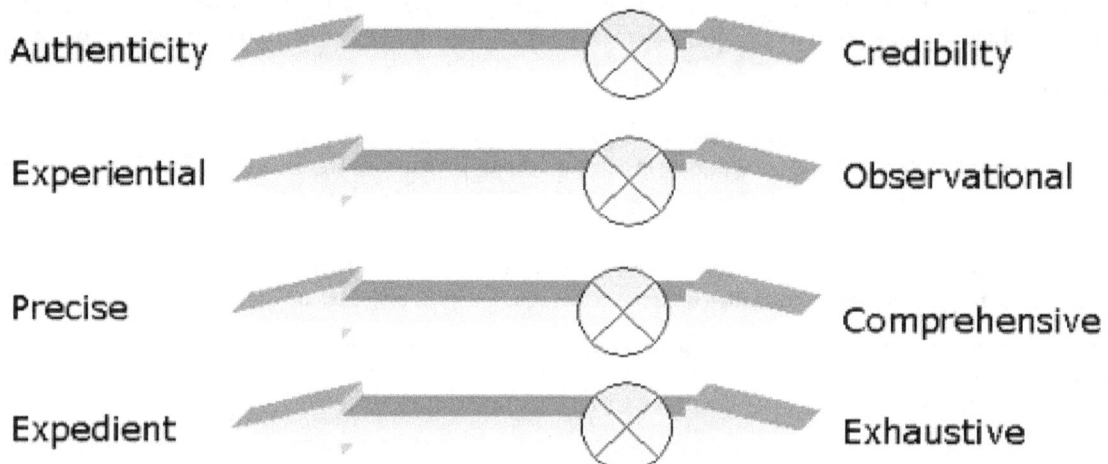

Third parties are two steps removed from the action. Third parties have the luxury of *taking in* or *thinking through* the issues of the day from the heated rhetoric and vested opinions of conflicting views and opposing camps.

FIGURE 4.12: Word Algebra Highlights the Possessive Attachment of These Detached Third Parties

```
"(analysts | researchers) * cover" ~compromise ~credible intitle:financial
```

About 152,000 results (0.37 seconds)

[PDF] The Rodney L. White Center for **Financial** Research Analyst ...
File Format: PDF/Adobe Acrobat - Quick View
by L Fang - 2004 - Cited by 10 - Related articles
compromised when the pressure for generating underwriting revenue, ... possibility that banks and **analysts tend to cover** and (are chosen to) ...... Michaely, Roni and Kent L. Womack, 1999, Conflict of Interest and the **Credibility** of ...
finance.wharton.upenn.edu/~rlwctr/papers/0424.pdf

[PDF] The Rodney L. White Center for **Financial** Research Analyst ...
File Format: PDF/Adobe Acrobat - Quick View
by L Fang - 2005 - Cited by 10 - Related articles
analysts tend to cover firms for which they hold favorable views, ...
finance.wharton.upenn.edu/~rlwctr/papers/0507.pdf

⊞ Show more results from upenn.edu

Shifting fortunes: The political economy of **financial** ...
by L Howard - 1997 - Cited by 36 - Related articles
Badly overextended, significantly **compromised** and eclipsed by presidential ..... A survey by industry **analysts Agusto Co., cover** ing 56 banks, ... Consequently, there is no **reliable** data from which to gauge the shift by firms from ...
linkinghub.elsevier.com/retrieve/pii/S0305750X9600085X - Similar

[PDF] WFC **Financial** Instruments Comment Letter
File Format: PDF/Adobe Acrobat - Quick View
Aug 19, 2010 ... and the professional **analysts who actually cover** the industry, all of whom oppose ... These highly subjective valuations will **compromise** the integrity and ..... Accordingly, it is not possible to obtain **reliable** evidence ...
www.fasb.org/cs/BlobServer?blobcol=urldata&blobtable...id...

Competition and Opportunistic Advice of Financial Analysts: Theory ...
by E Sette - 2007 - Cited by 2 - Related articles
of optimism of affiliated **analysts. When more analysts cover** a stock, ... to misreport information and in equilibrium their **credibility** could be **compromised**. ... When recommendations are **credible**, and only the message of the ...
papers.ssrn.com/sol3/Delivery.../SSRN_ID965861_code451678.pdf?...1

Google output in 2010.

UNIT FOUR: Sense-making Through Information Context | Page 4:29

Google   "(analysts | researchers) * cover" ~credible ~compromise intitle:financial

All   News   Images   Shopping   Videos   More   Settings   Tools

About 30 results (1.24 seconds)

[PDF] **Growth and Risk in Financial Analysts' Stock ...**
https://pdfs.semanticscholar.org/.../bcfb4f586b9ab3b29a1887375a008213... ▾
compromise between (1) having enough observations to avoid excessive ..... services is not large enough (28 observations) for making reliable .... study are driven by firms with high analyst following or by analysts who cover a particularly.

[PDF] **Financial Fraud and Analyst Reputation - Editorial Express**
https://editorialexpress.com/cgi-bin/conference/download.cgi?db... ▾
Jan 31, 2014 - credibility of the analyst's forecasts and consequently rely less on her ... by showing that financial analysts, particularly when they compromise .... Therefore, in our empirical analysis below, we focus on analysts who cover ...

Open PDF in Browser
https://papers.ssrn.com/sol3/.../SSRN_ID2924661_code102678.pdf?...1...
We also provide evidence on several plausible mechanisms through which industry ..... compromise analysts' willingness to be effective monitors if their monitoring may .... Average number of firms followed by analysts that cover the.

[PDF] **Industry expertise and monitoring effectiveness of financial ...**
www.fmaconferences.org/Orlando/Papers/analystmonitoring.pdf ▾
by D Bradley - 2015 - Cited by 12 - Related articles
relationship could compromise analysts' willingness to be effective monitors if their monitoring may .... "Conflict of interest and the credibility of underwriter analyst ...... Average number of firms followed by analysts that cover the subject firm.

The same query in 2019. Note the diminishing presence of related articles, academic citations, and the disappearance of the cascading "Show more like this or "- Similar" articles from referring links.

Searching Out Loud: Giving Voice to Independent Investigations | Marc Solomon

Discussion Points

- With the advent of social media, this kind of trend-watching is becoming more widespread and applied to smaller, discrete groups. Rather than income, race, or age, all one needs are the collective histories that enjoin us in our social networks.

- What kind of history? As investigators we should aim our search target sites on the fixations and passions of first parties. Any obsession will do – especially a common interest that clarifies and isolates the priorities of a single issue, shared interest, or common threat.

- How do we leverage third parties as the standard-bearers for credibility? The more active version of third parties involves observers who deliberately keep their professional distance from the first parties they assess. Research organizations, rating agencies, and government oversight functions, for example, are third parties whose influence is determined by how credibly they maintain their independence from the leaders and organizations they evaluate. The moment that distance is impugned by a conflict of interest, they lose their independence as well as their authority.

- Can we as investigators rig the deck? 'Course not. We can no more speak for third parties as we can effectively arbitrate on brokering the best programs, most influential networks, or visionary leaders. What we can do is tap our query formation tools to track the arguments being made and the opinions being swayed. What we can do is measure the messages sent by first parties and those sent by second parties. Want a formula for credibility? It's there in this comparison.

Credibility is about Independence

We often overhear how certain messagers and public figures see their reputations and fortunes rise and fall according to their credibility. In this light, a provider's ability to be taken at their word, in fact taken seriously at all, is based on the highly intuitive choices we make to pay attention to or tune out from what the messenger is providing us.

With so many competing messages and channels for receiving them, credibility is not just a stronger hand for making speeches or taking positions. It is a precious asset that information providers forfeit at their own peril.

Credibility for Message Receivers

Investigators share this critical dependence on the virtue of being credible. To lose credibility is not just to be perceived as less knowledgeable or attention-worthy. It is an indictment on the investigator's judgment – our critical ability to process events and analyze outcomes. Our analysis runs independent of how this impacts the persons and groups standing to gain or lose from the conclusions we reach.

Independence is not only critical to an investigation. It is often the only factor working in favor of the investigator. That's because the players we engage through our web searches and subsequent interviews will regard us as complete strangers – not only to them personally. It's also to the loyalties they may be honoring with their actions.

The most effective way to be less invasive or threatening? Come to the table with an open mind. Easy enough? Not exactly.

Often our background research or cursory understandings lead us to harbor suspicions that preclude alternative explanations or more complete understandings. These instinctual perceptions are a huge threat to our credibility. The last way we want our interviews to go is for the entire discussion to be about what we investigators intend to do with the information we're given. That guarantees two outcomes: (1) inaccurate and/or misleading statements from, (2) folks who have little to say about subjects they know entirely well.

That's why the background work we do prior to direct questioning of a witness, expert, or potential team member is foundational to the success of the investigation. It's not that search engines find us the guilt, innocence, or suitability of the folks we google first before we meet. It's that our web investigation is the strongest case we can make for our own credibility because:

1. An expanded knowledge of our search targets keeps the focus away from ourselves; and
2. Exposure to the differing views within our PCF helps us to keep perspective (and a healthy distance from the issue in question)

The second point is all the more critical when we're called in 'to keep tabs on someone' or inform a decision based on the need for *closer* scrutiny.

- When do thoughts *not* occur to us?
- When do we believe invalidated evidence?

Typically, it's not when we're drawing in that evidence but when we're drawing unsupportable conclusions. We're rushing to judgment when we shouldn't be rushing or judging. The more we identify with a victim or a cause, or a policy position, the more we compromise our effectiveness to lead or manage independent investigations.

There is perhaps a third point for using credibility to keep us researchers honest and on track. And it goes like this: We don't compromise the evidence by oversimplifying issues or fixating on a single person or party.

That's the need to thread together our people and topic searches. Our web investigation should set its sights on search targets that include both people and the ideas that galvanize them. It's rare that we will ever focus exclusively on an individual, or say, a public policy. In fact, often when we hit a failsafe, it's because we've failed to balance the larger social dimension of an elusive person or the personal aspects of a broad policy issue. Both targets support the overall research aim. For example, we witness...

- Irregularities in how an executive handles their company's operations
- How a criminal network perpetrates hoaxes, scams, and frauds on unsuspecting consumers

CREDIBILITY AS SOCIAL DYNAMIC

So what happens when the credibility questions shifts back to the information provider? First of all, researchers are compromised when we're considered actors or participants in the cases we're trying to uncover. Secondly, we want to find search targets that share the same need for perspective that we do. That doesn't mean we both share the same understandings, knowledge, or perspectives. It simply means they can see the people and topics we pursue from both a vested and detached perspective.

Where do we find such people?

Perhaps an ideal blend of direct experience and elevated perspective exists with former employees. Members of an extended social network like LinkedIn may be willing to talk about their past encounters with our search targets. They are speaking from first-hand accounts of the person's job performance, sense of team play, and even their personal quirks and work habits. The level of candor increases in these situations precisely because ex-employees are free from the threat of reprisals or political infighting that results from (1) exposing a colleague, or (2) voicing opinions that would otherwise attract public attention to a private matter.

This kind of impunity can also be found on a group level where organizations are largely self-supporting. Also, its members are brought together through a more sustaining purpose than individual financial gain. A phrase like "one of the most influential organizations you've never heard of" draws a compelling picture of a group whose effectiveness is based on a *mission* or higher calling. Such groups carry more credibility because they are free of the need to keep up a public appearance. Most commercial success is dependent on public recognition. Hence, the need to attract attention through marketing or lobbying efforts.

Grounded (and Unfounded) Suspicions

When do we know credibility is in short supply? When do we need to sprout our antennas to pick up the credibility signals that others miss? That depends in large part on who's doing the talking and who they're communicating to. A dead giveaway that the hounds are on the prowl? When we come across requests for anonymity in the media. This tells us that either the information provider...

- Is talking to imaginary people and making the whole thing up, or themselves, or
- An insider has the need to make a statement they can't bring themselves to stand behind for fear of facing legal retribution or the angry mob with pitchforks assembled outside their corner office

Going on the record could mean our whistleblower is...

- A person of strong character and integrity
- Surrendering names to authorities in the hope of getting leniency in their sentencing
- Disclosing a selective version of past events to distract investigators from other details they wish to remain suppressed
- All of the above

The Candor of Strangers

Our more savvy friends and business contacts know where to find our buttons and how to push them. They know how to curry favor, sing our praises, or even voice their displeasure that grabs our immediate attention. But when perfect strangers exchange their views, their opinions pack an impact that the folks we know really can't match. Ever find yourself talking to a total stranger on an airplane?

Assuming this is a one-time meeting, they have no incentive to tell us anything but the unvarnished truth about how we appear, or what they perceive about us. Impersonal intimacy happens in the virtual world when we inspire total strangers to post responses on our Facebook pages, or engage us on discussion boards. It's not the ulterior motives of those in our networks but the power of an idea that helps us see buttons we are pressing, without even knowing it – and then – boom! Out of nowhere a dialog ensues about how someone else relates to what we're sharing.

The Guise of Celebrities

Unlike that stranger slumped into seat 22C on your last flight, celebrated newsmakers like entertainers and athletes operate within the staged distortions of the public spotlight. Our BS detectors must be calibrated to the amplification of otherwise mundane asides. These trivial personal details become bold social declarations when the media juxtaposes an absent-minded comment with the macro trend it reinforces: Think male politicians referring to the female reporter at the press conference as 'sweetheart.' The upshot? A Knowledge-ABLED investigator cannot take celebrity interviews at face value because of the potentially explosive nature of these off-the-cuff comments.

And it's not just the whiff of scandal that our BS sniffers are sensing in these public displays. The intent to diffuse controversy or disarm a potential adversary is no less a distortion than a less-than-innocent gaffe. Here are some potential signs that an on-the-record exchange reflects the back-channel coaching our celebrated witness received than the actual transcripts we're reviewing:

1. **Intimacy** – The celebrity confides something to this drone reporter he would never spill on the lap of the competing story producer.
2. **Regret** – The big name embraces the faceless reporter as a confidante – not just a mere immortal cigar-puffing hack.
3. **Gratitude** – The star is uncomfortable conferring credit unto himself and directs the reporter to give his teammates equal billing. Deities of choice may rank even higher.
4. **Uncertainty** – Nothing is less natural for a drone reporter than to detect an air of uncertainty. The planting of doubt in all its tortured forms bears the very seeds of authenticity. It's the unresolved aspects of twists and turns that made great narratives in the past and in the foreseeable future.

SOURCING CREDIBLE REFERENCES

Don't go to the source. Go to the recipient. That's the rule for raising the credibility factor in our investigations. What am I getting at here?

Up until now, we've viewed the roles and responsibilities of second parties as reporters or agents for transferring the knowledge and affairs of first parties to third party publics and constituencies. They have another common, well-defined, and sincere role to play as receivers of first party goods and services. Yes, second party buying groups are customers too.

Who has our attention when we research a big ticket item and solicit authority opinions? Is it the supplier of the product? Is it the supplier's rivals or the broader industry they belong in? Vendors and the segments they compete in express views of themselves that are by definition self-serving, at best questionable, and more times than not, self-selecting.

Why is this a more credible position than what reporters provide? Customers are waging actual dollars by staking their fortunes to those of their suppliers. That kind of commitment is certainly more binding than the heresy of a second party reporter, or analyst who might not even use or understand the products they're retained to publicize.

Former U.S. Defense Secretary Robert Gates summed up the same sincerity rationale succinctly in the the aftermath of the WikiLeaks controversy in 2010 when he said:

> "The fact is governments deal with the United States because it's in their interest, not because they like us, not because they trust us, and not because they believe we can keep secrets."
>
> – Farhan (2010)[4]

LATERAL THINKING AS A CREDIBILITY CHECK

Lateral thinking is an approach to problem-solving where an indirect response provides the best answer.[5] Being one step removed from an information source removes the firsthand bias that compromises the perceptions of first persons and parties. We see this in our focus on credibility as the gold standard for assessing the quality of the evidence we're reviewing.

We can apply lateral thinking to our investigations when we do the following:

1. Blend firsthand experience (authenticity) and third-party observation (credibility) by focusing on second persons or second parties with direct (personal) experience of your primary search target.

2. Recognize that those with direct experience look at those individuals (our targets) through the performance of services and actions – not through self-promotion, self-referential words, or purchased endorsements.

The best way to trust the judgments we hear is to 'walk across the block' or extrapolate who stands to gain/lose from its investment in our search targets.

In that spirit, from a PCF perspective, consider these ground rules:

1. Always start from the premise that there is an interdependent relationship between first and second parties
2. Hear from an industry that enjoys a symbiotic link to the one in question
3. Examples of the most reliable (credible) sources to use when we're assessing an investigation target include these anchoring perspectives: Are they observers, participants and how vested are they in the outcomes of the targets they're tracking?

FIGURE 4.13: Symbiotic Relationships for Sourcing Credibility

Supplier (First Party)	Recipient (Second Party)
1. Public company profiles	Investment securities firms
2. Regulatory battles	Trade associations
3. Household appliances	Electric utilities
4. Retailers	Credit card issuers
5. Media	Advertising agencies / leading advertisers
6. Airlines	Hotels
7. Construction	Real estate
8. Consumer electronics	Batteries
9. Road food / highway construction	Truck drivers

Conjugating the Verbiage

The nine instances shown in Figure 4.13 above reinforce lessons drawn from the following materials:

1. Steps that involve combining search tools and source groupings, introduced in **Units Two** and **Three**

2. Ways to see through the dynamics of the message senders and recipients we've identified through provider conjugation, introduced here in **Unit Four**

3. Expanding our proficiency in interpreting and leveraging information sources according to their credibility and vested interests as information providers

Extrapolation in Action

We all know the cliche about elected leaders speaking their minds in public...

> *Question: What's the first signs that our politicians are not being entirely candid?*
>
> *Answer: When their lips move.*

We all know that banks get robbed because that's where the money is – even by their own bankers. Our powers of BS detection are tested and strengthened each day when elected officials, corporate leaders, and attention-starved celebrities keep two separate ledgers: (1) their words, and (2) deeds.

The paper-based journalism industry may never recover. But exposing hypocrisy is as much a winning business model as a self-protective impulse that keeps our *honest* doubts in line with our *reasonable* expectations.

So how do we keep our BS detectors in working order during our techie research missions? After all, there's so much to sift through that the volume of pros and cons overwhelms those vows we make to stand our middle ground. To see the trade-offs from false choices. To map those choices to our business, our values, our clients. Period.

In the technology business, it helps to lower the degrees of separation from trade show evangelists to the unassuming functional managers. BS levels drop when we're dealing with working stiffs, e.g. middle managers like me. That's because we don't seek the victory of a sales closing. We crave the solace of living within our system choices. That doesn't mean anyone manning the trade show booth has a used car they want to pawn off on those walking the hall.

But it does mean that the folks who earn their keep by holding costs down care more about war stories than case studies. They care about the unexpected experience than the full feature list. They couch those potential conflicts less in terms of how the program works and more in terms of the peers they'll have to work with. They are not looking outside for recognition, but within their organizations for the internal approval needed to pull resources and manage the project.

The Limits of Provider Conjugation

So far we've applied the PCF to each of the roles and situations that impact the sending and receiving of individual and group-based communications. We've reviewed this in terms of typical situations, dynamics and behaviors that occur within first, second, and third person and party contexts.

This model is useful – to a point. As we saw in souring credible references, PCF is key to ascribing motivations to senders and receivers alike. It's an excellent tool for measuring the self-interest of the message sender against the perceptions and sometimes conflicting agendas of those it reaches.

But PCF has the potential to create more confusion than it explains because it is context-dependent. We may be members of a trade association with inside knowledge of how a sister member from a separate industry operates. We might also be an individual consumer who makes purchases independently of whether or not that benefits our employer or the other trade group members. Sounds a bit dense, no?

The problem is that most of us dependent spirits take actions on behalf of ourselves and the groups we represent. Trying to untangle these arrangements would be challenging under the simplest arrangements and the most acute record-keeping. If a message is communicated in public, can we automatically assume it's a façade or intended to mislead a gullible set of recipients? Conversely, can we assume a conflict of interest if we later learn that an internal debate around that communication was hotly contested? No, we cannot put our own fears and suspicions above the body of evidence we're evaluating.

The upshot? Provider Conjugation makes sense to use in fixed, recurring situations where the roles are well-established and the rules of engagement are understood by all participants. For more fluid situations where the characters are harder to cast, the outcomes are more uncertain, and the ambiguities outweigh the absolutes, we apply another contextual tool – the Vectors of Integrity.

Analyzing Context: The Vectors of Integrity

- What is an integrity vector?
- How is this different than provider conjugation?
- Where and when do we apply it to validate the findings in our research?

When we first assessed some common information exchanges in the PCF model, we assigned information attributes to the motivation vectors of those exchanges. We looked at opposing forces that are neither uniformly positive or negative factors. Both feed the context of the evidence communicated in our investigations.

Two seminal and opposable forces we considered were credibility and authenticity. We also contrasted precision and comprehensiveness, loyalty and skepticism, etc. Independently, each factor sounds desirable. Can a researcher be too comprehensive in their research? Can an investigator really have too much credibility in their findings?

Well ... um ... in fact, yes.

It's not exactly that any body of knowledge yields an excessive and unhealthy dose of credibility. It's that the detachment it conveys requires the counterweight of authenticity in order to be both: (1) believed, and (2) acted on. Credibility on its own lacks the realism that can only be captured through a shared and vested interest riding on a tangible and specific outcome. Otherwise, it's too abstract. It's removed from the actual people that an exceedingly credible decision will impact.

That's where integrity strides in to vet the evidence we collect, the arguments that tunnel under our skin, and the doubts we face as second-hand witnesses to the persons, institutions, and records we investigate.

Integrity of Character

Think of a soldier-turned-politician who advocates for peace – someone who's lived firsthand what most of us can only invoke through metaphor and delusion. That's a person of impeccable experience and observation. Unlike the uncomplicated stereotypes we used in the PCF, our statesman example is not mapped to the extreme of either vector but rooted in the center.

He reflects back on his life in the balance when the bullets flew first-hand. But he also knows the need for protocol and temperance. He knows that passion around the negotiating table can be as much a liability to negotiation as going into battle without a weapon.

Now let's revisit some of those plot points we introduced in the earlier vectors. Where or how could integrity be located in the cross-roads of the following continuums? Here are the nine pairings:

FIGURE 4.14: The Vectors of Integrity

1. Authentic ← → Credible
2. Experiential ← → Observational
3. Loyal ← → Skeptical
4. Active ← → Deliberative
5. Strategic ← → Tactical
6. Structured ← → Flexible
7. Original ← → Tested
8. Precise ← → Comprehensive
9. Expedient ← → Exhaustive

The Political Dartboard

Now let's break it down into something real. Since we started out with our war hero statesman, let's stick with the same prism for applying integrity vectors in a sphere of influence even the most apolitical among us have a hard time escaping. The analogy is especially useful in the United States, given the country's two party political system which reduces the complexities of all policy issues to a single binary lens of:

5. Public or private

6. Red state or blue state

7. Caucasion or *of color*

8. For us or against us, etc.

If we look at the creeping influence of cable news channels, we see an accepted and instructive narrative in the undercurrent of nearly every news story. It's home team versus away team. It's Republican against Democrat. It's the right and left punching each other out in sound-bytes and competing narratives. Heroes and scapegoats are assigned credit and blame for the 'sound' policies they craft and promote and the 'failed' policies they trash and try to repeal.

Even political leaders who lack charisma or good debating skills can seize the limelight when the trashing becomes personal. The less principled and consistent the stances taken, the easier it is to cast the petty aspersions than to debate the great issues. But it's simpler to size up the person than to determine the future merits of an abstract policy. And it's certainly easier to spool campaign cash into ads that communicate on those terms. **(Frum, 2012)**[6]

On the political playing field, authenticity stems from absolutism. Staking out an absolute position is the equivalent to an exclusive showing of a house, an official sponsorship of an event, or an original work that can't be duplicated. Absolutism is on display in maniacal quests to be President, i.e. the *severity* of Governor Mitt Romney's conservatism in the 2012 Republican primaries. Positions on issues are rearranged around this priority, pretty much to the exclusion of the others (or that of future primary seasons).

From a policy perspective, that's what's known as a flip-flop. But from a character perspective, that's genuine authenticity. His accusers label him a fake because all his convictions dwell within this single aspiration. He can always rework whatever he rationalizes in public. Are his convictions baseless? Not if his resolute wish to be President forms the basis of his public life. That's fair game for satirists, historians, journalists, and ultimately voters. PCFs won't tip the election or even cast a judgment – other than we need to consider our political candidates as individuals, and as leaders, and decide: Can we live with the contradictions formed by these often diverging identities?

Integrity Vectors

Now let's apply the generalities of political reporting to each of the vectors. For each diametrical force, we will consider how integrity straddles the center, drawing strength from the extremes but not their excesses.

As we're about to see, each indicator in Figure 4.14 includes a range (continuum) to plot active and passive behaviors (observational and experiential vectors). Each continuum forms the context. What does that context tell us?

1. How integrity embodies the virtues of each opposable force, and
2. How its absence leads to an imbalance, posing a compromising influence of those same forces

Evidence our first indicator: The agenda vector.

VECTOR:	OBSERVATIONAL	EXPERIENTIAL
AGENDA:	Take nothing at face value	Take no prisoners

1) Authentic Versus Credible

Authentic candidates are seen as genuine and emotionally honest (if not steadfast in their beliefs). A candidate lacking authenticity is perceived as artificial, appearing more fickle and sensitive to the political winds than their own convictions and principles. But as we have seen in our PCF travels, pure authenticity can blind messengers who are completely beholden to their own subjective experience. Conversely, a credible messenger is open to a broad range of inputs and opinions. But a well-rounded perspective is an empty one, devoid of direct experience and personal connection.

Vector Positioning: Integrity stakes out the middle of the integrity vector. A person of integrity keeps enough distance from a decision to see the motivations and perspectives of clashing parties. But that distance is not so remote or *safe* that it's based on secondhand or purely observational evidence.

VECTOR:	OBSERVATIONAL	EXPERIENTIAL
Professional Virtue:	Credible	Authentic

2) Experiential Versus Observational

This is the old argument that one story is worth a thousand words – or perhaps a million numbers. For instance, it's easier for people to open their hearts (and wallets) when adversity can be personified through the bloated belly of a famished orphan. That's the subjective experience of suffering. It's raw and emotional, naked, and real. It's a mere drop in the quantifiable bucket of the ravages of poverty. But if our brains are told that five million African children go to bed hungry, guess what? That abstraction doesn't measure up to response drawn from the illustration of the personal – the indelible immediacy of one person's plight. (University of Oregon Study)[7]

At first glance, this makes no sense, says Jonah Lehrer, the author of **How We Decide**:

> "We should give away more money when we are informed about the true scope of the problem, not less. Why do we do this? The depressing statistics leave us cold, even when they are truly terrible."

And yet, concludes Lehrer, the good news is that we're still wired to care about each other:

> "We feel pleasure when someone else feels better."

Vector Positioning: The balancing of experience and observation is very much a balancing act. In his book **Adaptive Leadership**, Ronald Heifetz talks about the two perspectives that uphold our notion of integrity – the need for a simultaneous presence on: (1) the figurative dance floor and, (2) balcony of the public arena:

> "The 'balcony' (looking down on the 'dance') is where you get a larger perspective of what you're facing and how you are doing with your response. From here you do your observing of patterns, reflecting, option thinking, analyzing and monitoring of the change. When you take action and make an intervention, you have stepped onto the 'dance floor' and are participating in the dance. For example, you convene a meeting, announce a strategy, create a task force, restructure, and reassign some staff." **(Heifetz, 2009)**[8]

The point, Heifetz maintains, is that one needs to switch between roles – often with little warning and certainly without the time needed for full deliberation or engagement.

VECTOR:	OBSERVATIONAL	EXPERIENTIAL
Orientation:	Objective	Subjective

3) Loyal Versus Skeptical

Skeptical candidates are analytical creatures. They prioritize consistency of logic and credibility over faith and commitment. Loyalists stick to their hunches, espousing allegiance over skepticism, and action over deliberation. Loyalists are seen as pledged to authenticity virtue – even when the surfacing facts fly against the broader strategy that carries familiar and oft-repeated arguments and rationales.

Vector Positioning: Integrity insists on proof. It doesn't offer unconditional buy-ins for plans or rationales because they sound plausible or curry favor. But once proven, integrity holds to the conviction required to serve higher principles, at the expense of personal gains and self-preservation.

VECTOR:	OBSERVATIONAL	EXPERIENTIAL
Personal Virtue:	Skepticism	Loyalty

4) Active Versus Deliberative

A person of action wants their deeds to speak louder than their oratory or their intellect. Decisive commanders express confidence in their decisions and rarely look back. Action-based leaders favor a one-sided approach: Goal-oriented, sometimes to the exclusion of ambiguous feedback and dissenting views.

Deliberative leaders are more reflective, characterized by a process-oriented approach for reaching consensus, compromise, and resolution. They revisit past decisions and leave prior commitments open to question and revision, accused of indecision or saddled with *paralysis through analysis.* Integrity seeks a balance of planning and execution so that whatever unplanned outcomes result can be addressed – even after the initial plan is carried out.

Vector Positioning: Integrity blends the urgency to move forward with the willingness to take informed risks. Decisions are not impulsive and information-gathering serves a purpose. Collection is not for the sake of collecting. Listening is not to strike a thoughtful pose but to give fullest consideration.

VECTOR:	OBSERVATIONAL	EXPERIENTIAL
Process:	Analysis	Action

5) Strategic Versus Tactical

One common continuum used by students of leadership is the interdependency between the grand designs of strategy and the concrete steps of tactical advancement. In our earlier **Unit One**-based SPM model we see this trade-off in the relationship between purpose (the *why* in search project management) and objectives (the 'where' we're going aspect of SPM).

In politics, the strategist is the statesman – the analytically-inclined visionary who tends to favor strategies based on 'big picture thinking' and their global implications – even to the point of grandiosity. The opposing vector is held by the political operative. Operatives are the infantry. They are the boots on the ground in political turf battles. They focus on clear and present objectives and rarely stray from actions that trigger fixed and measurable returns.

Vector Positioning: Integrity seeks to stretch boundaries without pushing too far too fast. Cutting a deal must be based on: (1) the enlightened self-interest of opposing parties with *skin in the game*, and, (2) enough face-saving to provide political cover for the ground ceded by opposing parties.

VECTOR:	OBSERVATIONAL	EXPERIENTIAL
CONTRACT:	Investments & Partnerships	Pacts & Oaths

6) Structured Versus Flexible

Structured is a looser construct for the more politically-charged *idealogical*. It means that candidates see the world through a lens that gives consistency to their decisions. It injects an air of probability to anticipated responses of future events as they unfold. Structured leaders are often commanding in their leadership, especially when that candidate enjoys widely favored position. This position shields him from attack. A more precarious position describes traditionally sensitive *no-win* issues where the candidate is vulnerable for asserting any position.

Flexibility expands the range of options and the uncertainties that come with them. Flexible decision-makers engage in dissonant and complex issues. This pits them in the role of conciliator and broker of clashing parties. Flexible leaders are attentive listeners. However, a full appreciation for the stakes (and potential downsides) faced by competing interests poses additional risks to conciliators. They will be accused of abandoning the people, causes, and reneging on the commitments that first brought them to power.

Vector Positioning: A middle ground between these two extremes would blend the two-way dialog of more flexible thinking with the one-sided determination of the structured approach. The integrity of the two means a process-oriented style for reaching consensus, compromise, and resolution. There is no surrender to one's principles or the deal-breakers deemed to be off the negotiating table.

VECTOR:	OBSERVATIONAL	EXPERIENTIAL
POSTURE:	Impartial	Committed

7) Original Versus Tested

One of the most convincing ways a leader can play both sides of the authentic versus credibility card is to portray the role of the 'original' – someone who can't be held to the traditional rules of political gravity because *the mold was broken when they made [blank]*. That introduces the element of destiny to an otherwise routine checklist of candidate foibles and tendencies.

Originals are also Rorschach Tests – blank canvasses where voters can project their aspirations and desires for a better future. By design, these candidacies are untested. The intrusion of an actual track record steals the romance from incumbent candidates. The devil-you-know counterclaim? At least we know what we're getting.

Vector Positioning: Integrity doesn't dismiss the realities of the recent past nor the possibilities of a foreseeable future. How willing it is to honor the history and uphold the promise depends on how those understandings are reached. In this case, the two opposable forces on the vector are either legalistic and documentable, or more loyalty-based and confidential.

VECTOR:	OBSERVATIONAL	EXPERIENTIAL
WORLDVIEW:	"This is a complicated issue"	"This is a dangerous place"

8) Precise Versus Comprehensive

Precision is not in the engineering world where math calculations are peer reviewed and repeatable to the satisfaction of other practicing experts. In the rhetorical world, precision means striking nerves. Sometimes it's fact-based. But the evidence is highly selective and the delivery is equally important, hinging on the vocal inflection of the speech or sound byte it dwells in.

A comprehensive message is selling its attention to detail and the many ways a series of actions may play out in due course. Often the comprehensive pitch loses the comprehension of its intended audience. The need to *cover all bases* with its attention to process and method often clouds over the clear outcomes a comprehensive approach is intended to deliver.

Vector Positioning: Integrity doesn't over-rely on first impressions, gut instincts, or an inflated sense of its own judgments of character. But it doesn't farm out its bidding and jawboning to surrogates. An agreement without an emotional commitment is a hollow one, and prone to the rewrites of unreliable circumstances.

VECTOR:	OBSERVATIONAL	EXPERIENTIAL
OUTCOME:	Permission	Trust

9) Expedient Versus Exhaustive

There's the side that takes up arms. There's not a moment to waste or a resource to squander. And then there's the side that takes up time, digging in their dragging heels until the clock winds down. There's the force for change and the countervailing force of resistance.

The maniacal focus of journalists to referee these conflicts can compromise their judgment. Linguist Deborah Tannen calls this "a single-minded devotion to balance [that] creates the illusion of equivalence where there is none." **(Tannen study)**[9]

Political campaigns are all about two things. One (money) gets the glory and the other (timing) is scarcely mentioned. But it's through the scheduling that campaigns can revive neglected issues or recast and direct long-simmering resentments in newfound ways. Issue avoidance can lull voters into a false sense of security, just as a jarring recurrence can trigger a reflexive backlash. It is the wild card of unforeseeable events that force the hand of the best-laid campaign plans. It's the severity of external pressures that drive internal adjustments to the timing, emphasis, and pacing of campaign messages.

When to turn up the heat of campaign rhetoric, lower it, or turn it on in the first place? These are questions traditionally addressed in focus groups and phone polling. However, in the social media landscape, these scenarios can be factored into the temperature of hot button issues within any given location and electoral cycle.

A web-based sample of information providers can be used to gauge relationships, character perceptions, and the issues that frame them according to stakeholder perspectives. This wide-ranging group includes civic groups, advocates, enforcement agencies, commentators, media outlets, ad placements, and campaign forums. Regardless of the political turf or the interest of each player, there is a conjugal exchange to be mapped, and ultimately measured through our **Unit Four** modeling techniques.

Vector Positioning: When does Integrity cross over from the fact-finding and dot-connecting to close ranks behind a course of action? Typically that precipice is reached when our investment outweighs any second-guessing or foreseen doubts that would cause us to turn back or disown our own conclusions or decision-making.

VECTOR:	OBSERVATIONAL	EXPERIENTIAL
FINAL STATEMENT:	Draws conclusions	Makes decisions

The Verdict on Vectors

The occupation with politics and heads of state are not meant to limit all illustrations to its hyper-conflicted portrayal on cable news and Twitter. Politicians are but one form of celebrity that invites endless speculations between (1) what public figures say in prepared statements, and (2) how those posturings square with the unscripted, authentic selves that can only exist off-camera.

Relationship vectors are not some truth serum that uncovers falsehoods and seeds of corruption. They're a diagnostic tool that helps us to weigh the objective and subjective-based experience of our search targets, even how we're perceived by others in that pursuit.

Vector Positioning: Integrity is the first player to toss their hat in the ring and last player in the room to pick sides. As we saw in the active-deliberative vector, integrity means active listening without being drawn into factional disputes. Observer or participant – which direction do you naturally lean? I bet the answers are as subjective as the circumstances are unique!

VECTOR:	OBSERVATIONAL	EXPERIENTIAL
MEMBERSHIP:	"With us AND against us"	"With us OR against us"

FIGURE 4.15: Summary of Integrity Vectors

MODEL	OBSERVATION	EXPERIENCE
AGENDA:	Take nothing at face value	Take no prisoners
PROFESSIONAL VIRTUE:	Credibility	Authenticity
ORIENTATION:	Objective	Subjective
EXPECTATION:	Skepticism	Conviction
PERSONAL VIRTUE:	Skepticism	Loyalty
PROCESS:	Analysis	Action
CONTRACT:	Investments & Partnerships	Pacts & Oaths
POSTURE:	Impartial	Committed
WORLDVIEW:	"This is a complicated issue"	"This is a dangerous place"
OUTCOME:	Trust	Permission
FINAL STATEMENT:	Draws conclusions	Makes decisions
MEMBERSHIP:	"With us AND against us"	"With us OR against us"

SECTION 4:2 | The Value of Social Information

As we saw in **Unit Three**, the web as an information ocean has a simple ocean surface. It's called Google, or more precisely what is visible (indexed by search engines) or invisible (the **Deep Web**). That surface is what we referred to as the Internet Radar.

Now that we've introduced several analytical tools for evaluating our search results, we will revisit our radars and calibrate them to the settings of the PCF ("Provider Conjugation Framework"). That way we know what we can reasonably expect in managing the Resource-based **Information Types**, first introduced in **Unit Three**'s Project Resources section. Our new PCF tool reveals how far removed our search targets are from the actions under investigation. Moreover, we can apply this not just to targets, but also the actions and outcomes associated with them.

As we saw at the beginning of **Unit Four**, information exchanges are essential to understanding the comfort zones between information sources and recipients. The jarring reality of our radar screens is that many of our most intimate transactions are not only visible to others, but sequestered from us. This partition between what institutions know about us and what we know of ourselves is particularly insidious. It's not in the interest of those institutions to make these details available to us. How does that play out in our contextual frameworks? Actually, the less guarded we are about our personal identities, the more plentiful – and authentic – the information that can be collected for (and against) us.

Earlier in this unit, we looked at information exchange and how this impacts communications between individuals and other individuals, small and larger groups. What we didn't examine was the more daunting exchange between larger groups in communications about individuals. To harken back to our original insights in **Unit One** on blindspots, these communications about us are likely to exclude us. At least without the aid of a highly-skilled forensics expert or First Amendment attorney.

This is not the kind of a blindspot where our dentist tells us to wear out night guards, lest we grind our molars into nubs of their former selves. This is the kind of blindspot where nondisclosure of larger institutions is key to such evidence-gathering. In the case of private industry, that reason is to sell us more of what we want. In the case of governments, it's to protect us from potential enemies of the state. In either case, electronic eavesdropping is as much a given part of digital connectivity as our estrangement from the larger society when we go offline.

This book does not address the risk of our civil liberties or the need for their protection per se. There is nothing in these pages that shows how to hack into a resource, issue a DNS ("Denial of Service") order against blasphemous websites. We don't address staunching the flow of information that spreads far and wide to third parties we cannot verify, trust, or knowingly support. That is a decidedly off-radar form of information usefulness both in terms of its availability, application, and quite frankly, the extent of my expertise.

UNIT FOUR: Sense-making Through Information Context | Page 4:47

USING PCF TO RENDER RADAR SCREENS

In **Unit Three**, we caught a glimpse in Figure 3.36 of the great and sometimes blurry divide between above and below radar of project sources. We saw how genealogical milestones like births and marriages coincided with business and legal transactions like licensing, employment histories, and personal financial assets.

How hard it is to obtain these records is not a matter of subjective experience. It's evolving policies and technologies that cause the continual shifting of boundaries between what lies above and below radar. The lines drawn between personal and private are in constant flux. They depend on state regulations, court rulings, and the ability of marketers to mine the usage patterns and data trails of web consumers.

We can use PCF to model the inferential line that exists between public and private communications. As the mapping below indicates, that shifting radar floats on the backs of second persons and parties. Quite simply, it all boils down to this: Now that I know, am I a reservoir or a vessel — a container or a conduit? Do I sit on this information or pass it on?

FIGURE 4.16: Mapping Provider Conjugation to What's on or off the Radar

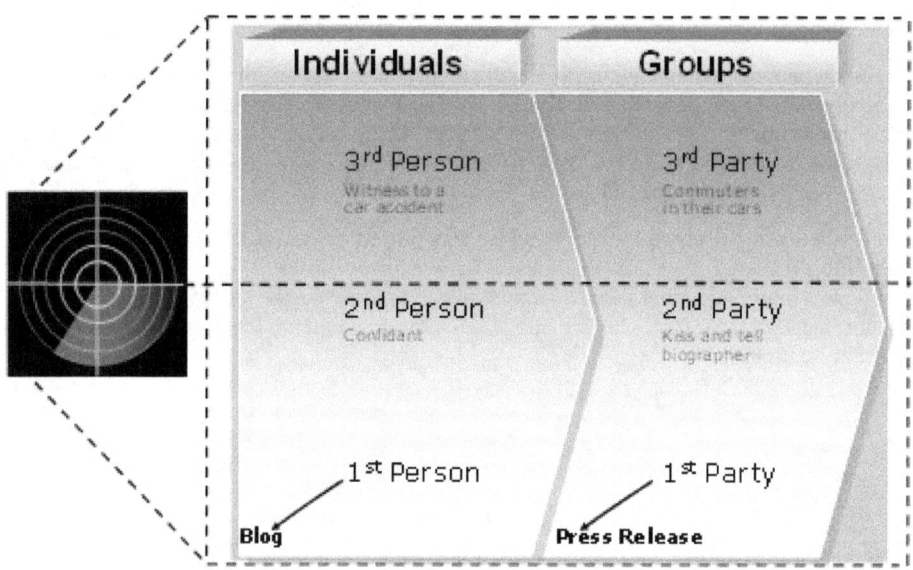

On/off radar is a simple distinction between what is documented and what happens beyond recall. Neither of these groupings is static although the more communications that are conducted electronically the likelier they move from the undocumented to documented column.

Searching Out Loud: Giving Voice to Independent Investigations | Marc Solomon

What does this mean for us as communicators and the extent of our participation? How does this influence our choice of communication for...

- Introducing ourselves to friends of friends?
- Delivering bad news to family members?
- Sending out invites to people who may not remember us?
- Giving a status on a project to a boss several time zones away?

Conversely, how does this change our approach as observers of our search targets? How does the mapping influence our choice of information providers? What are our stakeout positions for anticipating actions, interpreting outcomes, and even comparing notes with other members of our team?

Authenticity, Credibility, Conflicts of Interest

As we've established in the trade-offs between subjective and objective biases, we can move forward with our PCF mapping. That means placing more confidence that the information we receive is authentic when the source has...

- Firsthand knowledge,
- Personal involvement (first person/party), and
- Direct knowledge of the actions of others.

Likewise, we can be more certain that our evidence is credible when the source has not been personally involved, but has been an outside observer (third person/party).

Conflicts of interest exist when deals are made *under the table*, or when a person or institution tries to buy their way into credibility. It could mean sponsoring the work of third party research firms, laboratories, and other domain experts inclined to produce opinions and reports in their favor.

PCF reveals some common activities relevant to the vetting such conflicts, specifically in legal cases, and generally in most institutionally-sanctioned discovery pursuits.

Watchdogs and Regulators

The formal or institutional way that conflict-of-interest is exposed is through the government intervention and enforcement of public law. However, the powers of regulators are often compromised when they flirt with dramatically higher pay from the firms they're regulating. Rather than expose risks, they disguise them in legalese or bury them under the weight of vague claims or irrelevant details.

The discrepancy here is in stark display on our search logs. The stated objective would be to preserve the public interest so that investors are protected from the short-term gains of a select few. The clashing and unstated purpose would be for regulators to reap financial rewards far greater they could earn on the public payroll. The expectation we would gain as investigators is that the regulator protects those with political clout. Not the interests of the wider, less organized groups their agency is charged to protect.

The notion of checks and balances is the guiding principle for directing the legal authority of regulatory agencies and the public officials who lead them. The hypocrisy created by the need to protect the few at the expense of the many is as likely to be...

- Revealed in empty, oft-repeated statements, as it is to be...
- Discovered by stealth efforts to obscure, hide, or selectively enforce laws on the books.

For example, in late 2007 high ranking public officials would project the belief that the fundamentals of the economy were basically sound. This pretense services the notion that elected leaders answer to expectations in order to preserve order. Preserving confidence, even when that confidence is false is the appeal of the status quo. This appeal often overpowers all attempts to investigate, reveal, and fix the systemic breakdowns that helped foster the meltdown and the full-blown financial crisis that ensued.

*We first considered this in **Unit One** when we looked at the kinds of blindspots we might expect to encounter in our radar detection efforts when investigating institutional or group behavior.*

Smoking Guns and the Whiff of Hypocrisy

We all know when something doesn't smell right. This is when the righteous words don't support the wrongful deed. We tally the unfortunate outcomes against the isolated actions that led us there. And they don't add up. Our sniffers have led us to the doorsteps of hypocrisy. That might sound esoteric like a Greek tragedy. It's a paper we once turned in about a whistleblower who sounded off against a code of silence. In fact, it's one of the most popular and consistent narratives used by the media. It's a well-established journalistic practice to expose corruption by reporting doubts raised from the conflicting evidence between a person's individual deeds and their public statements – typically as a first party leader or group representative.

Everyone has their own reconstruction of events. Everyone has a selective version of what went down. Everyone has their own sniff test for what *doesn't quite smell right*. However, our own testing merits require us to introduce standards that are widely understood and evenly applied. We need to anticipate public, legal, and stakeholder scrutiny. Our protective instincts may suspect underhanded motives. But our better instincts acknowledge the role of our skeptics to responsibly question our conclusions and quite possibly the methods for our investigation. **(Lewis, Einhorn, 2009[10])**

One of the overlooked benefits of web investigations is this. Because they exist in the public domain, our strongest doubters and most skeptical adversaries can literally conduct the same tests and probes that we conduct – and achieve the same results. Arriving at the same conclusions is a completely different matter!

Figure 4.17 models some of the damning circumstances that we can use to test our hunches. Then we can either strengthen or toss out initial impressions of the people and groups we investigate.

Subjective Experience: The Changing Roles of Information Providers

The distinctions between self and group identification is based on some common roles that we all share as senders and receivers. In Figures 4.17 through 4.19, who is cast on which end of the exchange is highly contextual. Below, we see how those perspectives will shift based on who initiates each communication and the chain of reactions it inspires. The most important pattern? Whether those messages are communicated informally from person to person, or officially through group-based or more traditional media channels.

FIGURE 4.17: Mapping PCFs to Individual and Group-based Information Providers

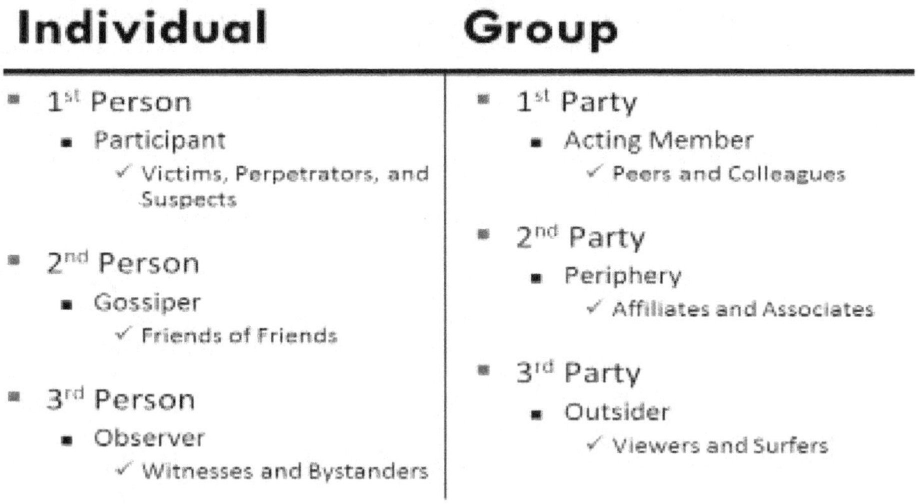

Individual	Group
■ 1ˢᵗ Person 　■ Participant 　　✓ Victims, Perpetrators, and Suspects ■ 2ⁿᵈ Person 　■ Gossiper 　　✓ Friends of Friends ■ 3ʳᵈ Person 　■ Observer 　　✓ Witnesses and Bystanders	■ 1ˢᵗ Party 　■ Acting Member 　　✓ Peers and Colleagues ■ 2ⁿᵈ Party 　■ Periphery 　　✓ Affiliates and Associates ■ 3ʳᵈ Party 　■ Outsider 　　✓ Viewers and Surfers

This diagram divides individual and group information exchanges according to the role of the information giver.

<u>Subjective Experience: Information Types and Purposes</u>

In addition to roles and responsibilities, we need to consider the types of information that are exchanged across the PCF playing field. We first addressed this earlier in **Unit Four** when we explored the forms and vestiges of informational artifacts – the physical or electronic containers that store the communication. We expanded the range to include overall purpose for providing information in the absence of a tangible container. Here is a PCF mapping:

FIGURE 4.18: Mapping PCFs to Information Types and Purposes

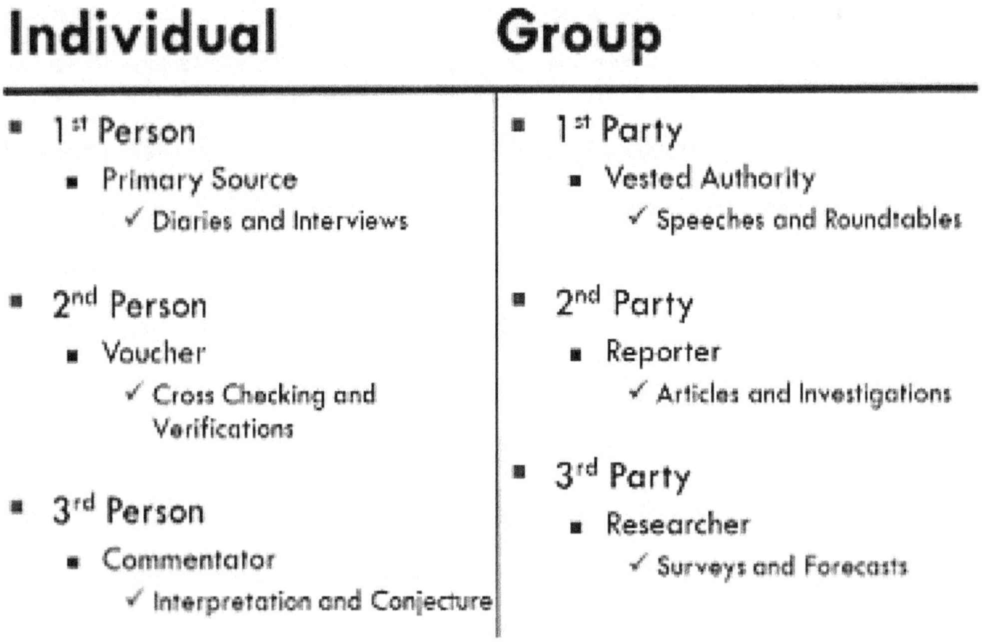

Individual	Group
■ 1ˢᵗ Person 　■ Primary Source 　　✓ Diaries and Interviews ■ 2ⁿᵈ Person 　■ Voucher 　　✓ Cross Checking and Verifications ■ 3ʳᵈ Person 　■ Commentator 　　✓ Interpretation and Conjecture	■ 1ˢᵗ Party 　■ Vested Authority 　　✓ Speeches and Roundtables ■ 2ⁿᵈ Party 　■ Reporter 　　✓ Articles and Investigations ■ 3ʳᵈ Party 　■ Researcher 　　✓ Surveys and Forecasts

This diagram divides individual and group information exchanges according to the form and purpose that the information provides us.

Subjective Experience: On/Off Radar

Consider the flip-side of provider conjugation – it's in the ear of the receiver. The switch happens when we revisit the framework from the perspective of the recipient. The official end of the spectrum floats to the top of the radar. The information or more private side lays low – below the radar. The zig-zag is not an exact calculation so much as a symbol for the slippery task of deciding what information is as likely to float above the surface or remain below.

FIGURE 4.19: Mapping PCFs to their Visibility Across the Internet Radar

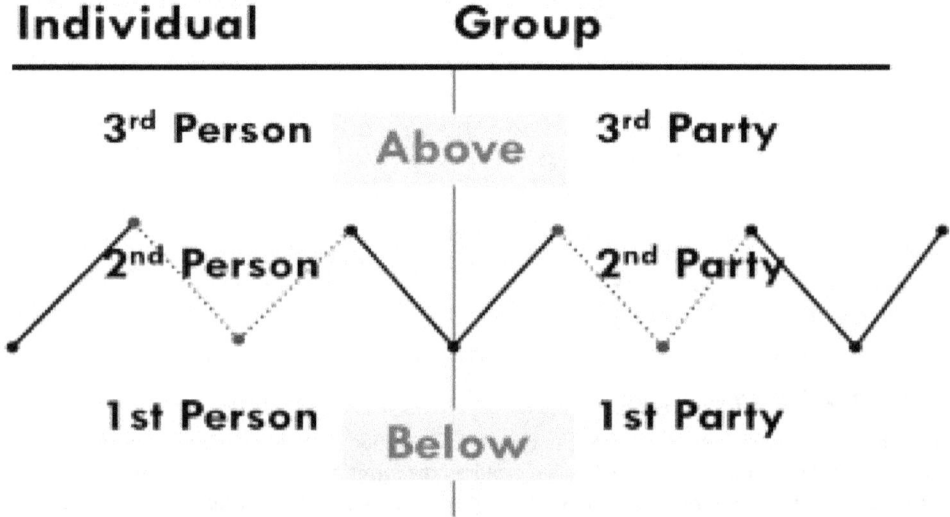

This diagram details the types of information we're exposed to as receivers of information exchanges. It shows the inferential line that exists between public and private communications typified by second person/party information exchanges.

WORKING UNDER THE RADAR

We now have a way of understanding what we reasonably expect to find on screens. We have a new mental model for tracking how information flows and how the direction of that flow will influence the interpretations, perceptions, and potential actions taken by its recipients. We can now see how this contextualization tool is situation-specific. It applies to us and our changing roles as providers or recipients. It also matters whether that communication is compelling us to act alone, or on behalf of a group.

We've also evidenced the limited explanatory powers of PCF in developing tools for analyzing context. That means addressing the numerous and sometimes conflicting forces we all need to reconcile as both providers and recipients. Hence, we've introduced the additional framework of Integrity Vectors to assess these complexities and the range of outcomes our search targets consider as they mull their options and followup actions.

What we haven't done is apply this mental mapping to real life scenarios. We haven't yet considered how to attack the kinds of questions that arise when dissecting a sequence of events, or understanding the underlying motives behind questionable activities. With that in mind, let's put what we've learned to work in the following web investigation:

Working Model: Search Target under Investigation

FIGURE 4.20: Search Target Suspect Profile

Suspect: Profile	Integrity Vectors	PCF Probes
Soloist or orchestrator	Tendency to act alone or in tandem	*Get a handle on socializing patterns through preferred hangouts, elixirs, and emotional range to detect any dramatic behavioral changes*
Exposure settings	Attention-grabbing or quiet (behind-the-scenes player)	*What does an individual or group do to call attention to themselves? When do they shed the limelight? Are they intent on demonstrating their grievances?*
Inspirations	Role models and scapegoats	*Who do they follow on social media settings? What are familiar targets for venting anger or praising – what are those beefs and virtues?*
Motivations	Competitive versus passive nature	*What is target's tendency to initiate communications? How much of their activity streams echo the posts and behaviors of their favored information providers? Are they more passive and likelier to play a supporting role?*
Transparency	Open and available versus secretive and remote	*How elusive or approachable is the target in their social media profiles? Do they attract virtual friends outside their immediate social circles?*

FIGURE 4.21: Search Target Suspect Eccentricities

Suspect: Eccentricities	Integrity Vectors	PCF Probes
Soloist or orchestrator	Temptations and vices	*Factor in past resentments for being passed over nd how those humiliations tempt a mastermind to proclaim their brilliance (and tip their own cover)*
Exposure settings	Perceived slights and vindications	*Consider the scores that were settled in pursuit of false accusations, petty jealousies, and otherwise avoidable past mistakes*
Inspirations	Rituals and habits	*Are there compromising or addictive behaviors that can be traced to social circles or through social media discourse?*
Motivations	Obsessive behaviors, (i.e. history of stalking)	*Does the target obsess on other individuals or groups? Where does the fluid distraction pass into static fixation? If a restraining order were issued, where would the target have crossed the line?*
Transparency	Impersonations, mimicry	*What are the behaviors of the target's heroes and praiseworthy members of the inner circle? When do those praises turn to taunts and ridicule?*

FIGURE 4.22: Search Target Suspect Resources

Suspect: Resources	Integrity Vectors	PCF Probes
Soloist or orchestrator	Expertise to carry out actions	*Take an inventory of financial assets, medical records, membership histories, academic and licensing credentials, and unique talents*
Exposure settings	Assets to finance operation	*Assets to consider from two countervailing angles: (1) What is the risk/benefit calculation for a target determining whether to engage in criminal activities; and (2) What assets need to be protected from potentially hostile actions of perceived adversaries?*
Inspirations	Long-term versus short-term associations	*Does the target share their goal orientation in the conduct of their social media profile? Are their communications more practical and immediate or focused on loftier goals?*
Motivations	Family history of bodily/mental illness	*What are the less-than-natural causes present in the demise of diseased or infirmed family members?*
Transparency	Family ties	*Does the target profile more as family or individually-focused? How much of that decision is based on the real need to break free from the circumstance of their upbringings?*

FIGURE 4.23: Search Target Suspect Network

Suspect: Network	Integrity Vectors	PCF Probes
Soloist or orchestrator	Unhappy investors	What assets are held (1) within the family, (2) on the periphery by extended members, or (3) intimate confidants outside that circle?
Exposure settings	Disgruntled employees	Focus on the enablers — who are the accomplices and go-betweens that function as conduits between the target and actions under investigation?
Inspirations	Marginalized family members	What are the weakest links in the family chain? Is the target the n'er-do-well asking for hand-outs? Are they the well-heeled benefactor leaned on for providing bridge loans? Do monetary disputes boil over in estate settlements?
Motivations	Online forums, discussions	How does the target perceive themselves Do they command the kind of respect from others that they confer onto themselves? What are they likely to repeat about how they define themselves? Are there any curious disclaimers that connect otherwise unrelated events and outcomes?
Transparency	Exposure to potential adversaries	How public is our target about expressing their displeasure and airing their grievances? Are they expressed at specific individuals or do these misgivings take on a more cultural or tribal tone?

FIGURE 4.24: Search Target Suspect Events

Suspect: Events	Integrity Vectors	PCF Probes
Soloist or orchestrator	Bargaining power	*What's the gap between personal wealth and what's projected in appearances? Where does target show painstaking control and what are they likelier to leave to chance?*
Exposure settings	Upsides and downsides	*Who might gain in prestige and reward from theft, rescue, sale, settlement, etc. Where are the potential blockers to cooperation such as indictment of family member of close friend?*
Inspirations	Expectations range	*What are the target's formative expectations, i.e. groomed as heir apparent? When do they expect to win outside approval or wield some new authority? Are these stepping stones based on privilege, popular will, individual merit, or outright coercion?*
Motivations	Work schedule and personal transactions	*Spot check for calendar events and changes like uptick in work hours. How do scheduling changes impact data trail: Purchase records, cell phone usage, security cameras, browser histories, etc.*
Transparency	Quid pro quos	*Are there back-scratchings, kickbacks, or pre-arrived reciprocal agreements? Is information suppressed to avoid media coverage and public scrutiny?*

SECTION 4:3 | Search to Converse —
How to Socialize What We Learn Through Networking

The social media section of **Unit Four** has two principle thrusts:

1. **Observation** – Approaching social networks as a researcher
2. **Participation** – Engaging them as a member, including how to screen, join, attract, and communicate through virtual communities

The slippery distinction between observer and participant is especially sensitive as we shift from the *searching* to *conversing* phase of our research projects. This section focuses on ways to trail and gather background details on search targets that generate digital identities through their social media profiles, networks, and posts.

The model we use for reading networks and acting on them is called the **Provider Conjugation Framework** or PCF. Like verb conjugation, this tool helps to establish the flow and context of how information travels and the perceptions it carries with it. We also apply it to ourselves as information providers in determining the perceptions we want to form about us. This includes the types of contacts we want to attract and build into our own networks – especially in reaching out to search targets that prove to be social media party animals, digital hermits, or somewhere in-between.

Social networks are important for tracing personal connections such as Facebook friends or LinkedIn connections but impersonal ones too. One's electronic network traces a person's media universe. Those horizons span well beyond access to cable or audio streaming to the experiential realm: Exposure to ideas and cultures that will present choices, and even shape behaviors.

The connection between impersonal information sources and personal decisions and priorities is not a subtle one. What we see, hear and read can influence what we say, think, and act upon. Understanding the electronic environment that surrounds an individual can be just as revealing as their DNA, school grades, and home address. Those influences are felt whether they're delivered through advertising, speechmaking, role models, or fashion statements,

The other direct connection here is that electronic media is our modern equivalent to presenting how society organizes itself into orders, groups, teams, and affiliations. Which of these groups count us as members is often similar to our personal networks. For instance, the sources we subscribe to may be indecipherable from the professional contacts in our smart phones. The causes and crusades that enlist our volunteerism and charity may well represent cures or advocacy for friends and family for which we pledge our unwavering support.

SOCIAL NETS: From Soul Searching to Virtual Searching

Nobody knows...

- The troubles you've seen?
- The trials you've faced?
- The journeys you've tread?
- The secrets you've held?

Certainly search engines are no exception. There is probably no day of reckoning in our lifetimes where search engines will replace confessionals or give psychotherapists cause to switch careers. Disintermediation means cutting out the *middle man* so that buyers and sellers can engage directly. In that context, the web has made mayhem of the career tracks of most travel agents, copy editors, and advertising directors from TV commercials to newspaper classifieds and those yellowing Yellow Pages.

But search engines can inform the question of how we appear as we're stepping and stressing through this world – from everyone else's perspective along the PCF spectrum. And while search won't put the kibosh on people who listen to our problems for a living, it unleashes two opposing forces: (1) It expands our appetite for connections, while (2) constraining pastimes formerly designed for *mixing things up*. It has made lasting changes to how career counselors, headhunters, matchmakers, and event planners design meetings and arrange situations between people and groups. Web-based research is a tool for building bridges and for the cementing of connections made within (1) these meetings, (2) panels they would host, (3) topics they anticipate, and (4) even interviews they might arrange through media covering the event.

Cutting Out the Second Party

Speaking of media, they are on the ultimate endangered list of communicators displaced by web technology, or to be more specific – the emergence of social media on the web. We all know that the infrastructure of our own virtual neighborhoods live on Instagram and Facebook – not in the pages of our local paper. From a PCF perspective, this means the elimination of second parties. Why go through a reporter or a news outlet when political leaders can reach voters directly on Twitter? Why sign with a record label when an established performer can distribute their songs directly to their fans?

We have scarcely begun to understand all the implications stemming from the displacement of second parties. Much has been made about the demise of traditional media and journalistic integrity. Little has been articulated about the opportunity this presents to Knowledge-ABLED investigators to provide the kind of vetting, fact-checking, and quality control services formerly the domain of news reporters. Even less has been written about the role of the Knowledge-ABLED as aggregators to (1) broker contextual meanings, (2) provider credibility, and (3) ultimately the integrity of the search targets and larger social forces they underpin.

But before we consider these downsides and opportunities, we need to focus first on social information: The fundamental (and overlooked) building block of all non-business model social media interaction. Without understanding social information, social media lacks context for us as researchers as well as group members of social networks.

The Role of Social Information

Think about primary intelligence-gathering. A seasoned investigator interviews a key witness. The examiner pays as much attention to the way the answers are delivered as to the answers themselves. Part of this evaluation is based on the source's social network. What are their family roots? Where do they go for a sense of community? Which of their own primary news sources will shape their sense of personal conduct from duty and obligation to individual liberty and social justice?

These are personal values that are woven into that external identity we share as citizens, fans, churchgoers, parents or any group affiliation that tells us the concerns, expectations, and commitments of its members. More than purchase histories and hobbies, the binding nature of personal networks leads the researcher to an unwritten code of priorities and value judgments we refer to as *the social contract*.

Now consider the witness's group affiliations and social circles. What are the key relationships that reinforce, contradict, or raise new questions about what our source decides to share in the interview? Is their version of events compromised by fears of retribution? Is bribery or some other form of coercion requiring them to ignore or downplay the guilt or responsibility of other suspects?

There is but one certainty when it comes to reading through the files of the evidence gathered by an experienced investigator: The relationships conjured up by their interviews weighs as critically as any quote that can be pulled from their interview, debriefing, or legal deposition.

Put another way, whoever we email and cc: on our correspondence, is often as important as the text contained in the body of that message. Who's aware of the issue under discussion is sometimes more critical than the topic itself.

So what exactly is social information? How is that different from social media or social networking? Social information is the context in which information is processed – not created, not delivered – but interpreted. The social value of information stands apart from its objective value as facts, opinions, and details. Social information addresses the subjective judgments and actions formed by the perceptions and values of information recipients.

How does this definition play out in the public spectrum? We'll use traditional media for context.

Traditional Media Bias

When the media is accused of bias, we can guarantee (1) a spirited debate, and (2) the opposite bias harbored in the information provider making the accusation. Left to its own devices, traditional media goes about each story it finds worth covering with the same foregone conclusions:

1. They've done their job correctly if we're still tuned in when the story's over.

2. How they keep our attention is not the lead story when it comes to media bias.

Here are some safe assumptions when learning about the same investigation in the papers, radio or traditional TV news: We're receiving a selective version of events chosen for us by familiar public figures who we have never met before. Their ultimate responsibility is nothing as lofty as an ultimate truth but to capture our attention long enough to sustain their popularity as news providers. Also referred to as secondary sources, we as passive news watchers are privy only to what the show's producer considers broadcast-worthy.

But we are not told how they landed those quotes, who tipped them off, and all those unnamed sources who don't wish to be held accountable for their all-knowing insights. So basically, much of the context or social value derived from the investigation is lost to the news consumer. From a social justice angle, this is a troubling part of news mechanics because a news organization can be subjected to the same coercions as our compromised witness. Only in the case of the news outlet, they are even more vulnerable to outside pressures. They have the added role of deciding not only the public's right to know but, what it, the media, considers worth knowing.

Anti-social Information

Newspapers, magazines, and TV news programs tend to squelch the social dimension of the news they report, on both legal and proprietary grounds. But all the personal networks, group affiliations, and bargaining that goes into deciding what and how to report news is now finding its way into the back corridors of sourcing a hungry investigation. From bloggers to grassroots sites and personal pages, much of the firsthand immediacy and even authenticity is generated by the postings of people with direct ties to investigations, sometimes with case-breaking specifics that would evade traditional news consumers.

Where does this leave us as intrepid Internet researchers? On a personal level, if we've read the blog, what's to stop us from emailing the blogger? What if we are an authoritative source ourselves? What if we've seen the news report? What will the traditional media producer say if we offer a competing version – say to a competing program? Now that the lines between news producers and consumers are blurred, traditional media outlets can ill-afford to pose as the final, definitive arbiters of the news that's fit to print, or the story that's worth watching.

In a broader context, the assessment tools we address in **Unit Four** will bring quantifiable proof to the way search targets and social topics are understood, perceived, and potentially acted on by a full range of information recipients. Increasingly, the web also feeds us full data sets of evidence that are both unfiltered by the providers, and the commentaries of mainstream news organizations. **(Arthur, 2010)**[11]

THE CONCEPT OF SOCIAL CIRCLES

The best way to understand the social dimension of information is through a variation on PCF called **Social Circles**. We can group social circles to map how information travels and what form its documentation takes (indicated by the right-pointing arrows in Figure 4.25). This is the experiential element of information – how it travels and where it lands.

The distinctions between senders and receivers include the following:

1. An individual or informal social circle represents communication attributed to a specific person.

2. Generally, the smaller the circle, the more sincere and authentic the communication as an extension of a person's individual will, personal preferences, and even *true intentions*.

3. A group-sponsored social circle refers to information provided by organizations, institutions or formally-delivered communications.

Because of their intimacy, core circles are useful for anticipating the upshot or aftermath of a compromising situation or awkward information exchange.

Social circles are also instructive for plotting that most vulnerable posture of all compromised communications – being blindsided. It is a universal reflex and personal affront to loathe learning through the widest of circles what we thought we should be told from a close friend or confidant.

Let's say we want to honor the request of not being blindsided by a boss or authority figure. Now let's assume that this person is busy, overbooked, and easily distracted. Is it better to send them emails directly (e.g., TO: boss) or indirectly (e.g., cc: boss)?

As we see below, social circles are concentrated and intimate at their core and diffuse and impersonal at the periphery. An inner circle is made up of long-time friends, esteemed peers, and contacts we are likelier to lower our guards in exchanging (and safekeeping) personal, off-radar information. We are connected to extended networks for their utility, i.e. suppliers, brokers, partners and other lateral relations share an indirect affiliation. The larger cultural dimensions on the outer layer are abstractions to us. There are no confidences, only perceptions shaped by information providers and forums in the larger social context.

FIGURE 4.25: Subjective Experience in the Form of Social Circles

Individual
- Extended Network → Instructions, Policies, Regulations
- Personal Network → Projects, Meetings, Advice
- Privileged Communication → Diaries, Therapy, Confessions

Group
- Culture & Society → Analysis, Expertise, Commentary
- Stakeholders → Debates, Deliberations, Consensus
- Inner Sanctum → Decisions, Influence, Power

This schematic groups the typical outcomes or by-products of common information exchanges. An individual or informal social circle is attributed to a specific person. A group-sponsored social circle refers to information provided by organizations, institutions or formally-delivered communications.[12]

SOCIAL NETS: From Searching to Conversing

The best virtual display of social circles is through Internet-based social networks. The pre-eminent social network is Facebook and its success at commandeering the attention of its members. This is a bias shared by many of its members who rarely wander off the Facebook ranch – a landlord "which chops infinity into an endless series of cul-de-sacs." **(Tyrangiel, 2010)**[13]

The second kind of social nets are the largely resume-based profiles submitted by professionals looking for new opportunities or looking to reconnect with former colleagues. Professional networking sites get you from the background research of your expeditions to the foreground engagement. This means approaching a key contact with a mutual aim:

1. Our research can help them, and
2. They can move us along in our careers and/or project work.

Professional Networks: LinkedIn

The dominant network for working professionals is currently LinkedIn.com. Unlike Instagram, Facebook, and sites that hold more media clips than career details, LinkedIn is a structured database of interconnected professionals complete with their key credentials, contact details, resumes, and endorsements.

The LinkedIn database is powerful. Remember each detail that it asks of you becomes a searchable field in your quest to find experts, hiring managers, and trade contacts. There is no expectation that we would use the vendor's process for approaching contacts that are more than one degree of separation from us.

Along with the structure, another big selling point is that members invest in their memberships. They spend more time and care in keeping their profiles current than what we might expect to see maintained by a corporate HR department. Endorsements are also welcome and there are built-in safeguards to validate the process. For instance, one can't endorse their own work although we can certainly trade on a quid pro quo with one of our network references. Sound like the laws of credibility calling?

Show You Mine, I'll Show You Yours

So LinkedIn is a massive database of self-administered professional life narratives. Access is determined by a network of click-happy connections: Show you mine if you show me yours (both the resumes *and* the contacts).

The database gets regular feedings and weedings because – hey – those are my bowling trophies and and inflationary job titles and biopic documentaries I put on my reality series reward card program. Psst... got any seed money?

What we're unpacking here through unlicensed metaphor is a database of resumes. The splendor of the architecture is that the profile templates are self-organizing. There are no semantic web quibbles over taxonomies versus folksonomies, what vocabulary is worth controlling, and which tag clouds deserve to float above the fog. In doing so, LinkedIn has achieved organic adherence to the age-old riddle:

> *How do I describe my uniqueness in the least invasive and most universal way possible?*

That vessel is the cross-fertilization of the knowledge garden we researchers, sales animals, and job-seekers can all cultivate, horse-trade, or hunt down. Whatever our motivates, we're sourcing the sprinkler system known as the LinkedIn advanced search feature.

FIGURE 4.26: LinkedIn's Advanced Search Features

One of my favorite applications of PCFs in social networks is the ability to search only former employees of a particular organization. This ensures that the person had firsthand knowledge of what was happening at their former employer.[14]

The Social Network Mating Dance

Perhaps we don't need to track down ex-employees when investigating the questionable practices of their former firm. Maybe we're looking up people we've lost touch with and want to reconnect? What a concept!

Recently I got pinged on LinkedIn by a former college cohort with a 1.5 separation degree of overlapping concentric social circles circa 1980-84. Who better than a fellow Hampshire College alumn and current job-seeker to put that ivory-coated knowledge harvest to the test?

My former college mate "Jon" writes:

> So, anyway, I want to harvest some of these connections. At first I thought I'd contact the person I knew, tell them who I was looking for and ask them to search the name and find the second degree connection. A little awkward and time consuming (for the person I'm asking the favor). Yeah, so then I see the "Get Introduced Through A Connection" link. I choose my connection, then I get this form:

FIGURE 4.27: LinkedIn's Awkward and Painful 'Getting Introduced' Request Form

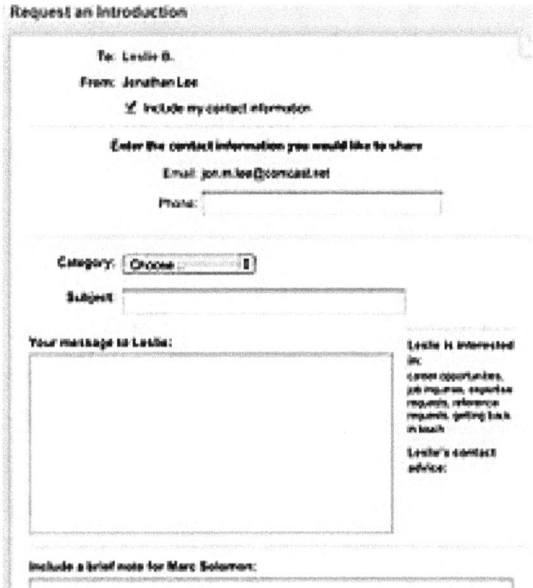

This is the way that LinkedIn implores a member to advance their networking opportunities through the intermediary – second person contact signifying the degree of separation between the member and the would-be contact.

His question is this: What happens ... how does this work?

> I hit send, a message goes to you. Do you only see my note to you - or the message to X (Leslie B. in this example) as well? And what about the person you know, who knows Leslie? How is that connection made? Automatically - or do you have to find the connection for me? Do they see my message to you, my message to Leslie?

The hypothetical scenarios go on for a few more paragraphs before the logic is tortured right out of the motivation for getting to the actual conversation stages – the linking out phase of the process. I appreciate these questions because they underscore the associative clunk factor of shuffling through an overloaded circuit of lateral connectors.

The community spirit of pay-it-forward reciprocity might work for random acts of kindness. But perhaps not so much for calculating and indiscriminate emails – especially from people we know more for their degree of separation than we do about them. Period.

The artifice of the social media back-scratch points to the exit ramp or the link-out. This is the realization that as gorgeous as that well-groomed garden is, all the growth happens within the narrow confines of Linkedin.com. It is a walled-in garden. That's why a thousand Facebook weeds makes more advertising perfume than the most painstaking bouquet of freshly cut resumes at LinkedIn.

We need to step on a few weeds, maybe even some poisonous ones, before any meaningful conversations can happen. That's where a nose for research meets an eye for opportunity and an ear for discussion. That kind of growth can only happen in soils and climates where the greatest variety of vegetation takes root.

The Cost of Free

While this resource is free, the vendor requests that we upload a listing of potential contacts from our own email directories that we can send invite to join LinkedIn. The benefit to us is that by expanding our network, we increase the size of the database. If we agree to sign-up we'll be able to search my network as well as those in your own who have already signed up with LinkedIn (or who you bring along).

There is also no requirement that you accept the invitation to join either. In the past, some may feel compromised or exposed for putting their credentials in the database. Some may have felt uncomfortable about asking their own contacts to consider joining.

These trepidations had died away by the teens decade of the 21st Century. In fact, any misgivings about surrendering private details have been overcome by social networks that promise an entire platform for hosting all varieties of virtual communications. The allure of viewing those carvings from the privacy of our imaginations is the trigger. And it works no matter what's hiding behind the password door.

Remember media bias? Think of that same partiality for attracting attention through social networks that a broadcast network can only dream about. The default setting for the platform version of Facebook is that social network-based information providers will swallow our personal histories whole for "posterity, police, and divorce lawyers." **(Gillmor, 2010)**[15]

It's up to the member to de-activate the archival function. Opt-in is set to the complete, if nakedly unabridged version. Facebook wants its members to spend the optimal spread of their waking hours on Facebook. Is this as sinister as it sounds? Or is a just reward for surrendering our personal privacy in exchange for citizenship in a virtual community?

The Downsides of Social Media

The most fundamental disconnect of current state web lies between our dual roles as content producers and consumers. It's one thing to shed aliases and handles as fluidly as we're pressed for passwords. It's quite another to be torn between our need for peer approval and self-protection. That's not a minor misalignment. That's a deep and impassable identity crisis. How the two are reconciled is not the next big app. It's the staging ground for the gathering storm perfection of...

- The rise of Facebook
- The fall of journalism
- The abyss of credibility

For the better half of two decades, we've been feeding the sociable media beast with friend affirmations. We want a sense of belonging, of inclusiveness. But if we pay for that community-building with back-scratches and platitudes that leaves a gaping hole between what we hope to be expressed and what we know to be true. It's not that Facebook praises are empty on arrival, but enforced by a culture of reciprocal transparency. As much as positive reinforcement is the elixir of choice for self-expression, it leaves us hungry for how others perceive us. It's tone deaf to the indifference of outsiders. Those are the potential employers who background check us out. But they're not looking for suitors, social circles, or listening to our echo chamber of megaphones.

They just want to know they can trust us and can't just take our word for it.

What would happen if none of us were allowed to post to our own social media profiles? Would our friends make up for the shortfall? Could our enemies commit *face crimes* and libel us with half-truths and fabrications? In a regulated web, non-vested observers would honor their own reputations by speaking to objectives, standards, and rankings – not how they've been blemished by greatness or influenced by the people they're profiling. Sounds like the ghost of journalistic myth-making? Sounds like a reason to pay for content in cash – not gratitude.

BUILD IT – AND THEY WILL DUMP

In the future, this darker Facebook would be compensated from both sides of the message exchange. Anonymous enemies would get to post unsubstantiated kiss-and-tells once they sign-up. Group members could pony up too. But they'd have to preempt these negative reviews with their own cathartic self-examinations. Posting enough of these face-saving gestures would earn enough credits to learn the actual identities of their blasphemers? No practicing journalist is in a competitive bargaining position in that business model.

The dark fantasy of an evil twin brother to Facebook may one day come to pass. It may inhabit a place once reserved for reporters who arbitrated once definable and containable questions like:

> *Can the public handle the truth about...?*

Facial truth may arrive without malevolent intentions. Some may even be noble in their naivete. For instance, it may be a libertarian impulse from Craigslist. If no one knows what breeds we kennel on the Internet, surely there's a universal understanding that flies under the longest of tails we wave. In the book of Craigslist, what people do in their uninhibited privacy is not only their own business but endows the publisher with the right of keeping their identities under the roof of one San Francisco-based Victorian.

This same Constitution that guarantees the right to free speech also protects the right to remain silent. Does that extend to the right to remain anonymous in our virtual identities?

It may be a social media partisan who believes that transparency, consensus, and may-the-best-idea win are all wrapped and sealed in the protective popularity of a Survey Monkey referendum. It most certainly is a loyal Wikipedia correspondent who adheres to the sacred tenets of Wikipedia editorial policies. Thou shalt do no original research (or synthesis of two or more existing ideas) in the unquestioning isolation of their passive voice and their hollow curiosity.

Can I Subtract You as My Enemy?

With those seeds in motion, would the particle-smashing collision that awaits this doubting world be that surprising? We would be spinning out of our social orbits by joining a site where...

- Alias predators post dubious half-truths
- These rumors require only a popular vote to become credible
- Such fabrications convince fence-sitters they're getting the whole story

How would we stop these allegations?

As Andrew Morris-Friedman speculates, the only way to lower the temperature without changing the subject is to post even more reprehensible stuff to attract even higher scores. In this dark counterweight to Facebook, one can't see their accusers unless they suffer the fools of self-effacement. That's how we actually identify our detractors in a world devoid of credibility – by being our own worst enemies.

What could be a more lucrative exercise in community damage control and shear predatory gawking? In such a fishbowl-like environment, partisans would queue for the chance to shape a fair and balanced view of our own profiles.

Approaching Would-be Contacts in a Social Network

Enough about dystopian social media scenarios. An important advantage to an investigator remains having a number of credible, reliable sources to depend on. Our existing social networks provides us with this. However, we should actively analyze our networks and work to expand them.

Consider that you are trying to get firsthand information about a target from a second party. By joining their social network, you move to infiltrating a professional network. From infiltration, you move to cultivation: Your goal is to find second-party sources with the exposure to be vested in an outcome (action). Self-preservation here is tempered with enough distance from the consequences to appear credible (observation).

We can see some of the limitations of looking to social networks as credible information sources. For now, let's shelve our research jerseys, and join the party in our dance outfits. *Putting yourself out there* is just the first step. We then move to infiltration – seeking a potential dance partner, ideally to glean first hand information from a second party.

When do we know we're dancing with flair and distinction? Those second party sources can speak, and do so, for first parties, i.e. employers. It's easier for most of us to start with a larger pool of potential teams or groups. We can then narrow down the individual members or those with specific skills, perspectives, prerogatives (like hiring us), or even the cachet of their own social networks.

Here are some helpful tips for reaching beyond our respective comfort zones and social circles.

Cultivating Contacts: Melting the Social Ice

Remember the last time you got spammed by a political party or special interest group? You might have felt taken down a notch in the social order. That's because there were probably many assumptions made in the communication that you didn't necessarily share or hold as priorities. Either way, direct marketing is a one-way conversation. That's not the goal of this exercise or of successful social networking. On the other hand, a few colorful teasers (like some current search projects for example) might be a good hook for luring the kind of attention and curiosity that would support a meaningful exchange.

Here's how that dynamic plays out in an active pursuit of new contacts:

> 1) **Try to focus on the ideal situation** *(not the perfect would-be contact)* – Instead of fixating on a particular individual, focus on groups that espouse a view we share, campaign we want to join, or even a firm or organization we want to work for. Consider eyewitnesses or first party members of a shared movement or interest.
>
> 2) **Play the outsider card** – Share with your contact what initially attracted you to them (from a distance). Because you are not yet acquaintances, you can speak with the candor and freshness that a close friend or confidant can't. Because you're a stranger, you speak for a very large and important group. Everyone your contact has yet to meet who share the premise from your original welcome email.
>
> 3) **Don't tell them your life story** – Keep the common ground you share to mutual experiences and/or contacts (people you both know in the same field). A long-winded introduction doesn't fly on email any more than it does in-person. I've also found that your gesture of reaching out is perceived with greater sincerity and receptivity when you're sharing something that happened to you, changed you, or inspired you to take action. It works in reverse when your patter becomes goal-oriented or future-directed.

4) Approach them as equals – No one likes to be seen as an object or an objective. Think of the last time you were *hit on* for money, personal favors, or the good of some self-interested group that would have otherwise ignored you if they hadn't jeopardized their own position. That's why most of us abhor the ultimate compromise – asking for things. It's in that compromised state where some of us equate the deep ancestral needs for companionship and sustenance to self-promotion and politicking. The truth is that you are horse-trading when you send a total stranger an invitation to join ranks. Playing the dance card is the reciprocal trading of networks through *connecting* or *friending*.

Don't Underestimate Your Own Worth

This is not a self-help book but...

As reinforcement for that last point, don't assume that the person you approach is assuming you're the question and they're the answer. Social networks can be excellent talent pools when you are trying to assemble an investigation team of diverse strengths and professional backgrounds. You may be knocking on someone else's door. That said, the door's likelier to open when the recipient can see how selling their own assets will form a mutual benefit.

It's easy when we're looking for employment to underplay our hands. We'll take a further look at this in **Unit Five** when we consider professional blogs as platforms for the domain expert we seek to interview. The long-term goal might be a string of consulting gigs or gainful employment. In the short-term? It's to convince our networking targets that they should be talking to you as much as you to them, no?

An interesting follow-up would be to play the academic card and talk with an established professional about the different aspects of an investigator's tool-set that you're covering in the course. A good opening line might be something like:

> "In your own career what would be hardest to teach someone else without experiencing it directly?"

> "What are some of the skills you'd like to brush up on, or find out that could complement the core assets you bring to the table?"

This is not a term paper assignment or a sales call. But I'm asking you to take the next step.

This request is based on the commitments you have already made by investing your time and effort in cultivating your own Knowledge-ABILITIES. It may not be apparent when we're knee-deep in query formations. The end-game here is not to become search whizzes but to let our research do the talking. Those are the talking points when we're opening up new doors and initiatives in the goals and objectives that inspired us to make these sacrifices in the first place. No website or Internet skill delivers that. It's ultimately up to us to get from searching to conversing.

Defining Boundaries and Failsafes

Just like the web that existed before social media, for every bullseye there are a thousand distractions that threaten to carry us past our original purpose and supporting objectives. That's why returning to the SPM ("Search Project Management") format is useful for grounding our network goals. It's focusing not just on people we'd like to meet but the specific interactions we're looking to conduct.

For starters, consider your SPM from both your target's perspective. Search targets are ruled by their own agendas and motivation vectors. The SPM is not a form of administration but an investigation's scope and boundaries — predetermined by objective measures (time, budget, goals). Here's an example of how that model shapes up in pursuing contacts within social media circles:

FIGURE 4.28: Applying SPM to Approaching Contacts in a Social Network

SPM step	Rationale	Positioning
Why: Purpose	Reason for the networking	You want to get paid twice a month, obtain affordable health insurance, have a place to go each day
What: Objectives and Expectations	Objectives are the supporting evidence Expectations anticipate available resources and likely constraints	You want to set up a series of informational interviews that may lead to opportunities not otherwise posted to job boards and company websites
How: Tools and Methods	Task and goal-based procedures	'Follow' contacts you aspire to meet but focus on the larger community of ideas, i.e. use your personal blog or page to showcase your research
When: Duration and Failsafes	Time commitment to search and noted failures to redirect project	You don't want to watch that kettle boil but you do want to track your overtures so you can drive the discussion if/when your targeted contacts circle back to you
Who: Offline follow-up	Who is a direct contact that will advance the goals of my project	Who, indeed? Informality is the operative goal here for getting new contacts to lower their guard, speak candidly, and provide instructive guidance

The mapping in Figure 4.28 does not imply that only contacts we actively pursue are the only ones worth pursuing, Many contacts happen serendipitously around less weightier conversation points than career goals. But a major benefit of social networks is often overlooked the moment we join them. Just because we want to be sociable doesn't means we put aside our research skills.

Let's leave jobs and potential income sources aside for a moment.

There are other goals achieved better through social networks than perhaps any other form of virtual communication. For example, investigators can create or develop a social network when we need to show the connections between the vested parties: suspect, victim, witnesses, legal counsel, etc.

As we'll do in **Unit Five**, even if we don't 'friend' a potential criminal, we can still map this type of network through the PCF and integrity vector models, and present it to clients. A social network shows the personal, first-party, authentic interactions between internal group members (family, interested friends) and external group members (law enforcement, public institutions, the media, etc.).

Social Network Assignment Checklist

Now that we have the format, how do we step through our networking paces with the full benefit of our Knowledge-ABILITIES? Here's one example checklist that I drafted for my students. This was the final assignment. However, the fruits of their social information efforts were intended to be timeless and self-sustaining. Long after any could recall their final grades, the lasting benefit is in the informed schmoozing practiced by all consummate networkers:

1) Join a social network. Determine a network and engagement strategy based on interview candidates you are considering from your background research.

2) Conduct interviews and searches for last class. Apply the lessons of perspective-taking to your candidate interviews and to the nature of the questioning done while conducting the primary information-gathering.

3) Determine what elements of your own career portfolio to publish on your page or blog.

4) Send invitations out to active contacts and extended community.

5) Select and perform one of these assignment options:

   a) Look-up three potential contacts within an organization who will help you secure employment within that organization. Conduct background research on all three.

   b) Reference experts in three different professions related to your ongoing investigation. Assess their credentials and their own professional networks, using the factors and metrics you learned in **Units Three** and **Four**.

   c) Bring the results of these activities to class.

6) Include background research and alerts/notifications.

Now let's organize those steps, using SPM:

FIGURE 4.29: Applying SPM to the Social Network Assignment Checklist

SPM step	Rationale	Positioning
Why: Purpose	Reason for the networking	You want to have meaningful exchanges with influential contacts whose whose reputations precede them (networking targets)
What: Objectives and Expectations	Objectives are the supporting evidence Expectations anticipate available resources and likely constraints	Demonstrate your use of query formation in **Unit Two** (syntax, semantics, operators...) by using a commercial search engine to locate affiliated members within your network and theirs Use this same approach to highlight special skills or unique insights that will help you advance goals addressed in your search target's work and expertise
How: Tools and Methods	Task and goal-based procedures	Use a search engine other than Google or Bing that helps to connect this goal of yours with your networking targets SUGGESTION: Social bookmarking sites like Delicious are helpful for finding specialized search engines that focus on your area of interest
When: Duration and Failsafes	Time commitment to search and noted failures to redirect project	Use your research to write an email that will trigger a positive response from your search target. It's up to you if you follow through, then drop it (and don't wait out Twitter for the next tweet to land!)
Who: Offline follow-up	Who is a direct contact that will advance the goals of my project	It's always a bonus to pick folks who are within driving range for that follow-up coffee or the chance to intercept at speaking engagements

SEARCH TO CONVERSE

We create or develop social networks when we need to show the relationships and connections between the vested parties. One example is in a case: suspect, victim, witnesses, law enforcement, etc. We can map this type of network through models like PCF and SPM and present it to our clients.

In such a mapping, a social network shows the personal, first party, authentic interactions between internal group members (family, close friends/advisers...) and external group members.

Search to Converse ("STC") is the orientation for honing our investigations. It means that the main purpose of our search projects is not to amass as much evidence as possible. It's to collect just enough to make it actionable – not collecting for its own sake.

STC involves mapping our evidence to the purpose and objective of the investigation. It includes the following elements and activities:

1. Alerts and notifications
2. Daily progress on blogs
3. Joining professional networks and cultivating contacts
4. Assessing social networks and public record searches

> **Definition: Search to Converse ("STC")**
>
> *A brief but compelling model for prior research on individuals that should be engaged directly to corroborate, dispute, and augment the evidence in question.*

Putting Networks in Play

Diagrams have their merits. They're visual and help us to work and document our work in an organized and systematic way. But the real pay-off is not filling in a bunch of boxes but engaging in the discussions that happen outside those boxes. How do we connect our research approach with an immediate and tangible goal, one that demonstrates the common ground we share with our potential networking targets?

So what did my students do? They found folks in each of their networks (LinkedIn, Twitter, Facebook, Instagram...) that work in their chosen field (professional investigations). Students then emailed and asked them to comment about their professional roles and how they assumed those roles.

Sometimes those emails can read as scripted, a little stiff. For instance, you're being too formal if a personal introduction reads like a cover letter for employment. Envision the fulfilling of your objective before trading war stories, cultivating contacts, or developing an expertise around collection agency operations. That's how you connect your background and education to the topics you showcase in your research practice – those bloggable topics where you seek to...

- Distinguish your expertise and be a beacon for best practices,
- Package a set of services unique to your offering, and
- Make the biggest impact in your own right.

The biggest redirect I give them is to broaden their focus – starting with the larger target like a group or organization first. Then we're narrowing down to a particular person because of their connections, accomplishments, shared interests, expertise, etc. Whatever draws you to that person is the *what* or objectives section of your search log.

Sound right to your ears?

Hurdles persist in the searching to conversing transition. Yes, these overtures connect to each student's own background. Yes, the intention is to bridge their prior experience to their new set of skills (or renewed appreciation of skills they had all along). However, that's no guarantee of an explicit connection between our networking goals and the current passions and/or positions of the networking target.

Don't hear back from your targets? The next time out, I recommend:

      1. Toning down the deafening ambition trapped in your brain, and

      2. Letting that ambition fuel the determination to rebuild the original grounds for a meeting.

Remember, this appointment is prefaced on a shared bond such as a vested interest, belonging to a common group, or unified by a shared goal. Presenting those agenda-setting bonds can lead to a rich exchange of views, contacts, job leads, etc. Often that extra distance means stepping back, not drilling down. For instance, one smart approach is the added perspective of working in multiple fields you share with your targets, not a single-minded pursuit of an unwavering goal.

Careful here. There is a risk of fixating too much on single individuals to the detriment of our larger networking goals. As we saw earlier in **Unit Four**, the referral requests on LinkedIn are clunky at best and invasive when the pursuit is through third or fourth degrees of separation. It's usually more productive to break through directly by using some of the query formation techniques and people finder tools we introduced in **Unit Three**.

Another approach is to contact alumni from the same academic programs. Seeking out contacts who document a career shift *after* completion of the program is a great way to substantiate their use of the same credential you're now pursuing as well.

When searching to conversing goes smoothly, it's rarely an effortless undertaking. Documentation manages to be exhaustive and airtight. There is not a single wasted description or idle observation. Overtures to targets is honest, compelling, fact-based, provocative – and completely worthy of a response. It's always a sensitive issue when we ask directly for professional guidance from an unknown actor. But this is no cold call. A consummate networker can diffuse the awkwardness. Referencing your relative distance from the field you're trying to crack is an invitation for perspective-gathering and engagement.

Determining Your Digital Identity

> *"We wouldn't worry so much about what people thought of us if we knew how seldom they did."*
>
> — Samuel Johnson

In **Unit Two,** we first explored the Query Formation equivalence for googling the babysitter. We used semantics to determine if I was in fact 'the Marc Solomon' – star of Internet research stage and screen. We further qualified my birth name with a list of possible area codes within the Boston Massachusetts metropolitan area:

> *"Marc Solomon" (617 OR 978 OR 508 OR 781) boston*

In **Unit Three**, we reviewed some common people finder tools for making accurate IDs, conducting background checks, and gathering contact information. We also considered tools that document the assets and properties of our potential search targets.

Now that we're beyond the mechanics of query building, we're at the point where it's actually getting personal: What is the difference between our Google profiles and our actual background and credentials? Or as someone who may have had vengeance in their hearts, and used a Facebook page for their catharsis...

- What are some of the distortions and where in the self-reporting do you see the compromises?
- Which of those pieces in our checkered pasts are better documented than others?

Perhaps, applying PCF is the best way to begin this deconstruction:

> *What would you like to change about what a third person rendering of you would look like?*

Passing through our own *looking glasses* may be advised here. And it's not navel-gazing or a walk on the wild side in pursuit of some low impact aerobics. Let's say we might one day wish to achieve some rather conventional life goals like marriage, family, and career success? In that light, we squint into the glare of violence, sex, and any inferences of criminal behavior under the lens of our digital identities. Questioning what we see *is* the point. We look into this mirror with the humility that we would extend the same unassuming hand of fair play and neutrality to the digital identities of our search targets.

To paraphrase Samuel Johnson, human vanity is a blindspot so large, we could fit love, ambition, and jealousy within its shadowing borders, and still have room for all our Facebook albums. There is no piety or superiority in stating the simple matter of fact that we all come to live in glass houses. The true test isn't how well we see through the glass. It's how well we hold ourselves up to the same judgments we make about those landing above our own personal radars.

Alerts and Notifications

In her book *Information Trapping: Real-Time Research on the Web,* Tara Calishain makes researching more efficient for the thousands of academics, journalists, scientists, and professionals for whom the Web is an indispensable tool – as well as bloggers, genealogists, and other hobbyists with a passion to pursue. She does so by teaching the latest techniques in creating ongoing information-gathering systems that are as automated as possible. Instead of the usual static, single instance of finding information, Calishain demonstrates how to use RSS feeds, page monitoring tools, and other software so readers can move from browsing to setting information traps.

These will notify you of changes to local communities and to individual websites.

FIGURE 4.30: Example of an Alerts and Notifications Interface

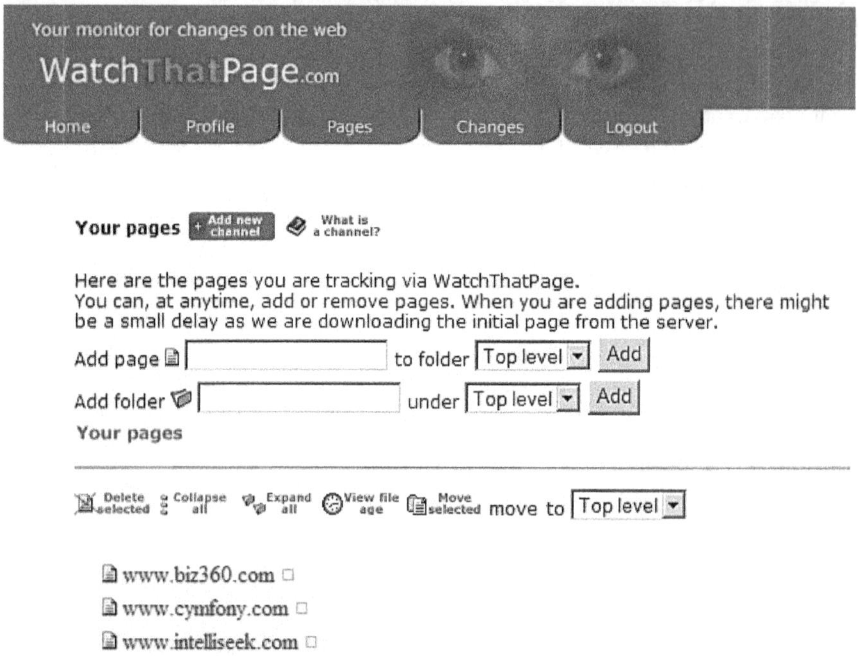

Watch that Page is an alerting service that notifies subscribers of changes to root domains and subdomains in a website of interest. This tool can be helpful on normally static company sites when a change in management or a particular alliance or product line is anticipated.

Tips for Searching Social Media Profiles

As we discussed in our introduction to the Deep and Invisible Web in **Unit Three,** it can be quite difficult to nail down fluid or continually evolving web pages, a.k.a. dynamic content. How do we know if we're trying to capture the proverbial lightening in a bottle? That's when the page in our browser ends with the following characters:

1. ?
2. %
3. +
4. $
5. cgi-bin

These pages could be flash demos, pop-ups or i-frames. In lay terms, this could be an ad that requires a cookie to generate or a travel reservation that only lasts for a specific duration. Without a static URL, the page cannot be tagged or regenerated without starting at the specific root site or database.

Fortunately, most digital credentialing is easier to pin down. In effect, the regular query formation rules apply. That means a combination of syntax and semantics can help generate lists of potential employees, experts, customers, or like-minded colleagues based on interest, location, experience, and any number of demographic qualifiers.

For example, one difference on Facebook between finding a potential date or new hire means means searching for 'women' in concert with 'diversity' in tandem with the sourcing 'location.' Those additional qualifications change the intention from a pick-up line to a prospect call. In terms of outputs, it helps to apply the information type filtering we learned in **Unit Two**. For instance, some social networks include such default fields as geography, employer, and alma mater as default outputs for their in-depth results. Sometimes those options change depending on network or our status within them.

If our major objective is name generation, we might not even bother with search pages. Lots of people are often highlighted as listings in directories contained within single PDF documents. Again, our ability to anticipate format types is key for informing the most most productive social media searches. Also, it sounds strange, but sometimes a straight forward professional search can become ensnared by the habits and preferences of SEO campaigns that distort your earnest intent. For instance, a search on 'nurse jobs' can turn racy with little qualification, or imagination for that matter.

FIGURE 4.31: Using Syntax and Semantics to Elevate Desired Working Terms in a Field of Choice

```
site:linkedin.com "knowledge management" relo package inurl:~job
```
About 97 results (0.36 seconds)

► Haak
I started my sales & marketing **career** in the Netherlands where I was responsible for .... cost of the proposed **relocation package** to the hiring executive. ...
www.linkedin.com/pub/dir/+/Haak - Cached

Associate Manager, Internal Communications at Blizzard ...
Nov 18, 2010 ... Location: Velizy (southwest of Paris) - a **relocation package** will be ...
Experience of **knowledge management** and / or business analysis ...
www.linkedin.com/jobs?viewJob=&jobId... - Cached

Sue anne
Title: **Recruitment** Sourcing Specialist at Research In Motion ... Manager - Channel Marketing, Indonesia (based in Indonesia) **Relocation package** will be considered. .... Title: EMEA **Knowledge Management**; Demographic info: Amsterdam Area, ...
www.linkedin.com/pub/dir/Sue+anne/+ - Cached

Lisa Blackmon | LinkedIn
Negotiated approximately 50 **salary** offers and dozens of sign-on bonuses/**relocation packages** annually at both ... The Braintrust: **Knowledge Management** Group ...
www.linkedin.com/pub/lisa-blackmon/08/B20/741 - Cached

Deepti Gudup - Project Manager at TechMahindra | LinkedIn
The Hague Area, Netherlands - Project Manager at TechMahindra
o Implementation of **work package** and Delivery closure formalities o **Knowledge Management** and transition to maintenance teams .... Jointly developed the web application to assist **relocation** of resources (employees and hardware assets) to ...
nl.linkedin.com/in/deeptigudup - Netherlands - Cached

Scott Gavin profiles | LinkedIn
Title: Expatriate **Recruitment & Relocation** Representative at Aramco ... current **jobs** or the **employment package**- contact me via LinkedIn or visit our NEW ...
www.linkedin.com/pub/dir/Scott/Gavin - Cached

SHUM
Senior Manager - Channel Marketing, Indonesia (based in Indonesia) **Relocation package** will be considered. If interested, kindly drop me an email at ...
www.linkedin.com/pub/dir/+/SHUM - Cached

Google Query in 2010. Note that keyword highlighting is in effect, even for term expansion phrases related to 'relo.'

FIGURE 4.32: The Changing Face of Using Search Engines to Network

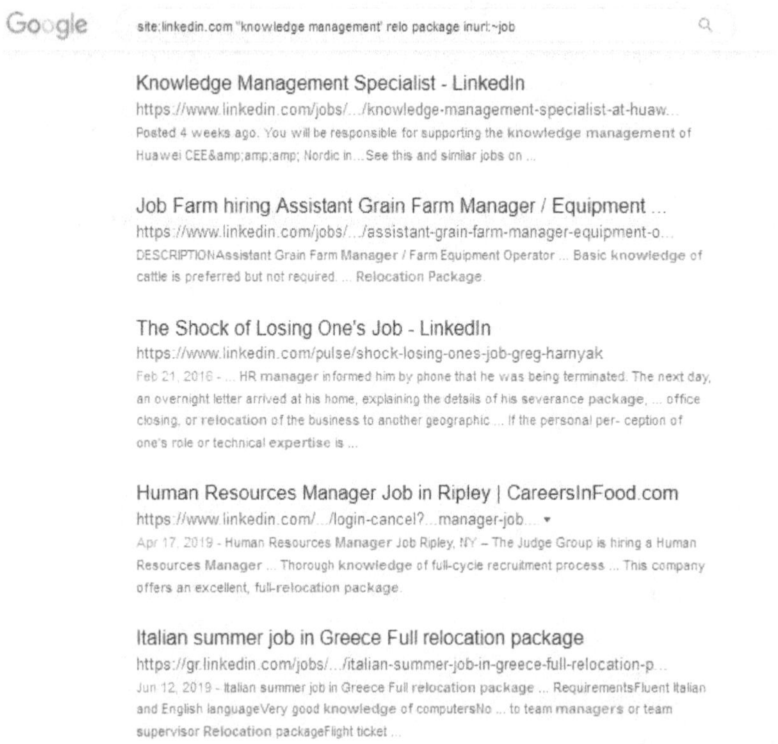

Google   site:linkedin.com "knowledge management" relo package inurl:~job

Knowledge Management Specialist - LinkedIn
https://www.linkedin.com/jobs/.../knowledge-management-specialist-at-huaw...
Posted 4 weeks ago. You will be responsible for supporting the knowledge management of Huawei CEE&amp;amp; Nordic in... See this and similar jobs on ...

Job Farm hiring Assistant Grain Farm Manager / Equipment ...
https://www.linkedin.com/jobs/.../assistant-grain-farm-manager-equipment-o...
DESCRIPTIONAssistant Grain Farm Manager / Farm Equipment Operator ... Basic knowledge of cattle is preferred but not required. ... Relocation Package.

The Shock of Losing One's Job - LinkedIn
https://www.linkedin.com/pulse/shock-losing-ones-job-greg-harnyak
Feb 21, 2016 - ... HR manager informed him by phone that he was being terminated. The next day, an overnight letter arrived at his home, explaining the details of his severance package, ... office closing, or relocation of the business to another geographic ... If the personal per- ception of one's role or technical expertise is ...

Human Resources Manager Job in Ripley | CareersInFood.com
https://www.linkedin.com/.../login-cancel?...manager-job... ▼
Apr 17, 2019 - Human Resources Manager Job Ripley, NY – The Judge Group is hiring a Human Resources Manager ... Thorough knowledge of full-cycle recruitment process ... This company offers an excellent, full-relocation package.

Italian summer job in Greece Full relocation package
https://gr.linkedin.com/jobs/.../italian-summer-job-in-greece-full-relocation-p...
Jun 12, 2019 - Italian summer job in Greece Full relocation package ... RequirementsFluent Italian and English languageVery good knowledge of computersNo ... to team managers or team supervisor Relocation packageFlight ticket ...

Here's the same query in 2019. Where are all the job candidates? Where are all the people? Where's the bleeping hit count?

SOCIAL BOOKMARKING: SOMEBODY KNOWS THE SITES I'VE SEEN

Unlike a professional networking site, a tagging or social bookmarking tool is focused less on finding people and more on discovering or recovering a useful site. Tagging is a productive and self-referential way to unify all the search experiences worth repeating.

Have you ever created a favorites placeholder in your web browser? Have you ever saved several if not dozens of bookmarks to record a visit to a page to which one day you might return (and never do?)

Can I ask you something?

How often do you even think of returning? If the answer is infrequently at best you're not alone. But if you think your isolation must persist, then you may find yourself alone fairly soon.

Drum roll please for social bookmarking.

I'll be honest. In some of my past classes the technology part of teaching Internet Research was a real hardship for some folks. You might have heard of the distinction between *digital immigrants* and *natives* to describe: (1) those of us who grew up with the web as a fact of life and, (2) those of us who are astounded every time we login. **(Prensky, 2001)**[16] The student I'm describing wasn't an immigrant but a digital *deportee*. They needed research to be tangible, linear, and fixed in one place. Virtual was not part of their dress code.

Core Social Media Technologies

Clearly, this factor is not in play with your sizable investment in making information useful. So here we go. I will be introducing you to three web technologies for documenting and presenting web-based investigations through social media – some of which you may already be practicing and observing:

> 1) **Social Bookmarking:** Fulfilling the promise of no memorization. Everything's activated when you need it.
>
> 2) **RSS Readers:** Realizing the need to boil the internet ocean down to a pond. Where the fish are plenty and they bite back.
>
> 3) **Blogs:** Your true calling put up in Internet lights for all to see. Especially the folks you want to converse with on future projects.

The one enduring benefit common to all three is the confidence that the roles they perform are not short-term or prone to becoming marginalized by the next big thing. That's because they can do something that's lost on trendsetters. They can't grasp the value in their sexy, top dollar devices because these technologies are about making information work for you.

The true power lies not in upgrading to the latest and greatest but managing our projects and attentions according to our own interests and priorities. That's what social bookmark sites (a.k.a. tagging engines), RSS Readers, and blogging platforms do for us — make information work for us and not the other way around.

The Benefits of Social Tagging

It's easier to show than it is to tell.

Yes, there are benefits for knowledge capture. We can recover not only pages worth revisiting but even the query language from instructive searches that led us there in the first place. But the biggest benefit is the network effect. That's the serendipitous spark that ignites when our crowdsourcing colleagues take the pain and effort to describe an experience worth repeating.

For us investigators, that's the very definition of search success. The key to repeating that success is to recall the paths we take to get from questions to answers. Each tag is a breadcrumb that jogs our memory for particular sources and/or searches that will help build on that knowledge (or avoid a past pitfall). This helps settle immediate scores and may well continue forward on future search expeditions.

Social bookmarking is a way of saving these places on a dedicated webpage that you control. Better yet, the upkeep is no more challenging than clicking an icon when a site worth saving passes through. If you care about your own time and managing your Internet-based research, then tagging is a big deal.

Tag Clouds

Before we get grounded in the practice of tagging as a daily practice, let's wander a bit in the tag cloud to understand some of the key distinctions and benefits.

FIGURE 4.33: Defining Tag Clouds

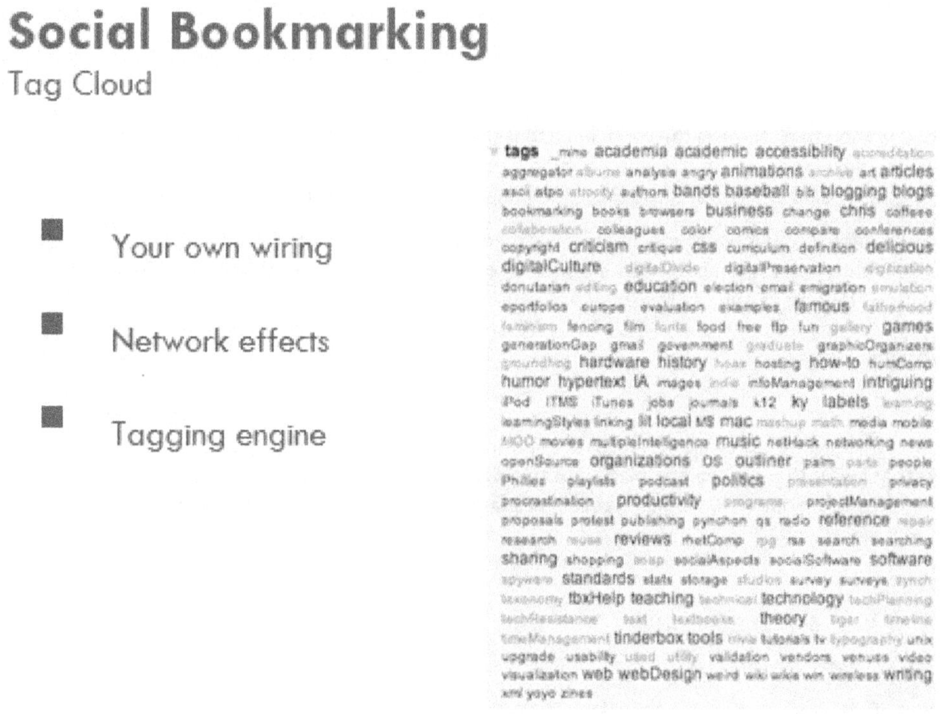

Social Bookmarking
Tag Cloud

- Your own wiring
- Network effects
- Tagging engine

This kind of indexing has long been the work of information scientists, taxonomists, and catalogers that adhere to the traditions of the disciplines they classify. In social bookmarking there are no such conventions – only the top-of-mind association that legions of searchers summon when they're looking to affirm the authority and 'aboutness' of a potential source of their investigations.

Let's look more closely at what goes into tag clouds and why this is a huge productivity gain for the **Knowledge-ABLED**:

> **1) Your Own Wiring** – Tagging enables you to recall productive sites and even search sessions according to the way you recall things. For instance, let's say you're tagging a database that yields some successful clinical trials for a rare disease that's anything but rare in your family. You will literally *save* that success according to the patient's name or referring doctor, or whatever detail is likeliest to conjure up your discovery process. That's the learning sequence you will not to revisit at a later stage of the trial, disease, and investigation.
>
> **2) Network Effects** – Tagging your work to a dedicated tagging site has the added benefit of leveraging the tags that have already been referenced by other registrants on the site. That means you can generate a listing of sites already tagged as well as the popularity of the site itself. A high number of tagging counts is an important validation that the source is frequently cited and/or productive in the investigations of others.
>
> **3) Tagging Engine** – The other important connection with tagging is that dedicated tagging sites organize the web around the respective vocabularies of every tagger who joins their network. Thus we can save terms to the words that we invoke to summon connections. But what about all the other terms that would never occur to us? Leveraging tagging sites as search engines produces high value results lists of potential resources, but also a richer yield of tags that are also relevant to our research.

FIGURE 4.34: The Network Effects Benefits of Social Bookmarking

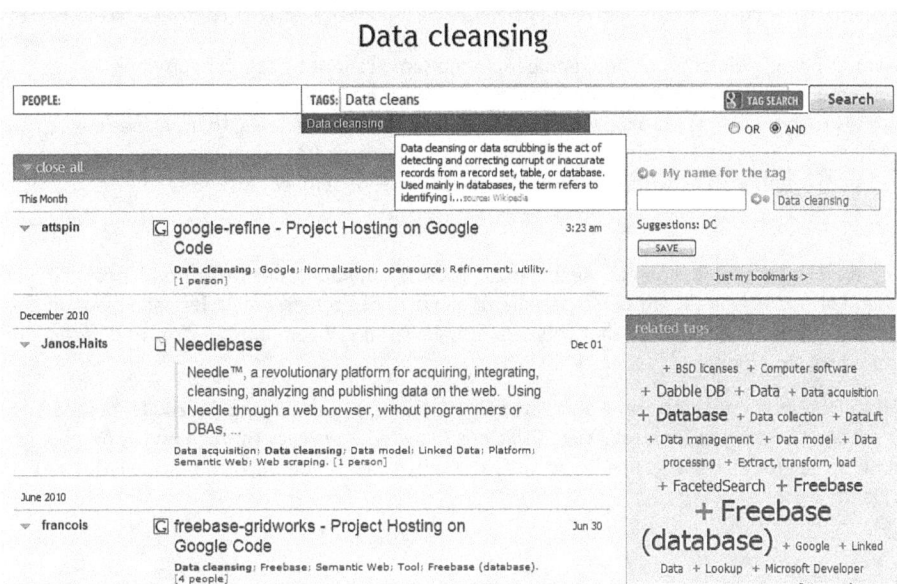

Social bookmarking helps us leverage the communal aspects of pooling resources together – certainly an improvement on the static nature of a favorites folder, as we see above in a tagging engine called Faviki, we can even summon on-the-fly definitions for the terms we're using in our tags.

The Limitations of Keeping Our Bookmarks Under Wraps

Bookmarking or what Microsoft refers to as a "Favorites Folder" is a traditional if somewhat static and inflexible way to store a list of websites worth remembering.

But there is no way to annotate these sites according to the experience they represent. Even though we've created a placeholder for archiving important discoveries, we can't reconnect them to our discovery process.

For instance, let's say that a database comprising the insurance records of physicians in Massachusetts were to be listed under health-related bookmarks. What if that site was also instructive as a tool for looking into malpractice claims on a doctor you're investigating?

This context introduces other dimensions that may be well worth exploring but obscured by the linear and cumbersome way that bookmarks are stored. In this illustration, the terms 'Malpractice' can be tagged. So can 'investigation' or 'Medical Errors' or any other noun or predicate that inspires us to remember the context for applying the bodies of knowledge documented in these resources. For the record, this documentation dynamic was begun in 2003 by the now dormant Del.icio.us. In its day, Del.icio.us was a magnet for leverage-worthy research links.

Additional Tagging Tips

1) Key words or noun phrases?

One distinction that is rarely addressed is that when we talk about key words we assume this includes compound words or multiple terms, a.k.a. phrases. For example, the American Dialect Society routinely includes hyphenates like 'game-changer' and 'shovel-ready' as nominations for its word of the year. Phrases referring to past political scandals or pronouncements like 'Zombie bank' or 'Smart power' are also fair game. **(Zimmer, 2009[17])**.

While this practice works fine in deliberations between people the same cannot be said for software programming. Just as nature abhors a vacuum, search engines despise the blank characters between words. Most social tagging sites treat any phrase broken with a white space as a separate tag. Other engines create lookup tables that match the tags we're considering with those already indexed. Some invite us to separate our tags with delimiters that treat phrases as separate terms such as commas or semi-colons.

2) One or many?

One thing we don't have to do is save a separate tag for singular and plural nouns, i.e. 'prison' and 'prisons.' Another is to use vague or overly general terms – especially when we're deepening our understanding of unique aspects of that topic, i.e. 'crime.' I recommend that you create single strings of compound words to differentiate the categories that are likely to emerge.

For instance, if we do a Delicious search on crime and entertainment we get a site tagged by 2000+ members called "Global Incident Map Displaying Terrorist Acts, Suspicious Activity." If we click through on the number of taggers, we'll see a full sweep for all the tags used to identify the site, a GPS rendering of Hazardous Material 'Situations and Incidents.'

The result is that we can create more purposeful headings like...

- CrimeMaps
- CrimeRetail
- CrimePredictions and so on...

Why no space between the terms? As we see below, if you use phrases in our tags then the tagging engines will list each term separately as its own tag. Not cool!

However, the engine will save as one tag if you create compound words from these noun phrases or add placeholders between terms:

```
SearchEnginesearch_enginesearch+engine
```

3) One or many?

Here's an important caveat about the pages you bookmark. They are bound to change no matter how thoroughly we document their temporary existence. News articles, calendar listings, or even transactional details like airline reservations are highly fluid, and resistant to any kind of placeholder. One workaround is to bookmark the cache result that is stored in the search index long after the same record is taken off the production server:

1. A referring link is broken now that the article has been removed...
2. However, the cache link of the same URL captures the removed article and is now taggable on a number of news sites that carried the same story

4) Drop anchor — tag away!

Finally, register with a tagging site like Digg, Reddit, StumbleUpon, or Diigo. Next, start tagging away on anything worth repeating. That includes webpages with explanations such as search engines with special features. It also includes the actual queries we create with semantic patterns and syntactic strings worth leveraging again. That means we're saving the roadmaps, not just the destination sites.

FIGURE 4.35: Saving Journeys – not just Destinations

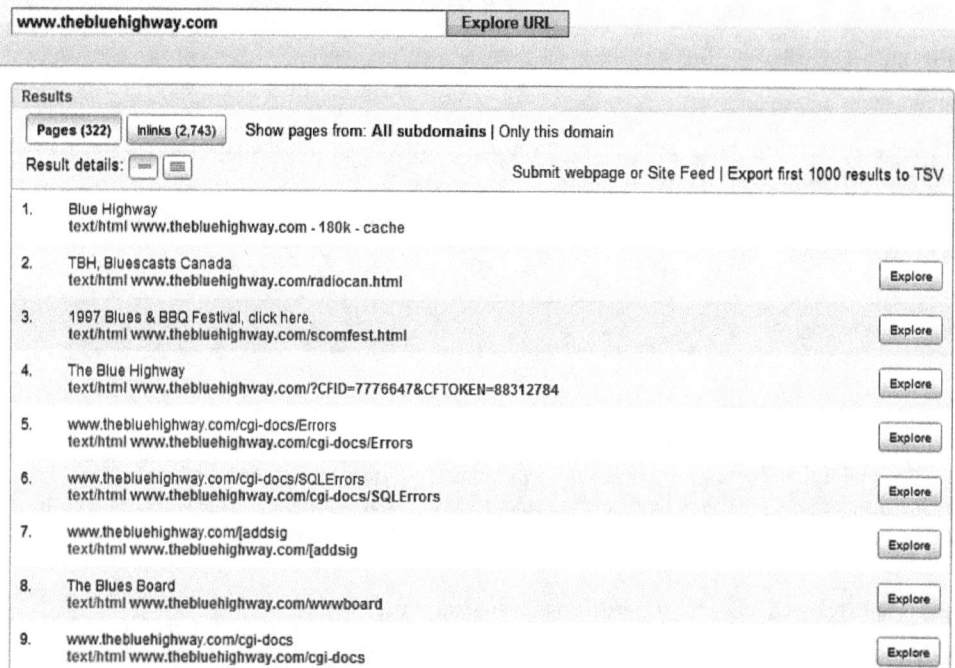

These examples of semantic searches are illustrations of success. Each one holds the particular tweaks for moving us from our original SPM objectives to 'how' we get at the evidence we're using to support our original purpose. Just a few more tweaks and we can apply the same queries to entirely new search projects.

See? It's not a wild leap from **Unit Two** to the socially-enabled sharing of endorsed content through tagging engines. Your hits should be smaller in number and higher quality than what you might expect with the bigtime engines. The reason is that Google is supply-driven. Everyone who covets 15 minutes of fame or a higher placement in its PageRank is concocting Google potions. That's the essence of commercial search. Tagging engines, however, are demand-driven. And that's music to the ears of most researchers. Any *hit* in a tagging engine search is a positive response – not a plea. And the response is ... hey, this is a repeatable experience.

At the risk of boring you I'll say it again: if it bears repeating, it's worth tagging.

SECTION 4:4 | Misinformation as an Information Source —

Misinformation: When Context Disappears

So far **Unit Four** has been about the perspective-gathering that we need for our research. This happens when our spyglasses focus in on (1) human affairs, and (2) why people do what they do. Modeling the motives of information providers is a decisive action for us observers. Piety is not commanding us to sit in the judgment of others. A healthy skepticism requires that we don't take one provider's perspective as the final, definitive word. Frameworks like PCF and the Vectors of Integrity are measurement tools towards that end. They gauge the distance between words and deeds: The universal metric for determining the level of attention (and often belief) we invest as message recipients.

Knowing the context doesn't just mean we can decide for ourselves. It gets us beyond the immediate *eye of the beholder*. It enhances what neuro-scientists refer to as 'theory of mind.' This concept addresses our ability to understand that others have beliefs, desires and intentions that are different from our own. **(Premack, Woodruff, 1978)**[18] It means we can see clear through the single-minded purpose of providers to the processing of those messages. We can assess how the layerings of meanings are sorted through, saved, discarded, and integrated into our existing world views, memories, and appetites for detail.

> *Definition: Theory of Mind*
>
> *The perspective-gathering that enables us to understand the priority scales, trust systems, and expectations that govern the everyday conduct of the individuals and group behaviors which we need to rationalize as researchers.*

But what happens when the force of a message is so great, it overpowers our reasoning? It overwhelms our ability to think critically. We can't anticipate. We can't process. We can only react. If it sounds like we've suddenly gone from dispassionate investigators to embroiled victims. That's not a trick of the light. That's the disarming nature of character assassinations: The demonizing of individuals and groups that stand in the way of the misinformation provider.

THE LIMITED PERSPECTIVES OF INFORMATION PROVIDERS

We now shift from the expansive context of recipients back to the more limited perspectives of providers.

Have you ever been on a call with someone you don't know? Have you ever been anxious about whose turn it was to speak first? Chances are, if the stranger called the meeting, you're not that concerned. You expect to be on the receiving end. Information providers are presenters and facilitators. Providers are on speaker. Information recipients are on mute.

Naturally, we all have a hand in both camps. It didn't take the advent of social media to blur the boundaries between content producers and consumers. The art of conversation is largely a study in switching off between both roles. But when that exchange happens in a set of search results and web pages, the conversation is strained and the information flows in one direction. This more traditional call and response pattern is similar to the economic model of supply and demand.

When we are providers, at least in more formal and binding communication channels, it's hard to escape this timeless and cautionary dictum:

> "Once it's out there, you can't take it back."

That's a recurrent question in our minds as individuals and as group members. Our communications are now recorded. From the most prolific political speech to the most casual off-handed tweet. Dialogs, monologues, blogs, search logs, and keystrokes of mental fogs: There's a digital recollection of what we've done with words and numbers.

However, that reminder for discretion may not lead to the reworking or even self-sensoring of material that finds its voice in forums, many extending well beyond the initial context. Anyone who's ever had an email of theirs forwarded to unknown individuals, knows this disorientation firsthand. The message goes out to others they either don't know or care to involve. That's when we grasp that loss of control: The realization that the follow-up interpretation may be quite removed from the original intention.

Now amplify the loss of context by the number of our followers, collaborators, and peers plugged into the same email servers that we are. That's a boat load of garbled communications, misinterpreted intentions, and unforeseen outcomes. Is my conclusion that public pronouncements and even private peer communications need to be better vetted? Say, the same way news articles were proofed by copy editors?

No, not because more attentive proofing isn't a good thing. It's not because *thinking*, even twice — before we *send* isn't a sound policy. It's because this is a book for researchers, not communicators. That's what we investigators must keep in mind as we begin to unpack passive, edgy, and downright hostile sources of misinformation, even intimidation. First and foremost in our thinking is that...

- Only the most thoughtful and deliberate providers actually think through the implications of what they communicate
- The clearer the motive for communicating, the less likely the information provider we're sourcing falls into this camp

Let me explain.

We talk about opportunities when we use information. We think in terms of risk when others do so. No risk assessment performed by an internet researcher is complete without considering misinformation – the unfounded hearsay that passes judgment as quickly as it spreads. So how do we pass better judgment and substantiate the information we pass onto our own peers, and clients, and networks?

The key to being Knowledge-ABLED is to steal a page from the PCF and Vectors of Integrity. We reapply the same principles used earlier to assess message recipients. Now we leverage them to weigh the merits of our sources. We can sort out what they're saying through three perspectives:

1. **Authenticity** – How directly an information source participates in the facts and opinions they produce.

2. **Credibility** – The difference between how a group describes itself and is depicted by others.

3. **Conjugation** – The distinction between interpersonal and group communications: How that impacts what, when, and to who digital information is communicated.

Don't Just Take My Word for it

Remember back in **Unit One** when we first broached the subject of blindspots? Rather than specific weaknesses, our blindness is rooted in our own oblivion. They may be personal shortcomings. They may be imperfections, or quirks that we choose to ignore. Either way, we are not the best communicators of our own impaired perceptions.

This design flaw is of particular note to information providers in the age of social media, especially in a medium that based on first person referrals to one's self. This is not narcissism or self-centeredness. These are the new rules of the game – the shared understandings between providers and recipients:

1. The first understanding is that I'm providing you with information about me.

2. The second less understood assumption is that I may not be the most qualified person to do this.

Once again, we're up against the integrity vector that spans from authenticity on one end to credibility at the opposite extreme. Can you trust me? Perhaps not. But understanding the inherent flaws of first persons and parties as the subject of their own messages increases confidence in our own Knowledge-ABILITIES.

FIGURE 4.36: Tracing the Source Origins of Information Providers Through Link Analysis

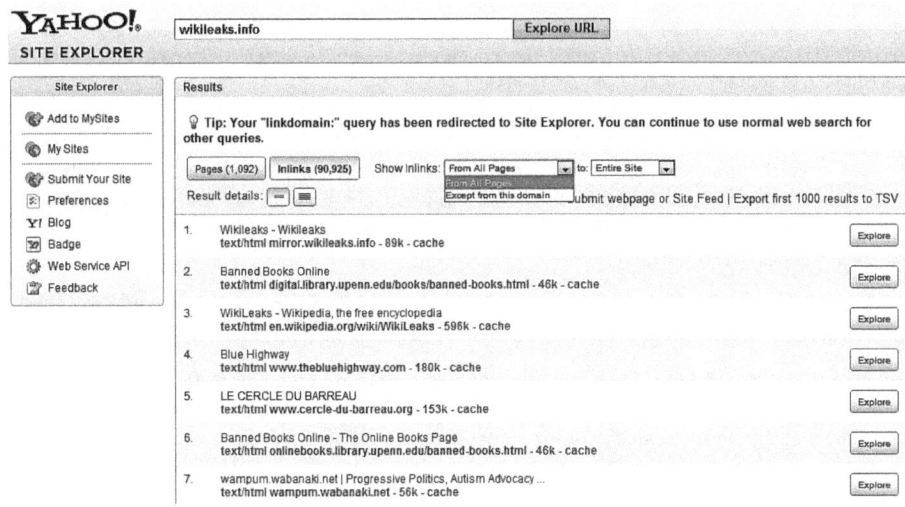

The linkdomain syntax lists all web pages that include hyperlinks to the target site root "wikileaks.info."

FIGURE 4.37: Focusing on One Prolific Linker to the Target Information Provider

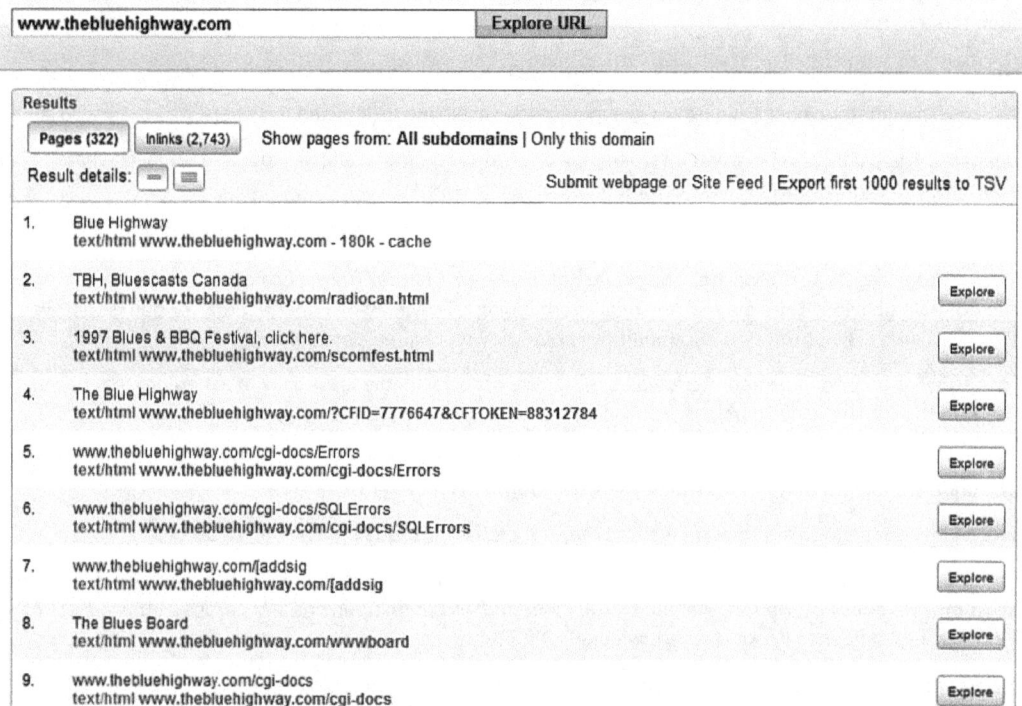

This screen capture illustrates the deepest of the most – the 322 individual webpages from the same site root (domain) that references the original search target (WikiLeaks.info). Link analysis like that performed here enables us to see not only referring links but the kinds of references our information providers cultivate to support their cases or even sell their products.

Going Negative

An old college friend of mine and I were watching one of our grainy college videos from the early 1980s. One production consisted mostly of off-air ads from the early 80s set to a David Byrne/Brian Eno-like avant guard collaboration. We were both taken with a fast food commercial where to pre-pubescent girls rode their bikes into town for an unstructured outing at the local McDonald's.[19] Chugging fries 'n cokes without a cellphone?

Imagine the consternation of letting a nine-year-old out on their own to experience retail commerce, moving traffic and total strangers? What parent 21st Century parental figure could ever live down the decision to let their own kids grow-up?

The other aspect of defensive behavior that's fascinating is the notion that people take these precautions for assertive or *control purposes*. It's easy to regard this aspect of human nature as an ingrained suspicion or pervasive social distrust. Perhaps. But I think it boils down to the fact that in the scarcity culture, most people feel more control over preventing sneak attacks than enabling a pleasant surprise. In the external world, negative information is processed much more quickly than positive news. It's the original homeland defense.

After my undergraduate video days, I moved into a post-grad political consulting program where we were taught that playing to peoples' fears was neither inherently evil nor virtuous. It depended on two factors:

1. Your candidate's base or loyalists will remain steadfast in their support.
2. The alienations you seed reverberate in the fears and doubts in what our professor called the *uncommitted middle* – the fence-sitters you're attempting to peel away from your opponent.

This tension between the power of the message and blaming the messenger is tracked assiduously by political media observers and influencers (they are often one in the same). That's why planting seeds of suspicion requires the messenger to disavow all authorship. Their effectiveness is neutralized once their messages are tainted by their own self-interest. The accusations and innuendos are much more convincing when the originator of the claims is not implicated by the reporters and pundits who broker the story. All credibility is gone when the messenger becomes the message.

A skilled political operative or public relations manager keeps their fingerprints off the revelations they leak to the news media. Assuming the reporter gets the scoop they were promised, this is a better than even trade for the leaker.

Once the story is delivered, the operative retreats to the war room to watch the sparks fly, their opponents squirm, track the implications, and stay ahead of the story. Whether having gone negative inflicts more damage than it sustains, both first party sides understand the third-party public the same way. The key determinants are no different for claiming victory than they are for escaping blame:

FIGURE 4.38: Gauging Reactions to Going Negative

Determinant: What's in it for me?		->What's it gonna cost?
1. NEGATIVE:	What's being taken away from me	->Who's it being given to?
2. POSITIVE:	What's being given to me	->What's expected in return?

Here's another campaign fundamental they drill into hired guns in training: A negative that's not responded to becomes grounded. The corollary here is that a negative with grains of reality becomes gospel truth. That reality cuts deep enough to trip any get-out-the-vote drive lacing up its campaign boots. Going positive might be riskier than playing defense.

The negative message is an economizing one. An accusation lands on its target and the audience processes the remark with only one question in-mind — how will the accused respond? A positive message takes much longer to be absorbed and believed. It's a defensive impulse that predates U.S. Presidential elections, perhaps even romantic betrayals.

That's because survival trounces reality. That's because positive news forms an instant response before a question can even form. That reflex says: *what's in it for you?* What potential conflict-of-interest lies buried in that cheery delivery of my selective facts?

The Best Defense

Up until now, we've spoken of *being used* by information in passive ways. We're enchanted with our gadgets or intoxicated with the access and control they afford us. But there are also intentional efforts to distort or devalue the original context of information. They're used to compromise an informant, an investigator, or persons whose knowledge may jeopardize the security and/or mission of a first party institution. We need to diffuse these risk factors before their detonation does harm to our families and friends, as well as our stature as investigators.

The increasing connectedness of porous, virtual borders is an opportunity to explore and test those connections. It is also threatens our ability to maintain confidences and hold secrets. So too, it endangers our ability to stifle unsubstantiated rumors. It removes the former safeguard of journalists to correct factual inaccuracies or quotes that may reflect the correct wording, but not the way the subject was trying to communicate their message.

Simply put, how do we set the record straight, when there are competing versions of the same record?

Such confusions and uncertainties are breeding grounds for misinformation campaigns. The campaigners conceal their attempts to mislead, distract, or misrepresent behind a self-selecting sets of facts supported by mounting bodies of dubious evidence.

Don't Believe Everything You Think

Misinformation is not always delivered through a diabolical intention. Sometimes our own assumptions blind us to the fact we are not our own best petitioners.

The most universal form of conflict-of-interest is the edict that one cannot confer credibility onto one's self. The information provider is compromised when they are the source *and* the story. Even highly confident and ego-driven type A personalities will instinctively seek professional representation through agents and brokers. This is preferable to representing their own interests directly. Is that because they're secretly bashful?

More than likely they've come to terms with the fact that they will be seen as one-sided versions of their own world views. They will not be perceived as impartial arbiters with the broader perspective needed to reconcile their self-serving interest with a more prevailing one.

Nothing Personal

The diffusion of risk factors means keeping a vigilant but dispassionate focus on misinformation as an information source. That means tuning into potential risks without rushing to judgments, falling victim to our own protective instincts, and seeing the paranoia in others for what it is: An unflattering blend of obsession, vanity and fear.

Obsessive behavior is a temptation when under attack. But paranoia is a luxury of the self-important. Wearing one's distrust on their sleeve can easily backfire – especially when acting wounded or defensive adds merit to the claims made against us. Is our outrage fueled by our sense of justice, guilt, or fear of what's to come? It's a dilemma few of us can sustain under the glare of public scrutiny. Self-defense shows us on our guard and shows our detractors that they may have knocked us off our game. We've lost all perspective between the evidence in question and our firsthand role in shaping the perceptions of the people who were not there with us.

For now let's assume that we're not under attack. Time is on our side. We know that the misinformers may not be all that informed of their own limitations as communicators. They might not even be aggressive or hostile so much as sloppy and oblivious of any unintended consequences.

There are three ways we will approach misinformation with deliberation and transparency, not defensiveness and firewalls! Misinformation providers earn our suspicions when they...

- Pay second parties to create a sense of false trust in the expectations and beliefs of third parties.

- Perpetrate fraud by projecting a sense of authority and confidence in times of turbulence and uncertainty.

- Game systems like Google's search rankings so that the gamers appear more legitimate or credible than their track record merits.

Here's how those defenses align.

1) Paying Others to do our Bidding: The Price of Social Media Admission

Nowadays, anyone cloaked in celebrity is a potential Trojan horse for peddling ads through micro-messaging platforms like Twitter. The brokers match the endorsers with the brands that match up best with their personalities. That match is critical if an endorsement is going to ring true in their tweets as well as their relationship to their fans and followers (recipients). **(Glover, 2011)**[20] The introduction of intermediaries is the newest wrinkle in the stealth marketing efforts of popular consumer brands. It's advertisers who began the practice of creating *buzz marketing* by paying bloggers to promote their firms or products without disclosing their motives for doing so. **(Gillmor, 2009)**[21]

These examples are a complete reversal of the subscription model where recipients once paid to receive ad-supported media. The reality of social media and the collapse of second parties is that the media is no longer ad-supported. The media is the medium and that medium is advertising.

The all-volunteer cadre of editorial staffers who safeguard Wikipedia presents a more insidious form of misinformation. They remove the the first-party distortions of vanity and self-protection. Wikipedia articles have their own self-selecting treatment of the subjects they cite. For instance, the fluid and transient tastes of Wikipedia's editorial staff skews the importance of group pastimes far beyond their merit as cultural influences:

> "Popular cultural looms large. The entry for the game Halo, for example, is significantly longer than the one for the Protestant Reformation." **(Bennett, 2011)**[22]

This kind of self-identity cuts us off from divinations that run deeper than any religious sect, let alone gaming application. The immediacy of now is tyrannical. There is no longer a grace period or a honeymoon. There is no requisite down time to take in the tumult of disruptive events and accord them the proportion, connectedness, and possible redress they deserve.

To its credit, those same editors are zealous enforcers of second party filtering between message senders and recipients:

> "Thanks to WikiScanner, software that cross-references the Net contributors of contributors, watchdogs have found that computers at ExxonMobil, Pepsico, and Diebold, among others, have been used to remove unflattering information from the companies' entries."

Devised by a CalTech student named Virgil Griffith, this safeguard is very much in keeping with the same credibility scoring we used to compare first and second parties. **(Borland, 2007)**[23] In this example, we compare a first party (Wal-mart) commenting on its own controversial employee healthcare policies with those of second parties. It's in that comparison that we can not only invite conjecture about motives but quantify the gap in these two perspectives. Our PCF-based perspective focuses on the disinterested third parties who have no personal or direct experience on either side of the debate.

FIGURE 4.39: The Hows and Whys Behind Misinformation Sources

Misinformation Provider	Intent	Blindspot	Consequences	Tools / Methods
Political operative going negative	Keep independent voters at home on election day	Can't get in front of story when messenger becomes the message	Distorting attachments	Use demagoguery to create false choices and over-simplify complex issues
Financial planner games the system	Fabricate expertise to an affluent and financially illiterate clientele	Clients' investments vanish as claims of fraud and lawsuits materialize	Inappropriate self-interest	Inflated PageRank commands in search results
Cyberbully contributor to 'honest' Facebook	Catering to a credibility gap between personal proclamation and perceptions of others	Anonymous sources are free to allege and insinuate with impunity	Character assassination – civility ceases when mutual admiration is no longer reciprocated	Only paid subscribers earn the right to 'free' speech
Trojan horse ad peddlers	Use known personalities to validate faceless merchandise and services	Celebrity discovered using a competitor's product	Publicists masquerade as news reporters when third parties are looking for honest brokers	Product placements via celebrity micro-blogging
Short selling day trader	Wants to inflate shares by inviting speculations of mergers and buyouts	Market chatter is not traceable to a specific provider	Unconfirmed rumors savage the share prices of worthy stocks – most are about stock sell-offs, not deal-making	Stocks plummet the day after the rumor passes

OVERCOME BY EVENTS (AND MISINFORMANTS)

Our deadline to respond is yesterday. Other people we care about are waiting on our decision. What would our information therapist say?

The most common ways that we as recipients are overwhelmed by too much information and thus prone to misinformants is that decisions must be made within a limited period. Time pressures created by short-term decisions concerning us seem even more pressing because...

- Big issues often play out in good and bad ways, but our ignorance of them means we must assume the worst.
- We may not grasp what's good for us...
- But we surely get what's good for the competing interest that the misinformant is demonizing to *clear the air* and *set the record straight*.

Misinformation providers are bound by the following aims:

1. They want to create a sense of certainty in the minds of their recipients.

2. The issues they address are a source of unresolved anxiety.

As recipients, we feel defensive and defenseless at the same time: Defensive because we're guarding against a negative outcome. Unwelcome surprises open us up to many more sources than we feel comfortable letting in. That explains to some extent why we drink from the fire hose of the emails and texts that come crashing down in our pockets and purses. It's not because we're convinced we can stay on top of everything. It's that we don't want *everything* to climb on top of us.

The defenseless side speaks to the turns and twists taken by our worst case scenarios around money, health, love, and social standing – all the likely culprits. That's when we're most vulnerable to messages that bring order and closure to these chaotic and control-resistant events. That's when misinformation carries the argument to us. Its eloquence lies in a simplicity so persuasive that we barely need convincing.

Tools of the Misinformation Trade

That's why misinformants take aim at complex and thorny topics with sweeping and conclusive messages. Misinformation tells us what we want to hear. It simplifies the details and permits us to move on: Either in deciding on a course of action (say, hiring an expert) or deciding to stand pat (sitting out an election). Misinformation finds its mark by taking aim at us in the following ways:

1. Replaying simple arguments with a limited range of predictable outcomes

2. Offering clear alternatives with positive or at least clarifying results

3. Requiring little or no additional input from the recipient

In this section, we'll consider several specific instances of misinformation campaigns. We will see how misinformants typically feast on our own insecurities – particularly when we spread our awareness into areas that impair our judgement. Broadly speaking, here's how that plays out in popular media channels such as the high-stakes political and financial arenas:

1) Guilt by association – Fixating on a sweeping conclusion that labels all affiliated members of one group as the *same*, meaning they...

    A. Hold to the same views and protect the same interests

    B. Harbor similar resentments

    C. Play by their own self-serving justifications and disregard for rules, mainstream views, etc.

2) Cover-up by smokescreen – Creating a fuss that overshadows any harmful exposure that may come to misinformants who...

    A. Implicate an adversary or potential enemy by leaking secrets about them they won't expose (alleged cover-up)

    B. Bluff reporters into accepting unsubstantiated rumors with a *scoop* that beats other providers to the punch

    C. Force a separation to avoid an implication by distancing the provider from deviant or controversial affiliates

3) Exaggerate by staging drama – Telling a narrative grounded more on attention-getting than sense-making where storytellers...

    A. Sensationalize an otherwise dubious claim or obscure topic with celebrity references and insinuations

    B. Inflate the dimension of ongoing disputes so that honest disagreements cascade into shouting matches

    C. Raise the suspicion that if opponents emerge victorious from an initial litmus test, it will trigger an irreversible trend, act as contagion, etc.

<u>Sources of Misinformation</u>

Who's likeliest to be the brainchild of a misinformation campaign? Whether we're talking about Machiavellian power magnet or market manipulators, their deceptions are intended to keep them a step ahead of their victims. This strategy serves the dual purpose of dictating the terms of a debate and the flash points of the conflict. The misinformant maintains the upper hand by keeping their opponents guessing where and when they'll be forced into a response.

Here are four types of misinformation providers, and the context in which they tend to flourish:

1. **Partisans and true believers** – Look hard at the principled stances held by rigid hardliners. They may have no intention of reaching a compromise, honoring a brokered truce, or even recognizing the legitimacy of dissenting views. How do we know? They're not looking to the next legal ruling or election cycle, but to the next round of doubts fueled in a counter-punch media offensive.

2. **Self-sanctioning experts** – Ever stuck in an information mess? What if we could pay a domain expert to plow us out? It's a common assumption that well-credentialed analysts are valued for advice. But the credibility afforded by their stature provides the justification for the groups who retain them to act in their own interests. In effect, they are providing political cover as well as advice. **(Weinberg, 2009)**[24] This form of credibility for hire is fraudulent whenever their fact-base is cherry-picked by their clients to fit the picker's own pre-determined objectives.

3. **Traceless originators** – The most popular author of accusations and slanderous defamations is named Anonymous Sources. Whether Sir or Madam Anonymous goes by *high level officials* or *secret admirers,* a protected identity is the surest way to grease the communication wheels. Anonymity lowers the risks to information providers for providing false and misleading evidence and groundless speculation. Case-in-point: The surest way to play the stock market is to assume that merger rumors are wrong and bet against them. That's because they rarely pan out. Instead the takeover buzz prompts a run on these stocks. Their corrective declines are soon to follow. **(Lachapelle, 2011)**[25]

4. **Trigger-happy journalists** – Not all misinformation is malicious or innately negative. As the self-appointed timekeepers of historic import, the media is the misinformed source that rushes to report on deaths greatly exaggerated (to paraphrase Mark Twain). Think of elections not officially won, e.g. the Florida vote in the Presidential Election of 2000. In such cases, the goal to be dull and accurate is overcome in the rush to be breathless and break the story.

Scams and Frauds: Who wants to be an authority?

As we saw with in the social media instances, the web offers information providers some novel approaches for manufacturing credibility. That's especially the case when the demand is for finding experts and the supply is a surplus of web hits. Scamming is about filling in the blank formed by that top qualification factor in all public reputations: "According to _____, everything we reported yesterday is wrong, now that we know _____."

FIGURE 4.40: Value Proposition for Experts

```
Higher the stakes + Lower our understanding
= the greater our desperation to fill this hole
```

The gamers' intent is to...

- Elevate themselves by substituting an impartial but convincing group of first parties (customers) and third-parties (experts) to sing their praises.

- Denigrate a rival or raise doubts about the competition in order to profit from the confusions and speculations of customers and investors alike. The role of hedge funds in major run-ups on the price of commodities and energy sources are prime examples here.

Of course, no one's going to read every single testimonial and vet the credentials of every party that petitions on the gamers' behalf. That's why a systematic ranking is so persuasive. It rounds up all the market noise signified in all the search results to a single, identifiable action plan: *"Go with _____."* Like the t-shirt says: *How can 77,000,000 Elvis fans be wrong?*

The effort to divert collective action away from a common purpose (what's available?) towards a specific outcome (buy my product!) is hardly a new phenomenon or limited to web searches. In a market-driven economy and culture, there will always be a competitive factor that attempts to redirect or overwrite any effort to define a common interest or greater public good.

Effective issues or policy-based research is not only about providing a balanced, objective, or impartial assessment of a public concern or resource. It's about resisting the efforts of private parties to coerce or bias the outcome in their own favor.

As public trust in institutions continues to erode, so too the temptation and ability to distort the notion of what's good for most or what's great for some grows in our digital discourse. The name for this subversive act is *gaming the system.* In this case, the game is fraud, and the system for perpetrating the scam is the Internet.

For example, what do we do when we're assaulted by information, convinced we have to act on this bombardment, and not certain how? We turn to an authority. We put our trust in a source that recipients know and trust and presumably share some mutual risk and potential gain – *if my source is correct, then we both win.*

Con artists understood this long before global trading and computer networks communications made the practice widespread. The huge gains in world financial markets made at the turn of the new century convinced many that we were living in a new golden age. This was to be an age of 'Frictionless Capitalism' — a world of unlimited wealth defying the normal laws of economic gravity. Ostentatious displays of well-heeled tycoons and the new super rich feasted on the dreams and insecurities of less shrewd and/or fortunate investors. Did I miss the boat? How could I too have the Internet punch my ticket to prosperity?

FIGURE 4.41: Debunking Tool Organized by Fact-checking Authorities

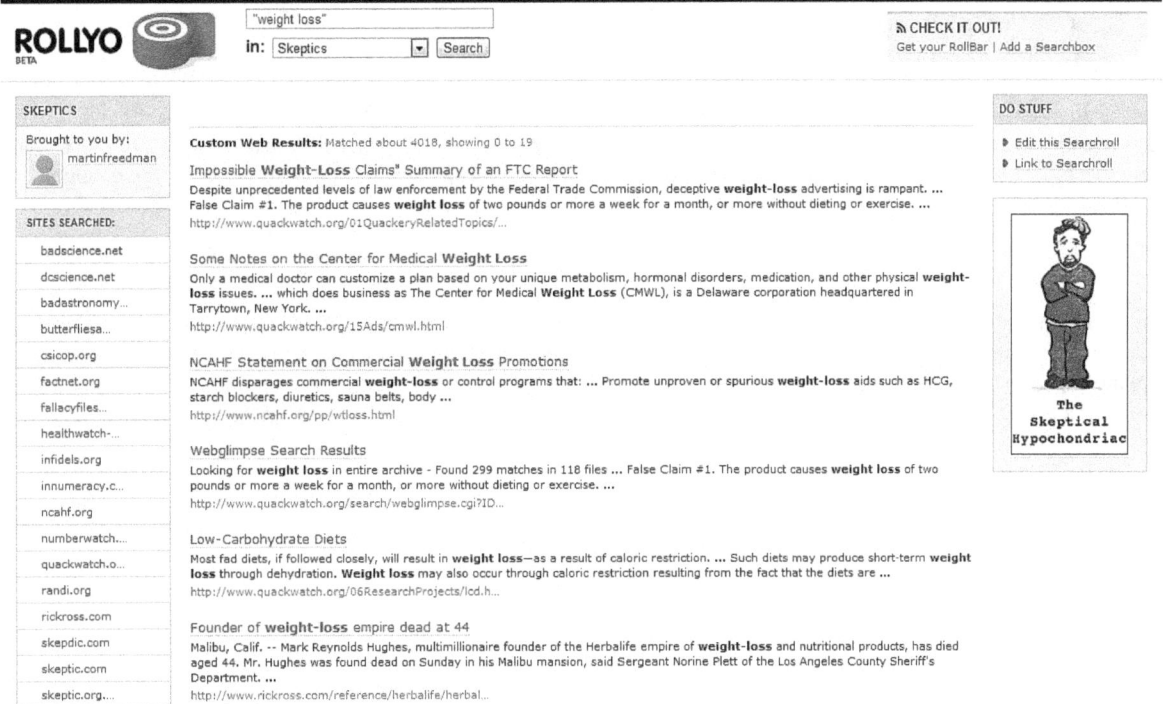

This screen capture references a search engine that combines dozens of myth-busting sites designed to set the record straight on familiar hoaxes and urban legends. This is a prime example of the OLP construct we first saw in Unit Two – in this case we're fishing in a relative pond for a well-documented fact base behind dubious claims related to dieting.

Scam Haven

Offshore islands like Swiss banks are tax havens where the powerful can shelter their incomes from the homeland authorities. The Internet is also a haven. It's not for concealing wealth but for forging identities, planting rumors, generating doubt or confusion, and most importantly, boosting the credibility of dubious groups and institutions.

How does this happen? What makes the web a haven for scams? Let's go back to a fairly common cause of information overload. No industry is capable of generating more excessive, unfiltered, and often conflicting information than the financial services industry. Indeed information is not only its primary resource but its chief by-product. After profits, the only tangible product it manufactures is ... that's right — a flood of information.

What happens when we go on overload about something that tests our understanding, and impacts us so directly? This happens when…

- We need to take action *before* we're ready.
- Dramatic shifts to the market and the stress this causes impedes our better judgment.
- We don't know much about the causes and effects of market gyrations.
- What we do know is that our reasoning abilities are compromised.
- We turn to financial experts.

What does this have to do with the web? Plenty.

Google is no more an information broker than Google is a mere search engine. It is the virtual friend and neighbor we turn to when the complexities of the world overwhelm our senses, over-match our knowledge, and even overpower the coping skills we use to handle high levels of uncertainty. Short of wishing the problem away, or reducing the confusion, is the enduring need to reach higher ground: The state of knowing when the bottom's dropped out or defining what it even looks like.

Then there's the reverse scenario. When giddy markets are buoyed by unbridled optimism. In times of prosperity, who is detached but also invested? Who can tell when soaring expectations crash past the barriers of reasonable rates of return?

What we want is a hedge against our loftiest dreams and our worst nightmares. What we want is a voice of reason. That's the persuasion that drowns out the endless sets of mediated search results and landing pages, crafted around our click histories — the messages and products we've bought before. And hearing is believing when the voice of reason doesn't come from the source. It comes from all the others who've benefited from a higher searching out loud reasoning.

Playing to the Crowd

As we know, search results include more unworthy hits than we can filter. What we can do is focus on the objective of the misinformant's deception — the third-party crowd in play for fraudulent provider.

Audience-directed praise and influence are expressed in one of two ways:

1. **Formal:** definitive endorsements based on orchestrated, fee-based campaigns through traditional advertising and media
2. **Viral:** in-process endorsements that are open to all and spontaneously formed through word-of-mouth and other free forms of expression

It is when we mistake the orchestrated campaign for the viral endorsement where the risk of fraud is greatest. Systems that create rankings or ratings through opinions and recommendations are especially prone to this kind of manipulation. Many of those impartial references are actually vested sponsors of the gamer. Sometimes, they are one in the same.

The engineering of search engine results is more than a lucrative cash cow for Google. It's the playing board on which the players (global Googlers) go to fill their gaping blanks (who gets my investment dollars). Assuming the name's familiar and the reviews are promising, the final verdict is in before the trading ticker refreshes.

These are the unregulated practices of gamers whose market fortunes rise in direct response to their search result positioning. Those are the rules to the game. And surprise ... the system is rigged. The facade of authority and the persuasion it confers is not only self-serving scheme but a self-fulfilling outcome. Appearances overwhelm reality until the bill comes due.

3) Gaming the Search System: Optimization at the Expense of Relevance

Another common form of distortion stems from feigning the popularity of websites by inflating the number of referring pages to raise a site's search position (or what Google calls its PageRank). With the emergence of search results as a marketing tool, more and more advertisers are trying to influence search terms in their favor.

Pay-per-Click (or "PPC") campaigns are an established way to achieve favorable positioning within the first set of search results. Matching a specific word or phrase they purchase from the search engine vendor promote their sites, services, and/or products. A landing page created by the advertiser either tops the results list and/or appears a noticeable area.[26]

UNIT FOUR: Sense-making Through Information Context | Page 4:101

Another way that marketers try to influence these outcomes is to bypass the search engine companies altogether. They try to artificially inflate their prominence and positioning through other means than direct advertising. This practice is referred to as search engine optimization (or "SEO").

One common SEO practice is to inflate the number of links between the pages each marketer is trying to boost in the search rankings. Sometimes this is done through reciprocal links exchanged between two cooperating entities. Other times a sole actor will artificially inflate their rankings by fabricating the popularity of their pages through a scheme called "link farms." The content of link farms is useless to anyone outside the group who creates them. Land in one and you've gotten that sinking feeling. Most of us have fallen into this familiar information ditch. The site we stumble on provides a keyword match to our concerns (and apparently everyone else's!) These sites exist for no other reason than to inflate the search ranking of the interests who generate them.

FIGURE 4.42: Carving up the First Page of Search Results (Circa 2010)

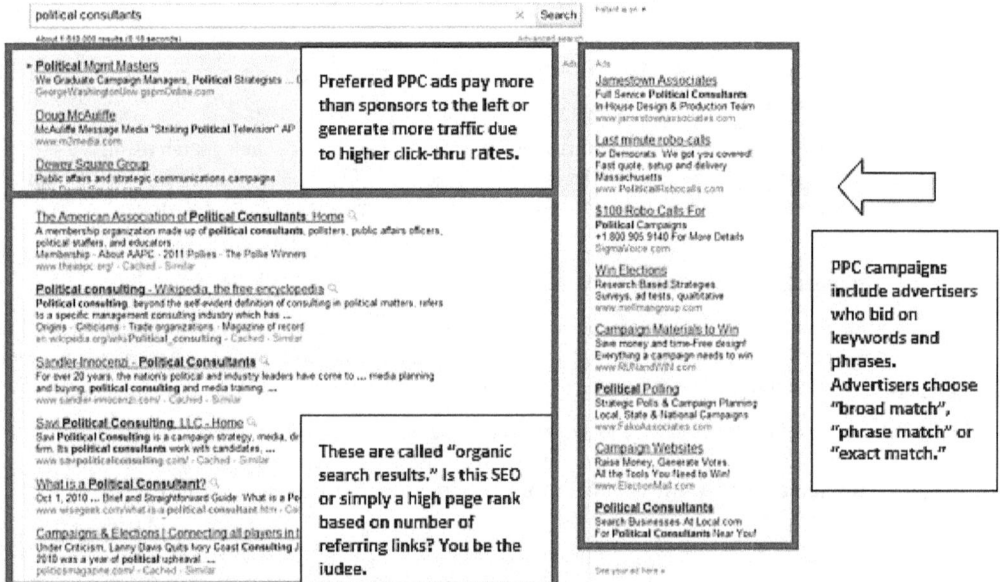

SEO is organic search – the main results that money can't buy. They represent 75% of all click-throughs. The other quarter is SEM on the right side of the screen. Many SEM click-throughs lead to landing pages (usually the ability to purchase the service advertised on the search results page).

Searching Out Loud: Giving Voice to Independent Investigations | Marc Solomon

UNIT FOUR: Sense-making Through Information Context | Page 4:102

FIGURE 4.42: Carving up the First Page of Search Results (Circa 2019)

Organic search results have been reduced substantially. They've been replaced by ads now appearing in the top three slots and by the featured snippet below them. This is a text box summarizing the topic that most closely correlates to the query. Other topic-related questions are stacked below a prominent trade association – the only organic search result in this example.

Searching Out Loud: Giving Voice to Independent Investigations | Marc Solomon

SCORING SYSTEMS THAT RATE THEMSELVES

Perhaps more than all the other potential conflicts-of-interest that investigators track, the outcome of gaming the system is an abuse that the digital world is well-equipped to document. After all, once news gets out, it can only travel fast. And the speed is based less on what the news is, and more about how it spreads virally – through the web like wildfire.

Contriving to win a contest by turning the rules of the game against itself is a fantasy sport witnessed firsthand in every set of returning search results. Coercive schemes like link farms exist solely of sites that link to other sites. Why? For increasing their link popularity score or PageRank in Google. Think of them as 'search spam.'

There are other ways to create false perceptions online. Much of the electronic trading done prior to the financial meltdown of 2008 concerns the fabricated credit default swaps. This is where short-sellers faked trades to incite market fears that the stocks of the companies they were selling signaled that these companies' fortunes were about to turn sour: A self-fulfilling prophesy.

Is there a role here for PCF? Can the query formation techniques that we introduced in Section 4.2 help us to make sense of system rigging?

First, we look for potentially false perceptions created by first persons or parties who manipulate scoring systems and institutional procedures to appear influential, respected, or unduly popular. Their fortunes rise in parallel with favorable search rankings or endorsed by the very rules they are trying to thwart.

This is particularly useful when we're trying to get a handle on the leading players in less established and fledgling markets. That's when we're likeliest to see a disconnect between a company's meager resources, and its formidable digital presence.

Everybody's Doing It

Another powerful use in the digital research of misinformation campaigns is to document awareness levels. Awareness could mean a lot of things from personal popularity to marketing campaigns and public policies. It is especially persuasive when we can connect awareness level to peoples' notion of choices they can take by acting on such awareness. This is not just about Coke and Pepsi or Democrats and Republicans. It's about something much more widespread and fundamental than who we vote for or even what goes in our shopping carts. It's about what's standard and what's deviant. It's about determining a normal from extreme that would otherwise go undefined.

For example, criminality is about deviance. The more prevalence we see in ruthless and self-serving behavior, the harder it is to punish someone for this kind of wrongdoing. **(Parloff, 2009)**[27] That doesn't mean that widespread brutality is an excuse for coldblooded murder. It does mean that the more commonly recognized that lying, cheating and stealing become, the more difficult it is to prosecute the guilty. This becomes important when authorities and leaders need to hold up the most egregious violators as teaching examples. The prevailing lesson here for the larger community is that such flagrant behaviors would no longer be tolerated.

In such cases it becomes essential to test some meaningful questions:

1. How widespread is the behavior?
2. Who crossed the line the most times or by the widest margin?
3. Who did it first (thus providing cover to all the subsequent copy-cats)?

Next Steps

As investigators it's a mistake to confuse disinterest with detachment. Playing the observer doesn't suggest a passive role or remaining in a reactive mode. That's when the impaired judgment rests with us and our own insecurities or haste for closure when certainty is a long way off. The better approach is to keep our sights peeled on providers and their motives for providing misinformation.

As we discussed in **Unit One,** the web is a great way to assess the social influences that surround people as search targets. From screening criminal suspects to potential hires, the web is a great way to test for blindspots and those areas most ripe for lapses in judgment. Questionable loyalties, compromised resources, and unmet obligations are all in play above our Internet radars, especially where social media is the information provider's milieu. Red flag conditions exist in all walks of commerce and levels of professional conduct. **(Campbell, Whitehead, Finkelstein, 2009)**[28]

Red Flag Conditions

What are some smoking guns? Where does our sniff test take us? Three red flags are frequently raised. The occasion? These are the most common lapses in the calculations of misinformation providers:

1. **Inappropriate self-interest** — The limits of our own personal experience prevent us from seeing how our actions impact others and their interpretations for what we do. Self-preservation erodes our ability to see our own biases, even when we petition on behalf of others. It is not by accident but design that in most high level negotiations we hire brokers to do our bidding. But when personal loyalties blind us to impartial observation, we lose the confidence of our professional peers. The *greater good* no longer prevails above the privileged concerns of the well-connected.

2. **Distorting attachments** — Personalizing adversity is an honest, authentic, and entirely human response to our own vulnerability. It is also nearly always unprofessional. Whenever we experience an emotionally-charged event, we are prone to raising the specter of that same threat in the future. Holding on to past grievances can often lead to future blunders. Instead of taking the long view, our search target fixates on some slight or wound inflicted from a feuding enemy.

3. Misleading memories — It's a standard assumption that someone with a track record of success is a better risk to build on that success than someone with less experience or a mixed record. The red flag rationale argues that success can breed overconfidence. If prior decisions turned out well, our target is blinded to key differences as conditions change and new conflicts arise. If the rewards of past smear campaigns eclipse the downsides, those approaches are likelier to repeat – if not the successes.

Who Fact Checks the Fact-checkers?

In the era of rapidly unfolding accusations and counter-punches comes the fact checkers. This is a research-based response to fill the vacuum formed between abject reality and the vested interests exposed in the electoral cycle. Fact-checkers scrutinize the dueling communication strategies of opposing campaigns. They are perceived to carry no personal biases and harbor or concealed motives other than (1) expand on the gap between an impartial observation, and (2) the distortions carried in campaign speeches, interviews, and news leaks.

They are sensitive to distinctions meant to objectify, marginalize, and ultimately demonize the, judgment, and character of the opposing camp. Conversely, an effective fact checker doesn't cross into the realm of advocacy. The fact checking lets the reader draw their own conclusions within the basis of facts, behavior, and perceptions evidenced by the research presented.

To the Knowledge-ABLED, this means handing over the ingredients and the recipe so that the message consumer (or voter in this case) can test *the same* set of facts. Recipients of all political stripes can dish out their own opinions — in their own kitchens.

One way to move beyond the emotional minefields of veiled threats and character assassinations is to steer clear of opinions entirely. Instead, focus on the more concrete aim of verification — specifically the degree to which evidence is being stretched to support the bias of the candidate. For instance, economic trends that underpin the policy changes favored by the campaign may align with a longstanding trend that's slowing, dormant, or even reversing in recent surveys. Another hotbed for skepticism is that the underlying logic of an argument is based on a faulty set of assumptions, or a choice of misleading comparisons. **(Kessler, 2016)**[29]

The Dubious Freedom of Anonymous Speech

One of the freedoms of a virtual world is that we get to play act or try out different sets of identities, based on the way we portray ourselves in simulated environments. We can try on new attitudes or assume personality traits and behaviors that are quite apart from our real-world identities and circumstances. That escapism is encouraged by the widespread use of 'handles' or so-called sock puppets — pseudonyms that shield recipients from knowing our contact information.

The liberation from our legal identities and actual places can also remove our sense of personal responsibility and fair play when we assume the role of information provider with impunity. There are no consequences for unfounded criticisms we find easier to make under the cover of an alternative and anonymous identity. The allure of a rich fantasy life masks the drudgery and unglamorous nature of daily existence. But it also confuses the balance between providing information and being accountable for the evidential details we share.

UNIT Four: Wrapping

Focusing on Information Context

Unit Four transitioned our Knowledge-ABLED approach to investigations from the usage phase of our research-gathering to the interpretive stages of our own weighing of the evidence. While **Unit Three** addressed the motives of information givers, **Unit Four** wrestled with the contextual merits of our evaluations process. We did this by focusing on follow-up actions and outcomes – namely how individual and group stakeholders process the digital content they both consume and produce through social media. Throughout this unit, we assessed how those deliberations should factor into our own analysis. **Unit Five** will square the substance of our research with the packaging and style requirements for best presenting these findings to our peers, clients, and stakeholders. Those presentation methods are critical, not just to our credibility as investigators, but as trusted advisers. Ultimately we are judged not by our findings, but by the recommendations we draw from our research.

[1] Kevin Maney, "The Ratings Game," The Atlantic, July, 2009
[2] Pennabaker, Chung, "Computerized Text Analysis," January, 2007
[3] Carl Elliot, "The Ghostwriter," The Atlantic Monthly, December, 2010
[4] Muhammad Farhan, "Cnewsworld, WikiLeaks Diplomatic Disclosures Cover all Full Report," December, 1, 2010
[5] An expression attributed to Edward de Bono, a psychologist, physician and writer.
[6] David Frum, "Severely Conservative?" The Daily Beast, February 10, 2012
[7] University of Oregon psychologist Paul Slovic conducted an experiment. He told undergraduates about a starving child named Rokia -- she lived in a crumbling refugee camp in Africa. His students expressed their sympathy with an outpouring of about $2.50 to a well-known charity. However, when it was communicated to a separate student group that over five million African children are malnourished -- the average donation dipped by half.
[8] Ronald Heifetz, The Practice of Adaptive Leadership, Harvard Business, 2009
[9] Professor Tannen remarks that news coverage of global warming actually ends up being biased because news reports of scientists' mounting concern typically also feature

prominently one of the few "greenhouse skeptics" who declare the concern bogus. This "balanced" two-sides approach gives the impression that scientists are evenly divided, whereas in fact the vast majority agree that the dangers of global climate change are potentially grave.

[10] Michael Lewis, David Einhorn, "The End of the Financial World as We Know It," The New York Times, January 4, 2009

[11] Charles Arthur, "Analysing data is the future for journalists, says Tim Berners-Lee," The Guardian, November 22, 2010

[12] Not all information sources within group circle consist of multiple persons. Sometimes a single individual may be responsible for speaking for a group, as is the case with corporate executives, elected officials, tribal elders, or even celebrities.

[13] Josh Tyrangiel, "2010 in Review," Businessweek, December 20, 2010

[14] The real payoff is that they are now free to speak their minds without the constraint of needing to speak on behalf of their former organization. If this blending of credibility and authenticity sounds familiar, it will ring more true the next time we reference the Vectors of Integrity from the prior section in this unit.

[15] Dan Gillmor interviewed by Brooke Gladstone, NPR's On the Media, November 19, 2010

[16] Marc Prensky, "Digital Natives, Digital Immigrants, On the Horizon," MCB University Press, Vol. 9 No. 5, October 2001

[17] Ben Zimmer, "Nominations for American Dialect Society Word of the Year, 2009," http://www.americandialect.org/Zimmer-2009-WOTY.pdf

[18] Premack, D. & Woodruff, G., "Does the Chimpanzee Have a Theory of Mind?" Behav. Brain Sc., 4, 515-526, 1978

[19] The term 'pre-teen' had not yet been coined in 1981.

[20] Ronald Glover, "And Now a Tweet from Our Sponsor," Businessweek, January 10, 2011

[21] Dan Gillmor, "Principles of a New Media Literacy," http://publius.cc/principles_new_media_literacy

[22] Drake Bennett, "Ten Years of Remarkable Detail: Wikipedia," Businessweek, January 10, 2011

[23] John Borland, "See Who's Editing Wikipedia - Diebold, the CIA, a Campaign," Wired Magazine, August 14, 2007

[24] David Weinberg, "Your Help with the New Expertise," KM World, August, 2009

[25] Tara Lachapelle, "A Winning Stock Strategy: Sell on the Rumor," Businessweek, January 13, 2011

[26] Advertiser positionig has changed over the years. What was formerly on the right-side of the results page has been made increasingly prominent. Sponsored links are located directly below the search box at the time of this writing.

[27] Roger Parloff, "Wall Street: It's Payback Time," Fortune Magazine, January 6, 2009

[28] Andrew Campbell, Jo Whitehead, Sidney Finkelstein, "Think Again: Why Good Leaders Make Bad Decisions," Harvard Business Review, May, 2009

[29] Glenn Kessler, "Here Are the Facts Behind that '79 Cent' Pay Gap Factoid," Washington Post, April 14, 2016

UNIT FIVE:
HOW TO PRESENT WHAT WE LEARN IN TEACHABLE WAYS

Investigation as Performance

In the first four units we have reviewed query formation, search mechanics, and some useful models for knowing how and where to address your research efforts. **Unit Five** addresses the more interpretive aspects of the research process. The analytical techniques we review here cut across all the various tools, sources, and commands we have addressed in the realm of web-based search. In fact, the analytical methods we introduce here can be applied in a larger context to your career and even more broadly: The lifelong ability to make sense of an often perspective-resistant world.

IN THE PAPERS

We don't act in isolation. And we don't act before we analyze. And we don't analyze without information that clues us into the implications of our actions:

1. What's different about our case?

2. What's similar about everyone else's?

It all boils down to conformities and exceptions: How do we stand out? How do we fit in?

The same questions apply to the information we seek for our clients, our families, our social networks, and ourselves:

1. How do my search projects validate, augment, or conflict with what I knew before I started?

2. How do my new understandings influence the people and groups I need to inform?

Unlike the searches we do, the pages we visit, and the content we stream or download, the value we derive from these collection efforts resists any kind of standard *value add*. We are no smarter or further along based on the volume of keywords, web pages, or research hours we burn on behalf of our research objectives.

Nevertheless, we don't need to become super searchers, let alone mind readers, to draw some universal appraisals:

1. What's analysis without consultation? Let's ask our trusted advisers for second opinions about our first impulses. The initial whim to see ourselves as conspiracy victims or crowning victors is how our egos attempt to boost our personal stake in the outcomes of our search results, and the big, impersonal worlds they represent.

2. A *gut check* from advisers and friends can preview the impact of our pending actions on the outside, measuring personal contributions within the larger communities we value.

3. This rationale applies as much to the business community as it does our personal affairs. Most of us don't buy stock simply because we think the company deserves our dollars. We buy because we think that others will soon act on the same whim, and nudge our net gain upward.

4. Analysis is inherently social. It is not limited to personal gain or self-discovery. Public perceptions and peer pressure inspire our analytical drives as much as any personality traits or naval-gazing tendencies. There's only one problem for us Knowledge-ABLED investigators. Web search does little to advance these research goals. Social media, with its commercial agenda and feeble search tools, offers even less.

UNIT FIVE LEARNING OBJECTIVES

Let's take a glance back at the foundational settings from **Unit Four** that will be foundational to the presentations we'll be building in **Unit Five**:

- We considered the guiding principles of group-based information – how the need for group discipline compromises personal loyalties and public credibility.
- We assessed individual-based information – including the sincerity of personal communication, its predilection for authenticity, and the limitations of its candor.
- We used common social media platforms to contrast the roles and priorities of individual and group site members.

Unit Four enabled us to master the motivations of content producers who use the web as their primary distribution. In effect, we can address the most important and elusive piece of the search log collection method we first introduced in **Unit One**. Topping of the list: Why information providers supply the material we access through digital research tools and methods.

Understanding this is critical to the fundamental goal of the Knowledge-ABLED. Not only the quality of these materials, but how they inform our cases: The recommended actions to take from our investigations.

Upon completion of this unit, you should be able to present your findings through the following three stages:

1) Analysis and Report Delivery

- Select appropriate presentation methods to map findings to follow-up actions

3. Use the metrics introduced in **Unit Four** to assess the volume and nature of attention paid to the case and the broader policy issues it addresses

2) Search Project Integration

- Join a social network and conduct background searches and interviews
- Map discussions to community awareness and broader public deliberations

3) Presenting the Results

- Present the final search project
- Project components (including project setup, search logs and conclusions/recommendations)

SEEING THE WORLD THROUGH THE PERSPECTIVES WE RESEARCH

How do we give life to idle facts?

How do we define the marketplace of ideas, the radar of public awareness, or the boundaries between common knowledge and inside information?

We need to see our activities in context, not isolation. Corporate librarians and professional researchers are still called upon to scour premium databases for marketplace changes. But without analysis, this is a latent function of marginal value, or enduring interest.

Worse, to the people who don't know us (say, our boss's boss), subscription databases are an unrecoverable expense. Market watcher OVUM Research makes this point:

> "Very few individuals are able to generate business value from the act of searching for information."

There is no value, not without connecting external situations to internal implications. Not without weaving a common thread between events running their course.

The purpose of news creation is to inform. First, we focus on who did what to whom, where, and when (the core details). Then comes the speculations over why (opinions and commentary). Now apply that formula to today's Times – then to tomorrow's Journal. How much of this is what happened yesterday? How about last month? The wires have already filed those stories.

Day after day, stories are filed that focus on coming weeks or prior quarters. Major media sources cannot republish restatements, or they too risk becoming the publisher's worst fear: *Yesterday's news*. A Biggest Picture perspective enables us to frame the context of marketplace changes for any client so they can better understand the fundamentals:

What the news means to them

…. as well as how this helps them develop their own media strategies:

What they mean to the news

Put another way, external monitoring cuts two distinct ways:

1. **The opportunity:** How do I get my name *out there* (by standing out), or

2. **The risk:** How do I protect my good name (by fitting in or just lying low)

Offering this perspective means looking at the practical considerations of market realities through the client's eyes:

4. **Limelight:** Are we the center of attention – on the periphery, off radar completely?

5. **Influence:** What's the prevailing wisdom – who carries the most sway?

6. **Control:** What seismic shifts are beyond our grasp – what's within our resources?

7. **Momentum:** How do we set the agenda so that rivals are on the defensive? Unlike the examples in the **Unit Four**, momentum is not the sole province of misinformants!

These are not theoretical quandaries. These calculations factor into every marketer looking to gain executive approval, or internal decision seeking to curry market favor.

The media is full of assumptions. This conventional wisdom is based more on convention than astuteness. These are sweeping conclusions that fit the narrative of a particular commentator or viewpoint. Such posturing is common, rarely questioned, and sounds something like this...

- When are moments 'defined'?
- Where are careers 'made'?
- How are reputations 'shaped'?
- What are the 'best-known' 'best known for?

These parenthetical questions are answered squarely in the gut, not in the head. It's the smaller picture perceptions we all know. Yet we extrapolate them to contain the same known universe we commonly accept as the marketplace, the business world, the competitive landscape, etc.

Another downside to gut checks is that they wear out their welcomes. There are no numbers to pad seat-of-the-pants decision-making. So there are no results to test the impact, and the need for re-sets and adjustments. It's not that marketers shy away from facts and figures. It's that no one knows quite how to measure bloated search indexes, unaccountable sources, and competing points of view.

These are vestiges of information glut, a condition that impairs our clients' ability to be well-informed. Without the bigger picture, it also threatens our status as knowledge providers to others. It overwhelms organizations with news developments they are not neither prepared to exploit or avoid.

It guilts them into an obsessive drive for detail that causes the loss of perspective (and valuable time) in the process.

Internal policies aside, the success of our digital investigations hinge on this Biggest Picture perspective: How campaigns are received beyond the marketing teams who conceive, approve, and execute them.

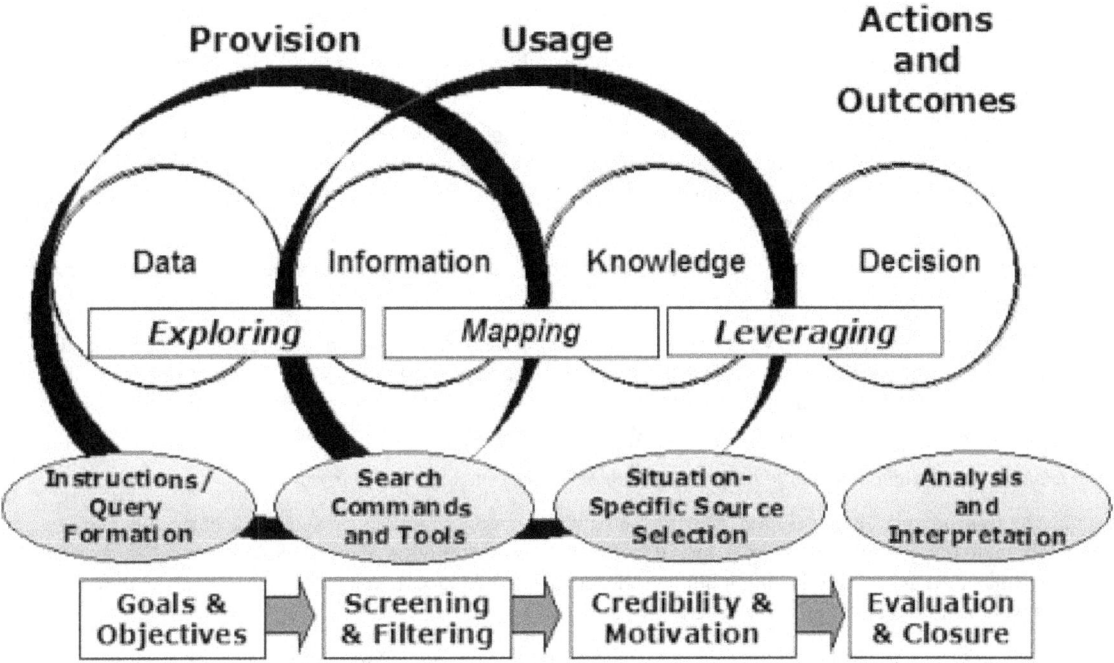

Along the Knowledge Continuum we are now in the evaluation and closure phase of the knowledge continuum, prioritizing the quality information we deem worth acting on or advising as part of a larger decision process.

<u>Unit Five Destination: How to Connect What We Learn to Useful Outcomes</u>

Unit Five takes us from the w*hen* to *why* steps of the SPM process. That means that we're finally ready to connect dots, draw conclusions, and offer advice. These are the recommendations supported by the evidence we've collected and filtered in **Units One** and **Two**, and analyzed in **Units Three** and **Four**. Each time through the explanatory power of Knowledge-ABLED models and frameworks.

We talk about opportunities when we use information. We think in terms of risk when others do so. **Unit Five** focuses not only on what we learn but how this works in relation to what others know and perceive. How can we as messengers assess the nerves we strike, and the buttons we push — the impact of our research.

The first four units focus on how to gather information and act on it. **Unit Five** is about how others will act on the research we deliver. How will these responses resonate through social media? More formally, how will they play out through reports and presentations to peers, clients, and other audience groups? How will our findings be interpreted and acted on? They key is in the how: *How* we deliver them is every bit as important as the presentation itself.

Unit Five brings together the search project management steps, query formation, quality controls, source fluency, and information conjugation methods to deliver our research to the clients, colleagues, and communities we're supporting. Our presentation methods will demonstrate to our project recipients how our informed use of web research tools and practices is bringing value, economy, and even closure to complex and resource-hungry investigations. Then we turn our attention to the report itself. The presenter has come to grips with the news being delivered, the sense-making of their analysis, and the changes they're proposing. That dynamic forms the core of **Unit Five**.

How our findings are interpreted and acted on is perceived through three common reasons why our audience will be captivated by the presenter:

> 1. **The Powerful:** We focus on those who control our destinies in order to know what to anticipate. This is research done about those in authority that our attendees don't know personally or deal with directly. Predicting what will happen and when is the first step towards turning the recommendations we provide into the actions mulled by our stakeholders. **(Sutton, 2009)**[1]

> *The powerful – People pay attention to those who control their outcomes in order to know what to prepare for and when it will happen.*

> 2. **The Explainable:** Insight and validation so that we know we're not alone. That through coordination and planning, we can accomplish mutual goals. A strong presenter doesn't assign blame or issue all-or-nothing ultimatums, but posits a range of options that the audience desires. All are practical considerations, preferably choices where stakeholders are predisposed to committing the resolve and resources to see it happen.

> *The explainable – Insight and validation to potentially influence outcomes in our favor.*

> 3. **The Unexpected:** Change is hard. Making the right adjustments depends on avoidance of the number one threat to our control – complete surprise! Nothing grabs the attention of our audience faster than hearing what we didn't expect to happen during our investigations. Nothing focuses the mind more sharply than reasoning how to handle changes on achievable terms.

> *The unexpected – Humans react negatively to unexplained events. The tendency is so widespread that it's preferable to give a negative reason than none at all.*

Unit Five Benefits

Unit Five shows participants how to proceed from the analytical to the presentation phase of their search projects. These are the conclusions that us Knowledge-ABLED investigators reach in order to inform clients, decisions, policies, and the communities worthy of our involvement, concern, and influence.

At the close of **Unit Five**, we should be able to determine what to include and discard. We will determine compelling ways to present the findings and recommendations informed by the contextual factors evidenced in prior units — namely PCF ("Provider Conjugation Framework") and VOI ("Vectors of Integrity").

Our allegiances are personal. The methodologies we consider in **Unit Five** are anything but subjective. But we aim as presenters to stand above the preferences and loyalties of any specific influencer: Be they information provider, digital marketer, or web researcher. They are presented as a means to transcend the limitations of self-referential assertions and individual biases.

We'll learn how to eliminate the guesswork for determining source selection, query formation, and the kinds of questions answered by **The Biggest Picture**. The Biggest Picture ("TBP") is a data-driven and repeatable way to quantify media perceptions of events, issues, and campaigns. While the results are repeatable and fixed, the target we're scoring is a moving target. Such are the outcomes wishing to be achieved, rivaled, or avoided altogether by our TBP clients.

We saw in **Unit Two** how SEO ("search engine optimization") decodes the keyword patterns in the top-of-mind associations of Internet users. In a comparable way, TBP models what information providers supply in the way of...

- Topics,
- Relationships, and
- Even explanations for connecting news with newsmakers.

The results drawn by our Biggest Picture provides a narrative for walking clients through their own best intentions and worst nightmares that live at the behest of the external world.

Searching Out Loud

SECTION 5:1 | Quantifying Knowledge–

The Survey-Making Nature of Internet Search Results

"My toaster is more powerful than my computer ... when it comes to making toast."

– Stephen Landsburgh

THE BIGGEST PICTURE

Think of search engines before you started to search out loud. Think of how you may have googled without factoring in some query formations of your own making? That's the level of competence we expect from our layperson search peers. They don't delve further than top-of-mind keywords. Therein lies an unsettling question at the core of the most innocent query: How far down do we submerge before we've settled a score, arrived at a decision, or exhausted a topic?

It's that difference between what we uncover, and what a casual user experiences from that same block of research time. That difference is important for two reasons:

> 1. It helps justify the time we spent investigating – especially when we're billing that session back to our clients.

> 2. It helps us anticipate any notable gaps in awareness between surface landings and our deeper excavations.

The second point is absolutely critical to unraveling the greatest mystery in the delivery of any consulting service. The suspense rarely lies in what we're delivering. It's how our delivery pushes on one sensitive button: (1) What the client already knows, and (2) what they're hearing for the first time.

If we're unsure, then the chances are much greater of *showing them up* for not being *in the loop* or *in the know*. Even worse, we can presume that clients don't need filling in or a fuller context because (1) they're too stressed already to absorb more details, or worse, (2) that they know it all cold, and that their preconceptions are as immutable as the facts we're revisiting together.

<u>Airtight interpretations</u>

Many of the deliveries we'll be making in **Unit Five** are shaped by what that client is prepared to receive. That's valid whether (1) we've found eyewitnesses that will testify on their behalf, or (2) that a loved one is suffering from a life-threatening illness. Whatever arrows are carried in our quivers, we need the evidence gathered to be accurate and timely. But it also needs vetting for its credibility, authenticity, and perspective. That kind of presentation is not referenced in any search sites or web pages. It's the meanings derived from our findings that draw clients into the often anxiety-ridden zone of acting on a pressing decision.

Our interpretations don't need to be airtight. Giving our imaginations, license to explore is granted by the fact base of our investigations. Factoring in the motives of our information providers is a tool to help our clients form their own opinion, or gauge their agreement level. They may conclude differently, but it will be based on the same evidence, and understanding about the sources who provided it.

Organizing Principles

Content analysis means taking a sample and measuring it in the aggregate. This is in much the same way a survey measures the pulse of collective opinions. It hasn't gotten any harder to collect samples through the web. What's difficult is ascribing motivations to specific editorial communities within those content groupings. Assembling news in the mass media period meant that certain rules and customs were followed. Guarding a news division from charges of libel or slander was an operational necessity for all publishers, no matter whose reputation they were denigrating, or higher truth they were defending.

There are no longer these shared motivations across the political spectrum for defending these First Amendment freedoms. In today's climate, it's hard containing one agenda to a specific website, let alone a region, an ownership ring, or a media genre. Regardless of vested interests and political persuasion, how can we hope to apply uniform standards across the board? We don't factor in every public company to determine how well the market performed today. We don't poll every voter to forecast an electoral outcome.

So where do the **Vectors of Integrity** kick in if we're gauging moods and detecting trends? We need a survey sample that's representative of the whole, not the definitive word on every last news source. That's how content analysts can answer these concerns: Navigating the sources that others find too voluminous to organize, and too jumbled to navigate.

SCORING FORMULAS

The world's message supply is unlimited, and will only expand as the web becomes more *worldwide* or fractures into spheres of influence. But all those messages encounter a fixed number of waking hours. Attention divides where messages compound. Here's the formula:

Attention Supply ÷ Attention Demand = Message Value

Start with the total content supply or story counts as the baseline. This helps determine how the media world parcels out its cumulative focus. Let's break it down.

Attention Supply

You would think everybody in the public arena wants attention. Honestly? Let's consider how most organizations go about trying to acquire it. Each advertiser boasts about its stature. Each company proclaims to be a market leader. Have you heard this all before? We may have never visited their website, downloaded their app, seen their ads, or heard of their products. And we can still recite their goal of world conquest without remembering the details for how they get there. That's because our ears glaze over from every press dispatch ever released in the annals of publicity-seeking.

Press releases, for example, try to confer authority and status on the same people who approve them. Before social media, they were ridiculed outside the PR trade as self-serving, delusional. That assumption surfaces whether the information provider is communicating about themselves or not. Such are the perils of open platforms and publishing on demand.

Press releases were always seen as literate spam – an orchestrated way to stage a one-way public conversation. Even today, they're an accurate way to assess how organizations see themselves in the milestones they find worthy of announcing:

1. Who are their most prized customers?
2. Who are their most valued contributors?

The external side of internal recognition is critical for assessing how strongly those messages permeate and are reflected back or even shared at all by the wider community.

Attention Demand

Face it. The market does not care what a company thinks of itself. But it may devour information on what sets that company apart – if it comes from someone outside the company. Whatever the reaction, verdict, or decision, the response will be delivered via demand-based media. The impact will be measured in the differences between push and pull: Supply and demand-based media.

In the former, supply-demand cycle information suppliers would peddle their wares to their editorial customers. News and feature editors would *buy the argument* that at least some of these noisy, boastful press releases contained (1) information their readers wanted to see, and (2) that it was worthy of their attention. It was believable, at least once it saw the light of day in print.

Fast forward to today and credibility is still the lifeblood of reporters, analysts, and public leaders. At least in any field where success hinges on the ability to speak plausibly, to and for one's peers. This is the essence of PCF-based group identity. This is what we introduced in **Unit Four** as first, second, and third party provider conjugation.

The same holds true for our survey sample. We need to establish source credibility as we shape our demand media sample. We'll be doing so by piecing together the coverage patterns of disinterested third-parties. That primary motivation remains reaching the widest audience, not in carrying the narrowest message.

Message Value

Think of message value as our credibility gauge. Message value is critical if our client's executive or marketing team is concerned about protecting assets, gaining traction, or just plain campaign success. Here a TBP perspective can cast a clarifying light on these otherwise murky calculations.

Message value hinges on the extent that third parties (bloggers, journalists, op-ed editors, pundits, etc.) cite the search target in our media sample. We arrive at message value by dividing attention demand into message supply:

1. The greater the content supply, and the less the media demand, the lower the message value
2. The lower the supply, and the greater the demand, the higher the value

Another way to frame high message value is to determine how little *push* is necessary to sustain the most *pull,* or gain the most traction. It is one calculation in a series of analytical ratios to measure the heavy, often unforeseen hand of external pressures, and influences of the marketplace.

MANAGING THE PROJECT

For years, managers of all stripes have exploited standard operating procedures ("SOP") to measure corporate performance. The rationale is this: While all organizations are unique, each competes for attention, resources, and revenues or funding in 'lines of business' or services with 'layers of management' or operations.

Here's what's not so rare. Relationships are formed between *vertical* industries and the *horizontal* functions filled by the organization's employees. Those bonds contain a finite set of arrangements and outcomes. These are interactions between the organization and marketplace that unfold over a business cycle, or a social calendar.

How stable or transitory a period are our clients cycling through? Set up a query that monitors management changes over quarterly periods. Just how sleepy a lull or tumultuous a shake-up can be quantified. TBP applies a consistent method for addressing horizontal business functions over a fixed time interval, and set of information providers (demand media).

The content supply is the total number of these interactions. Tracking them is a fixed number of messengers – that's our demand media grouping. They assemble a finite set of outcomes (speculations and results) from a menu of milestones (staged and unplanned events).

Setting up the Model

Measurement standards can emerge from this Biggest Picture method for rating the market presence of organizations and the nature of their public identities. That's a broad perspective. But the model can also focus on more precise impacts:

1. The record of a specific business unit within a company,
2. The consequence of a leadership change, or
3. The impact of a recent merger on the overall brand, etc.

Conversely, the search target can shift to the internal impact of an external event, i.e. the repercussions of a high profile law suit.

The best way to answer generalities with specifics is to draw a content sample within a meaningful timeframe. We can then parse the sample by how the content addressing our search target collects inside content sources, industry segments, and management functions. We can establish who discusses our search targets, and the intensity of that discussion, by understanding how the model captures these outputs.

Looking for Relationships

Secondly, we'll want to mine those same outputs for bloggers, reporters, analyst organizations, and content-producing channels who contribute(1) the bulk of coverage volume, and (2) the 'opinion weight' about our search targets. Opinion weight determines whose influence tracks most closely to the transcendent themes, and issues surrounding the public identities of target organizations.

It's one thing to measure indiscriminate hit counts. It's quite another to score the influence and impact of public debates, issues, campaigns, and relations. That's why knowledge of content sourcing is critical for assembling a TBP-based content analysis. It equips us to assess the strength of marketing affiliations and the antagonisms formed in public clashes. That's because we can track the size and scope of the content providers that cover our targets and weigh-in on these topics.

Such an analysis can draw a complete picture of an organization's stakeholders and social networks. One that deviates dramatically from the carefully scripted first party communication of a company website, press release, or annual report.

Telling the Story

Content analysis frameworks like **The Biggest Picture** define relationships by translating transactions into story lines. A sound methodology assures our clients that they can be market listeners as well as leaders. Their vested interests won't skew the sample we've assembled. Conversely, the sample can suggest remedies and next steps if the results reveal problems that were otherwise dormant or unaddressed.

Most of us are familiar with the sports metaphor of the 'corporate playbook' for implementing organizational strategies. But the content analyst augments this with a storybook for telling the narrative of the study to the client:

1. Stories create message retention, generating interest in themes and affiliations beyond the main target.
2. Stories 'unfold' – keeping our clients riveted to the next unforeseen or continuous plot twist.
3. Stories clarify the complexities of conflicting numbers and create the consensus necessary to initiate, mend, extend, or dissolve all kinds of relationships.
4. Stories compel their listeners to action – honoring this newfound consensus and the deadlines these decisions entail.

Think of our own organization's fortunes. In corporate marketing it goes something like this:

> *Quarterly plots consist of a sequence of events or actions that move the story forward by introducing conflicts (say, competing product launches), adding complications (changes in the management ranks), and providing resolution (winning new business).*

That sounds repeatable and formulaic. Now how come we can't get Google to connect these dots for us? The problem isn't in our skills as storytellers, or business analysts, but in the garbled way we piece our narratives together.

WHEN CLIENTS COME KNOCK-KNEED

We need to consider this: We resist the temptation to start counting before we can deliver credible numbers about a company's reputation.

First things first. We ask ourselves: What flurry of events would conspire to have a CXO or a marketing genius, or the agencies they retain seek outside counsel about…

- Something they know a lot better than us – their organization
- Something they are powerless to prevent – an encroaching set of unfavorable conditions

Weathering a crisis is the only kind of climate worthy of adaption. To do this may require nerves of steely resolve, and unblinking acceptance of one's faults and frailties. But it absolutely means grounding where an organization has landed to other hardship cases. Such comparisons invite baselines and benchmark evaluations long before an opportunity for the group to regain their footing and eventual stature. It takes numbers.

Here are a few assumptions we can make:

1. The group in question is either under attack, or expects to be within a rapidly closing window of safety.
2. Fear of *where this can all lead* is impeding the leadership from behaving responsibly and working things out as a group.
3. The executives believe they will become the butt of talk show monologues and that they will be blamed for circumstances far beyond their control. Write this off to the conceits of paranoia: Good or bad, it's all about me. Especially the bad!

Insiders like our business leader cracks the door open for outsiders like us during a crisis. Crisis counselors are in the reassurance industry. Executives pay to be told that their darker instincts are clouding their judgments, and that it's not the end of…

- The world they have known,
- The business they've built,
- Growth they have promised, or
- Distant horizons they envision.

But their need for reassurance needs to rest on facts – not on our abilities to console or placate them.

This is where a little perspective goes a long way. A baseline that compares the current predicament to pre-crisis levels of scrutiny and exposure is the first step. This is the foundation for understanding thresholds, precedents, and anticipated trends. That's where the reassurance can begin. It's what the client should expect should the crisis run its course. Perhaps that includes some preemptive moves which could accelerate the healing process or resolution of the crisis.

UNIT FIVE: How to Present What We Learn in Teachable Ways | Page 5:14

Once the pre and current baselines of client media coverage are established, the same sample sizes will need to be scoped to the topic in question. Our first use case features the before and after effects of a high profile lawsuit filed against a national food chain on grounds of misleading consumers (target crisis). *Note:* **Unit Six** *is a use case that plays out where we, the Knowledge-ABLED, are both the consultant and client.*

UNIVERSE OF CLIENT

Cyclical tracking is useful for determining a baseline of news coverage and comparing crisis periods to more benign news cycles. Firestorms come and go. Search targets will forever be staked to standard time frames.

FIGURE 5.1: All Mentions of Taco Bell in Google News for the First Half of 2011

Note the custom range parameters in the box on the lower left. Date ranges are essential for creating a meaningful sample for applying a 'Biggest Picture' analysis of a search target's media exposure.

Universe of Topic

Next, we need a handle on the larger pool or context that frames the organization's mission, business segments, stakeholders, and communities of interest. This sample ensures that the actions and outcomes discussed in the media are addressing a major policy or public concern of interest to our search targets and/or clients.

FIGURE 5.2: All Mentions of Food Safety, Poisoning, or Food Contamination

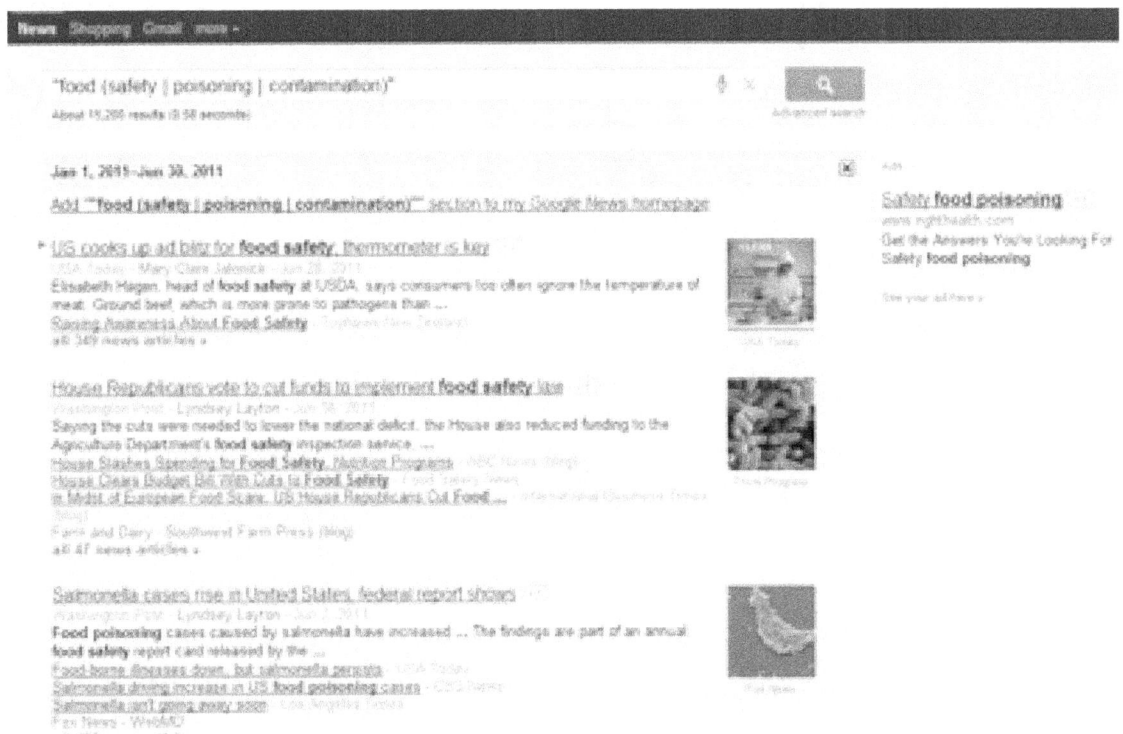

This results page represents Google News for the first half of 2011. Note the usefulness of semantics in the form of word algebra for generating a targeted range of outcomes from which to test the public standing of the search target (Taco Bell).

Cross references

We note very little overlap when we merge the topic and client samples. Does that mean Taco Bell is rarely mentioned in the same breath as food safety concerns? Yes.

Does that also mean that our search target is in the clear, regarding public health concerns and its menu of products? Absolutely not.

This is the stage where we need to analyze the cross references for clues about where Taco Bell's reputation can be further compromised. Just because little coverage is generated in our topic universe doesn't mean related issues are not in play. It's also conceivable that Taco Bell's products may be implicated in other controversies.

FIGURE 5.3: Cross Reference of Client Mentions and Topic Universe within Same Timeframe

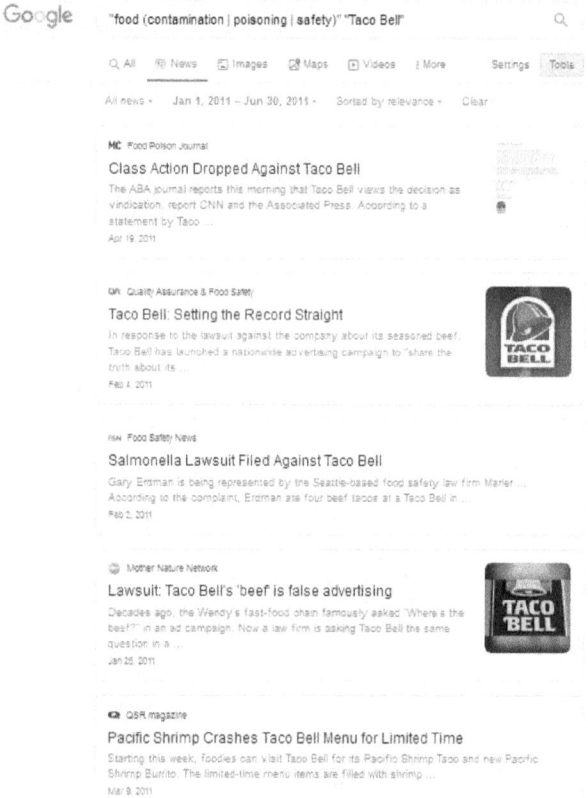

Parting the Clouds of Judgment

Nothing scrambles our perspective more than a judgment clouded by preparing for an attack, a siege mentality. If one's guard is up, so are the distortions in our mirrors, and sense that we need to marshal our powers of self-preservation.

The Biggest Picture creates a statistical framework for calculating the extent of that attack both as a looming possibility and as a foregone conclusion. The fact that it's possible to slide between prologue and postscript is a simple framing of the time intervals we're sampling through the date range feature modeled in Figure 5.1.

Beyond analytics and reporting, being able to test past history, track current trending, and hypothesize around future scenarios has another positive impact. That's the ability to add perspective to clients inclined to inflate their impacts, both pro and con, on the markets they serve.

Conversely, as a participant, this broader perspective can breed more engagement than detachment. Tracking scores unfold. Clients ponder what finer points to cultivate, tweak or even trash: A Market heats up, a crisis winds down, a theory runs its course.

It's a fairly common consulting tool to benchmark a standard business practice. This is so the client can assess their relative standing among their peers. Their relative stature determines where to *raise their game*, or alternatively, to recede back *into the pack*. For example, "here's how you're doing on eight dimensions of risk" is just the kind of value proposition that a benchmarking outfit will pitch to the leadership of an operational function within a larger organization.

This kind of orientation is the performance measurement fare we'd expect to see in assessing the internal productivity of a business unit. What about outside perceptions? What if the weakest link in that same unit's supply chain causes concern about the quality of its products, or the legitimacy of its services? Such doubts can ripple through the longstanding reputation of well-established brands with undiscriminating haste.

Ironically, those on the receiving end of public scandal are no better informed or reasoned than the customers who move quickly to do business elsewhere. One way to lower the stress level is to conduct a post mortem of a crisis event. Like the more traditional benchmarking of internal functions, a perception-based survey like TBP is a sober, clear-headed, and repeatable way to gauge the after-effects, the settled perceptions in the post event aftermath.

Post Mortems

That post event reckoning is not limited to damage assessments. Counter measures can be just as meaningful. For example, it's a fair question to ask how effective were the responses to an original threat. In the case of Taco Bell, the parent Yum Brands insisted on a public apology in a Wall Street Journal ad. This message was aimed at the illegitimate claims of Taco Bell's detractors.

So what gets measured in this counter-measure? The key indicator is not about the intensity of the resulting press coverage. It was about how the brand's exposure to risk was lowered or not, depending on the shift in the post event numbers.

It's a familiar story. A dubious claim with a speck of veracity arrives from nowhere: Taco bell = sawdust. Freaked-out executives switch to reactive mode. Their tepid responses are tentative and slow. They are the butt of late night talk show jokes by the end of the next news cycle. The top brass circles the wagons:

> 1. We're getting killed – really? Is this how it feels or is that how it is?
>
> 2. Did sales really go down?
>
> 3. Could the same be said of Yum Brands' capacity to absorb the unexpected?

Reference points must be determined and tested before inviting any further comparisons. It's not me and you against the world. It's not within a world where every element is boiled down to good or bad. We need to correlate concerns and interests against other externalities that we'll detail in the next 'Likely Suspects' section. Before we internalize a threat, we need to catalog it, score it, and connect it to a larger playing field of risks and opportunities. Before we determine what scores to settle, we need to establish the scoring system.

We now need to cultivate a range of potential influencers capable of impacting the stakeholders and communities representing or served by the target in question. Sound familiar? These are the groups or parties diagrammed in the PCF.

How do we do this? Before we proceed, we need to better understand this other pre-existing universe.

Likely Suspects

It's critical to generate a meaningful volume for determining the baseline or pre-event level of media exposure. But it's equally important to test the nature of the coverage – specifically what connections are being made and the strength of those relationships.

A baseline is essential to calculate the swelling of post event fallout. The nature of the coverage helps us to characterize negative connotations such as the distortions, innuendo, and scapegoats. It can also offer a positive contrast in more favorable coverage.

Those linkages can take many forms. Here's a listing of some reliable associations and the entities they include:

- **Events**
    - Milestones
    - Cyclical rites (awards, ceremonies)
    - Meetings (communities, trade groups, negotiations)
- **People**
    - Executives/Owners
    - Spokespersons
    - Reporters/Bloggers
    - Witnesses/Experts
- **Roles / Responsibilities**
    - Stakeholders (board members, customers, employees)
    - Competitors
    - Elected Officials
    - Legal Parties (regulators, judges, law enforcement)
- **Locations**
    - Venue (sports, entertainment)
    - Physical (crime scene, rights-of-way)
    - Region (host community, civic associations, town/city boosters)

As we will see, most reporting is less easily regarded as positive or negative. This is particularly true as we factor in the PCF framework and the multiple, sometimes conflicting ways that different receivers perceive information providers and their messages.

Hidden Assets

The extended circle of likely suspects is not only key for connecting the analytic *dots,* but for deciding which aspects of the survey to communicate in the findings and recommendations. Most organizations wrestle with some universal questions around the ways in which they're perceived within an external context:

1. What attention am I being paid?
2. How do I use that attention?
3. Which of my reputations are by my design?
4. Which ones do the media identify with?
5. What's the bottom-line and how do we measure up?
6. What's the prevailing wisdom and who carries the most sway?

We understand what's worth pursuing in our recommendations to the client once we've mapped our information providers to this wider community of stakeholders. Remember, we will turn up a lot of new connections and under-appreciated associations by keeping our search terms more generalized and action-based. Figure 5.4 showcases how a Biggest Picture approach demonstrates the public strength of our clients' most overlooked jewels.

FIGURE 5.4: Matching Client's Marketing Assets to Benefits of TBP Methodology

Asset	Approach
Branding Properties	Launch impacts, footprints, stature…
Suppliers & Partners	Relationship strength – the companies we keep
Executives/Thought Leaders	Experience quantifiers – (who's who in which and where…)
Experience-Based Promotions	Contests, conferences, awards, perennials…
Message Projection	Aspirations, tag lines, value propositions, endorsements…
Risk Assessment	Protecting the public identity of private or safeguarded assets
Serendipity	Overlooked venues to position core strengths through joint ventures, cross-marketing and under-leveraged equities

Now let's return to that sub-set of food safety stories mentioning Taco Bell.

LOOKING FOR TROUBLE IN ALL THE RIGHT PLACES

Now that we know who's who, we can see set our sights to these wider and diverging perspectives. That means coming up with a more relevant set of topics for tracking Taco Bell.

What it doesn't mean is fixating on specific events or actors who are likely to change or recede as coverage patterns evolve. It's the nerves they strike and the alarm bells they sound that we're looking for here.

FIGURE 5.5: Sample Page from Prior Cross References

So what's in play here? For starters we've got a regulatory entity (the USDA) and an accusation of a code violation by two law firms. This is a complex matter.

The article opens more questions than it answers. We don't know the relationship between the two law firms or even whose interests prompted them to file the lawsuit. Also, in addition to our client and topic, we've got two additional perspectives to consider:

1. Taco Bell franchisees
2. Taco Bell customers

The main concern for us at this point is to create a more meaningful test for tracking public perceptions of our search target. Now an interesting thing happens. We add the four keywords:

USDA | filling | lawsuit | misleading

We keep our target and our time frame and our hit counts soar from 22 to 191. Additionally, nine of the first ten stories on our Google search page cite the original legal action referred to in Figure 5.5:

FIGURE 5.6: Reformulated Query of Cross References

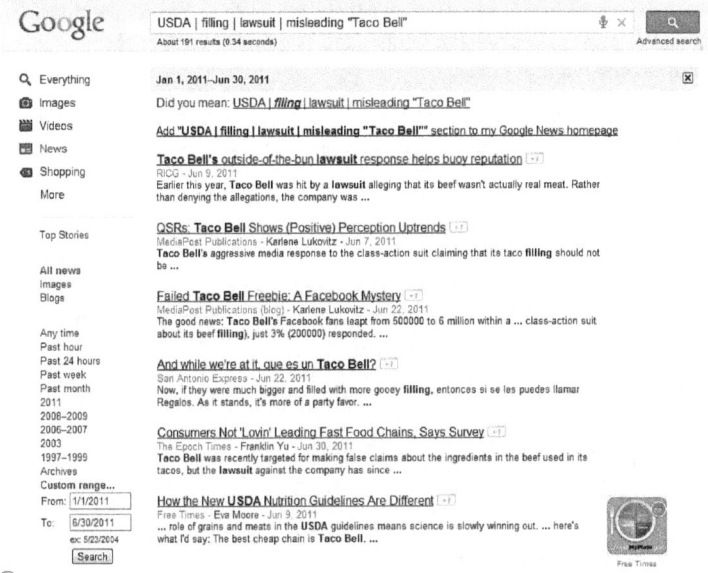

Note that this search was conducted after the half year mark for an event that occurred close to the beginning of the same cycle. This suggests that 'the story has legs' or that the issue is still active.

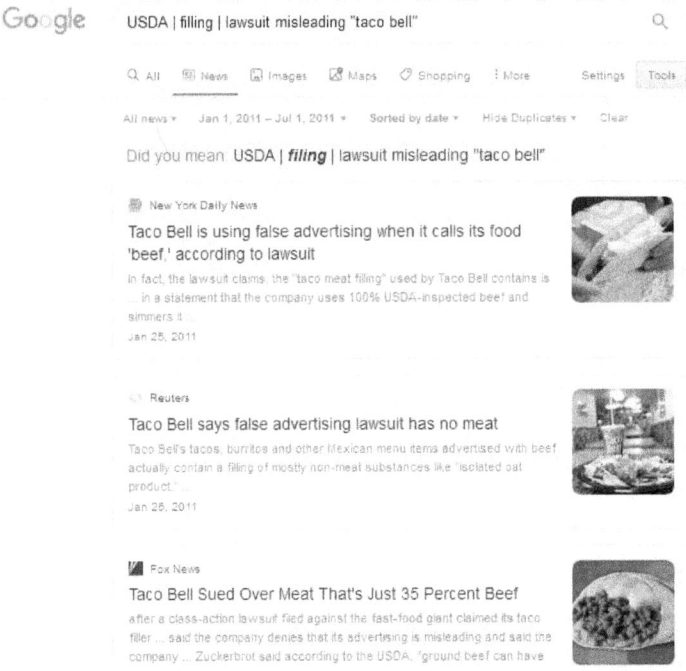

The same query in 2019. Note that the story counts are missing below the query statement.

But just how important are the actual numbers? How significant is it Google indexes 191 instances of web pages from what it deems news sources over six months that mention both our target and topic?

Not much.

We must connect events to outcomes in order to create valid comparisons and viable conclusions. We must channel this activity around the media exposure of Taco Bell's peers. We must map coverage upticks and downturns to the specific adjustments it makes to address all the market commotion beyond its control.

Unlike internal goals where it's about *making our numbers*, the external side is scoped by non financial metrics. Defining a target's media performance is largely based on benchmarks – peer comparisons that shed light on perceived threats and opportunities unique to the peer group.

MEDIA PERFORMANCE BENCHMARKING

Topical terms are invoked In order to validate each target. For instance, a term set consisting of the terms restaurant, food, chain, or burger means that McDonald's doesn't track the surname 'McDonald.' Now we overlay five negative outcomes for each food chain consisting of: **scandal | controversial | misleading | lawsuit | complaint**.

FIGURE 5.7: Benchmarking Negative Media Coverage through Peer Comparisons

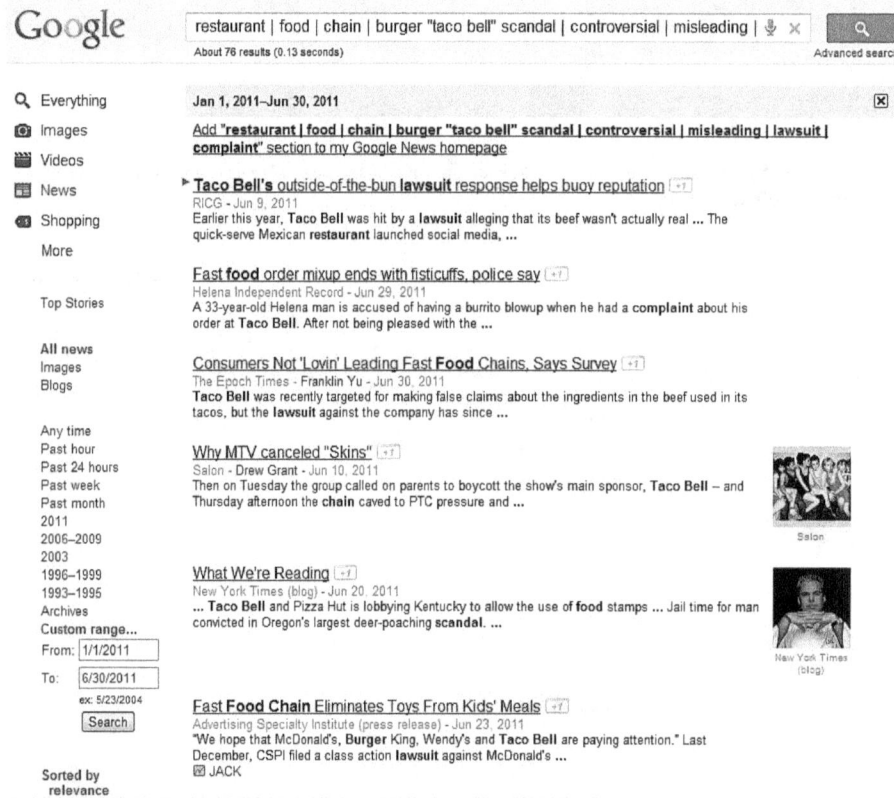

The term 'filling' is omitted from the benchmarking sample due to its specific Taco Bell connotation.

Here are the tallies based on the leading brands within Taco Bell's market segment:

FIGURE 5.8: Benchmarking Scores of Leading Fast Food Chains

Peer Member	Hit Counts
McDonald's	43
Burger King	125
Wendy's	35
Taco Bell	76
Pizza Hut	44

Now again, these hit rates have limited value without gauging the overall footprint each brand carries within its own client universe. We more clearly see the level of negative press each property generates when we add the total counts for each property:

FIGURE 5.9: Benchmarking Scores of Negative Media Coverage

Peer Member	Hit Counts	Total Counts	Negative coverage score
McDonald's	43	7580	0.6%
Burger King	125	4710	2.6%
Wendy's	35	1970	1.8%
Taco Bell	76	1110	6.8%
Pizza Hut	44	1830	2.4%

The results indicate two clear findings:

1. Team McDonald's is the brand to beat – not just for sales, but for the volume and nature of its media coverage.
2. Taco Bell hit a rough patch that began at the beginning of the reporting cycle, and persists throughout the study period.

So, how do we deliver these results to a client, especially when the news is not exactly flattering?

Here are two presentation factors worth considering:

1) Transparency

Transparency is critical. The client needs less to own the process and more to trust in it. That means our clients get the same results we do. This worthy goal is made all the more elusive in the post standardized results page era of filter bubbles. **(Pariser, 2011)**[2] We're not out to impress an opinion-maker, or an audience panel. We're leasing them a model that will deliver the same repeatable answers when they pose the questions, just as we have in **Unit Five**. Now that's empirical transparency.

The emphasis is overdue. The adoption of open and repeatable standards is no longer a luxury we can do without. That's because the more customized the survey, the more questionable the results. Doctored results cast doubt and destroy credibility. Ironically, such surveys have little merit outside the companies who contract to produce them.

2) Quantification

Media performance is not a direct survey of a primary respondent. It's hit counts – the number of pages matching our search criteria. That's not always clearly understood by the client who may have a more conventional understanding of surveys.

The benefit for them is clear. This is not a new survey methodology, but a quick and demonstrable way to quantify the volume and nature of news coverage. The vehicle is Google, so they are applying a tool they use every day in a deliberate manner.

Another potential point of confusion is that we are using relatively high sample sizes to test subjective versions of a media-based reality. Many business and even marketing folks assume traditional polling methods when one wants to test consumer perceptions. Figure 5.10 suggests ways to communicate TBP benefits to clients, new to media performance benchmarks:

FIGURE 5.10: Merits of Anecdotal Versus Quantitative Surveys

Anecdotal	Aggregation
Qualify	Quantify
Verify	Validate
Consider	Conclude
Speculation	Proof
Squishy	Accountable

Follow-up

Remember the three levels of quality control we explored in **Unit Three**? They include:

1. **Level 1 | Big Picture** – The hit counts of carefully formulated queries used to score the media coverage of search targets.

2. **Level 2 | Street Level** – The site contributing those counts – typically the aggregator or original publisher of the content provided.

3. **Level 3 | Microscopic Level** – This is the actual page within the provider site where the details of the story, the news correspondent, and her interviews reside.

It's time to drill down on the more qualitative distinctions, once the initial benchmarks are established on level 1. Here are two potential next steps for to assess the scoring, and analyze the patterns they yield:

1. In Level Two, source the site roots in order to classify the audience reach and impact of Google News providers. The Wall Street Journal and the Podunk Bulletin & Trading Post may count the same on Level One, but they are not media equals by any measurable standard.

2. Trace the story lines in Level Three that emerge and distinguish what the search engine cannot. This is where the search target is the instigator or main subject (active narrative) versus a bystander or implication (passive narrative). In the case of Taco Bell, think about street crimes reported in the parking lot of a local franchise.

As we also saw in **Unit Three**, sourcing is not just about points of origin, but intentionality: The motivations for informing *who* about *what* that are harbored by all information providers. This is the most dominant factor in our Knowledge-ABLED presentations for two reasons:

1. Knowing the larger social purpose of providing information is the single easiest way to influence its impact.

2. Conferring this to a client is the single greatest value add we can provide, and bill for, as investigators.

THE VIEW FROM BELOW

Up until now, we've been interfacing with the upper echelon. Those are the folks above the folks who sign our checks. Count a fair number who have an ongoing need to know market risks and opportunities. These are the folks in a position to act on them. But it's not all shareholders and venture equity. It's also the folks who pay their bills directly. That means considering the way line managers assess the credibility of their suppliers and bosses. Generally speaking, line managers are the lower level minions who keep operations running smoothly, or retool specific functions to improve those operations. It's this reason our PCF analysis include the internal perspective, not just the market focus.

If there is an inherent bias of using PCF, it's that we're never more than a chance connection removed from testing a theory of hypocrisy and corruption:

1. We all know the first signs that our politicians are not being entirely candid – when their lips move.

2. We all know that banks get robbed because that's where the money is – even by their own bankers.

3. Our powers of BS detection are tested and strengthened each day when elected officials, corporate leaders, and attention-starved celebrities keep three separate ledgers, including (1) their words, (2) deeds, and (3) the difference (a.k.a. hypocrisy).

The journalism industry may never recover. Exposing hypocrisy is as much a winning business model as a self-protective impulse. It keeps our *honest* doubts in line with our *reasonable* expectations.

So how do line managers keep their BS detectors in working order? Let's say they're in fact-finding mode for upgrading the software required to run their business functions. Let's assume there's much to sift through. So much that the volume of pros and cons overwhelms those vows they make to stand their ground.

That position, let's assume, lies somewhere in-between a wholesale upgrade of the latest version, and business-as-usual. Our operations guy needs to see the trade-offs with the options at-hand: To map those choices to their business, their values, their clients. Period.

In the technology business, it helps to bypass the trade show evangelists and seek out those unassuming functional managers. BS levels drop when dealing with working stiffs (like me). That's because operations folks seek not the victory of a sales closing. They crave the solace of living within their system choices.

That doesn't mean anyone manning the booth has a used car they want to pawn off on those walking the hall. But it does mean that the folks who count themselves as payroll costs care more about war stories than case studies. They care about the unexpected experience than the full feature list. They are not looking for outward recognition. They're pursuing the internal approval needed to pull resources and manage their projects.

Those outside vendors will show up on The Biggest Picture radar. Any technology marketer worth their salt is tracking media mentions in trade journals. Preferably, these outlets cater to the function-happy folks and not just to the technology crowd.

Also, that every day experience of the line manager extends beyond reporting structures and project management. It scales not only to her unit and organization, but how that entity is perceived in the wider market. Marketers call this 'brand stature.'

Before we get there, we need to take a step back. Let's review the tools and methods we've already introduced for delivering these Biggest Picture benefits.

INSTITUTIONAL CREDIBILITY

In **Unit Four**, we assessed information context through the lens of two new frameworks: PCF ("Provider Conjugation Framework") and VOI (the "Vectors of Integrity"). These models help us to see the ways our search targets receive and interpret information providers.

We also looked at social information. Here, the perspective of second persons and parties are removed from the path between information providers and recipients. Social media is the most vivid example of this. We then considered the conditions where the coercive elements of misinformation can flourish, true especially where the misinformant is free from divulging one's identity, along with their news.

But what about the messages that are paid for by message providers? What about keywords that are auctioned through the Google Ads program?

1. Do we take a step back as researchers when providers have no other use for us (other than as message consumers?)
2. Do we discredit them because they have the ulterior motive (getting us to buy their products, or sell their arguments?)

Most of us are not such information purists that we must remove all self-serving motives from (1) our search results, (2)database providers, or (3) RSS feeds. But we need to include motivation in the mix when we're sourcing the very evidence we're using to recommend or act on. This question is foundational to The Biggest Picture approach needed to contextualize our search targets. That context covers markets, operations, and stretches over the wider public realm of media scrutiny.

DETERMINING INSTITUTIONAL CREDIBILITY

Here in **Unit Five,** we assess and measure **four motivation levels** used to define credible news-making communications. Each motivate is evaluated according to its surface news value. TBP is there to test the rationales that explain the deeper, implicit understandings between message senders and receivers.

As we saw in **Unit Four**, there are several steps in-between the spinning of *set results* into *net results*. The same dynamics apply whether we apply this to individuals, as we did earlier, or as groups as we address here. In effect, they will learn how to interpret set results based on the guiding principle of credibility. Unclear about the motives of information givers? Look no further than who they're giving out to.

When determining the institutional credibility of a website's content, we need to...

- Anticipate the format,
- Know the media grouping that identifies its readership (local, trade, weekly, etc.), and
- Recognize the sources' self-interest.

Here are three group-based assessment methods available to us.

1) Common interest and word of mouth

One of the clearest ways to define self-interest is to consider its opposite – common interest. A common interest is genuinely forged through conversation, typically between two people sharing experience and advice. Sometimes one person imparts the same with several people. If this form of trusted communication sounds familiar, maybe you're familiar with its marketing identity: Word of mouth.

Word of mouth is a conversation if we reference the PCF model: One to one with common interest. That intimacy is corrupted when that transfer becomes a many-to-one discussion, with a commercial or self-serving first party interest. Think of the word of mouth being swapped out for the word-of-sponsor.

Why do so many institutions rise and fall based on word of mouth? Their success depends on the participation of others, with their time, money and attention. Like the stock market, if a trading system appears rigged, fewer people invest in it. If members of a religious order do not abide by the church's own ethics, fewer people come to worship. Only when we as participants have no other choice is there a public tolerance – if not resigned acceptance – of the institutional corruptions inspired by self-serving behavior. Our longstanding national addiction to oil recalls a lack of choice in America's participation in politically unstable areas of the world. It's a quandary that continues in spite of American energy independence. Astonishing.

One of the interesting aspects in the rise of bloggers and web-based self-publishing is this: Marketers are in less control of word of mouth communications than ever. The many-to-one word from our sponsor cannot compete with the one-to-one word of mouth. A commercial can never be a conversation. We as participants think twice before buying into information that serve the self-interest of companies we do not know, politicians we would not elect, or institutions that have no place in our own value systems.

As information consumers, we understand that the information supplied us on the web is often tainted. Yes, by self-interest but also by institutions posing as *real people* and *trusted advisers*. Such inputs and opinions are swayed, even purchased, by the institutions, corporations and products they steer us towards.

2) Self Interest and media incest

The easiest way to specify something so pervasive and universal as self-interest is to revisit the role of information providers during the infancy of television broadcast:

> *Dateline: New York World's Fair, April 1939.*
>
> *Place: RCA Pavilion*
>
> *"Cue General Sarnoff and action!"* **(Bilby, 1986)**[3]

The first event TV ever covered was the birth of itself.[4]

Love at first sight.

Like all industries, the media's primary business purpose is not to educate, orchestrate or distract but simply to sell more media. Unlike all other industries, the media is entirely comfortable in front of a camera as well as behind one. In how many industries does the annual awards dinner attract a third of all U.S. adults?[5]

The difference between our trophies and theirs is that they don't even acknowledge a camera presence until their acceptance speeches.

So what do we mean about the *incestuous* state of media relations?

One way that the broadcast and cable media is like any other business community is that its members are acutely aware of what each one of them is saying. In fact, stories about media people are easy to deliver:

1. Readily recognized name
2. Little to no background digging
3. Someone whose job security other media folks either want to...
    - Test by questioning their personal choices, or
    - Test by asking for a professional favor

It's all pretty transparent stuff. But like any self-serving fabrication, it's also unbelievable. All the *like this* Facebook approvals can't mask the artifice of backscratching and self-congratulations.

The question isn't who do we believe, when we're all beholden to our own interests. The more interesting problem here for us is to build a rationale. This is the explanation for why and how stakeholders interpret and act on *the news* based on who presents it, and how it's presented to them.

3) Self Importance and media delusion

How do we measure respect?

Every media season witnesses an award overdose. Each year, the industry hands out thousands of trophies at hundreds of ceremonies. Incest abounds as TV broadcasts of Oscars, Grammy and Tony Awards all win Emmys.

Not surprisingly, of all industries the business segment the media is most inclined to cover is ... well ... the media. The self-referential nature of broadcast media is an accepted fact of broadcast content. We expect to hear *plugs* of new books, movies, dieting plans and moral crusades. Self-promotion satisfies the dual need to fill *air* time with the persuasion of coming attractions.

Thus, it's not really news when our media celebrities broadcast their deeply-held beliefs that they are not only informing us, but *speaking for us*. Otherwise, why would they be permitted to hold so much attention within such a public space? The argument for the separation of news-gathering and opinion formation is both world-weary and unwinnable.

Can the two really be isolated? That the self-selection of certain facts and the exclusion of others is not its own form of commentary – a game of tele-prompting through TelePrompTers?

But just because talking heads on cable networks take personal liberties to mold or fabricate our public discourse doesn't disqualify them from competing for our attentions.

Their reputations may suffer. Their influence may wane. But these are addressed in The Biggest Picture model. These are not just nagging questions but receptive to responses. TBP enables answers as calculable as the formulas that aid and abet the delusions we've endured as passive viewers for over half a century.

The Biggest Picture too harbors its own biases. Like most other scoring formulas, it has an implicit goal in moving us from a wider awareness to corrective action. That's prodding our clients to see, understand, and address the kinds of big picture connections CEOs, elected officials, and decision-makers generally make in isolation.

METHODOLOGY

Every survey model comes with its own set of terms and conditions, a.k.a. survey methodology. In addition to statistical ranges of accuracy, a methodology establishes *the how* of the data collection, especially the *how big* size of the sample. Sample credibility for perception measurement is defined by the requirements for painting *the biggest picture*. This means building a successful demand-based content analysis practice.

A demand-based system measures total media attention paid to the issues, commercial assets, and personalities that drive market opinion over months, years and decades. The results speak for the markets – not the marketers. The orientation is based on how stakeholders see the market players. What won't we see in a TBP methodology? How individual companies view their own isolated actions.

Supply media is beholden to the specific aims of a single client function – PR. Want to prove coverage volume is up? You don't need The Biggest Picture to prove out an increase in press mentions. The demand model its based on responds directly to the entire organization. TBP is a reporting and analysis tool to understand and manage the heavy, unforeseen hand of *external factors*. External here is a vague label used to group everything from media hysteria, to crisis communications, and legal counsel.

Defining The Biggest Picture

So how do we put The Biggest Picture into practice?

First let's more clearly define the vision. The Biggest Picture is: a conceptual framework that...

- Defines resonance and context from the fleeting and fuzzy onslaught of commercial messages
- Imposes a structure on horizon gazing – shifts in the competitive environment, management fads and cultural norms
- Creates a numbers-based perspective on non-quantitative information

Now, let's bring it down to daily news cycles and media consumption. We know the feeling of being stressed out by too many incoming messages. We can only assume that information glut once lived the nitty gritty details buried in newspaper text and broadcast noise. The advent of screens in our grasps has exploded the noise level well beyond human cognition. It may sound like the survey-taker would need to barricade such explosions. Actually, instead of trying to contain them, the broadest, breathtaking views can be had from scaling these walls of information.

Problems with Content Analysis

Most content analysis distorts the media it measures by reducing all relevant messages to a simple 'hit count' of pre-considered targets. This is done by polling organizations, market research firms and PR agencies to assess how the media influences public perception of their clients and key competitors, campaigns, events or policy issues. Yet few news stories can be judged as definitively good or bad for a company's short or long-term prospects. It's even harder to shade coverage in terms of *partial* goodness, or *potential* fallout.

Furthermore, predetermining who or what to monitor skews the results in favor of pre-test assumptions. The most sincere, accurate, and credible way to score how these messages perform in selected media is to constrain our analysis. That means limiting the scope of target messages, time frames, and the media they're grouping in.

One must resist the temptation to pre-determine a target company, opinion leader, consulting group, or editorial slant based on a vested outcome. A stakeholder can hold The Biggest Picture up to their own self-reflections. But that mirror image must reflect the same results when a disinterested observer applies the same method to the same sample.

This hands-off approach permits a more credible means to quantify category leaders, media perceptions, message shapers, and the ancillary messages that spin off from the original. It also turns up what we weren't looking for, but needed to find out – a promising indication of useful research.

Universal Laws of Self Interest

As a PCF analysis indicates, the coverage patterns of news topics by news groupings is far more useful than the first-ten-hits-or-bust approach to conventional search engine analytics. Looking out over the entire provider pool is critical for isolating common stories from unique viewpoints about those developments. In other words, it often depends more on where those search findings are *dropped* than where they're *found*. For instance, who's picking up the tab for delivery through leaks and other backdoor influences.

The universal laws of self-interest apply to groups and individuals alike under the media glare. Credibility, authenticity, and integrity all share ringside seats at the Biggest Picture:

1. Airing one's laundry in public loses credibility, the more the launderer likes to hear their name.
2. A *truth-teller* whose main virtue is their authenticity, think whistle blowers, cannot claim to speak-out as an independent voice.
3. Any witness whose testimony rides on altruism (put group interests ahead of own, etc.) will be discounted, without an audit to determine the personal cost of their admission in blood, treasure, and social hardship.

Post Social Media Fallout

Before the advent of social media, it was easier to define direct from indirect relationships. They were traditional boundaries that separated actors from audiences and primary or firsthand observation from secondary research. Roles played formerly by publishers are less distinctive now that the world can legitimately beat a path to a Facebook page.

So too, the viral nature of social media clouds former distinctions between self and public interest. Connecting to a celebrity's twitter feed is a personified form of self-selection. Membership is not compelled by an overarching duty or requirement to act on behalf of the group for whom one now belongs. The attraction of social media fame could well be triggered by vanity and voyeurism as much as a crusade appealing to a higher calling.

What's the unifying factor that helps us clarify the motivations and behaviors of either extreme? *Self-preservation* seems to have held its breath long enough to outlast most other forms of characterization. That's the perennial force we can use to align information providers with...

- The content they supply,
- The sources they bypass, and
- The ultimate editorial priorities that service their business model.

The Rise of the Web Curator

Supply doesn't drive demand anymore.

It's as true with information as it is with hard goods. The best way to sell in a buyer's market is to not flood the market with more messages, but to figure out the ones being consumed – and acted on.

On the demand side, people don't know their way around much of the information that could otherwise serve them. Accelerating access to news is outpacing people's ability to make sense of it, let alone apply it to their personal and professional lives.

This is not just about consumers but producers. Witness the workspace.

Knowledge workers are pelted with e-mails, interrupted by video chats, and inundated with databases they're blocked from accessing. The insult to the injury here is that any attempts by the outside world to fight to the top of our in-boxes are dead on arrival without a welcoming format. Define attractive? Let's deliver a summary of all relevant data points stakeholders need to gain clarity on their markets, firsthand knowledge on their customers, and, influence in their companies.

This is an invitation for curators to design radars for tracking news flashes and coverage patterns. But it's also an opportunity to harness the explanatory power of PCF to analyze information providers: The *what's-in-it-for-them* equivalent to radars.

That's what we began to explore in our reference to Google Trends, and what we'll refer to as the Knowledge-ABLED framework of a credibility index. This diagnostic spells the difference between...

- Supply-side wire coverage that generates self-proclamations and selling arguments), and
- Demand-side exposure that confirms third party validation and the figurative *buying* of those same ideas.

Trade editors ordain what's news, not just a vendor or PR agency's attempt to create news. The result: An air of respectability is imparted to the *plugged* product or positioning.

The Death of King Content

Every day it becomes more difficult to assess the impact of each competing message. How much of the original message survives? What unforeseen events change the story around? How does one assert authority, let alone authorship, when the story-telling medium is the host to over a billion competing publishers?

For most of the Twentieth Century, an information supplier was a publisher whose most prized piece of hardware remained the printing press, a Fifteen Century invention. Vested subscribers would pay for these paper-based information products – honest! This is a world in which leading publishers bought in to the success of this business model as they grew to believe that...

> Content is king.

It meant that select groups of people paid for the information they supplied with their dollars and attention. It meant that the publisher received a double-dip from the advertisers they attract who were chasing the same set of readers.

Content is no longer king.

There is no longer a premium on being the first to know. The future lies in being the first to understand in a way that draws others to that same understanding, (and their own conclusions). That's the manifesto for curators.

Content is a stammering, mucus-laden *umm* among the miscellany of unfiltered search results and anonymously-authored articles in your news feed. In a world where pocket devices are publishing platforms, scarcity isn't measured in speed, access, or being connected, but in making connections. Enter the sense-making territory of the web curator.

Knowledge Demand = Web Curatorship

Imagine we're on the exhibition floor of the social media event of the century: Information surplus? Meet knowledge deficit! That introduction is being brokered by a knowledge planner – someone who can reconcile information supply with knowledge demand by anticipating...

- How news travels,
- In what circles, and
- Where that impacts most.

The cultivations of web curators are based on the three pillars of interpretation — context, context, and context. Tell me who said it, who heard it, and where, and what they said becomes immaterial. Tell me the way in which an appeal was made, and the call to action falls by the wayside.

As the PCF demonstrates, show me the eyewitness who lived through the event she's recounting, and...

- We see her authenticity implicitly,
- We infer her emotional investments, and
- This leads us to question her disinterested bystander status.

An accomplished curator is not simply a message interceptor or re-transmitter, but a temperature gauge. This is the pulse taker that assesses the bursts and slowdowns of message traffic within the personal radar frameworks we discussed in **Unit One**.

Nice-to-know works for birthdays and extended voicemail greetings. It doesn't cut it for web searches, where we're operating on a need-to-know-basis. If it lands off radar, it never happened in the first place. Our attentions don't shift.

In this tree-falls-in-the-forest scenario, a web curator is the best defense against the maladies of information fog such as A.D.D., insomnia, the blurring of professional and personal affairs, and disengagement: The anxiety, and periodic paralysis associated with device-enabled availability.

That doesn't mean farming our calendars out to a personal attention manager. That happens in a decade or two. But it does mean answering to the contextual value of our personal mental space: WIIFM ("What's in it for me")?

THE MARKET FOR CURATORS

So how does the curator find their niche? Being all things to all content consumers is about as relevant as trying to bury one's subjective point of view. The new transparency isn't about leveling the playing fields of opinion. It's about linking to sources. **(OnPoint Radio, 2011)**[6]

Unlike the ad-supported models of SEO campaigns, a curator is not a human lynchpin for converting click-happy consumers. Idea people are not buying merchandise. They are buying arguments – those that support the rationales for the advice they sell. Perhaps the killer app here is rediscovering the art of disengagement: Finding no surprises when we reconnect because the curator has our back at all times. Imagine the liberation it gives this over-achieving, insecure, multi-tasking taskmaster:

> "She tries to communicate a need for balance to employees who report to her, too. "I worry about the speed at which they are going," she says, adding that she wants them to "shut down" when needed, for the sake of their families and their health." **(Meese, 2011)**[7]

Assuming we know what keeps our clients up at night, what kind of radar-building equipment serves the needs of curators?

That's where grounding in advanced search commands and even tired, old traditional media segments come in handy. As we saw in **Unit Three**, using a custom search tool like Google CSE Search to bundle sources, helps to differentiate, quantify, and validate our pet peeves, hot stock tips, and celebrated rumors on the news horizon.

Run those queries in the form of event-based trip wires, and the daily counts form the aggregated patterns of what coverage blows hot and cold. Google Trends runs the media pick-up patterns in tandem with the same terms in Google searches. In effect, we have that same handshake from the trade expo: Media supply meets (or misses) user demand.

These radar constructs are good for high visibility issues that soar and plummet from year-to-year. But many of our search targets would go undetected atop such public radar. For that we need to scale down to a more street level view through localities, community members, and more niche or locally based organizations. That's where an RSS reader like Feed Demon shines as a personalized approach to event tracking and the aggregated coverage patterns – the iPhone equivalent of Google Trends as a personal radar.[8]

FIGURE 5.11: Comparing Content Supply to Knowledge Demand through Google Trends

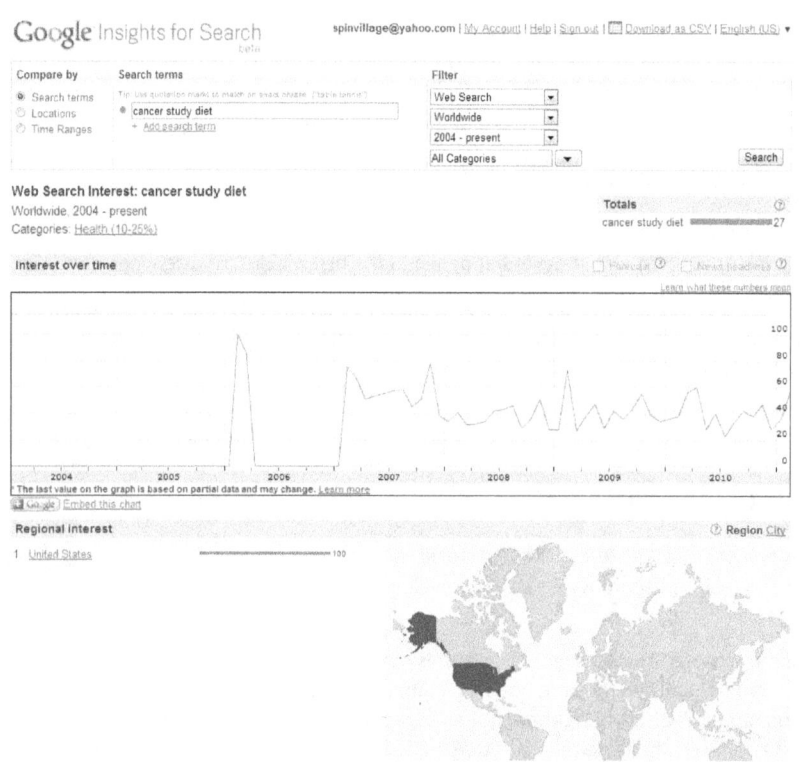

These consecutive screen captures display time series analyses of demand-side or pull-based content sourced through Google's search logs. The web search volumes are then compared in the second graph to the supply-based volumes of media references to the same keywords over the same time period. The latter graph also includes milestones or key events that may have led to spikes in news coverage on the topics in question.[9]

The Value of Curatorship

Finally, curators should sell their quantifiable benefits to a confused and distracted market. That sales pitch starts with single examples. Abstractions like what the best-known are best known for might be a starting point for idea people. For more grounded folks, it boils down to this: One purposeful, unitary artifact that reveals the telling quote, table, framework or footnote – diamonds in the ... umm ... content *rough*.

The bigger picture benefits will emerge once these evidential building blocks become ingrained in our web-based discovery process. That might be sweet music to sleep-deprived crisis managers. It may be a threat as well to the scientists of external risk assessment who traffic in the language of hysteria. This is the paranoid leading the para-blind down an alley of would-be prowlers and invaders. No one likes to depart from the script. No one makes time for interruptions. They arrive unannounced. Their departure comes in its own time.

The impulse to panic is an age-old temptation not restricted to unsuspecting widows or defenseless victims. Is the concentration level thick with anticipation? Is it diffused through false alarms and unmet expectations? Is this...

- A wave of consensus,
- A squeaky wheel,
- A whistle in the dark, or
- A charging stampede?

What are the measured responses that address tangible perceptions – not last night's bad dream but tomorrow's realities, in the light of day?

A curator can discern the strength of association, and tell us where our clients are in their perceived crises. Are they floating near the bottom of a deep-sea, or being washed into shore escorted by the storm surge itself?

These are searches out loud that commercial search engines are not configured to deliver. They are speechless, both in posing the questions, and in tracking the volume and nature of the responses. The old Irish expression is that if you want a crowd, start a fight.

And when our clients do, they'll be needing numbers to back them up, not just attorneys and personal body guards. At the very least, they'll need a web curator who can point out who's in the audience, and why they're there.

Questions Answered by The Biggest Picture

So what are the implications now that we've established a methodology to address content analysis? What are some of the more vexing questions that surround issues of public reputation, perception, and the impact to organizations of largely subjective assessments?

For starters, we remove the 'subject' (the target organization) from the 'investigation' (Biggest Picture methodology).

That objectifies the sample so the results are attributable to sources other than the target. That doesn't mean all media impressions are containable to disinterested observers and non-vested parties. It's still possible that the marketing efforts of the target organization have a hand in the survey outcome. Private interests can rebrand their outbound marketing campaigns as news sites that have no visible tie to their original sponsors. Target organizations can and do hold financial ties to the information providers who cover their activities, or withhold such coverage, depending on their incentive structure.

But The Biggest Picture is not about ownership structures. It's not an under-the-surface investigation. It's the reality of the marketplace perception – an aspect of modern corporate life every bit as skewed as the veiled agendas of political elites, corporate media, and the digital giants.

Choosing Our Battles Wisely

Our target organizations take daily stock of the proverbial news radar. Partly, they're hoping to confirm that positive messages are getting out, and that negative ones don't escape into the headlines.

Perception metrics address the risk factors inherent with crisis communications and market disruptions by determining:

1. What's beyond our target's control and what's within their grasp?

2. What keeps an opportunity open without having to be the driving force?

3. What do they need to know without needing to know it inside out?

The term 'crisis' infers a lack of control over events conspiring to create doubt and uncertainty about an organization's well-being and reputation. It is a gathering momentum that demands an immediate response to preempt further surprises and unexpected market shifts.

It's Always About 'Our' Targets (– isn't it?)

Conversely, questions used to measure market success are wrong. It's not based on what our targets spend. It's based on how they look and to whom. Here's how that perspective-gathering plays out in the context of the wider marketplace perception. *They* in this case refers to how non-vested third parties view our first-party based organizations (and clients).

It's not about...

- The media they place.
  It's about the media they're placed next to.

- The attention they deserve.
  It's about the attention they're paid (whether or not they deserve it).

- The promotions they give away. It's about the company they keep.

- The loudness of their announcements.
  It's about how well they listen for the marketplace response.

- Reaching demographic audiences.
  It's about reaching understandings with the people they want to engage.

- The name they made for themselves.
  It's based on who's introducing them within the forums they address.

Capitalizing on The Biggest Picture

Now let's alter the perception, so that 'they' is now 'us.'

That's the internal discussion we're about to have about acting on the findings of a perception measurement survey:

1. What are the questions these results are raising?
2. What lines of attack are open? First, for further study, and then for followup?

In a first person plural setting, followup is typically for outbound teams to pursue, including sales, marketing, corporate communications, and public relations.

FIGURE 5.12: First Party Perspective – Connecting Corporate Positioning to Public Perception

COMPARISON	LINGERING DOUBT	BUSINESS SOLUTION
ORGANIZATION	Are we listened to?	Reveals sphere of influence status based on our commentator status
	Who is listening?	Vividly quantifies our stakeholders and degree of their stake in us
	Are we believed?	Contrasts ratio of push to pull coverage – what's self-proclaimed and what's conferred
	Are we noticed?	Indicates that our message is out there; how it resonates
	How are we different?	Tests for what propositions have saturated the market and message projection; confirm registering of key differentials
	What's our biggest distraction?	Shows where internal resources are sapped / prone to external pressures
	What's the biggest impact on our organization?	Exhibits dominant theme in terms of internal functions
	Who do people think we are like and in what way?	Capture brand attributes according to the relationships and experiences they connect on
	Are we making an impact?	Weekly movements in perception metrics correlate internal performance goals to the outcome of campaign launches and marketing events

Now let's cast our net beyond the self-referential, and expand it to our stakeholders – anyone likely to benefit or suffer from our market standing:

1. What's the consensus out there when this combination of customers, shareholders, rivals, reporters, and analysts share their collective impressions of what we bring to market?
2. How much are these perceptions justified by the facts on the ground?
3. How much carries forward from past slights, misperceptions, and petty scores not yet put to rest?

FIGURE 5.13: Second Party Perspective – Connecting Market Reputations to Peer Recognition

COMPARISON	LINGERING DOUBT	BUSINESS SOLUTION
PEER GROUP	Are we a player?	Tells us how well we compare against established rivals and peer sets
	Is anybody in our space listening?	Reveals gap between aspiring messages and tonality of resulting press and research pick-up
	Is anybody repeating our mantras?	Shows key influencers and their residual off-spin
	Is it being misinterpreted	Shows how detractors dredge up unresolved grievances
	Who else is saying the same thing in our space?	Document leadership status when wannabes try to steal our thunder and cachet
	Who do we think we are associated with and are not?	Compare internal channel relationships with how they play out publicly
	Who is talking about us the most?	Use commentator types to deduce our biggest stakeholders
	Do we command the stature of a company our size?	Alerts us to changes in our week-to-week market presence as well as which organizations or brands exhibit best-in-class scoring by peer grouping as well as overall
	How do our customers see us?	Reveals what media circles we travel in, erasing the blindspots that plague brand-weak organizations who need to better position their products and services.
	Who do people think we're like?	Shows our media distribution by stakeholder

Finally, let's consider saving a seat at the table for strategy. In corporate-speak this is the aspiration-based question we come to once we *make our numbers*, fill a key position, or dispel a rumor. We're over the humps and the horizons beckon: What are those broad strokes or visionary missions that will trigger fundamental market shifts and even summon new ones?

The Biggest Picture can inform tactical choices on our marketing calendars, but its sights are set on helping shape emergent terms and conditions. From a third-party perspective, this means gauging (1) the expansion, (2) maturing, or (3) decline of target markets. It means establishing a baseline for determining the historic intensity of key events that rally and hold the interest of the stakeholders we're trying to attract.

FIGURE 5.14: Third Party Viewpoint – Connecting TBP Perspectives to Long-term Goals

COMPARISON	LINGERING DOUBT	BUSINESS SOLUTION
UNIVERSAL	*What kind of visibility do we want to have?*	Enlists best-in-class brands and overall industry leaders for pace-setting purposes
	How can we stand out?	Lends proof that media distortions warrant changes to our current press coverage
	Who are the cool brands / companies?	Measures category-defiant brands
	What trend can we take full advantage of?	Demonstrate corporate, lifestyle and policy trending from their defining moments to groundswells, herd mentalities and market shifts
	Who is different from us saying the same thing?	Find unexpected friends and adversaries who deliver similar value propositions in unexplored segments
	What space are we associated with that is not our space?	Overlooked markets that suggest a comfortable fit for your natural strengths

SECTION 5:2 | Information Bartering –
When Passwords Fail to Connect

In the days before social media, there was a common distinction between being on and offline. First, we would gather information and then logoff, applying what we learn second-hand from published sources. The subtle difference here is *published* since we could still consider phone discussions or face-to-face interviews with experts and eyewitnesses to be first-hand intelligence-gathering. In pre-social times, we interviewed the computer. We were one step removed in receiving information directly from our intelligence-gathering sources.

But the simple assertion that humans = primary sources and machines = secondary sources holds no longer. Tweeting a celebrity with my blogging homage to their latest album, book, movie, or media tour is not really firsthand or secondary.

Social media has stretched the boundaries of who we touch, while shrinking the effort required to extend ourselves. Moreover, the chance our overtures will be heeded by people we've never engaged directly is no longer a freak occurrence. But we've paid for these additional points of access by diluting the intimacy of our exchanges: Yes I know *of you* but the reference is indirect. It's reliant on multiple degrees of separation, and resistant to our immediate recall.

One constant remains in a world of apps for meet-ups, group gaming, and vocal-free exchanges. Primary intelligence gathering involves information bartering: The act of trading on know-how. This doesn't necessarily mean that money changes hands. Instead, we have information that no one else has – at least no one in the networks where we operate. A capable information broker understands that the value of bartering comes when we trade information to find out what others know (and whether it's our business too!)

Sometimes the trading can bypass the very sources we're investigating. We'll demonstrate one of the least risky and most productive forms of information bartering: The translation from search results to list-building for the ultimate purpose of marketing to specific social networks.

CONVERSATIONAL ICEBREAKERS – BREAKING THE CASE OPEN

What are some key differences between query formation (interviewing computers) and interviewing people?

This question is best addressed from the vantage of the best post social media forum we have for using our investigations. This channel exists not just to do research, but to attract would-be peers, persons of interest, and even opportunities in the form of investors, partners, and hiring managers. That would be the now well-established act of self-publishing, through social media posts, blogging, and ebooks.

Blogging could be a cathartic way to unleash frustration. Nothing except self-restraint will keep us from posting or even over-sharing our pent-up furies. But with a little discipline, blogging can also be a way to build stature. A deliberative approach resists the role of the *wannabe authority*. Publishing as the Knowledge-ABLED investigator means (1) build bridges of understanding, and (2) cases for recommending courses of action through our research findings.

Every bridge built is a potential bartering situation that hinges on the familiar building blocks of social networking. If they seem familiar in an offline way, that's because they mirror the same engagement mix we'd expect to see when we're the targets: Think customer outreach in the toolbox of traditional marketing formulas, such as...

- Name dropping (testimonials)
- Expertise (FAQs)
- Dos and don'ts (checklists, red flags)
- Case studies (demonstrations)
- Product reviews (brokering producer-vendors)
- Customer surveys (brokering user-consumers)

So let's see how these approaches play to the strengths of Knowledge-ABLED bloggers like us.

Name Dropping (testimonials)

There's no shorter distance between two people than a second person connection. Getting from a third-party affiliation like a former company or location to a mutual acquaintance is a time-honored conversation starter. Well-connected blogs combine this *friend-of-a-friend* dynamic with an even more universal element for gaining market visibility and traction. That's the vanity of having one's name both mentioned and cemented to their own virtual outposts.

Look at any well-trodden blogging forum and we're likelier to take in news feed dynamics than static essays on our personal career choices. The only animals on Planet Blogosphere are the ones who check the indexes for their own appearances.

Expertise (FAQs)

"Frequently asked questions" or FAQs are a handy way to handhold the novices who are new to our sites and services. FAQs are an easy way to tell visitors not only what they need to understand as a layperson, but how they can get the most out of us, ideally as a client. That client perspective looms especially large here. FAQs are a necessary writing exercise for anyone who's ever had a hard time generalizing their special skills, or summarizing what they do.

FAQs are useful forums for accentuating our assets as service providers. But they're also a tool for initiating the relationship-building phase of potential allies and peers. Any recent task completed on a project worthy of repeating can be rephrased as an FAQ. Another opening ripe for FAQ fulfillment are lists such as dos and don'ts, and red flags. Again, they comport to any checklist that's generic enough for use as a general introduction to our skills and service offerings.

Case Studies (demonstrations)

There's no substitute for experience, but the runner-up is living vicariously through the episodic accounts of life in the trenches. In consulting circles and geeky-leaning market segments, these narratives stories are elevated as *success stories*. Such use cases confer status on both the narrator, her set of tools, and the larger team that completes a project. Hint: It helps build interest to introduce some well-plied narrative devices such as ingenuities inspired by scarcity, adversities. READ: Project team invents a novel approach while deploying it on a shoestring budget and unforgiving timeframe.

Ironically, the whole idea of success is such a subjective standard that any self-referential case study can ring false and self-serving. This perception prevails even when real and lasting value is delivered through the talents of these storytellers. Bloggers would do well to factor in community skepticism. This is the wariness groups develop when being pitched at the same moment they're comparing study results against their own requirements and experiences.

For that reason, focusing on what goes wrong speaks with greater directness and persuasion to our influence circles. War stories are the way to go here. They calibrate our BS detection settings. And if we're the survivors, we can speak with third-person objectivity, and first-person authenticity. Just because a fact-finding mission is about reaching a sensible decision, doesn't mean we only buy into level-headed rationales. I'm much likelier to believe a partisan who alternatively both loves and hates the product in question with the passion of a user, and producer ... AND implementer. War veterans bear the scars of their own misadventures. The cost of guessing wrong is an investment beyond the terms of any purchasing cycle or licensing deal. But an expert blog can shield readers from the same potential pitfalls, or even their own naivete.

Product Reviews (brokering producer-vendors)

One of the best ways to barter our direct experience with extended communities is to document our trials and errors with the tools of our trades. It's perennial marketing gospel that motivated customers are likelier to buy from direct recommendations (word-of-mouth) than from the indirect suggestions of promotional media (advertising). Blogging represents a wider, more persistent opportunity, short of sharing a first-person affiliation with an active user of the service/product under consideration. Blogging provides a total third-person stranger (us), with no direct stake in their decisions, other than to be cited as a trusted adviser in future buying cycles.

Consummate experts can leverage their independent authority status as brokers for would-be customers in the evaluation stages of their pending purchases. That role of influencer can be expanded to include both product vendors and service providers as well, depending in no small part on the level of traffic directed to the reviews we post.

Customer Surveys (brokering user-consumers)

One of the benefits of any sound diagnostic is not only to identify what customers want, but their perceptions (what they think they want). The Biggest Picture is a credible way to add context and volume to weigh the specific features or assets our clients offer against the demands of the marketplace. Tapping into those preferences is doubly desirable when those requests can be satisfied today. It's not on the drawing board for a next release. It's a tool ready for the using, and a finding ready for acting on.

A TBP approach is especially useful as a substitute for close-ended questions normally found in marketing surveys. Typically, perceptions are searchable when the content producer is not limited by a set of predefined choices, or multiple choice responses. The respondent is free to communicate in an open-ended way that may or may not match any of the pre-canned responses.

The Pulse-taking Virtues of Research Blogs

Demonstrating our research acumen is another essential ingredient of building a following as researcher-bloggers.

One way to use social media tools, deviating from the personal updates, is to substitute topic-based events of greater consequence. RSS is the streaming tool for tuning us into the disjointed and often inane details of those slipping in and out of real-time texting consciousness. But the same medium can track unfolding events of interest to us and our communities while *keeping the lights on,* even if we skip a cycle in our own updates or publishing schedules.

One thing to remember is that blog posts are rarely read out loud – let alone discussed in public. It is the internal workings of one's ruminations given the posterity of our life's recordings. Our every move captured between <send> commands has the potential to gain the affirmations or disapprovals of people with whom we share no other histories. In the following excerpt, the author, Vicki Abelson writes of the cascading effect of a checkbox change to the marriage status panel on her Facebook Page:

> "I took to snooping to see what he was up to. He was 'interested' in women. And men. But, women, first. I never quite got over that. I don't think he meant anything by it, but it seemed a disrespect. At least I perceived it that way. In response, I removed 'Married' from my info (because I'm mature that way), not realizing that it would post on all of my friends' news feeds. I was instantly deluged with, 'What happened?' Little did they, or I, know at the time – a lot. I reposted 'Married' later that day, but it never meant quite the same thing again. **(Abelson, 2011)**[10]

The real tease in this passage is the notion that the simple transacting of a change to a digitized form could spiral into such a defining moment in the estrangement of two people. That simple signal change did the job that first launched a force much bigger than the news business. That would be the syndication industry. But we no longer need to rely on the kindness of press agents. We've hatched a whole new reward system for passing messages with RSS.

Good news for us knowledge-ENABLED news aggregators. It's a system dependent on our query formation skills. What it's not is beholden to information providers!

Dynamic Blogging

One of the merits of blogging is that we need to solder the pipes once. The plumbing should work fine after that, whether we have something new to post or not. The tools themselves will pull the content in based on the news feeds we stream. Unlike working on our desktop, we don't have to create new material, update our interests, or be on-the-hook for every new development in our fields.

Dynamic blogging refers to the hands-off approach of piecing together updates to time-sensitive topics that appeal to our site visitors. It's hands-off because a successful RSS query practically feeds itself without our intervention. If this concept sounds familiar, think back to the event triggers that resonated in The Biggest Picture groupings we framed for the corporate and marketing functions within Taco Bell. These triggers can be pulled for designing RSS queries too. Here is a sampling of action-based queries with an emphasis on the semantics used to anticipate these finely-tuned news feeds:

FIGURE 5.15: Sample Event Triggers in Criminal and Civic Crimes for Content Aggregation

Criminal Cases	Civil Cases
"missing (child OR teens OR children OR person) (police OR manslaughter OR murder OR homicide OR suspected)"	"(misled OR misleading OR misinform OR misinformed) (customers OR clients OR shareholders OR employees)"
"missing (neighbors OR loved OR family OR persons) OR disappearance (family OR loved) -war –disaster	"(overstated OR overstate OR overstating) (revenue OR earnings OR revenues OR income)"
"police (raids OR raid)"	"(punitive OR disciplinary) (actions OR action)" (corporate OR company OR business OR industry)
"street gang" OR "street gangs" OR "gang (shooting OR violence OR warfare)"	"(siphoned OR siphon OR rip OR ripped) off"
("organized crime" OR mafia OR mobster OR mobsters)" OR "crime (bosses OR boss)"	"(windfall OR excessive) (sales OR profit OR profits OR margins)" OR profiteering OR profiteers OR "price gouging"
(allegations OR accused) "(sex OR sexual) (crime OR assault OR harassment)" -military -defense –sports	"collar (prison OR prisons OR crime OR crimes)" OR "executives * (incarceration OR incarcerated)" OR "minimum security"

On the Job Blogging

The guarantee of lifetime employment vaporized in the recession of the early 1990s. **(Pozen, 2012)**[11] Since then, the economic reality of the great foreseeable future is that most of us need to diversify our income sources, regardless of our job titles, client rosters, salary histories, or earning potential. There is no corporate belt-slackening that awaits the next post recession rebound. For professionals dependent on salary income, continuous improvement is not an option.

The precarious state of the economy on job security is a kick in the pants for all of us. One response is to use our blogging mediums to raise our research games in meeting these professional challenges.

FIGURE 5.16: Research Blog in Support of Investigative Practice and Research Services

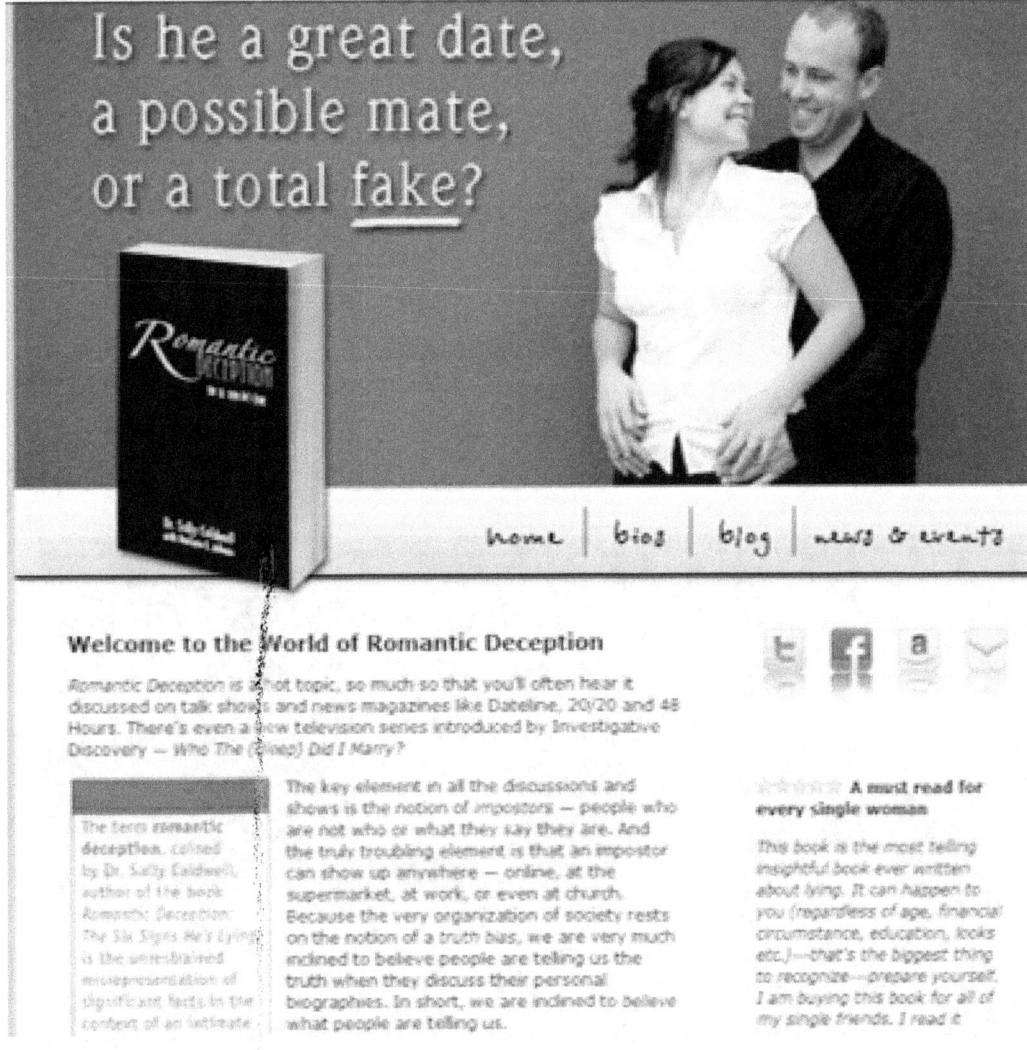

Here, former student and author Darlene Adams profiles her seminal work on patterns of betrayal in romantic deception. It's an expertise she continues to ply through her blogging topics.[12]

It's no secret that a shaky economy is unspoken code for going back to school to bump-up in credentials and upgrade job skills. There is no unconfirmed rumor leaking here that social networking sites now define the crossroads for matching client and job leads to project requirements and hiring managers. Another fertile opportunity open to the Knowledge-ABLED is the research blog as a showcase for our investigations: Be it as a job applicant, business consultant, or ranking expert in our fields of interest.

Using Blogs as a Research Medium

For much of this book, we've taken a dim and even elitist view towards web-based marketing. The abstraction of increased understanding takes a backseat to the concrete goal of generating sales. Most of this book has been polemical in nature. That means writing not only a how-to book but why becoming Knowledge-ABLED is an essential 21st Century skill, regardless of our vocational directions and career choices.

Searching Out Loud: Giving Voice to Independent Investigations | Marc Solomon

Okay. So being a skillful researcher has two immediate paybacks:

    1. We can background check our future employers and clients like it's nobody's business.

    2. We can showcase those skills as educators and consultants for hire.

Do you detect a subtle shift here? We're moving our background checks into the foreground. We're not just practicing our craft, but communicating it to a potential audience. These recipients are our peers. Hopefully, they get both our blogs and the fact they can benefit directly from collaborations with us.

One thing prefaced in final course assignments with my student investigators was dedicated to blogging goals and objectives. I prefaced the final project with these two questions for them as aspiring PIs:

    1. How can you break into a new profession?

And if you are an established professional...

    2. How do you hone your act, or create a new niche to your best advantage?

To my students, a PI-related blog was their calling card for hooking up with other PIs on the cases they tracked, the skills they cultivated, and, the job opportunities likelier to arise from networking than from scanning job sites or company websites.

FIGURE 5.17: Research Blog Transformed from Victims' Rights Examples to a Cross-cultural Exchange between Communities

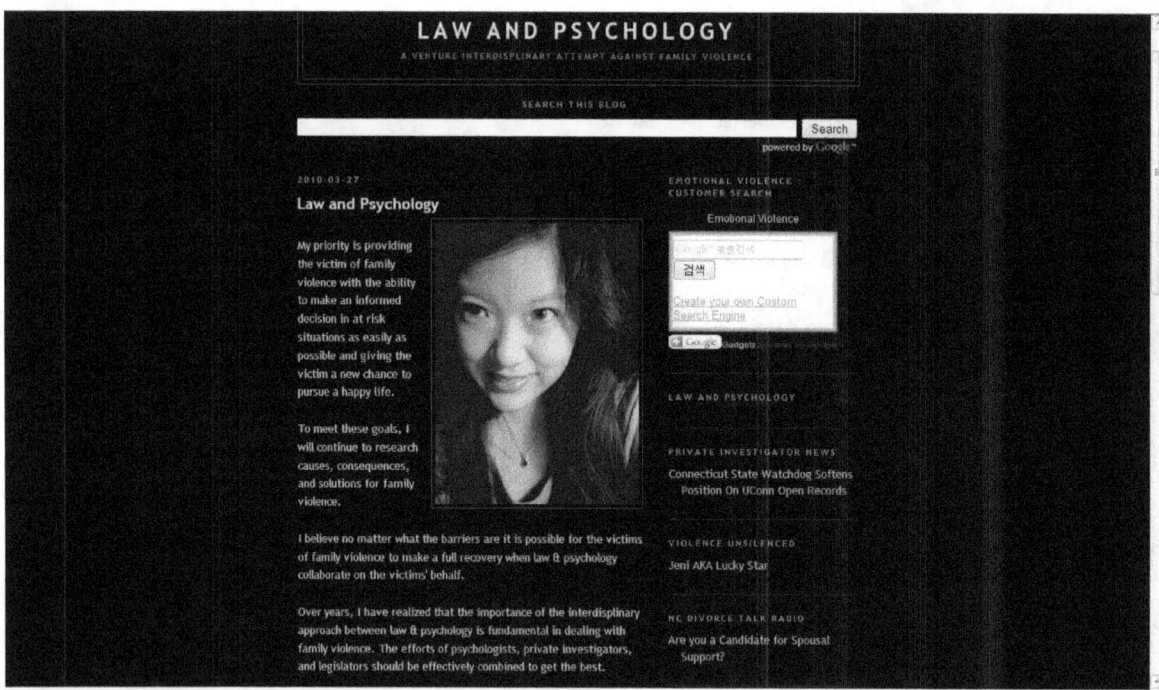

Above, a former student identifies some of the common misconceptions about legal protections and loopholes and enriches the forum with a CSE ("custom search engine") that captures topical feeds in her native dialect.

These breakthroughs were once attained by playing *the media card*. That means writing a freelance article for a trade periodical. Here the writing project is the excuse for beginning a dialog with a subject expert or potential colleague. We put ourselves out there. They accept our invitations for an interview.

Blogs however, are not necessarily about interviewing experts. They can be linked to those search targets. Those links are especially germane when picking topics to write about where we share a mutual interest with the leaders in our fields. So blogs are good for attracting the attention of the folks we need to meet. In my case, they were also useful for giving my virtual learners a meaningful grade for participation in my courses!

That demonstration included how well they integrate some of the lessons we've already completed into the making of our blogs. For instance, the social bookmarking tool we're now acquainted with for capturing useful websites was repurposed as a blog-based content source. Their choice of topic was also important – not so much *what* subject they chose but how well their blog page connects with the topicality of their subject expertise. Finally, their ability to reflect on these developments in their postings was the single most unique way to make their own contribution. Singling out opinions about news, commentary, and the evidence used to support them.

THE CATHARTIC BLOGGER

Recent behavioral studies suggest that blogging has emotional benefits for bloggers. Micro-blogging on Twitter with its 140 character limit is even more of a rush. Dispense with the laws of rhetoric, and all that's left is us trusting our guts.

Don't think you're being heard about a particular grievance? Pontificate freely. In cyberspace, no one's going to curtail the right to rant (whether anyone hears your rant or not).[13] Need to share some inspiration or shed some light? Go for it. These positive impacts are similar to more traditional forms of record-keeping like a diary. Only the Internet transforms a personal medium into a social one. Every keystroke is recorded and shared within a self-selecting audience.

It's the size of that audience that inspires the commercial voice of blogging: Here's how to attract visitors and harvest their emails, here's how to become a megaphone in the blogosphere, here's how to increase your income by allowing advertisers on your site, etc. Sound familiar? Maybe you're old enough to remember the snake oil salesmen who bid up the price of internet domain names?

Our non-merchandising motivations for blogging are twofold:

1. The community aspects of blogging enables us to extend our relationships from our immediate circle to a virtual one (and if we're lucky a virtuous one as well). This is a group of peers limited only by a common language and a common interest. Done right, it is that community that will expand to suggest new career horizons, maybe even our own career paths.

2. It is the calling card aspect of blogs that enables the would-be contacts we've come to know through our own research. Research blogs enables the people we approach to get up-to-speed on (1) mutual interests, (2) common goals, (3) professional contacts, and (4) uniquely held opinions, priorities, and forms of expressing them.

That's our primary reason for using our blogs as platforms for staging our Knowledge-ABLED assets. It's not to rise in the ranking formulas, but first to find our own voice in the research we do, and second, to have the work speak for itself.

Picking a Blogging Theme

As an investigator, we typically use blogs to cover a particular *beat* or interest that attracts or keeps us in our selected profession. Maybe it's an issue actually related to the digital world such as fraud detection and identity theft. Maybe it's a round-up of specific crime-fighting resources that the public can use to solve crimes, address legal problems, or petition on their own behalf. Maybe it's a pursuit of the details about local crimes and tracking them to trial. Maybe it's about the virtual presence of other investigators, and how they market themselves to the very communities you know or aspire to join?

Blogging themes are only limited by your imagination: Summoning a common experience worth sharing inside a virtual community. For our purposes, *the what* of our research blog addresses the types of reporting methods you'll enlist on your site. There are three common approaches and you are not limited to picking only one. In fact, a hybrid of several methods might improve our calling card status as a research blogger:

1. **Opinion-editorial:** This is the most common and popular approach to blogging. The blog becomes a *soap box* or launch pad for our take on recent noteworthy events. Op-ed blogs are especially prevalent in the political arena. From our perspective, your own political affiliation is not important. What is critical is that we cite other published sources that both inspire and support our passions and skepticisms. Supporting evidence and research methods should be out in front. This is our contribution to shaping current debates, dialogs, and inevitably the laws and policies we aspire to influence.

2. **Events and developments:** This is the correct card to play once we're comfortable with the kibitzing and bartering that happens between members of the same or related communities. First is the quiver in the bow of all barterers: Knowing how and where to anticipate the unexpected before it becomes breaking news. The second step is to set information traps loose on your blogging site. Tools such as RSS feeds and email alerts are especially helpful for building event listings based on topics, locations, and institutional calendars, i.e. legislation or legal proceedings. In **Unit Six**, we'll try our hand at **Information Trapping**, and the role of RSS feed readers as one way to tease out details lost in ad hoc site-by-site capture.

3. **Summaries and tools:** Summaries take a page from op-ed and event-based blogs to round-up sites and pages that serve specific professional circles. The goal of a summary provider is less to assess the quality of each resource, and more to classify these links in a useful way for our site visitors. Another tool we introduced in **Unit Two** are customized search engines ("CSEs"). Building our own CSE enables blog visitors to classify the content they find according to the search groupings we configure.

BLOGS AS CALLING CARDS

As I've tried to suggest in these bartering arrangements, blogs are not just excuses to vent or glad-hand the folks we're hoping will return our calls.

Blogs are a showcase for experience. A resume is static and self-contained. A media kit or backgrounder on your services and references is out-of-date the moment it's ink or paper. A blog is dynamic. The deeper our involvement, the more dynamic it becomes, and, the likelier we'll attract others to it by connecting...

- What's happening on the web related to our professional goals and personal interests, and
- The extended community of peers we're trying to reach, build, or augment.

The research blog can tap into digital news, opinion and media (videos, podcasts, slide presentations, etc.) that concern us. But how do we get from a casual to an ardent interest? How do we go from an occasional way of becoming informed, to a systematic capturing of the subject domain we're trying to master?

Does it means attending webcasts, subscribing to journals, and getting updates to every last word on our field of interest? If the answer is yes, I promise you two things: you will fail, and you will lose interest before that sense of failure takes hold.

That doesn't mean we need to throw cold water on our investigations every time we miss a blogging cycle:

1. What if we could be exhaustive in our research without suffering mental exhaustion in the process?
2. What if we didn't need to check every conceivable source, and could still account for each one?
3. What if we could filter what each source was saying, spared the distraction of redundant and irrelevant information?
4. What if we could tweak our query refinements so that only importance passes through them?

Pulling Selective Content Towards Us Through RSS

You wouldn't need to spend extra time and resources to transition from blogger to researcher. But you would need two points of information:

1. What are RSS feeds, and
2. How do I put them to work?

RSS is the way any web-based publisher can package and send updates about the content they publish: Be it news site, marketing campaign, or blog post. Also RSS is flexible. It's not just a conduit for articles. Yes it includes traditional content we might have subscribed to in the offline world of newspapers and magazines. But much of what's carried never existed in print form. Episodes from broadcast media programs, education-based tutorials, and entertainment-based outlets from film, the performing arts, and popular sports are all fair game for RSS feeds.[14]

Do you review your email or familiar sources with a weary feeling that the meaning behind what you're reading can be measured in fractions instead of volumes?

I know what you're thinking: I can barely keep up with my email. How can I possibly open another towering in-box of messages demanding my attention? I thought you said RSS would mean spending less time on screens!

I did. But you need to define your content turf. You also need a good set of controls for tuning the kinds of feeds you get back, let alone the kind you too would find worthy of publishing in your blog. That tool is called a feed reader and we'll get to those.

Our event triggers in the form of news feeds, our commentary, and our social circles now travel in a style that research bloggers are accustomed to. And it's called RSS.

But first here's something else to know about RSS. It's not just about pushing more content than we can handle in our face. Yes, it will do that if we let it. But we can also use RSS as a pull mechanism. *Pull* means that we've already screened a selective chunk of material and we've decided to share it with our site visitors. RSS enables us to see not only oceans of content but the gold nuggets worthy of interaction.

Let me explain.

FIGURE 5.18: Research Blogs Worthy of Subscribing

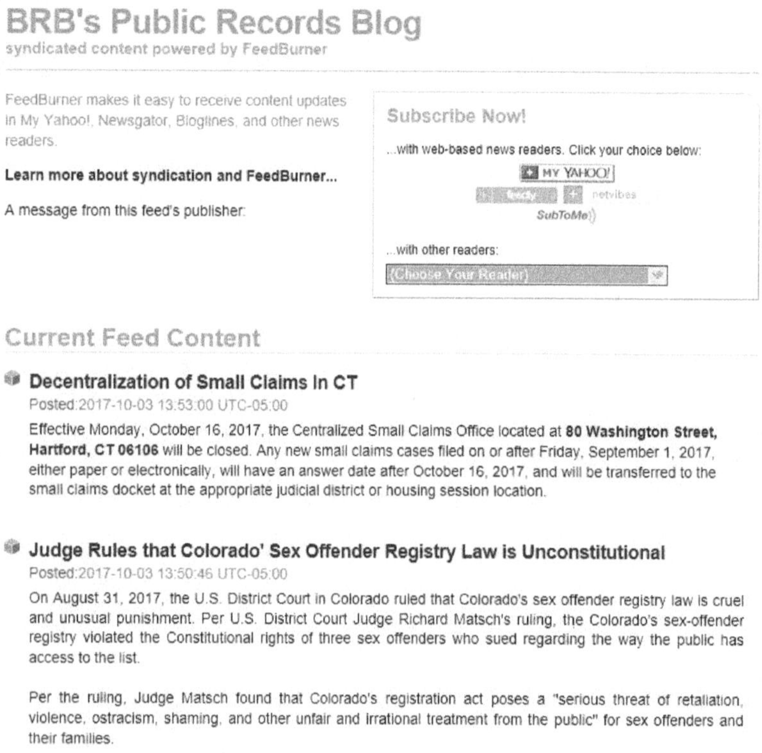

BRB's Public Records Blog
syndicated content powered by FeedBurner

FeedBurner makes it easy to receive content updates in My Yahoo!, Newsgator, Bloglines, and other readers.

Subscribe Now!
...with web-based news readers. Click your choice below:
MY YAHOO!
feedly   netvibes
SubToMe

Learn more about syndication and FeedBurner...

A message from this feed's publisher:

...with other readers:
(Choose Your Reader)

Current Feed Content

Decentralization of Small Claims In CT
Posted:2017-10-03 13:53:00 UTC-05:00

Effective Monday, October 16, 2017, the Centralized Small Claims Office located at **80 Washington Street, Hartford, CT 06106** will be closed. Any new small claims cases filed on or after Friday, September 1, 2017, either paper or electronically, will have an answer date after October 16, 2017, and will be transferred to the small claims docket at the appropriate judicial district or housing session location.

Judge Rules that Colorado' Sex Offender Registry Law is Unconstitutional
Posted:2017-10-03 13:50:46 UTC-05:00

On August 31, 2017, the U.S. District Court in Colorado ruled that Colorado's sex offender registry law is cruel and unusual punishment. Per U.S. District Court Judge Richard Matsch's ruling, the Colorado's sex-offender registry violated the Constitutional rights of three sex offenders who sued regarding the way the public has access to the list.

Per the ruling, Judge Matsch found that Colorado's registration act poses a "serious threat of retaliation, violence, ostracism, shaming, and other unfair and irrational treatment from the public" for sex offenders and their families.

All blogs are subscribable (just like news feeds on all social media sites). Whether they're worth tracking relates to their thoroughness and the dynamic nature of the turf they cover. In this case the BRB news feed is tracking the complex and fluid nature of public records access on a state-by-state basis.

One common use of RSS feeds is to stream or pull the sites we flag in a social bookmarking tool like Reddit out to our blogging site. Another tool called a news aggregator enables us to submit articles we find important, endorse the submissions of others, and comment on the news items we flag with our own unique perspective.

Another benefit of a decent RSS reader is to flag items. While it's helpful to assign stories to our reading pile, there's an added benefit for bloggers. The main reason for the clips is to handpick specific stories that we'll want to showcase in reposting to our own sites. This feature enables us to be both filters, and amplifiers for our own readership.

The Complementary Nature of Blogs and RSS

We're coming to the end of our presentation cycle. But the main agenda item here is not blogging, actually. It's about the symbiotic relationship between blogs and RSS ("Really Simple Syndication"). In addition to social bookmaking and blogging, this business of RSS feeds (Feed Demon) will be helpful to us in a number of ways.

Query formation is designed to produce *aboutness*. Aboutness implies that our search results actually address the issue that inspired the search. RSS is aboutness plus timeliness. It's what's going on in our field which is not just topic-related but you-specific – READ: Your own niche. *Niche* here covers your blog as personal branding statement, and how others will come to know you. This is number one Google hit, with a bullet now.

RSS is for people who don't like to search. Instead of formulating new queries every time out, think about this: The liberation of creating the definitive tweak and have new dividends arrive each day that reaffirm this pay-off. That's what happens when our searches product 70% or better aboutness. The context is true to our intentions. We want to connect that confidence to one specific location. Where the only information that's allowed in is the result of our own discriminating filters.

UNIT FIVE: How to Present What We Learn in Teachable Ways | Page 5:52

We've caught lightning in a bottle. But in the case of RSS it can strike often, depending on how exacting or specific we are about what we're trying to catch.

FIGURE 5.19: Research Blog as a Subscribable News Feed

We've just hit the subscribe button. Here's what an XML script looks rendered as an HTML page in a browser. News readers are tools for assimilating news feeds into searchable and categorical archive.

Searching Out Loud: Giving Voice to Independent Investigations | Marc Solomon

Along those lines, the RSS reader is really *our pond.* That's where we're likeliest to run into the kind of developments that not only grab our attention but implore us to take action. Once we can establish a meaningful stream of news, site updates, and trackable events, it follows that we plan calls, emails, webcasts, and social calendars around the rhythms of the RSS reader.

So how do we capture lightning in a bottle?

It might make sense to come up with RSS sources related to our investigations. As we'll see in **Unit Six**, one painless way to do this is to...

- Click on the [File] dropdown in an RSS Reader called FeedDemon.
- Select 'Find New Feeds.'

I put in the phrase "public records" and got back some spot-on reports, directories, and trackers about what law and licensing records are coming online as well as some neat CSI ("crime scene investigation") mapping tools vis-a-vis Google Maps.

One other no-brainer is to seek out others that we want to reciprocate fellow bloggers, either by commenting on their posts, and/or including them in our blogrolls.

Blogrolls

Another benefit of a news aggregation site pertains to another RSS mainstay called a blogroll. Blogrolls are links to your favorite bloggers that can travels dynamically to our research blogs via RSS. Blogrolls are an especially good way to create a community presence, and the sense of respect, comity, and peer review suggested by these assemblies. Another benefit of blogrolls is that no two bloggers have the same take on the same subject (Twitter bots withstanding).

One blogger may be focused on case law involving child abductions. Another might be tracking law enforcement efforts to coordinate efforts around state boundaries. Yet a third may be looking at the reporting of Amber Alerts, along with their completeness, accuracy, and effectiveness of databases listing these abductions and their status.

From a topical perspective, blogrolls represent a cross-section of domains that all share a mutual goal or common interest. What lies at the center of that interest? That's where our blog needs to be...

- In the topics we address
- The sources we draw from
- The views we espouse, and most importantly
- The expertise we're cultivating

Another use of RSS is to generate customized search results that signify a string of significant developments that address our blogging topics. Here's where we Knowledge-ENABLE those assets we've assembled in units past through our...

- Understanding of query formation through syntax and semantics,
- Expectations around sources through oceans, lakes and ponds, and
- Motivations ascribed to sources through the **Provider Conjugation Framework**.

Each of the models can be instructive for site visitors – particularly for our more engaged peers. Those user-producers we introduced earlier in this section.

Works in-progress

Let's say for instance if you want to display a feed of reported Amber Alerts by region. A series of Google queries uses a mixture of syntax and semantics such as [local:Massachusetts] and the following search statement:

> *"(issue OR issues OR issued OR issuing) * amber alert"*

The asterisk is the placeholder for any number of possible terms that can appear between the predicate, and the objective phrase here, our targeting of Amber Alerts.[15]

We can reject Google's definitions around news providers if we want to apply some basic OLP ("Oceans, Lakes and Ponds") principles. Instead, we can create a CSE with our own Google account that's based on our own sets of information providers.

One grouping could be local university pages where we're interested in tracking job openings or courses being offered in our interest area. Another could be local media sources where we're tracking the coverage of a highly-charged murder investigation. Still another? A series of highly influential blogs, all attempting to influence the outcome of an ongoing dispute, policy, or looming election.

That last example begs an important question: How does one determine the popularity of a particular blogger? It's hard to know who to pay attention to with the barrier to entry so low, and breadth of blogging topics. Reddit communities, Twitterers, and Facebook manifestos all compete for attention by posting the stories they find, commenting on them, voting for other posts, and forming networks in the process. That's the dynamic at work in news aggregation sites. That's where the popularity of our search results are driven by the dedication of a core group of daily participants, the first-person power users.

How do we find them?

There's no shortage of algorithms all chasing the golden fleece of social media supremacy. An ideal tool would integrate...

- Usage, including other stories they've submitted along with their comments
- That slippery, defining metric called 'authority' based in part on the number of links to a particular blog site from other referring winks, prods, and actual commentary
- Instances where our work has been cited by other bookmarking sites, news communities, personal pages, and tweets?

That's always a plus, right?

What does this say about our own blogging efforts?

Should we invest every idle moment in becoming a disciple of the viral marketing bug? The fervor that resides in social media junkies in order to place their discoveries in some select tier of elite influencers?

That's for you to decide.

But aside from questions of status, influence, and reputation, it certainly helps to familiarize ourselves with the tools and practices needed pull up X chair at Y table. That's no arranged seating plan. That's us developing a grasp, a voice, and eventual discussions with potential allies and colleagues through the virtual presence of the blogosphere.

Custom Search for Blogging

As we just intimated, another way to point your engine in the direction of the right collection is to determine that ourselves. Specialty or custom search enables us to literally perform a search within a search. Here the engine can trap useful sites by limiting the search to specific site domains or URL terms.

The CSE accentuates our skills as content curators, as well as query formation developers. We can introduce entirely different angles to a news feed based on the conventions followed in these different publishing traditions. Case-in-point: Looking for name droppings due to promotions and announcements? Then the script favors the targeted job titles of appointed executives in the industries we're tracking.[16]

Wire Services
- upi.com/*
- reuters.com/*
- ap.org/*
- businesswire.com/*
- prnewswire.com/*

If we're partial to more assessment-minded and analytical fare, then we want to separate pull media from push. This is the kind of information that we used to pay for. Occasionally we still do. That means focusing on major business media sources:

Major Business Media
- inc.com/*
- fastcompany.com/*
- economist.com/*
- businessweek.com/*
- forbes.com/*
- ft.com/*

We can always encircle those old standby networks in the antiquated world of broadcasting. Here we cast our horizons on a national level to see how widely spread an awareness is our search targets:

Broadcast Media
- cnbc.com/*
- abcnews.go.com/*
- cbsnews.com/*
- msnbc.com/*
- bbc.co.uk/*
- npr.org/*

If we seek a more local flavoring, our event triggers will accentuate those functions through the regional business press and the business section of local metro dailies. Think local when considering regional business community, lobbying efforts, business permits, seed funding, and connections to related academic and non-profits:

Newspapers
- latimes.com/*
- nytimes.com/*
- washingtonpost.com/*
- chicagotribune.com/*
- wsj.com/*
- Crains[*changes by edition for given locality*].com/*

The overriding point here isn't that media groupings have their own rhythms in the form of their turfs, news selection priorities, editorial leanings, and presentation styles. It's that tools like RSS and custom search engines enable the news junkies in us to be both discriminating curators, bloggers, brokers, and yes, investigators.

SECTION 5:3 | Message Delivery–
The Presenter as Exhibit

We've accumulated lots of information heading into that client presentation, final dissertation, or job interview. Our local drive, note-taking apps, and Google Docs are jammed with search log tracking of queries, results, and sources to evidence patterns. They contain what we've investigated, how we've done so, and hopefully, a range of outcomes about where it all leads.

This information is in the form of opinion, data, and perhaps additional people to interview, actions to take, or mysteries that will go unsolved. These findings will be presented to the client along with recommendations in the final report.

We've finally come to the final research frontier. No, it's not unmasking the wizard behind the smoke and mirrors. It's showing our cards. It's placing the unvarnished truth on the meeting table so that our associates, students, supervisors, clients, and community peers can decide for themselves:

1. Do they see how we traveled from our original premise to our final conclusion?

2. Do they buy it?

3. Do they see a personal upside for following through on our recommendations? How about for increasing their own commitments?

4. Are there overlapping interests here – can they be unified in pursuit of a common goal?

It all boils down to this: How our research informs and influences their thinking, behavior, and ultimately their actions. How do we close that distance between *our* words, and *their* actions?

In this section we stop weighing the evidence. We start weighing in on the facts, opinions, and supporting details worth evidencing. We begin with the selection process: Which facts? Whose opinions? What order? When to conclude? Where to end up?

CONFIRMABLE FACTS, EDUCATED GUESSES

Confirmable facts and educated guesses result when we apply the three levels of **Quality Control**, which allow us to...

- Offer our best *guesstimate*
- Base our hunches on hard evidence
- Resolve competing claims colored by perception and/or self-interest and self-preservation

What do we learn in our interviews and research that we can incorporate into our final client presentation? Are there staggering revelations that linger on well past the point of discovery, of self-evident explanation?

Is it a dead match between our original expectations and our final conclusions? It usually helps to put away the iPhones and Androids when we count in the *surprise factor:* How much the outcome deviates from the core thesis or assumptions made at the beginning of the project.

The greater the surprise, the closer to the front of our report that surprise should be placed.

Then there are results that are neither dutiful confirmations, nor shocking revelations. But they still warrant the *front page* treatment. Maybe our findings are not unexpected. Could be this is just yesterday's news to the client. Perhaps our conclusions will have a familiar ring.

But what if we propose a big departure from business-as-usual? What if it has an unfamiliar ring, or even a disruptive one? We might become implicated in our own investigations when we go poking our sniffers into unsuspecting places. Here our research credibility may take a hit. One case-in-point: Our research pops open the trial balloon our client was floating about a potential business partner, maybe even a suitor of their C-suite?

Here are a few sounding bells to consider:

      1. Do we shift the emphasis away from the big pay-off of a long-shot opportunity, and revisit the original premise?

      2. Do we plant some alternatives that deviate from our initial assertions?

      3. Do we expand the investigation to include competing theories and explanations?

When Judgment Calls

These are judgment calls. They rely as much on our skills of correctly reading client hopes and aspirations as drawing out any specific finding or conclusion. Are we confirming what they believed before our search project? Are we delivering on their prior expectations – or dashing them? The only way to know for sure is to trace the mission to its source. That means we already know our client's motivation. We knew the *why* before we got to work on the research.

Motive is not a given. It's the exception when intentions *don't* leave us in the dark. Our clients don't want to give us any preconceptions about what we'll find. They don't want to confuse our fresh perspectives with their own hardened biases or presumptions. They might not want us to know their motives because they would feel compromised. Most core motivations stick close to home.

Most reasons that drive an investment in research are self-serving ones, revealing more about selfish impulses than about the bigger picture of who else wins or loses from the impact of the answer. Regardless of the question, that's the card the Knowledge-ABLED are left holding.

THE POWERLESSNESS OF NUMBERS

Then there are groups. There's another distinct possibility why we're kept in the dark if we're presenting to a board, panel, or committee. The person contacting us to do the work doesn't know either. They are a funnel between the original question-poser and us. Theirs is not to question why but often to shield the identity of their superiors. Trying for motive, seeking priorities, or even clarifying objectives can be at best a waste of our time, or worse, a fight we did not intend to pick. Challenging a funnel to be more forthcoming is a fight the researcher does not win.

So getting to motive can be unflattering to our client. It can be frustrating to deal with surrogates like funnels who know little beyond protecting their bosses. What's the reward for us as the researcher?

The number one question for any investigator has little to do with social networks, access to resources, or even topflight interview skills. It's not about asking informed questions — unless they lead to a determination of what the answer is worth. That is the researcher's motivation. And by *worth,* I don't mean self-worth, or even a more social context like worthy or commendable. I mean literally the commercial price that the client has factored into the calculation they made before calling on us.

Here is the basic reduction of the *worth equation*:

Worth = outcome + fee

Say for instance that casting doubt on your client's connection to a criminal action has this upside: The potential to save them both criminal penalties and some potentially hefty fees in mounting their legal defense.

What the answer's worth to a client will not only help you set a fee, but inform the extent you're willing to go. Equally helpful, motive can tell you where you will go astray looking for superfluous information that costs time, materials, and conceivably your reputation as an investigator.

Knowing why is not a failure-proof formula. It doesn't always translate the answers we give into dollars and per diems. For instance, let's say our client is a restaurant owner. She's reasonably certain she is being ripped off by her employees. But she has no clue just how widespread the problem is. Does that mean the burden of education falls to us? Does that mean we need to first investigate the numbers to measure the risks for a business of her nature and size? That may be a risk worth *our* taking.

As we educate our client, we're also informing ourselves. It's earnings from learnings. Not only are we learning about what we're helping to prove, prevent, debunk, or confirm. Most importantly, we're here to help recoup the payback for our clients' investment in our investigative services.

Decision-making Traps

> *"Beliefs without decisions are just sterile."*
>
> **— Nassim Nicholas Taleb, the Black Swan**

We talked earlier of the necessity for action in our delivery of search results and client recommendations. We also spoke of the need to understand client motivation which informs...

- How we present our findings,
- How we maintain distance from our investigations, and
- Even how much we bill for them.

But it's not just positive strokes or clear actions we're out to communicate with our findings. In fact, our quest for the former can undermine our status as researchers. It's the oldest sellout in the annals of consulting. Yes, our own self-interest can easily compromise the validity of the research.

Who knew!

Pre-drawn conclusions and overlooked assumptions are the telltale signs of undue diligence and flawed rationales. But those warning bells ring across the presentation table as well. In fact, it's easy to dismiss research that doesn't account for ulterior motives: What our audience hopes to gain from our labors. **(Morville, 2005)**[17]

The term 'professional researcher' is about as exploratory as the range of topics and outcomes we are collectively called on to investigate. But one universal dictum is that commercial gain and self-interest do not compromise our investigations. Can different researchers come to different conclusions from the same body of evidence?

Heck, yeah.

If anything, we can be less skeptical around competing explanations than those drawn from a single, uniform, unquestioning point-of-view.

Methodologies as Quality Checks

However, this healthy diversity of opinion does not hold in the evidence-gathering of the research. Opinion surveys are believed when there are fewer opinions about how that survey was conducted. The methodologies we use to draw our samples and test hypotheses should be transparent. They should bear repeating, just like the air pressure in our tires, or the blood pressure in our veins.

A gauge is not a reliable measurement tool if it is based on intuition and individual preference. So too, with the research we present. There must be no doubt that the same search stands up to repeated observation by similarly skilled and resourced professionals.

In real life, we do not care about simple, raw probability. We worry about the consequences. We fret over the magnitude of an event once it occurs. As Nassim Taleb points out in his polemic *the Black Swan,* our clients need to move beyond the mitigating muddle of true/false into if/then: What are the probabilities for understanding each possibility we consider as...

- The consequence of the true
- The severity of the false **(Taleb, 2007)**[18]

The Nerves We Fray

This larger dimension of usefulness takes on a whole new life, when we consider what our clients and peers, will do with our investigations. Our case might be winding down, but their sleeves may first be rolling up. In fact, now that they've heard from us, the very notion of how close or far the client is from their ultimate goal may shift as well.

We may never know the loops we're closing or the mysteries we're exposing. We may well remain in the dark once the projector light dims. We may surrender our badges to building security, no closer to understanding what we've done to...

- Shape our clients' perspectives,
- Weigh their priorities,
- Confirm their intuitions and biases, and
- Trigger their initiatives.

But the investigation itself is not compromised just because our research is transparent and our clients' end game is opaque. Keeping their cards hidden doesn't absolve our need to anticipate how these implications can play out. We can't insist on correct interpretations. We can't *impose* a set of recommendations. But we need to step through the minefields with the understanding we may not step deftly over every improvised explosive.

Can we reel in the very same forces we're about to unleash? This is an off-stage question best raised before the final presentation is even scheduled. Here are three examples of dialing back on the buttons we're about to push, and nerves we may well fray:

1. **Raising Doubts** – Be careful not to confuse unexpected survey results with hypothetical scenarios. This broader perspective can come uncomfortably close to a client's traditional allies and partners. *Spooking* our clients can overshadow our informing them. Present a doomsday scenario that falls outside the sponsor's imagination, and we risk dooming the presentation too.

2. **Idle Speculations** – Don't engage in presenting simple true or false guessing games. Leave the logical problems to the theoreticians. A Knowledge-ABLED investigation is about getting our presentation audience off the dime. Not detachable speculation and abstraction, but informed commitment and action.

3. **Shock Factors** – Know our client's expectations coming into the presentation. The greater the surprises we come to share, the greater the distance the audience needs to travel to grasp, let alone digest, buy into, or follow-up on the assertions we're making.

Losing Our Sway

No piece of client intelligence is more important than cycling through what the client tells themselves without prompting. The revelation clients are hoping to learn isn't new to their thinking. It's to confirm what they want to believe:

> *"See? I told you so!"*

That's the reflexive posturing known as confirmation bias. If the evidence supports it, then our client was right at first sight: The empress sees herself in the mirror – and a dazzling outfit on has she! **(O'Toole, Bennis, 2009)**[19]

If case evidence refutes confirmation bias, what does this portend for us? What happens if we refuse to dress or redress this naked truth? Do we paint the *yes men* as suitors, seeking favor as informants? Are they selectively providing only counsel that supports our clients' deeply held convictions? How strong a hold? Strong enough to reinforce their own frame of reference – that much is clear.

Uninvited Guests

Not all stakeholders gathered around our presentation table are invited guests. In fact, a few of them don't even have Facebook pages. There manage to sneak in regardless of how well we prepare. So don't be surprised. But do sit up and pay attention when the following meeting crashers slip through the conference door:

1. **Anchoring** – Our minds are more welcoming when we come to an issue fresh. Once an initial impression is formed, it's harder to maintain a detached perspective. Sometimes we're joining in momentarily. Other times, we're jumping in with both feet. We expect *a return*. We've invested, sometimes, without consciously knowing it.

2. **Memorability** – We are unduly influenced by the tyranny of immediacy. We must instantly stop what we're doing. Here's the newest blip that some messenger slipped under the door where we hung that Do-Not-Disturb sign. No consequence is too mundane. There is no history or future. There is only the presumption of the most pressing issues at the moment.

3. **Status Quo** – Figureheads and institutional managers tend to let decisions languish, preferring incremental changes to sweeping transformations. This is especially true of institutions that pay with their mistakes through their exposure to risk. That potential far outweighs any potential gains from shaking things up. Risk aversion is often masked by an aggressive research effort: We look for reasons to do nothing.

4. **Sunk Cost** – How well do we know our presentation guests can certainly influence how much we disclose what we know *of them*? The more removed we are from their networks, the more clearly we can objectify them. We see them as part of a crowd, a breed, tribe, or trend. But that detachment makes a stakeholder more reluctant to move beyond the past and steer clear of lingering questions, competing explanations, and conflicting evidence. As we saw in first party PCF, decision-makers remain vested in their past decisions.

5. **Biology** – Psychologist and author Daniel Kahneman connects the weight our bodily needs place on our critical judgment. Nature calls in more varied and subtle ways than our non-presenting selves might stop and consider: Low blood sugar, for one thing. Kahneman points to the increased leniency among Israeli parole judges after a lunch break. Just before snack time? Not the optimal time to have one's case reviewed. **(Speed of Thought, 2011[20])** Before we connect the dots for our clients, let's draw one between direct causes and their effects: In this case, the lowering of glucose levels and admission of these uninvited guests at our meetings.

PROGNOSTICATIONS

The annals of record-keeping are more about keeping history, than making it or predicting its course. More than researchers, fact checkers, and evidence-gatherers, our clients harbor a not-so-secretive desire. They wish that we were bona fide time travelers. Our time travel credentials can remove all doubts and apply all-certain approvals. We are fortune tellers disguised as investigators. This delusion needs to be understood and appreciated from the clients' perspective. A bias towards closing loops, and completing them within one's incomplete experience is what Taleb concludes in the Black Swan:

> "We are too narrow-minded a species to consider the possibility of events straying from our mental projections." **(Taleb, 2007)**[21]

It is not our job to be soothsayers. But that's what we do every time we're asked to place a bet, or handicap the probabilities of what we'll encounter down the road. The one thing that we can do as researchers is take the client outside their own self-referential views of the world. We can increase their appreciation for the great number of unknowns.

Still, who wants to be shown their own insignificance in the wider scheme of things? Wouldn't hard knocks afford us this free education, without paying a researcher to serve up the same humble pie?

Here we are with the biggest of pictures. If our clients don't see themselves, they might not see their competitors either. And that may prove no small consolation for a group looking to break-out from a listless and unassuming market. Maybe, the biggest jump on the competition is about timing: Knowing when to strike *when* the coast is clear? Put another way: Demonstrating market disinterest is the green light for rallying the release of our client's ambitions. Whether it's a campaign or a product, here's the cover we afford them:

1. They can act with impunity: What are better grounds for action than a chaotic muddle as camouflage for skirting the law?

2. They can see a world of possibility: Seeing a greater range of actions and outcomes is the basis for forming a better perspective on the *fathomable* than on the *familiar*.

3. They can prioritize: Detachment from the short-lived distractions of the moment enables clients to remain both focused on long-term goals and flexible on short-term adjustments.

So that's the value we're offering. We're showing our clients how they can put themselves in situations where favorable consequences loom larger than negative ones. That doesn't mean we know the odds. But it does mean we can foresee the impact on our clients and how those consequences should influence their decisions, their meaning, and even guiding them to see...

- What decisions are worth deciding, and
- What's better tabled because (a) the chances are remote, or (b) its beyond our reach, our sphere of influence.

Ah, the analytical luxury of pure speculation!

RESEARCH PROJECTS AS INSURANCE POLICIES

Humans react negatively to unexplained events. The tendency is so widespread that it's preferable to give a negative reason than none at all. The most popular explanation is the one that answers why sh*t happens: Why events don't play out in our favor. As Nassim Taleb likes to point out, the evocative events that we dread can cause us to *overestimate the unusual* or lie in wait for cataclysmic events:

> *"Which ... is how insurance companies thrive."* **(Taleb, 2007)**[22]

Like delusions of grandeur, these darkest wish fulfillments share a common bond with their rosier counterparts on the daydream ledger: They don't come true.

There are defining moments ingrained in our minds. The calamitous nature of a past disaster enables them to burrow deeply. They can grip the public imagination, indeed the course of history itself. Nassim talks of the *hedgehogs* that fixate on the inevitability of an unprecedented, sweeping, and odds-defying catastrophe:

> *"Falling for the narrative fallacy that makes us so blinded by one single outcome that we cannot imagine others."*

Seeing the wider playing field might intimidate some clients. Others see advantages in this great expanse of uncertainty. They look for contingencies and alternatives. They don't fixate on the precision of models and relative certainty of the known unknowns, a.k.a. probabilities.

Ray Kurzweil has said that technology is growing exponentially. And our intuition about the future is linear. To paraphrase Steve Jobs, perhaps this is why we don't expect innovation from focus groups:

> *If you asked a group of early 20th Century consumers what kinds of transport will make their lives more traveled and their schedules busier, they might suggest faster horses. No one would have clamored for horseless carriages before any roads were paved. But that didn't kill the car in its cradle – only the forecast for fast horses.*

To riff on Nassim Taleb, (who's borrowing from Warren Buffet)...

- Don't ask the barber if you need a haircut
- Don't ask an academic if what he does is relevant
- Don't rail against political ads and then donate money to politicians

Self-interest is frowned on in public. It is pervasive in private. Hence, the strong association of the Knowledge-ABLED prevails between harboring suspicions and confirming them through unauthorized access or *overheard remarks*.

Presentation Voice

The first rule of presentation etiquette is the use of the first party voice by the presenter.

The *Informal We* is a casual way to infer a shared understanding or priority. It's an understated way for bringing clients into tacit agreement:

> We have a common history and a mutual aim to this project. Therefore, 'we' respond similarly to the evidence presented and conclusions drawn.

However, it's positively toxic to those questioning their membership in this agreement circle. The Informal We backfires when the speaker presumes a false unity, an overreach of who we're speaking for.

The *Royal We* is a rhetorical device that moms used on their kids to school them in the etiquette of the social courtesies and graces upheld by the family name. This possessive flourish comes across as stuffy and elitist to our presentees if we...

- Act like know-it-alls,
- Can substitute our experience for everyone else's, and
- Are too proud to endure opinions that conflict with our own.

The Informal We is not self-important. It does not presume to be the final word. It's an opening for an informed discussion about the state of the market, or the pulse of a community. It's keeping careful watch on the players and connecting the dots as a trend-watcher. That's when the 'Informal We' is the way to go for presenting a base of facts that confers both openness and authority.

What about when the Knowledge-ABLED are not only the presenters but presenting original research? We are the source of the trends that we present on our blogs and to would-be customers. We're also the authors behind the numbers. Are we buttoned down and inscrutable? Mad scientists? A dash of the *Royal We* here benefits us as presenters in three ways:

1. Presenters are perceived as doers.[23]
2. It scales the size of our operations in the minds of our audience to a larger, more established firm.
3. We're seen as delegators, conferring authority, stature.

Personality Types

Over the course of this book, we have witnessed many dichotomies. We've considered opposable forces or diametrical conditions, representing different ends of a spectrum of outcomes. We think of the continuums of credibility and authenticity, or the fork in the road between the fact and opinion-based questions we first encountered in **Unit One**.

The left and right brain forms another powerful dialectic. As presenters, we need to engage both modes of thinking as complementary to our problem solving. Here's how those forces play out in terms of evidence-gathering:

FIGURE 5.20: Left and Right Brain Evidence-gathering

Left brain	Right brain
Rational	imaginative
Linear	perceptual (metaphorical)
Logical	intuitive, whimsical
Sequential	visual (pictures, gestures)
Literal	ambiguous, paradoxical
Objective	subjective
time-sensitive	time-free
Accurate	Approximate

An important takeaway for researcher-presenters is not to favor one approach over the other. Instead we encourage both sides to remain on speaking terms: Supporting one another for testing rationales and weighing outcomes.

The key is knowing when we're favoring one side at the expense of the other. For instance, shortchanging a multitude of viewpoints because of a dominant view demonstrates a lack of curiosity and a face value acceptance of the status quo. That's a left brain approach to a right brain exercise. In contrast, an unquestioning acceptance of one's direct experience is no substitute for well-established laws, measurements, and patterns governing the physical world.

The trick is understanding where to strike the balance between longstanding precedent and the specific circumstances where we need to apply our sense-making.

FROM HOMEWORK TO BILLABLE WORK

Do we enlist the hard left and the soft right of our brain matter in our problem-solving? Either way, our presentation chops are best served by going the distance, and then some. That means proving our mettle by playing out alternate scenarios. This is different than taking in conflicting arguments, or clashing views. This is investing in several plausible outcomes, with no allegiances to any specific agendas, or priorities of the people involved.

One way to address this is to revisit our old crony, mister risk. This means talking through the uncertainties that our clients must confront.Those are concerns where the rosy forecasts and the fundraising goals fall short. Presenting a glass half-full and half-empty scenario is critical for connecting the research we've done to the results we're trying to help our customers achieve.

Playing out best and worst case scenarios not only proves that we know our stuff. We're also pragmatists who can adjust our services to fit fast-moving and complex situations. Scripting these two different outcomes also shows that we don't just want *in*, but are willing to put ourselves on the line for clients.

For instance, we might share the risk by reducing our upfront fee with the agreement of a greater upside, should the client's program meet or exceed its goals. This shows that we not only have skin the game, but stand behind a performance-based commitment.

It's all Black and White (and partly gray)

Now let's go from the abstraction of brain cells to the bare details of our case. There are many factors involved with any investigation. At the outset, let's consider what we know for sure and where the speculation ensues. That's when conclusions start to form and our work begins: How we substantiate our own conclusions about the case. Here's where those less-than-foregone conclusions coalesce around those inexhaustible details:

FIGURE 5.21: The Continuum of Uncertainty

Certainty	*Uncertainty*
Names and dates	Interpretations
Crime scene evidence	Perceptions
Personal records	Motivations & influences
Past deeds	Personal values and judgments
Rules and laws	Personal reward and justice system

REASONABLE CERTAINTY AND HONEST DOUBTS

As any veteran will tell you, a case brimming over with detail does nothing to guarantee that the evidence is mounting in favor of a specific outcome or conclusion. At a certain point, we need to take a hard right turn from the left brain exhibits of crime scenes and ballistics analysis to the right brain of probable motives and pay-outs. That means a most decidedly *third person* perspective on our *first person* search targets.

For example, one of the best pathways into the intentions of case-relevant suspects is to examine their frame of reference. This means looking at the personal networks and extended communities of those under investigation. Judging a suspect's ultimate intention straddles the line of *knowing the unknowable*.

Looking more broadly at our target's frame of reference is a useful, if not foolproof way to understand their influences, and reward system for carrying out potentially criminal actions.

FIGURE 5.22: The Continuum of Reasonable Certainty and Honest Doubt

Reasonable Certainty	*Honest Doubt*
Community Awareness	Self-Justification
Common Knowledge	Self-Deception
Advice and Guidance	Intuition
Safe Harbor	Self-Image
Community Interest	Self-Discipline

SECTION 5:4 | Project Presentation –
The Presentation as Exhibit

So we've arrived at game day ... the unveiling ... the truth-letting

The sudden death overtime round where we show our cards in arrangements made to help our clients play their own hands, whether the stakes are around...

- Weathering a crisis,
- Gaining first mover advantage, or
- Sizing up the probable motives of a person of interest in a murder plot.

There are three irreducible factors from which all final presentations are judged: (1) The client's prior pre-existing knowledge, (2) new awareness we provide, and (3) investment in the outcomes we recommend. These success factors are tempered by our own...

- **Obstruction:** We're not being told the whole story – at least how our clients understand it.
- **Transparency:** Our clients hold a layperson's view from outsourcing their research process to Google.

Marking the distance we traveled between an unaided Google search and the value we're providing, is one roadmap worth pulling out *before* we share our findings. In fact, it's every bit as important as retracing our first tentative footsteps, from before we familiarized ourselves with our search targets, topics in play, and details pertinent to our cases.

We would be doing our clients and ourselves a disservice if we don't capture the original inferences that fall into our laps. The comparison is this: Simple keyword searches processed through complex algorithms, versus the value provided by the tools and frameworks we apply as Knowledge-ABLED investigators.

MARKING THE DISTANCE

One of the best ways to guide the client through our investigative process is to track our progress through the SPM sequences we established back in **Unit One**. A well-documented SPM form will include (1) the unfolding of our query formations, (2) tool selection, (3) source inventory, and (4) key indicators such as a list of pointers and/or project corrections prompted by our failsafes.

How do we evidence this? We can showcase the value of our services by demonstrating how we use query formation to cut through the generalities to the most salient, accurate, and ultimately useful findings. For example...

- Assessing the uniqueness of the target (how easy is it to google the person?) and commonality of search terms
- Judging the difference between what individuals or organizations say about themselves, versus what others say about them, e.g., credibility testing
- Comparing the priorities and references used by clients with the popular associations cited by other stakeholders, including rivals, customers, and other channels of opinion

The next step is to show how the background research extends into the foreground. That means how our digital investigations prompt us to seek out, and conduct primary interviews and fact-finding:

1. What were the interview questions we drafted?

2. How were they based on our background checks?

3. Where do those interviews fill in the loose-ends and conjecture from our search logs?

INTEGRATING THE PIECES, PACKAGING YOUR PRESENTATION

Research is often just one aspect of an investigation. In some cases, it is the sole reason behind a client's request. In both cases typical reports often contain specific sections.

1. Statement of Investigation Objective

The baseline that sets that roadmap in motion is a restatement of the project aims as well as any revised or adjusted scopes of the work. This is a contractual pledge to the client. It's also a binding commitment by the consulting researcher to maintain professional standards. The researcher will work within established ethical guidelines while understanding that...

- No protocol or set of responsibilities can directly address all actions, outcomes, and issues that are brought to bear in the conducting of any given investigation.
- The researcher will endeavor to avoid relationships or circumstances that would jeopardize her independence or rigor of the methods used to capture, disseminate, and analyze the findings contained in her report. **(Mitchell, 2011)**[24]

2. Information Supplied by the Client

Another table-setter is the opportunity to restate the significant client discussions and conferrals after the original premise for the project was reached. This is an essential reckoning of a fixed objective with the fluid and dynamic nature of independent investigations. Two additional dynamics are at play here:

1. Being *listened to* is a big deal. Seeing our requirements and consultations in writing is an important reminder of agreements made prior to the project.

2. It's also a reminder to the client which aspects of their prior knowledge they decide to share on background with the project team.

3. Methodology Section

This is the least requested and most often referred to section on projects that involve client larger groups, often with competing agendas and uneven participation. The methodology section does not change. It helps inform or reacquaint team members with the approaches used to secure the findings presented. In the Methodology section, it helps to explain to show how we'll arrive at conclusions before we draw them by...

- Referencing the tools and frameworks we've applied as Knowledge-ENABLED investigators to maintain our independence.
- Doing this without sacrificing diligence, or succumbing to the self-selecting nature of personal biases, i.e. the need to be right.
- Sequencing the repeatable steps used to test assumptions and assimilate new findings.

4. Findings

The results we choose to include in our discussions or slides should be actionable or supportive of our conclusions and recommendations. There's always room to append the raw data, and unabridged evidence in a separate file. In the Findings section there are various perspectives from which we can address our presentations. These include:

1. Quantification (counts specific to search targets based on the source selection and time frame comparisons we saw in a survey model like **The Biggest Picture** in Section 5.1)
2. Project tracking (event-specific alerts and source-specific notifications)
3. Precedents and baselines (comparing this investigation to similar probes based on norms and expectations)

5. Conclusions

There's always a temptation to over-explain the validation process: Why we come down on one side or another. The explanatory power evidence of *conclusive evidence* releases the intoxicant we call *near-certainty*. Never underestimate the value of reducing uncertainty – even when those reductions may not be where the client is pinning their hopes. The Conclusion section states your confidence level based on what the search results tell you about the case you're conducting:

1. When you are uncertain, your confidence level is *hypothetical*.
2. When you are sure, your confidence level is *conclusive*.

6. Recommendations

A good consultant proves their mettle by attempting to put themselves out of business at the project close. Most clients (paying ones anyway) have their attention on our presentations. They also keep one eye on any scope creep required to nail down the loose-ends we can't resolve in this phase. That's why the recommendations section should resist any attempt to speculate beyond the evidence contained in the report at-hand.

There needs to be *enough to go on* even if we're suggesting an expansion of the existing effort. If not, a delay of the meeting date may be the best revised scheduling.

7. Repeatability

It's the omission of showing the panel, the client, the board, city elders or whoever has enough skin in this game to realize it's not just us. It's not just the case we're making. It's that anyone else without a vested interest in the outcome could reach the same conclusion.

The web is especially persuasive if we can prove that we're not gaming systems, or tipping our hands. We're simply assembling what any bystander with our research skills could figure out, without the lawyers and the news reporters. The flip side is that we need to make this as plain and obvious to our audience as it may have been difficult and even painstaking to produce.

Did I mention that can sometimes be a challenge?

Getting Input from Collaborators

Up until now, the journey of the Knowledge-ABLED has all the trappings of a solo mission. Even when we introduce the more social elements of our investigations, we are striking a largely independent chord in our singular pursuit of unvarnished evidence. Searching by nature is an introverted pastime. Searching out loud is the way we question search engines. That said, conversations between researchers and the databases they converse with are largely solitary, telepathic affairs. At least until they see the light of day in the presentation of their findings.

The lone researcher slaving away at an unblinking screen is a plausible scenario for most the work we've done together in **Units Two** and **Three**. That convention goes out to the window once our BS sniffers are pressed against the window of our presentations. That window is not restricted to the clients who've retained us. In fact, the more solo our journey, the more incentive we have to open that window to colleagues and associates. Who specifically are sound candidates for this collaboration?

Ideally, they have a domain expertise that's relevant to the (1) topics, (2) locations, (3) policies, and/or (4) client objectives you've been retained to investigate, or even support. But that association could backfire if the connection extends to the actual case, social networks, and communities impacted by the findings. Professional interest and personal detachment will ensure the trust required to build on the feedback and suggestions one anticipates in pre-presentation mode.

PLANNING THE PRESENTATION

Verbalizing our patter is quite a different calculation from tabular graphics, and color palettes. However, it's the single biggest non-editorial presentation decision we'll make. Do we fly solo through the final ascent? Would a co-pilot or at least a co-presenter reinforce the degree of diligence and care we've exerted for the duration? The camaraderie alone may prove a welcome respite from the relentless pursuit of a disciplined, but often isolating discovery process.

If so, has our co-presenter bought into our findings? Can they add their own convictions to the resonating strength of our recommendations?

It helps to do a hand-off, not just in terms of voices, but in stepping through a workflow process. The most compelling presentations give the audience a sense of the interplay. This is the back-and-forth that happens between a stakeholder with an issue or a question, and a subject expert with an answer or an approach. Hearing different voices also keeps sessions varied and interesting. Pad your presentation with invitations for responding. Structure interaction time into each section.

What about our own presentation style? Body language aside, there are some generic flourishes that cut across most presentation deliveries. Whether we're teaming up or soloing, we'll need to modulate our voice, and maintain eye contact across the room (especially with those distracted by texts and smart phone prattle). Avoid the temptation to read the bullets verbatim off presentation slides, use some well-executed hand gestures to underscore points. Take extra care to smooth the sectional transitions, with responses or without.

Logistics

There's the additional dynamic of the room we'll be working in addition to our voicing:

- ■ **Room Setting** – Can you select the room set up to meet the interactivity needs of your presentation? It's a long shot we'll have a say in room size, acoustics, seating arrangements, and white, unwelcome noise, e.g. the droning of the overactive air conditioning units.

- **Group Size** – How many and who will be in the audience? Audience size determines the level of interactivity. Typically any room with 25 attendees or greater requires that the Q&A be delayed until the end of your talk. For smaller groups, it may be advisable to capture feedback in real-time on a flip chart. Then re-engage those questions and comments on the back-end of the discussion. For larger groups, repeat questions before answering them. Viola! All participants hear the same question. Repeating it buys you time to compose your answer.

- **Prior History** – How well will the audience know the topic? For example, will there be various levels of knowledge: Beginner, intermediate, advanced? Can we draw the audience out with a polling topic to involve them? Eyeballing the number of hands raised helps us to figure out awareness levels and exposes the audience to the same real-time responses.

- **Texting Questions** – For the larger audiences, invite Q&A in advance. In public settings, text questions to a pre-selected phone number or Twitter feed. This spares the clumsy orchestration of having audience members step to a microphone to fire off an off-color or politically-loaded question.

- **Oprah Moves** – Be mindful about leaving the podium if you are serving on a panel. We don't wish to show-up our fellow presenters. On the other hand, if *we have the floor*, then working the room may be an appropriate way to capture the audience, and keep them engaged.

THE ABILITY TO INFLUENCE

So those are the building blocks of presenting our research. One aspect not typically addressed in the elements of effective presentation styles are the outcomes we're trying to reach. Think of it a Dale Carnegie advice bible on *how to win arguments and influence people*.

It's not just enough to access data. It's not just about having a seat at the table. It's not even enough if you have the authority to ask the tough, direct questions to commanding figures. Those are the luminaries that are squirming in their witness chairs, hoping you won't ask them. What does help is eye contact. What helps is when your eyes are persuaded by your own words. Remember, your eyes have the capacity to talk, along with your voice *as* you're presenting.

Launching a web investigation implies the use of tools and resources that anyone could use at that same witness table or from a WIFI-enabled cave around the globe. That common virtual touch is both the greatest challenge for virtual investigators and our greatest opportunity. With that said, here are those trade-offs. How to overcome the obstacles and ride the advantages, without missing a beat:

1) Stand up to Information Overload

There is a direct connection between too much information and too little forethought. Mainly, it's what to do when the overload hits. Anxiety has a way of ruling out options. That stress is magnified when we feel like an answer or a resolution is at-hand. It's just buried under a blizzard of databases and websites.

Rather than step back and regroup, it's often tempting to retreat into the very habits that caused us to freak-out in the first place. One of these havens is not so much a habit as a fantasy. It's the temptation of succumbing to the information myths that cloud our thinking, and pressure us into the poor choices we make when we're *used* by information.

Remember, being Knowledge-ABLED is both a defense against information glut, and a rally cry. It means we're an ally to our collaborators, clients, and communities in the quest to take informed action within a clarifying set of foreseeable outcomes.

2) Defy the Oversimplification of the World According to Google

One of the all-time leading urban legends is the notion that Google and the web are interchangeable. Need a free piece of information? Give Google a few hints about the person and their whereabouts, and Google will breathlessly deliver their every mention.

What does hold some water is the notion that until something better comes along, Google is the de facto radar for establishing what a casual search can yield in the way of public knowledge about everyday people – particularly those with uncommon first names and surnames.

3) Don't Overreact

One common and counterproductive information strategy is the tendency to over-communicate. This tendency is inspired by the false assumption: For every incoming message, there is an outgoing response.

Think we owe it to every tree that ever fell in any forest to read all our correspondence? We can't let it manage us if the ultimate goal is to stay on top of our workload. It's not as if the world is waiting on our immediate response. No one is going to need an ambulance if we don't answer straight away. Separate the urgency of the matter, from the desperation of the person provoking us.

If that's easier in theory than practice, consider this escape hatch: One liberating aspect of RSS readers is that we can let hundreds, even thousands of posts pile up without the fear that we're flushing down some unrecoverable treasure. Another great thing about RSS feeds is that we can search the granular details without needing to read, scan, or even browse through pages of search results. Web pages bearing no resemblance to our priorities or even passing interests.

Information needs to make time for us.

4) Getting a Grip on Attention Surplus Disorder

This made-up malady is the common impulse of triggering a refresh on your favorite communications tools to steal attention away from the task-at-hand. You need to disconnect from the web if you need to focus on presenting your thoughts in an original way. Presenting arguments, supporting claims, and analyzing reams of evidence means one thing for certain: Synthesizing many ideas and inputs. Many of us can't do this through screens for the single reason that the temptation is too great to dodge headlong into ... more inputs!

It is necessary to transition from the collection to the analytical phase of your research so that you can process, interpret, and prioritize the information you've synthesized into that range of clarifying options. Those next recommended steps that underpin your own unexpected findings, measured conclusions, and plausible outcomes.

Approaching this transition with a sense of closure and completeness is what we mean by *logging off* with confidence. So remember – you *do* have to clear your head – maybe even turn off your iPhone, and go for a stroll.

5) Dealing with Continuous Partial Attention

Another affliction on the receiving end of attention surplus is "continuous partial attention." That's what happens when your audience is tapping its collective fingers on the cracked knuckles of their smart phone keys.

We're talking about an impairment that runs deeper than the most uncooperative witness, or the most elusive search term. That's the inability of your audience to stay with you through an extended discussion, complex argument, or drawn-out sequence of events and speculations. At the same time, the group you're addressing is not being rude on purpose.

They are not tuning out. They may even be keeping up with you (and other pressing concerns simultaneously). Continuous partial attention is that clashing combination of connectedness and distraction. The key to combating it? Finding the correct mental file drawer where our audience puts information they will access *after* the presentation.

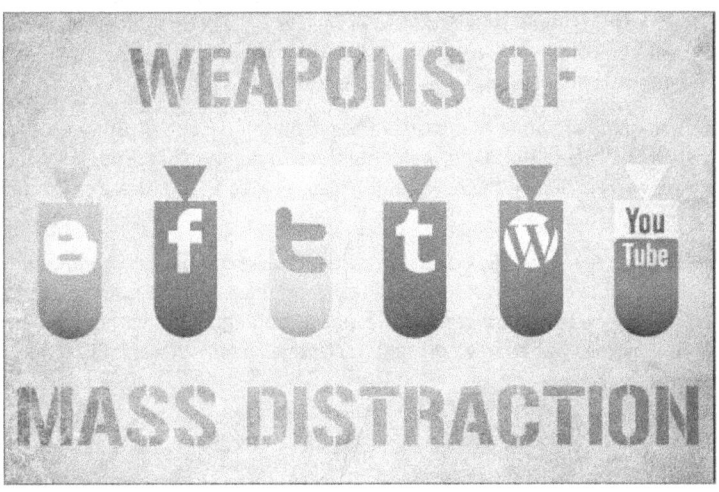

6) Failure is an Option

"Fragmented stories of partial failure create more learning than formal documents summarizing best practice."

– David Snowden

Fear of failure is a great galvanizing tool. Unnecessary risks and avoidable blunders are two surefire ways to sharpen the listening capacity of our audience members. On the subject of failure, let's own up to ours. Let's avoid terms like *success* and *wins,* and all things triumphant.

That doesn't mean we have to talk down our accomplishments or use false modesty when we deliver great value. It means that failure is not only an option. It's a requirement. Mistakes are not just something to own up to. They are worth taking credit for. Learning happens by design – not accident. Mistakes are neutral. Learn from them and they're highly instructive. Repeat them and we deserve to lose our presenter license. The worst repeatable error is that the same person makes the same mistake time and time again. The second worst error is to pay for the same learning over and over.

7) Seeking out Apparent Conflicts of Interest

The greatest contradiction between people and how they use information is conflict-of-interest. The notion that what they say in public runs contrary to what they do in private. Hypocrisy is often associated with the variance between how people behave as figureheads in their professional roles, and as individuals in their personal lives. Often this means taking their lofty titles and leadership roles to speak for the group they represent, when their private dealings advance their own interests ahead of the organizations they represent.

Not all hypocrisies are deliberately self-serving. Sometimes they are based on self-deception. Sometimes these escapes are willful flights of fantasy. As we saw in **Unit One**, we're oblivious to our own blindspots. Sometimes we invent our own histories, not because we're deluding ourselves, but because we're all too aware of the social demands of the workplace.

For example, our resumes are self-constructed upwardly-advancing career projections based on merit and well-deserved promotions. Such fabrications often cover over our flaws, skill gaps, unceremonious firings, or other disconnects that cast doubt and confusion on the image we're projecting as potential hires. Other common social rituals like the filing of tax returns are another way that we present a selective fact base to an official authority, as a way of offsetting another societal obligation.

8) We're all Subjective Experts

While appearing well-accomplished to one audience, we show our destitute side to the government. Is it a conflict of interest to pay lower taxes? How plausibly can we plead poverty to the tax collector? These are subjective questions, dependent on who you ask. Behaviors that govern conflict-of-interest are a more reliable bellwether. They have as much to do with the audience, as the actors for whom they sit in judgment.

Put another way, most of us *fudge* a little on our tax returns. The more productive result in your conflict-of-interest investigation comes when you ask how the institution handles this common practice. When does one person's fudging land themselves at the top of the suspected cheaters pile? When do the actions of an individual taxpayer trigger counter-actions – an IRS audit for example? Conducting conflict-of-interest investigations are not limited to retrieving the public, legal, and financial records of one individual. If that were so, anyone with a credit card and a open browser window could meet the challenge. A Knowledge-ABLED investigator anticipates the actions an authority may take based on the way it handles the case in question.

9) Gathering an Influential Perspective

This kind of analysis is not limited to brushes with the law and the work of enforcement agencies. Sometimes the potential range of outcomes is not about serving jail time. Maybe it's not punitive at all:

1. Perhaps you're estimating the kind of professional fees you command as a subject matter expert?
2. You're in the running for a job whose funding depends on sources outside of the hiring organization?
3. Maybe you need to weigh treatment options for a loved one, afflicted unexpectedly with a serious illness?

Regardless of the particulars, our investigation skills will help determine an outcome for our clients and ourselves based on: (1) The outcomes our sponsors can expect, and (2) our own negotiating position with the groups and institutions we are trying to influence.

This is not a *me or you* proposition. This is a how-do-I-fit-into-the-broader-scope-of-what-can-happen-given-past-history orientation. Ultimately we all want the higher-paying position. We want the cure to heal our loved ones. But these aspirations are not ranked highest, or even buried in search results. Your influence will be felt when you can speak with authority about the greater concerns and priorities on the minds of the hiring managers, funding sources, and clinical trial sponsors: In short, the decision-makers who would weigh in your favor.

And regardless of what *that* message is, your outsider status makes you the ideal messenger.

10) Don't Let Google Over-complicate Your Own World

As we saw in Section 1.4: Becoming Knowledge-ABLED, the standard version of Google departed from the reality stage in 2012. This rendered all search results as subjective. No two user sessions were certain to produce the same outcomes. Ever since, virtual investigators have been left to ponder:

1. How can we be offering transparency when an algorithm is intercepting our searches?
2. How can we promise repeatability when our click patterns and profile data skew our results away from those of our presentation audience?

The answer is that a promising number of search engine alternatives have cropped up. They not only refrain from tracking us, but enable the same queries to produce the same outcomes, regardless of who's formulations they are. Duck Duck Go, Wolfram Alpha, MetaGer, and Disconnect Search all deliver the benefits of search syntax, semantics, and operators without the need to sacrifice granularity, or surrender personal data. Best of all, you can turn the URLs generated by your queries over to your clients (the way search logs were intended). Scooch over to the passenger seat, and watch their personal investment in the project soar.

FIGURE 5.23: Elements of Presentation Style

Element	Presentation Goal
Audience	The Statement of the Investigation Objective will rehash the explicit goals of the assigned research. The remainder of the report is governed by an implicit goal – anticipating the reader's needs.
Tone	Research is delivered even-tempered and even-handedly. The researcher is dispassionate, reserved, never shrill, and resists the temptation to exaggerate, editorialize, or accept unsupported evidence.
Movement	Like our own learning curves, a decent presentation progresses from initial impressions to tested assumptions. It's not static and doesn't restate idle facts. There is a sense of order without contrivances or forced narratives.
Format	A winning presentation looks smart on the page. That means being easy to absorb, skim quickly, and extract salient information. It refrains from unrelenting text and includes tables and graphics to summarize findings, generalize patterns, and support conclusions.
Investment	How much time will they spend reading our document once we're done presenting? Consider this when deciding how much detail to communicate through supporting charts and addendums.

The Experiential Side of Presenting

It's not an accident than SPM reflects the cardinal rule of reporting: The journalism convention for constructing a news article, covering the *who, what, when, where, why,* and *how* of the events we're chronicling. While the sequence has been reordered, the retelling of our research can be conveyed through our discovery process: Where we are, and how we got there, follow the same script. That makes it easier to share our discoveries and the spirit of discovery in our presentations.

Think of it as comparing notes rather than favoring one competing version of events and their significance. That means capturing first impressions as a basis for involving the client in our collective research experience. It's also a compelling reminder for how off we may have been on our original hunches.

Naturally, it helps to humanize the data side when we're summarizing the stories that numbers can tell. But behind every persuasive analyst is a healthy, lucid comparison, relating tables and charts to the people and anecdotes they address.

FIGURE 5.24: Journalism 101: Unpacking News Reports through the Inverted Pyramid[25]

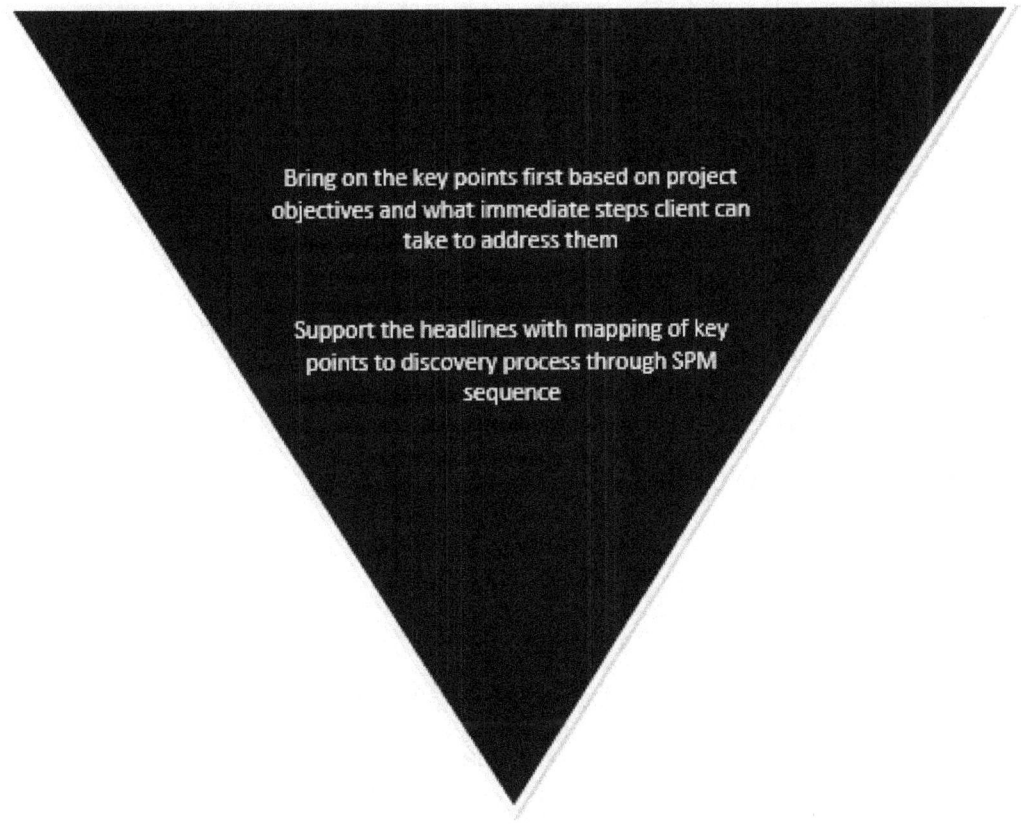

UNIT FIVE: Wrapping

Focusing on Presentation

Unit Five tied together the collection, filtering, and evaluation methods introduced and modeled in the first four units. Those practices were surfaced in a survey or quantitative approach to capturing search-based outcomes ('The Biggest Picture'). We then looked at the social currency of our research findings through the information bartering opportunities afforded by blogging communities and domain experts. In Section 5.3 we examined some intentional ways to involve our social circles in the packaging of our research. We finished the unit with the mechanics of delivering these reports to our clients and communities.

In **Unit Six**, the book's curriculum will conclude with a Knowledge-ABLED use case based on the professional transformation of a commercial video producer to an educational media consultant. This use case guides us through the false starts and initial frustrations to the firmer footing and ultimate confidence-building that comes with being Knowledge-ENABLED.

All relevant practices, frameworks, and search strategies in the case study are referenced to the specific units and chapters where they're introduced and demonstrated. For instance, our use case subject entrepreneur plots out his research goals and supporting tasks through the **Search Project Management** model.

Our protagonist applies the principles of **Site Selection** and **Oceans, Lakes, and Ponds** to determine his sources, generate business leads, and build his understanding of the market and its growth potential. Finally, our practitioner uses the **Provider Conjugation Framework** as a way of engaging the very same business contacts that first landed on his radar as search targets.

[1] Robert I. Sutton, "How to Be a Good Boss in a Bad Economy," Harvard Business Review, June, 2009
[2] Eli Pariser, "The Bubble Filter," TED Conference, February 2011
[3] Kenneth M. Bilby, "The General: David Sarnoff and the Rise of the Communications Industry." New York: Harper & Row, 1986
[4] Andrew Morris-Friedman, "Hindsight of the Future," Hampshire College, 1984
[5] This was a reliable audience size for viewing the Academy Awards prior to the arrival of social media.
[6] Onpoint Radio, "iPad & The Daily, AOL-HuffPo: Reading The Media-News Future," February 7, 2011
[7] Mickey Meese, "Who's the Boss, You or Your Gadget?" New York Times, February 5, 2011
[8] Feed Demon has a notable presence in Unit Six's Knowledge-ABLED Case Study.
[9] Google Insights for Search was discontinued in 2012.
[10] Vicki Abelson, "Divorce Internet Style," Huffington Post, December 28, 2011
[11] Robert Pozen, NPR, OnPoint, "The Economy in 2012 and Your Money," January 3, 2012
[12] Darlene Adams, "Romantic Deception: The Six Signs He's Lying," Dr. Sally Caldwell and Darlene E. Adams, CreateSpace, 2010
[13] Assuming we acknowledge the line between civil liberties and hate speech.
[14] However, it's no accident that RSS is ineffectual for tracking news feed activities on social

media. Such monitoring would pose a commercial challenge to social media platforms.

[15] To restrict all information providers to Bay State-based publishers.

[16] The forward slash and asterisk indicates that all indexed pages are included under each site root.

[17] Ibid, Morville

[18] Nassim Nicholas Taleb, "The Black Swan," Random House, 2007

[19] James O'Toole, Warren Bennis, "Culture of Candor," Harvard Business Review, June, 2009

[20] "Fast and Slow: Pondering The Speed Of Thought," NPR, October 27, 2011

[21] Ibid, Taleb

[22] Ibid, Taleb

[23] This stands in contrast to us thinker-researchers, crunching the numbers in the back office.

[24] Bill Mitchell, "Ethics Guidelines for Poynter Publishing," March 3, 2011, http://www.poynter.org/archived/about-poynter/20209/ethics-guidelines-for-poynter-publishing

[25] Note that we considered another pyramid inversion in **Unit Three**: Figure 3.45: The Pyramid of 20th Century Institutional (Source) Credibility. This infographic correlates the stature of traditional media sources with their circulation numbers.

UNIT SIX:
THE KNOWLEDGE-ABLED COOKBOOK | WORKING CASE STUDY

Stirring Things Up

In the first two units, we learned how and where to find information more quickly that we can act on right away. We used SPM ("Search Project Management") to organize the research-gathering before launching our investigation. We applied the concept of OLP ("Oceans, Lakes, and Ponds") to determine which digital tools to use for the job at hand.

We learned how to tune our searches. We used syntax, semantics, and search operators to reduce our hit counts, and filter out bogus sites and distracting details. We sharpened our whereabouts through the information types in **Unit Three** that oriented us to our points of entry and helped us navigate and reduce fruitless searches. In **Unit Four**, we administered the sniff test to determine the credibility of our information providers, and conjugated those providers to make sense about who's communicating, who they're intending to reach, and why.

That's a lot to absorb. But remember the primary benefit of becoming Knowledge-ABLED: The point is not to collect information but to apply it— be it facts, opinions, or even the details of its capture. That's where turning theory into practice can jumpstart our thinking about how others connect their own Knowledge-ABILITIES to practical problem-solving situations.

In **Unit Six**, cooking is our navigation tool and research metaphor. Like meal preparation, research is the blending of utensils (tools), ingredients (sources), and spices (filtering). The results nourish our bodies (minds). A maestro researcher shares two other qualities of a master chef: (1) A thirst for knowledge, and (2) an appetite for learning. This holds true no matter how finicky the customer or time-sensitive the answer. The questions are timeless.

As we see in our growing **Source Fluency**, it's not about memorizing the recipe or storing every ingredient. It's about meeting the challenge with what's ahead and what's at hand. Think about it. Are the best chefs the ones with the largest refrigeration units or most plentiful spices? It may just be that they know their way around an array of combinations, substitutions, and prepping. Together, they can summon the most complex flavors with the simplest of ingredients. Breathe in, deeply!

In the research kitchen, the difference between inventory and fluency is this: Sources are dynamic. Archives are not. Websites launch, die, atrophy and refresh in a continual cycle of change. How to analyze, interpret and attract the sources you need to fill your search objectives does not change very often. It means adopting and tweaking a few basic approaches that can be used over and over again. And while an engrossing investigation will never be as absorbing as a sumptuous gravy, there is recipe-making in the steps to satisfy our learning desires: They are not buried in secret sauces, or guarded by proprietary algorithms.

Not if you're Knowledge-ABLED.

Unit Six Learning Objectives

If we want to put our knowledge abilities to the test, we need to start thinking about our research combos, tools, and time elements as real projects. There's nothing abstract about search tools, query formation, quality controls, and that hard stop to end all reality checks — deadlines.

Here is a set of five culinary metaphors that liken food preparation to the search syntax and operators we first addressed in the Query Formation section of **Unit Two**.

Unit Six Destination: Food for Thought— You Are What You Eat

There are parallels between creating clear, repeatable successes in our culinary practices, and in our research projects. Both cooking and researching engage (1) our need for quality in the ingredients we use, (2) fitting utensils to task, (3) tasting as we go to bring out the natural flavors, and (4) the energy boost it brings to deliver an experience worth building on.

Think about it. Cooking is all about recovering time-honored traditions to service two of our most persistent hungers – sensual pleasure and life-sustaining energy. The formulas for serving information share common ground as well:

> 1. **Combinations** — What blends well with what else – what fails to work together?
> 2. **Utensils** —Which is the right tool for the job – what tools are multi-purpose and which ones have only a dedicated use?
> 3. **Durations** — How long do you cook them together – what are the signs that serving time is near?

FIGURE 6.1: Assembling the Meal

MAIN INGREDIENTS	MEAL TYPES	CUISINES	COURSES	COOKING METHODS
Chocolate	Breakfast	African	Appetizers	Advanced
Dairy	Brunch	American	Beverages	Bake
Fruits	Lunch	Asian	Breads	Broil
Grains	Supper	Caribbean	Cheese	Fry
Meats	Dinner	Continental	Cocktails	Grill
Seafood	Snack	Eclectic/Fusion	Desserts	Marinade
Nuts	Ceremonial	Jewish	Hors d'Oeuvre	Stir Fry

All of the five query methods introduced in Figure 6.1 get served up in our first information recipe. We'll see them in action later when we break down the query formations used to establish a sole proprietor in a promising new business opportunity. Now here's how those metaphors get baked into the kinds of queries we'll see in our first information recipe (case study):

FIGURE 6.2: Gathering the Research

KEYWORDS	PROMINENT TERMS	LANGUAGES / LOCATIONS	PRESENCE	FORMATS
Clearly described search targets	*Domains, anchors, titles, recurrences*	*Dialect, physical distance, site location*	*Content neutral site factors*	*File type for storing pages and content*
Authors	Companies	near: (proximity)	Advertisers	MS Excel
Buzzwords	Consortia	inurl: (site root)	Solicitations	Adobe PDF
Technologies	Public Agencies	loc: (publisher HQ)	Reciprocal links	Flash
Jargon / acronyms	Creative Works	lang: (vernacular)	Non-reciprocating	CSV
Process methods	Sponsored Events	"(in OR near) [place]"	links	CGI

1. **MAIN INGREDIENTS – The recipe for success:** As you can see from the list in Figure 6.3, main ingredients headline the chapters of most cookbooks. Chocoholics aside, they comprise those four basic food groups we first learned about in grammar school. Keywords are the building blocks of effective query formation – the jargon, technologies, descriptive phrases, and familiar methods you use as conversational ice-breakers with your search engine. The same terms you use to *season* your shoptalk.

FIGURE 6.3: Main Ingredients

MAIN INGREDIENTS	KEYWORDS
Chocolate	Experts
Dairy	Authors
Fruits	Buzzwords
Grains	Technologies
Meats	Jargon / acronyms
Seafood	Process methods

2. **MEAL TYPES** – Time, place, and distance forms the context for understanding: The type of meal we're preparing is the context we're seeking in **Unit Four**. Instead of a light dinner or a late night snack, we're clued into where keywords appear and what they say. Is our person of interest the author, main topic, an offhand reference? Is the story we're following the main event, side show, part of tomorrow's news, or ancient history?

FIGURE 6.4: Meal Types

MEAL TYPES	PROMINENT THEMES
Breakfast	Job titles
Brunch	Private Companies
Lunch	Consortia
Supper	Public Agencies
Dinner	Creative Works
Snack	Sponsored Events

3. **CUISINE** – The location of web-based research: Cuisine is the tradition behind the preparation of those main ingredients. Caribbean or electric fusion style plays out literally in terms of language choices. Not just dialects, but more subtly when the foreign tongue is an unfamiliar topic, event, or practice. Command of digital languages helps us to become quick studies, even when the landscape is littered with buzzwords only a native speaker could readily decipher.

FIGURE 6.5: Cuisine

CUISINES	LANGUAGES / LOCATIONS
African	allinanchor:school district test scores
American	near: (proximity)
Asian	inurl: (site root)
Caribbean	loc: (publisher HQ)
Continental	lang: (vernacular)
Eclectic/Fusion	"(in OR near) [place]"

4. **MEAL COURSES** – The reputation of information providers: The meal course you're serving is carried by the reputation of the messenger. How are they seen by particular groups and audiences? That depends on the recipient. Presence focuses on the social dimensions of your information providers. Their virtual identities are carried through their page rankings, link shares, site visitors, traffic patterns, sponsors, web marketing campaigns, and related sites.

FIGURE 6.6: Meal Courses

COURSES	PRESENCE
Appetizers	GPS coordinates
Beverages	Advertisers
Breads	Solicitations
Cheese	Reciprocal links
Cocktails	Non-reciprocating links

5. **COOKING METHODS – Preparations for serving client information needs:** Finally, our ovens, stoves, grills and their settings parallel how information is packaged or served up. Is it that you're looking to crunch numbers so you're looking for a spreadsheet? Is it a statute or a section of the law? Is it a job resume? Bets are it's available in read-only form as a PDF. What if it's a tutorial that steps you through a process you'll need to master? Then steer clear of static pages that turn soggy and stale when they're not refreshed. Focus instead on flash files and video demos. Regardless of the mission, these data wrappings are specific information types that assure us the content we need comes in a format most useful to our purpose.

FIGURE 6.7: Cooking Methods

COOKING METHODS	FORMATS
Bake	MS Excel
Broil	Adobe PDF
Fry	Flash
Grill	CSV
Marinade	CGI

Unit Six Benefits

In the digital-kitchen, what a researcher delivers to their recipients depends as much on what they have to work with as it does what the client's requested, or even what the recipe calls for. That's why these case studies can't be expressed in terms of specific sources. Likening search tools to ingredients or utensils doesn't guarantee a repeatable outcome any more than a set number of information providers delivers a fixed number of viewpoints.

As we did with information types in **Unit Three**, the different dimensions of a common experience like cooking comes with its own process guidance. That getting from our grocery bags to our dining tables is more complex and nuanced than microwaving an instant entree. The recipe-making in **Unit Six** is based on the models we've been using throughout this book. From the step-by-step sequencing of the search log, through the ways that OLP informs where we search, our cook book will show how those combos, utensils, and durations come together.

Searching Out Loud

SECTION 6:1 | Transitioning from Commercial Clients to Nonprofits – A Knowledge-ABLED Case Study

The recipe we'll be dishing up profiles a small business owner and client of mine named George Reis. Like many small business owners / service providers, George has seen the silver lining of an economic down cycle as an opportunity to enter new markets by offering his services for free or discounted rates.

This use case will unfold in three sections:

- ■ **Part One: The Diagnosis** – We find out what makes our entrepreneur tick, how he's transitioning careers, and his challenges both as a researcher and a marketer.
- ■ **Part Two: The Search** – We apply the models and methods introduced in the first five units of the book to help scale the virtual research walls that were blocking the entrepreneur in Part One.
- ■ **Part Three: The Engagement** – We see the pay offs from the results of this unit's Part Two section through our subject's ability to generate business leads, develop networking contacts, and narrow down to a selective and promising market niche.

Like many passion-driven entrepreneurs, George never warmed up to having a boss or a regular pay check. To him servicing a generic and predictable market was never the right challenge for growing his business, his skills, or his ability to deliver added value to his customers. As a video producer, he was also frustrated by the tired, repetitive nature of the infomercials he scripted, shot, and packaged. When the economy hit the skids, George didn't see the downturn as an excuse to do more of the same. He wasn't interested in pitching new customers on the same overused marketing concepts.

There's one other thing you should know about my friend George before we begin. He may be a little restless, even a bit edgy. But he's not caught up in being edgy or trendy.

He isn't interested in change merely for change's sake. But if the resulting blend of his plied trade and newfound skills treads new market territories, George is up for the exploration.

SECTION 6:2 | The Diagnosis –
Re-engaging the Same Internet that's Failed Us Before

George Reis has been *around the block*. He's not interested in abandoning ship or starting from the ground up. He wants to enter the nonprofit sector. He sees nonprofits on more stable footing than his familiar corporate clients, a first impression he will question later on. Job security aside, he's primed to gain a foothold in an underserved niche poised for rapid growth.

Reis is motivated by the idea of giving back to a community in need. He's also drawn to the challenge of working in an unsettled area. What he calls a *less established market* with a wider range of opportunities. He is especially hooked on working alongside social workers and educators: *"People who work with people– not suppliers, wholesalers, and producers."*

Initially George swallows his fees in exchange for some hands-on experience. He agrees to assist a local, all voluntary group involved in job placements and career counseling for teens diagnosed with a high-functioning autism spectrum disorder ("ASD") called Asperger's Syndrome.[1] Asperger's includes a wide range of behaviors and learning disabilities. One binding element is that 'Aspies' store large volumes of arcane information and that they are challenged to share this knowledge in a broader context or community.

George puts together a topnotch production on a shoestring. It documents the inspired stories of the program's students who overcome their social deficits to make worthy contributions to area employers. The piece is shown at community forums and professional conferences. And while the work attracts raves for the students, the video itself raises far more public awareness than it does private funding.

In a nutshell – George knows where he wanted to be. Getting there requires a read on people, a quick study on markets, and a clear focus on how to apply his ample talents and meager resources. George is ready and willing. But is he Knowledge-ABLED?

INITIAL INTAKE: COMING TO TERMS WITH INTERNET CONFUSION

When George first comes to me, he is suffering what he calls *the curse of internet confusion*. He isn't bewildered by the technology. He can certainly retrace his way from Google to the websites of organizations with whom he became acquainted in his pro bono work.

George searches the web everyday across multiple devices, a healthy connection speed, and the latest version of everything. "What am I missing here?" he asks. When we move onto where he's stuck it starts with the question about which nonprofit sector to focus on.

George understands that cracking into unexplored territory is largely a numbers game:

- The more qualified prospects, the better
- The more knowledge about autism, the more options about where to focus
- The more he can see what passes for *good* production, the easier it will be to sell his superior wares in this neck of the nonprofit woods

The problem is that he didn't know how to qualify them without spending resources he doesn't have.

"I'm not getting answers," George says. "I'm getting thousands of search results – leading nowhere – at least no place I want to be."

The confusion isn't just the scarcity of answers but that the outcomes are cloudy. They can't be reduced to a simple yes or no, or even a straight-forward best or worst case. In effect, George can't base any follow-up actions on his searches. He's not looking for pages. He's looking for people, or at least pointers to resources. But he doesn't have the time to track every lead or vet every site.

"So here's a novel idea," I say to George. "Let's forgive search engines for being poor interpreters of our desires. Let's assume they can't read our minds, and that's probably a good thing."

Instead, I suggest that George learns to speak the language of search.

He's not buying it. He doesn't want to become a programmer, he says: "I'm not into writing code. That would be somebody else's career switch."

I assure him that I'm no programmer and I'm not trying to make him one either. I tell him this isn't some foreign dialect he'll be learning. It means expressing his business requirements in ways that get him answers – pronto. I offer one other assurance:

"This is not the final word on your definitive questions. This is an invitation to continue a discussion we can steer in your favor. Yes, a discussion with the very same Internet that's failed you before."

Defining the Boundaries

It certainly helps that George has already defined to a large degree what he's looking for. These are more than the purely fact-based questions we first considered with Information Types section in **Unit Three**. He wants to know which names are worth the investment. A related issue is how he'll connect to those prospects through a common purpose, a definable event.

But there's something even more fundamental going on than too many searches and not enough time. The problem isn't about prospects, target markets, or learning new languages. The problem is that his to-do list is overwhelming, even before the internet confusion is ready to kick in.

I tell George that his tendency to do too much at once is a common flash point for internet confusion. He's cornering the need for niche marketing in the same breath as cultivating experts. He's grappling with accreditation for ASD programs while trying to tackle lead generation. Wearing many hats in the middle of a career switch is par for the course. But the ease of searching multiple subjects all at once can lure us into the false expectation that acting on the search results should happen with the same swiftness and deliberation. The desire to treat a research project like the check-off box of groceries is a recipe for doing too much at once – and not doing justice to any of the items on the list.

So we don't get too hung up on query formation, or the finer points of search refinements like unique IDs and pointers. Instead, we head straight for site selection with OLP leading the way to some concrete and instructive project tasks for George:

1. Generate leads for potential buying groups and individual experts and influencers (oceans)

2. Identify fast growing segment of a stable, established market (lakes)

3. Develop unique sales proposition to would-be buyers (ponds)

Once OLP kicks in, we can begin writing George's **Search Project Management** plan ("SPM") to guide his research efforts.

Better Business Targeting Through Site Selection

Let's start with oceans. Just because George's intentions are clear doesn't mean this makes a stitch of sense in any search language. That's because the most straightforward business plan overwhelms the logic of the most sophisticated algorithm (search programming). And as basic as these requirements sound to our ears, they are completely foreign to the average keyword matching query formation *(see **Unit One**, Section 1.3 – blindspots –– Gateways to knowledge awareness)*.

Secondly, Reis needs to get from an ocean to a pond so that he's sourcing potential business contacts in his search results, not in his dreams. That means using a top level search tool like Google, Bing, or some of the privacy engines we reviewed in **Unit Two** to mine social networking sites for profiles that fit his lead generation criteria. The same combination of semantics and syntactical commands will help fetch structured contact lists that have already been compiled. Most likely this will come in the form of a spreadsheet that he can integrate into his own contact management program. But that's a bit *downstream* from here.

First, he'll need to bridge the distance between his former identity as the President of Reis Productions, and his new professional role. But before he can ingratiate himself with a new crowd, he needs a reliable way to open those first doors. This is not about mounting a full-fledged *search expedition*. This is about generating a list of business leads. And this is not just any list. Those who land on it will be conferred status and prestige for *making the cut*.

The best way to qualify leads is not whether they keep Facebook pages. Anyone can do that and the barriers to entry are too low to establish credibility or a meaningful track record. Instead we determine the legitimacy of the organizations they lead through information lakes. Business portals, tagging sites, and subject directories will point the way to trade groups, industry experts, and third party research providers.

These are the **Quality Controls** that address priority #2 – the market research that not only defines, but confirms the business opportunity George is about to jump on *(see **Unit Three**, Section 3.2 – Quality Control – Knowing Where to Invest Your Attention)*.

BUILDING CREDIBILITY THROUGH REPORTING REQUIREMENTS

Besides solid contacts, George needs credible sources to warm up his cold sales calls. He bases his initial list-building on government reporting requirements. That means the research is based on a legal framework – not a marketing imperative. The pay-off to Reis is that the information is *clean*. 'Clean' means it's legitimate. It's not subject to tampering. There are no improprieties through back-channel dealings or other potential conflicts of interest between George's business leads and the information providers he uses to source them. Bottom line: **Source Fluency** in **Unit Three** teaches us we don't need to be subject experts to know how to leverage authoritative information sources.

The other benefit about sourcing this way is that legal frameworks (like needing to file publicly available disclosure forms) often leads to marketing imperatives anyway. Typically, this means tracing the people mentioned in the reports. From them, George can use provider conjugation to source the second person donors who champion the causes he's searching – first as an outside acquaintance, then as a player.

In this case, insiders are either trustees, board members, or executives drawing salaries from the budgets of these organizations *(see **Unit Four**, Section 4.1 – Provider Conjugation – How to Determine the Motives of Information Providers in Groups and as Individuals)*.

Finally, George needs to season his initial findings with a common set of circumstances that tell both he and his prospects: Hey, we might just have a match here.

The unique specifics are often spelled out by the leading example that inspired this marketing campaign:

1. Why was the first project successful?
2. Which success factors can be modeled and repeated?
3. What benefits did George Reis deliver that the customer considers a commodity (all competitors supply this) versus value-add (unique to Reis Productions).

Site Selection According to Sources

The next framework is figuring out the *how* for getting to the *where* part. That's what oceans, lakes, and ponds are about. In Figure 6.8 here's how that OLP structure will play out in terms of what tools George uses. More importantly than specific search or websites, this site selection table maps George's OLP choices to the project tasks (actions), and business goals (outcomes) they're designed to support:

FIGURE 6.8: Mapping OLP to Actions and Outcomes

Scope	Resources	Actions	Outcomes
Ocean	Google, Yahoo, Bing	Search **news collections** with 'expansion/growth' semantics for defining events and 'non-profit' syntax as the subject filter in his search statements Search **blog collections** to identify most influential bloggers that address health topic directly and the local hospitals and lab facilities where current research is being conducted	Tune search results to fit desired business results by filtering out garbage and factoring in motives of potential allies, rivals, and customers Establish independent voice for news, commentary, and dialog on Autism Spectrum Disorder issues where George is resource to community
Lake	Delicious, Biznar, LinkedIn, Face Book, Google keyword Tool	Search tagging engines for material already vetted by domain experts Use web utilities to validate nonprofit sites for consistency, traffic, link analysis, and related sites Mine public interest in business services, related topics to target market Bypass permissions for viewing social media profiles by searching social networks via major search engines to establish leads through targeting criteria such as location, employer, and job title	Vet source providers for their authenticity, credibility, and visibility within ASD community Avoid fail-safes like link farms and SEM ("Search Engine Marketing") ads looking to cash in on explosive interest in ASD issues and misinformed use of the web Attract silver bullets like big picture stories and forecasts that give scale and perspective on looming and widespread changes to the target market
Pond	SCIRUS, GuideStar, LII ("Librarian Internet Index"), AcronymFinder, Feed Demon (RSS reader)	Source experts from management, scientific, and academic circles as professional references and potential interviews for George's blog Search individual databases not indexed by major search engines but referenced in deep web search directories such as the Librarian's Internet Index (LII) maintained by the California State Library Association	Yield premium database results at no cost through deep web sources focusing on social networks and non commercial repositories of public records and personal profiles Tap utilities like RSS readers to trap event-based information and begin tracking the most important players, alliances, programs for servicing the community and most successful methods for establishing them Use RSS readers to shadow lead generation contacts

Self Evaluation Through Blindspots

Next we revisit another screening tool introduced in **Unit One** – an inward and outward quest for blindspots. The framework we apply is the Johari Window, with an unflinching eye towards the risks that come with career transitioning. Factor in George's personal vulnerabilities and inexperience. This speaks to his lack of any formal medical or therapeutic training. He has no formal health care, child care, or teaching experience to fall back on *(see **Unit One**, Section 1.3 – Blindspots –- Gateways to Knowledge Awareness)*.

We then refocus the question from the outside in: How can he position his inexperience as a networking asset? There may be an opening in a community where the lead question is not about how *well* you're doing, but by the good you're doing others. Perhaps it's a connection formed between informed and community-minded service providers that are drawn to his hard-headed business sense?

We consider ways that George could strengthen his hand by reaching out to established experts. I ask George who he might reach out to, and what direction that conversation could take. He envisions several potential openings. These could lead to collaborations with experts in the ASD community. We sketch them out together, with an eye toward what's double.

George decided to try the easy stuff first. These are the kind of exchanges that don't require a big upfront commitment in time, or attention. (Note how commitment and trust levels increase with each opening):

1. Talk about their own opinions or concerns about teaching aids they currently use
2. Refer George to research institutions that could support such efforts through grants and endowments
3. Advise him on potential scripts for future productions
4. Become part of the production, either as off-camera consultants or on-screen in their client interventions
5. Invest in whatever product he ultimately develops
6. Serve to distribute the product

That's a lot of conversation points – even with just one potential collaborator. For now, George knows the mountain isn't coming to him. He has to do his homework first and find potential allies inclined to join forces in some way, if only to refer him along to a better qualified business lead.

Secondly, he needs to scope out the success stories in this niche. How involved were their alliances and the outfits that staged these productions? What were the creative outlets for developing videos and the commercial outlets for selling them? Could he use social media to shadow them in a noninvasive way?

Next, how could he begin to line up potential suitors. Larger, established organizations that would benefit from his fresh perspective and superior production skills. He knew he'd done a lot better reaching out to actual people – not to the gatekeepers of large organizations. Some might be even flattered to be asked. Groups might be noncommittal if providing a group response. Some might pass on the request. Few would engage directly *(see **Unit Four**, Section 4.1: Bartering Information between Groups and Individuals)*.

Finally, how could George both stay informed about daily changes and new developments and put this knowledge to immediate use? Themes were now beginning to emerge:

1. From educational campaigns to celebrity endorsements
2. From charity events to FDA approvals
3. From professional associations and trade meetings to influential studies mentioned in prestigious medical journals about new treatments and studies

How to stay on top of it all? More importantly, how not just to be well-informed but well-regarded, and ultimately put to work where he can do the most good?

The best thing about seeing blindspots is that it helps George to realize the need not only to stay on task but resist the temptation to bunch them together.

Once the SPM is addressed, we'll be off and running.

Scoping Out the SPM to Keep the Project Online and in Line

Okay, George admits, he's beginning to see a connection between how he interacts with digital technology and how he'll begin approaching potential partners and customers. The list build is helping us to circle back to the original premise of where George is taking his business.

We can now map his project goals to his research methods. We use the SPM form to document (1) query formations, (2) search tools, (3) information providers, and (4) a sampling of what we'll see in the first-pass of search results. Next, we'll consider how the results of his lead generation campaign impacts his business development plans.

FIGURE 6.9: Search Project Management Plan for George Reis Productions

LESSON	KNOWLEDGE-ABLE BUSINESS DEVELOPMENT
What are we gaining (Skills):	George will learn how to use advanced search commands as screening tools to both narrow a pool of prospects and build potential bonds with those contacts
What are we delivering (Requirements):	Translate the goal orientation of potential customers into a rich list of contacts whose inclinations for action are supported by George's search findings
Why are we motivated (Purpose):	Confidence of meeting a soaring need in an under-served market and providing a social benefit in the process
Where is this going (Objectives):	<ul><li>Pre-qualify the organizational assets of potential customers</li><li>Scope out the appeal of proposed offering</li><li>Enlist potential collaborators and distributors of proposed offering</li><li>Draw lessons learned from current entrants and emphasize key competitive differentiators and benefits to potential customers</li></ul>
What are some reasonable outcomes (Expectations):	Potential purchasing groups and collaborators researched according to organizational assets, key constituents, philanthropic roots, ties to public funding sources, and inclination to innovate – specifically try out fresh approaches to social kills educational for students impacted by ASD

LESSON	KNOWLEDGE-ABLE BUSINESS DEVELOPMENT
Which positive signals do we see (Silver Bullets):	• Social media presence and campaign approaches of vendors who service this niche • Comparisons such as rankings, ratings, or demonstrated rivalries between prolific funders of interventions for ASD populations (particularly students, teens) • Studies and forecasts that 'size' or quantify the developmental needs for ADS students as they transition to adulthood • Respected therapists and clinicians that critique the shortcomings of current instructional media offerings targeted to the ASD population • Spike in downloads or sales of video, DVD, or any interactive format used to support academic, clinical and community-based ASD programs • Influential people with high public profiles who have firsthand experience with ASD issues through personal and family connections
Which negative signals do we see (Fail-safes):	• Too wonky – political pundits involved in the policy side of public debates, offering complex and detailed arguments about which programs to fund • Too local – Events and initiatives that are too specific to a particular region to have greater meaning beyond the organizers or the venue • Too preachy – Similar to policy wonks but more emotionally-charged and polarizing • Too geeky – The web is home turf for software developers so there's always the risk of distraction posed by their homegrown programs • Too pricey – That would be any information whose cost exceeds the price of this book

SECTION 6:3 | The Search –
Learning How to Swim in the Deep End

George is now ready to implement the search plan. He cultivates a variety of keywords in support of his query formation. As a culinary metaphor, keywords and phrases are his main ingredients. Effective keywords are the seasoning: The jargon, technologies, descriptive phrases, and familiar methods we use to pepper our shoptalk.

The ocean is the place where keywords not only play but pay the search companies their primary source of revenue. Buy a keyword and the purchaser fuses the connection between knowledge demand (the searcher) and content supply (what ever the keyword holder is selling). But there's more to keywords than the ads that appear in our search results. There's some great pay-offs here for the Knowledge-ABLED.

Because the indexes of commercial search engines are so vast, it gives us ample lee-way to test search terms and word patterns, both in our own search results and in the popularity of what's being searched. Let's talk a little bit about the latter, and why this is not only good science but savvy marketing.

An ocean-sized index gives us a lot more room for matching suitable word combinations and unique identifiers not found in a smaller pool. Even if Google came with no syntax or the secret sauces that influence the results rankings, the enormity of its index cinches the deal. It increases the odds that we'll graze, if not collide directly into inviting search targets.

Reproduction of our discoveries is another distinct advantage of documenting our work through popular search sites. The proof in any virtual pudding is empirical transparency: That whatever results or rationales we share with our peers are not only supported by a fact base or a well-vetted resource. It's that our colleagues, clients, and communities could repeat our experiments, and replicate the same results.

Searching Out Loud: Giving Voice to Independent Investigations | Marc Solomon

Using Term Expansion to Segment Markets

As we discussed in **Unit Two**, term expansion serves two important purposes:

> 1. It improves our own query formations by leading us to like-minded terms we might have otherwise overlooked.
>
> 2. It tells us what terms others are using to approximate the same search targets as ours.

Now let's put term expansion to use.

Here's what George has gathered before we meet. He googles the terms 'nonprofit' and 'market' and finds out from the first set of hits that there are roughly 1.5 million nonprofit organizations (NPOs) in the U.S., with about $1.6 trillion in aggregate revenues. It sounds promising. In practice, he's hard-pressed to put these numbers into action. He seeks to pattern off the success of some pro bono work his production company did to bring public attention and policy debate to an important health care issue.

So far, so good.

Now, how do we put these priorities into terms a search engine understands?

Imagine the world's largest and most popular restaurant where there is no menu. The waiter comes over to your table and asks without presumption or prejudice: "What is it you would like?" Now imagine that order taken over several billion times every day in every corner of the world. This is an apt description for the **Google Keyword Tool**: An index that helps marketers match popular query terms against their own goods and services.[2]

George starts out with 'video' as a keyword – the single term that sums up what he brings to the marketplace:

Figure 6.10: We Can See the Flurry of Related Interests and Concerns Triggered by Keyword Research

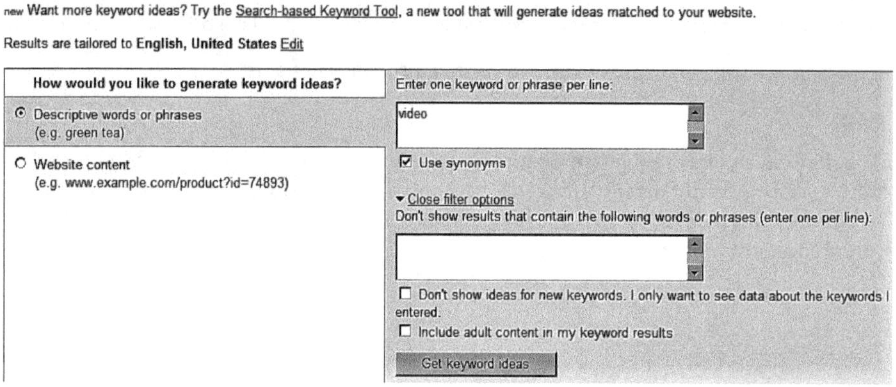

Figure 2 Here are the results when we add 'autism.'

Keywords	Advertiser Competition	Local Search Volume: May	Global Monthly Search Volume	
Keywords related to term(s) entered - sorted by relevance				
video		226,000,000	414,000,000	Add
music video		24,900,000	13,600,000	Add
music videos		5,000,000	5,000,000	Add
videos		68,000,000	185,000,000	Add
video clips		1,830,000	2,740,000	Add
mtv video		165,000	301,000	Add
watch video		673,000	550,000	Add
vidio		550,000	3,350,000	Add
free video		6,120,000	13,600,000	Add

Note that under the term expansion options, the original keyword fails to appear – even once. Here's what happens when George cross-references his service offering with his niche target:

Additional keywords to consider - sorted by relevance				
pdd		90,500	165,000	Add
asperger's		246,000	368,000	Add
asperger		246,000	550,000	Add
aspergers		368,000	450,000	Add
asperger syndrome		110,000	110,000	Add
asperger's syndrome		135,000	201,000	Add
aspergers syndrome		74,000	90,500	Add
pervasive developmental disorder		18,100	14,800	Add
learning disabilities		201,000	201,000	Add
pdd nos		22,200	60,500	Add
social stories		33,100	40,500	Add
asperger's disorder		9,900	12,100	Add
aspergers diagnosis		2,400	2,900	Add

Searching Out Loud: Giving Voice to Independent Investigations | Marc Solomon

Now George adds 'autism video' to his list and compares it to the most common search term associated with autism:

adhd asperger	▨▢
pdd video	▢
aspergers social skills	▨▢
asperger sindrome	▨▢
autism video	▨▢
asperger characteristics	▨▢
aspergers syndrom	▨▢
asperger spectrum	▨▢

Figure 3: The magnetic pull of 'videos' is now apparent.

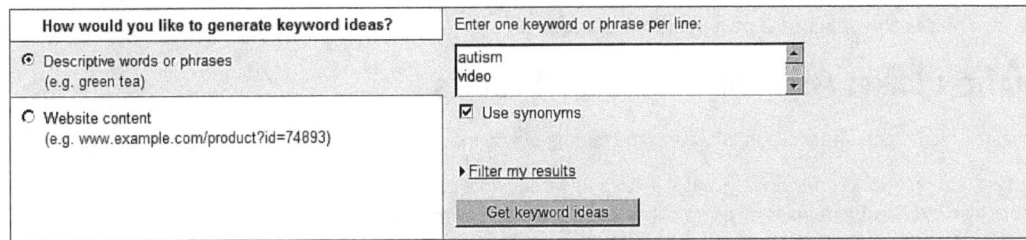

Figure 4: 'Autism Video' is nearly as popular as the diagnosis.

Keywords related to term(s) entered - sorted by relevance				
autism		2,740,000	2,740,000	Add ˅
autistic		450,000	368,000	Add ˅
autism society		33,100	33,100	Add ˅
autism video		12,100	9,900	Add ˅
autism spectrum		60,500	49,500	Add ˅
autism symptoms		74,000	60,500	Add ˅
autism awareness		40,500	33,100	Add ˅
autism children		110,000	49,500	Add ˅
videos		68,000,000	185,000,000	Add ˅
autism child		49,500	14,800	Add ˅

What we're seeing is a large drop-off in keyword demand for what George believes to be his key value-add for competing in this market niche. He has two choices:

1. Corner a market for services no one is demanding, or
2. Change direction towards better established business segments.

Given his core audience (medical researchers) and his marketing budget (non-existent), he chooses the latter. Key to this shift will be George's ability to capture the high demand segments that best fit his core services.

IF AT FIRST WE DON'T SUCCEED...

Once George realizes that fundraising for nonprofits is a non-starter, he begins looking in a smaller pond. This is where his prior work and current skills will accent his strengths. He becomes a *bigger fish*. He focuses on autism – the theme of the pro bono work that originally led him down the nonprofit path.

The cross-referencing of autism and video leads him away from fundraising and towards educational DVDs that teach children with Asperger's Syndrome – the high functioning form of autism we described in the Diagnosis Section. His is struck and captivated by what binds the learning needs of all Aspies: To engage the daily events that most of us routinely navigate without a plan or a lesson.

George watches a sampling of these social skills learning aids on a YouTube channel created by a prolific producer. It includes her own line of streaming media for sale to schools, special education teachers, therapists, and parents.

Off the bat, George draws three conclusions:

1. He's impressed with 'the mission.' A lot of kids could be helped by this kind of instructional media.

2. He's not exactly *blown away* by the level of production quality.

3. He believes he can do a more customized product based on the individual experience and aptitude levels of each student.

He decides to make a hard turn off the video fundraising highway. The Google Keyword Tool is ample proof that it's the wrong entry point. But before he can get up to speed on this new pathway, he needs to (1) piece together the potential market, and (2) his own pluses and deficits for best positioning within it.

THE INFORMATION LAKE: ASSESSING MARKET STUDIES

So why is George best served by an information lake for determining which market he should enter?

As we saw in **Unit Two**, subject directories are a great way to cultivate sources already vetted by domain experts and researchers. They are also excellent gateways or portals into the deep web sources that evade ocean searches. That's because they are invisible to the detection methods of commercial search engines.

George is looking for a big picture view to evaluate existing conditions and the projected fortunes of established and emerging markets. Even seeds of new growth that have yet to be spotted or formally recognized. That kind of perspective doesn't typically exist as an isolated website, news article, or press release. Traditionally, this kind of knowledge commands a premium and is delivered through a paid subscription or ad hoc research report. There are other workarounds to avoid these fees. For now, let's assume George is looking for the business forecasts and market predictions one is likely to learn though a research report or market study *(see **Unit Two**, Section 2.3: Tool Selection – What research tool to use and for which job)*.

This kind of information exacts a premium. It's designed to give its customers an edge on less attentive market watchers. It offers first movers the green light, or conferring nod to shape and exploit a business opportunity before it fully blossoms.

From an epicurean perspective, market studies are the elaborate dishes that research organizations publish. The better studies insure a broad enough interest spread out over the longest sales cycle or 'publishing run.' The cooking methods used to deliver market research reports are proprietary. The secret sauce for most study makers are the statistical models they apply to their forecasts and recommendations. Researchers need to be retained. Opinion shakers need to be shaken. Analyses need to be written – and justified. But what justifies the cost of buying a study? Why the fuss?

In George's case, there is no valid reason. That's because breaking into a niche-based service business is low. He doesn't need to outfit his production company with new equipment. He doesn't need to pre-purchase supplies. He probably doesn't even need to complete a licensing procedure or file papers with a regulatory authority.

On the other hand, his capital investments would be higher if he needed to retool his shop with the latest machines. If he was considering whether to sell products, the cost of supplies and assembly would warrant knowing where those material costs are headed: Is this is a good time to take that plunge? The investment outlay could easily recoup the expense on research. But that's not the kind of research George needs.

The Research Study Flea Market

One of the reusable skills of becoming Knowledge-ABLED is the ability to uncover and connect prior research. It's akin to the shopping skills of a vintage store owner rifling through a pile of pre-owned garments or house-wares at a tag sale. Even though we're not getting the freshest material, it may be just as relevant with age – and cost-free.

First, I advise George to check out a deep web resource called Biznar. It's a portal of business media and market research firms that publish lots of industry analysis and forecasts. The faceted view of its search results enables George to drill down on the commercial aspects of servicing his potential niche.

Figure 6.11: Biznar is a prime example of rummaging through dated research reports

There is no formal category called the 'Autism Market' as you can see from the query. Why? Because it's too unsettled, ill-defined, and there are ethical questions. Think of the criticism aimed at drug companies in referring to at-risk populations as market segments. (Referring to a medical condition or an 'underserved market' is another matter). But because George is using a resource dedicated to making business assessments, he can view the marketplace from a variety of perspectives. This includes drug-makers, insurance providers, educators, behaviorists, and the need for developing new clinical interventions, and support services for the 1 of 150 children who fit this diagnosis.

This resource opens George's eyes to a whole new wrinkle: The swelling ranks of mid-career professionals enrolling in a growing number of universities that offer ABA or 'Applied Behavioral Analysis' programs. This is the therapy of choice for the growing ranks of children with autism.

What did this tell George? The trend confirmed that these newly certified therapists are positioned in a seller's market, regardless of the larger economy or its impact on donations to nonprofits.

Information Packaging – It's All in the Delivery

If market research is about a labor intensive recipe for producing a premium slice of forward-looking information, then the delivery itself is another important ingredient. Let me explain.

In his first market assessment, George was looking for a fully prepared meal. This means that a single market study would focus on specific segments that are both ticketed for growth and where George can add the greatest value. As we saw with the Information Lake examples such as **Biznar**, the likelihood that George is going to find a pre-packaged answer to his highly customized search criteria is remote at best *(see **Unit Two**, Section 2.2: Natural Language Search Engines)*.

We already know George is not about to pay a third-party for their research reports. He's certainly not about to hire a professional to gather primary research about his dedicated topic. He's going to have to cobble together facts and assessments that weren't made public for his direct benefit. He's got to think about who and why information providers make their findings available to us through the web. Is it through public reporting requirements? Is it pure ego, force of habit? Is it that other like-minded denizens are trying to build communities just like George?

Where's a good place to start? Crunch, crunch, crunch – that's the sound of the numbers he needs to support his gut hunch: The need for interactive media to support the growing target market ... a soaring ASD population.

Another lakeside companion is the popular outpost of **YouTube**. George explores what nonprofits are doing with video to promote their causes and advocate for at-risk communities. The video collections of major search engines form a superior lake for sourcing instructional materials as well as more market-focused appeals. These dedicated searches function as portals into multiple video sites.

Figure 6.12: YouTube Video Channel

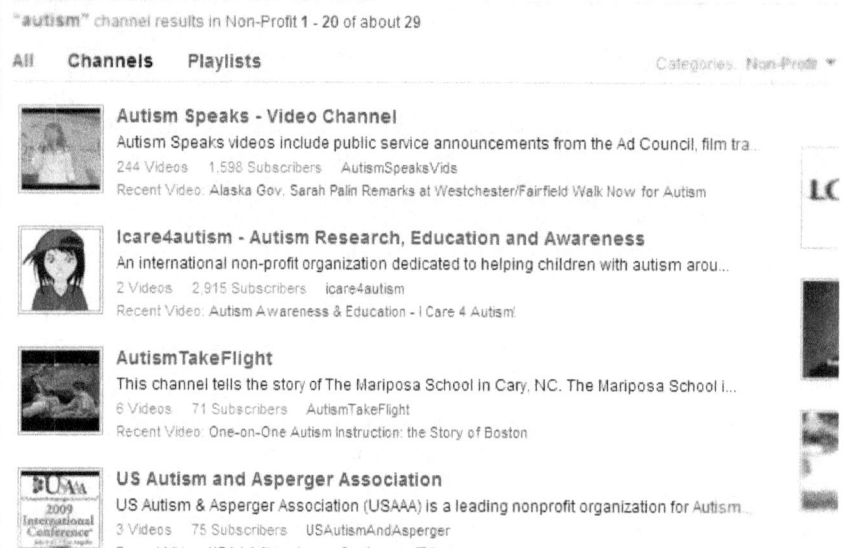

The advantage to focusing on a single video site like YouTube is that George can leverage its channel structure and the added filter of nonprofits for keeping tabs on the top performers according to page views.

Switching Between Oceans and Lakes

Next, George leaves the vast ocean for the more selective focus he'll find on the information lake. He samples a well-stocked subject directory called **Scirus**. Scirus focuses on academic and technical literature that addresses many disciplines within the sciences – including references to health care and the prestigious **Medline** database. George is not looking for people but qualified references to experts.

Figure 6.13: Qualifying Experts

Here he stems the term 'autis*' ... so that he can pick up both 'autism' and 'autistic' in the titles of the works.

George also considers the refinement list of related terms. What's the difference here? Our old pals syntax and semantics are back from **Unit Two.** They're here to help George revisit the question of list generation. He can do this with keywords that enjoy wider recognition in the networks he's pursuing and trying to infiltrate.

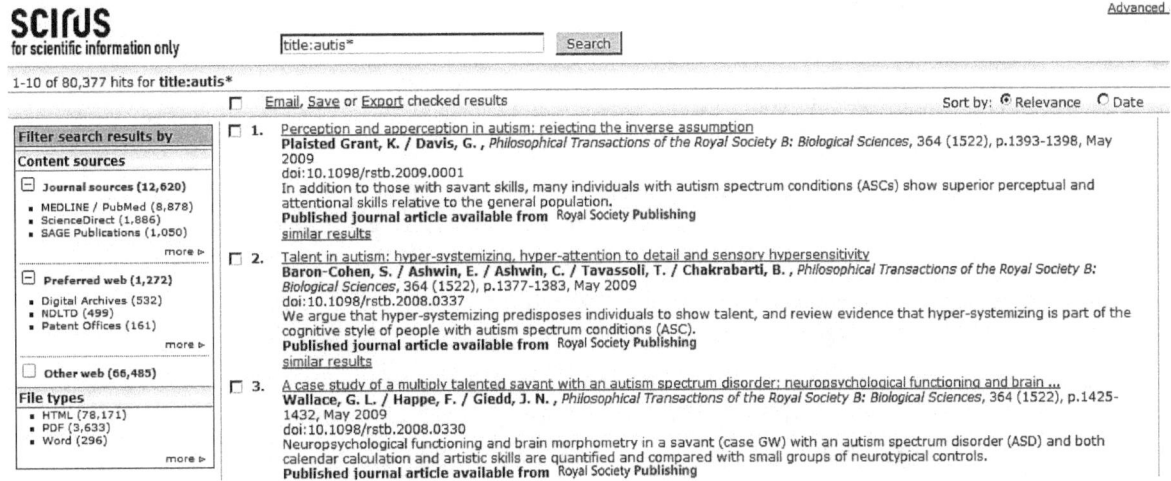

George then combines the new expansion terms with a more professional-leaning social network. But instead of searching in a pond, George jumps again back into the ocean (in this case Google). That's because the search engine results by-pass the security structure imposed by the networking site. In other words, the search engine ignores the barriers imposed by social networks around access to profiles. Also, note how George includes both keywords and a large subset of unique IDs that he can use to isolate licensed service providers from laypersons with the same subject interest.

Here's the breakdown:

1) Data source (pond) –

> "Site:linkedin.com

2) Keywords addressing target niche –

> autistic OR autism OR aspergers OR "developmental (disabilities OR disorders)" OR "social skills""

3) Keywords addressing professional accreditation –

> phd OR psyd OR "ccc-slp" OR "ms-ccc" OR bsc OR lcsw OR msw OR lmft OR mscp)

Searching Out Loud: Giving Voice to Independent Investigations | Marc Solomon

He further develops the list with a database of acronyms:

Figure 6.14: Advanced Degrees

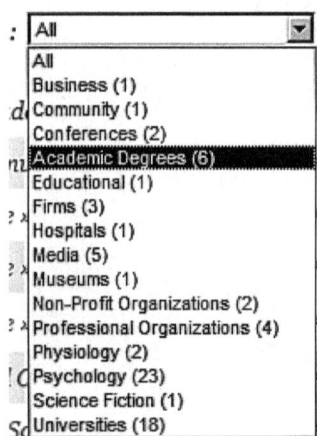

Here we see groupings to define academic degrees with the term 'psychology' as the defining keyword.
This approach enables George to pre-qualify a list of vested practitioners. This is not a simple keyword match. It's a filter for professionals licensed to provide clinical and therapeutic services that are widely needed, but not always funded or publicly available.

George lingers a bit longer in the ocean, this time choosing **Yahoo** as his window into the same social network he googled earlier. With a few minor tweaks, this is the same search strategy we broke down on the preceding page.

Figure 6.15: Domain Experts

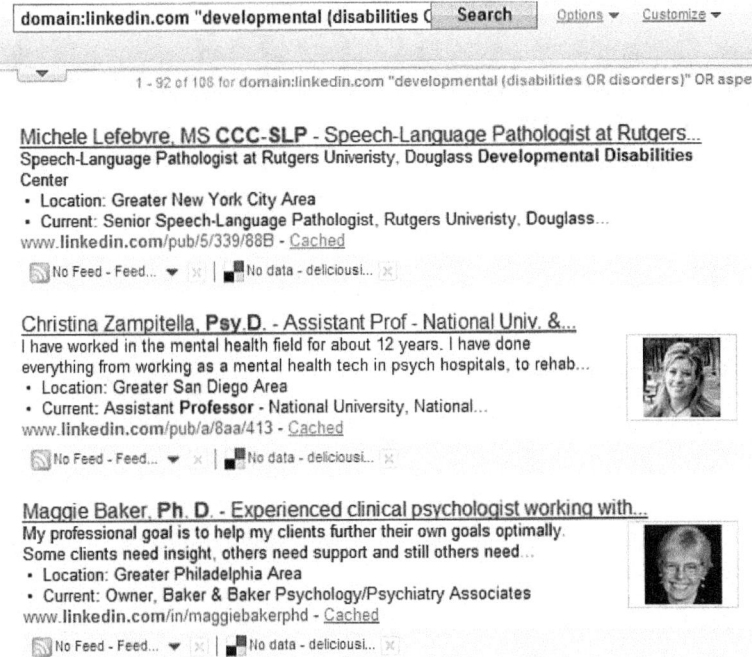

Note that 'site:' is referred to as 'domain:' on Yahoo. These kinds of syntactic discrepancies are frustrating and to be expected from competing search standards. While the syntax and results pages change between the different search engines, the logic used to pull key details while suppressing bogus ones remains the same from tool to tool.

As you can see in the output, what changes dramatically is the way each search tool presents the results. It's also important *not to* assume that just because a particular detail is captured doesn't make it searchable through the interface displaying it.

For example, the geographic field of 'Location:Massachusetts' is just as likely to pick up 'Massachusetts Avenue' in Washington, DC as the state of 'Massachusetts.' There is no additional benefit for using syntax that's not supported by the search tool selected.

UNIT SIX: The Knowledge-ABLED Cookbook | Page 6:29

domain:linkedin.com "(learning OR developmental)(disorder

Web Images Video News More ∨ Anytime ∨

Ad related to: domain:linkedin.com "(learning OR developmental)(disorders OR disabilities)" "

LinkedIn Learning Classes | Learn Anytime, Anywhere.
www.linkedin.com/Online-Courses
linkedin.com has been visited by 100K+ users in the past month
Learn Business, Creative & Tech Skills With Online Video Tutorials. Start Today!

LinkedIn Learning	Online Business Training
Learn The Most In-Demand Business, Technology, & Creative Skills.	Acquire New Skills. Do Great Business. Advanced Your Career!
Enhance Your Tech Skills	Courses For Educators
Strengthen Your Tech Skills & Expand Your Opportunities.	Discover New Ways To Create Dynamic Learning Environments. Start Today!
Online Creative Courses	Solutions For Teams
Design With Confidence & Bring Life To Ideas. Begin Your Free Trial!	Personalized eLearning For Every Employee. Request A Free Demo!

Learning is a complex process - linkedin.com
www.linkedin.com/pulse/learning-complex-process...
Learning is a complex process that can be shaped and reinforced through variable aspect. Understanding the nature of **learning** complexity, its risks and influences help to establish methods, tools ...

Ad related to: domain:linkedin.com "(learning OR developmental)(disorders OR disabilities)" "

LinkedIn Learning Classes | Learn Anytime, Anywhere.
www.linkedin.com/Online-Courses

Here's the same query conducted nine years later in Yahoo. As we see there is no other purpose for the results other than to generate ads.

Searching Out Loud: Giving Voice to Independent Investigations | Marc Solomon

CONNECTING PEOPLE TO GROUPS

After George captures a list of professional contacts, he wants to expand the pie from individual practitioners to particular groups. His wants to expand the original list with an ear out for associations, charities, and educational organizations such as institutional alumni and policy groups. These organizations share that the goal of increasing public awareness around autism and related learning disabilities.

George includes stable storage formats such as PDFs and spreadsheets. He expresses his preference for definitive documentation and focuses on programs and learning aides designed to reach the public through toolkits and reference guides.

His last flurry of keywords is skewed towards adding more qualified professionals to his list – especially where there was an organizational entity to target *(see **Unit Two**, Section 2.1: Query Formation – What to ask and how to ask it)*.

Here's the breakdown:

1) Type of document –

> *(filetype:pdf | filetype:xls | filetype:xlsx*

2) Prominence on web page –

> *(intitle:contact | intitle:resource | intitle:directory | intitle:attendees*

3) Keywords addressing target niche –

> *(autism | asperger's | autistic | nonverbal | "(learning | developmental)(disorder.*. | disabilit.*.)"*

4) Keywords addressing group role –

> *"board" "president" "treasurer "secretary"*

5) Filter out lists of publications –

> *-inurl:catalog*

Figure 6.16: Combining Job Titles with File Formats

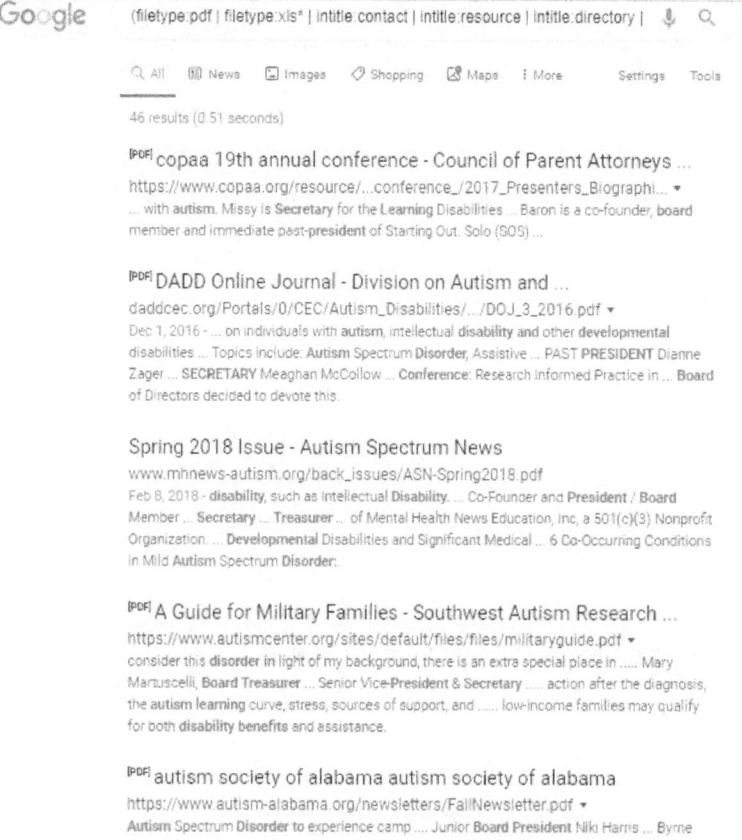

Combining file formats with targeted job titles and meeting venues is a sound strategy for list development.[3]

Another resource for groups is to pursue rankings. Those are the *best of the best*. Think of the magazine rack or your doctor's office waiting room. Now think 'special issues.' What makes them special? Most times the occasion is marked by a ranking that confers some status for *topping the list*. The top polling positions are in fact *the prizes* pedaled by publishers and coveted by award seekers, and often, those publications' advertisers.

To the Knowledge-ABLED, best of lists are also screening devices used by publishers to throw their media cachet around. Usually there is a formal methodology that legitimizes the ratings used to qualify the top selections. It's critical to the information provider's credibility that the list be perceived as reflecting the popular will of its readers, or the merits of the list members. Not as a vehicle for favoring their advertisers, or ignoring groups with no business ties to the publisher.

In Figure 6.17, we see the added deference researchers give the search results from the former social bookmarking site **Delicious**. Each reference is based on a page visit worthy of revisiting – hence the tag.

The number in the blue box on the right side of the results is the number of members who have bookmarked the same resource.

Figure 6.17: Lists and Rankings

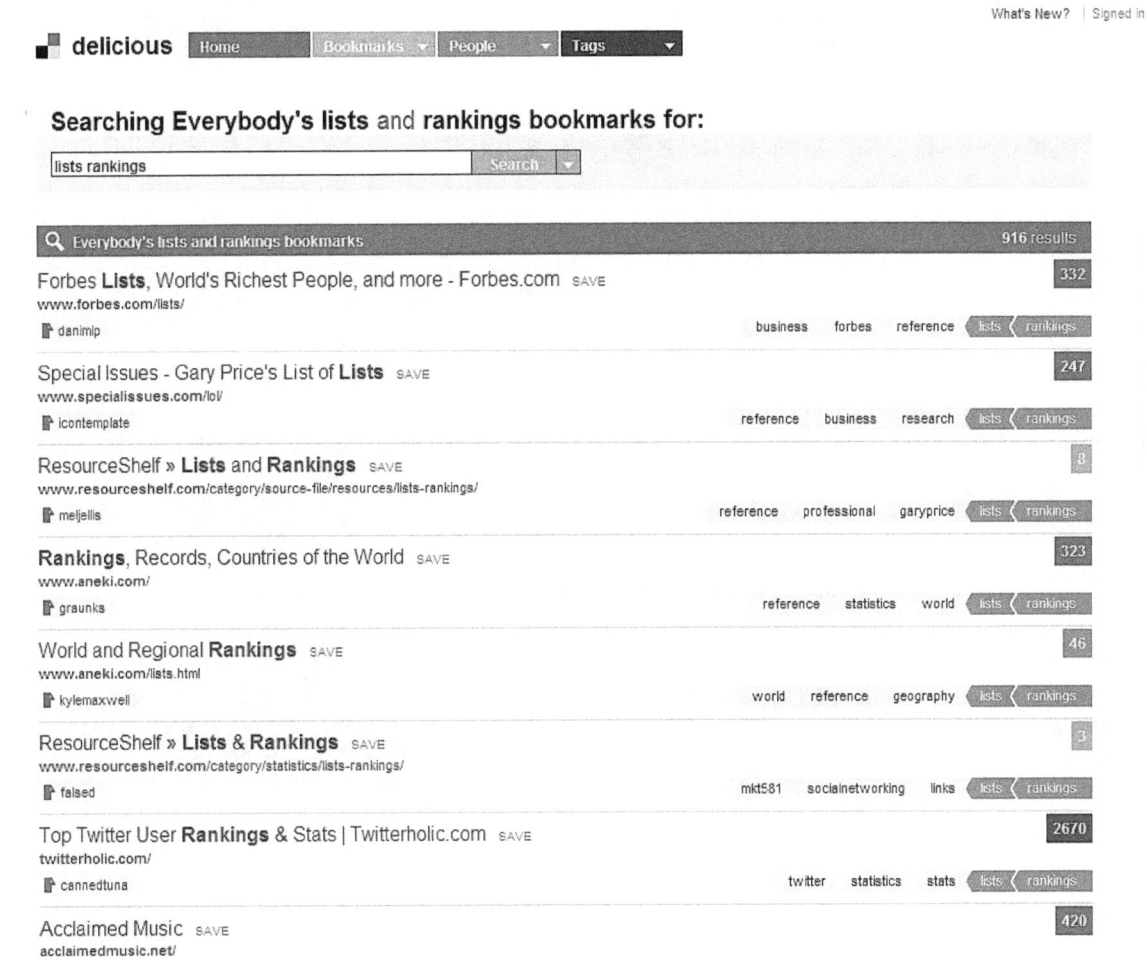

George references the social bookmarks tagged by Delicious members and comes across a pond-sized resource called 'The List of Lists' from a respected librarian, domain expert, and independent authority on sources named Gary Price.

USING LAKES TO VET SOURCES

In the nonprofit world, another pond for sourcing and evaluating George's target groups is the **GuideStar** database for researching public philanthropies. George works the same calling card here that succeeded in his last pond search and *stems* the word root for autism:

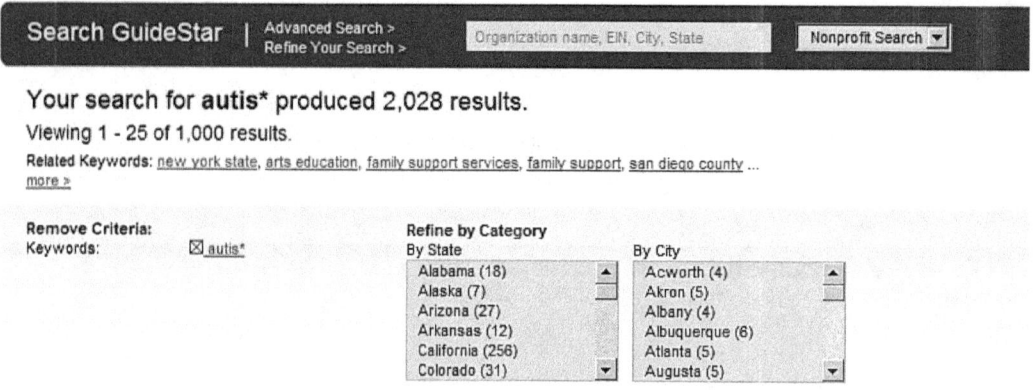

The excessive number of hits gives him some discretion on the types of organizations he needs to target. We can see who George has in his sights by the refinements he makes in his second pass:

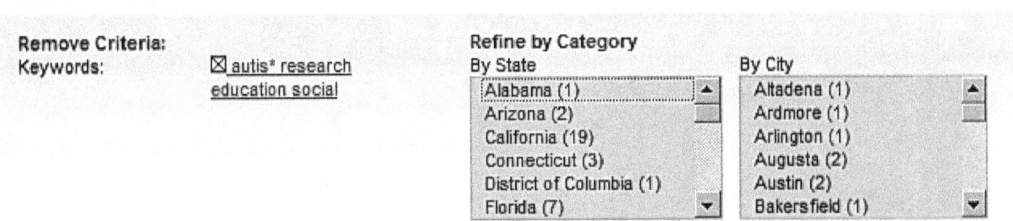

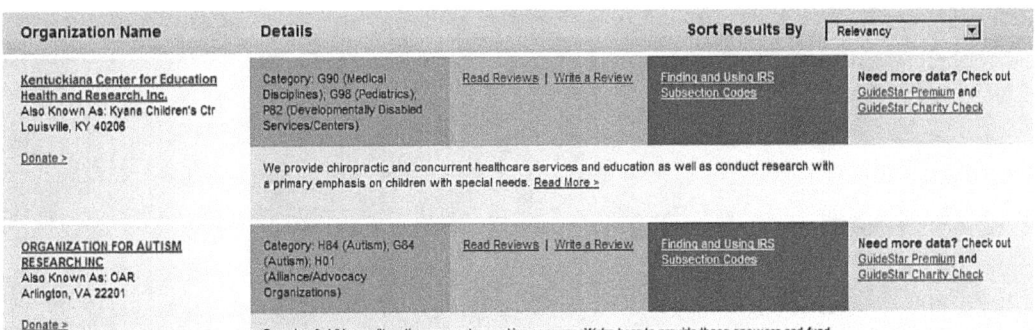

George leverages unique classifications from a pond resource. Here he cross-references the codes in the database that signify 'specialized schools' and 'autism.' By adding these three additional terms to the mix George is sharpening his sights, better qualifying his leads.

Working within the limitations of a single source like GuideStar is especially useful for comparing and contrasting peer organizations. A specialty database like GuideStar may include unique classifications. These take the guesswork out of search terms and even the name-dropping that happens later at the conversing stage when calling on these groups.

On the other hand, ponds offer none of the filters we're used to seeing in ocean-type searches. Also, with the exception of geographic breakouts on top of the results page, there are no facets for groupings these 118 organizations into meaningful categories *(see **Unit Three**, Section 3.2: Source Fluency – Applying the concept of OLP).*

> Category: G90 (Medical Disciplines); G98 (Pediatrics); P82 (Developmentally Disabled Services/Centers)
>
> We provide chiropractic and concur[rent...] a primary emphasis on children with [...]

> Category: H84 (Autism); G84 (Autism); H01 (Alliance/Advocacy Organizations)
>
> Parents of children with autism neve[r...] studies that provide practical informa[tion...]

> Category: B28 (Specialized Education Institutions/Schools for Visually or Hearing Impaired, Learning Disabled); B94 (Parent Teacher Group)

In this case, the last example for provider conjugation is also critical to non-profit success. It can be adopted for private sector lead qualification too. That's the idea of board membership or flipping the question so that we're searching for people in groups (as opposed to groups and their members).

Again, it helps to go to the source and review the required filings for the groups on GuideStar that catch George's interest. But there are risks to playing the role of painstaking researcher:

1. A case-by-case review is time-consuming.

2. Most filings are issued in a read-only format so that each relevant contact is keyed into George's contact management program.

3. The filing may not be up-to-date.

On point three, there is little or no notification capacity in pond sources so that the currency or timing of new filings is left to chance. (As we'll see next in sourcing ponds, RSS feeds enable us to be thorough and up-to-date in our tracking efforts).

A small infusion of semantics in George's query construction gets us back on track for conjugating groups. Semantics help George to register movers and shakers with the boards they serve on. By *small*, we sense that even the greatest of lakes are tiny compared to their ocean counterparts. This means that we don't want to introduce too many requirements in lake-centered search requests. For example, we could base a query formation in Yahoo – traditionally the largest lake directory on the web like this:

> *Autism video "board member" OR boardmember OR "member of * board"*

This construction is too elaborate for most ponds but could be applied to a lake-sized resource like a popular social network site, similarly to what George did in his ocean-based lead qualifications.

The Information Pond: Where the Fish Bite Back

The last goal George outlined in his SPM is the elusive talent for remaining informed without becoming inundated. We can stay on top of fluid events. But we can just as readily identify the distractions that use us, rather than be effective users of our own research findings.

Welcome to the world of RSS that we first explored in **Unit Five**. RSS is a meal type, capable of serving up three squares and all the in-between snacking we can handle. There is no more effective way to prevent drowning in an ocean of search results than setting up a series of news trackers that capture the daily flow of updates to targeted topics through RSS feeds. Instead of viewing them as an endless parade of diversions, they concentrate the mind because they allow us to...

- Perform a search within a search (limit your results to the feeds themselves)
- Prepare our own filters that capture critical details as they unfold

Being informed is more than not being blindsided by the unexpected. It's more than being able to hold up one's end of a chance conversation. Ultimately it means putting RSS to work as a survey tool. The question is:

"What's going on in the market of late?"

The answer is our project goals. In this case the answer is George – specifically what he will do to improve the range and level of services provided to the ASD community *(see **Unit Four**, Section 4.1: Applying Provider Conjugation Frameworks to social media)*.

Information Trapping

Pioneered by the research blogger and author Tara Calishain, information trapping is a method for staying informed without becoming (1) overwhelmed by the web, or (2) corrupted by social and search media providers. Calishain's work is instructive for helping George determine set-up his feeds through (1) some pretty reliable milestones, or (2) event triggers that *trap* the kinds of details that might otherwise be buried in a results list. For instance, one important sign of change involves how, when, and from where special education programs receive their funding. A similar question might be what numbers turn up in surveys and forecasts to quantify the demands for such services. George expresses the business case in an RSS feed in a news collection:

> *"special (needs | education)" (aspergers OR autism) (funding | forecast | demand | budget | trend | market)*

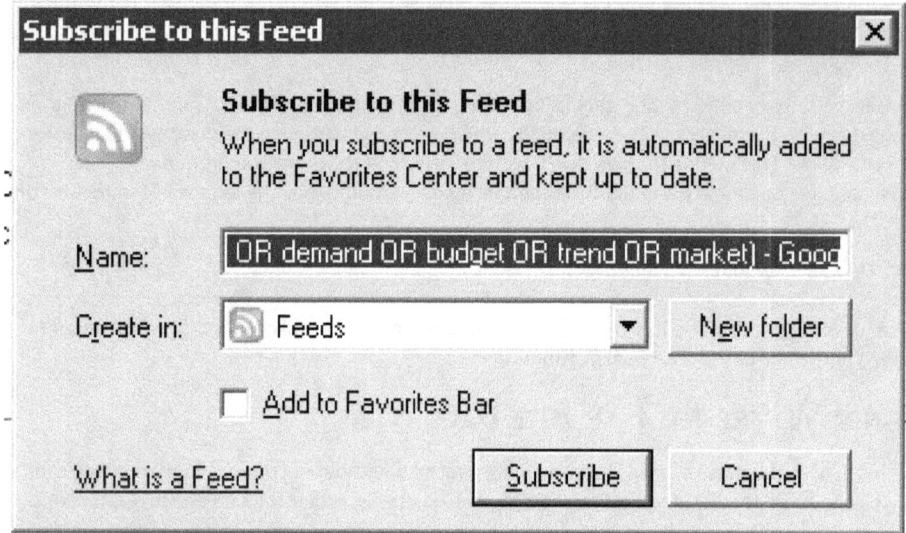

He then creates four additional event triggers:

1. Special events for tracking promotional campaigns, celebrity endorsements and other high profile sponsorships.
2. Transition planning to capture programs designed to help students on the autism spectrum to lead independent and productive lives as adults.
3. Funding to track Grants, Foundations, and Institutes which are active, what kinds of programs they fund, and what kinds of alliances they're forming to sustain their efforts.
4. Autism videos include any documentaries or instructional media used to help students build social skills or train facilitators on specific interventions.

What's going on here?

From Trapping to Acting

George is setting up his filters, as he puts it: *"I catch the fish in the ocean, instead of the ocean in the fish."*

He's referring to the role of each search string in filtering out the failsafes that he'd documented in his ocean and lake-based explorations. These query formations have the double benefit of generating news feeds based on specific changes to the topic, market, and/or community in question. In other words, depending on what net snags them, George already has some idea of the actions taken to route them to the destination in his feed folder. These are the five event triggers.

He can then anticipate his own follow-up efforts once these daily changes hit these profiles:

1. **Pearl Culturing** – Go back to GuideStar to check status of new organizations that turn up in the event triggers.
2. **Deadline Notices** – Apply for grants and other funding announced through feed #4.
3. **Market Reassessment** – Readjust his target niche based on new projections and forecasts fed through feed #1.
4. **Evergreen Folder** – This practice refers to a time-honored tradition of journalists and adopted by bloggers to address topics in the news that hold their relevance longer than the novelty of a more dramatic front page story.
5. **Fallen Trees-in-the-Forest** – This monitoring practice surfaces what's not happening. That's important for proving that critical, shared priorities are not being met (such as the transition planning services tracked in feed #3).

Sourcing RSS Feeds

Of course, not all RSS feeds have to come from information traps set to the news collections of search engines. **Topix.net** was one pre-Reddit example. Smaller lake-based sites package topic-based news feeds that carry the added value of...

- Pre-arranged groupings by their own feeds such as 'autism discussions' and 'autism feeds' below.
- Source stories from providers not picked up by the search news collections.

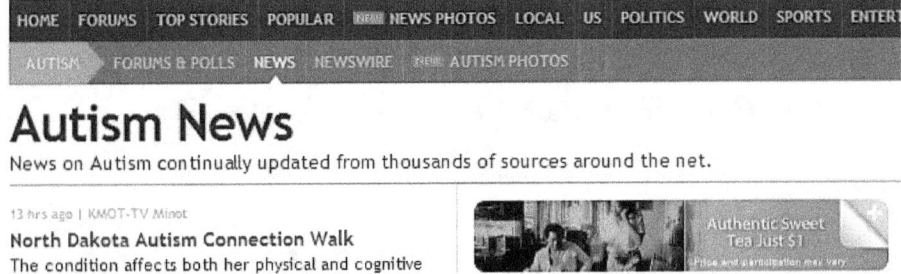

George changes the feed location to a simple title for tracking all related events by topic and saves it to his subject folder – 'Autism.' Topix.net switched to an all-entertainment format beginning in 2015 as Topix.com.

Traditional media sites, like broadcast, newspaper, and print magazines, are another rich source for RSS feeds. Most of them can be subscribed to through RSS. Some may even have specialty feeds that track topics where they provide original coverage: Think of trade and industry developments covered in the business section of the local paper.

The Book on Feed Readers

Once the feeds are created, they need to be acted on. The best way to do this is through a dedicated feed reader that lives as a separate application on the desktop and updates whenever we hit the refresh key. Why is separate better? Two reasons:

1. **Cognitive** – When it comes to remaining on task the web is a trap door. Maybe it's a set of revolving trap doors when we're multi-tasking through so many sites. The more divided our attentions, the more challenging it is to focus and prioritize.

2. **Functionality** – Web browsers were built as viewers, not as data-handling or analytical devices. They were designed as windows on the web, not as tools for assessing the information that pulses through it. A capable feed reader functions as both a measurement tool and a micro lens for uncovering the details we lose in our browsers and the limitations of HTML.

Where does this leave George? Instead of reviewing each feed in his browser George downloads a dedicated feed reader with the advanced search filtering he required for his information trapping efforts. First, he subscribed to the RSS feed (event trigger).

We can see this through the interface of a free RSS reader called **Feed Demon**, below.[4]

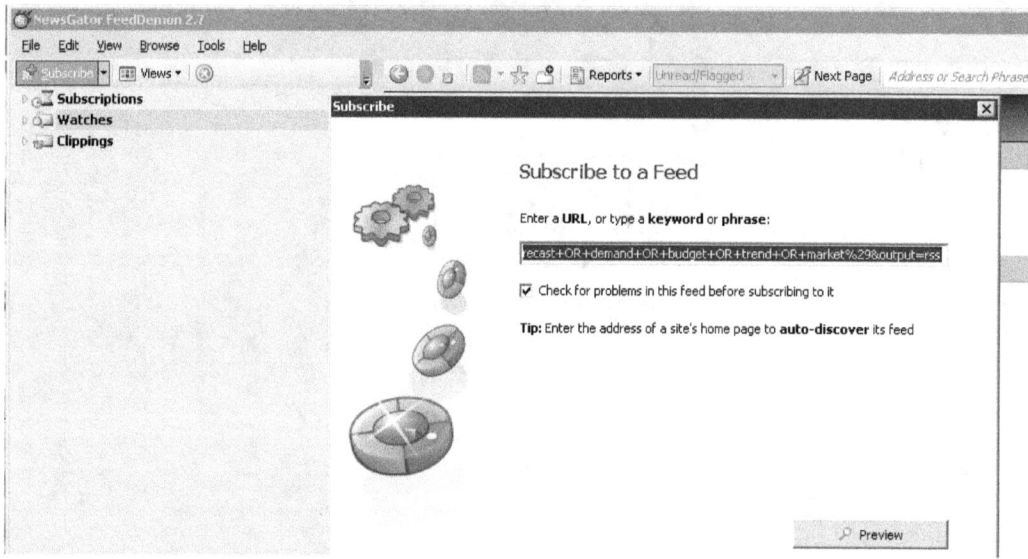

The feed is automatically saved to the RSS reader.

Next, he labels the feed by the type of events he's tracking. Remember his five event triggers? He stores all five in a folder dedicated to his targeted market:

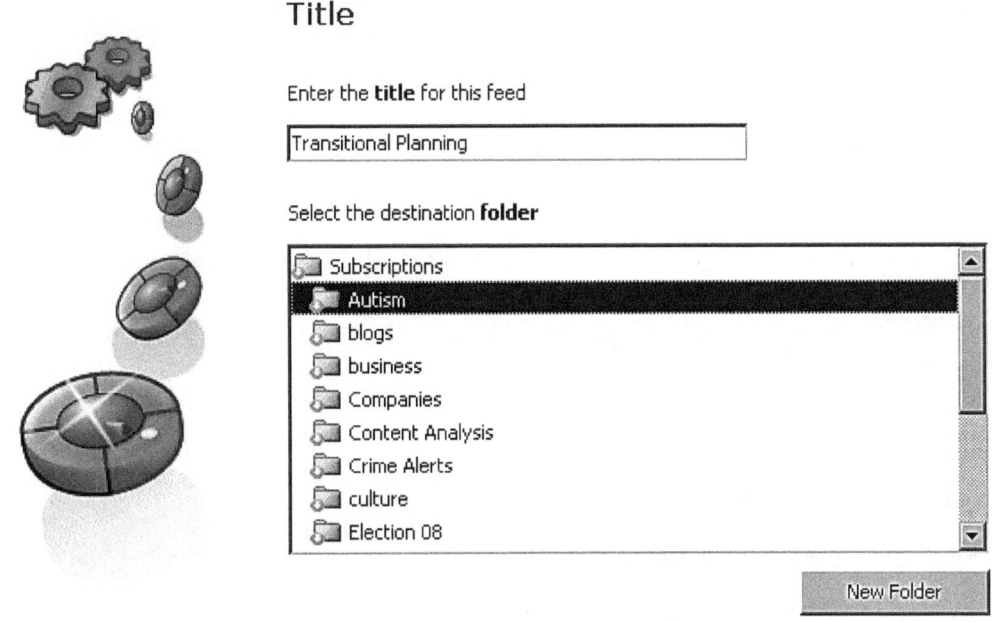

He titles each feed and saves them to his home folder on all market developments specific to Autism.

Here's what the Autism folder looks like once he opens it. The counts refer to number of unread feeds in each event trigger or subscription:

The counts next to each event trigger indicate the number of new articles that match each trigger.

FEED READER FUNCTIONS AND BENEFITS

We talked a little about the added functionality of feed readers. What exactly do they add that web browsers can't? Here are three. In addition to RSS subscriptions and news-trackers, readers can slice and dice search results like the razor-sharp Cuisinart. We'll explore further through local search, watch lists, and clip folders.

Local Search

Local search is very much what we mean by getting from oceans to ponds. Instead of contending with billions of web pages, we're looking at several thousand or fewer news feeds. They're showing up in our readers because they're pre-qualified to be there. Conducting a search within a feed reader has the added sway of confirming what's in our guts. It green lights us to go ahead: Make those connections and contacts we were mulling over, but hesitated without some kind of independent research or validation.

Once his event triggers are in place, George can add refinements to the information traps that he's set. First, George performs a search within a search. The RSS equivalent of getting from an ocean to a pond.

In the following local search results, we see seven news feeds with an important keyword: Language. 'Language' is not present in any of the event triggers set by George. On the left side, George is telling the reader to search his Autism folder exclusively for any mentions of his keyword. On the right, we see both the context and the event trigger from which the matches occur:

UNIT SIX: The Knowledge-ABLED Cookbook | Page 6:42

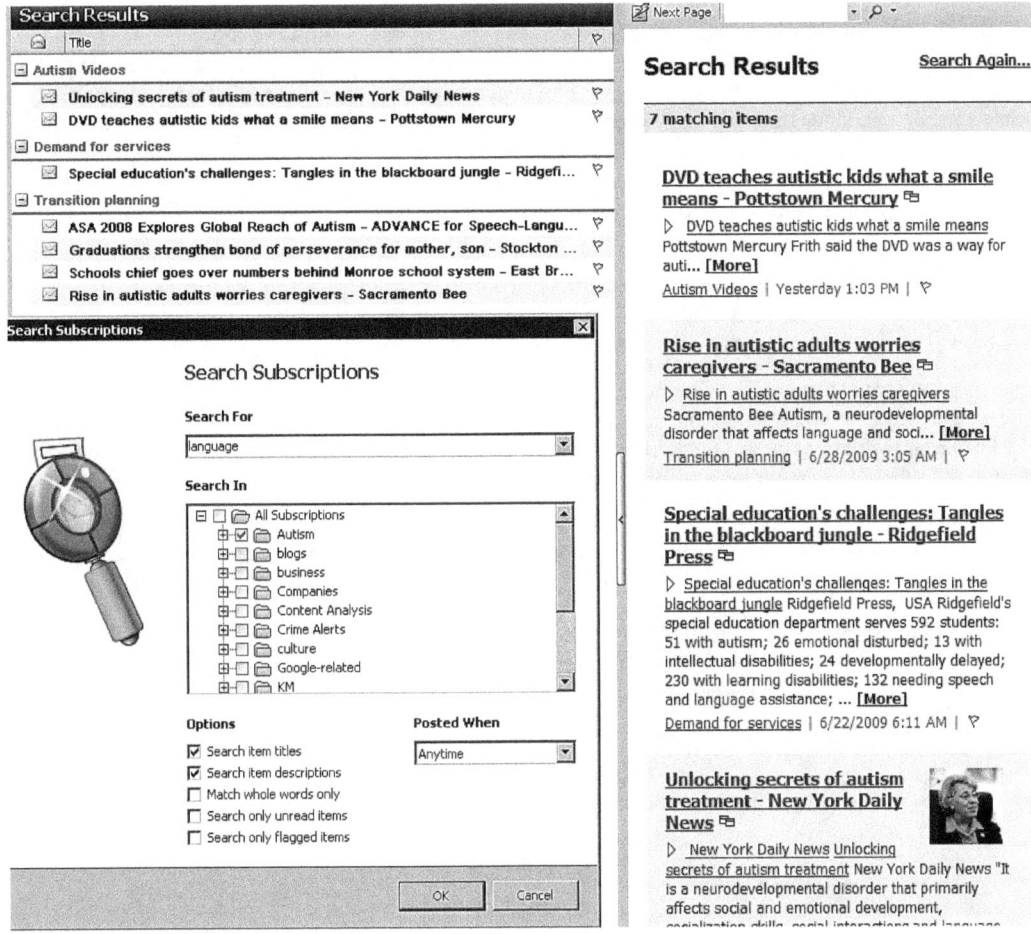

All instances of the term 'language' appear in feeds that collect in Autism event triggers only. This is an example of 'searching within a search.'

Searching Out Loud: Giving Voice to Independent Investigations | Marc Solomon

Selective use of local search spells the difference between sinking in a black hole of information and spotting some golden opportunities inside the very same onslaught of news and events. The opportunities lie not in *what* George has access to, but *how* he does the accessing. The proof is in the confidence it gives him to approach the very same newsmakers with some news of his own: Mainly the unmet needs that fall into George's information traps, and his ability to meet those demands.

Watch Lists

Finally, George sets up a Watch List in anticipation of the critical and timely details that he'll need to track as his project unfolds.

Watch lists are our fishing nets in our information ponds. We set the bait with a series of key terms that match the results being reeled in by the news feeds. The Watch List only looks at the phrases that feed into the subject folder, ensuring that each story addresses both autism and the groups George is targeting.

As with local searches, it's important to remember whether our pond is restricted to one folder or includes all the feeds in our readers. Because we may have set-up other folders for other projects, we need to tune them to the correct requirements. In other words, we'll fill our nets with hundreds of unfiltered articles if we create a watch list with a single unspecified term like 'learning' or 'education.' Why? These feeds won't contain our *must-have* keywords like 'autism' or 'video.'

Watch Lists are good for bringing in the *prized catch* or to trawl entire schools of fish. Basically, they can be used as micro filters for tracking specific groups and individuals. But they're also invitations to create a range of outcomes, without becoming trapped or fixated on specific targets.

Below, we see where George will build his list of organizations. Their names are unique enough to exact match the group George is tracking. We evidence this by the six common keywords below:

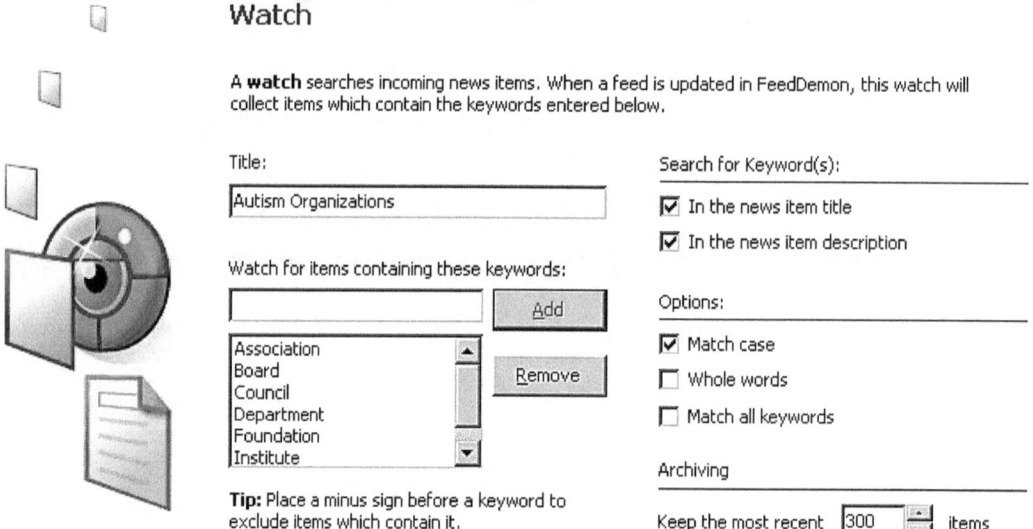

Note that none of his keyword phrases includes a specific organization. This is a sound demonstration of the law of unintended targets (see Unit Four, Section 4.1, Provider Conjugation).

As we notice straight away, there's no shortage of groups landing on George's group radar. More importantly, George knew nothing of these groups prior to setting up the Watch List. Because he was careful to stay on topic, George is able to use a more open-ended approach for mining new prospects:

The Watch List snags 22 new articles. George finds most of them worth a read-through:

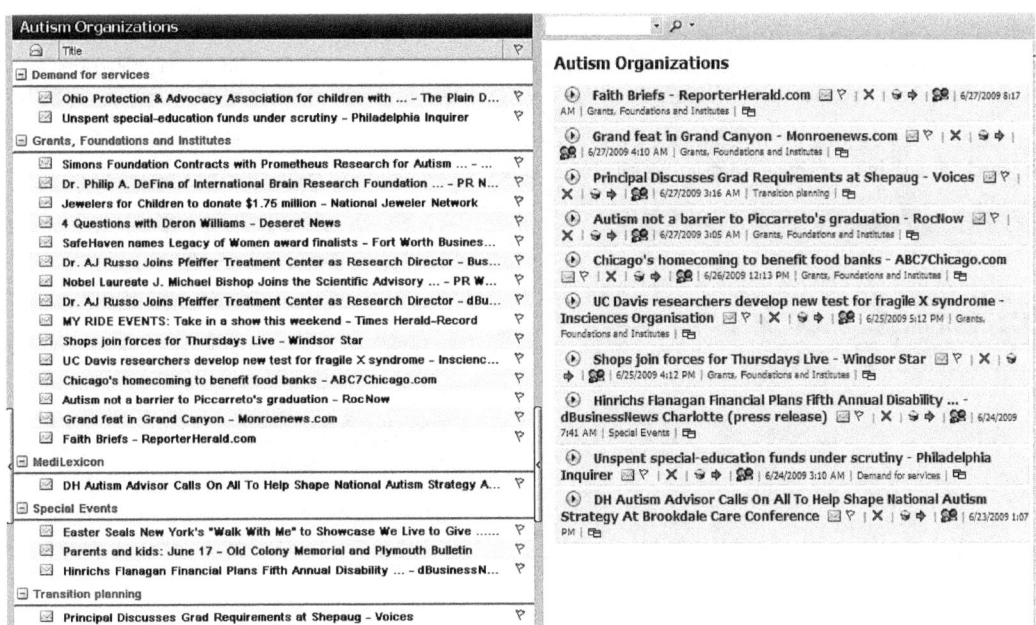

Watch List results are saved to the specific event triggers that George saves to his Autism folder – representing his target community.

This is the process of letting a search *breathe*. It means applying a partial filter that keeps focus on our questions, but allows for people and groups unknown to us to complete our puzzles. For instance, each event trigger is an empty bucket before the news feed is activated. Now we see those buckets beginning to fill with organizations we barely know. But we're drawn to their work. The feeling may yet prove mutual.

"This is a smart, noninvasive way to know what's going on in my target community," says George:

> "Not only does it keep me on task and time-effective but it pulls in people and groups I'd otherwise never known about. And me to them for that matter."

Each feed is triggered through a unique combination of keywords and wildcards. By using an RSS Reader, the details find George automatically. Trapping means *finders keepers* in the search world. Using the Watch List, those countless results pages disappear as well.

Clip Folders

Fewer searches and better search results are hard to argue with. But what about the stuff you want to hold onto? After all, news feeds like any feed stocks have a shelf life. This ain't the National Archives. They don't remain forever, like the files on some decommissioned server in the bowels of the back office. That's where Clip Folders can help. They don't expire. Try to find a feed reader that allows you to file away specific web pages for safe-keeping. Here's how George puts clip folder to work:

1. If he gets an idea or draws on a connection from something he's read, he can reference it for future discussions.

2. If an upstart organization like George's proposes a value proposition or new business model, he can capture these go-to-market strategies as clip folders, and then revisit these ventures as they develop.

3. If an important degree program or academic credential emerges from his education research, he can perform a local search, and then drag those items into a clip folder. *See the example from ABA below):*

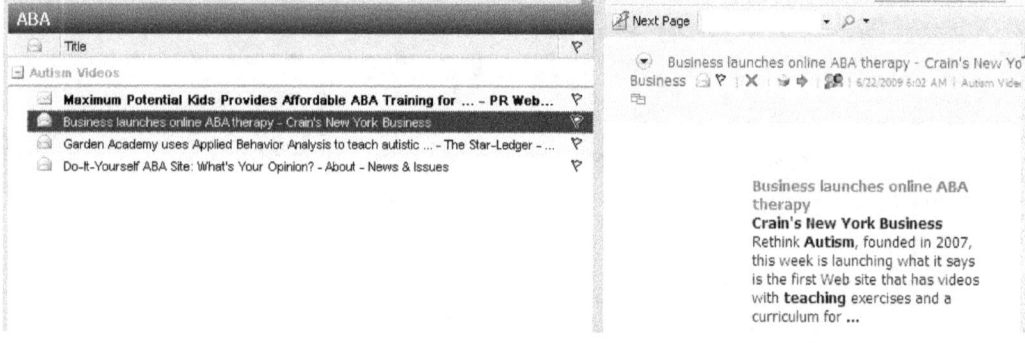

Business launches online ABA therapy

Access to trained providers is a constant worry of parents of autistic children. One intervention method, Applied Behavior Analysis, can cost as much as $70,000 to $100,000 per year for the prescribed 25 to 40 hours per week of therapy. Insurance coverage for the treatment is limited.

A Manhattan company sees a business niche that capitalizes on the high cost and limited availability of ABA treatment, fueled by the growing number of families affected by autism. Rethink Autism, founded in 2007, this week is launching what it says is the first Web site that has videos with teaching exercises and a curriculum for autism treatment. Parents can access treatment online for their children, with videos that teach academic, social, emotional, language, motor, play and daily-living skills. The company recently hired Jamie Pagliaro, former executive director of the NYC Charter School of Autism, as its business development executive.

Rethink Autism filmed the videos in its own Manhattan production studio, asking parents to volunteer as subjects in exchange for free services from therapists who conducted the exercises. Hundreds of video-based lessons and assessment tools will be uploaded. The site will also offer scheduling, data tracking, progress reporting and access to e-mail support from trained therapists at the company. Parents can access the site for $125 a month—roughly the cost of one hour of therapy by a professional ABA consultant.

Rethink Autism expects thousands families to use the program in the first year. "In addition, based on interest to date, we expect hundreds of organizations [school districts, social service agencies, early intervention centers, etc.] to be using our product as well," says a spokesman for Rethink Autism.

The Web site is www.rethinkautism.com.

Here is an example of the kind of innovation George hopes to capture for his own set of interactive video services. Those services will be marketed to both educators and directly to the larger autism population. *Note that this clip includes a value proposition (a specific dollar value) based on the cost reduction of the new delivery method for the ABA therapy.*

SECTION 6.4: The Engagement –
Searching for Conversing

In the last section, we pressed our search pedal to the metal. In Part Three of this case study, the rubber meets the road. And this is one pathway George needs to travel down with his roadmap and without his gadgets. Yes, it's show time. It's time to logoff, and start engaging people, and not machines.

George has his fact base in order. He's ready to make networking overtures. He's primed for attracting potential partners, investors, and customers. That reservoir of event triggers starts to fill. George is able to see connections and ultimately make them. His new contacts come to rely on his perspective: How the latest news impacts the many overlapping players he's identified. All have their own skin in the same game. The name of the game is this: Teaching extraordinary kids the practical business of getting along in a world they find alien and stressful.

His new contacts begin to see him as a player but not a threat. They see him as a member of an extended community that they have an equal stake in. Most importantly, they see how their association with George can help their own goals.

Of course none of these sources, tools, and methods for applying them count for very much if they don't help build the networks, get the interviews, or position George for the major career transition he's undertaking. That doesn't happen in the research. It happens in the outreach. So how do we get from preparing, collecting, analyzing, and synthesizing to the actual conversation with the folks and groups we've been researching?

As we saw in **Unit Five,** these pointers are key for any entrepreneur looking to market their services in new and unfamiliar niches. Our roadmap there are the same frameworks that brought us this far:

> 1. The site selection methods first introduced in **Unit Three,** and
>
> 2. The same provider conjugation framework we began using in **Unit Four.**

It's all about evaluating the interests and networks of information providers. The difference now is that George is no longer the outsider. In Part Three of **Unit Six,** George *has become* that provider *(see **Unit 4**, Section 4.3 – Search to Converse).*

LETTING THE MARKET SPEAK FOR ITSELF

Finally, George leans on his Knowledge-ABILITIES, confronting his ultimate research goal: Making the case for his services to the market he's trying to track. How can George convince the ASD community that advocating for the educational needs and social skills and his own business goals are one in the same?

He can't. But it's nothing personal. As we saw from introducing provider conjugation in **Unit Four**, the best delivery method is a credible messenger, and we can't confer credibility on ourselves. But that doesn't mean he can't petition on his own behalf.

He needs to drive home his own unique value proposition when he's going up against other media producers and educational consultants. He needs to reinforce this with would-be customers that may be convinced they could perform the same job in-house.

What Reis can do is show how few of the needs he's addressing are currently being fulfilled in the news blurbs that cross his radar screen (RSS reader). Those core offerings become key advantages when they're expressed by the community through word-of-mouth – not the service provider through advertising and paid promotions.

Feed readers also afford an enhanced perspective that's too often missing in a rapidly-paced and competitive world of broadcast media. In the 24/7 news cycle, being the first to know takes priority over having the time to reflect and assess the bigger picture. Feed readers not only cut down on the distractions and the ads, but let us dwell on news and events that impact us directly.

Here's how those advantages play out when we're attentive to a market that speaks for itself:

> 1. We saw George use his reader as a kind of microscope for uncovering players, events, and trends that served to confirm his own hunches and ground his optimism in supportable facts and numbers.

Searching Out Loud: Giving Voice to Independent Investigations | Marc Solomon

2. We saw how George learns about private training firms that are marketing affordable ABA ("Applied Behavior Analysis") training to staff, teachers, therapists, and caregivers from school districts to family clinics.

3. We even saw how RSS readers are open windows into how providers price their services. How his prospects bill clues him in on their cash flows and funding models. It tips him off on what the other providers are charging, so he can price his own offerings competitively. (Hint: pricing is a great way to differentiate any offering and it doesn't mean having to work pro bono again!)

From Catch-of-the-Day to All-You-Can-Eat

Fishing in a pond helped to move George from finding marketing leads to business prospects. The next step is a qualified prospect where the conversation goes from one to two-way – an active dialog with potential customers about specific business opportunities uncovered in the research.

George can speak with greater authority about these opportunities because of his ability to better define markets and listen to them. He's positioned to connect his services to the realities his prospects are facing. He has a much sharper understanding...

- Who are his best prospects based on his site visitors, and the feedback he gets on his blog posts and newsletters?
- What appeals to them such as their business goals, project priorities, shared contacts, and experiences?
- Their major pain points and anxieties such as the loss of a large donor, cutbacks in state-funded programs, or a program alternative more competitive than their own.

George seeds his requests for follow-up discussions with the invitation to review his prospects' aspirations and their concerns. He proposes to lead with the current state of the prospect, and their perceived place within the autism community. Within the present situation, he reminds them how his offering will help them.

It's not because of a startling new invention. It's not even because he can crank out cheaper, faster, better widgets. It's because his pitch is all about his prospective customers. His offering will solidify their reputations as responsive and forward-looking leaders of a growing and resource-hungry market. This market extends from practitioners, to caregivers, and to receivers from all age groups across the autism spectrum. George sees the opportunity. And so do they.

He seals the pitch with...

- Third party market research that forecasts and validates the need for (1) both the prospect's core mission, and (2) George's own monitoring efforts.
- Second parties that would vouch for the quality, value, and innovation he delivers as a service provider.

He confirms an exploding interest in interactive education as a prime enabler for serving the new market requirements, revealed through each of the event triggers George used for stocking his RSS pond.

Listening to Markets

Part of developing a keen market sense is listening for what people are asking for – especially when those requests fall on deaf ears. George returns to the Google keyword tool to better understand what his targeted market niche is demanding. Three core target terms of 'Aspergers', 'autism', and 'training' are organized below by popularity. But note how steeply the counts drop when two or more terms are combined:

Figure 6.18: Diminishing Search Returns

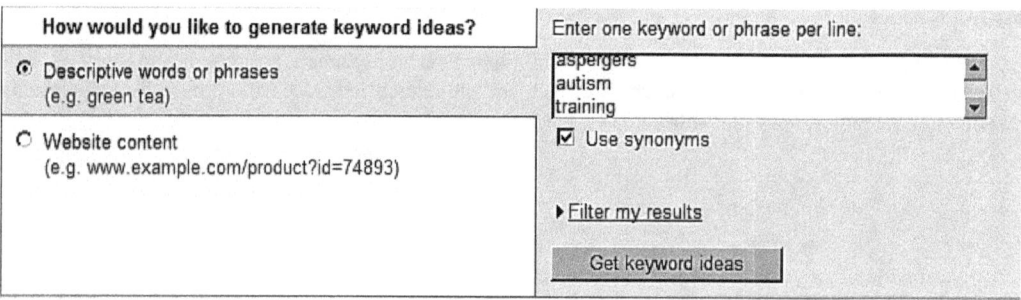

The steady decline between simple terms and phrases is on vivid display here – a demonstration of the law of diminishing search returns.

When George tests 'training' as a keyword, he sees that many of the most popular searches are completely irrelevant to his community. In SPM terms, these terms are failsafes. Their only useful purpose is to avoid repeating them. He picks up the distracting terms in the broad match results that Google applies. He then filters out terms like customer, 'HR,' 'IT,' 'dyslexia,' 'deaf,' 'dog,' and 'corporate.' He filters out additional noise words pulled in by his three core keywords of 'training,' 'autism,' and 'Asperger's.' The superfluous keywords are *negative* match types:

Figure 6.19: Working with Stop Words

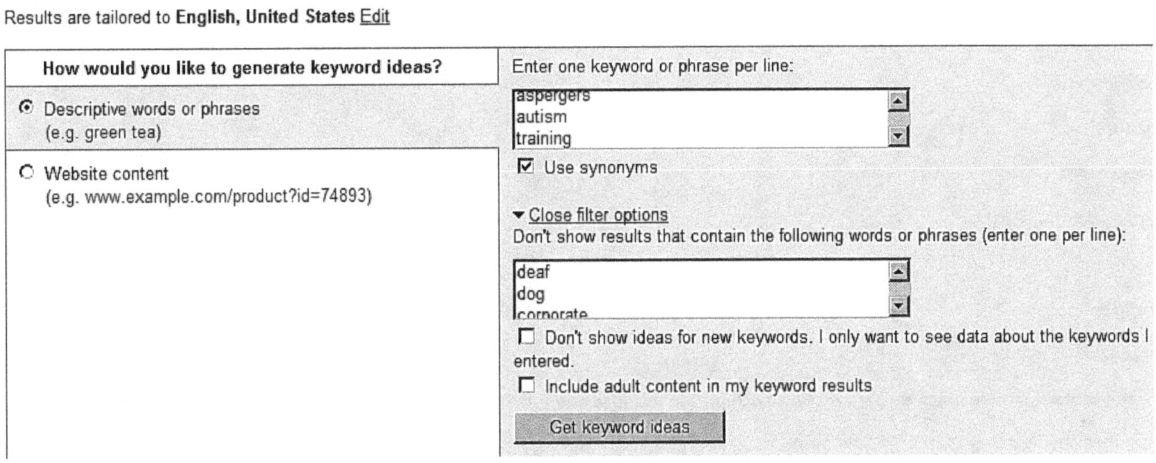

These are the false hits or stop words that George can eliminate from keyword consideration as he refines his keyword sets.

Next, he focuses on exact matches and suggested pattern matching types. These terms indicate what specific services are being requested, and ways of requesting them not evident in the keywords George was applying. For example, broad matches include autism therapy, language training, and interactive learning. Each combination includes a description of the market and a means to servicing it.

They also include signs, causes, and symptoms of autism, suggesting a strong need for diagnostic guidelines and testing:

"autism symptoms"

"signs of autism"

"language training"

"training development"

"interactive learning"

"communication training"

George also reviews suggested keywords that were not part of his original keyword analysis. He finds a strong undercurrent of 'self-help' where practitioners are looking for continuing education credentials or parents are looking for a more direct role in their kids' ASD interventions.

Figure 6.20: Term Expansion for your Watch List

"school"

"development"

"courses"

"certification"

"parents"

"assessment"

"apprentice"

"coaching"

"seminar"

"Trainers"

Note the term expansion going on here — how each phrase includes one term that George specifies and a second that he hasn't.

To explore this, George performs the same local search capabilities we saw earlier. His list of keywords is taken from the same term expansion method he used earlier to shift gears, from fundraising videos to autism training and interactive tools. In each case, the market had spoken. In each one, a call for the kind of support that George is poised to provide.

Interestingly, his new 'Market Speaks' Watch List is quiet on the subject of the most prevalent keywords assessed by Google.

Why is that?

Is it confirmation of an unmet market need? Is the pond too small to be catching multi-term queries? Could a half billion Google users be wrong? It's probably a mix of being ahead of the curve, but also a useful example of the law of diminishing returns – how the number of results thins dramatically when we move from two to three or more terms per Watch List profile.

It's true that none of the stories trapped by the RSS feeds includes any of the keyword matches provided or suggested by the Google keyword tool. It's equally true that the Autism Folder in George's feed reader only has several hundred news feeds. In search terms, that's more like an *information puddle* than a pond. A Watch List that runs empty for a week or more means dialing back on the specificity. That means refraining from the use of phrases. It means querying one keyword at a time.

Figure 6.21: Letting Stemming Run its Course

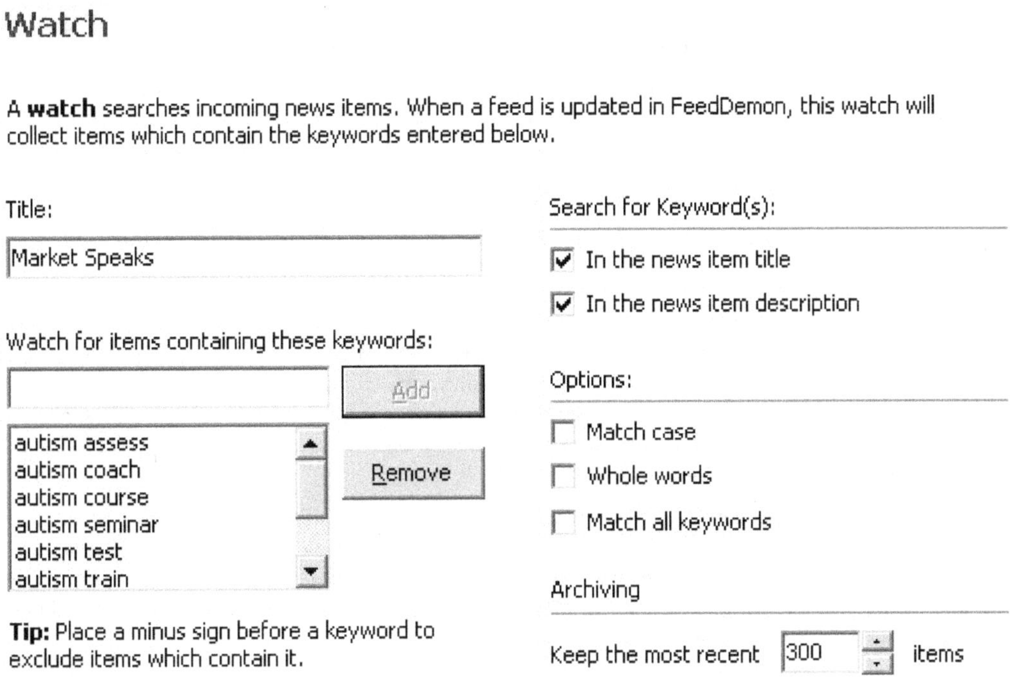

Watch

A **watch** searches incoming news items. When a feed is updated in FeedDemon, this watch will collect items which contain the keywords entered below.

Title: Market Speaks

Watch for items containing these keywords:
- autism assess
- autism coach
- autism course
- autism seminar
- autism test
- autism train

Tip: Place a minus sign before a keyword to exclude items which contain it.

Search for Keyword(s):
- ☑ In the news item title
- ☑ In the news item description

Options:
- ☐ Match case
- ☐ Whole words
- ☐ Match all keywords

Archiving: Keep the most recent 300 items

Note how none of the option boxes are checked, allowing for full stemming of each keyword.

What does this tell us about fishing in ponds? As we experienced in applying ocean-based queries in smaller collections, we were much too specific for the size of the database we were searching. The smaller the database, the less picky we can afford to be.

How Site Selection Opens the Door to New Business

We need to review where he enters the picture before we see where George stands in the eyes of those he's approaching: How he's ready to insert himself into the same conversation he first overheard online. He's no longer the novice, but an authority in the niche of his choosing. His Knowledge-ABILITIES make him the *go to* guy for his specialty. That sweet spot where market forces (think event triggers) conspire to raise his profile not as another vendor, but an expert in his space. Certainly, blogging is one way to elevate our profiles as authorities in our fields of choice. We'll begin to see how George establishes this as a second party information provider.

Fishing in oceans, lakes, and ponds does not guarantee George will land *the big one*. But it does expand, accelerate, and sharpen his efforts to get those first *tugs on the line*.

How did OLP move George from finding marketing leads to business prospects?

Oceans

George Reis used ocean searches to establish some key market demands in terms of keywords and phrases. The ocean was where he narrowed down his general interest in nonprofits to a core niche to focus on. He used the broader word patterns as a term expansion tool for setting the information traps (event triggers) in his RSS reader.

Most importantly, he used the enhanced search capabilities of oceans to search inside the lake-sized social networks that turned up important leads of potential allies and customers.

As a researcher, Reis understood the way commercial search engines work. He used their vast indexes to be picky about the quality and purpose of the information providers his searches produce. As a marketer, George built his networks with the same tools he used to build-up his understanding of this new niche. He seeded his queries not with random keywords, but with the right mix of syntax, semantics and site selection methods. Instead of being on the receiving end of pay-per-click web ads, George served his own marketing requirements, mining the right sites to find qualified leads, and the prospect of future meetings.

Lakes

Portals and social networks helped George in his market research. Wikipedia gave him some working definitions. These terms helped him to understand the different kinds of diagnoses across the autism spectrum, as well as the most common forms of intervention. Specialized directories like **GuideStar** documented the mission, staffing, and financial footing of thousands of nonprofits that serve the autism community. In a lake, sources can be vetted. Groups are classified. Categories are defined. Comparisons can be made. Lakes can do this. Oceans and ponds cannot.

Oceans can't because they're too deep and prone to incorrect word matches. Ponds are one-trick ponies. They're great for nailing down a fact, or confirming a result. But they're too shallow to contain any context or assumptions made by third parties. An astute researcher can draw their own conclusions based on what they see. But that's the first-hand interpretation of an analyst, not a search result from inside a database. Lakes on the other hand, are expansive enough to hold meaningful comparisons but restrictive enough to prevent tangential or off-topic associations.

Because of his ability to better define markets and listen to them, George spoke with greater authority about these opportunities, and is positioned to connect his services to realities his prospects are facing.

Ponds

Ponds were the final step prior to his campaign launch. Ponds are where George began filling in the missing blanks from his ocean and lake-sized efforts. How many of these organizations were not only listed but really out there – active in the community, and sensitive to getting their name out? Where were the intersecting interests between the different stakeholders?

This kind of awareness can only happen in a pond setting. The background noise is filtered away. As we saw with the event triggers, a pond is where the narrative unfolds for emerging trends. It gives George a depth and clarity that sets him apart from a *sales guy,* who knows how to drop names, but not build a trusted relationship.

George used lakes to group the top players and segment the market. He used ponds to connect the dots between motivated groups and the influencers that that lead them. He now has a list of qualified prospects. The conversation is poised to go from one to two-way: An active dialog with potential customers about specific business opportunities, uncovered in his Knowledge-ABLED efforts.

Now George can tell...

- Who are his best prospects and how to approach them – doctors, therapists, academics, researchers, etc? They each have their own professional standards, expertise, and biases (many of them having family members with autism!)
- What appeals to them within the current state of their financial resources, project priorities, shared contacts, and experiences.
- Where they feel their pain points and anxieties such as the loss of a large donor, cutbacks in state-funded programs, or a program alternative more competitive than their own.

PROVIDER CONJUGATION FRAMEWORKS

Finally, it's time to plug the personal and group dynamics back into the equation. Just who will George approach and how will he engage? As the following PCF tables suggest, the connection between background research and foreground discussions is not limited by source access, chance meetings, or conference schedules. It depends mainly on our willingness to try and apply Knowledge-ABLED tools and methods.

First Person

As discussed in **Unit Four**, first person conjugations are the most intimate and informal of any communications channel on or off the web. They are authentic and expedient. Think of diaries. It's rare to find a team of lawyers and fact-checkers filtering a self-referential document, unless it's a last will and testament. Also, because only *writers* are pulling the strings, we are the trusted readers – their confidants. This gives us sway to both flatter them and cite other views beyond their personal awareness or professional boundaries.

George plays the first person card in the blogosphere. Posting feedback on their sites flatters them with outsider attention, and strengthens his connection to the medical research community – an important influencer group on the hospitals and labs he's targeting. He also decides through his tracking efforts that one target is too big. The nonprofit group **Autism Speaks** is head and shoulders above any other organization. It is too big a fish based on George's modest starting position. Instead, he focuses on upstarts, insurgents, and contrarians looking to contrast themselves with the big fish. Most importantly, he doesn't beat his head against the wall trying to infiltrate an entrenched incumbent.

Figure 6.22: First Person Singular Provider Conjugation

Degree of separation	Sender and Receiver	Actions	Outcomes
1st person	George in the blogosphere	George finds stakeholders that tend to blog about their own innovations and breakthroughs, e.g. scientists that discuss their lab work ahead of their findings He avoids both obscure and elite bloggers who are either lacking bandwidth (overcommitted) or influence (under recognized)	He becomes a resource to the same community he's trying to join He posts responses to key influencers that prompt dialog and budding alliances He builds community presence with a community support blog and offers password-only access to RSS-generated research for qualified prospects

Second Person

The second person is our confidant. Free of all professional duties and institutional boundaries, their only loyalties as message receivers are to the first parties they're engaging. The second person is also the home of WOM ("word of mouth"). WOM is the most praiseworthy endorsement a first party organization can command because of its authenticity.

As a marketer, George needs to play this one carefully. He can't talk up his own accomplishments and expect his legend to spread. He can hear things through the grapevine. He can be on the receiving end of what his network delivers, in terms of new contacts and opportunities. He needs to enter from a credible position for any doors to open. One potential *in*: The track record he's already established as a commercial video producer.

Figure 6.23: Second Person Singular Provider Conjugation

Degree of separation	Sender and Receiver	Actions	Outcomes
2nd person	George and his network	George uses his own social network to see who's most tied into target niche based on indirect participation – as a former employee, member, or stakeholder of a group in the niche George is targeting	George cross-references contacts who have worked both in his core industry (video production) as well as in his targeted niche (nonprofit groups in health care research)

Third Person

The third person is the friend of a friend. When something happens to a third person, we know whatever that is can happen to us too – whether the odds are remote (winning the lottery), or inevitable (losing a loved one). Third persons are not third parties: The traditional definition for groups with no vested interest in the markets and companies they assess. Instead, third persons are our neighbors down the street that we may know of, but are not personally-acquainted.

Remember the candor of strangers in the last unit? Well, those are third persons. They're observers with no particular agenda in mind or goal to reach. Because of their detachment, they are highly credible but not authentic due to the same factor: Their lack of direct involvement. George tries out some common icebreakers with his efforts to name-drop, and focus on the personal nature of a shared community. Especially the common goals and frustrations of people on the autism spectrum.

Figure 6.24: Third Person Singular Provider Conjugation

Degree of separation	Sender and Receiver	Actions	Outcomes
3rd person	George and his extended network	The friend of a friend circuit reveals the personal side of professionals belonging to ASD affinity groups or discussion boards. How so? They are the parents, relations, and/or are themselves diagnosable on the autism spectrum	This unifying bond breaks down the resistance that would normally prevent an outsider from infiltrating a tight-knit and somewhat guarded community of peers

First Party

First parties are the meeting channel. First parties are where we seek communion, consensus and commiseration with our fellow and sister group members. But it's also where individuals temper their own desires and principles for the common aims and priorities of the greater organization. Our memberships bind us to behaviors and loyalties that test our ideals, and sometimes compromise our principals. First parties also deliver professional recognition from the...

- Titles we hold, and
- Companies we represent, to the...
    - Roles that we play,
    - Rules we observe, and
    - Codes and doctrines we pledge to uphold.

First parties cast George in the role of the outsider. His goal is to crack organizational codes. That doesn't mean hacking through the corporate firewall, dumpster diving for shredded documents, or eavesdropping on closed door meetings. It means...

- Understanding the standards that govern how the group operates,
- The results its leadership expects, and
- Particularly how the organization sees itself relative to stakeholders (shareholders, customers, rivals, etc.)

It's especially helpful for understanding how the group wields authority when venturing outside its own circle. For instance, many of George's corporate clients were engineers by training. They had little charisma or marketing smarts. But George always marveled at how they could gain the trust of their clients without representing themselves well. Their work did the communicating, serving the higher truth of immutable laws that determine sound principles of design and construction. As George learned, deep trust in a role can be a substitute for personal experience on an individual level.

This lesson was not lost on George as he began targeting the health sector. His prior work helped him to understand how profession-based sales targets like doctors and therapists bridle at the very idea they are a market. Why? It undercuts their patients' trust, and casts doubt on the professional standards they've pledged to uphold.

Figure 6.25: First Party Plural Provider Conjugation

Degree of separation	Sender and Receiver	Actions	Outcomes
1st party	His search target and their qualification	George uses search syntax to identify databases of public records containing the contact details of executive directors at nonprofits in his target market and territory He focuses on sites dedicated to promoting philanthropic giving by documenting the track record of charitable institutions. (Operations of groups in this sector are more open because their work is regulated as a 501c3 corporation and must file a 990 form with the IRS to maintain its tax exempt status)	He transfers those records to his contact management program along with giving histories and group members he's now connected to through social networks He bases his call list of prospects on growth organizations looking to surge further in local region with shared missions and goals for communicating them He's sensitive to the various protocols and codes that physicians and therapists use in care-giving and advocating in their patients' interests

Second Party

Second parties are group-based intermediaries. If this sounds academic or abstract, let's shorten it to its popular nickname – *the media*. Second parties confer status to first parties. They set the bragging rights, pecking orders and industry perspectives, i.e. who's ahead? Second parties are not just about microphones and press credentials. This channel also includes an extended community of business partners, shareholders, regulators, customers, and rivals. All have one stake in your organization's success, and at least two stakes in their own.

Second parties are where George can open first party doors by playing the second party media card. As an outside reporter, he can lavish attention on the leaders and innovators that inspire the groups he's targeting. In return, he can wrap that message around the reputations of the folks he interviews. Another second party benefit is the schmooze factor. That means welcoming professional journalists to the fold. Unlike his interview subjects, networking with trade reporters means going *off record* to gain a more personal or authentic view than the official record provides.

This helps George break through the veneer of group politics and talk with reporters as people who share a community stake in the same community.

Figure 6.26: Second Party Plural Provider Conjugation

Degree of separation	Sender and Receiver	Actions	Outcomes
2nd party	His search target and their motivations	George creates a customized search engine that tracks specialty media for success stories, industry trends, and case studies for modeling innovative deal-making between nonprofits and video production services	The search tool highlights the work of trade editors and communications professionals that George can approach for story ideas and business referrals. It also yields an evergreen file of topics worth covering on his blog

Third Party

When a first party communicates through a second party, typically it's to reach the third party. Why? They want to win more votes, sell more products, or simply to gain greater advantage, with or without the participation of the larger society.

Third parties are the faces in the crowd who cast their votes, respond to surveys, and don't get hung up on their fifteen minutes of fame. Instead, they have fifteen minutes per day that they use to read or hear about the fame of celebrities they follow. Third parties are the audience that assembles to hear speeches, follow celebrated Twitter accounts, and consume the latest fashions.

The media keep their finger on the pulse of third parties to determine social trends and cultural dimensions of what's falling in and out of favor. With the advent of social media, this kind of trend-watching is becoming more widespread, and applied to smaller, discrete groups. Rather than income, race, or age, all one needs are the collective histories that enjoin us in our social networks.

What kind of history? Any obsession will do. Especially a common interest that clarifies and isolates the priorities of a single issue, shared interest, or common threat.

The more active version of third parties involves observers who deliberately keep their professional distance from the first parties they assess. Research organizations, rating agencies, and government agencies, for example, are third parties. Their influence is determined by how credibly they maintain their independence from the leaders and organizations they evaluate. The moment that distance is impugned by a conflict of interest, they lose their independence as well as their authority.

George is mindful that he can't rig the deck. He can no more speak for third parties as he can effectively arbitrate on brokering the best programs, most influential networks, or visionary leaders. What he can do is stay out in front of the pack,

with a comprehensive, exhaustive, and credible radar screen called an RSS reader. His event triggers, watch lists, and clip folders help connect the dots. Now George can piece together first parties. His Knowledge-ABILITIES reveal how his prospects' efforts are being communicated by second parties, and ultimately received by the third-party communities they are trying to mobilize and serve.

Figure 6.27: Third Party Plural Provider Conjugation

Degree of separation	Sender and Receiver	Actions	Outcomes
3rd party	His search target and their reputation	George uses an RSS reader to filter new feeds and trap items worth monitoring, including individuals, nonprofits, and trade associations he has initially approached about his service offerings and potential business alliances	He traps he sets reveal many high profile events and promotional opportunities – most of which are triggered by the same private sector markets George once serviced

Searching Out Loud

---

[1] In 2013 the American Psychiatric Association and its Diagnostic and Statistical Manual of Mental Disorders changed Asperger's from a single diagnosis into a wider set of autism spectrum behaviors.
[2] In 2018 the Google Keyword Tool and AdWords were rebranded as Google Ads.
[3] List results are based on the following query formation: (filetype:pdf | filetype:xls* | intitle:contact | intitle:resource | intitle:directory | intitle:member | intitle:attendees | intitle: confere (autism | aspergers | autistic | nonverbal | "(learning | developmental)(disorder.*. | disability.*.)
[4] Support for the Feed Demon news reader ended in 2013.

Searching Out Loud: Giving Voice to Independent Investigations | Marc Solomon

UNIT SEVEN:
Epilogue | Searching Out Loud in Unreasonable Times

Giving Voice to Searching Out Loud

When it comes to searching out loud there is nothing to buy.

There is nothing to upgrade.

There is no think-for-yourself-app to download.

Becoming Knowledge-ABLED doesn't create more Twitter followers. Plotting our position on the vectors of integrity doesn't make us more attractive to advertisers. It could speed our way out of jury pool contention the next time we're summoned to serve. Maintaining the independence of our investigations doesn't open up the doors of power to more influential networks. In fact, it may well block our access.

Also, all the tools at our disposal won't save us from the darker forces that cloud over information transparency, compromise the social trust, and threaten our investigative freedoms. Our searching out loud provides a voice to call out the rise of emerging power structures that are shaping social norms and behaviors in sweeping and largely veiled and unspoken ways evidenced in...

- Self-serving algorithms
- Faith in social networks
- The growth of big search and social media interests
- The increasingly fluid state of information

Being Knowledge-ABLED does not influence the pacing or direction of these changes. It does however enable us to document the conflicts of interest that form when those recently entrenched interests create and maintain the information that provides their power.

Since the initial draft of Searching Out Loud, search technology has marched ahead. Many of the resources discussed in the second and third units are now decaying in the Internet bone yard of once cool technologies and failed business models. Some familiar landmarks have been spared:

1. The uninhibited freedom of hyperlinking across the information commons of the World Wide Web endures.

2. Much of the syntax and search operators still guide the boolean logic of the manually written commands we performed in the query formation section of **Unit Two**.

3. We can still configure the custom search capabilities we explored in **Unit Four**.

4. We can still use syntax to isolate specific sites without the search restrictions they impose from within their own domains. However, we can no longer probe the deeper pattern-matching once revealed in the data mining of academic studies and vocations in the archives of career sites like LinkedIn.

A Shared Understanding of Facts

We turn those same tools on our search targets throughout this curriculum. And our tools, frameworks, and presentation methods provide our clients, peers, and communities with the basis for deciding the cases we investigate.

At the beginning of this book's writing we were able to achieve this goal through something unremarkable and expected: A shared set of empirically settled facts. However, that same expectation is now a mission. It is an extraordinary realization to consider just how daunting and necessary this challenge has become.

Our pursuit of an information commons for sourcing experts, surfacing inferences, and testing assumptions has led to something very specific – the systemic capture of those digital learnings by big tech. *'Big'* here describes a massive accumulation of data about us that has been converted into a juggernaut of online ad revenues. For the past ten years we have seen the crunching of our click patterns, demographics, and personal finances siloed into proprietary databases.

These massive repositories profile our digital lives and promise to shadow them in the future offline world. The conversation between big tech and little user is largely silent but might go down like this in the transcription:

1. You want to use our services? | Fine.

2. Sign our terms and conditions. | Scroll down page. See that you service 'user' is now sold 'product.'

The how-we-got here-justification is glossed over by the tabling of an even bigger question: what alternatives do we have?

In his 2017 polemic, *Deep Work: Rules for Focused Success in a Distracted World,* author Cal Newport chronicles the unquestioning acceptance of big tech through the emergence of the *technopoly,* a term coined by media historian Neil Postman to denote its pervasive influence and insidious nature:

> *"Technology eliminates alternatives to itself in precisely the way Aldous Huxley outlined in Brave New World. It does not make them illegal. It doe not make them immoral. It does not even make them unpopular. It makes them invisible and therefore irrelevant."* **(Postman, 1992)**[1]

The simple absolute power of the technopolist to steamroll over the pre-technopoly world enables us to look with clear eyes again at the ability of search tools to sharpen our attention rather than divert it. It also gives us perspective on the evolving role of the information provider:

A time before...

- Smart phone use cultivated a lifestyle that never logs off and pinned us against the vague and insistent threat of 'FOMO' if we do (the *"fear of missing out"*).
- Where the heavy lifting of deep work was occasionally interrupted by the need for distraction. **(Newport, 2016)**[2]
- Offers of "unlimited minutes" actually prompted us to change cell phone service providers!

This re-appraisal of the digital world through offline eyes can be traced to a spate of books, articles, and diatribes inspired by the tenth anniversary of the Apple iPhone. All trying to come to grips with the 'rewiring' of the human brain. Brains with insatiable expectations for novelty triggered by an addiction-inducing social media. Cal Newport is one voice among the recriminations that sought the sensible and proactive way to nurture introspection. This means re-balancing our virtual lives without a wholesale rejection of the diversions posed by unrelenting connectivity.

His solution?

> *"Instead of scheduling the occasional break from distraction so you can focus, you instead should schedule from focus to give into distraction."* **(Newport, 2016)**[3]

In effect, Newport is reversing the psychology of being plugged in so that adherents are the active sources and not the passive recipients. The fruits of their labors lie in the more lasting connections and reasoned arguments to be made through deep work — a point not lost on a pre-iPhone understanding of the evolving information order and power structure. Knowledge-ABLED tools and approaches flourished in a pre app-for-that Internet that's still widely accessible today.

Accessing our powers of concentration by limiting our connectivity to investigation-based evidence was a time management tip in 2007. In the late 2010s, it's foundational to the execution of Knowledge-ABLED practices.

ELEMENTS OF SUBSTANCE

We Knowledge-ABLED sorts are substance people. That's not a pat on the back. That's not a misplaced sense of vanity, some inflated sense of importance. Okay...

- Perhaps substance over style indicates a certain nerdy preoccupation with knowledge as a destination as well as journey.
- Maybe self-identifying with the term 'researcher' as opposed to 'user' shows a bias towards acting on what we learn in our investigations.

But is substance coming back into style? Has it ever? A bias towards substance leaves us open to the blindspots posed by big tech. That's to say we're less concerned with how our apps blink or our screens pop than we are with the merit of an argument or the validity of a conclusion that we may view online or off.

Independent Thinking (in these dependent times)

But you'd have to be off the grid completely to miss this post mobile computing reality: We're hard-pressed to recognize an offline world. In our tethered state, independence of thought runs counter to our need to be connected. Our persistent need of validation and praise compromises the freedom required to nurture (1) curiosity, (2) reflection, (3) focus, and (4) pursuit of the evidence we gather... wherever it may lead both online or off.

On first glance the recent turbulence for information providers seems entirely predictable and can be summed up in three widely-accepted interpretations of the way we assemble and draw from an Internet-based public record:

1. The demise of print media, including print media hosted websites
2. The rise of social media, especially the one-way mirror of Facebook
3. The rush to fill the news void formerly held by journalists with algorithm-based news feeds

What tends to escape these three 'given' tectonic shifts in the media landscape is the disappearance of a common, real-time information experience. They used to happen as routinely as the viewing of a top-rated prime time sitcom. Nowadays it takes a presidential election, a Super Bowl, a celestial sky-watch, perhaps an epic terrorist event to...

- Forge a national identity,
- Burnish collective memories,
- Reinforce widely-held beliefs, or
- Trigger a common response to an existential threat.

Okay, so why am I not nostalgic for the return of a more collective information experience? That sounds like old news. Why can't I just aim my BS detector at my own news feed and decide for myself?

Granted, the idea that someone knows better than me what my information needs are sounds positively quaint by 21st Century standards and stuffy to my ear as well. The reality is that the news is no longer experienced as...

- Coming from a singular, authoritative source whose brand confers trust, and
- A transparent, non-interpretive, and open truth served up by partisan-free reporting.

The crumbling of these journalistic myths may have influenced our own wavering standards as news consumers, a once glorified act of staying informed as (1) a responsible citizen, and (2) in the service of a wider public interest.

A Run on News Feeds

Fifty years ago the anchorman was the supreme vessel for channeling the outside world into our personal understanding of a public awareness. Today that understanding is no longer shaped by humans in news organizations but by algorithms developed by the search and social media. It's the machine learning of our consumption habits that drives our understanding of the foreseeable future and the channel it's on is no channel at all but the news feed.

The news feed is the single indivisible unit of individual communication in the social media age. The print, radio, and TV channels of mass communication have no such claims to our attentions or their influence on our behaviors through the transactional logs of web browsers. For the Knowledge-ABLED, news feeds pose a number of daunting challenges.

For starters, there is more doubt now in what defines 'news' and how those definitions indulge the appetites we're feeding. To be logged in is to be on the receiving end of a news feed. But the other truth that comes with their prevalence is the secrecy of their construction. They are opaque to all — except the engineering team attending to the algorithm that convert our digital behaviors to those news feeds.

What we can say with confidence is that news on a national, state, or local level is not the same news on a personal level. With every refresh of an update we're on the verge of a dopamine rush. A change in your number of followers? An uptick in the number of likes? In a world awash in smart phones are we really news junkies or addicted to the pay-off of instant rings, a steady hum of vibrations, and an honor roll of badges to award our virtual personas.

This definition is not tethered to a thirst for learning and discovery. It's pegged to the insatiable appetite for influence and the desire to seek out connections — a very different goal orientation than those running an independent investigation or an empirical research study.

The implications are vast. Seeking approval from those we're inclined to favor runs counter to the thankless gathering of evidence that may run counter to our personal allegiances and even core beliefs. Relying on the business model of a social media powerhouse to provide our news feeds is a visceral gratification: Of course we're right!

What could be a more intuitive indulgence than aligning the world views we hold with the world we experience? Passive acceptance of our own pre-formed opinions and facts is the black hole of blindspots. It's the same delusional trap in the warning sign's of Postman's technopoly: For the Knowledge-ABLED, unqualified acceptance of algorithm-charged information comes at the expense of the thoughtful, detached analysis we imply with well-informed choices. Choices we surrender to news feeds.

How do we force those choices back open? How do we make real the compromises to our society and communities the quality and value of information that vanishes in a sea of feeds? How do we move beyond the dire predicaments to the firmer ground of the investigative traditions we espouse?

Let's begin with stories – not an actual tales or legends but the *concept* of stories.

RE-IMAGINING THE NEWS AS NON-FICTION STORIES

Storytelling has a perennial value for holding our collective interest. From the proverbial fire pit to the TV blue light of the projection screen, stories don't just keep us focused but also guessing about the next plot twist. The Knowledge-ABLED are well-advised to play the non-fiction story telling card. Some of the benefits run parallel to literature in that we're extending the attention of information consumers. But it's more than that:

> *"History seems to be a pointless parade of insignificant events until we shape it into something that has significance for us, until we build myths out of it, until we begin using it to make up stories."* **(Smith, 2016)**[4]

Stories transcend the indifference created by the web's information density. It's a slippery blur that masks the origin and certainly the intention of the originators. It marginalizes the difference between authoritative sources with reputations on the line and anonymous ones with obscure and often dubious motives.

Think about awakening to tomorrow's recounting of tonight's election results.

There's the basic math of the ballot counting. Look past the raw numbers and there's a metaphor lurking behind each percentage in every exit poll. You can hear the breathless announcer hyperventilating over the booming loudspeaker...

- The neck-and-neck jockeying for advantage in the homestretch.
- The front-runner's inside track versus the outside chances of the dark horse.
- We're glued to the photo finish of any down-to-the-wire race that's too close to call.

Each of those flourishes are established well before race time. It's set in the odds-making that determines who's on the ticket. Our experience of the external world is one of a hotly contested power struggle. The story-making of that struggle is how we come to understand its winners, losers, heroes, villains, and how those understandings shape the internal worlds of the story's audience.

The story telling personifies the struggle through this familiar cast. It's the characters in the fight and not the abstractions of what's being contested preserved in the power of narrative. Of particular interest to the Knowledge-ABLED: How the story is received by audience members outside the spotlight's glare. The folks hanging on every twist who have no direct stake in the outcome. They may not be part of the story but their reaction to it is still party to our investigations.

Sorting out differences in interpretations is typically traced to the source fluency we considered in **Unit Three**. What if we knew who was spiking the news feed punch bowl? Transparency on its own may help us understand motivations but it also serves to filter out arguments that clash with our views and does little to shape a conclusion already formed.

The vetting process we learned in **Unit Three** remains an essential tool for the Knowledge-ABLED. There will always be hidden agendas that pair with revealing details just as certainly as alterior motives drive the public release of private concerns.

However, knowing the source is only half the story. Fact-checking the news statement by counterclaim may cast light on the biases and selective references of a source's editorial tendencies. This is inside baseball for political elites and press critics. It has only limited use for those of us more interested in holding the powerful accountable than in holding power. That fuller story requires we understand how the communities and groups we investigate connect the news to their own priorities, perceptions, and binding purpose.

A winning story line focuses attention without needing to win us over. Persuasion may follow but only as an outcome of the curiosity, caring, and deliberation inspired by a well-spun narrative:

> "It might feed the paranoia of some contemporary politicians to note how often professional reporters, supposedly skilled in exhaustive fact-gathering and dispassionate narrative, have proved to be good at making things up." **(Turow, 2016)**[5]

The Media That Chooses Us

Why is this temptation to appear authoritative, influential, or just plain convincing more than just a deviant impulse? If some propagandist crosses the line why can't they be outed and marginalized by an informed, vigilant, and skeptical band of subject matter experts?

Is it because the skeptics can't agree? Agreement assumes that we're all starting with the same clean slate and not nursing some long-held grudge, unwavering opinion, or suspicion of facts — regardless of who's revealing or vetting them.

Is it because individuals lack the trust once showered on traditional mainstream news sources? There has long existed an incestuous relationship between those surfacing the facts and those holding them up to the cameras and microphones. We see this dynamic in partisan attempts to both elevate and denigrate scientists — the star witnesses on the side of the fact tellers:

> "Both mistrust of scientists and other 'experts' and mistrust of the mass media that reports what scientists and experts believe have increased among conservatives (but not among liberals) since the early '80s. The mistrust has in part, at least, been deliberately inculcated. The fossil fuel industry publicizes studies to confuse the climate change debate; Big Pharma hides unfavorable information on drug safety and efficacy; and many schools in conservative areas teach students that evolution is "just a theory." The public is understandably confused about both the findings and methods of science." **(Ehrenreich, 2017)**[6]

This uneasy relationship between chosen facts and accepted narratives transcends media brands and polling numbers on most trusted authorities. The most irrefutable facts stand on the shakiest ground because conservatives and liberals seem to hold different beliefs about what constitutes 'truth' regardless of the evidence presented:

> "Finding facts and pursuing evidence and trusting science is part of liberal ideology itself. For many conservatives, faith and intuition and trust in revealed truth appear as equally valid sources of truth." **(Ehrenreich, 2017)**[7]

Sound familiar? This is the same pattern we see resonating in the integrity vectors in **Unit Four**. Going with intuition has an innate pull on our authenticity strings. The more deliberate empiricism trusted in liberal arguments is not only perceived as inauthentic, but potentially hostile to a conservative mindset.

All the familiar mainstream news sources have been forced to show their true partisan colors in the post mass media environment. The New York Times David Leonhardt reasons that we've worked our way through the collapsing of former bastions of news. We've transitioned through the passing of Saturday Evening Post, Life magazine, live radio broadcasts, and more recently the news divisions of the three major TV networks.

© Joe Haupt: Vintage Marvel Transistor Radio

Replacing the old dinosaurs with new sources for news is one thing. But we've never had to fill the vacuum left by the demise of an entire news medium. We've never had to adapt to a news environment with our own labeling, frames of reference, and installed our own BS filters. The fact that Facebook has filled the breech so expediently in cost and scale inspires a greater commitment to Facebook earnings than the loftier ideals expressed in the aspirations of good journalism. Is it because the First Amendment was never built to withstand the ultimate freedom of speech — the untraceable speech-maker? Or the ultimate cynicism of a disputed claim — that no one can be trusted?

Before we can figure out the clashing interests of compelling storytellers and independent fact finders, we need to establish that the latter are focused on the whole story. That the whole is not limited to one storyteller, source, or perspective. If the Knowledge-ABLED are to survive in the world to come, we must resist the emotional grip of narratives and the temptation to predefine the conclusions of an active investigation.

Beating the Competition to the Narrative

Information quality was once assessed to a large degree by the number of folks paying for it through subscriptions and newsstands. Would-be novelists were lending these talents to media organizations hungry for the editorial edge of their sense-making, pattern-matching, and even the unwitting use of character development in the nonfiction newsmakers they covered. These attributes are what gave news organizations a competing edge over their rivals.

Then came the advent of 24/7 news cycles. Cable news cornered the market on fast-breaking news but the bragging rights for the deeper narrative remained with the lottery tickets and candy on the neighborhood newsstand. It was the depth and clarity of the content which supported both a sustainable business model and laudable public role for the print media.

In the late teens of the 21st Century, being *scooped* is more akin to the milliseconds between synthetically engineered financial trades than the gap between public events and our awareness of them. In the last ten years the news industry has shed two of every five journalists and editors from their payrolls. The commercial rationale is that the middleman has been cut out with the ad dollars now flowing to the search and social media. In fact half of all digital revenues worldwide were now captured through the duopoly of Google and Facebook. **(Samuels, 2016)**[8] The single biggest investment for capturing this windfall? It wasn't the cost of developing the code or even marketing it but $2.7 billion Google set aside to settle antitrust charges from the European Union for privileging its own shopping service in its search rankings. **(Reuters, 2017)**[9]

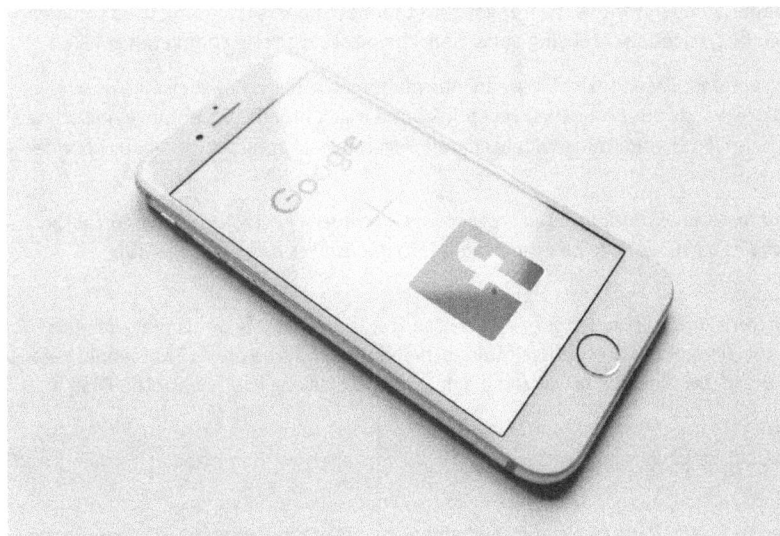

© www.quotecatalog.com: google facebook

The New Kings of Content

In the mass media model, both content and distribution were handled by print and broadcast media outlets. In social media times content is the new *talk*. It's cheap, abundant, and practically self-generating. Anyone with a Facebook page has a license to publish their thoughts, feelings, and opinions as readily as we used to consume news, sports, and weather. Regardless of mood swings and weather patterns, it's distribution that lords over content.

The Google and Facebook grip on distribution has marginalized the quality of content. This is not wistful nostalgia. This is the sobering and dated idea that content quality could ever again serve as a sustainable business model in an information distribution system powered by proprietary news feeds.

The reversing fortunes of social media and newspapers are causal in nature – a one-way ticket of redirected ads to a seismic shifting of eyeballs. But what about that one-way street? Is the reshaping of the digital news infrastructure also warping expectations of media organizations, (traditional, search, social or otherwise), as stewards of the public trust?

The bold and declarative use of live-streaming over Facebook, Twitter, and YouTube is in stark contrast to the tentative positions of social media executives and their editorial policies. It makes business sense for Facebook Periscope to foist responsibility for that to its *"citizen journalists with live-broadcast cameras in their pockets."* **(Sullivan, 2016)**[10]

Being accountable for the diverging appetites of 1.6 billion users is not a battle Facebook wants to fight any more than they wish to compensate an editorial staff. One executive told the Washington Post that *"we are not in the business of picking which issues the world should read about. We are in the business of connecting people and ideas — and matching people with the stories they find most meaningful."* **(Sullivan, 2016)**[11]

Don't Mind Me — I Was Only Streaming

It's curious that Facebook is not playing the same don't-shoot-the-messenger card that newspapers have long used to defend themselves against charges of bias and libel. In fact, Facebook is shying away from the messenger role completely.

Partly this is a reflection of the shear message volume. Facebook's role as an information provider is not the same as a news-gathering organization. Where the news industry weeds out non-news, Facebook has a much broader acceptance, including news under a content banner that includes material designed to be widely shared, regardless of accuracy, origin, or provider intent. This includes content that...

"[H]as been, and will be, immune from current 'fake news' critiques and crackdowns, because it never had the opportunity to declare itself news in the first place. To publish lies as 'news' is to break a promise; to publish lies as 'content' is not." **(Herrman, 2016)**[12]

How long this new positioning of content matchmaker can stand in for news messenger is unclear. My bet is that only the threat of government intrusion will force big social media to defend itself under the banner of a free press. That would be an extraordinary retrenchment for Facebook — the globe's leading privatized big data snoop cloaking itself under the First Amendment.

So how does this play out in a world where would-be newspaper readers and TV viewers are now monetized as Googlers and Facebook friends?

1. Dwindling news budgets have led to foreign bureau closings and global events are being reported second-hand by off-site junior level reporters.

2. A decade-long downward trends show losses of one-in-five local television evening news watchers and one-in-three for the late news. **(Friedman, 2017)**[13]

3. The gap between how Americans get their news continues to narrow with digital consumption nearly pulling even with TV news. **(Bialik, Matsa, 2017)**[14]

The overwhelming conclusion? New digital realities have severed the economic dependency of social and search media consumers on media professionals.

Lingering Trust Issues

Still, short-circuiting the media industry doesn't curtail our love of narrative or curb the news consumer's appetite for sense-making. If anything, that hunger is spiking from a proliferation of anonymous, unsubstantiated, or questionable news sources underwritten under the cover of First Amendment protections to mask the underwriters.

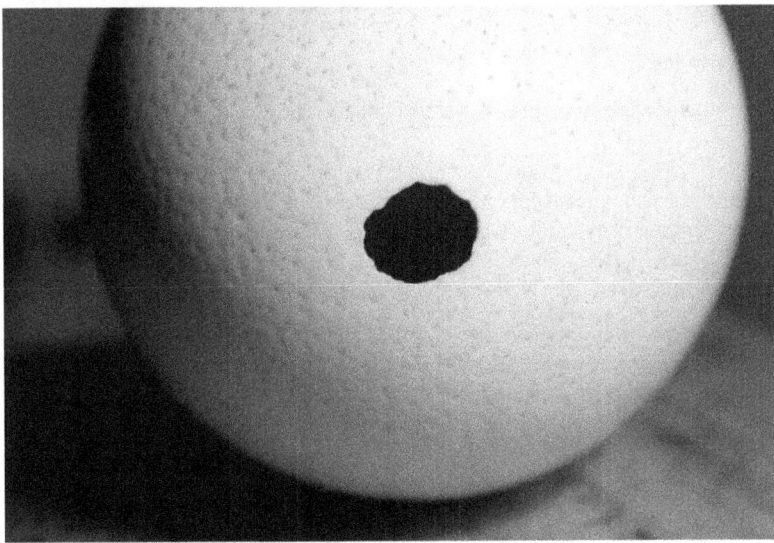

© Lynn Greyling: Pštrosí skořápky

Also, the unseasoned state of most reporters places an increased reliance on the front door of official, if unnamed sources such as White House spokespersons or military and diplomatic channels. In effect the power structure becomes the unchallenged selector of facts to support the outcomes they're driving. **(Samuels, 2016)**[15]

Not the surest foundation to foster independent thinking or credible investigations.

In the news gathering void of today, we substitute relatedness for relevance and influence for substance. A reporter dedicated to a story is no match for a celebrated Twitter account focused on their follower counts. In bygone days we saw news professionals as compromised by the institutional weight of their news brands. They made or suppressed headlines based on what their subscription base or viewers supported. Today that marketing tactic is no longer a source of temptation for wage-chasing journalists.

We assume everything about them now: Their politics, their sensitivities, their personal values and social judgments are wrapped tightly around their personal branding, social networks, and signature issues. How well they connect with like-minded affiliates in large part determines whether the role is self-supporting, an unpaid gig, or a voluntary display of self-expression.

But the status-shifting of news professionals means more than the career path detours of would-be journalists. The referral process used to shape news coverage has transitioned from fact-sorting and evidence-gathering to the worst excesses of the predisposed investigator:

1. Self-affirmation – Presumptions of guilt and innocence

2. Self-delusion – Unwillingness to revisit past assumptions

3. Self-fulfillment – Preaching to the converted

4. Self-assurance – Injecting certainty into uncertain outcomes as a shorthand for clarity

The Less Popular Public Imagination

In none of these cases is the investigator liable for their own preconceptions. In some circles the partiality is so dominant that an investigator and their stakeholders are oblivious to their own 'hardball' biases. In other instances, journalists are reluctant to tie events they cover to probable cause. They fall back on false equivalence. They exaggerate uncertainty instead of pressing the case to be made on reasonable grounds that 'A' knowingly brings about 'B.' **(Leonhardt, 2017)**[16]

All of this is reinforced by our means to channel social media as both consumers and producers. As we've seen with Facebook's to play the messenger, the information provider role that we explored in **Unit Four** is wide open and susceptible to any imposing and persuasive narrative willing to force itself onto the national stage:

> "He is both a creature and a creation of the media and the media will never own that."
>
> — Michael Moore, writing about the election of Donald Trump[17]

Why does the media back away from its own creations? Why does Facebook refuse to assume or even question its proper role as the dominant news outlet on the planet? Why are information providers alternately drunk with power and afraid of it at the same time? Nothing threatens that power more than the admission it comes from casting attention on the powerful. Acknowledging the symbiotic relationship between newsmakers and information providers could trigger an outcome worse than any negative press. In this scenario the fallen media is relegated to the same fate of Postman's technopoly — a forgotten remnant of the pre-connected world.

© shuets udono: Car accident in Japan

Attention-grabbing interactions such as likes, comments, and hash-tags are the replacement currency for subscribers and ultimately relevancy. The news industry's fortunes have always been tethered to the newsmakers they cover. That connection is only weakened by waning pay walls and non-paying subscribers.

Publishers' Remorse

These inhibitions are not new to declining revenues. They're rooted in outdated expectations of accountability. In the traditional media landscape, misinformation and libel were easily traceable to publishers, financiers, and partisan agenda-setters — their motives were as concrete and locatable as the presses that printed their invective.

Also, the separation of editorial from advertising was an established news business firewall that protected the credibility of the newsroom while sustaining the paper's financial position. The vanishing of that firewall is not just a collective aw shucks moment for Google, Facebook, and Twitter. It leaves a crack in our public discourse exploited under virtual cover by the unattributed claims of imposters, and hackers.

© c-span.org: The in-house counsel of search and social media giants in testimony before the U.S. Senate in October, 2017.

Part of these trepidations lie in the short but dramatic history of story-telling on social media itself. This is a narrative that began and ended within the confines of mostly Facebook pages. It was a transparent vessel (connecting with other members) within a sealed container (limited by the size of those connections), and 'friended' approvals generated subscriptions, a.k.a. news feeds. The news here is that subscribers now perform the dual role of content producers and consumers.

Those markings began to shift as 'likes' and 'shares' spilled over the boundaries of Facebook. It was no longer the fishbowl-like sensation of jumping between arranged carousels of Hallmark moments and photo opportunities. It was the wider web now curated by those same friends and family. Yes, it remained the same tight and familiar container. But now a growing legion of more global and mobile users were looking outward from the lens of Facebook. And it wasn't all baby showers and high school reunions.

© Mohamed Hassan: Facebook Ads

The news publishers wanted in. The news brokers were no longer network anchors or city desk editors but Aunt Suzie and Cousin Hank. Gaining a foothold through Facebook meant being one of the family – not one of the stringers holed up inside the asylum where the rioting was spiraling out of control.

Just as they had retooled their wares around search engine placement in the early 2000s, news publishers saw adoption and ultimately infiltration as the path forward. They tuned their headlines, images, summaries, video links, and even the story-lines to their Facebook reception. Some embraced the site as a primary source of visitors. Some enjoyed the revenue bump from an explosive rate of click-throughs. Some pursued this strategy into absurdity and exploitation. **(Hermann, 2016)**[18]

However, the ascendancy of social media has obscured once discernible links between libel, slander, and the legal recourse to combat it:

> "The decline of newspapers in physical form and their passing on to the internet puts them on all fours with the vast flows of information, fantasy, leaks, conspiracy theories, expressions of benevolence and hatred. There they have to live or die." **(Lloyd, 2016)**[19]

It's not just legal protections that have withered in the transition from broadcast to social media. It's the evidence-based reporting that formed the bedrock of print journalism and the basis of third-party credibility. In an era where journalists were accountable to their fact-base and their newspapers, journalists were not rubber stamps for untethered commentators or even fake Facebook accounts backed by unsubstantiated innuendo. It was not just an aspiration but the expectation that journalists secure the trust of their readers.

That relationship wasn't prefaced on circulation numbers or something as intimate as the reader's time spent with their periodicals. It was by acting as a public trust – by placing the public interest above the interests of the institutions they covered. When the Baby boomers came of age, most Americans got their news from a select group of media elites.

Nowadays the typical millennial consumers news stories like a rolling supply of virtual dating prospects — swiping left and right for rejects, placeholders, and keepers. That's where trust has traveled in the last generation — from the anchor seat at the national news desk to the purely instinctual responses of rapid fire digital stimulation.

By today's standards, is the trust factor still an attainable goal? Can the ethos of a well-informed citizenry be preserved as an internet-based business model? That chapter is yet to be written.

What we can do is consider the emerging obstacles and enablers for an independent and free press in a post social media age and for the Knowledge-ABLED as keepers of that mission. Our parade of challenges begins with the evolving role of the eye witness — the very essence of direct experience.

Figure 7.1: Searching for Eyewitnesses That Have Fallen Off the Radar

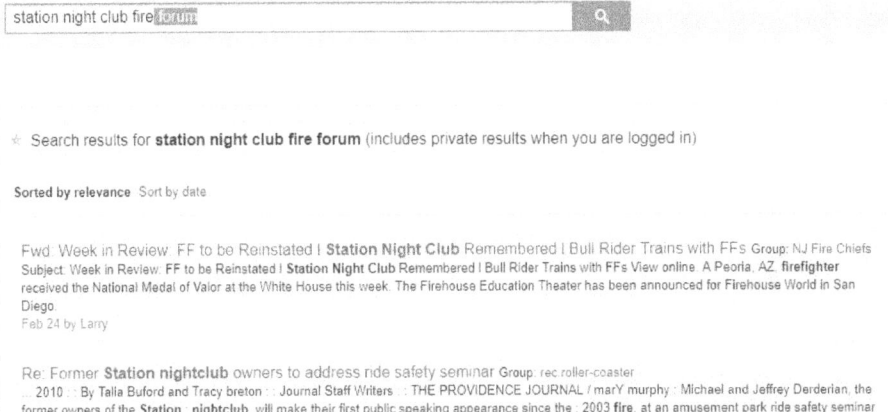

Note the disappearance of the the same date sorting option we saw in the Source Fluency (Section 3.2; Figure 3.18) involving a 2003 Yahoo search of the same topic. Understanding cause-effect conditions and unpacking the sequential movement of an investigation is not possible when archival searches have no date ranges. Also note the additional step of the required login before "private results" can be disclosed to an otherwise anonymous user.

UP IN THE CROWD

In 2016 the battle for the northern Iraq city of Mosul was live-streamed on Facebook.

Users in the audience showered the fighters on the ground with the favor of their emoticons. Each bullet fired and bomb detonation was intended to unleash chaos and carnage on the city and its citizens. Staging this in front of a live Internet audience produced a virtual cave painting of emojis rained down on the battlefield by the Facebook spectators.

Social media platforms are the new staging grounds for delivering the pain and suffering of soldiers and civilians to a global audience on demand. Some may be rooting for a home team. Some may be backing the visitors. Still others may question the legitimacy of the true natives and invaders. But many more may not have been united by social justice, land grab, or religious belief. Perhaps there were no greater causes or galvanizing forces than a primal urge of voyeurism — to seek a vicarious experience of unscripted violence?

Whether the Facebook faithful are even aware of of this impulse is unclear. What does resonate for those with direct recall of this event is that social media streams have blurred the line between fantasy violence and battlefield carnage — maybe even impairing our capacity to tell the difference.

No one equipped with a beer, couch, and subscription cable is a stranger to the performance factors that spark the appeal of live sports entertainment. The news is whether the same formula can be applied to armed conflict and other public acts of aggression — especially those that require the criminal justice system to determine questions of guilt, punishment, and liability.

In a media landscape that serves up warfare as a reality-based programming source, the need for the Knowledge-ABLED to define these new intrusions on eroding boundaries of what's real, fair, or private is critical to resolving real world conflicts — even when they're encouraged or inflamed by virtual actors. Recordings of criminal conduct whether channeled through Facebook streaming, the body camera on a state trooper, or mundanely captured by surveillance video all require an understanding of what ensues off-screen before and after the altercations in question.

© Mass Communication Specialist 2nd Class Zackary Alan Landers: Luzon Strait, Philippine Sea

Interestingly enough, you had to be there – at least on the live stream. The battle for Mosul doesn't share well. Your friends are not clicking on that gruesome account you tried to pass onto them after the latest siege:

> *"Most likely, unfiltered news will convey a negative aspect of society. Again, another revelation from The Intercept or ProPublica won't get many clicks."* **(Filloux, 2016)[20]**

This says that the prospect of witnessing history loses its allure once the outcome is determined — much like any competition already decided by the outcomes in our news feeds.

Privacy and the Public Mind

In addition to direct experience, another challenge for the Knowledge-ABLED is to sort through the thinning distinction between thought and action.

In pre-social media times self-contained introspection defined most internal considerations in human thoughts and thought patterns. Mental deliberations were conducted in the privacy of the mind – away from the din of the market, the judgments of peers, or the approval of the crowd. Diaries were not open books but an individual's way to record or even rationalize the struggles between their own thoughts, the sense-making, and the looming decision: Do I act on them or not?

Regardless of our urge to share experiences or document our thoughts, most of us led largely private lives. Most of us could determine how much we wished others to know us through the natural filtering of home, family, work, and community.

© Heather Cowper: Anne Frank Diary at Anne Frank Museum in Berlin

In our new world, the individual has been absolved from introspection. Thoughts and feelings are now routinely shared in posts and tweets. The need for privacy and autonomous control of our thoughts and feelings are challenged and perhaps being slowly overtaken by a competing need for connection and approval among our peers and leaders within our social circles.

This notion of social leadership finds its voice in emerging markets to tabulate the number of 'follows' or 'friend requests' to discern influence. But approval runs deeper than that. How widely shared are opinions are, by whom, and the associations they trigger are all in effect 'search targets' the way the issues and topics we weigh in on used to be the primary source of our search investigations before social media:

> "Our society has been woefully negligent about what in other contexts we would call the rules of zoning, the regulation of commercial activity where we live, figuratively and literally. It is a question that goes to the heart of how we value what used to be called our private lives." **(Bell, 2016)**[21]

Individuals are no longer self-contained by their thoughts but encouraged to float them in a trial balloon of social media speculation. The line between thought and action is receding – accelerated by the collapsing of the virtual and physical realities we see in mass shootings, hostage-taking, executions, and other existential threats designed for the social media stage.

It's not enough to lay the blame on social media for breaching the wall between public and private lives. There's also the surveillance actions of nation-states and cyber-criminals that compromise our private interactions — be it conversing with our friends, transacting with our financial institutions, or opining about the questionable judgment of our elected leaders. As historian Timothy Snyder reasoned to NPR's Robert Siegel, *"It can't be right, Robert, that every time someone hacks my emails, it's news for someone else."*

Snyder goes on:

> "Totalitarianism starts when the difference between your public life and your private life is effaced. If we can't have exchanges with our friends and family, with loved ones that won't at some point be made public then we can't have private lives. And if we can't have private lives then we're not really free people." **(Snyder, 2017)[22]**

The question of freedoms forfeited by our social media interactions boils down to writing on a web page in one's thinking-out-loud voice: Am I speculating on a chance future event? That leaves the conversation open for Facebook advertisers to satisfy the conditions the writer shares with their Facebook friends:

"I've been thinking about reading lamps for our night stand" is a green light for a Facebook advertiser to sprinkle the member's page with additional thoughts about lamps. There's the alluring floor model. Next comes an expiring coupon. It's followed by the tempting button to ingest your payment details. If we're taking strictly about products, one person's liberation from retail lighting stores doesn't become another's surveillance encounter.

But if we're talking about the expressing an aspiration or a passionately held conviction, then we have crossed into invasive new territory. That's how we learned retroactively that Facebook advertising moves opinion and ultimately voters, not just inventory.

© Ian Brown: First screen

The wish fulfillment of the speculative rhetoric found in social media posts is not just a potential sale but an investigation opening. It presents both a qualitative and quantitative research opportunity that the Knowledge-ABLED can use to inform the motivations of search targets. The complex and multi-dimensional nature of connecting personality to motivation is rendered less abstract by these new algorithms. In fact, a suspect in a shooting could express an affinity for firearms that could trigger multiple rounds of gun ads. The connection between thought and action could not be more direct.

That's why I suspect it's only a matter of time before investigators require the micro-targeted ads sent to persons of interest in the period leading up to the crime in question. It's not so hit or miss in the case of Facebook micro-targeting. The bar here is lowered even further for publishing falsehoods to a tribal universe of true believers.

Click Bait and Run

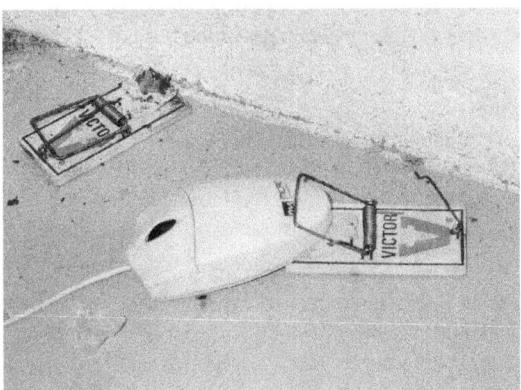

© Karen Rustad: Computer mouse caught in a mouse trap

In addition to thought and action, another former distinction between our public and private lives is collapsing before our senses. There is no longer a healthy gap between the reality of facts and the perception of emotions. Social media has blurred the lines between the fixed, static, and transactional nature of systemic facts and everything else. That includes the imprecise world of human resentments, anxieties, and expectations.

How do these flash-point perceptions track with the cold, sober facts?

It's the business model informing social media success that rewards Facebook, Google, Netflix, etc. for holding our attention – not for holding themselves to the standards once required of news-based organizations. It wasn't a deliberate coup, hostile takeover, or a concerted attempt to marginalize journalistic ethics. But it was and remains as lucrative as it is sensitive. And personal.

The Knowledge-ABLED can bypass the connection statistics that shadow our digital identities for the explanatory power of opinion-neutral metrics (government data, rainfall totals, calendar dates, etc.) The loosening grip of a fact-based reality is opening the door to an alternative one. However, a savvy public records search will pull-up the life-changing events and personal milestones that plot our biographies. It's up to the investigating biographer to sketch in the details.

That level of commitment to professional accountability is sorely lacking in a social web ingested with our personal details and affects now concealed from us. The insult is amplified by the low bar for publishing emotional charged and factually suspect news to a non-discriminating universe.

Historian Timothy Snyder speaks of a world of emotions and alternative realities where those power structures "manufacture lots of stuff that isn't true." This poisoning of the news well permits alternative news providers to paint all news as untrustworthy as "everyone is like this." Social media becomes the unwitting partner of the propagandist:

> "You spread this kind of cynicism that you shouldn't really trust anybody, everybody's just a partisan, [and] everyone just has their own skin in the game. And then once that belief spreads we're then in the world that I'm talking about, which is ripe for fascism." **(Snyder, 2017)**[23]

Fake It Until You Make It

Another challenge to the independence of effective investigation lies in the alienation of investigative sources as well as subjects. The neutrality of a detached examination can easily be construed as a threat a to the opposing sides of aggrieved parties. Simply put, it's an unwelcome advance on the truth when a third party group or individual is in the business of selecting facts without picking sides.

Detachment is daunting to political partisans because it carries the weight of privilege as well as alienation. Elitism has extended beyond the traditional boundaries of entitlement. In the past, elites comprised the clubs that wouldn't have us as members via birthright, well-connected access to capital, or academic pedigree from where the elites draw their intellectual stature. Admission privileges have been extended beyond this exclusive club. And their swelling ranks include an expanding threat – not just in numbers but in the strings pulled and affronts visited upon the raging populist ranks. The elites are not only the beneficiaries of a rigged system. They are its perpetrators.

Facebook's ascendance as the nation's number one news source has widened the circle of elites to include voters who insist on a body of evidence to support the allegations and assertions of the candidates they would elect. This change does more than marginalize the role of journalists or displace the mass media as pre-eminent news brokers.

From our perspective, the Knowledge-ABLED are privy to the greatest motivator for communicating power — the testing of one's influence through the act of self-justification. What we cannot do as investigators is to throw up our disbelieving hands as if now we've heard it all and rest our judgment on our own instincts.

For that we may take our cues from Georg Hegel.

In his day the philosopher Georg Hegel observed that *"Reading the morning newspaper is the realist's morning prayer."* There is a wistful quality to Hegel's quaint assertion in the perception-focused world that dominates our news and politics.

© Jakob Schlesinger: Hegel-Porträt

Social media has fundamentally changed our relationship to news from a question of facts and opinions to a world in which all facts are injected with opinion, including which facts to include or ignore, and thus subject to change on the whims of the information provider. For example...

- It has been reported that the 45th President of the United States routinely reports his net worth based on his mood at the time, rather than relying on Generally accepted accounting principles ("GAAP") to provide that calculation. **(Peterson-Wirthorn, 2016)**[24]
- Spreaders of unverifiable claims are not interested in clarity or engaging in debate. The goal is not to support the familiar us-versus-them narrative of the oft-repeated call-to-action. It's to push the message receiver past the point of keeping score or even caring because of the information provider's ultimate message: *"Don't trust anyone."* **(MacFarquhar, 2016)**[25]
- The broadcast media has compromised its own stature as a broker between public officials and the public interest by retaining political pundits for their insider perspectives and then giving those consultants access to that network's televised debate questions. The result? A rigged contest that advantages the pundit's own candidate-clients. **(Gold, 2016)**[26]

THE REALITY OF PERCEPTION

Belief in the social media news provider rests on the provider's understanding of the recipient and the metrics that determine their news feeds — not in the actual story they're telling. In effect, it's no longer about perception versus reality. It's all perception. Reality's role is a limited one if only to assess the reality of the perception. It's no longer the distinction between personal experience and non-partisan ideal that *"everyone is entitled to their own opinion but no one is entitled to their own set of facts,"* as the former U.S. Senator from New York, Daniel Patrick Moynihan once surmised.

Moynihan couldn't anticipate a world where his conviction of fact-based standards would need to be followed up with the clarification of *whose* reality these facts were grounded in. It's as if his evidence-bearing notions of transparency weren't giving voice to social norms but an outdated and naive belief calibrated into its own filter bubble. What was once a standard of journalistic excellence had devolved into a misguided belief in the power of facts. This belief held that once established, facts did not rig elections or silence the opposition but raise pressing and unresolved questions, regardless of whose narrative was framing them.

© Marion S. Trikosko: Daniel Patrick Moynihan

This corruption of former decorums is not brought about by any single political view, belief system, hostile foreign power, or media empire. That would be a compelling narrative which misses a more grounded truth about the daily sinister threats we perceive in our news feeds:

1. We are all information providers.
2. Our news finds its ultimate validation in stories.
3. These stories are told through narratives.
4. These narratives don't merely support but surround us within the comfort of our ranks.

And if we can't be certain we can release our intentions on probable outcomes— the not-so-secret ingredients found in fake news and alternative facts.

What do these changes mean for the Knowledge-ABLED? Well for starters, in a world of perception-based reality there are no open debates or independent voices. There is no role for the humility and empathy that comes with reaching outside one's circle. There are only foregone conclusions resonating with (1) one's echo chamber of choice, or (2) irrefutable evidence cherry-picked from the same enclave. The news we see is true...

- Regardless of its factual accuracy
- If it rings true in the mind of the reader

We see these fallacies and delusions exhibited in the sunk cost rationale used to reinforce our own biases and preferences. We see this tendency exacerbated by our growing appetite for novelty. Partly this is explained with the banality of ever-shorter deadlines and time horizons in the 24-7 news cycle. But there's something more personal and even self-incriminating that drives our need for titillation.

Negativity Defenses

It's negative news that excites us in our fight-or-flight read of the news feed-based radar. Conversely good news bores us: "The opposite of a bad story isn't a good story. It's a non-story." **(Chait, 2016)**[27] That means us information recipients are predisposed to see all reported changes in our feeds both as potential conflicts on the larger political stage and threats to us on a personal level.

This defensive view is the way we rationalize the news as fitting a pre-existing pattern that confirms our suspicions. Being blindsided with negative news is reinforced by our own confirmation bias. In other words there is no longer a distinction to be made by how we organize our news and how we rationalize the world to justify the way we see things.

It's self-serving to social media subscribers alike when our preconceived biases are indulged by Facebook's reading of them. It's more insidious that we are now culpable for our own partisan pandering by way of those same algorithms. But that assumes there remains an agreed upon mainstream of news and opinion, if only to resist wading back into one.

Our collective digital identities have come to know a new, menacing interpretation of facts. This is the media landscape where sunk cost rubs shoulders with confirmation bias. This is a world free of the curiosity, experimentation, and open-mindedness that comes with an unfiltered view of the news.

It goes something like this:

1. I've invested time and effort for understanding my world.
2. That includes the news and opinions that inform these evolving views.
3. Each new event reinforces opinions that solidify with time: (History is on my side...)
4. So much that my world view is immutable and resistant to reshaping by future events.

We of the curious detachment sort must resist this intransigence — even when facing the stiff headwinds of cynicism and resignation. Like Senator Moynihan, our insistence on accountability means appealing to the closet truth-seeker that still resides within our own guarded, weather-beaten exteriors.

It's All Sunking In

This rationale isn't limited to individuals. Institutions operate under the influence of their own sunk costs and predetermined confirmations. Even authoritative news sources such as the New York Times will pre-ordain what kinds of stories make their pages well in advance of the events they cover. One former editor contrasted the ear-to-the-ground ethos of the beat reporter with the insular paper of record. He described the Times as more intent on following its own editorial priorities than the pursuit and reporting of unscripted events falling outside its predetermined editorial agenda:

> *"By and large, talented reporters scrambled to match stories with what internally was often called 'the narrative.' We were occasionally asked to map a narrative for our various beats a year in advance, square the plan with editors, [and] then generate stories that fit the pre-designated line."* **(Cieply, 2016)**[28]

How does this impact our search investigations? Will we find any substance when we pick through the rubble of the filter bubble? Probably not. We'll find the circular logic of self-referencing echo chambers. Plenty of righteous indignation. How about actual evidence?

Ultimately the Knowledge-ABLED will find most news feeds off limits for the production of evidence-based recounting of events. Gathering timelines of incidents, rounding up eyewitness accounts, or assessing the motives of the players involved is more substantive than supporting a hunch through a trusted source.

David Morris: April 28 the evidence

The gumshoe work typified by the plainclothes investigator is synonymous with working in the shadows. Our determination whets an insatiable appetite for details, and an unwavering commitment for piecing them together. For the Knowledge-ABLED, the dedication once reserved for staking out crime scenes, knocking on doors, and poring through stacks of requested records may now be available virtually. But the discovery process is no less painstaking.

We're not in the business of requesting victims to suspend their anguish at the consequences we're retained to assess. We don't ask them to swallow hard and be impartial. It's the authoritative impact of their direct experience that privileges their witness-bearing accounts of events. It's the scarcity of direct experience that will grow in value against the vast indirect experience of the tiny screen.

The Freedom to Explore the Investigation

That us-versus-them mindset keeps us anchored to the weight of our own egos. It narrows the range of arguments considered plausible by our peers, acceptable within our social groupings, and resonating within the belief structures of our cultural and religious tribes.

Investigators are told to double-down on evidence-gathering, fact-checking, and patterns of behavior. The Knowledge-ABLED go further and consider those findings within an elevated perspective of a collective experience. This means not just *"the facts, ma'am"* but the context that predisposes our stakeholders to accept or reject those facts. This elevated approach accommodates conflicting views of an investigation. The sense of being responsive to the concerns of those conflicting parties.

Jack Webb as Detective Joe Friday from the NBC crime drama, Dragnet

All of this requires the freedom of experimentation and trial-and-error as the glue for course-correcting the unforeseen. Investigation is the act of ruling out the implausible. But it also means factoring in diverging interpretations and clashing opinions. This act of inclusion says...

- Yes to include disputing versions of a single truth or clashing interpretations of the same event
- Yes to engaging all stakeholders directly – even the search targets. But also to laying out the recipe for explaining the discovery process so that anyone can step through the same pathways of learning
- Yes, without laying claim to discovering the trail or determining who's fit to follow our Knowledge-ABLED discoveries

That would not only mark an advance but a return to transparency that a single, global information network was designed to deliver. Is that an information ideal doomed to collapse under the collective weight of government censoring, multiple sign-ons, or a trillion news feed updates? Is it a promise worth keeping? **(Jeffries, 2014)**[29] The answer lies in the balance of whether information is *of use* to us – or whether we're *being used* by the same information.

Knowledge-ABLED to do List

© Elvert Barnes: 38a.FarragutNorth.BaltimoreMD.10April2018

Since you're an information nut, you've exposed yourself to the frameworks and methods in these pages: Search logs, blindspots, source conjugation, oceans, lakes, and ponds, and the biggest picture. Together they form the...

- ■ **Path to media literacy** — the critical analytical skills necessary to filter, disseminate, and assess what we experience on a screen from what we can tell of the world online *and off*.

- ■ **The tools and practices of the Knowledge-ABLED** – a practical means to apply your information geekdom in the service of research, consulting, and independent investigation.

Ultimately if the last ten years have foretold anything about the next ten, it's this:

1. The Internet is a hot communications medium and will only intensify. Hot media is that which engages one sense completely. It demands little interaction from the user because it 'spoon-feeds' the content. (McLuhan, 1964)[30] It is the tool for both capturing the emotional impetus and storing the social turbulence embroiled in human affairs.

2. Smart phones aren't merely personal digital assistants as they were originally conceived. The face-to-screen interaction is a facade-inducing masquerade. It's a showcase of fabrication, misinformation, and the capacity to weaponize the same websites once designed to foster community between groups.

The following ten to-do items are my answer to the challenges posed by the rise of big search and social media on small screens. This includes managing information quality, the credence we place in our sources, and the sourcing effort itself. Each item plays out the implications for independent investigations at the crossroads of Internet-based communication:

1. **Option #1:** Self-service model that upholds free speech as judgment-neutral distribution hub where each person should see as little objectionable content as possible. **(Zuckerberg, 2017)**[31]

2. **Option #2:** Transparent model that requires full disclosure of message providers and upholds quality standards of the information shared on and across platforms.

That either road taken presents a rocky climb is beyond dispute. Another irrefutable conclusion: It will take the media literacy skills and ethical compass of the Knowledge-ABLED to bring clarity and purpose to the new responsibilities of free speech that travels across search engines, social networks, and mobile applications.

This Knowledge-ABLED road taken is not some plaintiff offshoot of information overload or the inevitable stress that comes with rapid change. These to-do items are the macro forces the Knowledge-ABLED will need to manage, organize, and interpret for our peers, clients, and fellow citizen information providers and consumers. Each of those list items will be critical to helping us to...

1. Vet sources and assign motives
2. Reverse engineer the proprietary formulas that define our filter bubbles
3. Piece together the narratives that predispose us to accept the the information we consume via the search and social media
4. Determine the best-interest scenarios for making this information known to us — for instance, how our taken-for-granted loyalties as consumers benefit the providers

Here then in no intended countdown order are your ten assignments for the Knowledge-ABLED and navigated road ahead.

1) Track Your Pre and Post Knowledge Abilities

Success is not limited to learning these practices. It includes retaining the way you did research before you plied your knowledge trade. Count that as a success factor in two ways:

1. You are an ambassador of these methods to peers, clients, and students, applying your own experience to the methods you've learned here. And each new lesson is an opportunity to teach them to peers who not only value your input but want to practice with the same independence of mind.
2. You understand the difference between human and machine-based searches. The Knowledge-ABLED can spell that difference. How? By contrasting the surface understanding of an algorithm-based search with the deeper connections captured by an informed approach to query formation and source fluency.

This second success factor imparts the value you bring that we considered in **Unit Five**. It's also to mark differences in between how lay users and the Knowledge-ABLED approach digital content that's been machine-mediated to match our usage data and digital profiles.

What contrasts do we mean exactly?

Here's one you've probably experienced. It's entirely human to avoid messages that challenge our assumptions and pushes back on our perspective. It may take some effort to avoid these discomforts but it takes far more to actually challenge or even change the opinions of those who don't agree with us. In the summer of 2017 a Monmouth University Polling Institute study suggested that roughly three-in-five Americans agree that there is nothing the current U.S. President could do to change their minds — both in their support and in their opposition to the same polarizing figure. **(Vesey-Byrne, 2017)**[32]

Conversely, the President could change his own tune on a long-standing national issue or raise one out of nowhere and his supporters will shift along with him. For example, his supporters actually flipped from a favorable to unfavorable view of the National Football League. **(Roth, 2017)**[33] The country's iconic national sport and leading TV show lost its home team status after the President called out player anthem protests as unpatriotic. This culture war declaration reflects a siege mindset offering two limited options: (1) Fight, or (2) flight. Neither determination is willing to assume the perspective-taking needed to achieve mutual respect. It's a tolerance level that bottoms out during verdicts and elections and the honest disagreements that persist regardless of outcomes. That's nothing new. Neither is feeling defensive when having difficult chats with people holding contrarian views. Who hasn't been there, right?

© Patty Solomon

The challenge is to break from our own respective orbits, gaining an appreciation for social circles clearly outside our spheres of influence. Not only are they resistant to our views. They may well feel personally threatened by our raising arguments we consider settled or evidence we view as irrefutable. When those two sides to every argument are digging in their respective heels, what are the tools for digging out?

#1 TO DO: Do your background homework in advance of direct engagement.

First, we need to step back and understand the larger, unfolding information universe that blankets and tweaks those biases. Then we need to measure them.

Case-in-point: The power of Facebook's reach into the sympathies and attentions of its users are contingent on a single metric: Page views. Pages views come from sharing. Which page criteria lead to the best sharing volumes? The answer has less to do with what's being shared and more to do with who's doing the sharing:

> "Facebook has to severely edit its huge content fire hose in order to determine what is eligible to be shown in one's news feed. In doing so, the company chooses to give more weight to content originated by friends and family. So, sharing is key because it leads to higher page consumption which, in turn, leads to multiple bespoke advertising exposures." **(Filloux, 2016)**[34]

What does this mean for settling scores with people outside our social spheres?

Nothing.

We're not trying to entrap our search targets under false pretense with invitations to connect on social media. We're not ad hoc members of a surveillance state that blankets our digital behaviors. Investigations are not about settling scores. There are certainly investigators who combine the smear tactics of opposition research with the hot emotional properties of social media. But those efforts are in the service of pre-drawn conclusions by partisans with a direct stake in the outcome.

What does this mean for understanding the motivations and justifications of the individuals and groups we investigate?

Everything.

We don't need to hack into the social media profiles of our search targets to piece together their affiliations. We don't have to travel in their circles to loop in their influences, status, loyalties, and role models. This is a world where we're all defined by the worst things we've done. After all, who can trust vapid praise on social media? That's an excuse to double down on unguarded moments of past indiscretions. Again, to the exclusion of the fuller person that's not so easily vilified.

What's incumbent on an earnest investigator to do is our homework prior to engaging our search targets directly. That doesn't mean profiling per se. It may not even mean learning anything directly related to the reasons we're engaging them. What it means is paying them with our respect for their details, even if it's nothing more conversational than a job interview.

2) There is No Right or Left or Center
(When It Comes to Affinity Bias)

The second Knowledge-ABLED priority builds on the profiles of search targets by objectifying their groups and affiliations. Those distinctions are especially important in an era of bubble filters and the communities they strengthen.

© Martin Shovel

Thousands of people might agree with you. But that doesn't make them true, or a majority opinion. **(Tobias, 2016)**[35] Therein lies the affinity bias of social media:

> *"Before the Internet, crackpots were mostly isolated, and surely had a harder time remaining convinced of their alternative realities. Now their devoutly believed opinions are all over the airwaves and the web, just like actual news. Now all of the fantasies look real."* **(Andersen, 2017)**[36]

Affinity bias is a distortion greater than the most headstrong partisan, incensed inciter, or conspiricist whose allegiances are bound to the suspicions that they harbor. Affinity is an allegiance baked into the business model of Facebook. It means *"content that will comfort users in their opinions and feelings toward society or politics. On Facebook, you'll never be alone thinking or believing what you hold dear."* **(Filloux, 2016)**[37]

What we cherish is often more cathartic than endearing. In a polarized setting, opposing factions hold strong, impulsive affections for the vanquishing of the other. That otherness factor is not limited to hate groups. The sting of ostracism is as widespread in a global network as it is a universal emblem of social unrest. Regrettably, affinity bias leads to the splintering of an already alienated and distrusting mindset that transcends our political culture:

> *"The Russians appear to have insinuated themselves across social media platforms and use the same promotional tools that people use to share cat videos, airline complaints, and personal rants."* **(Confessore, Wakabayashi, 2017)**[38]

Those kinds of conclusions are distorted further by the kumbya message of the platform moguls. In his 'one Facebook' world salute in April, 2016, Mark Zuckerberg tooted his own business model horn. He elevated his company to the role of global unifier and its social mission to that of a governing body — channeling what most constitutionalists would refer to as freedom of expression:

> *"We stand for connecting every person. For a global community. For bringing people together. For giving all people a voice. For a free flow of ideas and culture across nations. (...) We've gone from a world of isolated communities to one global community, and we're all better off for it."* **(Zuckerberg, 2016)**[39]

Is Zuckerberg's global vision an aspiration toward a borderless agrarian community or a single target market? In one corner lies the cross-cultural flow of ideas, in the other, the spoon-feeding of information consumers. The flow of it is heading one way. And it ain't free once it flows back out.

That flow is what Facebook users metabolize in the form of pictures, likes, and posts. It forms the basis of what Shoshana Zuboff refers to as 'surveillance capitalism' — consumers grouped into product segments by their inherited demographics, self-identified affiliations, and credit histories. **(Zuboff, 2016)**[40] The shadow identity formed in the passive capture of actively engaged members of a search network. The same model applies to Google's search-based advertising services. But those factoids don't make the news feed — just more extra servings to Zuckerberg's 'global community' of low-stress messages delivered by favored messengers.

© Anthony Quintano

Facebook is made up of dozens of millions of groups carefully designed to share the same views and opinions. Each group is protected against ideological infiltration from other groups not sharing in the same affinity. Maintaining the integrity of these walls is the primary mission of Facebook's algorithm. **(Filloux, 2016)**[41]

And surveillance capitalism is not a wholly creation of a free market or a net neutral web. **(Lips, Taylor, Bannister, 2005)**[42] Consider how quickly we recoil at state-run programs designed to discriminate against, deport, or even ban targeted religions and nationalities. Zuckerberg's global community is drawn from the same discriminating behaviors commonly written into national by-laws: Racial profiling, religious intolerance, gender bias, etc. **(Feldman, 2017)**[43] Just as governments can screen travelers or round-up undesirables, Facebook customers can target, exclude, or otherwise isolate the very same citizens who would...

- Espouse the high-minded goals of an open and equal Internet for all, or
- Acquiesce to the parochial, censored nature of a Great Internet Firewall. **(E.H., 2013)**[44]

#2 TO DO: Don't objectify people. Personalize the groups they join.

Virtual profiles are impersonal – devoid of context. The most successful digital media companies all share a singular focus on using transactional data to enrich their revenues. This fixation misses the offline realities that confront independent investigators. Foremost on the Knowledge-ABLED agenda is the priority utmost on the minds of investigators: The question of motive and the explanatory power of sense-making.

As we've established, this falls flat as an engineering problem. The query of 'why' is alien to the search box. This is not merely a design flaw of software but a lost opportunity if the Knowledge-ABLED don't find the recoverable motives behind what are typically a questionable course of actions by our search targets:

EPILOGUE: Giving Voice to Searching Out Loud | Page 7:32

1. What are the situations our search targets come home to every evening?

2. What are the larger-than-life lessons that fuel the ambitions and visions of a better life for a person-of-interest?

3. What kinds of adversities confronted by a suspect in a case are binding and worthy of battling, which kinds are worthy of escaping or avoiding altogether?

© Jeremiah Solomon

This is an open invitation to the Knowledge-ABLED for revisiting the composite that envelopes person-hood, not consumption habits on two legs as depicted by the social and search media. There are limits to what we can find out about the button-pressing patterns of web-enabled humans organized into blocs of receptive message receivers. That's where underlying behavioral forces are in the driver's seat:

1. The responsibilities we take on

2. Our falling into the wrong crowd or rising in the right one

3. The activities that energize us (and the sustainability of that enthusiasm)

4. The conditions we tolerate (and the location of our breaking point)

These are not shopping carts, social memes, or like counts but the individual choices that define our highly personalized narratives. There's no more intimate way to hold our own pieties in check than to focus on our own values.

For a moment, let's consider us hot on the trail of ourselves as the search targets?

Taken on the face of our social media identities, BS detection isn't limited to those with our shared sense of smell. We're also the ones being sniffed. We align ourselves with employers, professions, interest groups, and causes. All our joining and belonging can imprint our scent on a trail of interactions — even when we move on from a severed association.

Even worse, disavowing those affiliations wraps us in the banner of a turncoat, hypocrite, or someone whose indecision is rooted in a weakness of character. It's a humbling position and one we'd be well advised to assume when placing our own targets under the scrutiny of our investigations.

3) Resist the Social Media Circus

In olden times there was a single arbiter for measuring how we valued the information we consumed. Money. Either the economics were gauged by (1) paid subscriptions and retail sales, or (2) the volume of viewers.

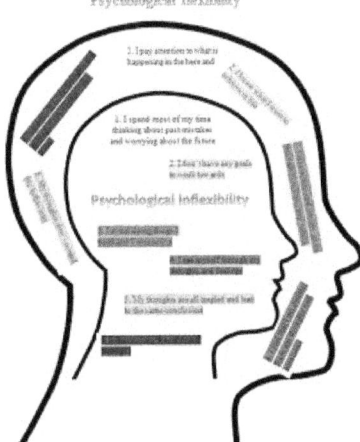

ACT *Psychological* flexibility vs inflexibility

This linear, repeatable gauge for determining impact, influence, and popularity is long gone. The idea of basing media reach on circulation numbers or newsstand sales is as relevant today as counting the passive consumers of staged events. Today, even the most conventional of news providers are almost entirely dependent on the ability to build and sustain a business model that captures what we spend in time facing a screen — not in dollars confronting a purchase.

Our wallets are secondary to our browser histories, a byproduct of our attention. That's where the time goes. It gets crunched into our consumption habits. It gets further refined by our virtual behaviors. Then, in the case of search media, it gets sold to message senders or auctioned to advertisers:

> "If you walk the floor of a modern newsroom, you will most likely see journalists staring at real-time charts flickering with numbers, and dials telling editors where readers are spending every second of their time." **(Bell, 2016)**[45]

What does this have to do with being an effective investigator? Absolutely nothing. That's right. The carnival-like experience of cloying ads and slow-loading news websites that feature auto-playing videos is not budgeted into our SPM logs ("Search Project Management"). Not now. Not ever. These distractions are only relevant if...

- ■ **Distraction 1:** They engage us in a game called *Made-You-Look* and they won by hijacking our attention.
- ■ **Distraction 2:** They provide a baseline for blindspots – the differences between what media we consume based on our affinity biases.

#3 TO DO: Unlearn the need for distractions. Learn what to ignore.

In response to distraction #1, learn what to ignore. Understand the sapping potential of transient information. Impose outside standards on content otherwise compromised by the advertising goals of big search, big social, and web analytics.

In terms of distraction #2, we can leverage **Unit Five's** The Biggest Picture framework for puzzling through the divergences and overlaps between opposing ends of the political spectrum. Understanding what's covered, overlooked, or suppressed between affinity groupings is the goal. It's also a benchmark for blindspots, one sorely lacking in an outside assessment of our collective media consumption. There is even a name for this blindspot. The *technopoly* coined by Neil Postman paves over the social norms it replaces before we can even detect their removal.

The media-literate consumer may not be immune from distraction. But independent-minded investigators are best advantaged to use Knowledge-ABLED frameworks for detecting and tracking affinity bias.

4) Use Google (Manual Edition)

© //searchengineland.com. Is Obama.

Remember that every single use of syntax is a manual override of the auto pilot formed by our consumption of type ahead suggestions. Our comfort with being taken to a pre-delivered outcome should not be the foregone conclusion of our query formation options. It's one thing when our browsers ask us if we want our saved profiles to auto-fill across repeating transactions. It's quite another when a rush of pre-sold Google AdWords storm in to fill a momentary hesitation in our own keyword choices.

There's a technopoly-induced acceptance that several billion Google users can't be wrong. There's a more urgent desire to uphold our independence in a world *"where the algorithmic nano-targeting of electronic media knows our desires and impulses before we know them ourselves."* **(Bell, 2016)**[46]

All the more reason for us to go off-road. All the more incentive for us to apply our query formation approach to our virtual investigations. Disabling the search suggestions happens automatically when you invoke syntax and semantics in your queries. At some future date, assuming Google continues to support manual search, we may also need to prove we're not some form of automation ourselves.

#4 TO DO: Turn-off auto search.

© image.freepik.com: Girl sitting on the floor chained to tablet

Those overrides are not limited to the syntax and semantics of query formations. They include the need to steer clear of default Google sources. We are accepting an algorithmic interpretation of information providers whenever we search without telling Google *where* to search.

Remember how news feed algorithms exploit our self-selecting behaviors — especially those that validate our opinions and beliefs? It's no different for the source selection in Google searches. That's why source fluency coupled with query formation increasingly holds the key to effective search strategies. Query formation is the manual override of search media filtering, ranking formulas, and the ad-triggered sponsor links embedded in their calculations. Source fluency enables us to assign motives to information providers, determining a best-interest scenario to the availability, suppression, or even likelihood of what we'll find before we go in search of it.

That said, the Knowledge-ABLED can demonstrate our value-add to clients even without a foreknowledge of our search targets and topics simply by tracking the differences between our mediated searches and what Google sends us. That distinction resembles the same affinity bias that we surface in social media communities — our click patterns organized into a labyrinth of groupings based on the binary logic of...

- good/bad
- hot/cold
- black/white

and extended into the emotional wilderness of...

- hate/love
- freedom/control
- nationalistic/global-minded, etc.

The Knowledge-ABLED also form groupable lists inspired by affinity bias. But we do it according to information providers — not consumers. By organizing results by sources, we can account for...

- **Variations of news coverage:** Grouping factors are key for determining any variations across the awareness spectrum on topics and stories. Mapping the media sources cited in our search results to their audiences is akin to understanding the information-sharing properties within social media communities.

- **Fact selection:** Which details are elevated or squelched — particularly in comparing coverage of the same events by competing interests. What leaps out as a genuine example of what the reporter has learned since their last post and what about it inspires them to educate us in the same way?

- **Depth of detail:** To what degree is first person and first party engagement factored into each news item? Was original research conducted? Was the accounting corroborated by providers outside the same media grouping? Could the entire premise been invented by the source in question?

- **The experts and organizations contributing their analysis:** An ambitious (and sometimes arduous) way to circumvent the echo chamber between sources, and the sometimes incestuous nature of reporters and the newsmakers they cover. This requires going a level deeper to focus on the groups referenced as background sources in the news stories. These less visible influencers can broker arrangements between news sources, facts selected, and level of validation required to present them as such.

5) Practice Source Fluency by Exposing Your Sources

As much as Google type ahead can hijack our investigations, this loss of control pales when compared to Google's coercion of sources — the information providers that represent the search results addressing the response to our searches. It's one thing to infiltrate our query formations with spoon-fed phrases designed to auto-complete our searches. It's another to selectively highlight or suppress sources based on our search habits and click patterns.

© [LEFT] Leandro Mazzini:Charge de ALIEDO [RIGHT] Harry R. Hopps: Destroy this mad brute Enlist - U.S. Army

One can argue that Google type ahead is a less serious threat to our Knowledge-ABLED practices because we can observe it directly. We can accept or steer clear every time Google generates related phrases or cuts to the chase of a conclusion we find distracting or irrelevant. But limiting the scope of sources to those providing acceptable answers or agreeable assertions or shared perspectives is not a preference we register in our browser settings. We are destined as passive consumers to receive the response we're conditioned to handle — unless we seek out a broader range of responses.

It's not enough to base accuracy on verification alone. A verified news source stretching credulity isn't breaking the rules, be it an Instagram post, a government official, or a celebrity with a high follow count. So long as they vouch for their actual authorship, they have a wide license to misrepresent, distort, and even invent the facts. A bar set this low seeks elevation if we are to bring accountability to the vetting process.

#5 TO DO: Be the source of credibility, not its recipient.

Don't take someone else's recipe for creating a well-rounded or better grounded view of the world based on the smiley-face logic of a social media algorithm. Don't expect that the same warpened reality can deliver how others outside our social circles consumer their news, *"bursting the filter bubble that they helped create."* **(Hess, 2017)**[47] Live Tweeting a public hearing or political speech is not a substitute for empirical pursuits such as fact-checking, mining for blindspots in **Unit One** or the credibility we seek through integrity vectors and PCF ("Provider Conjugation Frameworks") in **Unit Four**.

Rather, base it on one source at a time. Reference the sources cited in **Unit Two's** Tool Selection where a list of specific URLs point to sources grouped by conventional forms of news coverage: Broadcast, wire services, management journals, financial media, etc. A more generic approach to sourcing is one way to keep the results focused on the research without fixating on news bias.

That said, creating our own news groupings offers clear comparisons of what stories get exposed, diminished, or emphasized according our coverage groups. The Knowledge-ABLED set up the experiment — not the algorithms created by the technologists.

6) SAVE THE PASSION FOR THE HUNT – NOT THE HUNTED

It's one thing to expose yourself to alternative opinions. It's quite another to approach one's smart phone notifications as an anthropological calling. There's no denying the benefits of seeking out the *other side* and bursting the filter bubble so that a broader perspective emerges. Even leading to an appreciation of opinions we don't happen to hold.

© Steven Marcus

But there's a detachment that's become increasingly rare in the bias debate and the hand-wringing over fake news and hyper-partisanship. An independent investigation requires an active interest in uncovering corruption and exposing injustice. But the independence comes with a price — that's the cost of an equally active disinterest in a particular outcome, verdict, or conclusion.

That means our focus is on the discovery process — not where those discoveries lead. That sounds simple and anyone who believes this is compromising their investigation from the start. If we're honest with ourselves, we'll concede that we want the good guys to win. We'll admit that our quest for truth answers to a range of conclusions, that may or may not be supported by our research. The ultimate test of our research mettle is whether our passions can exist outside the scales of justice. Any attempt to tip these scales will taint the most exhaustive investigators and sow doubt in the evidence we gather.

A healthy skepticism about the self-serving nature of message sending is critical to disinterest. It's the essential ingredient missing from the vested nature of a post social media news environment. Our clients, peers, and message recipients will come to the table with their own predispositions — each of these biases immediately informed by any social media search of us as information providers in our own right.

#6 TO DO: Carry a deep and abiding disinterest in your search targets.

If disinterest was a person they would undoubtedly be friended by their pal, depersonalization. That's right. The very same cold, off-putting way that your geeky nerd friends would rather cozy up to some lab results than some celebrated tweets might play better to the scientific method than to the heart-strings of a sympathetic audience.

But sympathy is not the correct device for promoting the kind of cold, unbiased outcomes delivered by an evidence-based investigation. That's why ginning up the emotional stakes undermines the very notion of independence. That's why the page-turning properties of a riveting narrative have no place in an effective investigation.

That kind of high-minded view of truth-seeking independence is easily humbled in the rush of an unfolding crisis. Those principled guidelines are crushed under the weight of a public emergency. There is no honor code for information providers as first responders. At the inception of the chaos forms the unconfirmed messages that attract our own predispositions to fill in missing details. These are not the cool, collected notions of the detached investigator but the insatiable appetite of hysteria. According to Dartmouth College Professor Brendan Nyhan...

> *Digital social networks are dangerously effective at identifying memes that are well adapted to surviving, and these also tend to be the rumors and conspiracy theories that are hardest to correct.*
> **(Carey, 2017)**[48]

Their staying power is traceable to our own shadow rationales to make sense of an unsolved crime or assigning guilt to a would-be perpetrator. In either case we are all prone to rushes in judgment in the heat of anxious moments. We seek to exact vengeance on an unwitting victim or in deference to a sympathetic cause:

> *"Purely from a psychological point of view, subtle individual biases are at least as important as rankings and choice when it comes to spreading bogus news or Russian hoaxes — like a false report of Muslim men in Michigan collecting welfare for multiple wives."* **(Carey, 2017)**[49]

How do we resist the simple human impulse to resolve these passions with readily-formed scapegoats who we hold responsible for outcomes far beyond the influence of a single actor?

An investigation based on the behaviors of institutions and the operations of systems is by nature an impersonal one. Unlike criminal investigations, no one actor is "the fall guy." No specific individual is the cardinal villain, absolving their subordinates of all wrongdoing and personal responsibility. By de-emphasizing the personal, we're able to encourage the self-correcting behavior of groups to honor their public spirit, reign in their members, and curb their own excesses.

7) Rinse and Repeat

At the core of the scientific process lies the same transparency we insist on with investigative reporting: Replication. That means that the recipe we use in our research kitchens would produce the same evidence in our investigations.

That doesn't necessarily mean the same conclusions but roughly the same facts to base them on. Only by using case notes like search logs can we move past the filter bubbles and the self-reinforcing agendas of information providers to focus on a body of evidence and the inferences we draw from it.

© Vitali Drabysheuski: Rinse and Repeat

Rinse and repeat bears reciprocal repeating. We should insist on the same documentation from other stakeholders with competing explanations for the same events, circumstances, or behaviors of the players involved. Insisting on a research recipe can create more suspicion than transparency from a peer investigator with no reference to search logs or an informed approach to query formation.

That stigma may wane if we respect contrarian natures, conflicting views, and argumentative dialog. Our role is not to stay ahead of the argument but to focus on the actual evidence through established fact-finding channels such as legal discovery. An informed and effective web-based search strategy is one such component and no less critical in an age of social media, smart phones, and algorithms designed to customize and ultimately isolate our information-gathering activities.

#7 TO DO: Perform the experiment in your kitchen but make sure to stick to the recipe (and share it).

We don't always sing from the same pew, talk from the same script, or land on or near the same interpretations of events. With all those chances to veer off the path of understanding, we owe those deviations and disconnects a simple courtesy. We need to document the path taken – if not the conclusion drawn.

The sequential nature of search logs are not so much programming instructions like you'd expect to see for developers in a code repository or for administrators in a user's guide. It's more of a road map piecing together how we follow a trail of evidence from a hypothetical assertion to a structured accounting of the actors and their actions. Along the way, the story our search log tells includes some validated assumptions, plausible explanations, and perhaps even an informed judgment or two.

© Joseph Gruber: Protest at the White House for Net Neutrality

The goal is not to create the ultimate search log. There will always be a search log less traveled and an alternative route that escapes the sights of the most accomplished investigator. Rather it's the transparency of the road map that transcends...

- The circular logic of gut checks, and
- The stubborn, longstanding disagreements of warring factions.

The searches we do and how we perform them won't carry a winning argument any more than we can define a source as definitive (and its word as 'final') based on its site traffic. What it can do is provide a level of accountability lacking in the reconstructions and logic flows of public officials, reporters, and the institutions they cover.

8) PUBLISH THE MAP – DON'T BURY THE TREASURE

The rinse-and-repeat cycle of the scientific method is an empty promise of transparency without the map. We need to include the sequence that connects our original premise to the evidence we gather, and where the evidence leads us. That journey invites the passenger-side participation of our clients who can either question or approve of our mapping. Either way, they're traveling alongside us.

It's important to make this a joint effort ahead of the destination — the sharing any overall assessments or conclusions on the evidence itself. Providing your clients and stakeholders with an open question is an open invitation to include your query formation elements ahead of any efforts to provide explanations and rationales.

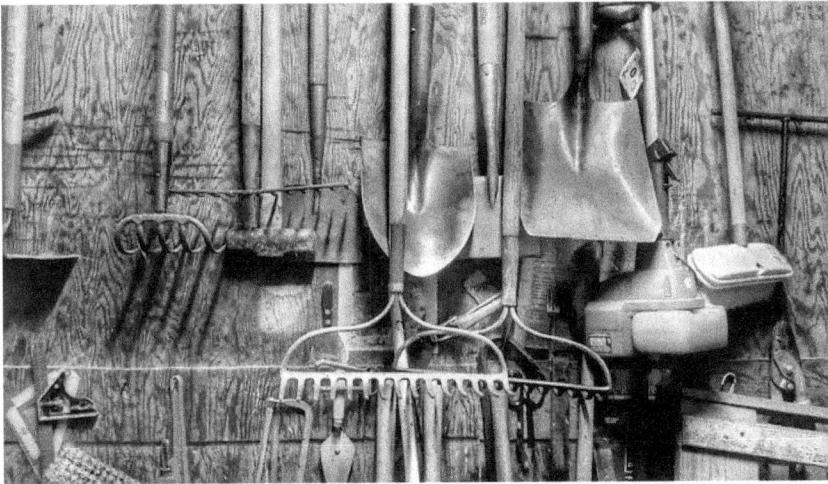

© Marc50: Garden Tools

Closure is not the guiding force for plotting the sequential nature of the discovery process. If anything, a series of competing interpretations and alternate scenarios should draw your stakeholders into an analytic process that is active, participatory, and ongoing as new evidence surfaces.

Coddling your inner archivist is an important corollary of this bread crumb trail-blazing business of map publishing. Leverage the cache-seeking potential of Internet archives like The Wayback Machine to bring transparency to Senator Moynihan's *unentitled* facts. These have been either buried, discontinued, or purged altogether from a medium that knows how to create distraction much better than it can shield us from obscurity. The Internet is complicit in Postman's Technopoly, abetting the quiet disappearances of embarrassing evidence. It's not your father's cover-up. It's more the promising leads put on ice by legally-binding non-disclosures. No-admission-of-guilt agreements in exchange for payouts to victims.

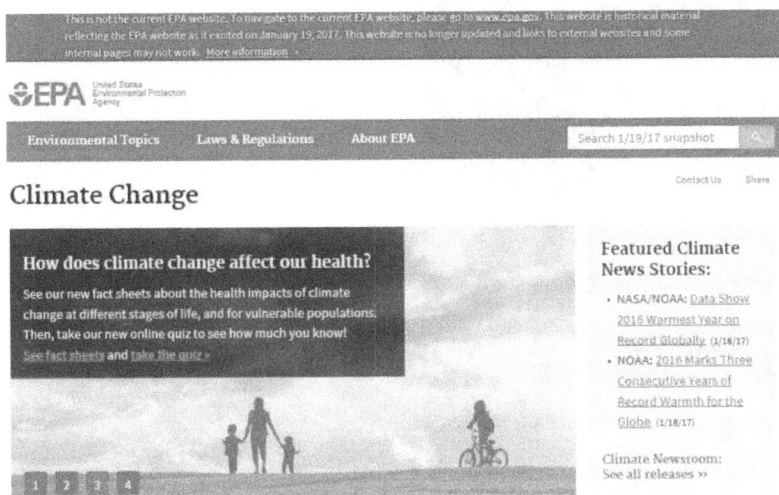

The policy shift on climate change by the Trump Administration prompted this holdover of a cached page documenting newly unsupported climate facts.

In addition to dedicated caching archives like Wayback, there is the slow but steady drumbeat of public records that are now accessible online. As documentation slips from stone tablets to parchment to notebooks to databases, the more our transactions go electronic, the farther back we can go. From legal decisions to ship manifestos, the digitizing of public records puts obscurity within reach.

Curiously, the term 'practical obscurity' refers to legal research in an analog world where the arduous task of combing fraying courthouse papers was considered a passive form of protection for our privacy. Before the Internet it was problematic to search the electronic stacks of legal, civic, and scientific record-keeping:

> *There were too many potential sources, and the volume of paper information was often unwieldy. Further, the information was frequently located at different places. Sometimes, the custodian of the information would put another subjective limit on access, i.e., the person behind the counter would be less than cooperative in providing the requested information. Moreover, once the information was located, it had to be copied. Under these circumstances, it was often only the most diligent seeker of information who would discover what the court had in its possession. These limits on access became known as 'practical obscurity.'"* **(DOJ v. Reporters Comm. for Free Press 489 U.S. 749, 1989)**[50]

#8 TO DO: Put your deciders in the driver's seat of your research.

The most effective way to give practical obscurity its proper due and burial is to share a working draft of the search project, prior to wrapping the investigation. At first this sounds like an awkward collaboration or a dodge from the autonomy of our independence. Let's think this through: A draft version leads to a final version. A recommendation rarely leads to the final word of a conclusive outcome.

Investigators are typically not the deciders at the decision table. That limitation on the powers of the researcher might be a sobering reflection on the limits of the Knowledge-ABLED. Conversely, it's a standing invitation to extend our influence as explainers, interpreters, clarifiers, and analysts to our clients, peers, and stakeholders.

© Marc Solomon, Hadley, MA

That means involving them in the discovery process to foster a better understanding of how we can open, throttle, or even distort channels of discovery through query formation and the source fluency that informs our counsel. That advice is premised on our status as research experts.

Searching Out Loud | Marc Solomon

But the recommendations we confer is not about forming better research statements but to resolve the issues that prompted our involvement.

Here's a suggestion: Revisit the search log to include three potential last steps. Each destination should suggest an alternative course of action. Leave room in the report recommendations for three distinct next steps based on the diverging outcomes suggested in the log. Ask the recipients to test each of these scenarios and see which option they find most plausible – regardless of their decision status.

9) NET NEUTRALITY IS THE NEW OBJECTIVITY

In addition to respecting the practice of impersonal judgment and the need for emotional distance, there is another emerging definition that must be factored into the objectivity goals of our investigations. Net neutrality is the term used to describe the principle that the Internet is a public utility just like water, gas, and electricity. As such its use as a public resource shouldn't be privileged or compromised in the private hands of ISPs ("Internet Service Providers"). The commercial interests who connect us are beneficiaries of global standards for browsing the web — not its builders or purveyors.

The Title II label below refers to the section of the Open Internet Order issued in 2015 that regulates what those owners of the information pipes do as they pump content across this public resource. Giving preferential treatment to some information providers over others is one example of an Internet fast lane. Not only do consumers pay for access but providers pay the same middle man for the right to distribute — sort of yesterday's cable TV version of tomorrow's Internet business model. What the title II detractors seem to be saying is that there can be no further separation between the Internet as a vehicle for commerce and its commercialization in private hands.

This argument led to a reversal of the Net Neutrality standard at the close of 2017.

© Fight for the Future: Fight for the Future net neutrality

Why is a regulatory skirmish between pro and anti-regulation forces relevant to our Knowledge-ABLED to do list?

This universality of an open web remains a point of leverage for those of us motivated by the research medium we engaged before the politics intruded. It's the Internet's enormity that provides researchers with a much broader spectrum to understand the impact of news. But it's not the news that's fit to print. It's news no longer without search habits, click patterns, and mutually-dependent social engagements such as liking, friending, sharing, and following. All of these interactions fuel algorithms designed to stroke our egos, endorse our preferences, and tickle our page-turning imaginations. The problem with engagement as a primary news determinant is that attention becomes the priority for its own sake — devoid of the context or its social impact:

> "A news feed that is optimized for engagement is essentially the algorithmic equivalent of 'it bleeds it leads' — this is problematic when journalistic due process is missing from a huge portion of web-based news." **(Tobias, 2016)**[51]

For starters, swapping out Net Neutrality for a more partisan model denies a fundamental civil liberty — equal access to the same level playing field — the Internet as public resource. The wider implication is this

That like your Google Search and my Facebook news feeds, that your Internet behaves differently than mine — at least for those of us who consider consider frozen screens and spastic lapses in page loads as grounds to close or tab, cancel a session, or close our browser outright. This is because that connection is not privileged by the ISP connecting us. Finally, in an Internet economy brokered by ISPs, many sites will be muscled out by their higher bidder competitors who ante up for the Internet fast lane.

#9 TO DO: The greatest hazard posed to freedom of information is free information.

She said, he said. You're with us. You're against us. Forces for good girding against a tide of evil. Whose side are you on?

Not all arguments are two-sided. Even in battle, the acceptance and rejection of ideas are fluid and interdependent. There is no wholesale acceptance. There is no wholesale rejection. This is not a zero sum game. Conflict is the one indivisible absolute.

One major advantage that the Knowledge-ABLED hold over the big social and search media is the ability to attract opposing perspectives. The independent investigator is not only free of group think but the two chief concerns of advertisers:

    1. Keep news consumers informed within their comfort zones, and

    2. Keep advertisers within range of those same consumers.

This freedom affords us to move our perspectives beyond partisanship and the clannish impulses of what we come to define in **Unit Four** as authenticity and credibility, its diametrical counterpart along the **Vectors of Integrity**. We can offer this perspective because media surveys across an open web can factor our our mental calculus as individuals and group members. We can invoke our basic human instinct for interpreting first person accounts against third-party reporting of the same events.

The recognition of these vectors in a scoring formula, (i.e. **Unit Five's The Biggest Picture**) is in itself the ultimate filter. It covers the very real divergences in awareness, attention, and ultimately predisposition to act on the news in our own self-curated media consumption.

This ability to step away from the noise of the crowd, commercial interests, and the intrinsic allure of bias itself all factor into the pulse-taking practices the Knowledge-ABLED and the benefit of carrying out these diagnostics in all walks of information-led exploration. The strength of these survey methods has yet to be tested in a post Net Neutral arrangement.

The Knowledge-ABLED will require backdoor arrangements to emulate an open web in the event of its demise.

© Marc Solomon, Springfield, MA

Searching Out Loud | Marc Solomon

10) MAKING-YOU-ACT IN THE *MAKE-YOU-LOOK*-ECONOMY

Perhaps the most exposed of human frailties isn't falling prey to hackers or spammers or trollers or bots or ransomware attackers or the next entrapment merchants scheming to separate our sense of honor and commitment from our credit lines and fiscal assets.

It isn't even being *hosed* by an unrelenting storm of noisy, undiscriminating news feeds, popup ads, spam-tinged calls to action, and a set of vaguely unsettling headlines, tickling our craven appetites with check-out counter-based formulas for capturing our wavering attentions.

What folks do with info provides us Knowledge-ENABLERS with endless fascination. There's a limit to the intrigue, however. That's the perishable state of our attentions.

© Lindsay Young Made you look, Banksy, is that you?

Our most common state of being compromised in a world of information by fire hose is to trust in the sprinkler system. That's when we fall prey to the assumption that all the days of our lives consist of...

- Roughly the same number of events
- Carrying about the same degree of historic consequence
- Sprayed into the media landscape with the same intensity by the same number of reporters on the same spray trigger

Ideally the Knowledge-ABLED carry a spray cap on that open hydrant of news feeds. It helps to irrigate us clear of the flood zone and keeps the proportion of news generation to our capacity for absorbing it.

But being an informed news junkie is not the same as being an astute researcher or an intrepid investigator. It helps to have a high threshold for consuming large news volumes. However, it's a whole different problem to transition from the detail-sifting to the pattern-matching required to connect-the-proverbial dots of an investigation.

#10 TO DO: Don't fall for the fallacy that a technological fix stands between us and all the world's social problems.

The Knowledge-ABLED don't subscribe to the no-news-is-good-news-feed. That's the information equivalent to questioning whether those forest trees topple down without a bias-neutral reporter to witness their fall.

One way to tell the news consumers from the data detectives is to uncover the filtering in that spray cap. In other words the screening criteria used to separate the signal from the noise in the particulars deemed relevant to the case. Is that a rationale formed by the researcher's own cunning and calculations? Or is it an algorithm more grounded in data science than the rationale of the human actors we're trying to rationalize through our research?

Algorithms are number-crunching programs designed to solve business problems like factoring for risk or calculating prices. What they should not be is construed as impartial or impervious to...

- The biases of the programmers who create them, or
- The companies that embed them in their products.

It can also be said that the Knowledge-ABLED are, a hedge against a romanticized view of algorithms. One where all investigative problem-solving is reducible to machine learning and codified outcomes.

Investigators don't typically farm out their search project priorities to a scoring formula. Like our big search and social media brothers, we too are focused, even fixated on the data trails of individuals and groups. But investigators don't regard their search targets as the sum of their preferences. A jury verdict or a legal decree is not reducible to a finite number of quantifiable conclusions.

Our justice system answers to a presumption of innocence. A principle at odds with systems designed to make predictive decisions based on large data sets. We don't cherry-pick our evidence the way an algorithm is designed to do for say high margin customers. The number-driven decisions of the market don't comport to the unstructured nature of independent investigations.

Yet there exists a Silicon Valley conceit that humans compromised by information overload require more technology to find their place within an emerging social order. It's an order prone to inversing our relationship with information from one of using it to one of being used by it. Can it be useful to us if it returns the favor by using us to its exclusive advantage?

Perhaps because those advantages were built to preserve the interests of its builders is reason enough that technology giants like Google and Facebook are both silent and oblivious to uniquely human intelligence factors.

That should alarm but not surprise us.

Nor can we claim to be misled or deceived by their need to closely guard the proprietary nature of their rationales for the ranking, scoring, repackaging, and ultimate sale of the products composed of our own data.

Our biggest challenge is not to face down the intimidation factor but to stand-up for human intelligence factors we otherwise take for granted, namely that blend of...

- Intuition,
- Creative problem-solving, and
- Experience-based learning we perform to decode other humans.

Human awe of technology doesn't just lead to lots of screens, apps, and forgotten passwords. It leads us to an overwhelming sense of doubt about our own unique capacities to create, innovate, analyze and problem solve. We see the daunting ability of technology to process raw data, identify patterns, and quantify all the formulas we throw at them. Is it any wonder reliance on our devices can lead to a vast overestimation of what mental work we can farm out to computers?

These calculations can be simple and mundane like understanding the body language of a fuming law enforcement officer. They can be advanced like piecing together the loose ends of the improbable events that challenge our powers of investigation. Either way there is no auto pilot, black box, algorithm, or inscrutable digital assistant that compares to the many aptitudes and continuums of human intelligence.

© theTrueMikeBrown

ONE FOR THE ROADMAP

The Great Logoff: Changing the Conversation on Big Tech

Even before social media, there was a great humbling of our individual uniqueness. This disquieting realization was brought to us by the number one search of all-time: Googling ourselves.

EPILOGUE: Giving Voice to Searching Out Loud | Page 7:48

Many, even most, found our names to be repeated properties across countless pages of search results. Our surprisingly common names assuring us that face-in-the-crowd obscurity for all but the most celebrated search targets.

Many of us continue to use Google not just as a search engine but as the sole arbiter of abstract cultural indicators such as public awareness or understandings and popular events and social memes. For potential holders of copyrights, trademarks, and business methods, this use of search media continues to be a deflating exercise given just how routine the co-opting of *exclusive* ideas can be across the web.

Since the first unaided attempt to own our naming rights to Google rankings, the technology has been blunt and unequivocal in its response:

> *Your uncommon identity is either shared or similar to the formulas, musings, and naming conventions of other strangers you're more likely to meet through a cease and desist letter than an actual customer wishing to pay for the fair use of your intellectual assets.*

Our singularity is further compromised in an even more basic machine transaction than the vanity search: The simple act of logging in to an online account. To big tech, the only unique attribute we possess are our user credentials — the passwords and IDs we use to vouch for the fact we are representing the human referenced on the account form, usually with some form of financial resources.

Misrepresentation doesn't carry the same set of risks for big tech that it does for financial services. One rarely hears of identity theft and the social or search media in the same breath. For the most part most Google or Facebook users are not their customers. Hardly surprising then that compromised identities don't carry much risk for either company. At least should their core business of selling our consumption and attention patterns go unabated.

© Erin Nekervis: In suspicion we trust

Searching Out Loud | Marc Solomon

At the time of this writing, a security breech in the search history of a Google user or their Facebook news feed is an unexplored realm of cybercrime. This is unlikely to be a risk exposure for big tech until prosecutors weigh in on the role of digital media assumption in the plotting of offline acts of subversion and violence, i.e. mass shootings. In the meantime, the cost to big tech for retaining us is largely a marketing concern: Developing habit-forming applications and reinforcing their attraction through convenience factors such as (1) site cookies, (2) prior social interactions, and (3) access to the back-end systems that record and store them.

Who knew how persuasive the saving of a password could be? Who knew we would surrender our privacy for so little in return?

The goal for the Knowledge-ABLED is to harness the power of inconvenience. Going rouge in our social and search media travels is not a violation of any law or a breach of any firewall. It's the simple assertion that our role as investigators requires our own imposed firewall between us and the extended big brother reach of the surveillance capitalism defined by Shoshana Zuboff *(see Page 7.30)*. It's also a warning that the society-wide default is now set to our unconditional love to the convenience of living virtually. And that loyalty is bending towards servitude.

Shoshana Zuboff

From this perspective, becoming Knowledge-ABLED is...

- ■ An earnest effort to use web-based research tools, archives, and frameworks to influence the decisions that bind the on and offline worlds together,
- ■ A first step towards drawing the line between the two for weighing trade-off s, and ultimately,
- ■ Balancing the power between the masters of internet capitalism and its citizen-users.

As a recent podcast series called the *Privacy Paradox* attests, our smart phones are tracking devices that leak our movements from our cars, homes, and offices. Such devices are not issued by "the State" or law enforcement. They're self-selected by a vast majority of smart phone owners. **(Zomorodi, 2017)**[52] Hence, we and not the info police are culpable for our own virtual jailing. Only when we see our smart phones with the same appreciation as our voracious data overlords will we see a clear, informed choice: (1) disable location settings, or (2) do nothing (default behavior). While we're in privacy settings, here's s another to-do under the disabled option: Insist on the digital liberties required to spread Knowledge-ABLED practices under the constitutional protections of the United States, and scaled to other global republics and democracies.

FINAL USE CASE

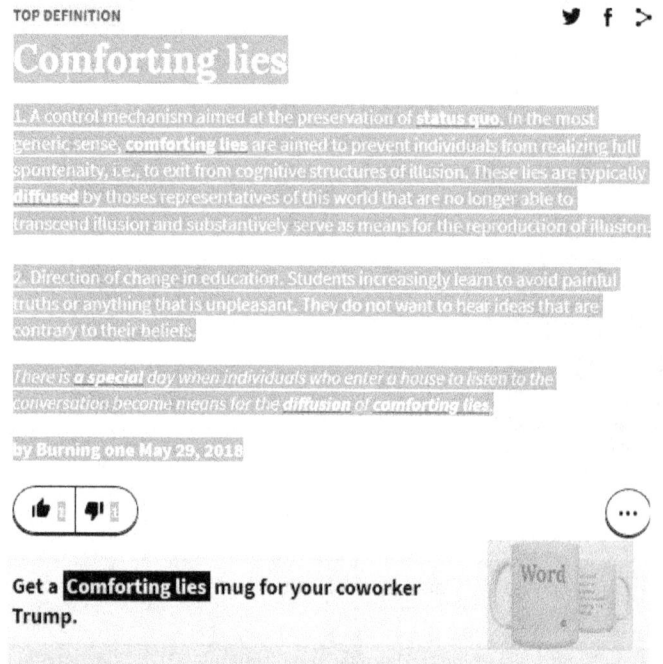

© Urban Dictionary: Comforting Lies

Are we consummate users of information or does information use us?

For the Knowledge-ABLED, the fight continues on for clarifying intentions, rationalizing motives, and clearly reading the perspectives of those we may share little in the way of experience or news feeds. And that piece is limited to what began in the 1980s as interrogating databases through search investigations. It's not just syntax, query formation, information types, or oceans, lakes, and ponds. It's the explanatory power of independent research as its own framework for understanding the dependencies of our human nature. Will it influence the folks we want to engage? Will it change the way technologists build logic into their algorithms and our devices? The outcomes could not be less certain or more relevant to our use case.

These changes impact the Internet not merely as an information network, commerce engine, and research medium. It's a reflection of how we relate to each other, both as a container and modeler of evolving behaviors. This is new territory in these last ten years. It's not a new variation on information overload or the stress of rapid change. It's not digital disruptions that describe the resiliency of organizations to unforeseen changes in their markets. It's not just the new normal of how we chose to draw attention, lost interest, harbor grievances, or censor our own trails.

I would argue that the entire range of these behaviors is *unexpected*.

There are no rules in our by-laws or decorum in our social interactions that reinforce a common set of expectations around our digitized personal conduct — whether we're dismissing the value of cat videos or accepting Bitcoin in the sale of illegal substances. I would also argue that the forces most rewarded on the Internet are the most reluctant to explore the impact and ultimate cost of what is now a commonly accepted and fully operational social experiment.

Becoming Knowledge-ABLED doesn't create more Twitter followers. It doesn't open up the doors of power to more influential networks. Also, all the tools at our disposal won't put any distance between us and the darker forces cloud over information transparency, compromise the social trust, and threaten our investigative freedoms. Our info-literacy provides the basis to call out these behaviors:

1. The logic of self-serving algorithms,

2. The conflicts of interest inherent in the information held by entrenched interests, and

3. The harm resulting from a naive faith in social networks.

At our most effective, Knowledge-ABLED frameworks provide the guidelines and test beds to assess the impact of private gain over a public resource. At a minimum, they instruct us on how to think like the machines programmed to marginalize the participation of citizen-users in the Internet as a public resource. From a human perspective, that kind of motivation is vastly preferable to the vengeance of an independently acting machine.

That is the path before us. This is a road less traveled by our colleagues and the communities we are supporting with our research. Partly because the free flow of information promised by the web has fallen into the private hands of propertied interests. Partly because the on-ramp to that original information superhighway has been detoured by the self-serving distractions of those same interests.

This book is not an argument for tighter regulation, a screed against privatization, whether you're frittering time away on social media, or a litmus test for determining how closely one's personal views align with the changing face of public perception. It is a sign post to the on ramp. It is the declaration that its passage is critical to future user-owners. Citizens of societies that honor transparency of sources and a common set of empirically settled facts. It is the confidence of knowing that our Knowledge-ABLED travelers will fuse the interwoven nature of continuous learning and independent thought into the communities they form.

As David Brooks writes in the pages of the New York Times:

> "The last few decades have been a social trust apocalypse. The only remaining bonds of trust are local and particular. But people are ingenious. They are figuring out how to build on those ties to weave and redeem the broader social fabric." **(Brooks, 2018)**[53]

© Rod Prouty: Autobahn A29 near Ahlhorn, Germany

[1] Neil Postman, "Technopoly: The Surrender of Culture to Technology," Penguin Random House, 1992
[2] Cal Newport, "Deep Work: Rules for Focused Success in a Distracted World," Grand Central Publishing, 2016
[3] Cal Newport, ibid
[4] Justin E.H. Smith, "No, He's Not Hitler. and Yet ...," The New York Times, June 4, 2016
[5] Scott Turow, "Laura Lippman's Wilde Lake," New York Times Book Review, May 31, 2016
[6] John Ehrenreich, "Why Are Conservatives More Susceptible to Believing Lies?" Slate, November 9, 2017
[7] John Ehrenreich, ibid
[8] David Samuels, "The Aspiring Novelist Who Became Obama's Foreign-Policy Guru -- How Ben Rhodes Rewrote the Rules of Diplomacy for the Digital Age," New York Times Magazine, May 5, 2016
[9] "Why Google and Facebook Prove the Digital Ad Market Is a Duopoly," Reuters, July 28, 2017
[10] Margaret Sullivan, "Face it, Facebook. You're in the News Business," Washington Post, July 10, 2016
[11] Margaret Sullivan, ibd
[12] John Herrman, "Facebook's Problem Isn't Fake News — It's the Rest of the Internet," The New York Times, December 22, 2016

[13] Wayne Friedman, "TV Stations' Local News Viewership Continues Decline," Television News Daily, July 14, 2017
[14] Kristen Bialik, Katerina Eva Matsa, "Key Trends in Social and Digital News Media," Pew Research Center, October 4, 2017
[15] David Samuels, ibid
[16] David Leonhardt, "Harvey and Human Activity," The New York Times, August 29, 2017
[17] Michael Moore. "Morning After To Do List," Facebook, November 16, 2016
[18] John Herrman, ibid
[19] John Lloyd, "Social media alone understood the Donald Trump story. The decline of newspapers puts them level with vast flows of fantasy and leaks," Financial Times, November 11, 2016
[20] Frederic Filloux, ibid
[21] Emily Bell, "The Price We Pay for an Ad-Powered Internet," The New York Times, November 11, 2016
[22] Timothy Snyder, "On Tyranny Explores New Threats Facing American Political System," All Things Considered, March 6, 2017
[23] Timothy Snyder, ibid
[24] Chase Peterson-Withorn, "How Donald Trump Exaggerates And Fibs About His $4.5 Billion Net Worth," Forbes, March 31, 2016
[25] Neil MacFarquhar, "A Powerful Russian Weapon: The Spread of False Stories," The New York Times, August 28, 2016
[26] Hadas Gold, "CNN severs ties with Donna Brazile," October 31, 2016, Politico
[27] Jonathan Chait, "The Case Against the Media. By the Media," July 25, 2016, New York Magazine
[28] Michael Cieply, "Stunned By Trump, the New York Times Finds Some Time for Soul-Searching," Deadline Hollywood, November 10, 2016
[29] Stuart Jeffries, "How the Web Lost its Way — and its Founding Principles," The Guardian, August 24, 2014
[30] Marshall McLuhan, "Understanding Media: The Extensions of Man," MIT Press, 1964
[31] Mark Zuckerberg, "Building Global Community," Facebook, February 16, 2017
[32] Joe Vesey-Byrne, "Donald Trump Commands Hearts, not Minds, According to This Poll," The Independent, August 14, 2017
[33] David Roth, "Trump Voters Say They Choose Trump Over The NFL," Deadspin, October 12, 2017
[34] Frederic Filloux, "Facebook's Walled Wonderland Is Inherently Incompatible with News," Monday Note, December 5, 2016
[35] Tobias Rose-Stockwell, "How We Broke Democracy (But Not in the Way that You Think)," Medium, November 11, 2016
[36] Kurt Andersen, "How America Lost Its Mind," The Atlantic, September, 2017
[37] Frederic Filloux, ibid
[38] Nicholas Confessore, Daisuke Wakabayashi, "How Russia Harvested American Rage to Reshape U.S. Politics," New York Times, October 9, 2017
[39] Mark Zuckerberg, "Facebook CEO Mark Zuckerberg at F8 2016 Day 1 Keynote," The Singju Post, April 18, 2016
[40] Shoshana Zuboff, "The Secrets of Surveillance Capitalism," Frankfurter Allgemeine, March 5, 2016

[41] Frederic Filloux, ibid
[42] Miriam Lips, John A. Taylor, Frank Bannister, "Public Administration in the Information Society: Essays on Risk and Trust," IOS Press, 2005
[43] Brian Feldman, "The Trouble With Facebook's Fake-News Data," New York Magazine, November 17, 2016
[44] E.H., "How Does China Sensor the Internet?" The Economist, April 22, 2013
[45] Emily Bell, ibid
[46] Emily Bell, ibid
[47] Amanda Hess, "How to Escape Your Political Bubble for a Clearer View," The New York Times, March 3, 2016
[48] Benedict Carey, "How Fiction Becomes Fact on Social Media," The New York Times, October 20, 2017
[49] Benedict Carey, ibid
[50] See U.S. Dept. of Justice v. Reporters Committee for the Freedom of the Press (1989), at 749 (holding that a citizen's interest in maintaining secrecy of his arrest and conviction records justified maintaining the records' "practical obscurity").
[51] Tobias Rose-Stockwell, ibid
[52] Manoush Zomorodi, "The Privacy Paradox: What Your Phone Knows," Note to Self, February 6, 2017
[53] David Brooks, "The New Power Structure," The New York Times, April 5, 2018

CURRICULUM GUIDE

Here is the structure used for organizing the book along with the chapters for delivering the methods and skills for becoming Knowledge-ABLED through the Searching Out Loud digital literacy curriculum.

===

UNIT ONE:
How to Turn Information into Knowledge
Preparing:
How to Project Manage Virtual Investigations

===

UNIT ONE SUMMARY

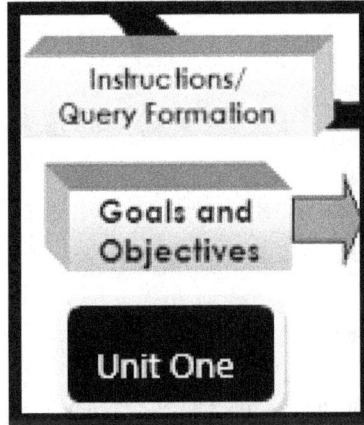

Our first section addresses search project management ("SPM"). SPM is based on the simple and often overlooked reality that being online costs a great deal; not in connect charges or even subscription fees but just by the shear amount of time we invest in searching, often with little to show for it.

Regardless of leaps in processing power, portability, and media convergence, there will remain a single problem reducible to two perennial questions: (1) what kinds of information are out there; and (2) how can what I'm looking for explain or even shape the decisions and actions I'll be making or revising?

SPM contains the discipline and focus that transcends technological change. In **Unit One** we apply SPM principles to recurring research assignments by setting out our information goals. To do this, we'll begin by defining what separates high from low quality information in pursuit of our project objectives. Then we'll decide on the appropriate research approach to our mission-specific projects. Finally, SPM gives us the focus to manage our search projects effectively so that the time and effort we invest is in line with the results we get online.

Unit One Section Structure

1.1 Search Project Management: How do we assess what we want from our research sessions before we log into them

    a. How information becomes useful knowledge in pursuit of project goals and search targets

    b. An overview of the digital discovery process from initial exploration to knowledge mapping and informed decision-making

1.2 Search Logs: How do we document the successes and failures of our research according to the goals and objectives of our investigations

- Pursuing search targets with discipline through selective documentation and action-based questions

1.3 Blindspots: What are some common traps and limitations that impede independent investigations and our effectiveness as researchers

- Setting our information radar to gauge the awareness levels and blindspots of our search targets

1.4 Becoming Knowledge-ABLED: What is our role in bridging the divide between the communities we serve and the technologies that serve us as researchers

    a. What do search engines do and how do they work

    b. How search engines process information, where they get their processing, and how we can get them to do our bidding

Unit One Benefits

- Learn and adopt SPM – A step-by-step process that helps us take control of Internet searches
- Set goals, milestones, and resource limits for finding and applying pertinent information to our research projects
- Build information radars that reveal where our search targets are spending their time and attention and where they're distracted or unaware (blindspots)
- Identify the culprits that steal time from our virtual investigations so we can bypass them when they next arise
- Figure in the time and expense we save by applying sound site selection practices
- Calculate the value accrued in billing for our research services

Unit One Tables

- The Knowledge Continuum – The challenge of using the web for research
- Search Project Management steps and examples - Putting our cards on the table through search logs
- Example search logs – Travel agents, caregivers, criminal investigators
- Google search trade-offs for researchers - Working within search engine limitations

UNIT TWO:
How to Search for Information That Informs
Seeking:
Using Search in Virtual Investigations

Unit Two Summary

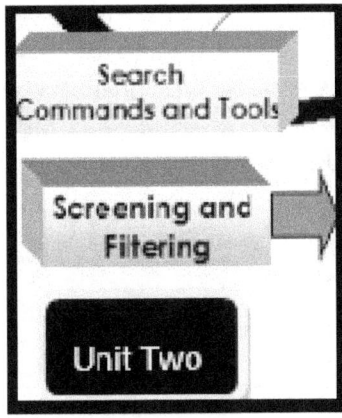

Unit Two is about tossing out the Driver's Ed instruction manual, getting in the car, and taking our established interests and new skills out for a test drive. **Unit Two** applies what we've learned about how search works to different engine and directory options. The goal is to conduct sophisticated, time-effective searches with a minimum of preparation and fees. Our priority is to focus on the best available tool and search strategy for the job at hand.

Having looked under the search engine hood in **Unit One**, we'll focus on tool selection, query formation, and refinement. We'll differentiate and select the right digital search and discovery tools, including visualization, cluster and NLP engines, as well as automated and human-filtered subject directories.

Next we start our meaningful exchanges with these tools by building effective queries. This means using the right search commands and word selection options for leveraging Internet resources, using correct syntax and semantics to express ourselves, and applying fact- and opinion-based guidelines to create productive outcomes.

Finally we draw on search operators, unique IDs, and pointers to either generalize or specify around the topics or our search targets – those events, policies, procedures, groups, or people in question. Our choices will depend not only on how but where we set our sights in the form of site selection.

UNIT TWO SECTION STRUCTURE

2.1 Query Formation: How to arrange, express, generalize, and specify our research questions

- a. What's a fair question and how to interview a search engine
- b. Conveying our intentions through syntax and search operators
- c. Refinements and corrections through term expansion and contraction

2.2 Semantics: What are the best terms for conducting research

- a. The role of informed word choice for building intentionality into search statements
- b. Applying unique IDs and verbatims to exact match and people searches

2.3 Tool Selection: What research tool to use and for which job

- a. Determining the right digital search and discovery tools for the questions we're raising, including visualization, cluster, metasearch and NLP engines
- b. Deciding on the right reference tools and recognized authorities in the fields we're searching including social media, portals, and subject directories
- c. Working with search engines, subject directories, or specialty databases when it's generalities, specifics, or somewhere in-between

2.4 Site Selection: Searching beyond search engines

- a. Where to do research and why size and location matters
- b. Determining the best starting point for the task at-hand
- c. Adjusting our approach to fit our resources

Unit Two Benefits

- Pose productive questions with a bias towards action
- Recognize appropriate search commands and word selection options for leveraging Internet resources
- Arrange and express effective search queries by using correct syntax and semantics
- Yield productive outcomes by applying fact- and opinion-based searches
- Generalize or specify around our topics and search targets by drawing on search operators, unique IDs, and pointers
- Overcome common pitfalls including familiar search detours, poor indexing, and character limits
- Reshape a misinformed question by redirecting our focus to more common problem sets and suggested searches

Unit Two Tables

- Defining what matters – The secret sauce of ordering search results through keywords, repetition, verbatims, and proximity
- Overcoming search limits – What we need to teach the search engine that it can't possibly know
- The haystacks and icebergs framework – Learning cues for opinion and fact-based searches
- Dialogging with search results through SEO (search engine optimization), unique IDs and pointers
- Answers, not documents – Defining natural language search engines
- Overlay of engines and directories – Precision versus recall

==

UNIT THREE:
How to Source Information That Instructs
Sourcing:
How to Evaluate Information Quality

==

UNIT THREE SUMMARY

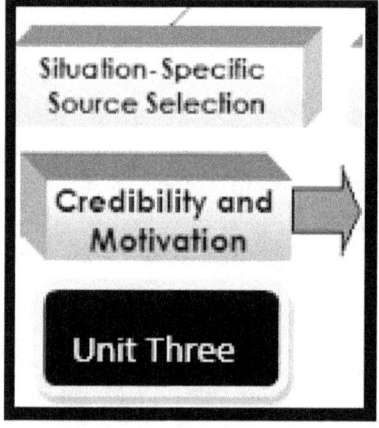

Unit Three focuses on acquiring source fluency and learning how to leverage those sources to improve the quality of the information you source virtually. The Unit starts by confronting the essential form of how information is delivered to us and the questions it inspires: Where is it located? What is it called? When was it done? Who did it? Why do I care? How do I find it again?

We can't possibly know everything and this is no less true for sourcing the world's knowledge. Committing an inventory of leading references and go-to experts on any subject is too daunting even for the reference librarians. Our goal is not to become librarians but to develop a skill called source fluency. Source fluency ensures that we're looking in the right place – even when we're a first-time visitor to unfamiliar topics. We'll set up a quality control process that not only reduces the search noise that clutters our screens. It also helps us to attract, analyze, and interpret the sources we need to fulfill our project objectives. We'll develop the quality of our findings on three levels: Search sets, websites, and individual pages (but only the ones worth opening)!

Unit Three is also devoted to unlocking the secrets, pitfalls and potentials of searching topic-focused Internet databases. Building on our **Unit Two** understanding of search engines (oceans) and subject directories (lakes), we'll dive into the information pond of more narrow and targeted specialty databases to uncover scarce and often overlooked information. OLP ("Oceans, Lakes, and Ponds") is the primary method for establishing: (1) source fluency, and (2) for determining *when* to pursue *what size* database in our virtual investigations.

UNIT THREE SECTION STRUCTURE

3.1 Information Types: How to integrate search findings into a useful form

    a. Surviving the search results page

    b. How information gets packaged in four dimensions – Entry-based, resource-based, view-based, and form-based

3.2 Source Fluency: How to cast our search nets for building source credibility and confidence

    a. Applying the concept of OLP ("Oceans, Lakes, and Ponds") to source the web

    b. Developing source fluency so we can apply sound sourcing methods no matter who's supplying the content

    c. How far to push and how deep to dig before drawing conclusions or reaching out to others

3.3 Quality Control: How to evaluate Information

    a. The three levels of quality control for skimming and assessing results sets, websites, and individual pages

    b. Determining when to use what source, including premium (fee-based) information and deep web (a.k.a. 'invisible web') sources

3.4 Managing Project Resources: How to price information's time and money dimensions

    a. Sizing up free versus fee – When it makes sense to use premium content and where to find it for minimal cost

    b. Using content groupings and specialty collections to narrow in on specifics or expand on topics

Unit Three Benefits

- Use appropriate techniques to analyze, interpret, and attract the sources you need to fulfill search objectives
- Regulate information quality – Focusing exclusively on sources worthy of our review
- Conduct an editorial check to qualify web-based publications
- Formulas to qualify resources, quantify our confidence in them, and avert the need to open individual pages
- Recognize where the likely boundary lies between public and proprietary information
- Know and apply the rules for uncovering overlooked information
- Reap the benefits of grouping sources for justifying our source choices
- Determine when the media becomes the story and not just the source of it

Unit Three Tables

- ■ Quantity controls for testing the waters – Ratio of key indicators including the Google sniff test, and signal-to-noise formulas
- ■ Link analysis for understanding the scope and reach of information providers
- ■ The deep versus the shallow web – Why two Internets
- ■ The media dietary chain – Recognizing source self-interest
- ■ Using premium databases for climbing out of an information ditch

UNIT FOUR:
Sense-making:
Focusing on Information Context

UNIT FOUR SUMMARY

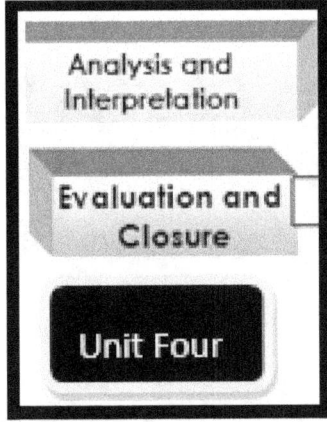

Unit Four has two principle thrusts: (1) Approaching research social networks as a researcher; and (2), engaging them as a member, including how to screen, join, attract, and communicate through virtual communities.

The slippery distinction between observer and participant is especially sensitive as we shift from the 'searching' to 'conversing" phase of our research projects. This section focuses on ways to trail and gather background details on search targets that generate digital identities through their social media profiles, networks, and commentary.

The model we use for reading networks and acting on them is called provider conjugation. Like verb conjugation, this tool helps to establish the flow and context of how information travels and the perceptions it carries with it. We also apply it to ourselves as information providers in determining the perceptions we want to form about us. This includes the types of contacts we want to attract and build into our own networks – especially in reaching out to search targets that prove to be social media party animals, digital hermits, or somewhere in-between.

UNIT FOUR SECTION STRUCTURE

4.1. Provider Conjugation: How to determine the motives of information providers in groups and as individuals

    a. Defining senders, recipients and audiences to understand the direction and speed that information travels

    b. Assessing the nature and trade-offs of individuals and groups as information sources

    c. Leveraging lateral thinking as a tool for conducting Internet research

4.2 Misinformation as an information source: How to use information rather than *be used* by it

    a. Taking the sniff test to grounded or unfounded suspicions

    b. Decoding the role that gatekeepers, watchdogs, and regulators play in scandal-making

    c. Picking up the scent of smoking guns – Red flag conditions for conflicts of interest

    d. Opinions online – How to know who is gaming the system or fabricating their credentials

4.3 The value of social information: Applying provider conjugation to social media

    a. Using social bookmarking to vet source experts

    b. Trapping information through RSS feeds to target new opportunities

    c. Building custom search applications to uncover key details

    d. Gaining media cachet through blogging and selective interviewing

    e. Joining a professional network, cultivating contacts

4.4 Search to Converse: How to get from reading about others to direct engagement

    a. The giant listening ear as a networking asset

    b. Bartering information among groups and individuals

Unit Four Benefits

- Background research the people you're going to meet – Deploy specialized search tools to gauge their web presence and digital identities
- Build a stable of advisers and referral networks for finding experts and second opinions
- Assess the differences between the way information is communicated informally through word-of-mouth and institutionally through groups
- Apply the Vectors of Integrity to determine the credibility of information providers and their own involvement in the issues they report
- Gauge the reputation of our search targets (it's not in the eye of the beholder)!
- Leverage social networking tools to raise our digital profile as an independent investigator
- Use alerts and notifications to stay on top of fluid and evolving situations
- Pick a blog theme that can be strengthened by our research

Unit Four Tables

- Social Networks – From soul searching to role seeking
- Using link analysis to determine social circles
- Common tagging concepts for breaking new ground and reclaiming past breakthroughs
- The Seven Vectors of Relationship Integrity – Using online communities to weigh objective and subjective-based experience
- Credibility Pyramid – The scale of public scrutiny
- Cultivating contacts – Defining boundaries and fail-safes

===

UNIT FIVE:
How to Present What We Learn in Teachable Ways
Presenting:
How to Connect What You Learn to Useful Outcomes

===

UNIT FIVE SUMMARY

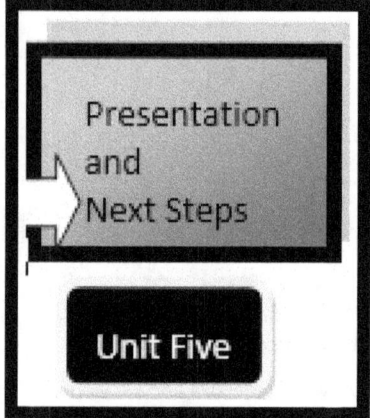

We talk about opportunities when we use information. We think in terms of risk when others do so. **Unit Five** focuses not only on what we learn but how this works in relation to what others know and perceive. How can we as messengers assess the nerves we strike and the buttons we push in the research we're delivering?

The first four units focus on how to gather information and act on it. **Unit Five** is about how others will act on the research we deliver through social media and more formal, offline channels: The reports and presentations to peers, clients, and groups (our "audience"). How will our findings be interpreted and acted on? How we deliver them is every bit as important as the research itself.

Unit Five brings together the search project management steps, query formation, quality controls, source fluency and information conjugation methods to deliver your research to the clients, colleagues, and communities we're supporting. These message receivers will clearly see how your informed use of web research tools and practices is bringing value, economy, and even closure to complex and resource-hungry investigations. We will then turn our attention to the report itself, coming to grips with the news we're delivering, the explanatory power of our analysis, and the changes we're proposing.

Unit Five Section Structure

5.1 Message Delivery: How to Knowledge-ENABLE our colleagues, clients and community through our findings, analysis, reporting, and recommended actions

    a. Confirmable Outcomes – Reducing uncertainty, building consensus, and making reasonable assertions from complex and resource-hungry investigations

    b. Results Verification — *Closing the loop* between the words and deeds as well as the facts and opinions documented through our search logs

5.2 Information Packaging: Bringing together the SPM structure, query formation, source fluency, and information conjugation to deliver winning reports

    a. Packaging the results – What they should contain, what to leave out, and how they should unfold as a learning narrative

    b. Assimilating search results, coverage patterns, and those elusive, missing pieces to draw meaningful comparisons and spotlight where the real story lies

5.3 Project Presentation: Conclusions, recommendations and next steps

    a. Drawing the line between independent investigators and the dependent actors we investigate

    b. Presenting clear and useful follow-up actions to clients and stakeholders without falling into decision-making traps

5.4 Post Investigation: Information-coping skills for self-managing our digital interactions

    a. Keeping the right doors open for continual discovery and professional growth

    b. Applying research disciplines to routines for managing our personal brands, virtual identities, and offline realities

Unit Five Benefits

- Differentiate deliberate from serendipitous discoveries
- Pinpoint conflicts of interest among our search targets
- Know where the bones are buried *before* you dig them up
- Legitimize the correct claims about conflicting facts and numbers
- Know and document the difference between confirmable facts and educated guesses
- Map research to primary intelligence and opportunities to barter information
- Assess the attention paid to our search topic and/or target and the broader issues they address

Unit Five Tables

- The certainty continuum for assessing the black and white (and gray)
- The candor of strangers and the corrupting influence of friendship
- The compromises to sound judgment posed by instant information
- Conversational icebreakers for breaking the case wide open
- Discussion maps for connecting the interests of our search targets to our project goals

===

UNIT SIX:
The Knowledge-ABLED Cook Book
Using Information:
A Recipe for Success

===

UNIT SIX SUMMARY

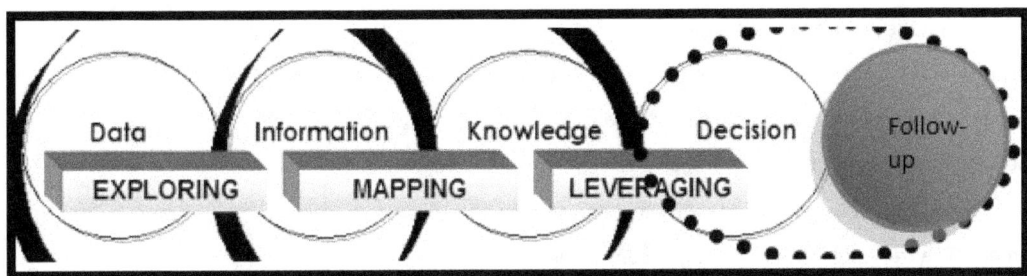

The book concludes with a Knowledge-ABLED use case based on the professional transformation of a commercial video producer to an educational media consultant. This use case guides us through the false starts and initial frustrations to the firmer footing and ultimate confidence-building that comes with being knowledge-ENABLED.

All relevant practices, frameworks, and search strategies in the case study are referenced to the specific units and chapters where they're introduced and demonstrated. For instance our use case subject entrepreneur plots out his research goals and supporting tasks through the Search Project Management model.

He applies the principles of site selection and Oceans, Lakes and Ponds to determine his sources, generate business leads, and build his understanding of the market and its growth potential. Finally he uses provider conjugation as a way of engaging the very same business contacts that first landed on his radar as search targets.

This journey is mapped out in three sections:

   1. **The Diagnosis** – We find out what makes our entrepreneur tick, how he's transitioning careers, and his challenges both as a researcher and a marketer.

   2. **The Search** – We apply the models and methods introduced in the first five units of the book to help scale the virtual research walls that were blocking the entrepreneur in the first section of **Unit Six**.

   3. **The Engagement** – We see the pay offs from the results of Part Two through our subject's ability to generate business leads, develop networking contacts, and narrow down to a selective and promising market niche.

Unit Six Section Structure

6.1 Introduction: Food for thought: you are what you eat

    a. Defining culinary metaphors and applying them to the research process, such as...

    b. Main ingredients, meal types, cuisines, courses and cooking methods

6.2 The Diagnosis: Assessing the goals and challenges of our case subject

    a. Initial intake – Coming to terms with internet confusion

    b. Better business targeting through site selection – Building credibility through reporting requirements

    c. Defining the boundaries – Scoping out the SPM to keep the project online and in line with our objectives

6.3 The Search: Matching the pursuit to the pay-offs

    a. The information ocean for generating and qualifying business leads

    b. The information lake for assessing market studies

    c. The information pond to get from trapping to acting on what we learn

    d. The book on RSS feed readers and their functions and benefits

6.4 The Engagement: The transition from searching to conversing

    a. Listening to markets – How to use RSS as a survey tool for mapping and confirming trends

    b. A review of the site selection techniques used to uncover the sources used in the case study

    c. The provider conjugation method for assessing the motives of information suppliers and how our subject is viewed by others as an information provider in his own right

Unit Six Benefits

- Use term expansion to segment markets
- Understand the situational specifics and efficiencies in the local search, clipping, and alerting functions of RSS readers
- Connect individual experts to their key affiliations and then learn which groups are worth approaching
- Generate feeds from news queries, news sites, and social media sources (event triggers)
- Design a proactive follow-up to business leads triggered by daily events

Unit Six Tables
- Assembling the meal
- Gathering the research
- Mapping OLP to actions and outcomes
- Search Project Management Plan for our use case, (a.k.a. "George Reis Productions")

While not part of the curriculum guide, **Unit Seven** *lays out next steps for applying the perennial lessons of Searching Out Loud in the changing dynamics between information providers and tomorrow's Knowledge-ABLED investigators.*

Symbols

123people| 3:78
1939 New York World's Fair| 5:28; see also History; Sarnoff, David, Gen.
24/7| i:6, 3:95, 6:46, 7:9; see also Timeframe
404 error| 2:42, 3:10, 3:12; see also URLs

A

Abbott and Costello| 4:19; see also wordplays
Abelson, Vicki| 5:43; see also Online Behavior
abstract| i:3-i:4, 1:6, 1:17, 1:24, 1:46, 1:76, 2:51-2:52, 2:54, 2:61, 2:99, 3:10, 3:12-3:13, 3:21, 3:27, 3:92, 4:36, 4:38, 6:2, 6:56, 7:18, 7:48; see also Opinion-based; summaries; theoretical
abuse| 2:37-2:38, 4:102; see also aggression; Power Structures
Academic| 2:20, 2:24, 2:27-2:28, 3:6, 3:26, 3:33, 3:56, 3:62, 3:94, 4:53, 4:69, 4:74-4:75, 5:55, 5:63, 6:12, 6:24, 6:43, 6:52, 6:56, 7:2, 7:20; see also curriculum; education; Learning; professors
 - academic journals| 3:34, 3:64; see also peer; review
 - academic papers| 3:57; see also annotate; Empirical; polemic
 - academicinfo| 2:87; see also Educational Resources Information Center (ERIC)
 - academics| 3:27, 3:95, 4:76, 5:64, 6:52; see also Contest; syllabus; technology, keeping current
 - diploma| 7:11; see also college; education
 - undergraduate| 4:90, 4:106; see also advanced degree; college; education
accidents| 3:48, 4:104, 5:75, 5:77; see also dangerous; Liabilities; probable cause; Risks
accomplices| 4:54; see also Affiliated; cohort; conspiracies; Criminal
accuracy| 3:63, 3:68, 3:70, 3:79, 5:29, 5:53, 7:10, 7:22, 7:37; see also approximate; chronology; Search Targets; Verification
Accusations| i:2, 2:85, 3:10, 3:62, 4:41-4:42, 4:53, 4:59, 4:91, 4:98, 4:105, 5:44; see also allegations; Blame; Judgment
 - accusers| 4:2, 4:39, 4:68; see also derail; detractors; doubters
 - resentment| 4:23, 4:43, 4:52, 4:96, 7:19; see also betrayal; Blame; Conflict; Disgruntled; marginalize
 - ridicule| 2:85, 4:52, 5:8; see also Blame; intolerance; marginalize; ostracism
Acronyms| 6:3, 6:26; see also acronymfinder; Regulations; shoptalk; shorthand; Unique IDs
 - acronymfinder| 6:12; see also Free, resources; pointers
actions and actors| 1:72, 2:43-2:44; see also Actions and Outcomes; noun phrases
Actions and Outcomes| 1:28, 2:5, 2:17, 2:37-2:38, 3:25, 3:88, 4:4, 4:46, 4:106, 5:14, 5:63, 6:12, c:17; see also closure; Oceans, Lakes, and Ponds (OLP); resolution
 - defeat| 2:67, 3:12; see also Contest; negative information; Perceptions; surrender; zero sum game
 - foregone| 1:2, 4:58, 5:15, 5:66, 7:22, 7:34; see also Expectation; inevitable; resolution
 - predetermined| i:16, 1:15, 1:18, 2:35, 3:61, 4:4, 4:70, 5:29, 7:23; see also Bias; Deceptions; foregone; presumption; rigged
 - range| i:9, i:13, 1:3, 1:8, 1:16-1:17, 1:24, 1:26, 1:36, 1:43-1:44, 1:47, 1:70, 2:6-2:7, 2:18, 2:23, 2:27, 2:29-2:31, 2:35, 2:37, 2:39, 2:48-2:50, 2:55, 2:67, 2:73, 2:85, 2:99, 3:5-3:6, 3:10, 3:23, 3:35, 3:38, 3:41, 3:76, 3:91, 4:4, 4:13, 4:39, 4:41, 4:43, 4:49, 4:51, 4:55, 4:59, 4:72, 4:95, 5:5, 5:15, 5:17, 5:28, 5:56, 5:59, 5:62, 5:74, 5:76, 6:8, 6:34, 6:41, 7:24, 7:36, 7:38, 7:44, 7:50; see also Continuum, the Knowledge; Perspectives, perspective-taking; Timeframe; Vectors of Integrity (VOI)
 - repercussions| 5:10; see also consequence; fallout; impact; implications
 - stake| i:7, 1:10, 1:61, 1:69, 2:31, 4:6, 4:18, 4:22, 4:39, 4:41, 4:97, 4:108, 5:36, 5:41, 5:68, 6:45, 6:56, 7:6, 7:29, 7:38; see also defend; proprietary; roles and responsibilities; Stakeholders
Addictions| 4:54, 5:27, 7:3, 7:5; see also abuse; Behaviors; Cognitive; Disabilities; impaired
 - compulsive| 1:36; see also Intuitions; reflexive
 - obsessive| 4:53, 4:93; see also Cognitive; impaired; reflexive
 - overdose| 2:38; see also Addictions; Excesses
Adobe| 6:5
advanced degree| i:4, 1:54, 6:26; see also Academic; diploma; education
advanced knowledge| i:4-i:5, 5:73, 6:5; see also Knowledge-ABLED
advanced search commands| 1:45, 1:65, 2:4, 2:68, 2:93, 4:63-4:64, 5:34, 6:37; see also query formation; search commands
adversaries| 1:11, 1:37, 4:32, 4:48, 4:53-4:54, 4:96, 5:38; see also Conflict; Opposition
advertising| i:5, 1:22, 1:26, 1:45, 1:65, 2:67, 2:71, 2:77, 3:50, 3:62, 3:72, 3:89, 3:93, 4:38, 4:89, 4:92, 5:8, 5:63, 6:12, 6:16, 6:46, 6:51, 7:10, 7:18, 7:33, 7:45; see also public relations; SEO (Search Engine Optimization)
Advocacy| 1:20, 1:25-1:26, 2:11, 3:73, 4:22, 4:37, 4:43, 4:56, 4:104, 6:23; see also grassroots; Influences; public interest
 - galvanize| 4:30, 5:75, 7:15; see also Campaigns; grassroots; persuasion; populist
 - grassroots| 4:59; see also Campaigns; neighborhoods; outreach; social circles
 - outreach| 5:40, 6:45; see also Campaigns; Organizations
Affiliated| 2:13, 2:45, 2:47, 2:67, 2:95, 3:34, 3:80, 4:72, 4:96, 7:11; see also Relatedness; Social Networks; strength of association
 - align| 1:19, 2:47, 3:35, 3:56, 3:93, 4:92, 4:105, 5:30, 7:6, 7:32, 7:51
 - ancillary| 2:59, 5:29; see also disconnect; dispersion; tangents
 - associate| i:13, 1:5, 1:66-1:67, 2:2, 2:16-2:17, 2:31, 2:54, 2:97, 2:107, 3:23, 3:37, 3:96, 4:45, 5:32, 5:37-5:38, 5:56, 5:71, 5:75, 6:19
 - cohort| 4:64
 - connectedness| 4:92, 4:94, 5:75; see also integrate, findings; Relatedness; tethered
 - gang| 5:43; see also accomplices; cavort; Code, of conduct; extortion; mobster; Violence
 - interconnected| 2:52, 4:61; see also interdependency; Relatedness; Social Networks
 - membership| 3:14, 3:26, 4:22, 4:53, 4:61, 5:64, 6:33, 6:54; see also Organizations
 - personal connections| 4:9, 4:12, 4:40, 4:48, 4:58; see also schmooze; Social Networks; strength of association
 - proxy| 2:69; see also Stakeholders; surrogate

affinity bias| 7:29-7:30, 7:34-7:35; see also Bias; filter bubbles; news feed
agenda| 1:15, 1:25, 1:59, 3:24, 3:52, 3:60, 3:63, 4:4, 4:13, 4:35, 4:39, 4:70, 4:74, 5:1, 5:3, 5:8, 5:35, 5:50, 5:65, 5:69, 6:54, 7:7, 7:13, 7:23, 7:31, 7:39; see also projects, client presentations
aggregate| 1:1-1:2, 1:27, 1:38, 2:72, 3:2, 3:13, 4:12, 4:57, 5:8, 5:23, 5:33, 5:42, 5:50, 6:17; see also RSS (Really Simple Syndication); sample
Agreement| i:1-i:2, i:4, 1:8, 1:15, 1:20, 1:75, 2:20, 2:36-2:37, 2:45, 3:20, 3:73, 3:89, 3:98, 4:18, 4:43, 4:55, 4:65, 4:106, 5:7, 5:64, 5:66, 5:69, 6:8, 7:7, 7:23, 7:28-7:29, 7:36, 7:41; see also cooperation; Interactions; Negotiations; pact; quid pro quo
 - arbiter| i:12, 1:3, 1:30, 3:50, 3:52, 4:29, 4:59, 4:67, 4:91, 6:57, 7:33, 7:48; see also broker; go-betweens; middleman
 - quid pro quo| 4:55; see also Agreement; Dichotomies; establishment; reciprocal; standard operating procedure (SOP)
Alert| 1:33, 2:47, 3:8, 4:5, 4:71, 5:47, 5:53, 5:70, c:11; see also Exposure
 - alarms| i:7, 1:34, 1:40, 5:20, 5:35, 7:46; see also Amber alert; red flag; Risks; shock; warning
 - emergency| 1:40, 7:38 - red flag| 4:103, c:10; see also Amber alert; Indicators; Radar; warning
 - reminders| 1:23, 2:16, 3:61, 4:87, 5:69, 5:78, 6:46; see also calendar; Memory
 - updates| 1:61, 2:42, 2:62, 3:13, 3:41, 3:54, 3:72, 3:94, 4:8, 5:42, 5:48, 5:52, 6:34, 6:37, 7:25; see also Alert; Radar; sequential; task; workflow
 - warning| i:15, 1:29, 1:40, 1:44-1:45, 3:25, 3:60, 3:74, 4:40, 5:59, 7:6, 7:49; see also alarms; dangerous; hazard; poisoning; red flag
Alexa| 3:64-3:66; see also advertising; Amazon; Quality Controls
algorithms| 1:4, 1:6, 1:55, 1:57, 1:62-1:64, 1:66, 2:45, 2:67, 3:3, 3:13, 3:31, 3:84, 5:54, 5:69, 5:78, 6:10, 7:1, 7:4-7:6, 7:18, 7:23, 7:27, 7:31, 7:34-7:35, 7:37, 7:39, 7:43, 7:46-7:47, 7:50-7:51; see also affinity bias; big data; Search Engine Marketing (SEM); Search Results
allegiance| 4:9, 4:40, 5:5, 5:65, 7:5, 7:30; see also loyalties; partisanship
AltaVista| 2:41; see also Discontinued Websites and Tools; Search Tools
Amazon| 2:15, 2:63, 3:19; see also Commerce; type ahead
Amber alert| 2:99, 5:53-5:54; see also alarms; Case studies; Law Enforcement; warning
ambiguity| i:11, 2:6, 2:15, 2:50, 3:9, 3:11; see also categorizing, human mediated; Confusion; disambiguation; Interrogation, humans of machines; machine-generated interpretations; machine-mediated human computer interactions; unclear
American Dialect Society| 4:84
analogies| 1:17, 3:29, 3:36, 3:82, 3:84, 4:39; see also comparison; correlation; Culinary; Fishing in a pond; meal type; Metaphors; roadmaps; symbols; trees-in-the-forest
Analysis| 1:21-1:22, 1:51, 1:58, 1:62-1:63, 1:66, 2:3, 2:19, 2:43, 2:60-2:61, 2:65, 2:107-3:1, 3:3-3:4, 3:13, 3:24, 3:50, 3:52, 3:54, 3:57, 3:62, 3:73, 3:88, 3:95-3:96, 4:2, 4:19, 4:25-4:26, 4:29, 4:33, 4:40-4:41, 4:44, 4:51, 4:68, 4:88, 4:96, 4:108-5:1, 5:4, 5:8-5:11, 5:14, 5:23, 5:29, 5:31, 5:37, 5:69, 5:73, 5:78, 6:1, 6:21-6:22, 6:45-6:46, 6:51, 7:42, 7:47, c:6-c:7; see also criteria; dissect; Evaluation; Indicators; Logic; outliers; rationale
 - contrast| 3:64, 4:9, 5:1, 5:17, 5:65, 5:80, 6:53, 7:10, 7:27; see also comparison; disparity; Evaluation
 - disparity| 2:49, 3:8
 - implications| 1:16, 4:22, 4:90, 4:96, 5:14, 5:57; see also Relatedness
 - review| 1:10, 1:12, 1:22, 1:47, 1:50, 1:63, 2:2, 2:6, 2:17, 2:33, 2:40, 2:61, 2:86, 2:88, 2:92, 3:1, 3:16, 3:24, 3:26-3:28, 3:48, 3:50, 3:55-3:56, 3:58, 3:61, 3:67, 3:72, 3:90-3:91, 4:33, 4:35, 4:42, 4:67, 4:75, 4:100, 4:108, 5:25, 5:40-5:41, 5:48, 5:52, 5:61, 6:33, 6:37, 6:46, 6:49-6:50, c:7, c:16; see also novelty; online forums; Overview; product reviews; summaries
 - revisiting| 1:5, 1:40, 1:54, 2:16, 2:45, 2:50, 2:99, 3:11, 3:87, 4:37, 4:40, 4:45, 4:50, 4:81, 5:27, 5:57, 5:65, 6:13, 6:25, 6:43, 7:12; see also course-correcting; examination; retrace
 - simplicity| i:11, i:16, 1:39-1:40, 2:9, 2:51, 3:26, 3:47, 3:95, 4:18, 4:26, 4:36, 4:38, 4:94-4:95, 6:1; see also Complex Context; Complicated Context; devotion; obvious; transparency
anatomy of a query| 1:61; see also query formation; technology, search
angle| 1:28, 1:43, 2:31-2:32, 2:56, 2:90, 3:94, 4:13, 4:53, 4:59, 5:54; see also Bias; Perspectives; scoop; slant
annotate| 2:67, 4:82; see also cite; Documentation; projects, client documentation
announce| 1:38, 1:42, 1:61, 2:17, 4:40, 6:36, 7:6; see also Alert; formal communication
Anonymity| i:2, 1:6, 1:10, 2:69, 3:18, 4:17, 4:31, 4:67, 4:105, 5:31, 7:6, 7:11; see also Credibility; First Amendment
 - anonymous| i:2, 1:10, 2:68-2:69, 3:19, 4:68, 4:95, 4:98, 5:32, 7:6, 7:11; see also default, privacy settings; Privacy; trade-off
 - faceless| 3:77, 4:32, 4:94; see also anonymous; Confusion; Distortions; impersonal; misleading
 - trace| 1:71, 2:72, 3:4, 3:18, 3:54, 3:63, 3:78, 3:86, 3:88, 4:1, 4:52, 4:56, 4:94, 4:97, 5:57, 6:11, 7:3, 7:7, 7:13, 7:38; see also Code, tracking; monitor; retrace
antennas| 4:31; see also blindspots; Public Awareness; Radar
anthropological| 7:37; see also Family; inherited; Social Networks; society
anti-trust| 2:62, 7:9; see also big search; duopoly; Regulations; technopoly
apology| 5:17; see also Intentions; Liabilities
Apple| 2:9, 2:35-2:36, 3:10, 7:3
Applied Behavior Analysis (ABA)| 6:22, 6:44-6:45, 6:47; see also Cognitive; diagnosis; methods
approximate| 2:18, 2:27, 2:59, 2:65, 3:10, 3:46, 3:77, 6:17; see also accuracy; educated guesses; Indicators
archives| 1:58, 3:6, 3:15-3:16, 3:18, 3:24, 3:29, 3:38, 3:42, 3:45, 3:81-3:83, 3:92, 4:66, 4:82, 5:80-6:1, 6:43, 7:2, 7:41, 7:49; see also Documentation; repositories
area code| 2:11, 2:27, 2:32, 3:70, 4:76; see also Code; Contacts; Location
artificial intelligence| 1:51, 1:56, 1:58, 1:65, 3:21; see also Humans; Machine-enabled
ascendance| 7:14, 7:20; see also ordering, search results
Ask.com| 2:50-2:51; see also Search Engine, NLP (Natural Language Processing)
aspiration| i:3, 4:70, 5:37, 5:45, 5:47; see also altruism; ideals; mission
Assets| 1:6, 1:13, 1:38, 1:61, 1:70, 2:49, 2:51, 2:95, 2:101, 3:1, 3:19, 3:27, 3:75, 3:77, 3:88, 4:29, 4:46, 4:53-4:54, 4:69, 4:75, 5:9, 5:18, 5:28, 5:40-5:41, 5:46, 5:52, 6:13, 7:45, 7:48, c:10; see also clients, financial incentive; personal assets; Risks; salary
 - personal assets| 2:101, 3:76, 3:78; see also Contacts; personal radar
 - personal finances| 1:6; see also credit histories
 - real estate| 1:73, 2:19, 2:55, 3:23, 3:47, 3:78, 4:24; see also household; neighborhoods
 - real property| 1:49, 3:46, 3:76-3:77; see also liens; reside
 - reward| i:6, 1:1, 1:47, 1:68, 2:39, 2:65, 2:85, 3:3, 3:24, 4:23, 4:47, 4:55, 4:62, 4:66, 4:104, 5:42, 5:58, 5:66-5:67, 7:19, 7:50; see also clients,

financial incentive; Contest; honor; merit; Recognition
assimilate| 1:72, 4:7, 5:70, c:13; see also integrate, findings
assumptions| i:15, 1:6, 1:18, 1:38, 1:47, 1:52, 2:14, 2:33, 2:62, 2:94, 3:12, 3:19, 3:58, 3:74, 3:89, 4:14, 4:16-4:17, 4:36, 4:60, 4:69, 4:73, 4:83, 4:92, 4:95, 4:97, 4:105, 5:23-5:24, 5:29, 6:9, 6:20, 6:27, 7:7, 7:11-7:12, 7:23, 7:28, 7:32, 7:34; see also Bias; Guesswork; presumption; Reason
attention surplus| 5:74-5:75; see also continuous partial attention; formula; Message Value
audio| 2:60, 3:19, 3:66, 4:56; see also Content Streaming
audit| 5:30, 5:76; see also Internal Revenue Service (IRS); Regulations
Authenticity| 1:18, 2:12, 4:2, 4:5, 4:10, 4:15, 4:23, 4:34-4:35, 4:38, 4:40-4:41, 4:46, 4:49, 4:61, 4:89, 5:2, 5:8, 5:31, 5:33, 5:42, 5:65, 6:12, 6:54, 7:8, 7:44; see also absolute; blunt; Credibility; first party; first person; loyalties; Perspectives; Vectors of Integrity (VOI)
 - candid| 4:35, 5:24; see also Authenticity; blunt
 - earnest| 1:57, 2:47, 2:63, 3:77, 7:29, 7:49
 - genuine| 1:20, 4:38-4:40, 5:26, 7:36; see also believable; blunt; earnest
 - honesty| i:16, 2:52, 3:6, 4:30, 4:35, 4:74, 4:79, 4:94, 4:96, 4:104, 5:24, 5:31, 7:28, 7:38; see also sincerity; transparency
 - sincerity| 1:16, 1:19, 2:63, 4:1, 4:15, 4:33, 4:60, 4:68, 5:1, 5:29; see also candid; genuine
author| 2:21, 2:57, 2:62, 3:13, 3:23, 3:26, 3:56, 3:58, 3:61, 3:72, 3:80, 3:93, 4:25, 4:39, 4:90, 4:97, 5:31, 5:42, 5:61, 5:64, 6:4, 6:34, 7:2, 7:37; see also domain expert
award| 1:38, 5:17-5:18, 5:27-5:28, 6:29, 7:5; see also Contest; Recognition

B

background checks| 3:70, 4:68, 4:77, 5:46, 5:70; see also finding people; public records; Search Targets; Semantics, finding people
backstabbing| 4:23; see also aggression; Coercion; extortion
balcony| 4:42; see also Perspectives, outsider versus insider
Bates, Mary Ellen| 2:93
Beginner| i:15, 1:8, 1:45, 1:53, 1:65, 2:18, 2:36, 3:1, 3:67, 4:45, 5:22, 5:45, 5:56, 6:14, 6:42, 7:2; see also ignorance; Learning; novice; Unknown Unknowns
 - novice| i:5, 1:1, 2:92-2:93, 3:31-3:32, 3:76, 5:40, 6:50; see also Naivete; Unexplored
Behaviors| i:4, i:7-i:8, 1:28, 1:33, 1:35, 1:38, 1:42-1:43, 1:52, 1:64-1:65, 2:47, 2:55, 2:69, 3:18, 3:28, 3:42, 3:47, 4:2-4:3, 4:5, 4:14, 4:36, 4:40, 4:53, 4:57, 4:76, 4:90, 4:104-4:106, 5:27, 5:31, 5:47, 5:57, 5:77, 6:8, 6:54, 7:1, 7:5, 7:24, 7:29, 7:31-7:33, 7:35, 7:39, 7:50-7:51; see also Addictions; ADHD (Attention Deficit Hyperactivity Disorder); autism spectrum; Group Behavior; Intuitions; Online Behavior; psychological
 - catharsis| 4:68, 4:76, 5:41, 7:30; see also Blogs
 - ego| 2:32, 4:25, 4:91, 4:102, 4:108, 6:23, 7:24, 7:43; see also conceit; dominant; Judgment; navel-gazing; personality; praise
 - hysteria| 5:28, 5:34, 7:38; see also anguish; Chaotic Context; upset
 - mood| 5:8, 7:9, 7:21; see also Expression; Intuitions; psychological; spirit
 - navel-gazing| 4:75; see also narcissism; subconscious; vanity
 - oblivion| 1:34, 2:47, 3:5, 4:88, 4:92, 5:75, 7:12, 7:46; see also ADHD (Attention Deficit Hyperactivity Disorder); blindspots; continuous partial attention; deaf; fuzzier
 - paranoia| 4:91-4:92, 5:12, 5:34, 7:7; see also fear; Self-delusion; suspicions
 - passive| 1:35, 4:8, 4:12, 4:15, 4:39, 4:51, 4:59, 4:67, 4:87, 4:91, 4:103, 5:23, 5:28, 7:3, 7:30, 7:33, 7:36, 7:42; see also complacency; indecision; Intentions; succumb; surrender; visitors
 - psychological| 2:51, 3:6, 7:3, 7:38; see also Behaviors; Cognitive; Rorschach; subconscious
 - self-assurance| 7:12; see also confidence level; Expression
 - self-fulfilling| 4:100, 4:102, 7:12; see also foreknowledge; prophesy
 - selfish| 1:19, 1:35-1:36, 5:57; see also self-preservation
 - technophobes| 1:70; see also technology, non-techies
Beliefs| 1:13, 1:38, 2:49, 3:18, 3:63, 4:2, 4:5, 4:10, 4:19-4:20, 4:40, 4:49, 4:87, 4:93, 5:29, 5:59, 7:4-7:5, 7:16, 7:19, 7:21-7:22, 7:35; see also Expectation; Judgment; loyalties; persuasion
 - bible| 5:72; see also authoritative
 - Buddhist| 2:50; see also Demographics
 - devotion| 1:24, 3:2, 3:24, 7:30, c:6; see also defend; loyalties; Perspectives, elevated; simplicity
 - divinity| 2:49
 - faith| i:2, i:16, 1:33, 1:35, 1:39, 1:53, 1:64, 2:90, 3:94, 4:7-4:9, 4:40, 7:8, 7:16, 7:51; see also Authenticity; devotion; loyalties; passion; pledge
 - gospel| 1:58, 4:90, 5:41; see also authoritative
 - piety| 4:75; see also Judgment; moral; righteous
 - preaching| 7:12; see also evangelists; gospel; outreach; persuasion
 - religion| 7:31; see also Demographics; divinity; faith
 - sacred| 4:67; see also devotion; Perspectives, elevated; revelation; worship
 - Scientology| 2:92; see also religion
 - spirit| 1:25, 1:39, 2:49, 3:49, 4:34, 4:36, 4:58, 4:65, 5:77, 7:39; see also bond; passion; willful
benchmark| 5:12, 5:16, 5:20, 5:23, 7:34; see also baseline; Best Practices; Metrics
benefactor| i:12, 1:65, 2:62, 4:54, 7:14, 7:20, 7:42; see also philanthropies; Stakeholders
Berra, Yogi| 1:69
Best Practices| 3:61, 4:74, 5:76; see also business leader; Case studies; Management, functions
 - business case| 6:34; see also Case studies; scenarios
 - gold standard| 3:63, 4:4; see also award; brands, best-in-class
betrayal| 4:22, 4:90; see also backstabbing; Deceptions; misleading; mistrust; words and deeds
Bias| i:1, 1:15-1:16, 1:44, 2:85, 3:62, 3:65, 3:90, 3:94, 4:5, 4:18, 4:34, 4:48, 4:59, 4:62, 4:67, 4:99, 4:105-4:106, 5:6, 5:25, 5:29, 5:58, 5:60-5:61, 5:63, 5:70, 6:52, 7:4, 7:9-7:10, 7:12, 7:22-7:23, 7:28, 7:31, 7:37-7:38, 7:44-7:46, c:5; see also assumptions; blindspots; confirmation bias; Intuitions; libel; Motives; subconscious

- inclined| 2:47, 3:83, 4:41, 4:47, 5:16, 5:28, 6:14, 7:5; see also predisposed
  - pre-drawn conclusions| 7:29; see also predetermined; Prejudice; presumption
  - predisposed| i:1, 4:6, 4:26, 5:5, 7:12, 7:22; see also inclined; Memory; predetermined; second guessing
  - presumption| 1:8, 1:28, 4:98, 5:7, 5:64; see also pre-drawn conclusions; predetermined; second guessing; unintended
  - slant| 2:28, 5:29; see also Perspectives
big data| 3:61, 7:10; see also algorithms; data mining; repositories
big search| 2:66-2:67, 3:47, 3:78, 7:1, 7:26, 7:34. 7:46; see also technology, business interests; technopoly
Bing| 2:39, 2:43, 2:66-2:67, 2:85, 2:90, 2:100, 2:106, 3:12, 3:82, 4:72, 6:10, 6:12; see also technology, search
biography| 2:33, 2:67, 2:101, 3:72, 3:74, 4:62, 7:19; see also past deeds; personal branding; personal narratives
Biznar| 6:12, 6:21-6:23; see also market research
black swan|1:44, 5:59-5:60, 5:63; see also 9-11 report; Disasters; Explanations; hysteria; known unknowns; Metaphors; unforeseeable
Blame| i:16, 1:9, 1:38, 4:90, 5:12; see also Accusations; allegations; Coercion; guilt; Liabilities; Perceptions
  - allegations| 3:9, 4:94, 4:96
  - aspersions| 4:38; see also dispersion; distractions; diversion; gossip; Speculation
  - scapegoats| 4:38, 4:51, 5:17, 7:39; see also Accusations; actions of others; grudge; otherness; ridicule
blindspots| 1:7, 1:29-1:31, 1:33-1:39, 1:43-1:44, 1:48, 1:50, 2:57, 3:5, 3:32, 4:14, 4:45, 4:48, 4:75, 4:88, 4:103, 5:37, 5:75, 6:10, 6:13-6:14, 7:4, 7:6, 7:33-7:34; see also conceal; Exposure; Hidden; Johari Window; Weakness
Blogs| 1:74, 2:84, 3:8, 3:18, 3:89, 3:94, 3:96, 4:5, 4:73, 4:79, 4:94, 5:39-5:40, 5:42-5:54, 5:79, 6:50, 6:53, c:10; see also first person; research blog; Search to Converse (STC)
  - blogger| 2:79, 3:18, 3:38, 3:46, 3:89, 4:59, 4:75, 4:92, 5:9-5:10, 5:27, 5:40, 5:42, 5:46-5:50, 5:52-5:53, 5:55, 6:12, 6:36; see also Search to Converse (STC)
  - research blog| 5:44, 5:47-5:48, 5:52; see also Blogs; Researchbuzz
bookmaking| 5:50; see also social bookmarks; tagging engine
Boolean logic| 1:55, 2:13-2:14, 2:16, 2:41-2:42, 2:59, 3:7, 7:1; see also AND operator; Logic; OR operator; search commands
Boone, Mary E.| 1:40, 1:42-1:43; see also Contextual
Brand| 2:30, 2:65, 3:61, 4:92, 4:102, 5:10, 5:16, 5:22, 5:25, 5:36-5:38, 5:50, 7:5, 7:8, 7:11, c:13; see also advertising; market segments; Popularity; Public Awareness; Reputation, company
  - brand stature| 5:6; see also Recognition; Reputation, company; spotlight
  - brands, best-in-class| 5:38-5:39; see also Best Practices
  - brands, consumer| 4:93, 5:17, 5:23; see also Reputation, company
  - brands, media| 7:8, 7:11; see also news organizations
  - personal branding| 5:51, 7:11, c:13; see also personal narratives
  - rebrand| 3:37, 5:35
Brand, Russell| 1:29
breach| 1:49, 3:75, 7:18, 7:48-7:49; see also Internet Security; personal data
breadcrumb trails| 2:12, 3:8, 4:80; see also navigation; User Experience (UX)
breathe, letting a search| i:11-i:12, 2:9, 2:66, 3:46, 6:42; see also database, searching; Quality Controls; refinement; second pass
Brinn, Sergey| 3:61
Broadcast Media| 5:56; see also radio; TV networks
  - abcnews.go.com| 5:56
  - bbc.co.uk| 5:56
  - cbsnews.com| 5:56
  - cnbc.com| 5:56
  - msnbc.com| 5:56
  - NBC| 2:35; see also TV networks
  - npr.org (NPR)| 4:107, 5:56, 5:80, 7:17
  - radio| 1:65, 4:59, 7:5, 7:8; see also podcast
  - TV networks| 7:8
Brooks, David| 7:52
Browser| 1:17, 1:61, 1:69, 2:1, 2:3, 2:39, 2:86, 2:95, 2:98, 3:7, 3:22, 3:27, 4:75, 5:73, 7:42; see also face-to-screen; User Interface (UI); World Wide Web
  - default, browser settings| 2:39, 2:69-2:70; see also Code, tracking; cookie
BS Detection| 4:34, 4:37, 5:25-5:26, 5:42, 7:4; see also evidence patterns; fact checkers; inaccuracies; Pattern Matching; Skepticism
  - smell test| 1:37; see also disinterested; Investigations; Skepticism; suspicions
  - sniffing| 1:44, 1:48, 2:50, 4:32, 4:48, 4:104, 5:57, 5:71, 6:1, 7:32, c:8, c:10; see also evidence gathering
Budget| 1:18, 3:2, 3:36, 3:50, 3:62, 3:92, 4:70, 5:41, 6:11, 6:19, 6:34, 7:10, 7:33; see also business plan; cost/benefit; overhead; planning
  - shoestring| 5:41, 6:8; see also containing costs; expenses; Free, resources; Research Projects
Buffet, Warren| 5:65
Burger King| 5:23
buried| 1:5, 1:25, 1:36, 2:103, 3:12-3:13, 3:23, 3:54, 3:73, 4:7, 4:18, 4:47, 4:90, 5:29, 5:32, 5:72, 5:76, 6:1, 6:34, 7:41, c:13; see also Exposure; Hidden; inundated; Obscurities
business community| 5:2, 5:28, 5:56; see also Major Business Media
Business Model| 1:1, 1:65, 1:69, 2:62, 3:75, 4:36, 4:68, 5:25, 5:31-5:32, 6:43, 7:1, 7:5, 7:9-7:10, 7:14, 7:19, 7:30, 7:33, 7:43; see also market research; planning; strategy
  - business plan| 1:3, 6:10; see also Forecast; market research; predefine; scenarios; Stakeholders
Businessweek| 4:106-4:107; see also Major Business Media
buzz| 4:92, 4:97, 6:4; see also conjecture; Google Keyword Tool; gossip; trends; viral
Byrne, David| 4:90

C

cache| 1:62, 1:71, 2:22-2:23, 2:42, 2:72, 3:9, 3:11, 3:16, 3:41, 3:54, 3:56, 3:64, 3:84, 4:84, 7:41; see also pages indexed; User Experience (UX)
calendar| 2:11, 3:38, 4:13, 4:55, 4:84, 5:9, 5:32, 5:38, 5:47, 5:52, 7:19; see also Timeframe
calibrate| 2:45, 3:34, 4:32, 4:45, 7:21; see also Indicators
Calishain, Tara| 2:30, 2:68, 3:12, 4:78, 6:35; see also Information Traps; research blog
CalTech| 4:94
Campaigns| i:2, 1:20, 1:42, 1:72, 2:31, 2:35, 2:52, 3:71, 3:78, 3:87, 4:38, 4:43, 4:68, 4:77, 4:90-4:91, 4:95-4:96, 4:100, 4:103-4:105, 5:4, 5:6, 5:9-5:10, 5:29, 5:32, 5:35-5:36, 5:48, 5:62, 6:4, 6:11, 6:14, 6:35, 6:52; see also Elections; pandering; persuasion; Public Opinion
- candidates| 2:44, 2:99, 4:19, 4:38-4:42, 4:71, 5:71, 7:20; see also applicant; Elections; entrenched; incumbent
- referendum| 4:67; see also ballot; grassroots; populist; public debate; Public Policies
- voting| i:2, 4:12, 4:18-4:19, 4:25-4:26, 4:38, 4:42-4:43, 4:57, 4:67, 4:90, 4:94, 4:97, 4:103, 4:105, 5:8, 6:56, 7:18, 7:20; see also Campaigns; democracy; Elections; override; referendum
cancer| 2:13, 2:16; see also Case studies
Careers| 1:3, 2:49, 4:57, 4:61, 4:69-4:71, 4:74-4:75, 4:108, 5:3, 5:40, 5:44, 5:46, 5:75, 6:7-6:9, 6:13, 6:22, 6:45, 7:2, 7:12, c:15; see also Professionals
- teaching| i:11, 1:33, 2:37, 3:26, 3:41, 3:94, 4:69, 4:75, 4:79, 4:103, 6:13, 6:20, 6:46, 7:7, 7:27, c:5; see also education; Learning; trainers
Carnegie, Dale| 5:73
Carrot2| 2:60; see also Search Engine, Metasearch; Search Engine, Visualization
case sensitive| 2:15, 2:17; see also query formation
Case studies| 3:22, 5:40
- 9-11 report| 2:44-2:46, 3:23; see also Clarke, Richard; Rice, Condoleeza
- accountability| i:2, 3:1, 3:50, 4:16, 7:13, 7:19, 7:23, 7:37, 7:40; see also Leaders; transparency; Verification; visibility
- climate change| i:7, 4:106, 7:7; see also Environmental Protection Agency (EPA); meteorological; Weather Conditions
- cyberbully| 4:95; see also cybercrime; Internet Security; Online Behavior
- eldercare| 1:24-1:26, 4:106, 5:70
- high fructose corn syrup (HFCS)| 2:65
- Hopi Indians| 1:75
- murder-mystery| 3:58-3:59, 4:103, 5:43, 5:53, 5:68; see also Criminal; fiction; gumshoe
- Sex Offender| 3:19, 3:31; see also abuse; Crime
- Station Night Club| 3:39; see also chronology; Crime Scene; Disasters; hysteria; personal injury
- stock market| 4:98, 5:27; see also cycle; momentum; monetary; publicly-traded companies; recession; shareholders; ticker symbol; trends
- Watergate| 4:8; see also Corruption; partisanship; public investigation; Scandals
catalog| 1:62, 1:65, 1:71, 1:73, 2:32, 2:63, 2:67, 2:85, 2:98, 3:10, 3:54, 3:87, 5:16, 6:28; see also Commerce; database, navigation; inventory; pages indexed; Websites, indexing
Categorizaton| 1:41, 1:43, 1:55-1:56, 1:61, 1:66-1:67, 2:7-2:8, 2:18, 2:28, 2:32, 2:41, 2:44-2:45, 2:57, 2:59-2:61, 2:86, 2:88-2:89, 2:93-2:95, 2:98-2:99, 2:103-2:104, 3:6, 3:9, 3:12, 3:18, 3:22, 3:27, 3:91-3:92, 4:83, 5:29, 5:38, 6:22, 6:32; see also aggregate; categorizing, defining boundaries; classification; Content Grouping
- categorizing, auto categorization| 1:61, 2:44
- categorizing, defining boundaries| 2:59, 2:103, 3:10, 3:92-3:93
- categorizing, field structure| 1:55, 2:7; see also field-based
- categorizing, human mediated| 1:41, 2:88-2:89, 3:7; see also human, filtered; machine-mediated human computer interactions
- categorizing, Information Types| 3:7, 3:9-3:10, 3:13, 3:16, 3:19, 3:23; see also Information Types
- categorizing, metadata| 2:59, 3:23; see also metadata
- categorizing, Relatedness| 2:45, 2:66, 2:95, 2:99, 2:103; see also Relatedness
- categorizing, role of word choice| 2:18, 2:93, 2:103-2:104, 4:84; see also ordering, word adjacency
- categorizing, searchable groupings| 1:56, 1:67, 2:8, 2:28, 2:41, 6:32; see also Content Grouping
- categorizing, subject directories| 2:86, 2:89, 2:93-2:94, 2:98, 3:28, 6:51; see also Subject Directory
cavort| 2:56; see also accomplices; plot
Censorship| 7:25, 7:31, 7:50; see also First Amendment; totalitarianism
- suppression| 1:39, 4:32, 4:55, 7:11, 7:34-7:35; see also Power Structures; totalitarianism
Center for Disease Control (CDC)| 3:61; see also National Institute of Health (NIH); public health
Central Intelligence Agency (CIA)| 4:107; see also Case studies; Surveillance
ceremonies| 5:17, 5:28; see also Recognition
character limits| 2:42, 3:13; see also query formation; suggestion search; threshold; Twitter
Character Traits| 1:25, 2:38, 3:50, 3:90-3:91, 4:18, 4:33, 4:37-4:39, 4:41; see also ingrained; Narratives; portrayal; Roles
- actors| 1:27, 1:48, 1:72, 2:37, 2:43-2:44, 2:60, 3:9, 3:20, 4:2, 4:31, 5:19, 5:30, 5:76, 7:16, 7:40, 7:46, c:13; see also actions and actors
- angry| 4:31; see also defiance; Judgment; otherness; passion; spite; vengeance
- evangelists| 4:35, 5:24; see also charisma; Influences; outreach; preaching
- heart| i:3, i:16, 1:32, 1:39, 3:27, 3:34, 3:59, 4:14, 4:39, 4:75, 4:102, 7:17, 7:38; see also desire; mission; overcome; passion; persist
- heroes| 4:22, 4:52, 7:6; see also aspiration; combat; Roles; winners
- humble| 1:32, 1:36, 2:47, 3:84, 5:62, 7:32, 7:38, 7:47; see also embarrassing; Expression; modest
- ingrained| 1:33, 1:40, 4:89, 5:34, 5:63; see also ancestral; Bias; inherited
- modest| 1:32, 2:49, 2:67, 5:75, 6:53; see also humble; subtle
- nerd| 7:4, 7:38; see also geeks; Technology
- stereotypes| 4:26, 4:37; see also cultural; ethnic; Perceptions; Prejudice; Roles; tribal
- strangers| i:5, 1:22, 1:28, 1:36, 1:38, 1:51, 1:61, 2:32, 2:54, 3:23, 3:55, 4:8, 4:15, 4:17, 4:29, 4:32, 4:68-4:69, 4:77, 4:86, 4:89, 5:41, 6:54, 7:16, 7:48, c:14; see also detachment; Observation; third person
- trait| i:16, 2:38, 2:51, 4:105, 5:1; see also impression; Roles

- winners| 1:14, 2:93, 4:35, 5:11, 5:24, 5:77, 6:29, 6:54, 7:6-7:7, 7:40, c:13; see also charisma; Contest; dominant; zero sum game
charisma| 3:46, 4:38, 6:28, 6:55; see also celebrities; convince; endorse; Influences; Leaders; persuasion
checklists| 1:26, 1:46, 1:69, 2:92, 3:25, 3:55, 3:76, 4:42, 4:71, 5:40, 5:42; see also guidelines; Procedures
Christian Science Monitor| 3:19; see also news organizations
chronology| 2:29, 3:10-3:11, 3:37, 3:78, 3:86, 4:1; see also sequential; story lines; Timeframe
civic| i:1, 3:91, 4:43, 4:45, 5:17, 5:80, 7:42-7:43; see also Freedoms, constitutional; protests; public interest
clannish| 7:44; see also tribal
Clarke, Richard| 2:44; see also 9-11 report
classification| 2:12, 2:26, 2:32, 2:40, 2:44, 2:55, 2:86, 2:88, 2:95-2:97, 2:106, 3:31-3:32, 3:86, 3:90-3:92, 4:23, 4:57, 5:23, 5:47, 6:32, 6:51; see also catalog; Categorizaton
cliche| 1:16, 4:35; see also Excesses; Exposure
Clients| i:4-i:5, i:11, i:13-i:14, 1:2-1:6, 1:10-1:16, 1:20, 1:24, 1:38-1:43, 1:45, 1:47, 1:50-1:52, 1:59, 1:73, 1:75-1:76, 2:3, 2:5-2:6, 2:39, 2:47, 2:62, 2:106, 3:1, 3:3, 3:13-3:14, 3:16, 3:24-3:25, 3:30, 3:50, 3:52, 3:54, 3:74, 3:90-3:91, 3:93, 3:96, 3:98, 4:2, 4:6, 4:11, 4:35, 4:70, 4:72, 4:87, 4:94, 4:96, 4:105, 4:108, 5:2-5:7, 5:9-5:14, 5:16, 5:18-5:19, 5:22-5:24, 5:28-5:29, 5:33-5:35, 5:40-5:41, 5:43-5:45, 5:56-5:66, 5:68-5:72, 5:76-5:79, 6:5-6:8, 6:13, 6:16, 6:55, 7:2, 7:21, 7:27, 7:35, 7:38, 7:40, 7:42, c:12-c:13
  - clients, added value| 1:59, 1:73, 1:75, 3:2, 3:56, 5:19, 5:25, 7:35; see also derive; projects, client billables
  - clients, conflict of interest| 1:20, 1:51, 3:94, 4:97, 5:44, 5:59, 7:21; see also Conflicts of interest
  - clients, financial incentive| 1:38, 3:75, 4:95, 5:59; see also Cost of Research
  - clients, hiring a researcher| 1:5, 1:11, 2:3, 5:41, 5:58, 5:70; see also Researchers
  - clients, legal consulting| 1:14, 4:12, 5:59; see also lawsuit; lawyer; pro bono
  - clients, motivations| 1:13, 1:15, 1:39, 2:3, 5:7, 5:34, 5:58-5:60; see also Motives; projects, clients expectations
  - clients, perspectives| 1:6, 1:42, 3:17, 3:31, 3:53, 5:4, 5:8, 5:11, 5:17, 5:20, 5:30, 5:41, 5:60-5:61, 5:63; see also Perspectives, research
  - clients, project delivery| i:14, 1:43, 1:45, 3:91, 3:97, 4:8, 4:88, 5:6, 5:8, 5:12, 5:23, 6:5, 7:40, c:12-c:13; see also projects, client presentations
  - clients, project development| 5:44-5:46; see also Research Projects
  - generate leads| 6:10; see also Search to Converse (STC)
  - clients, project roles| 5:14, 5:44, 5:59, 7:27; see also roles and responsibilities
  - clients, project trust| 1:15, 1:24, 3:51, 4:1, 4:36, 5:12, 5:23-5:24, 5:64-5:65, 5:69, 6:55; see also handshake; projects, clients expectations; Trust
  - clients, validation| 1:41, 1:75, 5:35-5:36, 5:62; see also Reinforcement
  - integrate, findings| 3:22; see also projects, client presentations; Researchers
Clinton, Hillary R.| 1:49
cloud computing| 3:24; see also big data; personal data
Code| i:15, 1:18, 1:32, 1:34, 1:62, 1:65-1:67, 1:73, 2:11, 2:19-2:20, 2:25, 2:27, 2:30, 2:32-2:34, 2:65, 2:68, 2:83, 3:11, 3:69, 4:19, 4:22, 4:48, 4:58, 4:75, 4:79, 5:44, 6:9, 6:55, 7:9, 7:38, 7:40, 7:46; see also Behaviors; classification; database, structure; markup language; Unique IDs
  - Code, access| 1:18; see also password
  - Code, legal| 2:32, 2:35; see also Forbidden; restrictions; rule-making
  - Code, limitations| 1:65, 2:32; see also machine-based limitations; technology, limitations
  - Code, of conduct| 4:80, 6:54-6:55, 7:38, 7:47; see also ethics; professional standards
  - Code, secret| 1:34, 4:23, 4:49; see also Privacy; secrets, keeping
  - Code, software| 1:62, 1:65, 7:9, 7:40; see also markup language; programmer
  - Code, tracking| 2:68, 3:12, 7:9; see also cookie; personal data; Privacy
  - Code, unspoken| 4:49, 5:45; see also Implicit; tacit
  - Code,IDs| 2:8, 2:19, 2:32, 2:34; see also Unique IDs
Coercion| i:15, 2:45, 4:17, 4:56, 4:59-4:60, 4:99, 4:103, 5:26, 7:36; see also Deceptions; misleading; predatorial; threats
  - brutality| 4:103; see also abuse; Coercion; threats; torture; Violence
  - predatorial| 2:68, 4:67; see also Coercion; exploit; threats
Cognitive| 3:98, 5:29; see also Disabilities; Intuitions; top-of-mind
  - brain, left and right| 5:65-5:66; see also right brain
  - conscious| 1:30, 1:35-1:36, 5:42, 5:61
  - continuous partial attention| 5:75; see also ADHD (Attention Deficit Hyperactivity Disorder); distractions; diversion; impulse; invasive; obsessive
  - hardwired| 1:4; see also impulse; reflexive
  - linear| i:13, i:15, 1:1, 1:8, 3:18, 4:79, 4:83, 5:63, 7:33; see also Cognitive
  - memorization| i:11, 1:7, 3:24, 4:7, 6:1; see also recall; rote; verbatims
  - narcissism| 4:89; see also Addictions; conceit; navel-gazing; Self-delusion
  - non-linear| i:15, 1:8; see also evidence patterns; inconsistencies
  - nonverbal| 6:28; see also Disabilities; Expression; sensual; telepathic
  - subconscious| 1:33, 1:44; see also dream; fantasy; Johari Window; psychological; Rorschach
  - top-of-mind| 2:6, 2:62, 3:57, 5:7-5:8; see also Intuitions; suggestion search; type ahead
Coke| 4:90, 4:105
Collaborative| 1:30, 4:15, 4:87, 5:72, 6:14; see also cooperation; crowdsourcing
  - sharable| i:4-i:5, 1:3, 1:8-1:9, 1:14, 1:19, 1:32-1:35, 1:47, 1:49-1:50, 1:53, 1:61, 1:70, 2:24-2:25, 2:31, 2:63, 2:71, 2:90, 2:101, 3:23, 3:38, 3:50, 3:66, 3:74, 3:76, 3:90, 3:93, 3:96, 4:1, 4:4, 4:6, 4:8, 4:12-4:13, 4:16, 4:18, 4:22, 4:28-4:29, 4:31, 4:36, 4:48, 4:53, 4:58, 4:60-4:61, 4:68, 4:73-4:74, 4:88, 4:94, 4:98, 4:105, 5:8-5:9, 5:30, 5:37, 5:42, 5:46, 5:49, 5:52, 5:60, 5:63-5:64, 5:66, 5:68-5:69, 5:77, 6:1-6:2, 6:4, 6:8, 6:16, 6:28, 6:36, 6:46, 6:52, 6:54, 6:56-6:57, 7:2, 7:10, 7:13, 7:16-7:18, 7:26, 7:28, 7:30-7:32, 7:36, 7:39, 7:42, 7:48, 7:50
college| 2:28, 2:104, 3:69, 4:64, 4:89; see also Academic; advanced degree
colloquialism| 2:51; see also Jargon; Language; slang; vernacular
columnist| 3:59; see also journalist; Newspapers; Opinion-editorial (op-ed); reporter
Commerce| 1:71, 4:90, 4:104, 7:43, 7:50; see also Companies; Trade
  - buying| i:14, 1:34, 1:45, 1:49, 2:12, 2:51, 2:62, 2:85, 2:89, 3:30, 3:60, 4:8, 4:33, 4:40, 4:47, 4:57, 4:97, 5:1, 5:9, 5:25, 5:27, 5:30-5:32, 5:41, 5:56, 5:60, 6:9-6:10, 6:21, 7:1; see also customer; merchandise; price

- commercial| i:1, 1:8, 1:54, 1:56, 1:65, 2:2, 2:15, 2:36, 2:39, 2:43, 2:69, 2:85, 2:88, 2:94, 3:4, 3:13, 3:18, 3:25-3:26, 3:30, 3:41, 3:50, 3:58, 3:63-3:64, 3:74, 3:81, 3:83, 3:85-3:86, 3:91, 4:31, 4:57, 4:72, 4:85, 4:89, 4:101, 5:1, 5:26-5:29, 5:34, 5:46, 5:58-5:59, 5:79, 6:12, 6:14, 6:16, 6:20-6:21, 6:51, 6:53, 7:9, 7:17, 7:42, 7:44, c:15; see also advertising; customer; Trade
  - franchise| 5:19, 5:23; see also retail
  - merchandise| 1:71, 1:73, 2:15, 2:48, 2:62, 3:8, 3:60, 5:32, 7:45; see also inventory; shopping cart
  - resellers| 2:24, 2:66; see also Commerce; retail; Trade; wholesale
  - retail| 1:27-1:28, 2:31-2:32, 3:54, 3:60, 4:89, 7:18, 7:33; see also customer; merchandise; shopping cart; Trade
  - sell| 1:6, 1:19, 1:38, 1:54, 1:61, 1:65, 2:6, 2:39, 2:51, 2:62, 3:73, 4:25, 4:42, 4:45, 4:57, 4:61, 4:69, 4:94, 4:102, 5:25, 5:27, 5:30-5:32, 5:34, 5:58, 6:8, 6:14, 6:16, 6:21-6:22, 6:56, 7:48; see also retail; Trade; wholesale
  - SKUs| 3:50; see also Code, tracking; retail; Trade
  - wholesale| i:17, 3:56, 3:62, 3:64, 5:24, 6:8, 7:3, 7:44; see also containing costs; retail; Trade
common interest| 1:13, 1:59, 2:9, 2:11, 2:18, 2:30, 2:37, 2:62, 3:6, 3:33, 3:54, 3:72, 3:88, 3:98, 4:103, 5:3, 5:26, 5:68, 7:1-7:2, 7:31, 7:50; see also Collaborative; public interest
communities of practice| 3:16, 4:16; see also Collaborative; Expertise
Companies| i:1, i:6, i:18, 1:10, 1:16, 1:34, 1:42, 1:54, 1:56, 1:62, 1:65, 1:67-1:69, 2:31, 2:39, 2:48, 2:52, 2:64-2:66, 2:68, 2:71, 3:14, 3:60, 3:64, 3:72, 3:77, 4:17, 4:25, 4:30, 4:34, 4:70, 4:93, 4:101-4:102, 5:1, 5:8-5:10, 5:12, 5:18, 5:22, 5:27-5:29, 5:31, 5:35, 5:37-5:38, 5:40, 5:43, 5:45, 5:63, 6:4, 6:16-6:17, 6:21-6:22, 6:54, 7:29-7:31, 7:46, 7:48; see also Management, functions
  - buyouts| 4:94; see also corporate mergers; takeover
  - conglomerates| 2:30
  - corporate mergers| 4:95, 4:98, 5:11; see also Assets; revenue; shareholders; takeover
  - headquartered| 2:29; see also corporate; Location; workplace
  - IPOs| 3:95
  - profit| i:17, 1:2, 1:10, 1:19, 1:34, 1:59, 1:65, 2:11, 2:71, 3:13, 3:17-3:18, 3:26, 3:53, 3:91, 4:97, 4:99, 5:43, 5:55, 6:12, 6:33; see also revenue
  - revenue| i:8, 1:69, 2:36, 2:62-2:63, 2:67, 3:14, 3:74, 3:93, 5:9, 5:43, 6:16-6:17, 7:2, 7:9, 7:13-7:14, 7:31; see also corporate; profit
  - shareholders| 1:34, 4:22, 5:24, 5:37, 5:43, 6:55-6:56; see also board; publicly-traded companies; Stakeholders; upper management
  - takeover| 4:97, 7:19
  - upper management| 1:34, 2:17; see also Management, functions
comparison| i:7, 1:10, 1:15, 1:22, 1:60, 1:70, 2:34, 2:50-2:51, 2:53, 2:56, 2:86, 2:90-2:91, 2:100-2:101, 3:10, 3:13, 3:19, 3:52-3:53, 3:55, 3:69, 3:98, 4:29, 4:47, 4:93, 4:105, 5:6, 5:12-5:13, 5:16, 5:20, 5:37, 5:41, 5:68, 5:70, 5:78, 6:19, 6:32, 6:34, 6:51, 7:36-7:37, 7:47, c:13; see also Analysis; contrast; correlation; criteria; Evaluation; outliers
Competence| 1:33, 5:7; see also acumen; Best Practices; domain expert; mastering; professional standards
  - acumen| 5:42; see also professional standards
  - astute| 1:38, 4:17, 5:3, 6:51, 7:45
  - mastering| 1:31, 3:32-3:33, 3:70, 3:88, 4:1; see also problem-solving; skills; talent
  - professional standards| 5:70, 6:52, 6:55; see also clients, project trust; ethics; protocol
  - savvy| i:7-i:8, 2:40, 4:32, 6:16, 7:19; see also acumen; Expertise
compound words| 2:17, 3:47, 4:84; see also Grammar; phrase
compromise| 1:2, 1:14, 1:19, 1:29, 1:36-1:37, 1:48, 1:54, 1:59, 1:68, 2:2, 2:54, 2:69, 2:90, 3:9, 3:11-3:12, 3:41, 3:74, 3:76, 4:6-4:7, 4:14, 4:30-4:31, 4:33, 4:39-4:40, 4:42-4:43, 4:47, 4:52, 4:58-4:60, 4:65, 4:69, 4:75, 4:91, 4:96, 4:99, 4:103, 5:1, 5:14, 5:57-5:60, 6:54, 7:1, 7:4, 7:6, 7:11, 7:17, 7:21, 7:33, 7:38, 7:42, 7:45-7:46, 7:48, 7:51, c:14; see also concede; Negotiations; Weakness
conclusive| 1:47, 2:3, 2:5, 2:40, 3:20, 3:63, 4:96, 5:71, 7:42; see also Actions and Outcomes; arguments; boldness; closure; overall; resolution
confession| i:1, 4:7, 4:57; see also absolve; catharsis; diary; first person; modest; sins
confirmation bias| 5:61; see also Bias; blindspots; clients, validation; sunk cost
Conflict| 1:19-1:20, 1:48, 3:62, 3:98-4:1, 4:4, 4:19, 4:35, 4:43, 4:47, 4:102, 4:104, 5:11, 5:75, 6:11, 7:1, 7:16, 7:22, 7:44, 7:51, c:10, c:13; see also disagreement; disputes; Intentions; Opposition; Resistance
  - antagonisms| 5:10
  - clash| 1:19, 3:6, 3:48, 3:62, 4:16, 4:39, 4:41, 4:47, 5:10, 5:65, 7:7-7:8, 7:25-7:26
  - combat| 4:22, 7:14; see also defiance; struggle; Violence; warfare
  - Conflicts of interest| 1:13, 1:19, 3:94, 4:5, 4:20, 4:30, 4:37, 4:48, 5:76-5:77, 6:11, 6:57-7:1, 7:51, c:10, c:13; see also Corruption; dubious; embarrassing; hypocrisy
  - disagreement| 4:18, 4:96, 7:28, 7:40; see also confront; disprove; disputes; Resistance
  - misguided| 1:39, 2:85-2:86, 4:87, 4:97, 5:37, 5:43, 6:12, 7:21, 7:46, c:5; see also disagreement; original intent; Perceptions
  - misunderstandings| 2:50; see also clash; cultural; disconnect; Interpretations; intolerance; misguided
  - obstacles| i:9, 5:72, 7:15; see also Disruptions; distractions; diversion; roadblock; Stop
  - struggle| 1:33, 7:6, 7:16; see also Addictions; dedicated; Fight-or-flight; mission; Opposition; Resistance
  - turf| i:7, 3:88, 3:94, 4:41, 4:43, 5:49, 5:55; see also localities; neighborhoods; parochial; territory
  - zero sum game| 7:44; see also adversaries; Opposition; ruthless; winners
conform| 3:11, 3:23, 4:13, 4:19; see also Code, of conduct; Group Behavior; protocol; rule-making; uniformity
Confusion| i:9, i:17, 1:1, 1:5, 1:35-1:36, 2:29, 2:49, 2:62, 3:23, 3:56, 3:93, 4:91, 4:97, 4:103, 4:105, 5:34, 5:57, 5:60, 7:7; see also evidence gathering; Misinformation; Sense-making
  - confounding| 3:25; see also defying explanation; elusive; unresolved
  - convoluted| i:5, 2:2, 2:20, 2:24, 3:31, 3:47, 3:83; see also Explanations; incoherent; indecipherable
  - tangle| 1:8, 1:13, 2:69; see also Chaotic Context; skirmish
  - unclear| 2:3, 3:64, 7:10, 7:16; see also entangled; incoherent; missing details; Obscurities; omission; vague
  - vexing| 1:34, 2:49, 2:53, 3:9, 5:34; see also alternative explanations; competing explanations; unsolved
conjugal| 4:10, 4:14, 4:26, 4:45; see also Provider Conjugation Framework (PCF)
consensus| i:2, 1:37, 1:41, 4:15, 4:22, 4:40, 4:42, 4:67, 5:11, 5:34, 5:37, 6:54, c:13; see also galvanize; majority opinion; Negotiations; outreach; prevailing
consequence| 1:39, 1:64, 2:3, 3:37, 3:58, 3:89, 4:8, 4:26, 4:68, 4:92, 4:105, 5:10, 5:42, 5:59, 5:61-5:62, 7:24, 7:45, 7:48; see also Actions and

Outcomes; impact; repercussions
Consulting| i:11, i:14, 1:3, 1:18, 1:40, 3:13, 3:94, 5:13, 5:44-5:45, 5:70, 5:79, 6:13, 6:45, 7:21, c:15
  - advice| i:4, 1:34, 2:12, 2:16, 2:93, 3:93, 4:5, 4:9, 4:12, 4:15, 4:73, 4:75, 4:96, 4:105, 4:108, 5:4, 5:26-5:27, 5:32, 5:41, 5:72, 6:21, 7:6, 7:32, 7:42, c:11; see also clients, validation; Expertise; therapy
  - confer| i:11, 1:2, 1:18, 1:38, 1:58, 3:10, 3:14, 3:62, 3:91, 4:32, 4:54, 4:91, 4:100, 5:8, 5:36, 5:41, 5:64, 5:69, 6:10, 6:21, 6:29, 6:45, 6:56, 7:5, 7:42; see also advice; Interactions
  - contractor| 1:73
  - freelance| 5:45; see also contractor; journalist
  - management consulting| 1:4; see also clients, legal consulting; projects, client benefits
Contacts| 1:22, 1:69, 2:19, 2:27, 2:30, 2:32, 2:61, 2:73, 2:98, 3:19, 3:60, 3:72, 3:83, 4:2, 4:12, 4:32, 4:56, 4:60-4:62, 4:64-4:65, 4:68, 4:70-4:75, 4:105, 5:46, 5:71-5:72, 5:79, 6:7, 6:10-6:12, 6:28, 6:33, 6:39, 6:45-6:46, 6:52-6:53, c:9-c:11, c:15; see also acquaintances; Personal Identity; Social Networks
  - badges| 1:70, 5:59, 7:5; see also personal branding
  - reside| 2:27, 2:32, 2:88, 3:46, 3:66, 3:69, 3:82, 4:1, 5:23, 7:23; see also household; neighborhoods
Content Grouping| 1:62-1:63, 2:23, 2:29, 3:2, 3:53, 3:76, 5:9, c:7; see also categorizing, defining boundaries; categorizing, human mediated; classification
  - bucketed, content| 2:2, 2:45, 2:47, 2:65, 2:90, 3:66, 4:39, 6:42; see also classification; Search Engine, Custom (CSE)
  - subgrouping| 2:47; see also categorizing, searchable groupings; classification
Content Streaming| i:13, i:16, 1:42, 2:36, 2:93, 3:12, 3:19, 3:61, 3:63, 3:73, 4:51, 4:56, 4:75, 5:42, 5:50, 5:52, 7:10, 7:15-7:16
  - movie| 2:65, 3:58, 5:28, 5:39; see also Roles; script; story lines
  - MP3| 3:19; see also audio
  - podcast| 5:48, 7:49; see also Topic-based
  - video| 1:8, 1:42, 1:62-1:63, 2:47, 2:66-2:67, 3:19, 3:21, 3:66, 4:6, 4:89-4:90, 5:48, 5:79, 6:5, 6:7-6:8, 6:14, 6:17, 6:19-6:20, 6:23, 6:34-6:35, 6:41, 6:44, 6:49, 6:53, 7:14, 7:16, 7:30, 7:33, 7:50, c:15; see also audio; YouTube
  - webcast| 5:53
content weight| 3:55-3:56, 3:71; see also new-to-known; pages indexed
Contest| 1:15, 1:46, 1:49, 1:67, 3:17, 3:98, 4:36, 4:102, 5:18, 7:6, 7:21; see also award; rivals
  - compete| 2:85, 4:34, 5:10, 5:28, 5:54; see also adversaries
  - disqualify| 5:28; see also prevention; Stop; tainted
  - rivals| 1:15, 1:42, 2:24, 2:31, 2:67, 2:71, 3:98, 4:22, 4:33, 4:97, 5:3, 5:6, 5:37, 5:68, 6:12, 6:55-6:56, 7:9; see also adversaries; compete; Opposition
  - stalemate| 1:17; see also Negotiations; obstacles; paralysis
  - success| i:10, i:14, i:18-1:1, 1:10, 1:13-1:15, 1:21, 1:24, 1:39, 1:59, 1:65, 1:69, 1:73, 2:7, 2:12, 2:40, 2:45, 2:59, 2:61, 2:63, 2:65, 2:90, 3:27, 3:60-3:61, 3:66, 3:68, 4:4, 4:22, 4:30-4:31, 4:61, 4:68, 4:75, 4:80-4:81, 4:104, 5:4, 5:9, 5:26, 5:28, 5:31, 5:35, 5:41-5:42, 5:68, 5:75, 6:2-6:3, 6:11-6:12, 6:14, 6:17, 6:31, 6:33, 6:56, 7:19, 7:27, 7:31, c:2; see also Best Practices; winners
  - surrender| 1:24, 1:34, 1:38, 2:11, 3:6, 3:15, 3:31, 3:79, 4:42, 4:65-4:66, 5:12, 5:59, 5:77, 7:6, 7:49; see also defeat; resignation; retreat; succumb; warfare
Contextual| 1:3, 1:18, 1:29, 1:39-1:43, 1:64, 1:66-1:67, 1:72, 1:74, 2:6, 2:19, 2:26, 2:31-2:32, 2:34, 2:38, 2:45, 2:47, 2:55, 2:64, 2:86, 2:93, 2:104, 3:10, 3:17, 3:56-3:57, 3:87, 3:91, 3:96, 3:98-4:2, 4:4, 4:6, 4:8-4:11, 4:13, 4:35-4:36, 4:39, 4:51, 4:56-4:60, 4:83, 4:86-4:87, 4:91, 4:96, 4:108, 5:2, 5:7, 5:13, 5:18, 5:25-5:26, 5:29, 5:32, 5:35, 5:41, 5:50, 5:58, 6:4, 6:8, 6:39, 6:51, 7:17, 7:24, 7:31, 7:43, c:9; see also Intentions; Perspectives; Sense-making; simplicity
  - Chaotic Context| 1:43-1:44; see also Unknown Unknowns
  - Complex Context| 1:41-1:44; see also Unknown Unknowns
  - Complicated Context| 1:40-1:41, 1:44; see also Confusion; entangled; known unknowns
  - connotation| 2:15, 2:21, 2:25, 2:30, 5:17; see also implications; literal
  - known knowns| 1:39-1:41, 1:44; see also obvious; Simple Context; simplicity
  - known unknowns| 1:29, 1:40-1:41, 1:43-1:44, 5:64; see also black swan; Complicated Context; Johari Window
  - Simple Context| 1:39-1:40, 1:44; see also known knowns
  - Unknown Knowns| 1:41-1:44; see also blindspots; Johari Window
  - Unknown Unknowns| 1:29,1:36, 1:39, 1:43-1:44; see also black swan; unforeseeable
Continuum, the Knowledge| 1:1-1:2, 1:54, 2:3, 2:5, 2:8, 3:74, 3:97, 4:4; see also Frameworks; Search Project Management (SPM); sequential
contracts| 1:13, 1:67, 2:53, 3:19, 4:2, 4:58, 5:22, 5:69; see also Disclosures
Contrarian| 1:75, 4:19, 6:54, 7:28, 7:39; see also evidence patterns; Pattern Matching
  - contradict| 1:34, 1:44-1:45, 1:75, 2:40, 2:99, 3:62, 4:18, 4:58, 5:75, 6:53, 7:28, 7:39; see also competing explanations; defying explanation; hypocrisy
  - disprove| 3:69; see also reversal
  - reversal| i:11, 1:29, 1:50, 2:12, 2:38, 3:26, 3:36, 4:68, 4:92, 4:99, 4:105, 7:3, 7:10, 7:43; see also irony; Legal; opposite
conviction| 2:38, 4:38-4:40, 5:60, 5:71, 7:18, 7:21, 7:56; see also disambiguation; Intentions
convince| 1:36-1:37, 2:5, 2:56, 2:71, 3:70, 4:42, 4:67, 4:69, 4:90, 4:95, 4:97-4:98, 6:45, 7:7, 7:30; see also Influences; opinion-maker; persuasion; rationale
cookie| i:10, 1:54, 1:61, 2:69, 4:78, 7:49; see also algorithms; Browser
Cookin' with Google| 2:75-2:76, 3:29; see also analogies; Culinary; Google CSE (Custom Search Engine)
cooperation| 1:41, 4:46, 4:102, 7:42; see also Agreement; align; Collaborative; Interactions; reciprocal
copyright| 2:30, 7:48; see also cease and desist; infringement; Legal; proprietary; trademark
Copyscape| 3:63; see also plagiarism
corporate| 1:34, 2:31, 2:62, 2:65, 3:60, 3:62, 3:77-3:78, 4:35, 4:61, 4:106, 5:9, 5:11, 5:24, 5:35-5:36, 5:38, 5:42-5:43, 6:8, 6:48, 6:55; see also Companies; Management, functions; publicly-traded companies; takeover
corpus| 2:97; see also database, index; repositories; search index
correlation| 2:23, 2:65, 5:16, 5:36, 5:80; see also criteria; Evaluation; Relatedness

Corruption | 4:18, 5:26, 6:34
- blackmailed | 1:37; see also Coercion; Disclosures; extortion
- bribery | 4:60; see also Coercion; kickbacks
- collusive | 4:24, 4:26; see also conspiracies; plot; secrets, keeping
- gaming the system | 2:24, 3:64, 4:99, 4:101, 4:104, 5:71; see also rigged
- kickbacks | 4:55; see also bribery; Crime; extortion
- rigged | 4:100, 4:102, 5:26, 7:20-7:21; see also conspiracies; Corruption; cynicism; gaming the system; Scandals

Cost of Research | 3:74; see also projects, client billables
- containing costs | 2:32, 3:2, 4:36, 6:2, c:7
- cost effective | 3:32, 3:35
- cost free | 3:68; see also free versus fee; public domain
- cost related | 3:74
- cost/benefit | 3:2; see also measurable; Metrics; projects, client billables
- expenses | 1:7, 1:21-1:22, 1:37, 2:15, 3:1, 3:26, 3:31-3:32, 3:69, 4:18, 4:22, 4:40, 4:48, 5:2, 5:65, 6:21, 7:6, c:2; see also cost related; cutbacks; eliminate; free versus fee
- out-of-pocket | i:10, 3:2, 3:75; see also Budget; containing costs; projects, client billables
- outlay | i:10, 6:21; see also projects, client billables; sunk cost
- overhead | 1:51, 4:8, 4:29, 5:63, 6:50; see also administrators; bureaucrats; cost related
- sunk cost | 1:38, 5:62, 7:22-7:23; see also Exposure; Motives; overreach
- surcharges | 3:73; see also fee-based; pay walls

counterclaim | 1:45, 4:44, 7:7; see also debate; derail; disclaim; dismiss; dispel; distractions
counterpart | 4:36, 4:43, 4:53, 4:67, 5:63, 6:34, 7:44; see also Opposition
Craigslist | 2:73, 4:69; see also Commerce; Online Behavior
crawl | 1:61-1:63, 1:68, 1:71, 2:42, 2:57, 2:66, 2:80, 2:85-2:86, 2:90, 2:98, 3:9, 3:11, 3:29, 3:31, 3:56, 3:91, 3:96; see also spidering
Credibility | 1:4, 1:18, 1:46, 1:70-1:71, 2:9, 2:49, 2:92, 2:107-3:1, 3:25, 3:34, 3:50, 3:62, 3:64, 3:72, 3:78, 3:88-3:89, 3:93, 3:95, 4:23, 4:25, 4:29, 4:33-4:36, 4:39, 4:44, 4:47, 4:67-4:68, 4:88, 4:92, 5:12, 5:25-5:26, 5:29-5:30, 5:80, 6:11, 6:45, 6:53-6:54, 6:57, 7:11, 7:26, 7:37, c:11; see also Provider Conjugation Framework (PCF); third party
- believable | 1:44, 5:9; see also plausibility; portrayal; transparency; Trust
- conceivable | 1:26, 3:60, 5:4, 5:14, 5:48, 5:58, 7:26
- disbelieving | 7:20
- discredit | 5:25; see also Confusion; counterclaim; debunk; detractors; dispel; doubters; smear; undermine
- dispassionate | 4:87, 4:92, 5:78, 7:7; see also detachment; disinterested
- fathomable | 5:62; see also believable; plausibility; scenarios
- institutional credibility | 3:94, 3:96, 5:26-5:27; see also Group Behavior; Perspectives; pyramid, inverted; third party
- plausibility | 1:21, 1:44, 1:66, 1:70, 4:40, 5:9, 5:65, 5:71, 5:76, 7:24, 7:40, 7:42; see also Actions and Outcomes; believable; conceivable; fathomable; planning; possibility
- unbelievable | 5:27; see also Bias; exaggeration; Interpretations; slant; spin; suspicions

credit | i:6, 1:52, 1:71-1:72, 2:12, 2:93, 3:25, 3:73, 3:76, 3:79, 4:32, 4:38, 4:67, 4:93, 4:102, 5:75-5:76, 7:30, 7:45; see also Recognition
credit bureau | 3:74; see also credit histories; Personal Identity
Crime | 1:26, 2:49-2:50, 2:56, 3:58, 3:73, 3:93, 4:4, 4:7, 4:66, 4:103, 5:23, 5:43, 5:47, 5:66, 7:17; see also cybercrime; damages; Forbidden; fraud; infringement; libel; manslaughter; slander
- kidnapped | 3:9; see also invasive; ransomware; terrorism
- manslaughter | 5:44; see also Crime Scene; evidence gathering; homicidal
- stalking | 4:54; see also eavesdropping; spy; Surveillance

Crime Scene | 1:26-1:28, 2:55-2:56, 3:47, 3:59, 5:18,5:53, 5:67, 7:24; see also GPS (Global Positioning Satellite); Location; neighborhoods
- CSI | 5:53; see also Crime Scene; criminal evidence; homicidal
- fingerprints | 1:47, 4:90; see also criminal investigation; evidence gathering; Personal Identity
- forensic | 1:27, 1:59, 2:1, 2:49-2:50, 2:75-2:76, 3:74, 4:47; see also Empirical; evidence patterns
- stakeout | 4:49; see also Crime Scene; Professional Investigator (PI); raid

Criminal | 1:17, 2:55-2:56, 2:60, 3:10, 3:46, 3:59, 3:74, 3:94, 4:54, 4:71, 4:76, 4:104, 5:44, 5:59, 5:68; see also Forbidden; indictment; suspects; violator; wrongdoing
- criminal case | 3:10, 3:39; see also allegations; indictment; legal proceeding
- criminal evidence | 1:27, 4:8; see also Evidence; exposing corruption; forensic
- criminal history | 1:17, 1:70; see also background checks
- criminal investigation | 1:49, 4:3, 4:11, 7:39, c:2; see also Investigations; public investigation
- mobster | 5:44; see also accomplices; conspiracies; extortion; gang
- notorious | 1:54, 2:10, 3:11; see also Criminal; Reputations; villains
- offender | 1:43, 3:30; see also Accusations; adversaries; violator
- perpetrate | 1:20, 2:12, 4:7, 4:30, 4:92, 7:20, 7:38; see also Crime; mastermind; plot
- violator | 3:37, 4:103; see also offender; punishment; villains; wrongdoing
- wrongdoing | 1:20, 3:9, 3:37, 4:48, 4:103, 7:39; see also Accusations; allegations; indictment; punishment

crisis | 1:44, 3:60, 5:12, 5:34; see also Risks; Unknown Unknowns
cross-reference | 1:58, 1:75, 2:19, 2:73, 2:87, 2:90, 3:78, 4:2, 4:94, 6:19-6:20; see also categorizing, Relatedness; Relatedness
crowdsourcing | 4:16, 4:81; see also Collaborative; Group Behavior; Online Behavior
crusade | 4:18-4:19, 4:56, 5:28, 5:30; see also Beliefs; evangelists; galvanize; mission; persuasion
Culinary | 2:75, 3:28, 6:2, 6:16, 6:39, c:16; see also analogies; Cookin' with Google; meal type; Metaphors
- bake | 1:54, 4:102, 6:3, 6:5, 7:30
- barbecues | 3:27
- beverages | 6:5

COMPLETE WORKS: Units One Through Seven | Unabridged Index:10

- boiled| 2:76
- bread| 6:5, 7:41
- breakfast| 6:4
- brunch| 6:4
- casserole| 2:76, 3:29
- chef| 6:1
- cocktails| 6:5
- cook| 1:42, 2:76, 3:66, 6:1-6:45, 6:47-6:57, c:16
- epicurean| 6:21
- flavor| 2:75, 3:15, 5:55, 6:1-6:2
- food preparation| 2:76, 6:2
- fried| 2:76
- grill| 6:5
- main ingredients| c:16; see also Reis, George (case study)
- marinade| 6:5
- meal type| 6:34, c:16
- no fat| 2:76
- recipe| i:16, 2:75-2:77, 3:22, 3:66, 4:105, 6:1, 6:3, 6:6-6:7, 6:9, 6:23, 7:25, 7:37, 7:39; see also Reis, George (case study)
- seasoning| 6:16
- spices| 6:1
- utensil| 3:6, 6:1-6:2, 6:6; see also tools for the job

cultural| 2:50, 3:50, 3:59, 4:5, 4:27, 4:55, 4:61, 4:94, 5:30, 5:46, 6:57, 7:24, 7:30, 7:48; see also pulse; social norms; society; strength of association; tribal
curatorship| 1:3, 2:50, 2:74-2:75, 5:31-5:35, 5:55-5:56, 7:13, 7:44; see also Content Grouping; database, specialized; skim; specialized collections
curiosities| i:1, i:5, i:9, i:15, 1:56, 1:67, 2:17, 2:40, 2:67, 2:85, 3:54, 4:54, 4:67-4:68, 5:65, 7:4, 7:7, 7:10, 7:23, 7:42; see also discovery; Learning
curriculum| i:15, 1:3, 7:2, c:17; see also education; Learning; syllabus
customer| 1:65, 2:62, 2:68, 3:14, 3:74, 3:94, 4:22, 4:33, 4:77, 4:97, 5:8-5:9, 5:16-5:17, 5:19, 5:31, 5:37, 5:40-5:41, 5:43, 5:64-5:65, 5:68, 6:7, 6:12, 6:14, 6:21, 6:45-6:47, 6:51-6:52, 6:55-6:56, 7:31, 7:46, 7:48; see also advertising; Commerce; complaints; price
cutbacks| 6:46, 6:52; see also containing costs; eliminate; recession; state-funded
cycle| i:1-i:2, i:7, 1:3, 1:12, 1:21, 1:23, 1:43-1:44, 1:50, 1:53, 3:10, 3:15, 3:19, 3:24, 3:95, 4:43, 4:96, 4:104, 5:9-5:10, 5:13, 5:16, 5:22, 5:29, 5:41-5:42, 5:48, 5:50, 5:60, 6:1, 6:7, 6:21, 6:46, 7:9, 7:22, 7:40; see also evidence patterns; momentum; Pattern Matching
cynicism| 2:63, 7:8, 7:19, 7:23; see also fake news; mistrust; Skepticism

D

dangerous| 4:42, 4:44, 7:38; see also precarious; Risks; threats; trouble
Dartmouth College| 7:38
dashboards| 3:18; see also intensity; Metrics; scorekeeping
data mining| 1:47, 3:61, 7:2; see also algorithms; big data
Databases| i:10, 1:5, 1:18, 1:22, 1:50, 1:60-1:61, 1:63, 1:69, 1:73-1:75, 2:3, 2:40, 2:57, 2:85, 2:89, 2:93, 3:2, 3:10, 3:16, 3:22-3:24, 3:27, 3:29, 3:32, 3:67, 3:74, 3:81-3:86, 3:97, 5:2, 5:31, 5:52, 5:71-5:72, 6:12, 7:2, 7:41, 7:50, c:4, c:6, c:8; see also deep web; lakes; Subject Directory
- database, Deep Web| 3:85-3:86, 6:12; see also Deep Work
- database, differences| 1:73, 3:23; see also contrast; database, searching; Websites, evaluating
- database, government| 3:68, 3:83-3:84; see also government websites
- database, index| 1:61, 1:66, 1:74, 3:55; see also directory indexing; subject indexing
- database, navigation| 1:53, 3:30, 3:84, 4:78, 4:82; see also navigation
- database, searching| 1:18, 1:63-1:64, 2:18, 2:85, 3:17, 3:31-3:32, 3:84-3:85, 7:50; see also Search Within a Search; topical searches
- database, size| 1:61, 1:74, 2:2-2:3, 3:3, 3:28, 3:64, 4:63, 4:66, 6:50, c:6; see also Oceans, Lakes, and Ponds (OLP)
- database, specialized| 1:16, 3:3, 3:11, 3:22, 3:25, 3:33, 3:68, 3:82, 3:86-3:87, 4:62, 6:24, 6:26, 6:31-6:32, c:5-c:6; see also specialized collections
- database, structure| 1:55, 1:74, 2:50, 2:57, 3:10, 3:24, 3:28, 3:30, 3:83, 3:85, 3:92, 4:62, 4:66; see also categorizing, searchable groupings
- database, subscription (premium)| 2:43, 3:42, 3:75, 3:77, 3:79, 3:88, 5:3, 7:2, c:8; see also fee-based
- database, topic-based| 1:69, 2:89, 2:93, 2:95, 2:98, 3:3, 3:34, 3:83, 4:83, c:6; see also Topic-based
deadline| i:9, 1:9, 1:61, 3:1, 3:17, 3:38, 3:92, 4:95, 5:11, 6:2, 7:22; see also journalist; scoop; Timeframe
debate| i:3, i:7, 1:42, 3:62, 3:89, 4:18, 4:26, 4:36, 4:38, 4:58, 4:93, 4:96, 5:10, 5:47, 6:17, 7:7, 7:21-7:22, 7:38; see also counterclaim; disclaim; honest disagreement; Rhetoric
Deceptions| 1:35, 3:9, 3:50, 4:18, 4:96, 5:75, 7:46; see also guise; hypocrisy; Misinformation; misleading
- camouflage| 5:63; see also Hidden
- cloaked| 4:92, 7:10
- façade| 4:36; see also Perceptions
- guise| 4:34; see also Hidden
- pretense| 3:31, 4:14, 4:48, 7:29; see also guise
- veneer| 6:57; see also Hidden
decisions| i:1-i:2, i:6-i:7, i:9, 1:2-1:3, 1:8, 1:15, 1:17, 1:31, 1:37-1:39, 1:44, 1:64, 1:69-1:70, 2:62, 2:95, 3:24-3:26, 3:30, 3:36, 3:38, 3:87, 3:90, 4:6, 4:9, 4:19, 4:22, 4:25, 4:30, 4:36, 4:39-4:41, 4:43-4:44, 4:53, 4:56, 4:89, 4:95, 4:104, 4:107, 5:3, 5:5, 5:7, 5:9, 5:11, 5:41, 5:58, 5:61-5:62, 5:71, 7:16, 7:41-7:42, 7:46, 7:49, c:1-c:2, c:13; see also Actions and Outcomes; clients, validation; criteria; Intentions; projects, client recommendations; Reason
Decline| 3:62, 4:97, 5:38, 7:13-7:14, 7:53; see also downturn; downward; Narratives; plummet; Weakness
- collapse| 4:92, 7:8, 7:17, 7:19, 7:25; see also downward; monetary; Perceptions; unfortunate
- crash| 2:51, 2:54, 4:99; see also debt; monetary; stock market
- demise| 2:106, 4:53, 4:57, 7:4, 7:8, 7:44; see also downside; Narratives; unfortunate

Searching Out Loud: Giving Voice to Independent Investigations | Marc Solomon

- plummet| 4:94, 5:33; see also descending; unfavorable
decode| 1:16, 1:34, 1:50, 1:64, 2:51-2:52, 2:107, 3:54, 4:7, 5:6, 6:4, 7:47, c:10; see also Code; Pattern Matching
dedicated| 2:50, 2:67, 3:1, 3:31, 3:33, 3:77, 4:80, 4:82, 5:45, 6:2, 6:22-6:23, 6:37-6:38, 7:11, 7:41; see also roles and responsibilities; vigilance
deep web| 1:73, 3:16, 3:30, 3:68, 3:83-3:86, 4:47, 6:12, 6:20-6:21; see also database, Deep Web; database, government; invisible web
Deep Work| 7:2-7:3; see also Disruptions; Newport, Cal
deference| 6:30, 7:38; see also protocol; public discourse
Del.icio.us| 4:72, 4:74, 4:84, 6:12, 6:31; see also Discontinued Websites and Tools; social bookmarks; tagging engine; Websites, bookmarking
delimiters| 2:41-2:42, 4:83; see also File Formats; Information Types, formats
Demand-based media| 5:10-5:11, 5:32; see also calculable; premium content; pull and push; Supply Media
 - attention demand| 5:9-5:10, 5:50; see also attention supply; content supply
 - content demand| 4:1-4:2; see also calculable; content supply; Supply Media
 - demand-based, content analysis| 5:29, 6:34, 6:51; see also The Biggest Picture, content analysis
 - demand-based, methodology| 5:29; see also formula; methods; The Biggest Picture, methodology
 - knowledge demand| 1:45, 4:4, 4:86, 4:98, 5:33-5:34, 6:16, 6:47; see also curatorship; projects, clients expectations; The Biggest Picture, client deliverable
Demographics| 1:61, 3:78, 4:13, 4:78, 5:36, 7:2, 7:30; see also advertising; cultural; customer; Family; Influences; micro-targeting; society; trends
 - adult| 2:67, 6:35
 - affluent| 4:95; see also pedigree; philanthropies; Power Structures; wealth
 - baby boomers| 7:14
 - boys| 4:22
 - caucasian| 4:38
 - gender| 7:31
 - income| 2:49, 3:8, 4:28, 4:70, 4:99, 5:43, 5:46, 6:57; see also disparity; neighborhoods; wealth
 - lifestyle| 5:39, 7:3; see also cultural; customer; society; trends
 - men| 1:16, 1:58, 1:69, 2:9, 2:13, 2:15-2:16, 2:21-2:22, 2:24-2:25, 2:28, 2:31, 2:37, 2:55, 2:62, 2:65, 2:86, 3:11, 3:83, 3:98, 4:43, 5:14, 5:18, 5:20, 5:25, 5:28, 5:40, 5:42, 5:60, 5:70, 5:73, 6:11, 6:14, 6:39, 7:38
 - millennial| 7:14
 - minority groups| 1:35; see also ethnic; Public Policies; racial profiling
 - Muslim men| 7:38
 - protestant| 4:93; see also religion
 - teen| 2:48, 4:65, 4:107, 5:43, 6:8, 7:3, 7:9; see also education
 - upscale| 3:78; see also Elite; pedigree
 - white collar| 1:43, 2:49-2:50
 - women| 1:58, 4:77, 5:42
Denial of Service (DNS)| 4:47; see also Errors; Internet Security
depiction| 2:54, 3:38, 4:88, 7:32; see also Narratives; scenarios
Devices| 1:45, 1:56, 1:58, 2:9, 2:16, 2:39, 2:56, 2:68, 2:85, 4:4, 4:8, 4:58, 4:79, 5:31-5:32, 5:46, 5:64, 6:29, 6:37, 7:38, 7:47, 7:49-7:50; see also face-to-screen; User Interface (UI)
 - Androids| 5:57
 - cellphone| 4:89
 - desktop| 5:43, 6:38; see also workplace
 - gadget| 1:3, 1:5, 1:51, 4:92, 6:46; see also User Interface (UI)
 - iPad| 5:79
 - iPhone| 5:34, 5:57, 5:75, 7:3; see also Apple; Smart phone
 - iPod| 1:51
 - laptops| 1:47, 1:51; see also workplace
 - PCs| 3:23; see also laptops
 - Smart phone| 4:25, 7:3, 7:26; see also Androids; iPhone
devise| 1:30, 3:62, 3:78; see also innovation; planning
diary| 5:46, 6:53; see also confession; first person; Social Media
diatribes| 7:3; see also Accusations; arguments; rant
Dichotomies| 5:65; see also cause-and-effect; Fight-or-flight; opposite; polar; Relatedness; yes or no
 - deficit and surpluses| i:4, 1:45, 4:98, 5:33; see also attention surplus; Dichotomies
 - diametrical| 4:39, 5:64, 7:44; see also opposite; polar; Relatedness
 - dynamic and static| 3:9; see also dynamic information
 - opposite| i:3, 1:75, 2:95, 3:6, 4:26, 4:58, 4:88, 5:26, 7:22; see also Contrarian; debate
 - polar| i:3, 7:28, 7:30; see also confirmation bias; Contrarian; echo chamber; enemy; opposite; tribal
 - reciprocal| 3:72, 4:55, 4:65-4:66, 4:69, 4:94, 4:101, 5:52, 7:39; see also equivalence; Interactions; mutual; quid pro quo
 - words and deeds| i:17, 1:15, 4:3, 4:87, c:13; see also Dichotomies; hypocrisy
 - yes or no| 1:52, 1:70, 3:49, 6:9; see also decisive; Logic; reciprocal
Did you mean| 2:44; see also Intentions; misspellings; SEO (Search Engine Optimization); suggestion search; type ahead
Diebold| 4:94
diet| 2:76, 3:19, c:8; see also Culinary; Metaphors; recipe
Digg| 4:85; see also curatorship; Perspectives, social media
Diigo| 4:85; see also social bookmarks; Websites, bookmarking
Diplomacy| 7:52; see also align; counterpart; Government; Negotiations; protocol
 - country| i:2, 1:24, 1:42, 3:53, 4:38, 7:28; see also Government; province; region
 - deport| 4:81, 7:31; see also dismiss; Government; Reject
 - overseas| 1:42; see also foreign

- passport| 2:33; see also foreign; overseas; Personal Identity
direct experience| 3:90; see also experience-based learning
dirt| 2:64, 3:8, 3:30-3:31; see also gossip; innuendo; negative information; smear
Disabilities| 6:8, 6:25, 6:28; see also Addictions; Cognitive; impaired
  - ADHD (Attention Deficit Hyperactivity Disorder)| 2:37; see also Cognitive
  - autism spectrum| 6:8-6:9, 6:12-6:13, 6:20, 6:23, 6:25, 6:28, 6:34, 6:45, 6:49; see also Cognitive; Intuitions
  - deaf| 4:66, 4:74, 6:47-6:48; see also nonverbal; oblivion
  - dyslexia| 6:48; see also Cognitive
  - impaired| 3:48, 4:88, 4:95, 4:103, 5:3, 5:74, 7:16; see also Addictions
disambiguation| 3:10-3:11; see also clarifications; Intentions
Disasters| 5:44, 5:64; see also black swan; crisis; hysteria; Risks
  - apocalypse| 7:51; see also doomsday; fallout; nightmares; Power Structures; warfare
  - calamitous| 1:43, 5:63; see also consequence
  - cataclysmic| 5:63; see also black swan; mayhem
  - catastrophe| 5:64; see also mayhem; Surprises
  - doomsday| 5:61; see also apocalypse; Cassandra; Chaotic Context; fallout; nightmares; society
  - epidemic| 3:61; see also Center for Disease Control (CDC); invasive; symptoms
  - hurricanes| 2:102; see also Weather Conditions
disciplinary| i:13, i:16, 1:9, 1:32, 1:41, 2:47, 2:89, 2:93, 3:1, 3:6, 3:13, 3:17, 3:60, 3:87, 4:1, 4:4, 5:1, 5:40, 5:43, 5:71, 6:24, c:1-c:2, c:13; see also crackdowns; public service; punishment; threats
disclaim| 1:41, 4:54; see also discredit; reversal; sabotage; uncertain
Disclosures| 1:16, 3:18, 4:2, 4:22, 4:92, 5:61, 6:11, 7:26, 7:41; see also debrief; divulge; dossier; headlines; leak
  - divulge| 1:14, 2:54, 3:64, 5:25; see also whistleblower; WikiLeaks
  - leak| 2:36, 4:90, 4:96, 4:104, 5:30, 7:14, 7:49, 7:53; see also breach; divulge; newsleaker
disconnect| 1:65, 3:38, 4:66, 4:102, 5:73, 5:75, 7:39; see also ancillary; evidence patterns; tangents
Discontinued Websites and Tools| 2:27, 2:62, 2:106, 3:12, 3:56, 3:97, 7:41; see also decommissioned; obsolete
  - decommissioned| 2:42; see also 404 error; obsolete
  - defunct| 3:9; see also archives; broken links; obsolete; outdated
  - Google Video| 3:66, 3:96; see also YouTube
  - obsolete| i:7; see also defunct
discovery| i:17, 1:11, 1:15-1:16, 1:18, 1:36, 1:43, 1:57, 1:69, 2:53, 2:107, 3:4-3:5, 3:14, 3:29, 3:78, 3:84, 3:98, 4:3, 4:79, 4:82, 4:94, 5:54, 5:68, 5:77, 6:16, 7:25, 7:38, 7:42, c:13; see also experimental; Learning; proof; realization
discussion boards| 1:26, 1:72, 2:86, 3:16, 3:62, 4:7, 4:16, 4:33; see also communities of practice; informal communication; listserv; newsgroup; online forums
disputes| 1:13-1:14, 1:19, 1:68, 2:42, 3:35, 3:37, 3:62, 4:3, 4:13, 4:44, 4:54, 4:73, 4:96, 5:53, 7:8, 7:27; see also arguments; Conflict; controversial; dissension; doubters; Legal; misunderstandings; Opposition; provocation
Disruptions| 3:9, 4:93, 5:35, 5:57, 7:50
  - distractions| i:6, i:9, 1:2, 1:7, 1:37, 1:45, 3:37, 4:32, 4:60, 4:91, 5:27, 5:34, 5:48, 5:71, c:2; see also continuous partial attention; dispersion; diversion; downplay; Exposure; Hidden; intrusion
  - diversion| 1:52, 3:25, 3:93, 6:34, 7:3
  - intrusion| 2:88, 4:42, 7:10, 7:16, 7:43; see also distractions; invasive; raid
disseminate| 2:57, 5:69, 7:26; see also curatorship; editor; journalist; skim
Distortions| i:16, 1:36, 2:24, 4:13, 4:91, 4:98, 5:29, 7:30, 7:37, 7:42; see also Excesses; fake news; Misinformation; outliers; propagandist; unfounded
  - delusion| 1:39, 2:68, 4:37, 5:8, 5:28, 5:62-5:63, 5:75, 7:6, 7:12, 7:22; see also dream; fallacy; myopic
  - fantasy| 3:58-3:59, 4:67, 4:102, 4:105, 5:72, 5:75, 7:14, 7:16, 7:30, 7:53; see also dream; fallacy; fiction; symbols
  - myopic| 3:27; see also delusion; navel-gazing
DNA| 4:58; see also ethnic
Documentation| 1:8, 1:10-1:11, 1:21, 1:26, 1:41, 1:45, 1:53, 1:61, 1:63, 1:72, 2:2-2:3, 2:6-2:7, 2:19, 2:22, 2:26, 2:45, 2:48-2:49, 2:57, 2:60, 2:76, 2:100, 2:107, 3:6, 3:23-3:24, 3:31, 3:37, 3:45, 3:50, 3:52, 3:56, 3:72, 3:76, 3:78, 3:81-3:82, 3:93, 4:11, 4:13, 4:42, 4:73-4:75, 4:77, 4:83-4:84, 4:102-4:103, 5:41, 5:68, 5:75, 5:77, 6:8, 6:14, 6:28, 6:35, 6:51, 6:53, 6:55, 7:1, 7:17, 7:39, c:2, c:5, c:13; see also archives; dossier; public records; recording
  - cite| 2:15, 2:49, 2:77, 3:60, 4:82, 4:93, 5:9, 5:20, 5:41, 5:47, 5:53, 5:68, 6:53, 7:35, 7:37; see also credit; original sources; point of origin; quote
  - correspondence| 4:59; see also Documentation; email; interplay; Search to Converse (STC)
  - debrief| 4:16, 4:58; see also Disclosures; interview
  - dossier| 1:6, 2:12; see also debrief; Disclosures; Overview
  - summaries| 1:71, 2:40, 2:52, 2:98, 3:12, 3:21, 3:57, 3:59, 3:70, 3:76, 5:31, 5:40, 5:47, 5:75, 5:77-5:78, 7:14; see also background checks; snapshot
  - texts| 1:38, 3:85, 4:25, 4:95, 5:42, 5:71; see also face-to-screen; Interactions
  - transcript| 2:60, 4:32; see also recording; unscripted; verbatims
Dogpile| 2:57; see also Search Engine, Metasearch
dopamine| 7:5; see also Cognitive; Intuitions; psychological
dormant| 1:44, 4:83, 4:105, 5:11; see also evidence patterns; static information
download| 1:51, 3:17, 3:22, 3:73, 4:108, 6:37, 7:1; see also Content Streaming; uploads
drama| 1:26, 1:40, 1:44, 1:48, 2:18, 2:31, 2:49, 2:72, 2:103, 3:89, 4:47, 4:51, 4:96, 5:10, 6:27, 6:36, 6:49, 7:13; see also episode; fiction; Narratives; story lines; unscripted
dream| 2:90, 4:66, 4:98-4:99, 5:34, 6:10; see also delusion; fantasy; nightmares
drug| 2:37-2:38, 3:60, 6:22, 7:7
dubious| 1:1, 1:46, 3:18, 3:61, 3:70, 4:18, 4:67, 4:91, 4:96, 4:99, 5:16, 7:6; see also authoritative; embarrassing; fake news; hypocrisy; suspicions; unsubstantiated

DuckDuckGo| 2:66-2:67, 2:71, 5:78; see also Search Engine, Privacy
duopoly| 7:9; see also anti-trust; technopoly
duplicated| 4:38; see also redundant; rehash; revisiting
dynamic information| i:15, 1:24, 1:40, 2:73, 3:4, 3:13, 3:15, 3:22-3:24, 3:61, 3:84, 3:91, 4:16-4:17, 4:25, 4:35, 4:68, 4:76, 4:83, 5:5, 5:40, 5:47, 5:52-5:53, 5:69, 5:71, 6:1, 6:52, 7:7, c:17; see also cgi; dynamic and static; fluid intelligence; static information

E

eavesdropping| 1:51, 3:7, 4:8, 4:45, 6:55; see also discrete; Surveillance; wiretaps
eBay| 3:59; see also Commerce
Economics| i:3, 1:19, 2:11, 3:25, 3:36, 3:49, 3:63, 4:13, 4:48, 4:86, 4:90, 4:97-4:98, 4:105, 5:5, 5:43-5:44, 6:7, 6:22, 7:10, 7:33, 7:43, c:12
 - monetary| i:11, 1:6, 1:38, 1:45, 1:47, 1:65, 2:10, 2:51, 2:63, 3:13, 3:36, 3:41, 3:50, 3:76, 4:19, 4:35, 4:39, 4:43, 4:54, 4:62, 4:69, 4:95, 5:24, 5:26, 5:39, 5:63, c:7; see also recession; stock market; Trade, financial
 - recession| 5:43; see also Decline; downturn; monetary; Scarcity; unemployment
ecotourism| 2:20; see also Case studies
EDGAR| 3:83; see also Securities and Exchange Commission (SEC)
education| 1:7, 1:31, 1:73, 2:8, 2:20, 2:22, 2:24, 2:27-2:28, 2:49, 2:72, 2:85, 2:89, 2:106, 3:12, 3:22, 3:24, 3:26, 3:53, 4:3, 5:27, 5:45, 5:56, 5:58, 6:8, 6:22, 6:44, 7:36, c:13; see also Academic; Learning
Educational Resources Information Center (ERIC)| 3:16
; see also academic papers; Cost of Research; Free, resources; public domain
Elections| 1:68, 4:8, 4:19, 4:35, 4:43, 4:48, 4:104, 4:106, 5:8, 5:24, 5:28, 7:17; see also Campaigns
 - ballot| 7:6
 - incumbent| 4:42, 6:53, 7:29; see also entrenched; establishment; Power Structures
Elite| 5:35, 5:54, 7:7, 7:14, 7:20; see also affluent; pecking order; Power Structures; wealth
 - echelon| 3:77, 5:24
 - pedigree| 7:20; see also Elite; Family; inherited
 - privilege| 1:26, 2:83, 4:8, 4:11, 4:13, 4:22-4:23, 4:25, 4:55, 4:104, 7:9, 7:20, 7:24, 7:42-7:43; see also disparity; echelon; Power Structures; self-preservation
 - tycoons| 4:98; see also mover; shakers; venture
Ellerbee, Linda| 1:36
email| 4:15, 4:26, 4:59-4:60, 4:65, 4:73, 4:95, 5:52, 7:17; see also anxiety; hygiene, electronic; spam
Empirical| i:1, 1:39, 4:10, 7:2, 7:5, 7:8, 7:37, 7:51; see also Evidence; Logic; scientific method
 - scientific method| 7:38-7:40; see also evidence gathering; Verification
Employment| i:11, 1:16, 1:19, 1:49, 1:59, 2:30-2:32, 2:39, 3:15, 3:69, 3:75-3:76, 3:80, 4:9, 4:16, 4:19, 4:31, 4:36, 4:54, 4:64, 4:66, 4:68, 4:77, 4:93, 5:9, 5:17, 5:32, 5:43, 5:45, 5:58, 6:8, 6:12, 7:32; see also Careers; Jobs; nondisclosure; salary
 - headhunters| 1:50, 4:57; see also broker; Careers; Jobs
 - labor| 2:86, 2:88, 3:60, 3:94, 5:59, 6:23, 7:3; see also horizontal business functions; Jobs; workplace
Encouragement| i:17, 1:30, 1:36, 2:63, 2:67, 2:69, 2:74, 3:12, 3:26, 4:4, 4:105, 5:65, 7:16-7:17, 7:39
 - elevate| i:1, 1:36, 2:65, 3:56, 4:16, 4:22, 4:31, 5:41, 6:50, 7:7, 7:24, 7:30, 7:36
 - embrace| 2:37, 2:66, 3:74, 4:2, 4:32, 7:14
 - enthusiasm| 2:63, 7:32; see also embrace
 - rally| 3:77, 4:8, 5:38, 5:62, 5:72; see also Campaigns; grassroots; Politics; protests; vocal
encryption| 1:16, 3:75; see also Code, secret; email; indecipherable; Internet Security
encyclopedia| 2:90; see also Wikipedia
endorse| i:13, 1:38, 4:18, 4:33, 4:61, 4:85, 4:92, 4:100, 4:102, 5:18, 5:50, 6:14, 6:35, 6:53, 7:43; see also celebrities; Influences
English| 1:55, 2:8, 2:48-2:49, 2:52, 3:7-3:8, 3:13; see also dialect; Grammar; Language; vernacular
Eno, Brian| 4:90
entrepreneur| 5:79, 6:7, 6:45, c:15; see also business plan; innovation
entry points| i:9, 1:1, 1:60, 1:66-1:67, 1:72-1:73, 2:32, 2:34, 2:72, 2:88, 2:90, 2:100, 3:7, 3:11-3:12, 3:21-3:22, 3:28, 3:32, 3:38, 3:52, 3:63, 4:1, 4:13, 4:93, 5:53, 6:1, 6:10, 6:20; see also Information Types
equality| 1:11, 1:20, 1:28, 1:35, 1:38, 1:41, 2:3, 2:68, 4:25, 4:32, 4:42, 4:69, 5:17, 5:23, 5:26, 6:45, 6:49, 7:8, 7:31, 7:38, 7:43; see also public interest
Errors| i:11, 1:9, 1:24, 1:41, 1:58, 1:66-1:67, 2:42, 2:61, 3:9, 3:11, 3:55, 4:83, 5:41, 5:75, 7:25; see also broken links; inconsistencies; missing details; misspellings; mistake
 - incorrect| 2:3, 3:60, 6:51; see also inaccuracies; misleading; mistake
 - mistake| i:6, i:16-i:17, 1:11, 1:21, 1:38, 1:46-1:47, 2:14, 4:52, 4:100, 4:103, 5:61, 5:75; see also inaccuracies
Escape| 1:11, 1:27, 1:31, 1:36, 2:15, 2:56, 2:93, 3:11, 3:54, 3:58-3:59, 4:17, 4:22, 4:38, 4:74, 4:87, 4:90, 4:105, 5:35, 5:73, 5:75, 7:4, 7:32, 7:40; see also Exposure
 - elusive| 1:76, 2:61, 2:64, 3:25, 3:45, 3:78, 3:89, 3:91, 4:30, 4:51, 5:1, 5:22, 5:74, 6:34, c:13
esoteric| 2:39, 2:50, 4:50; see also polemic; Rhetoric
ethics| 1:39, 5:69, 5:80, 6:22, 7:14, 7:23, 7:27; see also Code, of conduct; professional standards
ethnic| 1:35, 3:76; see also cultural; Demographics; dialect; family roots; inherited; tolerance; tribal
European Union| 7:9
Evaluation| 1:19, 1:24, 2:98, 3:4, 3:10, 3:50, 4:1, 4:13, 4:25, 4:29, 5:26, 6:20, 6:57, c:7; see also Analysis; anomalies; calculable; conclusive; correlation; criteria; diagnosis; dissect; Indicators; rationale; refactoring
 - assess| i:16, 1:3, 1:6, 1:10, 1:35-1:36, 1:43, 1:45-1:46, 1:49, 1:68, 1:70, 1:73-1:74, 2:16, 2:36, 2:39, 2:65, 2:97, 2:101, 2:107, 3:2, 3:4, 3:6, 3:12-3:13, 3:15, 3:22, 3:51-3:52, 3:58, 3:62-3:64, 3:67-3:68, 3:72, 3:88-3:89, 3:91, 3:95-3:96, 3:98-4:1, 4:6, 4:9, 4:29, 4:33-4:34, 4:36, 4:51, 4:59, 4:86-4:88, 4:98, 4:103, 4:105, 5:1, 5:4, 5:8-5:10, 5:16, 5:23-5:26, 5:29, 5:31-5:32, 5:34, 5:47, 5:54, 6:22-6:23, 6:37, 6:46, 6:49, 6:54, 6:57, 7:9, 7:21, 7:23-7:24, 7:26, 7:34, 7:40, 7:51, c:2, c:7, c:12, c:14, c:16
 - cause-and-effect| i:15, 1:39, 2:52, 3:92; see also Dichotomies; equivalence; reciprocal

- criteria| i:1, 2:35, 2:41-2:42, 3:4, 3:32, 3:71, 5:23, 5:76, 6:10, 6:12, 6:23, 7:28, 7:46
- diagnosis| 2:37, 3:60, 6:8, 6:22, 6:51; see also Analysis; cross-reference; Indicators; methods; vital data
- downstream| 6:10; see also cause-and-effect; consequence; fallout; impact; interdependency
- examination| i:7, 1:15, 3:61, 4:1, 4:45, 4:58, 5:66, 5:79; see also Investigations
- gauge| 1:11, 1:28, 1:63-1:64, 2:49, 3:3, 3:55, 3:89, 4:5, 4:25, 4:43, 4:86, 5:7-5:9, 5:16, 5:22, 5:32, 5:38, 5:59, 7:33, c:2, c:11; see also Guesswork; Indicators
- litmus test| 3:13, 4:97, 7:51; see also Indicators; Politics; proof
- mull| 2:56, 4:53, 6:40; see also deliberate; review; theoretical
- predefine| 2:85, 3:30, 3:66, 5:41, 7:8; see also Bias
- probable cause| 1:8, 7:12; see also possibility; Probabilities; scenarios
- refactoring| 1:11; see also revisiting; second guessing
- Rorschach| 4:44; see also Behaviors; beholder; connectedness; examination; psychological

Evidence| i:2, 1:26-1:27, 1:38, 1:40, 2:34, 2:70, 3:11, 3:88, 4:1, 4:4, 4:39, 4:51, 4:104, 5:5, 5:56, 5:65, 6:48, 7:1; see also Crime Scene; criminal evidence; self-evident; tampering
- circumstantial| 2:56; see also criminal evidence; implications; random
- discrepancy| 3:64, 4:47; see also inconsistencies; missing details; omission; unexplained
- dissect| 1:23; see also Pattern Matching
- evidence gathering| 4:13; see also Crime Scene; exposing corruption; homicidal; manslaughter
- evidence patterns| i:6, 1:5, 4:3, 5:27, 5:57; see also Evidence; inconsistencies; Sense-making
- puzzle| 1:10, 2:32, 3:76, 6:42, 7:34; see also clue; gap; missing details; mystery
- self-evident| 1:39, 5:56; see also Empirical
- tampering| 4:9, 6:11; see also poisoning; tainted; witness
- unresolved| 4:32, 4:95, 5:37, 7:21; see also mystery; unexplained

Exalead| 2:41, 2:102; see also Search Engine, Metasearch

Excesses| i:15, 2:92, 3:56, 4:36, 4:39, 4:99, 5:43, 5:66, 6:32, 7:12, 7:39; see also Distortions; unsubstantiated
- exaggeration| 4:97, 5:77, 7:12, 7:53; see also abuse; Influences; persuasion; provocation
- overreach| 4:19, 5:64, 5:73, 7:17; see also aggression; exaggeration
- overstate| 3:75, 5:44; see also Reinforcement

exclude| 1:46, 1:48, 2:9, 2:12, 2:14-2:15, 2:19, 2:22, 2:37, 2:76, 3:9, 3:31, 3:35, 3:62, 3:86, 4:38, 4:40, 4:45, 5:28, 7:29, 7:31; see also evidence gathering; evidence patterns

excuse| 4:103, 5:45, 5:47, 6:7, 7:29; see also permissible; rationale

Expectation| 1:33, 2:45, 2:48, 3:8, 3:46, 3:70, 4:44, 4:90, 5:12, 6:55, 7:2; see also research preparations; Surprises
- immediacy| 1:33-1:34, 1:40, 1:44, 1:75, 2:33, 2:88, 3:71-3:72, 3:87, 3:91, 4:2, 4:12, 4:32, 4:39, 4:51, 4:53, 4:59, 4:73, 4:80, 4:86, 4:93, 4:95, 5:35, 5:39, 5:45-5:46, 5:61, 5:73, 6:14, 7:38; see also sequential
- original expectations| 1:10, 5:57; see also assumptions; course-correcting; gut check
- planning| i:11, 1:7, 1:24-1:25, 1:39, 1:56, 2:14, 2:99, 3:8, 3:38, 4:8, 4:40, 4:43, 4:57, 4:94, 5:5, 5:28, 5:32, 6:14, 6:35-6:36; see also predefine; Search Project Management (SPM)
- reliability| 3:50, 3:94; see also reliance; Sense-making; steadfast
- unexpected| 1:39, 1:44, 1:68, 2:54, 3:13, 3:37, 4:35, 5:5, 5:16, 5:25, 5:35, 5:38, 5:47, 5:57, 5:60, 5:76, 6:34, 7:50; see also crisis; red flag; Surprises

experimental| 2:12, 2:81, 4:106, 6:16, 7:37, 7:39, 7:50; see also discovery; innovation; scientific method

Expertise| i:9, i:13-i:14, i:16-i:17, 1:1, 1:15, 1:20, 1:24-1:26, 1:30, 1:32-1:33, 1:46, 1:65, 2:1, 2:8, 2:21, 2:67, 2:86, 2:88, 2:92-2:93, 3:1, 3:5, 3:10, 3:13, 3:17, 3:26, 3:31-3:34, 3:63, 3:72-3:74, 3:82, 3:85, 3:88, 4:2, 4:5, 4:9, 4:16, 4:19, 4:25-4:26, 4:30, 4:42, 4:45, 4:47, 4:61, 4:69, 4:71, 4:77, 4:95-4:97, 4:99, 5:17, 5:39, 5:41, 5:44-5:46, 5:71, 5:76, 5:79, 6:9-6:13, 6:20, 6:24, 6:27, 6:50, 7:2, 7:7, 7:36, 7:42, c:6, c:10-c:11, c:16; see also acumen; communities of practice; Wisdom
- advisor| 3:20, 4:12; see also Consulting; recommendations; retain
- authoritative| i:13-i:15, 1:44, 1:73, 2:89, 3:10, 3:95, 4:7, 4:29, 4:33, 4:48, 4:55, 4:60, 4:92, 4:97-4:98, 4:100, 5:5, 5:8, 5:31, 5:40-5:41, 5:53, 5:64, 5:72, 5:75-5:76, 6:21, 6:46, 6:50-6:51, 6:55, 6:57; see also domain expert; Influences; Power Structures
- domain expert| 1:33; see also Semantics, finding experts

Explanations| i:6, 1:3, 1:5, 1:12, 1:15, 1:20, 1:33, 1:51, 1:75, 2:34, 2:43, 2:57, 3:3, 3:17, 3:35, 4:2, 4:14, 4:30, 4:36, 4:51, 4:84, 4:87, 4:95, 5:4-5:6, 5:26-5:27, 5:31, 5:49, 5:56-5:57, 5:59, 5:61, 5:63, 5:69-5:70, 6:23, 7:19, 7:22, 7:25, 7:31, 7:39-7:40, 7:42, 7:50, c:1, c:12; see also diagnosis; Evaluation; Logic; rationale
- actions of others| 1:3, 1:33, 4:3; see also Blame; Motives; Perspectives, perspective-taking
- alternative explanations| 4:31, 7:40
- causal| 7:10; see also reciprocal
- caveat| 4:85
- clarifications| i:11, i:16, 1:14, 1:22, 1:31, 1:45, 1:51, 1:57, 1:68, 1:72, 2:2, 2:12, 2:40, 2:50, 2:104, 3:1, 3:8-3:9, 3:25, 3:32, 3:72, 3:90, 4:7, 4:28, 4:95, 5:9, 5:11, 5:22-5:23, 5:26, 5:29-5:31, 5:57, 5:61, 5:72, 5:74, 6:52, 6:57, 7:9, 7:12, 7:21, 7:27-7:28, 7:42, 7:50, c:12; see also narrow
- competing explanations| 1:20, 1:75, 4:15, 5:58, 5:60, 5:62, 7:39; see also Evaluation; extrapolate; Interpretations
- corollary| 4:91, 7:41; see also Logic
- corroborate| 1:27, 3:52, 4:73, 7:36; see also Reinforcement
- defying explanation| 1:33, 1:51, 5:6, 5:64; see also Confusion; mystery; unexplained
- explainers| 5:71, 7:42, c:1; see also rationale
- explanatory power| 3:4, 4:52, 5:5-5:6, 5:32, 5:71, 7:19, 7:31, 7:50, c:12; see also Influences; persuasion; Reason
- theoretical| 1:5, 1:38, 1:47, 1:70, 1:75, 2:30, 2:56, 2:61, 3:8, 3:33, 3:56, 3:94, 4:86, 4:107, 5:16, 5:24, 5:56-5:57, 5:73, 6:1, 7:7, 7:14, 7:38; see also abstract; conceivable; hypotheses; possibility; scenarios
- unexplained| 5:5, 5:63; see also conceal; mystery

explicit| i:7, 2:9, 2:14, 2:19, 4:76, 5:78; see also Implicit; inclusion; obvious; Search operators, exclusion

Explorations| i:11, 1:29, 1:73, 2:2-2:3, 2:47, 2:70, 3:1-3:2, 3:17, 3:19, 3:32, 3:34, 3:90, 4:49, 4:75, 4:83, 4:91, 5:7, 5:23, 5:31, 5:47, 5:59, 6:23, 6:34,

COMPLETE WORKS: Units One Through Seven | Unabridged Index:15

6:39, 6:49, 7:1, 7:12, 7:50; see also curiosities; discovery; serendipitous
  - hunt| i:6, 2:34, 2:45, 2:65, 3:36, 4:62; see also criminal investigation; Search Targets
  - pioneering| 2:70; see also discovery; novelty; Unexplored
  - uncover| 1:11, 1:27, 1:30, 1:71, 2:54, 2:56, 3:2, 3:4, 3:27, 3:77, 4:30-4:31, 4:44, 5:7, 6:21, 6:37, 6:46, 6:52, 7:38, 7:46, c:6-c:7, c:10, c:16; see also discovery; exposing corruption
  - venture| 3:74, 4:18, 5:18, 5:24, 6:43; see also cooperation; fund; Organizations
Exposure| 1:15, 1:20, 1:33, 1:37, 1:70, 2:67-2:68, 2:106, 4:23, 4:30-4:31, 4:35, 4:47-4:48, 4:51-4:56, 4:65, 4:96, 4:104, 5:59, 5:72, 7:26, 7:37-7:38, 7:45; see also Disruptions; Hidden; Obscurities; Paparazzi; Radar; visibility; warning
  - detection| 2:40, 3:60, 4:32, 4:51, 5:45, 7:34; see also event trigger; Secrecy; Surveillance
  - exposing corruption| 1:15, 1:20, 4:36, 4:48, 4:55, 4:97, 5:25, 7:38; see also Corruption; public investigation
  - fixation| i:11, 1:48, 3:11, 3:25, 3:27, 4:104, 5:63, 6:41, 7:46; see also compulsive; exclusive; obsession; Paparazzi
  - invasive| 3:46, 4:29, 4:62, 4:74, 7:18; see also Disruptions
  - marquee| 3:54; see also Fame; headlines
  - obsession| 2:31, 2:51, 3:28, 4:31, 4:54, 4:92-4:93, 5:5, 6:58; see also compulsive; Exposure; fixation; viral
  - overlook| i:9, 1:5, 1:8, 1:10, 1:36, 1:52-1:53, 1:71, 2:12, 2:40, 2:51, 2:68, 2:101, 3:2, 3:4, 3:11, 3:56, 3:68, 3:91, 4:1, 4:48, 4:57, 4:70, 5:18, 5:59, 6:17, 7:34, c:1, c:6-c:7; see also blindspots; discrepancy; inconsistencies; missing details; oblivion; overshadow
  - overshadow| 4:97, 5:61; see also dominant
  - spotlight| 1:26, 4:32, 7:6, c:13; see also celebrities; newsmakers; Radar; Recognition; stature
Expression| 1:47, 1:55, 2:10, 2:13, 2:21, 2:31, 2:33-2:34, 2:37, 2:43, 2:46, 2:62, 2:76, 3:14, 3:23, 3:58, 4:101, 5:27, 5:35, 7:30; see also Influences; Interpretations; Rhetoric
  - blunt| 2:15, 7:48; see also antagonisms; Authenticity; candid; honesty; tonality
  - boldness| 3:61, 4:32, 7:10; see also aggression; blunt; decisive
  - decisive| 1:18, 4:22, 4:86; see also Actions and Outcomes; deliberate
  - discrete| 1:15, 1:18, 3:31, 3:77, 3:93, 4:9, 4:31, 4:88, 6:13, 6:58, 7:29; see also backdoor; Intentions; secrets, keeping
  - sensual| 1:33, 6:2; see also Intentions; nonverbal; passion; persuasion; pleasure
  - tonality| 3:64, 4:54, 4:66, 5:37; see also impression; projects, client reports; vocal
extortion| 1:37; see also blackmailed; Coercion; Corruption; Crime; embarrassing; exploit; hostage; threats
ExxonMobil| 4:94
eyewitness| 1:16, 1:27-1:28, 1:65, 2:60, 5:33, 7:15, 7:23; see also Crime Scene; Observation; witness

F

Facebook| 1:38, 1:74, 2:12, 2:53, 3:10, 3:46, 3:54, 3:62, 3:77, 4:13, 4:32, 4:56-4:57, 4:61, 4:65-4:67, 4:73, 4:75, 4:77, 4:94, 5:27, 5:30, 5:42, 5:53, 5:61, 6:10, 7:4, 7:8-7:10, 7:12-7:16, 7:18-7:20, 7:23, 7:28-7:31, 7:43, 7:46, 7:48, 7:52-7:56; see also affinity bias; duopoly; hot media; micro-targeting; news feed; Perspectives, social media; pre-social media; Zuckerberg, Mark
  - Facebook page| 1:38, 1:74, 2:12, 2:53, 4:32, 4:75, 5:30, 5:61, 6:10, 7:9, 7:13; see also news feed; personal branding
faceted search| 1:68, 2:43-2:46, 2:69-2:70, 2:98, 6:21, 6:32; see also Content Grouping; Search Engine, Clustered
Fact-based| 1:17; see also accuracy; precise; proof
  - concrete| 1:19, 1:25, 1:44, 2:49, 2:56, 2:61, 3:6, 3:16, 3:19, 3:48, 3:80, 4:41, 4:105, 5:44, 6:10, 7:13; see also contracts; literal; persuasion; proof; tangible
  - exact| i:3, i:9, i:11, 1:24, 1:31, 1:68, 2:11, 2:14, 2:19, 2:23, 2:37, 2:43, 2:63, 2:88, 2:104, 3:7, 3:9, 3:17, 3:27, 3:48, 3:50, 3:54, 3:58, 3:69, 4:29, 4:36, 4:50, 4:58, 5:22, 5:52, 6:20-6:21, 6:39, 6:41, 6:48, 7:27, 7:38, c:4; see also granular; haystack; precise
  - fact checkers| 4:106, 5:63, 6:53; see also inaccuracies; Skepticism; Snopes; veracity
  - fact versus opinion| 2:100, 3:18-3:19, 3:49; see also Site Selection
  - factoid| i:9, 1:75,7:30; see also bogus; superfluous; trivial
  - factual| 1:47, 2:32, 4:91, 7:19, 7:22; see also BS Detection
  - specificity| i:9, 2:4, 2:6, 2:23-2:24, 2:42, 2:75-2:76, 3:2, 3:5, 3:28, 3:62, 4:47, 4:105, 5:17, 5:27, 5:71, 6:34, 6:49, c:3-c:5; see also granular; precise
fads| 5:30; see also fashion; intensity; memes; novelty; Popularity; trends
failsafes| 1:10-1:12,1:17- 1:18, 1:21-1:28, 1:46, 1:53, 1:69, 1:71, 2:49, 2:76, 4:71-4:72, 4:74; see also Search Project Management (SPM); Stop; time commitment; time, spending; useful, failsafes
fake news| 7:10, 7:22, 7:38; see also alternative explanations; Confusion; demagoguery; Distortions; distractions; diversion; fact checkers; filter bubbles; fog; hypocrisy; Misinformation; pandering; point of origin; pretense; propagandist; unsubstantiated
Fame| 1:35, 1:54, 1:65, 2:33, 3:11, 3:38, 3:74, 4:7, 4:26, 4:85, 5:30, 6:56; see also Influences; newsmakers; Recognition
  - celebrities| 1:33, 1:49, 1:67, 2:67, 3:77, 4:8, 4:32, 4:44, 4:92, 4:94, 4:96, 5:30, 5:33, 5:39, 6:14, 6:35, 7:11, 7:37-7:38, 7:47; see also admirers; cachet; Fame; newsmakers; personal branding
  - entertainers| 2:93, 3:35, 3:54, 3:58, 4:32, 4:83, 5:17, 5:48, 7:16; see also celebrities; omnipresent; personality
  - omnipresent| 2:66; see also Recognition
  - renowned| 3:34; see also celebrities; newsmakers; Reputations
Family| i:16, 1:19, 1:23-1:25, 1:33, 1:38, 2:12, 2:35, 4:15, 4:47, 4:53-4:56, 4:58, 4:70, 4:73, 4:75, 4:81, 4:91, 4:108, 5:32, 5:43, 5:64, 6:46, 6:52, 7:13-7:14, 7:17-7:18, 7:29; see also Relatedness; tribal
  - ancestral| 3:18, 4:69; see also anthropological; History
  - brother| 4:67, 7:46, 7:49
  - child| i:16, 1:35, 1:49, 2:48, 4:39, 4:106, 5:43, 5:52, 6:13, 6:20, 6:22
  - cousin| 1:54, 3:14; see also Relatedness
  - daughter| 1:35
  - family history| 4:53; see also cultural; inherited; neighborhoods; region
  - family reunion| 2:86; see also annual; Milestones
  - family roots| 4:59; see also ingrained; inherited; tribal
  - genealogy| 3:79, 4:46, 4:75; see also Family; finding people; inherited; maiden name; surname

Searching Out Loud: Giving Voice to Independent Investigations | Marc Solomon

- mother| 2:56, 3:69
- parents| 1:35, 3:15, 6:20, 6:49; see also hierarchy; inherited
- reunion| 3:46, 7:13; see also annual; Milestones; Trade, shows
- sister| 4:36, 6:54
- spouse| 1:39, 3:6

FAQs| 2:50, 3:8, 5:40; see also QueryCat; useful answers; useful websites
fashion| 1:75, 4:26, 4:56, 4:79, 6:56; see also memes; Public Awareness; trends; viral
favor| i:9, i:15-i:17, 1:3, 1:38, 1:44, 1:47, 1:52, 2:9, 2:30-2:31, 2:37, 2:49, 2:51, 2:74, 2:100, 3:10, 3:19, 3:56, 3:64, 3:72, 3:86, 3:89, 3:94, 4:18, 4:26, 4:29, 4:32, 4:40-4:41, 4:47, 4:51, 4:64, 4:69, 4:79, 4:98, 4:100, 4:102, 4:105, 5:3, 5:5, 5:17, 5:27, 5:29, 5:52, 5:54, 5:60, 5:62-5:63, 5:65-5:66, 5:73, 5:76, 5:78, 6:8-6:9, 6:29, 6:57, 7:5, 7:15, 7:28, 7:30, 7:46; see also Influences; Negotiations
fear| 2:51, 3:64, 4:31, 4:36, 4:58, 4:90-4:91, 4:102, 5:2, 5:73, 7:3; see also Liabilities; Motives; Risks
fee-based| 1:1, 1:8, 1:18, 1:23, 1:56, 2:36, 3:1, 3:4, 3:14-3:15, 3:24, 3:36, 3:41, 3:73, 3:75, 3:78-3:79, 3:81-3:82, 3:86, 3:91-3:95, 4:1, 4:100, 5:58, 5:66, 5:76, 6:8, 6:20, c:1, c:3, c:7; see also Cost of Research; free versus fee; premium content
Feed Demon| 5:33, 5:50, 5:52, 6:12, 6:37; see also Reis, George (case study); RSS (Really Simple Syndication)
- watch list| 1:35, 6:40, 6:42-6:44, 6:50, 6:58; see also Alert; event trigger
- watchwords| i:14; see also categorizing, role of word choice
Feed reader| 6:46; see also news feed; RSS (Really Simple Syndication)
fiction| 3:58, 7:6; see also fantasy; narrator
File Formats| 2:42, 3:57, 6:5, 6:29; see also database, structure
- aspx| 3:22
- CSV| 6:5
- docx| 2:26
- field-based| 1:58, 1:62, 1:64, 2:26, 2:30, 2:41-2:42, 2:51, 2:59, 2:77, 2:79, 3:23, 3:56, 3:83, 4:9, 4:74, 4:77, 5:32, 5:42, 5:44, 5:46, 6:50, c:4; see also categorizing, field structure
- filetype| 2:26-2:27, 2:35, 6:28; see also Information Types, formats
- xls| 2:26-2:27, 6:28; see also MS Excel; spreadsheet
filings| 1:70, 2:72, 3:38, 5:2, 5:13, 5:75, 6:33; see also Documentation; Regulations; tax
filter bubbles| 2:66, 7:21, 7:23, 7:27, 7:29, 7:37, 7:39; see also affinity bias; algorithms; micro-targeting; Surveillance Capitalism
Filtering| 1:35, 1:51, 1:56, 1:58, 2:3, 2:5, 2:7, 2:9, 2:15, 2:19, 2:21-2:22, 2:29, 2:32-2:33, 2:40, 2:42, 2:88, 3:24, 3:28, 3:30, 3:96, 4:1, 4:15, 4:25, 4:100, 5:4, 5:48, 5:50, 6:1, 6:12, 6:26, 6:32, 6:34, 6:41-6:42, 6:48, 6:52, 7:7-7:8, 7:21, 7:23, 7:26-7:27, 7:29, 7:37, 7:39, 7:44, c:3; see also pearl culturing; query formation; refinement
- human, filtered| 2:86, 2:88, 3:28, c:3; see also categorizing, human mediated; Humans
- parse| 2:58, 2:67, 5:10; see also classification; Grammar; Syntax
- second pass| 2:8; see also pearl culturing; refinement; search logs
- trawl| 2:95, 2:99, 3:55, 3:81, 3:83, 6:41; see also Oceans, Lakes, and Ponds (OLP); retrieval
- winnowing| 2:13, 2:16; see also narrow; refinement
Findability| 1:76; see also aboutness; prominence; Relevance; searchable
finding people| 2:18, 2:89, 3:75, 3:80, 4:74-4:75, 6:43, 7:8; see also alias; background checks; genealogy; maiden name; Semantics, finding people; surname
Findlaw| 2:93; see also Legal; Subject Directory
Firefox| 3:72; see also Browser
firewall| i:15, 1:59, 4:92, 6:55, 7:13, 7:49; see also infrastructure; insecure; Internet Security; Workarounds
First Amendment| 3:50, 3:91, 4:45, 5:8, 7:8, 7:10-7:11; see also free speech; Freedoms, constitutional
- civil liberty| 7:43; see also Freedoms, constitutional; libertarian
first party| 4:21-4:23, 5:37, 6:54-6:55; see also plural; Provider Conjugation Framework (PCF)
first person| 1:25, 3:36, 3:76, 3:90, 4:3-4:4, 4:14-4:15, 4:22, 4:33, 4:37, 4:59, 4:68, 4:87, 4:92, 4:102, 5:30-5:31, 5:39, 6:53; see also Authenticity; catharsis; confession; diary; Provider Conjugation Framework (PCF); singular form
Flood, Barbara| 1:38, 1:76; see also Johari Window
focus groups| 4:26, 4:44, 5:64; see also advertising; market research; public perceptions; Surveys
folksonomy| 4:62; see also tagging engine; taxonomy
Forbidden| 2:92; see also heresy; Laws; rule-making
- heresy| 4:33
- incest| 5:27, 7:7, 7:36; see also Conflicts of interest; Relatedness
- trespasses| 3:73; see also illegal; unguarded; violator
Forecast| 1:44, 2:30, 5:8, 5:63, 5:65, 6:12, 6:20-6:21, 6:34, 6:36, 6:47; see also market research; Visionary
- future| i:14, 1:34, 1:45, 3:16, 3:88, 3:94, 4:32, 4:38, 4:41-4:42, 4:67-4:68, 4:79-4:80, 4:104, 4:106, 5:16, 5:31, 5:41, 5:43, 5:45, 5:61, 5:63, 6:13, 6:43, 6:51, 7:2, 7:5, 7:18, 7:23, 7:34, 7:51; see also 1939 New York World's Fair; envision; hindsight; History; Visionary
- prognostications| 5:62; see also foreknowledge; hypotheses
foreign| 3:13, 3:32, 3:55, 4:7, 6:4, 6:9-6:10, 7:10, 7:22; see also outsider; remote
forum| i:2, 1:30, 1:35, 4:12, 4:15, 4:43, 4:54, 4:60, 4:87, 5:35, 5:39-5:40, 6:8; see also agenda; online forums; venue
frame of reference| 1:29, 1:35, 1:47, 2:30, 3:6, 4:3, 5:51, 5:67-5:68, 7:8; see also Perspectives, perspective-taking; theory of mind
Frameworks| i:5, i:8, 1:1-1:3, 1:7, 1:10, 1:29-1:30, 1:38-1:39, 1:43, 1:72, 1:76, 2:2-2:3, 2:7, 2:39, 2:50, 2:86, 2:100, 3:5, 3:24, 3:32, 3:35, 3:51, 3:89-3:90, 3:95-3:96, 4:2, 4:4, 4:7, 4:9, 4:11, 4:50-4:51, 4:56, 4:86, 5:4, 5:11, 5:15, 5:17, 5:25, 5:29, 5:31-5:32, 5:34, 5:52, 5:68-5:69, 5:79, 6:11, 6:13, 6:34, 6:45, 7:2, 7:21, 7:26, 7:34, 7:37, 7:49-7:51, c:5, c:15; see also new-to-known; Oceans, Lakes, and Ponds (OLP); Provider Conjugation Framework (PCF); Search Project Management (SPM); The Biggest Picture (TBP); Vectors of Integrity (VOI)
fraud| 1:43, 2:1, 2:49, 2:88, 3:16, 3:45, 3:61, 4:30, 4:92, 4:94, 4:96, 4:98, 4:100, 5:47; see also Crime; Deceptions; Distortions; scammers; white collar crime
Free, resources| 1:1, 1:10, 3:16-3:17, 3:77, 3:81, 3:92, 3:95, 4:2, 4:34; see also Cost of Research
- free versus fee| 3:2, 3:15-3:16, 3:26, 3:79, 3:82, 3:95-3:96, 4:2, c:7; see also containing costs; database, subscription (premium)

Freedoms, constitutional| 3:31, 4:106, 5:9, 7:8, 7:30; see also civil liberty; First Amendment; guarantee
- free press| 7:10, 7:15, 7:42; see also First Amendment; Journalism
- free speech| 4:68, 7:26-7:27; see also civil liberty; Freedoms, constitutional
- uninhibited| 2:67, 4:14, 4:67, 7:1; see also innocence; unfiltered

friends| i:14, i:16, 1:38, 2:12, 2:47, 2:64, 2:71, 3:62, 4:1, 4:15, 4:32, 4:47, 4:51, 4:55-4:56, 4:60, 4:66, 4:68-4:70, 4:73, 4:89, 4:91, 4:99, 4:108, 5:38, 5:40, 5:42, 5:76, 6:7, 6:54, 7:10, 7:13, 7:16-7:18, 7:29, 7:38, 7:43, c:14; see also Affiliated; ally; camaraderie; interpersonal; social circles
Froogle| 3:8; see also Discontinued Websites and Tools
fudging| 5:77; see also approximate; Indicators; rounding
Full record| 3:21-3:22; see also public records

G

gatekeepers| 6:14, c:10; see also administrators; intermediaries; Roles
Gates, Robert| 4:34
geeks| 1:7, 1:59, 2:44-2:45, 3:13, 5:41, 7:26, 7:38; see also nerd; technology, professional roles
Gigablast| 2:37, 2:39, 2:59, 2:70, 3:22; see also Search Engine, Metasearch
Google Ads| 2:62, 3:93, 5:25, 7:34; see also advertising; duopoly; Search Engine Marketing (SEM); SEO (Search Engine Optimization)
Google CSE (Custom Search Engine)| 2:4, 2:75-2:76, 5:33; see also categorizing, role of word choice; Content Grouping; Search Engine, Custom (CSE)
Google Earth| 2:56; see also climate change; GPS (Global Positioning Satellite); maps
Google Keyword Tool| 6:17, 6:20; see also Search Engine Marketing (SEM)
Google Trends| 1:75, 3:78-3:79, 3:96, 5:31, 5:33; see also internet radar; The Biggest Picture (TBP); trends
Google type ahead| 7:36; see also Google AdWords; suggestion search
googled| 1:47, 4:75, 5:7, 6:17; see also finding people; vanity
Government| i:7, i:14-i:15, 1:38, 1:42, 1:73, 2:33, 2:66, 2:92, 3:37, 3:67-3:68, 4:33, 4:45, 4:86, 5:65, 5:76-5:77, 6:55, 7:30-7:31; see also database, government
- ambassador| 7:27
- bureaucrats| 3:37; see also administrators; public perceptions
- census| 1:27; see also Demographics
- Congress| i:7, 2:11
- federal| i:5, 1:40, 1:69, 1:73, 2:11, 3:67-3:68; see also Regulations
- government websites| 1:69, 2:26, 3:38, 3:67, 3:75; see also deep web; public domain
- governor| 4:38; see also public officials
- Senate| i:2
- intelligence, government| 1:29, 1:34; see also Central Intelligence Agency (CIA); secrets, keeping; Surveillance
- judiciary| i:2; see also Code, legal; court; review
- legislation| 5:48; see also Government; Legal
- public hearing| 7:37; see also Advocacy; equality; Interactions; Opposition
- public officials| 1:39, 4:36, 4:39, 4:49, 7:21, 7:40; see also bureaucrats; figureheads
- tax| i:10, 1:73, 3:67, 4:12, 4:99, 5:75-5:76; see also Internal Revenue Service (IRS); monetary; Public Policies
Government, forms of| 2:66; see also Elections; ideological
- democracy| 7:49, 7:54; see also Elections
- fascism| 7:19; see also authoritative; Power Structures; suppression; tyranny
- Surveillance Capitalism| 7:55; see also filter bubbles; personal data; Power Structures; predatorial
- totalitarianism| 7:18; see also Censorship; Government, forms of; suppression
GPS (Global Positioning Satellite)| 1:8, 1:13, 1:26, 2:56, 3:10, 3:46, 3:74, 3:96, 4:83; see also Google Earth; Location; Surveillance Capitalism
Grammar| 1:72, 2:37, 4:7, 4:11, 4:22, 6:3; see also particle of speech
- adverbs| 3:9; see also predicate
- colons| 4:83
- comma| 2:38, 4:83
- consonants| 2:62
- misspellings| 1:67; see also Did you mean
- paragraph| 2:7, 2:30-2:31, 2:37, 2:49, 2:51, 3:12, 3:61, 4:65
- parenthesis| 2:16, 2:30; see also verbatims; Word Algebra
- plural| 2:15, 2:37, 2:76, 4:7, 4:9, 4:12, 4:25, 4:83, 5:36; see also first party; Provider Conjugation Framework (PCF); second party; third party
- predicate| 2:6, 2:10, 2:37-2:38, 2:44, 3:9, 3:20, 4:83, 5:53; see also actions and actors; nouns and verbs; verbs, conjugation
- pronoun| 2:10, 2:38; see also noun phrases
Grievance| 4:51, 4:54, 4:104, 5:37, 5:46, 7:50; see also Accusations; Blame; complaints
- Disgruntled| 4:54; see also accusers; derail; disputes
- displeasure| 4:32, 4:54; see also diatribes
- upset| 1:44; see also Contest; Probabilities
Grote, Jerry| 1:33; see also blindspots; Memory
Group Behavior| 1:38, 4:1-4:2, 4:4, 4:13, 4:17, 4:48-4:49, 4:86; see also Code, of conduct; Collaborative; conform; dissension; tribal
- group communication| 3:15, 4:9; see also first party; official; spokesperson
- hive| 3:98; see also consensus; crowdsourcing
guarantee| i:2, i:10-i:11, 1:11, 1:33, 2:32, 2:38, 3:12, 3:91, 4:30, 4:58, 4:67, 4:74, 5:43, 5:66, 6:6, 6:50; see also absolute; certainties; possibility; Probabilities
Guesswork| 1:13, 2:11, 5:7, 6:33; see also Probabilities; Speculation
- educated guesses| 1:31, 2:106, 3:14, 4:4, 5:57, c:13

- guesstimate| 5:58; see also calculable; possibility; Probabilities
- inference| 3:48, 3:87, 4:8, 4:75, 5:68, 7:2, 7:39; see also extrapolate; Logic; rationale
- rounding| 1:61, 7:23; see also Probabilities
- second guessing| 1:37, 1:64, 4:45; see also hindsight; posterity

gumshoe| 7:24; see also Professional Investigator (PI)
guru| 3:94, 7:52; see also Expertise; genius; soothsayers

H

Hacks| 1:59, 2:43, 2:66, 3:11, 3:74, 4:32, 4:45, 6:55, 7:13, 7:17, 7:29, 7:45; see also breach; bypass; Internet Security; Workarounds
- mashup| 2:54-2:55, 2:91; see also programmer; synchronize; User Interface (UI)

Hagel, Georg| 3:93
Harvard University| 2:27, 3:97
haystack| 1:16-1:17, 3:20, 3:36, 3:48, 3:50, c:5; see also granular; Metaphors; precise
Haystacks and Icebergs| 1:16-1:17, 3:19, 3:35, 3:48-3:49, c:5; see also narrow; Term Expansion
- bullseye| 2:88, 2:93, 3:36, 3:77, 4:71; see also Metaphors; precise
- concept-based| 2:3, 2:101, 3:2; see also abstract; Opinion-based
- granular| 2:47, 2:57, 2:59-2:60, 3:22, 3:31, 3:52, 5:73, 5:77; see also precise
- recall| 1:30, 1:61, 3:6, 3:9, 3:36, 3:88, 4:11, 4:71, 4:80-4:81, 5:26, 5:39, 7:16, c:5

headlines| 3:90, 5:36, 6:3, 7:11, 7:14, 7:45; see also Exposure; Fame; newsmakers; prominence; Public Awareness; Radar; top-of-mind
healthcare| 1:16, 1:25, 4:93; see also medical malpractice; public health
Heifetz, Ronald| 4:41; see also balcony; Leaders
Hewlett-Packard (HP)| 2:22
Hidden| 1:27, 1:38, 2:26, 2:36, 3:6, 3:61, 3:72, 3:93, 4:4, 4:48, 4:65, 5:60, 7:7; see also Deceptions; Exposure; guise
- conceal| 1:1, 1:11, 1:14, 1:36, 1:53, 3:63, 3:73, 3:83, 3:93, 4:14, 4:91, 4:99, 4:104, 7:19; see also Deceptions; misleading
- disappearance| 2:59, 3:14, 3:21-3:22, 3:25, 3:78, 5:43, 5:52, 6:43, 7:4, 7:41
- incoherent| 1:45; see also Confusion; Expression; indecipherable; rant
- missing details| 7:38; see also discrepancy; evidence patterns; loopholes; omission; puzzle
- opaque| 2:67, 3:3, 5:60, 7:5; see also block; Deceptions; inscrutable; Radar; Secrecy
- unannounced| 1:61, 3:57, 5:35; see also Secrecy; unplanned
- unnamed| 4:59, 7:11; see also anonymous; Obscurities; secrets, keeping

Highbeam Research| 3:16
History| i:7, i:13, 1:10, 1:17, 1:38, 1:44, 1:49, 1:70, 1:73, 2:32, 2:36, 2:71, 2:86, 2:95, 3:19, 3:22, 3:37-3:38, 3:61, 3:64, 3:73-3:76, 3:83, 3:87, 4:28, 4:38, 4:42, 4:46, 4:52-4:53, 4:55-4:56, 4:58, 4:66, 4:97, 5:16, 5:38, 5:42-5:43, 5:61-5:64, 5:75-5:76, 6:4, 6:57, 7:2, 7:13, 7:16-7:17, 7:30, 7:33, 7:45, 7:48; see also ancestral; archives; Perspectives
- ancient| 3:37, 3:85, 6:4; see also ancestral; tribal
- bygone| 3:95, 7:11; see also Discontinued Websites and Tools; nostalgia; outdated; Perspectives; posterity
- modern| 4:56, 5:35, 7:33; see also lifestyle; Perspectives
- museums| 3:87; see also Perspectives, elevated
- predate| 1:11, 2:88, 3:96, 4:90; see also outdated; pre-social media; precedence; predetermined; predisposed
- retrace| 1:36, 3:5, 3:9, 5:68, 6:8; see also Code, tracking; course-correcting; social bookmarks; track; URLs

Hit Counts| 2:13, 2:18, 2:35, 2:54, 2:64, 3:14, 3:39, 3:69-3:70, 5:11, 5:21-5:22, 5:24, 5:30, 6:1; see also new-to-known; prominence; quantity controls; recurrences; Relevance; Search Results; signal-to-noise; The Biggest Picture, metrics
- False hit| 1:67; see also irrelevance; ordering, search results
- recurrences| 1:9, 1:26, 2:50, 3:63, 3:70, 4:36, 4:43, 4:87, 6:4, c:1; see also frequencies; quantity controls; verbatims

honor| i:1, i:8, i:12, 1:11, 1:19, 2:42, 4:42, 4:60, 4:66, 4:96, 5:11, 5:40, 6:2, 6:36, 7:5, 7:38-7:39, 7:45, 7:51; see also merit; Recognition
hot media| 7:26; see also McLuhan, Marshall
Hourihan, Judy| 3:29; see also Cookin' with Google
household| 3:17, 4:34; see also Demographics; neighborhoods; reside
HTC| 2:35
html| 2:26, 2:82, 3:12, 3:39, 3:57, 3:73; see also Code, software; markup language
Humans| i:7, i:16, 1:15, 1:17, 1:29, 1:41, 1:47, 1:51, 1:58-1:60, 1:65, 2:6, 2:26, 2:37, 2:44, 2:52, 2:86, 2:88, 2:90-2:91, 2:93-2:94, 3:13, 3:19-3:20, 3:28, 3:31, 3:34, 3:59, 3:92, 4:19, 4:23, 4:75, 4:86, 4:89, 4:104, 5:5, 5:29, 5:32, 5:63, 7:3, 7:16, 7:19, 7:26-7:28, 7:39, 7:44-7:48, 7:50-7:51, c:3; see also artificial intelligence; Machine-enabled; machine-mediated human computer interactions; technology, intimidation factors
- human intelligence| 7:46-7:47; see also Interrogation, humans of machines
- genius| 1:49, 3:20, 5:12; see also Expertise; guru; innovation
- Interrogation, humans of machines| 1:56, 1:58, 1:62, 1:66, 1:76, 3:18, 7:50; see also machine-mediated human computer interactions

Huxley, Alduous| 7:2
hygiene, electronic| 3:23; see also literacy, information
Hyperlinks| i:13, 2:7, 2:19-2:20, 3:62, 7:1; see also Allinanchor:; Allinurl:; broken links; Denial of Service (DNS); Inurl:; URLs
- embedded links| 1:59, 2:20, 2:36, 2:68, 3:21, 3:23, 3:38, 7:35, 7:46; see also Allinanchor:; Link analysis; Websites, ranking

hypocrisy| 3:89, 4:8, 4:22, 4:35, 4:48, 5:24, 5:75, 7:32; see also betrayal; controversial; Deceptions; fraud; words and deeds
hypotheses| 3:9, 5:16, 5:59; see also rationale; scenarios

I

IBM| 2:29
ice breaker| 1:54, 6:54, c:14; see also Search to Converse (STC); socialize
ID| i:10, 1:13, 1:47, 2:4, 2:6, 2:8, 2:30, 2:32-2:35, 2:101, 3:11, 3:69, 3:80, 4:75, 6:10, 6:25, 7:48, c:3-c:5; see also haystack; Unique IDs
Idealist.org| 3:19; see also Non-profits

Searching Out Loud: Giving Voice to Independent Investigations | Marc Solomon

COMPLETE WORKS: Units One Through Seven | Unabridged Index:19

ideological| 1:38, 4:41, 7:8, 7:31; see also Beliefs; Government, forms of; Power Structures
ideals| 1:15, 1:35, 2:1-2:2, 2:76, 2:85, 3:6, 3:30, 3:85, 4:13, 4:30, 4:56, 4:67, 4:70, 5:2, 5:31, 5:48, 5:73, 6:54, 7:8, 7:10, 7:30, 7:44, 7:48; see also altruism; aspiration; dedicated; kindness; mission; sacred
IMDB ("Internet Movie Database")| 2:91 indeed.com; see also database, specialized; entertainers
immigrant| 3:18, 4:26, 4:79; see also deport; Diplomacy; foreign
immune| 7:10, 7:34; see also Exposure; healthcare; impunity; oblivion
impact| i:8, 1:5, 1:15, 1:17, 1:24, 1:39-1:40, 1:64, 1:70, 2:3, 2:5, 2:65, 3:6, 3:14, 3:48, 3:62, 3:89, 3:98-4:1, 4:4, 4:23, 4:25, 4:29, 4:32, 4:35-4:36, 4:45, 4:55, 4:73, 4:75, 4:88, 4:99, 4:104, 4:108, 5:3, 5:9-5:10, 5:16, 5:18, 5:23-5:24, 5:31-5:32, 5:34, 5:36, 5:46, 5:57, 5:62, 5:71, 6:14, 6:22, 6:45-6:46, 7:23-7:24, 7:33, 7:43, 7:50-7:51; see also Actions and Outcomes; consequence; fallout; repercussions
impersonal| 1:37, 3:73, 3:93, 4:12, 4:17, 4:26, 4:56, 4:60, 4:108, 7:31, 7:39, 7:42; see also Credibility; Observation; superficial
Implicit| 1:1, 1:8, 1:34, 2:14, 2:22, 2:51, 3:12, 3:31, 3:37, 3:58, 3:98, 4:11-4:12, 4:70, 5:26, 5:28, 5:32, 5:50, 5:72, 5:77, 7:6; see also nonverbal; tacit
 - unsolicited| 1:48; see also Interactions; persuasion
inaccuracies| i:16, 1:27, 4:30, 4:91; see also accuracy; Errors; evidence patterns; fact checkers; Pattern Matching
inappropriate| 4:94, 4:104; see also Code, of conduct; Forbidden; misguided; violator
incarceration| 5:43; see also Crime; jail; Law Enforcement; prison
indecision| 4:40, 7:32; see also competing explanations; elusive; honest doubt; uncertain; unsure
Indeed.com| 2:73
Indicators| 1:17, 1:29, 2:29, 3:69, 4:46, 4:59, 5:22, 5:30, 5:80, 6:48, 7:4; see also bellwether; calculable; calibrate; correlation; Forecast; formula
 - bellwether| 3:55, 5:76; see also Forecast
 - course-correcting| 7:26; see also criteria; readjust; refactoring; revisiting
 - eyeballing| 4:17, 5:72, 7:10; see also approximate; educated guesses
 - fuzzy| 1:75, 2:33, 2:99, 3:7, 5:30; see also approximate; confidence level
 - obvious| i:11, 1:36, 1:38, 1:53, 1:58, 2:6, 2:50, 2:61, 2:76, 3:25, 5:70; see also clarifications; explicit; no brainer; resemblance; self-evident; simplicity
 - outliers| 3:61; see also anomalies; evidence patterns
 - outweigh| 3:14, 3:60, 4:36, 4:43, 5:61; see also Evaluation; overpower; quandary
 - readjust| 3:55, 6:36; see also course-correcting; refactoring
 - threshold| 1:65, 1:68-1:69, 3:12, 3:14, 3:67, 5:12, 7:45; see also Laws; machine-based limitations; restrictions; rule-making; technology, limitations
individual-based| 4:1, 4:4, 4:6; see also catharsis; confession; diary; first person; Freedoms, constitutional; libertarian
Influences| i:4, i:7, 1:6, 1:15-1:16, 1:35, 1:44, 1:60, 1:64, 1:70, 2:3, 2:7, 2:36, 2:85, 3:16-3:17, 3:52, 3:60-3:61, 3:63, 3:72, 4:2, 4:9, 4:17-4:18, 4:23, 4:25, 4:29, 4:38-4:39, 4:47, 4:50, 4:56, 4:66, 4:93, 4:100-4:103, 4:108, 5:5, 5:9-5:10, 5:24, 5:28-5:31, 5:36, 5:41, 5:53-5:54, 5:56, 5:61-5:62, 5:66-5:67, 5:72, 5:76, 6:16, 6:57-7:2, 7:5, 7:11, 7:17, 7:20, 7:23, 7:28-7:29, 7:33, 7:39, 7:42, 7:49-7:50, c:14; see also Advocacy; Coercion; persuasion; Power Structures
 - catering| 4:94, 5:25
 - espouse| 4:40, 4:68, 5:52, 7:6; see also Advocacy
 - lobbying| 2:11, 4:16, 4:18, 4:31, 5:55; see also Campaigns; compliance; Government
 - mover| 5:68, 6:21, 6:34; see also Leaders; provocation; shakers
 - pandering| 7:23; see also affinity bias; Campaigns; catering; Rhetoric
 - shakers| 6:21, 6:34; see also opinion-maker
Infomine| 2:87, 2:90, 3:16, 3:28; see also librarian; specialized collections
information architecture| 2:56, 4:63; see also categorizing, field structure; navigation; unstructured information
Information Overload| 1:52, 3:1, 3:25, 3:70, 4:100, 5:73, 7:27, 7:46, 7:50; see also Confusion; distractions; face-to-screen; fog; impersonal
 - fog| 1:9, 1:31, 4:64, 4:88, 5:33; see also Metaphors; search logs
 - inundated| 5:31, 6:34; see also Confusion; Information Overload
 - unfiltered| i:7, 2:5, 2:94, 4:59, 4:99, 5:31, 6:41, 7:16, 7:23; see also antagonisms; blunt; Filtering; Information Overload
Information Providers| i:8, 1:38, 1:41, 1:47, 1:65, 1:67, 2:24, 2:29, 2:44, 2:52, 2:55, 2:66-2:67, 2:80, 2:106, 3:4-3:5, 3:16, 3:25, 3:37, 3:51-3:52, 3:72, 3:87-3:88, 3:90-3:91, 3:94, 4:2, 4:5-4:6, 4:8-4:11, 4:14, 4:23, 4:30, 4:36, 4:44, 4:48-4:52, 4:57, 4:60-4:61, 4:67, 4:87-4:89, 4:98, 5:2, 5:7-5:8, 5:11, 5:18-5:19, 5:25-5:26, 5:28, 5:32, 5:36, 5:43, 5:48, 6:1, 6:4, 6:6, 6:11, 6:14, 6:23, 6:46, 6:51, 7:4, 7:12, 7:22, 7:27, 7:35-7:36, 7:38-7:39, 7:43, c:8, c:10-c:11, c:17; see also aggregate; misinformation providers; Provider Conjugation Framework (PCF); Reputation, information providers
 - confidant| 3:46, 3:93, 4:9, 4:32, 4:54, 4:60, 4:68, 6:53; see also discrete; interpersonal; Provider Conjugation Framework (PCF)
 - external communication| 3:15, 4:13; see also formal communication
 - formal communication| 4:18; see also first party; official; press release; spokesperson
 - informal communication| 4:13, 4:49; see also conversational
 - Informants| 1:18, 3:3, 3:24, 3:46, 3:52, 4:9, 4:11, 4:91, 5:60; see also divulge; newsleaker; second party
 - whistleblower| 4:34, 4:50, 5:31; see also Law Enforcement; public agencies; public investigation; Scandals
 - word of mouth (WOM)| 5:27-5:28, 6:54; see also direct experience; first person; Reputations
information quality| 1:53, 2:40, 2:86, 3:19, 3:51, 3:56, 3:79, 7:26, c:7; see also hygiene, electronic; Quality Controls; Researchers
information science| 3:10, 3:21; see also categorizing, defining boundaries; categorizing, searchable groupings; database, differences; organizing principles
Information Traps| 5:48, 6:36, 6:39, 6:41, 6:51; see also Calishain, Tara; Reis, George (case study); RSS (Really Simple Syndication); Search Engine, Custom (CSE)
 - entrap| 7:29, 7:45
 - event trigger| 5:34, 5:43-5:44, 5:50, 5:56, 6:34-6:39, 6:42, 6:45, 6:47, 6:50-6:52, 6:57, c:16; see also RSS (Really Simple Syndication); time stamp
Information Types| i:9, 2:2, 2:72, 3:1, 3:3-3:4, 3:6-3:7, 3:9, 3:15-3:19, 3:22-3:24, 3:57, 4:2, 4:46, 4:50, 4:78, 6:1, 6:5-6:6, 6:9, 7:50, c:7; see also literacy, information; methods; Quality Controls; template
 - Information Types, entry points| i:9, 1:1, 2:34, 3:7-3:8, 3:13, 3:24, 3:29, 3:57, 4:2, 6:20; see also Continuum, the Knowledge; Search Targets
 - Information Types, formats| 3:7, 3:19, 3:22-3:23; see also template
 - Information Types, points of view| i:9, 1:44, 2:36, 3:7, 3:17-3:18, 4:2, 5:4, 5:33; see also Perspectives, research

Searching Out Loud: Giving Voice to Independent Investigations | Marc Solomon

COMPLETE WORKS: Units One Through Seven | Unabridged Index:20

  - Information Types, resources| 3:7, 3:9, 3:12, 3:14-3:17, 3:19, 3:23; see also Source Fluency
information, publicly accessible| 2:30, 2:37, 2:95, 3:28, 3:83-3:84, 3:92, 4:2, 6:26; see also Code, access; Open Internet Order; public domain; transparency
Infotrac| 3:42; see also database, subscription (premium); Library
infrastructure| 1:69, 3:94, 4:57, 7:10; see also information superhighway; Internet Service Provider (ISP); Trade
infringement| 3:74; see also Brand; cease and desist; Crime; plagiarism; trademark
ingredient| i:10, 1:64, 2:75-2:77, 3:28, 3:46, 3:50, 3:98, 4:105, 5:42, 6:1-6:4, 6:6, 6:16, 6:23, 7:22, 7:38, c:16; see also Culinary; meal type
innovation| 5:64, 6:44, 6:47, 6:56, 7:47; see also devise; discovery; entrepreneur; patent; Unexplored
insecure| i:13, 4:95, 4:98, 4:103, 5:32; see also anxiety; breach; Liabilities
Instagram| 4:63, 4:75, 7:37; see also curatorship; Facebook
integrity| i:1-i:2, 3:95, 4:33, 4:37-4:38, 4:40, 4:58, 5:31, 7:31; see also balcony; Character Traits; Vectors of Integrity (VOI); Wisdom
Intentions| i:1, 1:3, 1:13, 1:21, 1:32, 1:43, 1:46, 2:6, 2:13, 2:16, 2:34, 2:38, 2:48-2:49, 2:52, 2:61, 2:106, 3:5, 3:23-3:25, 3:56, 3:64, 3:71, 3:89, 3:91, 4:11, 4:30, 4:32, 4:36, 4:42, 4:51, 4:71, 4:77, 4:96-4:97, 5:57, 5:77, 6:1, 7:10, 7:15, 7:23, 7:27; see also arrogance
  - aggression| 4:92, 5:61, 7:16
  - bragging| 6:56, 7:9; see also conceit
  - complacency| 1:39, 1:44; see also passive; status quo
  - complaints| 1:65, 5:21, 7:30; see also Blame; customer surveys
  - conspiracies| i:7, 2:45, 3:16, 4:24, 4:26, 5:1, 5:13, 5:36, 6:50, 7:14, 7:30, 7:38; see also accomplices; criminal evidence; public investigation; Self-delusion
  - deliberate| i:2, 1:3, 1:58, 3:4, 4:22, 4:29, 4:40, 4:44, 4:83, 4:87, 4:92, 4:105, 5:1, 5:23, 5:40, 5:75, 6:9, 6:57, 7:7-7:8, 7:16, 7:19, c:13; see also Vectors of Integrity (VOI)
  - discouraging| i:17, 1:5, 1:38, 2:24, 3:26, 3:76, 4:18
  - pressure| i:2, 1:20, 1:33, 1:48, 4:13, 4:19, 4:43, 4:59, 4:95, 5:1, 5:9, 5:36, 5:59, 5:72; see also anxiety; nerve; stress
  - provocation| 1:69, 2:51, 4:74, 5:73; see also Conflict; predetermined; threats
  - ruthless| 4:103; see also demagoguery; Leaders; pandering; Power Structures
  - sinister| 2:62, 3:46, 4:66, 7:22; see also devil; evil; ruthless
  - unintended| 1:39, 1:43, 4:93; see also accidents
  - willful| i:15, 1:10, 1:14, 1:16, 1:18, 1:35-1:36, 1:38-1:39, 2:62, 2:71, 3:5-3:6, 4:31, 4:41-4:42, 5:58, 5:65, 5:75, 6:8, 6:52, 7:12, 7:28; see also deliberate
Interactions| i:15, 1:44, 1:49-1:51, 1:56, 1:65, 2:3, 2:48, 3:34, 4:12, 4:16, 4:70-4:71, 4:74, 5:10-5:11, 5:50, 5:72, 7:12, 7:17-7:18, 7:26, 7:32, 7:43, 7:48, 7:50, c:13; see also Agreement; interview; Negotiations
  - backchannel| 2:53, 3:89, 4:34, 6:11; see also Negotiations; Radar; secrets, keeping; unofficial
  - backscratches| 4:66, 5:27; see also admirers; charisma; Negotiations
  - camaraderie| 5:71; see also bond; embrace; interpersonal; Relatedness
  - conversational| 1:21, 1:52, 1:54, 1:59, 1:65, 1:71, 2:88, 3:76, 4:56, 4:69, 4:74, 5:39, 6:32, 7:17, c:9, c:16
  - dialog| 1:50, 3:76, 4:8, 4:32, 4:42, 5:5, 5:45, 5:47, 6:12, 6:46, 6:52, 7:39, c:5; see also conversational; Negotiations
  - encounter| 1:11, 1:46, 1:74, 2:3, 2:56, 3:32, 3:54, 4:31, 4:48, 5:8, 5:62, 5:64, 7:18
  - exchange| i:9, 1:15, 1:35, 1:38, 1:51, 2:1, 2:7, 2:27, 2:47, 4:1, 4:8-4:13, 4:15-4:17, 4:32, 4:36, 4:43, 4:45, 4:48-4:49, 4:60, 4:66-4:68, 4:72, 4:74, 4:86, 4:101, 5:39, 6:8, 6:13, 7:18, 7:41, c:3; see also cooperation; Negotiations; quid pro quo
  - face-to-face| 4:13, 5:40; see also direct experience; Humans; interpersonal
  - face-to-screen| 7:26; see also Devices; impersonal
  - intermediaries| 2:63, 4:1, 4:8-4:10, 4:14, 4:93, 6:56; see also second party; second person
  - interpersonal| 4:17, 4:89; see also conversational; face-to-face; Humans
  - interplay| i:7, 2:3, 5:71; see also dynamic information; multi-dimensional
  - mutual| 1:19, 4:15, 4:19, 4:61, 4:68-4:69, 4:94, 4:98, 5:5, 5:40, 5:46, 5:52, 5:64, 6:42, 7:28, 7:43; see also Dichotomies; Relatedness
  - telepathic| 5:71; see also Expression; interplay; subconscious
Internal| i:14, 1:41, 1:75, 2:31, 2:48, 3:13-3:15, 3:78, 3:83, 4:12, 4:18, 4:35-4:36, 4:43, 4:70, 4:73, 5:2-5:3, 5:9-5:10, 5:16, 5:20, 5:24-5:25, 5:36-5:37, 5:42, 7:6, 7:16, 7:23; see also first party; Perspectives, outsider versus insider
  - external and internal| 3:14-3:16, 4:13, 5:11, 5:21; see also Information Types; Perspectives, outsider versus insider
  - insider| i:16, 1:2, 1:14, 1:22, 1:28, 1:33, 1:43, 1:49, 2:30, 2:52, 2:76, 2:93, 3:13, 3:15, 3:20, 3:23, 3:31, 3:98, 4:4, 4:17, 4:31, 4:36, 5:2, 5:10, 5:35, 5:47, 6:11, 6:41, 6:51, 7:6-7:7, 7:14, 7:21; see also Bias; blindspots; privy
  - internal communication| 3:15, 3:79, 4:13, 5:37; see also informal communication
Internet| 3:24-3:26, 4:79, 4:87, 5:46, 6:8-6:9, 7:14, 7:49, c:16; see also interconnected; World Wide Web
  - intranet| 3:60, 3:81; see also SharePoint; Websites, company
  - Net Neutrality| 7:41, 7:43-7:44; see also Internet Service Provider (ISP); Public Policies; Regulations
  - online| i:4, i:8-i:9, 1:6, 1:45, 1:70, 2:54, 2:67, 3:73-3:74, 3:86, 4:102, 5:52, 6:50, 7:2, 7:4, 7:26, 7:41, 7:48, c:1, c:10-c:11, c:16
  - Open Internet Order| 7:43; see also Net Neutrality; Regulations
Internet Explorer| 3:72, 4:82; see also Browser
Internet Public Library (IPL)| 2:85, 2:87, 2:90; see also Library; specialized collections
Internet Security| i:15, 2:48, 7:48; see also breach; encryption; firewall; Hacks; insecure; password
  - adware| 2:68; see also cookie; invasive; malware
  - backdoor| 2:71, 5:31, 7:44; see also insecure; intrusion; loopholes; Risks
  - bot| 1:61, 3:31, 7:45; see also machine indexing
  - malicious site| 2:68; see also malware; ransomware; Websites, dubious
  - malware| 2:68; see also Code, tracking; cookie; ransomware
Internet Service Provider (ISP)| 7:43; see also Net Neutrality
Interpretations| i:1, 1:52, 1:59, 1:62, 1:64, 2:9, 2:37, 2:47-2:48, 2:65, 2:107-3:1, 3:3, 3:5, 3:7, 3:24, 3:35, 3:58, 3:96, 4:4, 4:13, 4:15, 4:19, 4:58, 5:4-5:5, 5:25-5:27, 5:74, 6:1, 6:9, 7:27, 7:42, c:6-c:7, c:12; see also Narratives; parse; philosophy; prism; Speculation
  - beholder| 1:38, 3:1, 4:5, 4:86, c:11; see also direct experience; first person; Perspectives; Rorschach

Searching Out Loud: Giving Voice to Independent Investigations | Marc Solomon

COMPLETE WORKS: Units One Through Seven | Unabridged Index:21

- honest doubt| 3:7, 4:36, 5:25, 5:68; see also BS Detection; dispassionate; fact checkers; Skepticism
- literal| i:8, 1:33, 2:11, 2:31, 2:36, 2:49-2:50, 2:52-2:53, 2:76, 3:16, 3:56, 3:58, 4:48, 4:81, 5:54, 5:58, 6:4, 7:17; see also concrete; Interpretations; tangible
- mimic| 1:54, 2:68, 4:52; see also Expression; ridicule
- momentum| 1:6, 3:10, 5:3, 5:35; see also Decline; Narratives; pulse; sway; trends
- myth| 2:69, 3:62, 3:88, 4:66, 5:72, 7:5-7:6; see also Beliefs; faith; fallacy; urban legends
- tangible| i:6, 1:39, 1:70, 2:48, 2:54, 3:18, 3:58, 4:36, 4:49, 4:73, 4:79, 4:99, 5:34; see also concrete; literal; proof; substance

interview| i:9, 1:13, 1:18, 1:24, 1:54, 1:59, 2:1, 2:47, 2:60, 2:99, 3:13, 3:78, 3:86, 4:8, 4:16, 4:29-4:30, 4:32, 4:57-4:58, 4:69-4:71, 4:104, 4:107, 5:1, 5:23, 5:39, 5:45-5:46, 5:56, 5:58, 5:69, 6:12, 6:45, 6:56, 7:29, c:4, c:10; see also debrief; evidence gathering; focus groups; Interactions; primary intelligence; Search to Converse (STC)

Intuitions| i:7, i:17, 1:30, 1:33-1:35, 3:14, 4:30, 5:60, 5:64, 5:66, 5:68, 7:6, 7:8, 7:47; see also Behaviors; Cognitive; Intentions; reflexive
- anguish| i:11, 7:24; see also dilemma; nightmares; predicament; suffer; unresolved
- anxiety| 4:86, 4:95, 5:7, 5:32, 7:38; see also insecure; Wurman, Richard Saul
- gut| 1:33, 1:48, 4:14, 4:43, 4:48, 4:108, 5:3, 5:46, 6:23, 6:39, 7:40; see also decisive
- gut check| 5:1, 5:4, 7:40; see also clients, validation; Intuitions
- impulse| 1:35, 2:64, 2:95, 4:6, 4:35, 4:41, 4:67, 4:90, 4:108, 5:24, 5:34, 5:57, 5:73, 7:7, 7:16, 7:30, 7:34, 7:39, 7:44; see also Cognitive
- nerve| 1:73, 3:58, 4:42, 5:4, 5:12, 5:19, 5:60, c:12; see also aggression; blunt; Cognitive; disputes; Motives; provocation
- serendipitous| 2:43-2:44, 2:47, 2:61, 3:5, 4:72, 4:81, 5:19, c:13; see also Explorations; random
- visceral| 7:5; see also gut check; reflexive

inventory| 1:21, 1:60, 1:62, 1:69, 1:71, 2:33, 2:65, 3:1, 3:4, 3:8, 3:23-3:24, 3:54, 4:53, 5:68, 6:1, 7:18, c:6; see also aggregate; Content Grouping; Search Engine, Custom (CSE); Source Fluency

Investigations| i:1-i:2, i:14, 1:4, 1:17, 1:20, 1:54, 2:107, 3:62, 3:64, 3:87, 4:5, 4:17-4:18, 4:29-4:30, 4:36, 4:94, 5:26, 5:30, 5:41, 5:69, 5:71, 6:12, 6:35, 6:39, 6:57-7:1, 7:4-7:5, 7:8, 7:11, 7:15, 7:20, 7:22, 7:26-7:27, 7:31, 7:34, 7:38, 7:42, 7:44, 7:46, 7:50-7:51, c:2, c:11, c:13; see also criminal investigation; evidence patterns; indictment; prosecute
- clue| 1:35, 2:40, 2:47, 2:51, 2:53, 3:7, 3:13, 3:23, 3:52, 4:108, 5:14, 5:58, 6:4, 6:46; see also criminal investigation; Indicators; mystery
- hint| 1:14, 5:73; see also clue; evidence patterns
- person of interest| 1:49, 2:64, 4:9, 4:34, 4:39, 4:41-4:42, 5:69, 6:4; see also criminal investigation; finding people; Search Targets
- practical obscurity| 7:42; see also Code, tracking; Journalism; Memory; personal data; public investigation; Surveillance Capitalism
- unsolved| 5:57, 7:38; see also evidence patterns

invisible web| 1:69, 1:71, 2:2, 3:74-3:75, 3:82, 3:85, 4:78, c:7; see also deep web
IP address| 3:47; see also Code, tracking; cookie; Net Neutrality; personal data; Whois
irrefutable| 2:56, 7:8, 7:22, 7:27-7:28; see also Fact-based; scientific method; self-evident
isolated| 1:14, 1:41, 1:70, 2:34, 2:60, 4:13, 4:49, 5:29, 6:20, 7:30; see also estrangement; evidence patterns; sequester; siloed

J

Jargon| i:16, 1:22, 2:18, 2:33, 2:98, 6:3, 6:16; see also Language; pointers
- slang| 2:18, 2:84; see also colloquialism; shoptalk; shorthand

jeopardy| 4:69, 4:91, 5:69; see also Liabilities; Risks

Jobs| i:2, i:7, i:9, 1:3, 1:5, 1:18-1:19, 1:21, 1:28, 1:35, 1:43, 1:50, 1:59, 1:70, 2:1-2:2, 2:17, 2:29-2:33, 2:53, 2:73, 2:85, 2:99, 3:3, 3:46, 3:69, 3:81, 3:90, 4:31, 4:58, 4:62, 4:70, 4:74, 4:77, 5:27, 5:42-5:45, 5:53-5:54, 5:56, 5:62, 6:1-6:2, 6:5, 6:8, 6:12, 6:20, 6:45, 7:29, c:3-c:4; see also Careers; Professionals
- applicant| 1:51, 5:44; see also candidates
- boss| 4:47, 4:60, 5:2, 5:24, 5:43, 5:58, 6:7; see also authoritative; executive; upper management
- hire| i:14, i:16-i:17, 1:6, 1:11, 1:14, 1:16, 1:31, 1:73, 2:1, 2:3, 2:17, 2:48, 3:19, 3:88, 4:19, 4:61, 4:68, 4:77, 4:90, 4:95-4:96, 4:103-4:104, 5:39, 5:44-5:45, 5:75-5:76, 6:23; see also clients, hiring a researcher; Employment; nondisclosure
- job description| 2:17, 2:73; see also Expertise; skills; task
- job interview| 1:59, 2:99, 5:57, 7:29; see also background checks; interview
- job offers| 1:50, 3:91; see also salary
- job openings| 1:3, 2:53, 3:82, 4:75, 5:45-5:46, 5:54; see also qualifications
- job security| 5:28, 5:44, 6:8; see also complacency; retool; skills; Social Networks
- job sites| 2:73, 5:46; see also Indeed.com
- job title| 2:30-2:33, 3:47, 3:70, 4:63, 5:44-5:45, 6:12, 6:29; see also Syntax
- jobseeker| 1:3, 4:63, 4:65; see also headhunters
- layoff| 4:25; see also containing costs; cutbacks; unemployment
- resume| 1:50, 1:74, 4:61-4:62, 4:65, 5:47, 5:75, 6:5; see also Careers; headhunters; personal branding; personal narratives
- unemployment| 1:19; see also jobseeker; layoff; recession

Jobs, Steve| 5:64
Johari Window| 1:38-1:39, 3:6, 6:13; see also blindspots; Frameworks; personal radar; Perspectives
Johnson, Samuel| 1:31, 4:77
Journalism| 4:36, 4:67, 5:25, 5:78-5:79, 7:8, 7:14; see also disseminate; editor; free press; news organizations; Newspapers; Opinion-editorial (op-ed); pre-social media
- press| i:15, 1:16, 1:37, 1:64, 2:9, 2:47, 2:79, 3:62, 4:2, 4:13, 4:32, 5:8-5:10, 5:16, 5:22, 5:28, 5:31, 5:37-5:38, 5:42, 5:46, 5:55, 6:20, 6:56, 7:7, 7:10, 7:12-7:13, 7:15; see also free press; Freedoms, constitutional; Newspapers
- scoop| 2:65, 4:91, 4:97, 7:9; see also deadline; event trigger; Radar; RSS (Really Simple Syndication)

Judgment| 1:17, 1:36-1:37, 1:44, 1:47, 1:58, 1:75, 3:34, 3:37, 3:48, 3:62, 3:73, 4:16, 4:22, 4:29-4:30, 4:34, 4:38, 4:43, 4:58, 4:75, 4:86-4:87, 4:91, 4:95, 4:99, 4:103-4:104, 5:12, 5:15, 5:57, 5:61, 5:66, 5:76, 7:11, 7:16-7:17, 7:20, 7:26, 7:38, 7:40, 7:42, c:14; see also Accusations; Character Traits; Intentions; leniency; Motives; righteous
- absolve| 1:35, 5:60; see also Crime; exonerate; innocence

Searching Out Loud: Giving Voice to Independent Investigations | Marc Solomon

- altruism| 1:19, 5:30; see also aspiration; ideals; Motives
- evil| 4:67, 4:90, 7:44; see also devil; moral; sins
- guilt| 1:39, 2:38, 4:30, 4:58, 4:92, 4:103, 5:4, 7:12, 7:16, 7:38, 7:41; see also Blame; catharsis; moral; presumption; trial
- hate| 2:67, 5:42, 5:80, 7:30, 7:35; see also Prejudice; unforgiving
- innocence| 4:30, 7:12, 7:46; see also Freedoms, constitutional; presumption; uninhibited
- moral| i:17, 4:25, 5:28; see also altruism; humility; Motives; righteous; sanity
- punishment| 4:103, 5:43, 5:76, 7:16; see also crackdowns; Laws; leniency; public service; sentencing
- sins| 1:29; see also confession; ego; moral; Weakness
- steal| 1:7, 4:42, 4:88, 4:103, 5:37, 5:73, c:2; see also Crime; time, spending
- truthfulness| 1:36; see also Empirical; Interpretations; scientific method; sincerity
jury| i:2, 2:38, 4:9, 4:17, 4:25, 7:1, 7:46; see also Judgment; legal proceeding; verdict

K

Kahneman, Daniel| 5:62
Kartoo| 2:53-2:54; see also Discontinued Websites and Tools; interconnected
Kavanaugh, Brett| i:2
Kayak.com| 2:73-2:74; see also aggregate; Portals
Keyword in Context (KWIC)| 1:66-1:67, 2:41; see also Contextual; keyword matches; proximity; query formation; Relevance
keyword matches| 1:67, 2:11-2:12, 2:16, 2:49, 2:52, 2:104, 3:14, 3:22-3:23, 4:102, 6:10, 6:26, 6:49; see also SEO (Search Engine Optimization)
kindness| 4:66, 5:43; see also deference; favor; humility; reciprocal; Wisdom
Knowledge-ABLED| i:1, 1:1, 1:6-1:8, 1:10, 1:43, 1:45, 1:47-1:49, 1:52-1:53, 1:59, 1:72, 1:74, 2:12, 2:43, 2:53, 2:71, 2:88, 2:95, 2:106-2:107, 3:2, 3:5-3:6, 3:50, 3:52, 4:9, 4:32, 4:57, 4:81, 4:88, 4:105, 5:1, 5:4-5:5, 5:13, 5:24, 5:31, 5:40, 5:44, 5:46, 5:57, 5:60, 5:63-5:64, 5:68, 5:71-5:72, 5:76, 5:79, 6:1-6:45, 6:47-7:1, 7:3-7:8, 7:15-7:16, 7:18-7:20, 7:22-7:27, 7:29, 7:31-7:32, 7:34-7:37, 7:42-7:46, 7:49-7:51, c:1-c:2, c:15, c:17; see also Continuum, the Knowledge; Investigations; literacy, information; Research Projects
  - Knowledge-ABLED practices| 1:74, 3:4, 3:63, 7:3, 7:36, 7:49; see also literacy, information
  - Knowledge-ABLED, advantages| i:16, 1:4, 1:62, 1:70, 2:30, 2:37, 2:45-2:46, 2:88, 2:95, 2:104, 3:58, 3:78, 3:91, 4:1, 4:25, 4:68, 5:3, 5:38, 5:45, 5:63, 5:68, 5:72, 6:16, 6:45-6:46, 6:56, 7:6, 7:21, 7:44, 7:46; see also Frameworks
  - Knowledge-ENABLED| 1:45, 5:69, 5:79; see also hygiene, electronic
Kohls| 2:31
Kurzweil, Ray| 5:64

L

lakes| 2:18, 2:44, 2:54, 2:72, 2:85, 2:87-2:88, 2:90-2:91, 2:95, 2:100-2:101, 2:107, 3:2, 3:13, 3:27, 3:31-3:32, 3:34-3:35, 3:48, 3:63, 3:66-3:67, 3:78, 3:82, 5:52, 6:10-6:11, 6:20, 6:23-6:24, 6:34-6:36, 6:49-6:52, 7:26, 7:50, c:6, c:16; see also Oceans, Lakes, and Ponds (OLP); Subject Directory
landing page| 3:8, 3:11; see also entry points; marquee; navigation; Websites
Language| i:8, 1:22, 1:35, 1:63, 2:11, 2:19-2:20, 2:26, 2:42-2:43, 2:47-2:49, 2:62, 3:38, 4:7, 4:11, 4:80, 5:34, 5:46, 5:71, 6:4, 6:9-6:10, 6:48, 7:47, c:5; see also Code, software; markup language; translation
  - dialect| 1:35, 3:27, 6:4, 6:9; see also American Dialect Society; colloquialism; Expression; nomenclature
  - markup language| 3:38; see also Code, software
  - nomenclature| 2:86; see also Jargon; shorthand; vernacular
Law Enforcement| 1:27, 1:58, 1:73, 2:98, 4:10, 4:44, 4:48, 4:71, 4:73, 5:18, 5:53, 5:77, 7:47; see also Criminal; guilt; police; prosecute
  - arrest| 7:56
  - cop| 1:48
  - indictment| 1:42, 4:29, 4:55; see also allegations
  - jail| 5:76, 7:49; see also incarceration
  - parole| 5:61; see also incarceration; Law Enforcement; offender; plead; punishment; sentencing; violator
  - police| 1:26, 1:47, 1:51, 1:55-1:56, 1:58, 1:72, 2:55-2:56, 4:66, 5:43, 7:49; see also cop; Law Enforcement
  - precinct| 1:27, 1:47; see also neighborhoods
  - prison| 4:84, 5:44; see also jail; parole; penal
Laws| i:7, i:15, 1:37, 3:81, 3:85, 4:14, 4:48, 4:61, 4:98, 5:30, 5:46-5:47, 5:65-5:66, 6:55, 7:31, 7:50; see also Legal; Regulations; restrictions
  - lawsuit| 2:65, 3:91, 4:95, 5:14, 5:20, 5:22; see also judges, courtroom; lawyer; legal proceeding; trial
  - penal| i:14, 5:58; see also incarceration
lawyer| 1:14, 2:32, 2:90, 2:94, 3:26, 4:11, 4:66, 5:70, 6:53; see also confer; counsel; Crime; Legal; pro bono; Professionals; prosecute
layout| 1:63, 2:54, 2:97; see also User Experience (UX)
Leaders| i:7, 1:11, 1:34, 1:37, 1:49, 2:31, 2:64, 3:46, 3:49, 3:77, 4:19, 4:22, 4:29, 4:35, 4:38, 4:40-4:42, 4:48, 4:57, 4:103, 4:106-4:107, 5:8-5:9, 5:11-5:12, 5:24, 5:29, 5:38, 5:46, 6:47, 6:56-6:57, 7:17; see also business leader; executive
  - business leader| 5:12; see also Companies; executive; Management, functions; upper management
  - CEO| 2:35, 2:63, 3:19, 3:94, 5:28, 7:55; see also business leader; Organizations
  - CFO| 3:95
  - decisionmakers| 4:41, 4:43, 5:28, 5:76; see also executive; figureheads; public officials; upper management
  - executive| 3:77; see also upper management
  - figureheads| 3:37, 5:75; see also public officials
Learning| i:12; see also experience-based learning; unlearn
  - experience-based learning| 7:47; see also Authenticity; communities of practice; immediacy
  - instruct| i:7, 1:73, 2:14, 2:37, 3:2, 3:13, 7:51; see also Procedures
  - syllabus| 2:87; see also Continuum, the Knowledge; curriculum; literacy, information
  - trained| 1:24, 1:41, 2:101, 3:20, 4:12, 4:90, 6:13, 6:46-6:49, 6:55; see also education; skills; syllabus
  - tutorial| 5:48, 6:5; see also curriculum; education; syllabus

COMPLETE WORKS: Units One Through Seven | Unabridged Index:23

  - unlearn| 7:33; see also Intuitions
Legal| 2:58, 2:89, 3:73, 3:81, 3:91, 4:47, 5:17, 7:41; see also Code, legal; Crime; impunity; indictment; Laws; permissible; sentencing; statute
  - cease and desist| 7:48; see also proprietary; secret sauce; Stop
  - counsel| 3:93, 4:12, 4:57, 4:70, 5:12, 5:28, 5:60, 6:8, 7:42; see also advisor; clients, legal consulting
  - court| 3:38, 3:73-3:74, 4:46, 7:42; see also judges, courtroom; trial
  - exonerate| 1:15; see also absolve; innocence; proof
  - illegal| 3:38, 4:27, 7:2, 7:51; see also arrest; wrongdoing
  - impunity| 4:31, 4:94, 4:105, 5:62; see also immune; license
  - judges, courtroom| 3:91, 5:18, 5:62; see also judiciary; Regulations
  - legal proceeding| 2:60, 3:70, 3:74, 5:47; see also indictment; lawsuit
  - plead| 1:36, 5:76; see also bargain; sentencing; Weakness
  - precedence| 1:53, 3:24, 3:88, 4:23, 5:13, 5:66, 5:71; see also establishment; organizing principles; Procedures
  - sentencing| 4:33; see also Crime; guidelines; indictment; judges, courtroom; verdict
  - statute| 6:5; see also Laws; Regulations; restrictions
  - trial| i:6, 1:9, 1:21, 1:24, 1:36, 1:72, 2:38, 2:61, 2:90, 3:38, 4:57, 4:81, 5:41, 5:47, 5:57, 5:76, 7:17, 7:25; see also criminal investigation; guilt; lawsuit
  - verdict| 2:38, 2:62, 4:19, 4:100, 5:9, 7:28, 7:38, 7:46; see also consensus; Elections; jury; opinion surveys; Public Opinion; sentencing; trial; unfavorable
leniency| 4:32, 5:61; see also discrete; Legal; rule-making; sentencing
leverage| 1:1, 1:61, 2:4, 2:30, 2:53, 2:66, 2:103, 3:2, 3:70, 4:15, 4:29, 4:35, 4:82-4:84, 4:88, 5:41, 6:11, 7:34, 7:43, c:3, c:5-c:6; see also Knowledge-ABLED, advantages; Negotiations; reusable; Useful; useful outcomes
LexisNexis| 2:30, 2:37, 2:87; see also database, subscription (premium)
Liabilities| 1:29, 4:37, 7:12, 7:16; see also Assets; Exposure; precarious; Risks
  - beholden| 1:54, 4:17, 4:41, 5:28-5:29, 5:44; see also compromise; debt; favor; Liabilities
  - damages| 1:1, 1:14, 3:18, 4:26, 4:67, 4:90, 5:16; see also Legal; Risks
  - debt| 3:20, 3:77; see also credit bureau; dependent; personal assets; poverty; Weakness
  - liens| 3:76; see also debt
  - personal injury| 2:94; see also Accusations; afflicted; lawsuit; Legal; Liabilities; suffer
  - precarious| 4:41, 5:43; see also dependent; elusive
  - trouble| 1:36, 2:12, 3:37, 4:57, 4:59; see also Conflict; dangerous; red flag; stress; threats
libel| 4:68, 5:9, 7:10, 7:13-7:14; see also slander; smear
liberal| 7:7-7:8; see also Politics
libertarian| 4:69; see also individual-based; Politics; unregulated
librarian| 2:48, 2:62, 2:72, 2:88, 2:90, 2:93, 2:95, 3:1, 3:22, 3:86, 5:2, c:6; see also Researchers
Library| i:10, 1:54, 2:18, 2:28, 2:98, 3:41; see also archives; Corporate librarians; specialized collections
  - lib,syntax| 2:18; see also Syntax
license| 1:65, 1:73, 2:33, 3:22, 4:46, 4:53, 5:7, 5:41, 5:52, 5:75, 6:21, 6:25-6:26, 7:9, 7:37; see also impunity; Procedures; Regulations
life-changing| 7:19; see also biography; Milestones; personal branding; Personal Identity; personal narratives; story lines
Link analysis| 2:29, 3:15, 3:63-3:64, c:8; see also Analysis; PageRank; Relatedness; strength of association; URLs
  - broken links| 3:50; see also 404 error; decommissioned; Denial of Service (DNS); URLs
Linkedin| 3:11, 3:47, 4:33, 4:63-4:67, 4:75-4:76, 6:12, 6:25, 7:2; see also Affiliated; job sites; personal branding; Social Networks
listserv| 2:84, 2:87, 3:16, 4:14; see also discussion boards; newsgroup; online forums; pre-social media
literacy, information| 3:62, 4:107, 7:26-7:27, 7:34, 7:51; see also curatorship; hygiene, electronic; Knowledge-ABLED practices
localities| 1:58, 2:55-2:56, 2:66, 3:54, 5:34, 5:54, 5:56; see also Crime Scene; GPS (Global Positioning Satellite); maps
Location| 1:58, 2:27, 2:29, 2:55, 2:66, 3:2, 3:10, 4:37, 4:72, 5:33, 5:55, 6:4, 7:13, 7:42, c:6; see also Crime Scene; maps; neighborhoods
  - landmarks| 1:27, 2:56, 7:1; see also Crime Scene; GPS (Global Positioning Satellite)
  - periphery| 3:77, 4:54, 4:60, 5:3; see also Crime Scene; proximity; tangents
  - province| 3:33, 3:87, 5:3; see also localities; territory
  - region| 1:27, 1:43, 2:27, 2:32, 2:42, 2:55, 5:8, 5:53, 5:55; see also cultural; dialect; province; tribal
  - remote| 1:23, 1:44, 1:70, 2:85, 4:39, 4:51, 5:62, 6:23, 6:54; see also Probabilities; workplace
  - venue| 4:13, 5:18; see also agenda; Trade, shows
  - vicinity| 1:26; see also GPS (Global Positioning Satellite); maps; proximity
Logic| 1:55, 2:41, 5:60; see also Boolean logic; Pattern Matching; rationale
  - binary| 2:7, 2:50, 3:13, 4:40, 7:35; see also Dichotomies; yes or no
  - calculable| i:17, 1:64, 5:17, 5:28, 7:44; see also rationale
  - circular| 1:23, 4:18, 7:23, 7:40; see also evidence patterns; redundant; revisiting
  - extrapolate| 1:58, 4:36-4:37, 5:4; see also analogies; Authenticity; equivalence; Provider Conjugation Framework (PCF)
  - formula| i:13, 1:26, 1:41, 2:7, 2:29, 2:31-2:32, 2:35, 2:42, 2:45, 2:51, 2:57, 2:65, 2:72, 2:107, 3:27, 3:64, 4:29, 5:2, 5:8, 5:28, 5:40, 5:46, 5:50, 5:58, 5:77, 6:2, 7:16, 7:27, 7:35, 7:44-7:48, c:8; see also methods
  - smiley face logic| 7:37; see also affinity bias; emojis; reciprocal; superficial
login| 2:21-2:22, 2:66, 3:81, 3:85, 4:79; see also Code, access; firewall; password
loopholes| 3:73; see also backdoor; discrepancy; gap; invasive; Legal
loyalties| 1:48, 4:1, 4:4, 4:9, 4:29, 4:36, 4:42, 4:67, 4:90, 4:103-4:104, 5:1, 5:5, 6:53-6:54, 7:27, 7:29, 7:49; see also Authenticity; Beliefs; Group Behavior; Trust; Vectors of Integrity (VOI)

M

Machine-enabled| 2:90-2:91, 2:93, 3:29, 7:27; see also artificial intelligence; Interrogation, humans of machines; technology, intimidation factors; technopoly

Searching Out Loud: Giving Voice to Independent Investigations | Marc Solomon

COMPLETE WORKS: Units One Through Seven | Unabridged Index:24

- machine-based limitations| 2:38, 2:51, 7:27; see also Perspectives, research; technology, limitations; threshold
- machine-generated directories| 2:44, 2:88, 2:90-2:91, 2:93, 2:98, 3:29; see also machine indexing
- machine-generated interpretations| 1:8, 1:75, 2:100, 3:13, 3:20-3:21, 3:36, 7:5, 7:27; see also disambiguation; human, filtered; Interpretations
- machine-mediated human computer interactions| 1:10, 1:51, 3:20-3:21, 5:40, 6:45, 7:51; see also Humans; technophobes
- machine-triggered human alienation| i:5, 7:46, 7:48, 7:51; see also technology, intimidation factors

Macys| 2:31, 3:51, 3:63, 3:89, 4:9, 4:18, 4:25, 4:32, 4:96, 5:16, 5:26, 5:39, 6:10, 7:15
Madoff, Bernard| 1:33, 2:10; see also ponzi scheme
Major Business Media|, 3:95, 5:55; see also business community; trade media
- businessweek.com| 5:55
- economist.com| 5:55
- fastcompany.com| 5:55
- Forbes| 5:55, 7:53
- ft.com| 5:55
- inc.com| 5:55

Management, functions| 5:11, 5:17, 5:37; see also administrators; horizontal business functions; roles and responsibilities
- horizontal business functions| 5:9-5:10
- payroll| 4:49, 5:26, 7:9; see also Budget; expenses; labor
- treasurer| 6:29; see also Trade, financial; upper management
- workplace| 5:76; see also Code, of conduct; Group Behavior; horizontal business functions; Management, functions

maps| 1:8-1:9, 1:26-1:28, 1:30, 1:34, 1:43, 2:5, 2:8, 2:25, 2:31, 2:34, 2:52-2:56, 2:65, 2:75, 2:86, 2:88, 2:106, 3:5, 3:7-3:8, 3:32, 3:34, 3:46, 3:66, 3:81, 3:83, 3:91, 4:9, 4:13, 4:35, 4:37, 4:43, 4:46-4:47, 4:49, 4:51, 4:59, 4:70, 4:72-4:73, 5:1, 5:18, 5:20, 5:24, 5:52, 6:8, 6:11, 6:14, 7:23, 7:40-7:41, c:2, c:14-c:16; see also Crime Scene; GPS (Global Positioning Satellite); Location; Weather Conditions

Market Demand| 1:42, 2:65, 5:42, 6:19, 6:34; see also advertising; Demand-based media; formula; niche; supply and demand; unmet
- industry sector| 6:8, 6:33, 6:55; see also business community; Commerce; market segments
- market segments| 4:33, 5:10, 5:13, 5:33, 5:38, 5:41, 6:19, 6:22-6:23, 7:30; see also industry sector; micro-targeting; niche
- niche| 3:63, 5:32-5:33, 5:45, 5:50, 6:7-6:9, 6:14, 6:18-6:19, 6:21, 6:25, 6:28, 6:36, 6:45, 6:47, 6:50-6:51, c:15; see also Demographics; Market Demand; market research; micro-targeting
- unmet| 4:103, 5:34, 6:41, 6:49; see also demand-based, methodology; niche; Scarcity

market research| 5:29, 6:10, 6:21, 6:23, 6:47, 6:51; see also customer surveys; Demographics; Forecast
mastermind| 4:7, 4:52; see also genius; guru
mayhem| 3:58, 4:57; see also Chaotic Context; crisis; Disasters; hysteria
McDonald's| 4:90, 5:22-5:23
McLuhan, Marshall| 7:26; see also hot media
Measurements| 1:1, 1:44-1:45, 2:36, 2:65, 2:85, 2:88, 2:107, 3:5, 3:17, 3:37, 3:69, 3:80, 3:97, 4:29, 4:35, 4:39, 4:43, 4:70, 4:86, 4:108, 5:3, 5:8-5:10, 5:16, 5:18, 5:26, 5:28-5:29, 5:31, 5:34-5:36, 5:48, 5:58-5:59, 5:65, 6:37, 7:28, 7:33; see also calculable; Guesswork; Indicators; Metrics; The Biggest Picture, metrics
- equivalence| 1:11, 1:14, 2:12, 2:107, 4:38, 4:43, 4:56, 4:75, 5:31, 5:33, 6:39, 7:12, 7:43, 7:45

media bias| 4:59, 4:67; see also Bias; public perceptions
media performance| 5:23; see also The Biggest Picture (TBP)
media, traditional| 4:58-4:60, 6:37, 7:4-7:5, 7:9, 7:13; see also pre-social media
medical malpractice| 2:13, 2:16, 2:49, 2:90, 2:93, 3:32, 4:83-4:84; see also Case studies
Medline| 6:24; see also PubMed; specialized collections
Memory| i:11, 1:33, 1:58, 3:19, 3:41, 3:84, 3:88, 4:80, 4:86, 4:104, 7:4; see also Cognitive; family history; recall; resonate
- Alzheimers| 1:26; see also amnesia; Cognitive; impaired
- amnesia| 1:31; see also Alzheimers; blindspots
- memorability| 1:44, 5:61
- memorable| 2:59; see also Milestones; significance
- nostalgia| 7:4, 7:10; see also Distortions; outdated; posterity; Self-delusion
- paraphrase| 1:46, 4:75, 4:97, 5:63; see also anecdotal; Expression; generalization; Interpretations; quote
- retain| i:11, 1:31, 1:38, 4:33, 4:96, 5:11-5:12, 5:71, 6:21, 7:21, 7:24, 7:27, 7:48; see also advisor; clients, hiring a researcher; Consulting; contracts
- rote| i:11, 1:33, 1:68; see also keyword matches; recall; verbatims

mercy| i:8, 1:30, 1:68; see also Beliefs; divinity; embrace; Judgment; kindness; leniency; sacred; Trust
Message Value| 5:9-5:10; see also attention surplus; calculable; deficit and surpluses; derive; measurable; Metrics
- message supply| 5:10; see also attention demand; supply and demand; Supply Media
- messagers| 4:29; see also Information Providers; recipients, message; sender; shoot the messenger
- micromessaging| 4:92; see also Twitter; visceral

messengers| 1:53, 2:15, 4:7, 4:22, 4:25, 4:29, 4:39, 4:90, 4:94, 5:4, 5:10, 5:61, 5:76, 6:4, 6:45, 7:10, 7:12, 7:30, c:12; see also Information Providers; Message Value; Provider Conjugation Framework (PCF); recipients, message; second party; second person; shoot the messenger
metadata| 1:61, 1:63-1:64, 1:73, 2:26, 2:36, 2:39, 2:41-2:43, 2:56, 2:59, 2:70, 2:86, 2:92, 3:22, 3:83; see also categorizing, metadata; metasearch results; query formation; Search Engine, Metasearch; Syntax; tagging engine
MetaGer| 5:77; see also Search Engine, Privacy
Metaphors| i:17, 2:2, 2:54, 2:75, 2:86, 3:10, 3:15, 3:27, 3:29, 4:37, 4:62, 5:11, 5:65, 6:1-6:3, 6:16, 7:6, c:16; see also analogies; black swan; personified
- Fishing in a pond| 6:47, 6:51; see also Oceans, Lakes, and Ponds (OLP)
- gardens| 3:87; see also curatorship
- information superhighway| 2:14, 6:46, 7:51; see also Internet; Net Neutrality; pre-social media
- trees-in-the-forest| 6:36; see also analogies; Fishing in a pond; Haystacks and Icebergs
- woods| 2:12, 6:8; see also Hidden; inundated; oblivion; Obscurities

Searching Out Loud: Giving Voice to Independent Investigations | Marc Solomon

meteorological| 1:27, 2:56; see also climate change; Weather Conditions
methods| i:6-i:7, i:10-i:14, 1:1, 1:5, 1:16, 1:21-1:22, 1:38, 1:46, 2:3, 2:5-2:6, 2:18, 2:24, 2:34, 2:40, 3:1-3:2, 3:25, 3:60, 3:71, 3:76, 3:93-3:94, 3:98, 4:4, 4:11, 4:13, 4:42, 4:48, 4:105, 4:108-5:1, 5:5, 5:10-5:11, 5:23, 5:25-5:26, 5:28-5:29, 5:34, 5:47, 5:59, 5:69, 5:79, 6:3, 6:7, 6:12, 6:14, 6:16, 6:20-6:21, 6:29, 6:34, 6:44-6:45, 6:49, 6:51-6:52, 7:2, 7:7, 7:26-7:27, 7:38, 7:40, 7:44, 7:48, c:1, c:6-c:7, c:12, c:15-c:16; see also Best Practices; diagnosis; Frameworks; standard operating procedure (SOP)
 Metrics| 1:75, 3:58, 3:70, 4:71, 4:86, 5:1, 5:20, 5:35-5:36, 5:53, 7:19, 7:21, 7:28; see also baseline; benchmark; Indicators; intensity; new-to-known
  - baseline| 3:54, 3:64, 3:98, 4:2, 5:8, 5:12-5:13, 5:17, 5:38, 5:69-5:70, 7:33; see also benchmark; Indicators
  - intensity| i:2, 2:30-2:31, 5:10, 5:16, 5:38, 6:23, 7:26, 7:45; see also dashboards; Exposure; scorekeeping; signal-to-noise
  - measurable| 4:41, 5:23
 middleman| 7:9; see also broker; conciliator; Interactions; resellers; Trade
 Milestones| 1:7, 1:15, 1:25, 3:19, 3:37, 3:73, 4:46, 5:8, 5:10, 6:34, 7:19, c:2; see also biography; family history; personal narratives
  - anniversary| 7:3; see also annual
  - birth| 1:34, 2:33, 3:19, 3:76, 3:80, 3:82, 4:46, 4:75, 5:27, 5:32; see also Personal Identity
  - death| i:16, 3:75-3:76, 3:82, 4:97, 5:68; see also mortal
  - divorce| 1:13, 3:73, 4:66; see also family history
  - mortal| i:4, 1:70; see also death; public records; vital data
  - resignation| 5:26, 7:23; see also decisionmakers; dismiss; executive; quit; Scandals
 military| 2:25, 5:43, 7:11; see also combat; Government; soldier; Violence; warfare
 minus sign| 2:9, 2:15-2:16; see also negation; Search Operators
 Misinformation| i:1, 1:14, 2:88, 3:24, 3:61, 3:78, 3:83, 3:89, 4:30, 4:36, 4:91-4:92, 4:95-4:97, 4:105, 5:3, 5:13, 5:19, 5:21, 5:43, 7:37; see also cynicism; inaccuracies; mistrust; propagandist; smear
  - fabricate| 3:88, 4:102, 5:28; see also Deceptions; fraud
  - misinformation providers| 4:93, 4:96-4:97, 4:104; see also fake news; propagandist
  - misleading| 1:14, 2:88, 3:25, 3:62, 3:79, 3:84, 3:90, 4:31, 4:37, 4:92, 4:98, 4:105-4:106, 5:14, 5:20, 5:22, 5:44, 5:46; see also Coercion; Deceptions; Distortions; fraud; Intentions
 mom| 2:32, 5:64; see also Family; moral; protocol
 Monmouth University| 7:28
 Moore, Michael| 7:12; see also hot media
 Morris-Friedman, Andrew| 4:69; see also 1939 New York World's Fair
 Morse, Stephen M.| 3:81; see also curatorship; genealogy; mashup
 Morville, Peter| 1:22-1:23, 1:38, 2:93, 5:60; see also information architecture; information science
 Mosul| 7:15-7:16; see also Case studies
 Motives| 4:13; see also Behaviors; Character Traits; desire; ego; praise; Roles
  - alterior motive| 7:7; see also personal gain; self-preservation
  - desire| i:16, 1:14-1:15, 1:24, 1:34-1:35, 1:39, 1:48, 1:53, 2:38, 2:47-2:48, 3:18, 3:50, 4:6, 4:15, 4:19, 4:36, 4:42, 4:86, 5:5, 5:41, 5:62, 6:1, 6:9, 6:12, 6:54, 7:5, 7:34; see also passion; visceral
  - grudge| 7:7; see also complaints; Grievance; Resistance; spite
  - jealousy| 4:52, 4:75; see also grudge; Reputations; rivals
  - passion| 1:7, 1:27, 1:37, 1:43, 1:48, 1:65, 3:30, 4:9, 4:28, 4:37, 4:74-4:75, 5:41, 5:47, 6:7, 7:18, 7:38-7:39; see also compete; desire; Expression; visceral
  - personal gain| 1:19, 4:41, 5:2; see also alterior motive; Self-interest
  - personal involvement| 4:47; see also direct experience; disengagement; first person; Provider Conjugation Framework (PCF)
  - pleasure| 1:14, 1:20, 4:40, 6:2; see also reward; self-fulfilling; wealth
  - praise| 1:49, 4:22, 4:32, 4:51-4:52, 4:66, 4:97, 6:53, 7:4, 7:29; see also endorse; Expression
  - revenge| 4:7; see also grudge; hate; passion; spite
  - root motive| 1:12, 1:29; see also ingrained; probable cause
  - spite| 5:27; see also Blame; Grievance; grudge; vengeance
  - vanity| 1:35, 4:76, 4:92, 4:94, 5:31, 5:41, 7:4, 7:48; see also conceit; narcissism; navel-gazing; Perceptions
 movement| i:2, 1:70, 2:35, 3:19, 3:61, 5:36, 7:49; see also Advocacy; grassroots; mission; momentum; Negotiations; Radar; track
 Moynihan, Daniel P.| 7:21, 7:23, 7:41; see also fact versus opinion
 Mueller Report| 2: 46
 multi-dimensional| 1:6, 2:49, 2:105, 7:18; see also Contextual; cross-reference; interconnected
 mystery| i:16, 1:25, 1:61, 1:65, 2:39, 2:49, 3:6, 3:46, 3:59, 4:7, 5:7, 5:56, 5:59; see also clue; Explorations; puzzle; unresolved; unsolved

N

 Naivete| 4:67, 5:41, 7:21, 7:51; see also Beginner; gullibility; ignorance; innocence; unexposed
  - fallacy| 5:64, 7:22, 7:46; see also scammers; urban legends
  - gullibility| 1:35, 4:36; see also fallacy; urban legends
  - ignorance| 1:31-1:32, 1:35-1:36, 1:39, 2:50, 3:6, 3:31-3:33, 3:37, 4:95; see also Beginner; Unexplored; unexposed
 name dropping| 2:15, 2:17, 3:52, 4:15, 4:93, 4:97, 4:106, 5:40, 6:7; see also ice breaker; Influences; newsmakers; social circles
 naming| 2:62, 3:23, 7:48; see also alias; allegations; criminal evidence; Disclosures; divulge; indictment; leak; Semantics, finding people; WikiLeaks
 Narratives| 1:8, 1:20-1:21, 2:53, 3:22, 4:14, 4:32, 4:38, 4:48, 4:62, 4:96, 5:3, 5:6, 5:11, 5:23, 5:41, 5:63, 5:77, 6:52, 7:6-7:9, 7:11-7:13, 7:21-7:23, 7:27, 7:32, 7:38, c:13; see also anecdotal; Interpretations; news stories; plot; theme
  - adverse| 1:44, 4:39, 4:104; see also Risks
  - afflicted| 5:76; see also abuse; disenfranchised; estrangement; marginalize; poverty; suffer
  - anecdotal| 3:20, 5:24, 5:79; see also annotate; episode; quote; Storyteller
  - backfire| 4:18, 4:92, 5:64, 5:71; see also reflexive
  - closure| i:16, 1:17, 1:20, 1:31, 1:39, 1:44, 1:70, 3:25, 3:36, 4:95, 4:103, 5:5, 5:74, c:12; see also conclusive; cycle; resolution; Stop

COMPLETE WORKS: Units One Through Seven | Unabridged Index:26

- dilemma| 2:38, 3:47, 4:92; see also confront
- doubters| 4:48; see also accusers; cynicism; detractors
- downside| 3:87, 4:18, 4:41, 4:55, 4:57, 4:104, 5:3; see also cost/benefit; implications; negative information
- downturn| 5:20, 6:7; see also demise; Economics
- downward| 7:10; see also pressure
- embarrassing| 2:10, 7:41
- eminent| 2:95, 4:61, 7:20
- entangled| 2:16, 3:62; see also Confusion; Obscurities; tangents; tangle
- episode| 3:74, 5:41, 5:48; see also Content Streaming; drama; story lines
- estrangement| 4:45, 5:42; see also isolated; restrictions; siloed
- fallout| 5:17, 5:29; see also consequence; crisis; Disasters; impact; negative information
- melodrama| 2:30; see also fiction; gossip; innuendo; Speculation
- personal narratives| 1:8, 7:32; see also author; biography; past deeds; personal branding
- post mortem| 5:16; see also death; Learning; mortal; story lines
- posterity| 4:66, 5:42; see also hindsight; History; post mortem
- predicament| 2:15, 2:38, 3:25, 5:12, 7:6; see also Liabilities; quandary; stress; trouble
- premise| i:5, 1:2, 1:13, 1:20, 1:24, 1:53, 1:67, 2:61, 3:54, 3:62, 3:87, 4:8, 4:22, 4:34, 4:68, 5:56-5:57, 5:69, 6:14, 7:36, 7:40, 7:42; see also hypotheses; scenarios
- rehash| 2:57, 3:30, 5:77; see also duplicated; rant; reaffirm; redundant; revisiting
- skirmish| 7:43; see also Conflict; confront; Contest; protests
- story lines| 5:12, 5:25, 7:7; see also anecdotal; biography; Character Traits
- suffer| i:3, 1:13, 4:39, 4:67, 5:28, 5:37, 5:48, 6:8, 7:15; see also afflicted; anguish; Grievance
- tragedy| 1:29, 3:37, 4:48; see also afflicted; anguish; Judgment; Roles; sympathetic
- uncertain| 1:4-1:5, 1:26, 1:44, 1:72, 2:6, 2:8, 2:50, 3:1, 3:36, 3:90, 4:16, 4:32, 4:36, 4:41, 4:91-4:92, 4:99, 5:35, 5:63, 5:65, 5:70, 7:12, c:13; see also insecure; Probabilities; Unknown Unknowns; unprecedented; unpredictable
- unfold| 2:85, 3:60, 3:78, 4:41, 4:104, 5:9, 5:11, 5:16, 5:42, 5:68, 6:7, 6:34, 6:41, 6:52, 7:28, 7:38, c:13; see also conclusive; momentum; plot; story lines
- unfortunate| 4:48, 4:100; see also calamitous; dangerous; Decline
- unscripted| 4:44, 7:15, 7:23; see also drama; impression; unfiltered

narrow| i:4, i:9, 1:47, 1:70, 2:2, 2:9, 2:12, 2:27, 2:50, 2:57, 2:60, 2:63, 3:1-3:2, 3:10, 3:19, 3:30, 3:48, 3:76, 3:82, 4:65, 4:68, 4:73, 5:9, 5:62, 6:7, 6:51, 7:10, 7:24, c:6-c:7, c:15; see also Filtering; granular; pearl culturing; precise; refinement
NASA| 3:83; see also government websites
National Football League (NFL)| 7:28; see also Contest; protests; spotlight
navigation| i:1, 1:27, 1:53, 2:2, 2:40, 2:88, 2:92-2:93, 2:104, 5:8, 6:1, 6:20, 7:27; see also dropdown; information architecture; site roots; useful websites; User Experience (UX); User Interface (UI)
negative information| 2:65, 4:27, 4:68, 4:90-4:91, 4:95-4:96, 4:98, 5:6, 5:18, 5:22-5:23, 5:36, 5:63-5:64, 7:13, 7:16, 7:22; see also Bias; fake news; public perceptions
Negotiations| 1:13; see also compromise; Interactions
- bargain| 4:56, 4:60, 4:68; see also alterior motive; containing costs
- barter| 1:34, 5:40-5:42, 5:48, 5:80, 6:14, c:13; see also exchange; Interactions; quid pro quo
- broker| i:1, 1:50, 1:60, 1:63, 2:62-2:63, 2:93, 3:73, 3:76-3:77, 3:79, 3:93, 4:29, 4:41, 4:60, 4:90-4:92, 4:94, 4:96, 4:104, 5:32, 5:39-5:41, 5:55, 6:57, 7:14, 7:20-7:21, 7:36, 7:43; see also arbiter; categorizing, human mediated; conciliator; machine-mediated human computer interactions
- concede| 2:57, 7:38; see also compromise; defeat; deference
- conciliator| 4:41; see also broker; reconcile
- deal| i:3, 1:32, 1:41, 1:49, 1:69, 2:9, 2:45, 3:16, 3:23, 3:25, 3:31, 4:2, 4:33, 4:35, 4:41-4:42, 4:47, 4:80, 4:94, 5:5, 5:24, 5:41, 5:58, 5:69, 5:75, 6:11, c:1; see also bargain; corporate mergers; Negotiations; price
- go-betweens| 4:54; see also broker; middleman
- handshake| i:7, 5:33; see also Agreement; symbols; Trust
- honest disagreement| 4:97, 7:27; see also Conflict; disagreement
- mediated| i:1, 2:67, 2:89, 7:27, 7:35, 7:43; see also broker; Interactions; reconcile
- offer| i:5, i:10, 1:45, 1:50, 1:74-1:75, 2:7, 2:15, 2:17, 2:21, 2:30, 2:48-2:50, 2:56-2:57, 2:67, 2:71, 2:85, 2:93, 3:6, 3:13, 3:72, 3:76, 3:83, 3:90-3:91, 4:1, 4:9, 4:16, 4:40, 4:59, 4:73, 4:97, 5:1, 5:4, 5:17, 5:40-5:41, 5:53, 5:62, 5:77, 6:7, 6:9, 6:18, 6:21-6:22, 6:32, 6:45-6:47, 7:28, 7:37, 7:44; see also Interactions; job offers; Trade
- pact| 4:43; see also Agreement; Diplomacy
- trade-off| 1:69; see also checklists; cost/benefit; Evaluation
- trading| 2:1, 2:33, 4:15, 4:69, 4:73, 4:98, 4:102, 5:26, 5:39; see also exchange; interplay
neighborhoods| 1:5, 3:77, 4:57, 5:43, 6:54; see also Crime Scene; GPS (Global Positioning Satellite); localities; Location; reside
New York Times| 2:23, 4:27, 7:8, 7:23, 7:52; see also news organizations; Newspapers
new-to-known| 3:55-3:56; see also content weight; Hit Counts; Metrics; Quality Controls; skim
Newport, Cal| 7:2-7:3; see also Deep Work
news feed| 1:51, 5:32, 5:41, 5:43, 5:50, 5:55, 6:35-6:36, 6:39, 6:49, 7:4-7:7, 7:10, 7:13, 7:16, 7:21-7:23, 7:25, 7:29-7:30, 7:35, 7:43, 7:45, 7:48, 7:50; see also filter bubbles; personal radar; RSS (Really Simple Syndication); Social Media
news junkie| 2:30, 5:54-5:55, 7:5, 7:45; see also curatorship
news stories| 3:10, 3:63, 3:67, 4:27, 4:39, 5:30, 7:14, 7:36; see also attention demand; headlines; Narratives; news feed; Public Awareness; story lines
newsgroup| 3:15, 3:60; see also discussion boards; pre-social media
newsleaker| 4:23; see also Disclosures; divulge; leak; Secrecy; whistleblower
newsmakers| 3:15, 3:90, 4:8, 4:32, 5:6, 6:41, 7:9, 7:12, 7:36; see also celebrities; Exposure; Fame; headlines; Influences; Information Providers; Paparazzi; Radar; renowned

Searching Out Loud: Giving Voice to Independent Investigations | Marc Solomon

Newspapers| 1:65, 2:65, 3:16, 3:52, 3:92, 4:9, 4:23, 4:25, 4:57, 4:59, 5:29, 5:48, 5:55, 6:37, 7:9-7:10, 7:13-7:14, 7:20, 7:33, 7:53; see also deadline; Journalism; news organizations; scoop
  - chicagotribune.com| 5:56
  - Crains| 5:56
  - latimes.com| 5:56
  - nytimes.com| 5:56
  - washingtonpost.com| 5:56
  - wsj.com| 5:56; see also Wall Street Journal
Non-profits| i:10, 2:14, 3:18, 6:7-6:8, 6:12, 6:17, 6:20, 6:22-6:23, 6:31, 6:51, 6:53; see also philanthropies; Public Policies; volunteer
  - charities| 1:19, 1:66, 2:32, 4:56, 4:106, 6:14; see also Non-profits; philanthropies; volunteer
  - fundraising| 3:77, 5:65, 6:20, 6:49; see also Non-profits
  - philanthropies| 6:31
  - pro bono| 6:8, 6:17, 6:20, 6:46; see also clients, legal consulting; Non-profits
nondisclosure| 1:5, 4:45; see also contracts; Employment; Legal; Privacy; whistleblower; workplace
Nouns| 1:72, 2:38, 2:43, 2:45, 3:9, 3:20, 3:69, 4:7, 4:83; see also actions and actors; Grammar
  - noun phrases| 2:43, 2:45, 4:84; see also actions and actors
  - nouns and verbs| 1:72, 2:43, 3:21; see also Dichotomies; Grammar
nuance| 1:10, 2:51, 2:88, 4:13, 6:6; see also discrete; subtle; vague
nudge| i:5, 5:1; see also opinion surveys; persuasion
nugget| 3:84, 5:49; see also granular; refinement
Nyhan, Brendan| 7:38

O

objectives| 1:3, 2:2, 3:1, 3:24, 4:1, 5:1, 6:2; see also planning; predefine; projects, clients expectations; strategy
Obscurities| 2:29, 3:73, 4:13, 4:83, 7:14, 7:41-7:42, 7:47, 7:56; see also Exposure; Hidden; practical obscurity; Search Engine, Privacy; Semantics, finding people
  - indecipherable| 2:37, 4:56; see also decode; encryption; inscrutable
  - murky| i:16, 1:44-1:45, 2:65, 5:9, 5:59, 5:62; see also Hidden; opaque; vague
  - vague| 1:25, 1:65, 2:3, 4:47, 4:83, 5:28, 7:3, 7:45; see also Deceptions; Hidden; inscrutable; opaque; subtle
Observation| i:2, i:4, i:8, 1:8, 1:34, 1:36, 3:11, 3:90, 4:1, 4:8, 4:15-4:16, 4:29, 4:34, 4:40, 4:44, 4:47, 4:56, 4:66, 4:79, 4:86, 4:90, 4:103, 5:29, 5:35, 6:54, 6:57, 7:20, 7:36, c:9; see also Evaluation; Indicators; strangers; unbiased; Vectors of Integrity (VOI)
  - audience| 3:8, 3:23, 3:63, 3:85, 3:91, 3:95, 4:8, 4:12, 4:14, 4:25-4:26, 4:42, 4:90, 5:4-5:5, 5:9, 5:22-5:23, 5:30, 5:34-5:35, 5:45-5:46, 5:59-5:60, 5:64, 5:70-5:72, 5:74-5:77, 5:79, 6:4, 6:19, 6:56, 7:6, 7:15, 7:35, 7:38, c:10, c:12
  - bystander| 5:23, 5:32, 5:70; see also eyewitness; strangers; third person; unbiased
  - camera| 1:35-1:36, 2:65, 4:8, 4:44, 4:55, 5:27, 6:13, 7:7, 7:10, 7:16; see also Exposure
  - onlookers| i:2, 4:23; see also third person; witness
  - voyeurism| 5:31, 7:15; see also Online Behavior; stalking
  - watcher| 1:48, 2:12, 4:28, 4:59, 4:89, 5:2, 5:64, 6:20-6:21, 7:10; see also advisor; Credibility; third person; watchwords
oceans to ponds, getting from| 3:31, 6:40; see also Location; narrow; refinement; Search Engine, Custom (CSE)
Oceans, Lakes, and Ponds (OLP)| 2:3, 2:50, 2:54, 2:86, 2:100-2:101, 3:4, 3:28-3:29, 3:31, 3:33, 3:52-3:53, 3:83-3:84, 5:54, 5:80-6:1, 6:6, 6:10-6:12, 6:32, 6:50, 7:26, 7:50, c:6-c:7, c:15, c:17; see also database, size; Frameworks; Quality Controls; Subject Directory; tool selection
official| 1:6, 2:34, 2:98, 3:17, 3:56, 3:88, 3:98, 4:2, 4:8, 4:11, 4:23, 4:25, 4:35, 4:38, 4:48, 4:50, 4:97, 4:106, 5:24, 5:28, 5:75, 6:56, 7:11, 7:21, 7:37, 7:40; see also first party; formal communication; public officials
oil| i:14, 2:16, 5:26, 5:46
Olympics| 2:35; see also Contest; Diplomacy
Online Behavior| i:8; see also affinity bias; Anonymity; face-to-screen; faceless; online forums; strangers; trollers
  - cybercrime| 2:49, 7:49; see also Internet Security; personal data; scammers
  - emojis| 7:15; see also shorthand; smiley face logic
  - fear of missing out (FOMO)| 7:3; see also anxiety; jealousy; Motives; Online Behavior
  - memes| 7:32, 7:38, 7:48; see also Exposure; viral
  - online forums| 4:54; see also discussion boards; listserv
  - viral| i:14, 2:37, 2:55, 3:61, 4:100, 5:30, 5:54; see also memes; pulse; spiraling; trends
ontology| 2:105; see also categorizing, Relatedness; semantic web; taxonomy
Open Directory Project (DMOZ)| 2:84, 2:86, 2:89, 2:91; see also Subject Directory
opinion weight| 5:11; see also Influences; Search Targets
Opinion-based| 1:24, 1:46, 2:2, 2:4-2:5, 2:49, 2:85, 3:18, 3:34, 3:49-3:50, 5:65, c:3; see also fact versus opinion; Fact-based; Haystacks and Icebergs
  - majority opinion| 4:20, 7:29; see also judiciary; prevailing; Public Opinion
  - opinion search| 2:52, 3:20-3:21, 3:36, 3:48-3:49, 3:59, 3:70, c:5; see also fact versus opinion; Haystacks and Icebergs; Opinion-based
  - opinion-maker| 2:36, 5:22; see also Influences; provocation; public relations
  - opinion-neutral| 7:19, 7:26, 7:45; see also Bias; detachment; disinterest
  - views| i:13, 1:20, 1:35, 1:74, 3:6, 3:17, 3:48, 3:72, 4:6, 4:22, 4:30, 4:32-4:33, 4:40, 4:74, 4:86, 4:91, 4:96, 5:29, 5:52, 5:62, 5:65, 6:53, 7:6-7:7, 7:23-7:24, 7:28, 7:31, 7:39, 7:51; see also Interpretations; posture; stance
Opinion-editorial (op-ed)| 5:47; see also Influences; Journalism; media bias; opinion-maker
Opposition| i:2, 1:20, 2:14, 2:65, 3:6, 3:16, 3:89, 4:9, 4:18, 4:36, 4:39, 4:41-4:42, 4:104, 5:64, 6:33, 7:4, 7:20, 7:30, 7:34, 7:44; see also Conflict; contradict; detractors; disagreement; Reject; Resistance
  - defend| i:5, 1:14-1:15, 2:46, 2:65, 2:85, 3:64, 4:89-4:90, 4:92, 4:95, 5:3, 5:8, 5:32, 5:34, 5:43, 5:58, 5:72, 7:10, 7:22, 7:28; see also ally
  - enemy| 4:18, 4:45, 4:66-4:67, 4:96, 4:104
  - offensive| 4:96; see also aggression; Conflict

- opponent| 4:90, 4:96; see also Contest
- undermine| 3:50, 3:89, 5:58, 7:38; see also backstabbing; contradict; derail; disclaim; discredit; refuted

orchestration| 4:51-4:55, 4:100, 5:8; see also agenda; fabricate; integrate, findings; Leaders; predetermined

Ordering| i:13; see also ascendance; Filtering; PageRank; Search Results
- descending| 3:61; see also reversal; spiraling
- ordering, events| 3:38, 3:53; see also chronology; Websites, ranking
- ordering, search results| i:13, 1:64, 2:10, 2:12, c:5; see also rank; Search Results
- ordering, word adjacency| 2:10, 2:13, 2:36, 2:38; see also Keyword in Context (KWIC); proximity

Organizations| 1:1, 1:3-1:4, 1:47, 1:71, 2:11, 2:15, 2:23, 2:27, 2:31, 2:34-2:35, 2:57, 2:60, 2:64-2:65, 2:72, 2:101, 3:1, 3:47, 3:49-3:50, 3:64, 3:73, 3:94, 4:15, 4:20, 4:23, 4:26, 4:30, 4:32, 4:36, 4:60-4:61, 4:69, 4:72, 4:74, 4:97, 4:107, 5:4, 5:9-5:14, 5:17, 5:19, 5:26, 5:29, 5:36-5:38, 5:69, 5:76-5:77, 6:8, 6:10-6:11, 6:14, 6:17, 6:28, 6:32, 6:36, 6:41-6:43, 6:52-6:57, 7:5, 7:9-7:10, 7:19, 7:36, 7:50; see also Companies; Leaders
- founder| 2:63, 3:60, 3:73, 7:53; see also Leaders
- mission| i:2, i:7, i:9, i:16, 1:9, 1:19, 1:24, 1:57, 1:60, 2:2, 2:12, 2:50, 2:88, 3:1, 3:26, 3:64, 3:68, 3:72, 4:22, 4:31, 4:35, 4:91, 5:13, 5:38, 5:41, 5:57, 5:71, 6:5, 6:20, 6:47, 6:51, 7:2, 7:15, 7:30-7:31, c:1; see also aspiration; Beliefs; Roles; struggle; theme
- news organizations| 2:72; see also Broadcast Media; Major Business Media; Newspapers; TV networks; Wire Services
- org| 1:26, 2:8, 2:25, 2:79, 2:89, 3:18, 3:26, 3:41, 3:53, 3:97, 4:107, 5:54-5:55, 5:80; see also Non-profits
- research organizations| 4:30; see also focus groups; opinion surveys; product reviews
- spokesperson| 3:60, 7:11; see also first party; formal communication; group communication; official; press release

organizing principles| 1:68, 2:73, 2:86, 2:94, 5:9; see also categorizing, searchable groupings; classification; Ordering; Pattern Matching

Origin| 1:3, 1:9-1:10, 1:20, 1:22, 1:25, 1:41, 1:58, 1:66, 1:68, 2:19-2:20, 2:24, 2:29, 2:52, 2:54, 2:62, 2:72-2:73, 2:87, 2:89, 2:92, 2:103, 3:3, 3:5, 3:13-3:16, 3:57, 3:61-3:63, 3:72, 3:88, 4:34, 4:42, 4:45, 4:67-4:69, 4:74, 4:77, 4:87, 4:89-4:91, 4:97, 5:16, 5:20, 5:23-5:24, 5:29, 5:31, 5:35, 5:47, 5:56-5:57, 5:64, 5:68-5:69, 5:73, 5:78, 6:14, 6:18, 6:20, 6:28, 6:37, 6:49, 7:6, 7:10, 7:26, 7:29, 7:36, 7:40, 7:51; see also Source Fluency
- derive| 2:44, 2:71, 3:82, 4:6, 4:59, 4:108, 5:7
- original intent| 1:3, 1:9, 1:22, 3:6, 4:78, 4:88; see also Intentions
- original objective| 1:10, 1:25, 1:68, 4:70; see also objectives
- original premise| 1:20, 4:75, 5:57-5:58, 5:70, 6:14, 7:40; see also Contextual
- original question| 2:52, 3:89; see also Documentation; original premise
- original research| 2:52, 5:65, 7:36; see also Perspectives, research
- original sources| 2:53, 2:72, 2:92, 3:5, 3:17, 3:62-3:64, 3:73, 4:3, 4:89, 5:24, 7:29; see also Vectors of Integrity (VOI)
- point of origin| 2:19-2:20, 3:15, 3:17, 5:25, 7:6; see also Information Types, entry points
- unfounded| 1:28, 1:35, 4:87, 4:105, c:10; see also anonymous; fake news; pretense

outsource| 1:50, 1:71, 2:66, 5:68; see also labor; overseas; Trade

Overview| 2:6, c:2; see also disseminate; dossier; market research; secondary information
- overall| i:14, 1:65, 1:74, 2:6, 2:90, 3:12, 3:32, 3:64, 4:30, 4:43, 4:49, 5:10, 5:22, 5:37-5:38, 7:40, c:2; see also Perspectives; snapshot
- snapshot| 1:61, 1:68, 2:22, 2:42, 2:69, 3:23; see also summaries; top-of-mind

OVUM Research| 5:3; see also market research; research organizations

P

page views| 7:28; see also Metrics; Search Engine Marketing (SEM); Websites, popularity; Websites, traffic

Page, Larry| 2:63; see also useful search results

PageRank| 1:62, 2:7, 2:42, 3:65, 4:86, 4:95, 4:101, 4:104; see also Google Keyword Tool; Search Engine Marketing (SEM); SEO (Search Engine Optimization)

paid subscriptions| 2:30, 2:37, 6:20, 7:33; see also database, subscription (premium); pay walls

Paparazzi| 4:24; see also celebrities; exploit; Exposure; Fame; fixation; omnipresent; spotlight

paralysis| 4:40, 5:32; see also impaired; partisanship; Resistance; stalemate

Pariser, Eli| 1:60, 5:24; see also filter bubbles

parochial| 7:31; see also grassroots; localities

particle of speech| 1:63, 2:38; see also adverbs; Grammar; noun phrases; verbs, conjugation

partisanship| 3:6, 7:38, 7:44; see also Accusations; echo chamber; Opposition; Politics; stalemate

partner| 2:6, 2:67, 4:22, 4:60, 4:68, 5:39, 5:57, 5:60, 6:14, 6:45, 6:56, 7:19; see also Collaborative; Stakeholders; venture

password| i:11, 1:6, 1:38, 1:53, 1:61, 2:21-2:22, 3:15, 3:74, 3:78, 3:81, 3:85, 4:65-4:66, 7:47-7:49; see also Code, access; Firefox; Internet Security

past deeds| 5:66; see also background checks; biography; personal branding; personal narratives

patent| 3:31; see also defend; discovery; innovation; proprietary; trademark

Pattern Matching| 1:5, 1:66-1:67, 2:47, 6:48; see also Logic; organizing principles
- anomalies| 3:10, 3:60; see also False hit; outliers; rare; uncommon; unexplained
- deviate| 3:12, 3:98, 5:10, 5:56-5:57; see also Logic; variant
- exclusive| 1:13, 1:20, 2:14, 2:33-2:34, 2:42, 2:76, 3:12, 3:26, 3:31, 3:66, 3:77-3:78, 3:86-3:87, 4:13, 4:30, 4:38, 6:39, 7:20, 7:46, 7:48, c:7
- fundamental| i:6, i:9, 1:27, 1:40, 1:52, 1:65, 2:40, 2:56, 3:17, 3:25, 3:93, 4:48, 4:57, 4:66, 4:90, 4:103, 5:1-5:2, 5:38, 6:9, 7:20, 7:43; see also establishment
- gap| 1:50, 1:66, 2:37, 2:40, 3:8, 3:10, 3:86, 4:2, 4:22, 4:55, 4:93-4:94, 4:104, 4:107, 5:7, 5:37, 5:75, 7:9-7:10, 7:19; see also evidence patterns
- generalization| i:16, 2:4, 2:6, 3:3, 3:9, 3:21, 3:27, 5:18, 5:40, 5:77, c:3-c:4; see also extrapolate; Haystacks and Icebergs
- inconsistencies| 2:71, 3:36, 3:91, 4:102; see also contradict; curiosities; defying explanation; hypocrisy
- novelty| i:6, i:17, 1:44, 1:52, 1:58, 2:2, 3:10, 3:14, 3:20, 3:28, 3:58, 3:70, 4:97, 6:9, 6:36, 7:3, 7:9, 7:22, 7:52; see also derive; fiction
- omission| 1:5, 1:29, 2:62, 5:70; see also discrepancy; missing details
- overlap| 1:42, 1:60, 2:104, 3:23, 3:63, 3:82, 4:64, 5:14, 5:56, 6:45, 7:34; see also cross-reference; multi-dimensional
- perennial| 2:31, 2:47, 2:49, 5:18, 5:30, 5:41, 7:6, c:1, c:17; see also annual; calendar; cycle; reminders
- similar| 1:75, 2:23, 2:34, 2:44, 2:59, 2:69, 2:88, 2:98, 3:26, 3:29, 3:63, 3:92, 4:56, 4:86, 4:96, 4:108, 5:38, 5:46, 5:59, 5:64, 5:70, 6:34, 7:48; see also common interest; comparison; Relatedness; resemblance

COMPLETE WORKS: Units One Through Seven | Unabridged Index:29

  - template| 4:62; see also Best Practices; Procedures; search logs
  - uncommon| 1:51, 3:54, 5:73, 7:48; see also gold standard; rare; unexpected
pay walls| 7:12; see also Cost of Research; premium content
pearl culturing| 2:42-2:43, 2:95; see also curatorship; Filtering; granular; refinement
pecking order| 2:36, 6:56; see also Group Behavior; hierarchy; ingrained; Power Structures
pendulum| 4:26; see also cycle; History; momentum; Sense-making
Pepsi| 4:94, 4:105
percentages| 1:23, 4:19, 7:6; see also approximate; educated guesses; indictment; Metrics; Surveys
Perceptions| i:8, 1:14, 1:32, 1:50, 2:106, 3:89, 3:98, 4:22, 4:29, 4:32, 4:39, 4:44, 4:53-4:54, 4:59, 4:66, 4:68, 4:91, 4:104, 5:4-5:5, 5:17-5:18, 5:20, 5:25, 5:34, 5:42, 5:64-5:65, 6:29, 6:46, 7:8, 7:22, c:12; see also Beliefs; Campaigns; frame of reference; Influences; Interpretations; Perspectives; posture
  - arrogance| 1:35
  - augmented reality| 2:56; see also artificial intelligence
  - conceit| i:1, 5:12, 7:46
  - controversial| 1:68, 2:12, 2:36, 2:65, 3:45, 4:32-4:33, 4:93, 4:96, 5:14, 5:21; see also hoax; hypocrisy; leak; provocation; Scandals
  - detractors| 1:1, 4:67, 4:92, 5:16, 5:37, 7:43; see also disputes; negative information; Opposition; otherness
  - impression| 1:33, 1:44, 2:100, 4:43, 4:48, 4:106, 5:35, 5:37, 5:61, 5:77-5:78, 6:8; see also Perceptions
  - inscrutable| 1:41, 1:59, 5:64, 7:47; see also Hidden
  - nightmares| 4:99, 5:6; see also anxiety; doomsday; scenarios
  - posture| i:1, 1:11, 1:20, 1:42, 1:64, 2:11, 2:63, 2:100, 3:2, 3:12, 3:48, 3:88, 4:15, 4:39, 4:41, 4:59-4:60, 5:22, 5:27, 5:34, 5:57, 7:3-7:5, 7:26, 7:44, c:14; see also Influences; opinion-maker
  - public perceptions| 5:2, 5:20, 5:30, 5:37, 5:64, 7:7-7:8, 7:51; see also affinity bias; focus groups
  - stature| 2:64, 3:3, 3:72, 3:89, 4:91, 4:96, 5:8, 5:12, 5:16, 5:18, 5:25, 5:37, 5:40, 5:64, 5:80, 7:20-7:21; see also brand stature; Recognition; Reputations; spotlight
  - stress| 1:24, 1:26, 1:45, 2:51, 3:6, 4:99, 5:7, 5:16, 5:29, 5:72, 6:45, 7:27, 7:30, 7:50; see also anxiety; insecure; pressure; shock
  - suspicions| 1:48, 2:50, 3:89, 4:30, 4:36, 4:92, 5:63, 7:22, 7:30, c:10; see also accomplices; raid; Resistance; suspects; Trust
  - sympathetic| 1:36, 7:28, 7:38; see also empathy; Expression; mercy; Perspectives, perspective-taking; tolerance
permissible| i:12, 1:68, 6:12; see also discrete; Legal; protocol; rule-making
Personal Identity| 2:27; see also acquaintances; Assets; Contacts; Milestones
  - alias| 3:61, 4:66; see also pseudonyms; shorthand
  - alma mater| 2:22, 3:78, 4:74, 4:77, 6:28; see also Affiliated; diploma
  - credit histories| 3:75; see also credit bureau
  - date of birth| 2:33; see also Milestones
  - employment history| 3:75; see also background checks
  - maiden name| 3:70; see also alias; finding people; genealogy; Search Targets
  - marriage| 3:46, 3:75-3:76, 4:46, 4:75, 5:42; see also Milestones
  - phone number| 2:33; see also Contacts; texts
  - pseudonyms| 4:105; see also alias; anonymous
  - Social Security| 1:49, 2:33; see also breach; personal data
  - surname| 2:10, 2:13, 2:27, 2:37, 3:66, 3:76, 5:21, 5:73; see also alias; Family; finding people; genealogy
  - wives| 2:50, 7:38; see also Family
personhood| 7:32; see also Personal Identity
personified| 4:39, 5:30, 7:6; see also Metaphors; Rhetoric; symbols
persons of interest| 1:49, 2:64, 4:3, 4:9, 4:33, 5:40, 5:69, 6:4, 7:18; see also Search Targets
Perspectives| i:1, 1:24, 1:29, 1:35-1:36, 1:40, 1:43-1:44, 2:64, 3:15-3:16, 3:18, 3:25, 3:33, 3:35, 3:38, 3:49, 3:51, 3:53, 3:73, 3:86, 4:2-4:4, 4:11, 4:13-4:14, 4:16, 4:18-4:20, 4:25, 4:27, 4:31-4:32, 4:35, 4:39-4:41, 4:44, 4:49, 4:51, 4:58, 4:69, 4:71, 4:75, 4:87, 4:89, 4:92-4:94, 5:1, 5:3-5:5, 5:8, 5:10-5:11, 5:13, 5:16-5:17, 5:20, 5:30, 5:36-5:39, 5:48, 5:51, 5:53, 5:61-5:63, 5:71, 6:12, 6:14, 6:21-6:22, 6:45-6:46, 6:56, 7:3, 7:8, 7:20, 7:28, 7:36-7:37, 7:44, 7:49-7:51; see also balcony; Contextual; Interpretations; Quality Controls; The Biggest Picture (TBP); Vectors of Integrity (VOI)
  - hindsight| 1:36, 3:39, 4:15; see also experience-based learning; posterity
  - microscope| 1:27, 1:29-1:30, 2:57, 2:60, 3:50, 3:61, 3:72, 6:46; see also exposing corruption; Metaphors; public scrutiny
  - outsider| 1:22, 1:29, 3:13, 3:15, 3:63, 3:98, 4:4, 4:17, 4:22, 4:66, 4:68, 5:12, 5:76, 6:45, 6:53, 6:55; see also Credibility; Observation; third party; third person
  - Perspectives, elevated| 1:36, 4:17, 7:24; see also guru; Wisdom
  - Perspectives, institutional| 3:18, 5:26; see also institutional credibility
  - Perspectives, outsider versus insider| 1:29, 3:16, 4:5, 5:25, 7:21; see also insider
  - Perspectives, perspective-taking| 3:26, 4:2-4:4, 4:24, 4:26, 4:72, 7:28; see also Johari Window; theory of mind
  - Perspectives, research| 1:43, 2:55, 2:66, 3:51, 3:60, 4:2, 4:5; see also Research Projects
  - Perspectives, social media| 3:53, 4:5; see also affinity bias; anxiety; gossip
  - prism| 1:25, 4:38; see also Perspectives, perspective-taking; Provider Conjugation Framework (PCF)
  - spectrum| 4:14, 4:50, 4:57-4:58, 5:8, 5:64, 6:8, 6:35, 6:47, 6:51, 6:54, 7:34-7:35, 7:43; see also autism spectrum
  - spyglasses| 4:87; see also icon; Metaphors; searcher
  - telescope| 1:29, 3:47, 3:62; see also Exposure; granular; Metaphors; precise
persuasion| 1:39, 1:49, 2:40, 2:62, 4:13-4:14, 4:95, 4:97, 4:100, 4:103, 5:8, 5:28, 5:41, 5:70, 5:72, 5:78, 7:12, 7:49; see also Campaigns; charisma; convince; deal; Influences; nudge; pandering; Rhetoric
philosophy| 1:25, 2:52, 3:72, 7:20; see also Beliefs; guidelines; Interpretations
pimagazine| 2:20, 2:24; see also Professional Investigator (PI)
Pipl| 3:78; see also finding people
pitchforks| 4:31; see also Opposition; protests; Resistance; vocal
Pizza Hut| 5:21-5:22

Searching Out Loud: Giving Voice to Independent Investigations | Marc Solomon

plagiarism| 3:63; see also academic papers; Copyscape; fraud; hoax; misleading
pledge| 4:9, 4:56, 5:69, 6:54-6:55; see also Authenticity; dedicated; fundraising; genuine; loyalties
plot| 3:32, 3:58, 3:75, 4:8, 4:11, 4:37, 4:39, 5:11, 5:68, 5:79, 7:6, 7:19, c:15; see also accomplices; cohort; conspiracies; Narratives; perpetrate
pointers| 1:60, 2:4, 2:8, 2:34-2:35, 2:39-2:40, 2:66, 3:16, 3:30, 3:66, 3:72, 5:68, 6:9-6:10, 6:45, c:3, c:5; see also Unique IDs; verbatims
polemic| 5:45, 5:60, 7:2; see also academic papers; arguments; persuasion; Reason; Rhetoric
Politics| 5:48; see also Campaigns; echo chamber; Elections; partisanship; persuasion; stalemate
 - conservative| 1:38, 4:39, 7:7-7:8
 - Democrat| 4:38, 4:103
 - Republicans| 4:103
poll| 3:78, 4:43, 5:8, 5:23, 5:29, 5:72, 6:29, 7:6, 7:8; see also feedback; Public Opinion; sample; Surveys
ponds| 2:12, 2:18, 2:28, 2:54, 2:63, 2:66, 2:75, 3:2, 3:13, 3:27-3:32, 3:35, 3:46, 3:58, 3:62, 3:78, 3:82-3:84, 4:79, 5:52, 6:10-6:11, 6:20, 6:25, 6:31-6:34, 6:39, 6:41, 6:46-6:47, 6:49-6:52, 7:26, 7:50, c:6, c:16; see also Metaphors; Oceans, Lakes, and Ponds (OLP)
ponzi scheme| 2:10; see also fraud; Madoff, Bernard; white collar crime
Popularity| i:2-i:3, 1:43, 1:46, 1:49, 1:64, 1:67-1:68, 2:18, 2:23-2:24, 2:29-2:30, 2:39, 2:52-2:53, 2:64, 2:67, 2:72, 2:93, 2:98, 2:107, 3:16, 3:30, 3:47, 3:58, 3:65, 3:69, 3:80, 4:26, 4:48, 4:55, 4:59, 4:67, 4:82, 4:92, 4:95, 4:97, 4:100-4:103, 5:26, 5:47-5:48, 5:53, 5:63, 5:68, 6:16-6:17, 6:23, 6:29, 6:34, 6:47-6:48, 6:56, 7:33, 7:48; see also Search Engine Marketing (SEM); Websites, popularity
 - bestseller| 1:49; see also Public Awareness; public perceptions; Reputations
 - rank| i:2, i:4, i:13, 1:6, 1:26, 1:46, 1:62, 1:66-1:68, 2:7, 2:15, 2:24, 2:29, 2:35-2:36, 2:43, 2:45, 2:57, 2:61, 2:66, 2:72, 2:85-2:86, 3:10-3:11, 3:17, 3:24, 3:37, 3:64, 3:93, 4:19, 4:32, 4:43, 4:48, 4:66, 4:69, 4:92, 4:97, 4:100-4:102, 5:11, 5:44, 5:46, 5:76, 6:4, 6:16, 6:22, 6:29, 7:9, 7:20, 7:22, 7:35, 7:38, 7:46, 7:48; see also ordering, search results; SEO (Search Engine Optimization)
popup ad| 7:45; see also advertising; Browser; i-frame; personal data; Search Engine Marketing (SEM)
Portals| 2:86, 6:10, 6:20-6:21, 6:23, c:4; see also aggregate; Information Types, entry points; useful websites
 - business portal| 6:10
 - gateway| i:9, 3:29, 3:31, 3:93, 6:20
portrayal| 4:42, 4:44, 4:105; see also believable; Character Traits; Expression; revisiting; role model; Roles; story lines
possibility| 1:18, 1:27, 1:43, 1:49, 1:53, 1:61, 2:14, 2:16, 2:32, 2:39, 2:53, 2:77, 2:85, 2:88, 2:101, 3:1, 3:10, 3:27, 3:36, 3:60-3:61, 3:79, 3:86, 3:90, 4:48, 4:62, 4:73, 4:75, 4:93, 5:15, 5:35, 5:49, 5:53, 5:57, 5:59, 5:62, 7:26, c:5-c:6; see also conceivable; Forecast; Probabilities; scenarios
Postman, Neil| 7:2, 7:6, 7:12, 7:34, 7:41; see also technopoly
poverty| 4:41; see also disenfranchised; Public Policies; tragedy
Power Structures| i:3-i:4, i:6, i:15, 1:21, 1:58, 1:60, 2:12, 2:17, 2:26, 2:38, 2:40, 2:60, 2:62, 2:65, 2:71, 2:81, 2:107, 3:2-3:3, 3:5, 3:9, 3:22, 3:57, 4:1, 4:7, 4:13, 4:18-4:19, 4:32, 4:35, 4:41, 4:47, 4:51, 4:55, 4:61, 4:79, 4:83, 4:90, 4:96, 4:99, 4:102-4:103, 5:4-5:5, 5:7, 5:15, 5:24, 5:31, 5:53, 5:64, 5:70, 7:1, 7:3, 7:6-7:7, 7:10-7:12, 7:19-7:22, 7:28, 7:31, 7:38, 7:42, 7:47, 7:49-7:51, c:1, c:12; see also consensus; entrenched; Influences; Motives
 - crackdowns| 3:37, 7:10; see also fascism; overpower; tyranny
 - disenfranchised| 4:27; see also abuse; poverty; racial profiling
 - dominant| 1:48, 2:81, 3:48, 4:61, 5:24, 5:36, 5:65, 7:12, 7:20; see also entrenched; suppression; tyranny
 - entrenched| 3:64, 6:53, 7:1, 7:51; see also Government, forms of; incumbent
 - impose| i:17, 1:35, 2:59, 2:88, 2:91, 2:107, 3:6, 5:29, 5:60, 6:25, 7:2, 7:12, 7:49; see also Power Structures; Reinforcement
 - overpower| 4:48, 4:86, 4:99; see also crackdowns; exploit; tyranny
 - override| 1:14, 1:20, 2:37, 3:82, 5:55, 7:34-7:35; see also majority opinion; prevailing
 - populist| 7:20; see also demagoguery; Elite; grassroots
 - powerless| 1:71, 5:12, 5:57; see also disenfranchised; disengagement; marginalize; poverty
 - wealth| 4:55, 4:98-4:99; see also affluent; charities; Demographics; stock market
prayer| 4:13, 7:20; see also Beliefs; devotion; Intentions; sacred; simplicity
precise| i:9, i:17, 1:8, 1:24, 1:36, 1:58, 1:61, 2:2-2:3, 2:12-2:14, 2:34, 2:39-2:40, 2:46, 2:57, 2:61, 2:64, 2:99, 2:101, 2:104, 3:3, 3:9, 3:11-3:12, 3:17, 3:19, 3:27, 3:36, 3:48, 4:31, 4:36, 4:42, 4:45, 5:10, 5:63, 7:2; see also Fact-based; granular; Vectors of Integrity (VOI)
Prejudice| i:1, 2:40, 3:26, 6:17; see also Bias; exclude; exploit; hate; marginalize; ridicule
 - intolerance| 7:31; see also Bias; Prejudice
 - ostracism| 7:30; see also disenfranchised; otherness; ridicule
 - otherness| 7:30; see also actions of others; fear; ignorance; marginalize; mistrust
 - racial profiling| 7:31; see also Crime; disenfranchised; marginalize; micro-targeting; otherness; poverty
premium content| i:10, 2:72, 3:1, 3:73, 3:78, 3:80, 3:86-3:87, 3:90, 4:1, 5:2, 5:31, 6:12, 6:20-6:21, 6:23, c:7-c:8; see also fee-based; free versus fee
Presley, Elvis| 4:98
press release| 3:18, 5:8; see also Wire Services
prevailing| 1:37, 1:70, 1:74, 2:3, 2:38-2:39, 2:107, 4:1, 4:23, 4:91, 4:103-4:104, 5:3, 5:18, 5:41, 5:47, 5:63, 6:49, 7:5; see also overcome; Popularity; Public Opinion; Wisdom
primary intelligence| 2:88, 4:59, 4:72, 5:40, 5:70, c:13; see also diary; direct experience; first person; Interactions; Search to Converse (STC)
print media| i:12, 2:30, 3:52, 3:62, 4:59, 5:9, 5:48, 6:37, 7:4-7:5, 7:9, 7:13-7:14; see also Major Business Media; Newspapers
Privacy| 1:38, 1:47, 2:27, 2:66-2:67, 2:69-2:71, 2:94, 3:30, 3:73, 4:65-4:67, 7:16-7:17, 7:42, 7:49; see also algorithms; data mining; filter bubbles; Johari Window; password; personal data; Secrecy; Surveillance Capitalism
 - default, privacy settings| 2:71, 4:67, 4:78; see also personal data; Surveillance Capitalism
 - personal data| 2:66, 2:71, 3:76, 3:78; see also breach; Hacks; Surveillance Capitalism
 - Privacy Paradox| 7:50; see also predicament; trade-off; vulnerability
 - privy| 4:8, 4:59, 7:20; see also gossip; insider; social circles
 - sequester| i:16, 4:45; see also debt; discrete; isolated; Secrecy
 - spy| 1:26, 3:60; see also counterpart; eavesdropping; Surveillance
Probabilities| 1:8, 1:29, 1:38, 1:52, 2:49, 2:56, 2:100, 3:20, 3:68-3:69, 3:93, 4:2, 4:57, 4:68, 5:59, 5:66, 5:68, 6:9, 6:21, 6:49, 7:12, 7:22, 7:28; see also calculable; Evaluation; Guesswork
 - absolute| 1:20, 1:36, 1:64, 1:75, 2:2, 3:5, 3:18, 3:34, 3:48, 3:70, 4:36, 4:38, 5:7, 5:12, 7:3, 7:44; see also Authenticity; Excesses; no brainer
 - certainties| i:1, i:16, 1:7, 1:11, 1:13, 1:15, 1:20, 1:32, 1:34, 1:38, 1:67, 1:72, 2:10, 2:12, 2:15, 2:20, 2:24, 2:39, 2:46, 2:48, 2:61, 2:85, 2:101,

COMPLETE WORKS: Units One Through Seven | Unabridged Index:31

3:16-3:18, 3:23, 3:26, 3:30, 3:34, 3:48, 3:54, 3:62, 3:91, 4:6, 4:29, 4:47, 4:98, 5:8, 5:28, 5:58, 5:62, 5:66-5:67, 5:73, 5:76, 7:4, 7:22, 7:50; see also confidence level; guarantee
- frequencies| 1:61-1:63, 1:66, 1:72, 2:42, 2:56, 2:60, 3:72; see also evidence patterns
- inevitable| 1:44, 5:47, 5:63, 6:54, 7:27; see also eminent; Expectation; foregone
- likelihood| 1:31, 1:40-1:41, 1:43, 1:46, 2:8, 2:33, 2:38, 2:62, 2:81, 2:90, 3:10, 3:55, 3:58, 3:74, 3:80, 3:93, 3:98, 4:13, 4:19, 4:51, 4:55, 4:60, 4:69, 4:81, 4:96, 4:102, 4:104, 5:40-5:41, 5:45, 5:47, 5:52, 6:23, 7:35; see also confidence level; Forecast; prediction
- no brainer| 5:53; see also absolute; certainties; self-evident
- odd| 1:30, 1:44, 1:47, 2:88, 3:16, 4:6, 5:62-5:63, 6:16, 6:54, 7:6, 7:46; see also contradict; outliers; possibility; unexpected; unexplained
- prediction| i:16, 1:1, 1:42-1:43, 1:68, 2:49, 3:6, 4:25, 4:95, 6:7, 7:4; see also Forecast; Visionary
- random| 2:12, 2:45, 3:21, 3:30, 4:65, 6:51; see also evidence patterns; unstructured information
- unpredictable| 1:42; see also crisis; random; Surprises
- unsure| 1:4, 5:7; see also anxiety; doubters; Indicators; uncertain; unresolved

problem-solving| i:11, i:14, 1:12, 1:15, 1:23, 1:45, 1:60, 2:3, 2:16, 2:90, 2:95, 3:11, 5:66, 7:46-7:47; see also Explanations; Knowledge-ABLED practices; mastering; skills; useful outcomes

Procedures| i:6, i:9, 1:9, 1:11, 1:16, 1:22, 1:69, 2:40, 2:85, 2:90, 3:60, 4:17, 4:70, 4:72, 4:102, 5:9, 6:21, c:3; see also indictment; Legal; methods; protocol; rule-making; sentencing
- Generally Accepted Accounting Principles (GAAP)| 7:21; see also audit
- playbook| i:5, i:7, 1:45, 1:70, 2:15, 2:103, 3:89, 4:11, 4:26, 4:29, 4:38, 4:43-4:44, 4:49, 4:51, 4:90, 4:100, 4:102, 5:11, 5:16, 5:28, 5:30, 5:32, 5:37, 5:45, 5:63-5:65, 6:11-6:12, 6:33, 6:45-6:46, 6:52, 6:56, 7:10, 7:23, 7:28, 7:33, 7:39, 7:43; see also guidelines
- protocol| 3:57, 4:19, 4:37, 5:69; see also Code, of conduct; guidelines; Procedures; rule-making
- standard operating procedure (SOP)| 1:69, 4:26, 5:10, 5:17; see also Management, functions
- task| i:11, i:13, 1:6, 1:26, 1:71, 2:2, 2:4, 2:9, 2:34, 2:66, 2:73, 2:79, 2:107, 3:6, 3:9, 3:22-3:23, 3:31, 3:33, 3:61, 4:40, 4:50, 5:32, 5:40, 5:73, 5:79, 6:2, 6:10-6:11, 6:14, 6:37, 6:43, 7:42, c:4, c:15; see also Management, functions; Procedures; template; workflow

product reviews| 5:41-5:42; see also comparison; cost/benefit; criteria; Evaluation

Professional Investigor (PI)| 1:4, 2:49, 2:54, 2:88, 2:94, 2:101, 4:74, 5:45-5:56; see also Investigations
- public investigation| 4:8; see also exposing corruption

Professionals| 1:4, 1:6, 1:10, 1:13-1:14, 1:16, 1:20, 1:32, 1:37, 1:49, 1:59, 1:65, 1:73, 2:30-2:32, 2:49, 2:54, 2:64-2:65, 2:89, 2:93-2:95, 2:101, 3:6, 3:10, 3:21, 3:25, 3:36, 3:46, 3:76, 3:78, 3:80, 3:86-3:87, 3:91, 3:93, 4:2, 4:5, 4:11-4:12, 4:14, 4:22, 4:29, 4:56, 4:61-4:62, 4:68-4:69, 4:71-4:75, 4:77, 4:79, 4:91, 4:103-4:104, 5:2, 5:27, 5:30, 5:32, 5:43, 5:45-5:48, 5:59, 5:69, 5:75-5:76, 5:79, 6:8, 6:10, 6:12, 6:14, 6:22-6:23, 6:25-6:26, 6:28, 6:52-6:57, 7:7, 7:10-7:12, 7:19, c:10, c:13, c:15; see also acumen; Careers; Jobs; Semantics, finding experts
- administrators| 7:40; see also bureaucrats; inventory; overhead; restrictions
- architect| 1:22, 1:34, 2:26, 2:56, 3:22, 4:62
- archivist| 1:58, 3:86, 4:84, 7:41; see also public records
- behaviorists| 6:22
- business analyst| 2:65, 5:12
- caregiver| 1:23, 1:25, 6:47-6:48, c:2
- Copywriters| 2:106
- Corporate librarians| 5:2; see also Researchers
- economist| i:7, 5:54
- editor| 2:19, 2:86, 2:90, 2:92, 3:92, 4:57, 4:87, 4:93, 5:9, 5:31, 7:9, 7:14, 7:23, 7:33
- engineer| 1:6, 2:50, 2:91, 3:19, 6:55, 7:27; see also programmer
- journalist| 2:21, 2:89, 3:26-3:27, 3:33, 3:62, 3:92, 4:8, 4:38-4:39, 4:43-4:44, 4:67-4:68, 4:75-4:76, 4:91-4:92, 4:97-4:98, 4:106-4:107, 5:9-5:10, 5:25, 6:14, 6:36, 6:56, 7:4, 7:9-7:12, 7:14, 7:20, 7:33, 7:37; see also columnist; deadline; editor; news organizations; Opinion-editorial (op-ed); reporter; scoop
- lobbyist| i:7, 1:6; see also Advocacy; business community; labor; loopholes
- nurse| 1:23, 1:25, 4:77, 7:7; see also healthcare
- physician| 1:10, 2:38, 2:86, 3:22, 4:82, 4:106; see also healthcare
- professors| 1:33, 2:32, 3:26, 4:90; see also Academic; college
- psychotherapist| 4:57; see also Consulting; healthcare
- publicist| 4:94; see also public relations
- scientists| 2:12, 2:50, 3:1, 3:10, 3:59, 3:92, 4:76, 4:87, 5:35, 5:65, 7:7
- therapist| 1:51, 4:12, 4:95, 5:12, 6:20, 6:22, 6:46, 6:52, 6:55; see also advisor; coach; psychotherapist
- trainers| 6:49
- travel agents| 4:58, c:2

programmer| 1:51, 1:58, 1:65, 1:69, 2:9, 2:19-2:20, 2:26, 2:48-2:49, 2:64, 2:70, 2:95, 3:13, 3:23, 4:83, 6:9-6:10, 7:16, 7:40, 7:46, 7:51; see also Code, software; Software Applications

prominence| 1:55, 1:63, 2:12, 2:19, 2:21, 2:28, 2:72, 3:54, 4:101, 4:106; see also aboutness; PageRank; recurrences; Relevance; top-of-mind; Websites, ranking

prone| i:5, 1:20, 1:30, 1:38, 1:53, 2:16, 2:46, 3:63, 3:98, 4:12, 4:19, 4:43, 4:79, 4:95, 4:100, 4:104, 5:36, 6:51, 7:38, 7:46; see also Liabilities; precarious

proof| 1:12, 1:15, 1:36, 1:45, 1:47, 2:6, 4:18-4:19, 4:40, 4:59, 4:87, 5:38, 5:58, 6:16, 6:20, 6:41; see also Evidence; Investigations

propagandist| 7:7, 7:19; see also fake news; Misinformation; Naivete

prophesy| 1:44, 4:102; see also prediction; Visionary

proprietary| 3:4, 3:15, 3:36, 3:76, 4:1, 4:59, 6:21, 7:2, 7:10, 7:27, 7:46, c:7; see also premium content; secret sauce

ProPublica| 7:16; see also Journalism; public investigation

prosecute| 1:14-1:15, 2:62, 4:103, 7:48; see also criminal case; Law Enforcement; Laws; lawyer; trial

protests| 7:28; see also confront; debate; Opposition; Public Policies; vocal

Provider Conjugation Framework (PCF)| 4:8, 4:10-4:12, 4:14, 4:17, 4:31, 4:35-4:40, 4:46-4:48, 4:50-4:58, 4:60, 4:71, 4:73, 4:76, 4:87, 4:89, 4:95, 4:103, 5:6, 5:10, 5:18, 5:25-5:27, 5:31-5:33, 5:62, 7:37; see also first party; first person; second party; second person; third party; third person

Searching Out Loud: Giving Voice to Independent Investigations | Marc Solomon

- singular form| 2:76, 4:10, 6:53-6:54; see also first person; Grammar; Provider Conjugation Framework (PCF); second person; third person
proximity| i:1, 1:27, 1:44, 1:63, 1:71-1:72, 2:12, 2:30, 2:32, 2:37, 2:85, 3:46, 3:48, 3:69, 4:7, 6:4, c:5; see also prominence
Public Awareness| 1:32, 2:35, 3:75-3:76, 3:79, 3:81-3:82, 4:5, 4:32, 5:3, 5:74, 6:8, 6:17, 6:28, 7:5, 7:48; see also attention supply; focus groups; memes; Popularity; Public Opinion; The Biggest Picture (TBP); top-of-mind
- public debate| i:7, 4:27, 5:11, 5:29; see also debate; echo chamber; partisanship
- public discourse| i:6, 1:30, 4:9-4:10, 4:13, 5:29, 7:13; see also continuous partial attention; debate; discussion boards; news feed; Rhetoric
- public figures| 4:1, 4:24, 4:30, 4:32, 4:45, 4:60, 4:98; see also celebrities; entertainers; newsmakers; public officials
- public identity| 2:12, 5:11, 5:19; see also Affiliated; Brand; Personal Identity; Reputations
public domain| 1:41, 2:101, 3:5, 3:16, 3:19, 3:61, 3:87, 4:41, 4:49, 5:10; see also database, government; Free, resources; government websites; Whois
Public Opinion| 1:15, 3:79, 4:20, 4:24, 5:48; see also Campaigns; Elections; Opinion-based; Public Awareness; Surveys
- pulse| 3:78, 4:26, 5:8, 5:32, 5:64, 6:37, 6:57, 7:44; see also public perceptions
- unfavorable| 5:12, 7:7, 7:28; see also negative information; persuasion; poll
Public Policies| 1:15, 3:31, 3:72, 4:31, 4:60, 4:104, 5:14, 7:56; see also Campaigns; equality; Government; Law Enforcement; legislation
- fund| 4:97, 6:35; see also Assets; fundraising; state-funded
- public interest| 1:34, 2:89, 4:48, 4:98, 5:31, 6:12, 7:5, 7:14, 7:21; see also Advocacy; civic; public investigation
- public service| 1:74; see also pro bono; punishment; Vectors of Integrity (VOI)
- state-funded| 6:53
public records| 1:6, 1:49, 1:73-1:74, 3:32, 3:35, 3:68, 3:74-3:75, 3:77, 3:80, 4:74, 5:53, 5:77, 6:12, 7:19, 7:41; see also background checks; Documentation; Milestones
public relations| 2:65, 4:91, 5:37; see also Brand; Reputations; Supply Media; Wire Services
Public Statements| 1:20, 4:3, 4:49; see also formal communication; official
- restatement| 1:49, 5:3, 5:70, 5:78; see also clarifications; Rhetoric
publicly-traded companies| 4:35, 5:9; see also Assets; Commerce; corporate; shareholders; stock market
publishers| i:8, 1:1, 2:23, 3:61, 3:63, 5:8, 5:30-5:31, 5:80, 6:21, 6:29, 7:13-7:14; see also Information Providers
PubMed| 2:88, 2:94; see also Subject Directory
pull and push| 5:10, 5:37, 5:55; see also calculable; Demand-based media; Dichotomies; Supply Media
purge| i:1, 1:34, 1:59, 7:41; see also closure; personal radar; repositories
purpose| i:1, i:4, i:6, i:17, 1:7, 1:11-1:16, 1:19-1:20, 1:24-1:25, 1:32, 1:36, 1:45, 1:59, 1:65, 1:69, 1:73-1:74, 1:76, 2:3, 2:34, 2:63, 2:81, 3:2, 3:5-3:6, 3:16, 3:60, 3:62, 4:11, 4:16, 4:31, 4:41, 4:47, 4:49, 4:69, 4:73, 4:83, 4:86, 4:89, 4:96-4:97, 4:102, 5:2, 5:24, 5:27, 5:34, 5:38-5:39, 5:47, 5:74, 6:2, 6:5, 6:9, 6:17, 6:48, 6:51, 7:7, 7:27; see also clients, motivations; Intentions; objectives; Search Project Management (SPM); theory of mind
pyramid, inverted| 3:96, 4:8, 5:79, c:11; see also Frameworks; institutional credibility; Journalism

Q

qualifications| i:7, 1:2, 1:35, 1:47, 2:1, 2:39, 2:88, 3:2-3:4, 3:26, 3:88, 4:1, 4:75, 4:77, 4:88, 6:8-6:10, 6:14, 6:24, 6:26, 6:28-6:29, 6:39, 6:46, 6:51-6:52, c:7, c:16; see also Explanations; job description; predefine; requirements
Quality Controls| 2:107, 3:2, 3:4, 3:17, 3:50-3:54, 3:57, 3:60-3:61, 3:65, 3:67-3:68, 3:71, 5:56, 6:10, c:7; see also Frameworks; Information Types; Metrics; new-to-known
- big picture| 3:1, 3:51, 3:53, 5:24; see also Perspectives, elevated
- micro level| 3:1, 3:53, 5:24; see also street level
- quantity controls| 3:59-3:62, 3:69; see also Hit Counts; Metrics; new-to-known
- street level| 3:1, 3:53, 5:24, 5:34; see also big picture; lakes
quandary| 1:34, 2:66, 3:48, 5:27; see also Confusion; predicament
query formation| i:10, 1:17, 1:21, 1:45, 1:47, 1:68, 1:76, 2:2-2:7, 2:17, 2:30, 2:39-2:40, 2:45, 2:69, 2:81-2:82, 2:100-2:101, 2:106, 3:3, 3:10, 3:21, 3:30, 3:53, 3:57, 3:70, 4:3, 4:30, 4:70, 4:75-4:76, 4:78, 4:103, 5:1, 5:6-5:8, 5:40, 5:43, 5:51, 5:53, 5:55, 5:69, 6:2-6:3, 6:10, 6:14, 6:16-6:17, 6:28, 6:34-6:35, 7:1, 7:27, 7:34-7:37, 7:39-7:40, 7:42, 7:50, c:3-c:4, c:12; see also advanced search commands; breathe, letting a search; database, differences; search commands; Search Operators; Search Results; Search Within a Search; second pass; Semantics; useful search results; Word Algebra
QueryCat| 2:50; see also FAQs; Subject Directory
Questionable Practices| 1:16, 4:65; see also Case studies; medical malpractice; unprofessional
- unlicensed| 4:62; see also unprofessional
- unprofessional| 4:104; see also ethics
- unqualified| 3:47, 7:6; see also Liabilities; unsubstantiated

R

Radar| 1:7, 1:29, 1:34-1:37, 1:47-1:48, 1:69, 2:2, 2:5, 2:57, 3:4, 3:15-3:16, 3:21, 3:29, 3:38, 3:74-3:75, 3:78, 3:80, 4:45-4:46, 4:48, 4:50, 4:60, 4:75, 4:103, 5:2-5:3, 5:25, 5:31-5:33, 5:35, 5:73, 5:79, 6:42, 6:45, 6:57, 7:22, c:2, c:15; see also event trigger; Paparazzi; Public Awareness; renowned; spotlight; top-of-mind; unofficial; visibility
- internet radar| 4:103; see also The Biggest Picture (TBP)
- monitor| 1:75, 2:87, 3:51, 3:60, 3:71, 4:4, 4:40, 4:75, 5:3, 5:10, 5:29, 6:36, 6:47; see also Alert; event trigger; Exposure
- personal radar| 1:29, 1:34-1:36, 1:47, 2:5, 2:57, 4:76, 5:33-5:34; see also interconnected; Johari Window; news feed; referral
- track| i:5, i:7, 1:2, 1:7, 1:16-1:17, 1:21, 1:26, 1:57, 1:67, 1:71, 1:75-1:76, 2:6, 2:11, 2:33, 2:36, 2:39, 2:53, 2:55, 2:59-2:60, 2:62, 2:68-2:69, 2:71, 2:101, 3:5, 3:11, 3:25, 3:45-3:46, 3:48, 3:60, 3:76-3:78, 3:90-3:91, 4:9, 4:29-4:30, 4:34, 4:42, 4:50, 4:57, 4:64, 4:70, 4:90, 4:92, 4:102, 4:104, 5:10, 5:13, 5:16, 5:19, 5:21, 5:25, 5:31, 5:33-5:34, 5:45, 5:47, 5:52-5:54, 5:68, 5:70, 5:77, 6:9-6:10, 6:12, 6:33-6:39, 6:41, 6:45, 6:53, 7:6, 7:19, 7:34-7:35, 7:49; see also dynamic and static; Unique IDs
raid| 5:43; see also criminal investigation; intrusion; sneak; stakeout
ransomware| 2:25, 7:45; see also backdoor; Internet Security; invasive; malicious site
rant| 5:46, 7:30; see also arguments; Blame; catharsis; diatribes; echo chamber; Expression; monologues; Rhetoric

rare| i:9, 1:6, 1:49, 1:52, 1:68, 2:3, 3:37, 3:56, 3:63, 4:30, 4:40-4:41, 4:61, 4:81, 4:83, 4:97, 5:3, 5:7, 5:9, 5:14, 5:42, 5:46, 6:53, 7:38, 7:42, 7:48; see also anomalies; calculable; Explorations; Scarcity; unexpected

rate| 1:10, 1:13-1:15, 2:15, 2:90, 4:99, 5:22, 6:7, 7:14; see also Evaluation; opinion surveys; rank; scorekeeping

RCA| 5:27; see also Sarnoff, David, Gen.

ready| 1:50, 1:76, 3:34, 4:83, 4:99, 5:4, 5:41, 6:8-6:9, 6:16, 6:45, 6:50; see also planning; research preparations

reality| i:11, 1:6, 1:8, 1:14, 1:20, 2:48, 2:54, 2:56, 2:93, 3:38, 3:58, 3:87, 4:45, 4:62, 4:90, 4:92, 4:100, 4:104, 5:23, 5:35, 5:76, 6:2, 7:4-7:5, 7:16, 7:19, 7:21-7:22, 7:37, c:1; see also Contextual; Interpretations; Perceptions

realization| 1:51, 3:52, 4:65, 4:87, 5:42, 5:70, 6:14, 6:20, 7:2, 7:47; see also discovery; hindsight; Learning

Reason| i:4, i:12, i:15, 1:3, 1:15, 1:33, 1:38, 1:43, 1:45, 1:54, 2:7, 2:27, 2:36, 2:86, 3:6, 3:8, 3:25, 3:74, 3:84, 3:88, 4:18-4:19, 4:25, 4:45, 4:66, 4:85, 4:99-4:101, 5:5, 5:7, 5:24, 5:41, 5:46, 5:50, 5:57, 5:61, 5:63, 5:69, 5:73, 6:21, 6:37, 7:8, 7:29, 7:34, 7:46; see also diagnosis; Explanations; Interpretations; philosophy; Sense-making

 - arguments| i:13, i:18, 1:15, 1:37, 1:39, 1:45, 2:51, 2:100, 2:104, 3:22, 3:24, 3:30, 3:93, 4:16, 4:18, 4:29, 4:36, 4:39-4:40, 4:95, 4:104-4:105, 5:9, 5:25, 5:28, 5:31-5:32, 5:65, 5:72-5:74, 6:43, 7:3-7:4, 7:7-7:8, 7:24, 7:28, 7:36, 7:39-7:40, 7:43-7:44, 7:50-7:51; see also conceivable; conclusive; disputes; persuasion; rationale

 - rationale| 1:15, 1:20, 1:22-1:23, 1:25, 1:27, 1:37-1:38, 1:50, 3:38, 3:61, 4:35, 4:41-4:42, 4:71, 4:73, 4:103, 4:105, 5:2, 5:10, 5:27-5:28, 5:33, 5:42, 5:60, 5:66, 6:16, 7:9, 7:22-7:23, 7:38, 7:40, 7:46; see also Analysis; conceivable; Explanations; inference; Logic

 - reasonable| i:16-i:17, 1:5, 1:10, 1:16, 1:23, 1:37, 1:41, 2:12, 2:101, 3:23, 3:74, 3:90-3:91, 4:6, 4:14, 4:18, 4:35, 4:45, 4:50, 4:86, 4:99, 5:5, 5:16, 5:24, 5:58, 7:3, 7:12, 7:17, c:13; see also clients, hiring a researcher; disinterested; dispassionate

 - reassurance| 1:24, 3:56, 3:92, 5:12; see also defend; job security; Reinforcement

 - sanity| i:12, i:14; see also compromise; dispassionate

 - sensible| 1:10, 1:40, 2:6, 2:40, 2:53, 5:41, 7:3; see also Empirical; modest; sanity

recipients, message| i:14, 1:64, 3:15, 4:6-4:7, 4:9-4:10, 4:33, 4:35-4:36, 4:45, 4:50-4:51, 4:58-4:59, 4:69, 4:86, 4:88, 4:92-4:93, 4:95, 4:98, 4:105, 5:5, 5:25, 5:45, 6:4, 6:6, 7:3, 7:21-7:22, 7:37-7:38, 7:42, c:10; see also attention demand; Information Providers; messagers; Perspectives; sender

Recognition| i:16, 1:30, 1:46, 1:65, 2:3, 2:72, 3:12, 3:34, 3:72, 4:96, 4:103, 5:27, 6:20, 7:4, c:4; see also admirers; award; celebrities; ceremonies; credit; Fame; opinion-maker; renowned

 - deserve| 4:62, 4:93, 5:1, 5:35, 5:75; see also award; honor; merit

 - merit| i:2, 1:6, 1:9, 1:38, 2:107, 3:3, 3:62, 3:96, 4:16, 4:18, 4:38, 4:48, 4:55, 4:73, 4:88, 4:92-4:93, 4:105, 5:22, 5:42, 5:75, 6:29, 7:4; see also Contest; deserve; reward

 - prizes| 1:39, 3:27, 3:31, 5:8, 5:31, 6:29, 6:41; see also Contest; Recognition

recommendations| i:13-i:14, 1:21, 3:10, 3:14, 3:20, 3:24, 4:74, 4:83, 5:1, 5:26, 5:40, 5:68, 5:70, c:13; see also projects, client presentations; projects, client recommendations

reconcile| 2:39, 3:10, 4:51, 4:66, 4:91, 5:32; see also Negotiations; rationale

recording| 1:10, 1:51, 1:53, 1:58, 1:62, 1:70, 2:5, 2:63, 3:5, 3:9, 3:22, 3:48, 4:8, 4:13, 4:87, 5:42, 5:46; see also archives; Documentation; History

Reddit| 4:85, 5:51, 5:54, 6:37; see also crowdsourcing; curatorship

referee| 3:62, 4:43; see also arbiter; Contest; Law Enforcement; unbiased

referral| 1:4, 1:20, 1:23, 1:25, 1:33, 1:38, 1:62, 1:73, 2:29, 2:88, 3:15, 3:21, 3:23, 3:29, 3:93, 4:5, 4:15, 4:60, 4:74, 4:82, 4:88, 5:35, 5:42, 6:36, 7:12, 7:30, 7:42-7:43, c:11; see also endorse; personal connections; Search to Converse (STC)

refinement| 1:70, 2:8, 2:40-2:41, c:4; see also Filtering; pearl culturing

reflexive| 4:43, 5:60; see also Contrarian; impulse; opposite

registrations| 2:26-2:27, 2:89, 3:29-3:30, 3:46, 4:82, 4:84, 5:36, 6:34, 7:36; see also IP address; public filings; Regulations; Websites, ownership; Whois

Regulations| 4:34; see also administrators; cost/benefit; Government; restrictions; rule-making

 - compliance| 3:71; see also Agreement; cooperation; Legal; precedence; tax

 - Department of Justice (DOJ)| 7:42

 - Environmental Protection Agency (EPA)| 7:41; see also climate change; federal; Regulations

 - Food and Drug Administration (FDA)| 6:14

 - guidelines| 2:4, 2:48, 3:61, 3:73, 4:17, 5:69, 5:80, 6:48, 7:38, 7:51, c:3; see also Code, of conduct; instruct; protocol; social norms

 - Internal Revenue Service (IRS)| 5:77; see also tax

 - National Oceanic and Atmospheric Administration (NOAA)| 3:83

 - oversight| 3:91, 4:29; see also guidelines

 - public agencies| i:14, 1:34, 1:73, 2:88-2:89, 2:94, 2:98, 3:50, 3:66, 4:29, 4:34, 4:43, 4:47-4:48, 4:73, 5:12, 5:29, 5:31, 5:76, 6:57; see also Law Enforcement; public hearing; watchdogs

 - public filings| 6:11, 6:23; see also Documentation

 - public health| 5:15; see also Center for Disease Control (CDC)

 - Securities and Exchange Commission (SEC)| 3:83; see also monetary

 - United States Drug Administration (USDA)| 5:19

 - unregulated| 2:66, 3:86, 3:90-3:91, 4:100; see also business community; conservative; disparity; lobbying; Power Structures

Reinforcement| 1:10, 2:30-2:31, 2:35, 2:63, 2:95, 3:22, 3:69, 4:32, 4:35, 4:58, 5:60, 5:71, 6:45, 7:22-7:23, 7:39, 7:48, 7:50; see also decisive; Influences; reassurance

 - echo chamber| 4:67, 7:22-7:23, 7:36; see also filter bubbles; Pariser, Eli; partisanship; pundit; redundant

 - reaffirm| i:1, 5:50

 - redundant| 1:34, 3:24, 5:48; see also Internet Security; rehash; Reinforcement

Reis, George (case study)| 6:7-6:8, 6:10-6:11, 6:15, 6:45, 6:51, c:17; see also Information Traps; RSS (Really Simple Syndication)

Reject| 1:68, 5:53, 7:14, 7:24; see also arguments; derail; detractors; discredit; Resistance

 - defiance| i:11-i:13, 1:41, 1:43-1:44, 1:69, 2:2, 2:6, 2:53, 3:17, 3:77, 4:22, 4:98, 5:38, 5:63; see also confront; protests; rally; Resistance; vocal

 - disengagement| 5:32; see also disenfranchised

 - dismiss| 1:35, 1:41, 3:16, 3:50, 4:23, 4:42, 5:59, 7:50

 - dissension| i:2-i:3, 4:18, 4:22, 4:40, 4:96; see also Grievance

 - eliminate| 1:61, 2:15-2:16, 2:29, 2:76, 3:90, 5:6, 7:2

COMPLETE WORKS: Units One Through Seven | Unabridged Index:34

Relatedness| 1:13, 1:17, 1:28, 1:32, 1:56, 1:67, 1:71, 1:73, 2:6, 2:8, 2:11-2:12, 2:17, 2:23, 2:25, 2:35, 2:37, 2:47, 2:49, 2:57, 2:59-2:60, 2:63, 2:65, 2:67, 2:69, 2:76, 2:86, 2:90, 2:95, 2:98, 2:101, 2:103, 3:3, 3:7, 3:13, 3:17-3:19, 3:30, 3:48, 3:60, 3:63, 3:72-3:73, 4:7-4:8, 4:15, 4:17, 4:23, 4:25, 4:32, 4:71, 4:82, 5:14, 5:45, 5:47-5:48, 5:50, 5:52, 5:55, 6:4, 6:9, 6:12, 6:25, 6:28, 7:29, 7:36, 7:50; see also Affiliated; correlation; Dichotomies; strength of association; theory of mind
 - bond| 1:25, 1:58, 2:86, 3:13, 3:50, 4:8, 4:12, 4:18, 4:74, 5:9, 5:63, 7:51; see also allegiance
 - dependent| i:2, i:16, 3:4-3:5, 4:29, 4:31, 4:36, 4:42, 4:68, 4:90, 5:5, 5:26, 5:30, 5:42, 5:76, 6:4, 6:6, 6:52, 7:4, 7:10, 7:33, 7:43, 7:50, c:3, c:13; see also Liabilities
  - hierarchy| 2:95; see also database, structure; ingrained; inherited
  - inclusion| 1:22, 2:9, 2:14, 2:18, 2:22, 2:42, 2:86, 3:36, 4:66, 7:25; see also OR operator
  - inherited| 7:30; see also family roots; hierarchy
  - interdependency| 4:34, 4:41, 7:44; see also cross-reference; multi-dimensional
  - resemblance| 2:32, 5:73, 7:35; see also comparison; connectedness; Family; Pattern Matching; similar
  - strength of association| 1:66-1:67, 1:75, 2:7, 2:65, 3:14, 5:11, 5:18, 5:35; see also connectedness; prominence; proximity; pulse; social circles
  - well-connected| 1:4, 4:105, 5:41, 7:20; see also Influences; social circles; strength of association
  - wired| 1:29, 4:40; see also Cognitive; Intuitions
Relevance| 1:61, 1:64, 2:36, 4:100; see also algorithms; Hit Counts; PageRank; prominence; sorting
  - aboutness| 2:40, 2:84, 2:93, 3:22, 5:51; see also Quality Controls; searchable; Sense-making
  - irrelevance| 2:15, 2:32, 2:43, 3:18, 3:72, 4:47, 5:48, 6:48, 7:2, 7:36; see also bogus; False hit; machine-based limitations
reliance| 1:2, 2:2, 2:12, 2:50, 2:67, 2:85, 3:7, 3:10, 3:25, 3:83, 3:87, 3:98, 4:13, 4:30, 4:35, 4:43, 4:104-4:105, 5:24, 5:27, 5:39, 5:42, 5:54, 5:57, 6:45, 7:4, 7:11, 7:21, 7:28, 7:33, 7:47; see also dependent; faith; Liabilities; loyalties; steadfast
renewable| i:3, 1:23, 3:16, 4:76; see also containing costs; leverage; reusable
reporter| 2:12, 2:72, 3:52, 3:98, 4:7, 4:9, 4:32-4:33, 4:57, 4:67, 4:90, 4:94, 4:96, 5:9-5:10, 5:37, 5:70, 6:56, 7:7, 7:10-7:11, 7:23, 7:36, 7:40, 7:45; see also deadline; disseminate; journalist; scoop; second party
repositories| 3:74, 5:50, 6:12, 7:2, 7:40; see also big data; cloud computing; public records
Reputations| 1:4, 1:6, 1:49, 2:64-2:65, 3:18, 3:60, 3:89-3:90, 3:93, 4:5, 4:26, 4:29, 4:66, 4:72, 4:97, 5:3, 5:12, 5:14, 5:16, 5:18, 5:28, 5:34-5:35, 5:54, 5:58, 6:4, 6:47, 6:56, 7:6, c:11; see also admirers; Brand; Perceptions; respect; Trust
 - cachet| 4:70, 5:38, 6:30, c:10; see also brand stature; charisma; Influences
 - establishment| 1:2, 1:27, 1:35, 1:38, 1:43-1:44, 1:64, 2:1, 2:3, 2:63, 2:85, 2:87, 3:7, 3:31, 3:34, 3:56, 3:63-3:64, 3:76, 3:87-3:89, 4:1-4:2, 4:36, 4:47, 4:56-4:57, 4:69, 4:100, 4:102, 5:9-5:10, 5:13, 5:16, 5:23, 5:28, 5:34, 5:37-5:39, 5:45, 5:52, 5:64-5:65, 5:68-5:69, 5:73, 6:3, 6:8, 6:10, 6:12-6:14, 6:19-6:20, 6:50-6:51, 6:53, 7:6, 7:8, 7:13, 7:21, 7:31, 7:39, c:3, c:6, c:9; see also premise; quid pro quo
 - Reputation, company| 2:64-2:65, 5:13, 5:15, 5:17, 5:36, 5:38; see also Brand; The Biggest Picture (TBP)
 - Reputation, information providers| 3:19, 3:90, 6:4, 7:6; see also Information Providers
 - tainted| 4:91, 5:28; see also Liabilities; Perceptions; tampering
requirements| i:1, i:6, i:9-i:13, i:15, 1:2, 1:9, 1:12, 1:17-1:20, 1:24-1:25, 1:33, 1:39, 1:42, 1:53, 1:67-1:69, 1:73, 2:7, 2:13, 2:15, 2:32, 2:39, 2:44-2:45, 2:47, 2:49, 2:60, 2:76, 2:93, 2:101, 3:1, 3:15, 3:17-3:18, 3:20, 3:22, 3:25, 3:27, 3:29, 3:32, 3:35-3:36, 3:48, 3:50, 3:52-3:54, 3:75, 3:77-3:78, 3:81, 3:85, 3:88, 4:2, 4:4, 4:9, 4:12, 4:26, 4:36, 4:40, 4:48, 4:58, 4:65, 4:67, 4:77, 4:86, 4:90, 4:105, 5:12, 5:24, 5:28, 5:30, 5:39, 5:41, 5:44, 5:69-5:72, 5:75, 6:8-6:11, 6:13, 6:23, 6:33-6:34, 6:37, 6:41, 6:47, 6:51, 7:4, 7:7, 7:16, 7:18-7:19, 7:25-7:26, 7:36, 7:38, 7:44-7:46, 7:49, c:16; see also assumptions
Research Projects| i:10, 1:1, 1:3, 1:7-1:8, 1:11-1:12, 4:53, 6:2, 6:9, c:2, c:9; see also blindspots; Clients; Continuum, the Knowledge; cross-reference; detachment; disinterest; Frameworks; Overview; Search Project Management (SPM)
 - projects, client benefits| 1:13-1:14, 3:14, 3:26, 5:3, 5:10, 5:20, 5:24, 5:35, 5:43, 5:63; see also clients, added value
 - projects, client billables| 1:52, 3:15, 5:8, 5:59, 5:66-5:77; see also clients, financial incentive
 - projects, client documentation| 1:10, 5:69, 5:78; see also Search Project Management (SPM)
 - projects, client presentations| 1:10, 1:50, 3:4, 4:71, 4:73, 5:5-5:6, 5:57, 5:69, 5:71; see also agenda; Overview
 - projects, client recommendations| 1:2-1:3, 1:47, 3:4, 5:7-5:8, 5:19, 5:29, 5:57, 5:59, 5:62, 5:66; see also clients, validation
 - projects, client reports| 1:3, 3:25, 3:91, 4:8, 5:14, 5:80, c:12; see also clients, project delivery
 - projects, clients expectations| i:14, 1:12, 1:15-1:16, 1:20, 1:40, 1:47, 2:39, 5:13, 5:58, 5:60-5:62, 5:71, 5:77; see also clients, project trust
Researchbuzz| 2:106; see also Calishain, Tara; research blog
Researchers| i:7-i:8, i:10, 1:1, 1:4-1:6, 1:8, 1:10, 1:15, 1:17, 1:20, 1:23, 1:29, 1:31-1:32, 1:36, 1:39, 1:41, 1:43, 1:45, 1:51, 1:61, 1:65, 1:67, 1:69-1:70, 1:72, 2:3, 2:12, 2:20, 2:23, 2:39, 2:44, 2:48, 2:53, 2:63, 2:67, 2:95, 3:1, 3:5, 3:11-3:13, 3:22, 3:31, 3:36-3:37, 3:63-3:64, 3:77, 3:82-3:83, 3:86-3:87, 3:89, 4:1, 4:4, 4:9, 4:15, 4:17, 4:30-4:31, 4:36, 4:56-4:59, 4:62, 4:85-4:87, 5:2, 5:5, 5:25, 5:42, 5:45, 5:48, 5:57-5:59, 5:62, 5:65, 5:69, 5:71, 5:77, 5:80-6:1, 6:6-6:7, 6:19-6:20, 6:30, 6:33-6:34, 6:51-6:52, 7:4, 7:42-7:43, 7:45-7:46, c:2, c:9, c:15; see also Cost of Research; Knowledge-ABLED; Knowledge-ABLED practices
 - research preparations| i:1, 1:8, 1:26, 1:40, 1:54, 2:1, 2:25, 2:75, 3:5, 3:28, 3:60, 4:12, 4:44, 5:3, 5:5, 5:7, 5:15, 5:61, 6:1, 6:4, 6:23, 6:45; see also agenda; Continuum, the Knowledge; search logs; Search Project Management (SPM)
 - searcher| i:11, 1:9, 1:24, 1:26, 1:62-1:63, 1:66, 2:59, 2:69, 2:74, 3:10-3:11, 3:27, 3:50, 3:52, 3:76, 3:93, 4:108, 6:16; see also discovery; Knowledge-ABLED; literacy, information
 - unbiased| 7:38; see also detachment; dispassionate; Perspectives, research
Resistance| i:12-i:13, 1:8, 1:20, 1:26, 1:33, 1:39-1:41, 2:27, 2:34, 2:65, 2:99, 3:57, 3:63, 3:82, 4:43, 4:84, 4:95, 4:98, 4:108, 5:12, 5:29, 5:39-5:40, 5:70, 5:77, 6:14, 7:8, 7:23, 7:28, 7:39; see also block; confront; dismiss; Opposition; pitchforks; Reject
 - block| 1:28, 2:55, 3:1, 3:22, 3:37, 4:1, 4:11, 4:19, 4:34, 4:55, 4:57, 5:34, 5:40, 5:72, 6:3, 6:7-6:8, 7:1, c:15; see also derail; dismiss; prevention; Stop
 - confront| 1:10, 1:25, 1:44, 3:11, 5:65, 7:31-7:32; see also Grievance; Opposition; pitchforks; Resistance
 - denials| 3:48, 4:18, 7:37, 7:43; see also 404 error; Contrarian; Denial of Service (DNS); elusive
 - derail| 1:45; see also detractors; sabotage; sandbag; Stop; subversion; undermine
 - Fight-or-flight| 7:28; see also aggression; combat; confront; Dichotomies; retreat
 - outrage| 4:92; see also angry; Expression; grudge; righteous
 - overcome| 1:67, 2:16, 2:29, 2:43, 3:8-3:9, 3:11, 3:37, 4:65, 4:97, 5:72, 6:8, c:5; see also obstacles; prevailing; struggle
 - persist| i:15, 1:40, 2:29, 2:49, 4:74, 4:79, 5:22, 5:41, 6:2, 7:4, 7:28; see also dedicated; overcome; time commitment

Searching Out Loud: Giving Voice to Independent Investigations | Marc Solomon

- quit| 1:1-1:2, 1:17, 3:36, 3:47; see also defeat; dismiss; prevention; resignation; Stop; succumb; surrender
- refuted| 3:11; see also arguments; counterclaim; debate; disprove
- unforgiving| 5:41; see also grudge; resentment; revenge; spite
- vengeance| 4:75, 7:38, 7:51; see also Motives; revenge; spite
- vigilance| 1:44, 4:91, 7:7; see also Opposition; prevention; revenge

resolution| i:13, i:16, 1:2, 1:13, 1:20, 1:22, 1:24, 1:37, 1:39-1:40, 1:45, 1:73, 2:62, 3:20, 3:25, 3:36, 4:38, 4:40, 4:42, 5:11-5:12, 5:70, 5:72, 7:16, 7:39, 7:42; see also closure; conclusive; Explanations

resonate| 1:47, 3:19, 5:4, 5:29, 5:36, 5:42, 5:71, 7:8, 7:16, 7:22, 7:24; see also Actions and Outcomes; convince; Memory; persuasion; retain

resourceful| i:12, 1:2, 1:5-1:6, 1:74, 2:72, 3:13, 3:30, 3:36, 4:11, 5:59, c:12; see also Knowledge-ABLED

respect| i:5, 1:19, 2:68, 2:95, 4:18, 4:54, 4:102, 5:28, 5:31, 5:52, 7:28-7:29, 7:39; see also admirers; Agreement; deference; honor; Influences; mutual; persuasion; reciprocal; Reputations; Trust

restrictions| 1:68, 2:18, 2:20-2:21, 2:24, 2:26-2:27, 3:29, 3:64, 3:69, 4:52, 5:34, 5:40, 5:71, 5:80, 6:41, 6:51, 7:2; see also Code, limitations; machine-based limitations; rule-making; technology, limitations; threshold

retool| 5:24, 6:21, 7:14; see also adult; Careers; Learning; rebrand; skills; trained

retreat| 4:90, 5:72, 7:10; see also Conflict; defeat; Perceptions; surrender; warfare

retrieval| 1:55, 1:66, 2:19-2:22, 2:25-2:26, 2:42, 3:11, 3:16, 3:84, 5:76; see also anatomy of a query; database, searching; Findability; Search Results

reusable| 1:21, 4:19, 6:21; see also leverage; renewable

Rhetoric| 4:7, 4:42-4:43, 5:46, 5:64, 7:18; see also Campaigns; esoteric; Expression; Influences; opinion-maker; pandering; persuasion; polemic; Public Awareness; public discourse

- demagoguery| 4:95; see also Misinformation; persuasion; Power Structures
- downplay| 4:60; see also diversion
- irony| 1:1, 1:33, 1:65, 3:47, 3:71, 3:87, 4:6, 4:14, 4:16, 5:16, 5:22, 5:41; see also Contrarian; hypocrisy; Motives; Surprises; unexpected; unintended
- marginalize| 4:79, 4:104, 7:6-7:7, 7:10, 7:19-7:20, 7:51; see also impersonal; Prejudice; Rhetoric
- monologues| 4:87, 5:12; see also Interactions; irony
- phrase| 1:49, 1:55, 1:59, 1:63, 1:70-1:71, 1:75, 2:6, 2:9-2:15, 2:17, 2:19, 2:21, 2:25-2:27, 2:30-2:31, 2:34, 2:37-2:38, 2:40-2:43, 2:47, 2:52, 2:54, 2:59, 2:63, 2:98, 3:7, 3:11-3:12, 3:30, 4:7, 4:31, 4:83, 4:100, 5:52-5:53, 6:3, 6:16, 6:41, 6:49, 6:51, 7:36; see also pointers; Semantics
- quote| 1:71, 2:15, 2:17, 2:20-2:21, 2:37, 2:43, 2:59, 3:52, 3:61, 3:63, 3:69, 3:98, 4:58-4:59, 4:91, 5:34; see also paraphrase; proverbial; Public Statements; tweet
- smear| 4:105, 7:29; see also slander; unsubstantiated

Rice, Condoleeza| 2:44; see also 9-11 report

right brain| 5:65-5:67; see also brain, left and right

righteous| 4:48, 7:23; see also Beliefs; hate; otherness; passion; Perceptions; piety

Risks| i:6, 1:12, 1:19, 1:29, 1:34, 1:43, 2:38, 2:65, 3:12, 3:14, 3:33, 3:50, 3:86-3:87, 3:89, 4:41, 4:45, 4:47, 4:53, 4:74, 4:85, 4:87, 4:90-4:91, 4:97-4:98, 4:100, 4:104, 5:2-5:4, 5:16, 5:24, 5:34-5:35, 5:39, 5:58, 5:60-5:61, 5:65-5:66, 5:75, 6:13, 6:22-6:23, 6:33, 7:46, 7:48, c:12; see also black swan; Disasters; Liabilities; personal injury; precarious; prevention; Probabilities; threats

- harm| 1:2, 4:91, 4:96, 7:51; see also dangerous; Disasters
- hazard| 1:6, 1:20, 7:44; see also Liabilities
- minefields| 1:24, 1:71, 4:105, 5:60; see also Complex Context; vulnerability
- peril| i:5, 4:29, 5:8; see also dangerous; hazard
- poisoning| 4:65, 7:19; see also food preparation; hazard; tainted; toxic
- toxic| 5:64; see also hazard; poisoning
- unguarded| 2:71, 7:29; see also embarrassing; trespasses; vulnerability; Weakness
- unrecoverable| 4:8, 5:2, 5:73; see also archives; closure; steal

roadmaps| 1:7-1:10, 2:7, 4:84, 5:68-5:69, 6:45; see also agenda; management consulting; planning; search logs; strategy

Roles| i:7, i:11, i:15, 1:3, 1:27, 1:33, 1:43, 1:70, 1:72, 1:74, 2:11, 2:21, 2:56, 2:107, 3:6, 3:62-3:63, 3:66, 3:89, 4:2, 4:4, 4:8, 4:10-4:12, 4:14-4:15, 4:17, 4:19, 4:26, 4:33, 4:35-4:36, 4:40-4:42, 4:48-4:51, 4:56-4:57, 4:59, 4:66, 4:73, 4:79, 4:86, 4:92, 4:97, 4:102-4:103, 4:105, 5:1, 5:17, 5:27, 5:30, 5:40-5:41, 5:47, 5:75, 6:10, 6:28, 6:33, 6:35, 6:49, 6:54-6:55, 7:3, 7:9-7:13, 7:15, 7:20-7:22, 7:26, 7:29-7:30, 7:39, 7:48-7:49, c:2, c:4, c:10-c:11; see also Character Traits; Expectation; Narratives; personas; Storyteller; theme

- Cassandra| 1:41; see also disbelieving; doomsday; prophesy
- coach| 2:15, 4:12, 4:32, 6:49; see also clients, motivations; Consulting
- culprit| i:5, 1:7, 1:28, 1:43, 4:95, c:2; see also perpetrate; suspects; villains
- devil| i:16, 1:20, 4:44; see also evil; Forbidden; sins
- layperson| 1:58, 2:32, 2:93, 3:17, 3:25, 3:54, 3:98, 5:7, 5:40, 5:68, 6:25; see also grassroots; User
- pariah| 1:41; see also ostracism; otherness
- personality| 4:102, 4:105, 5:1, 7:18; see also ego; ingrained; personas; predisposed
- personas| 7:5; see also Behaviors; Character Traits; psychological
- role model| 4:51, 4:56, 7:29; see also Character Traits; Reputations; resemblance
- villains| 7:6, 7:29, 7:39; see also Accusations; actions of others; Blame; conspiracies; Criminal; culprit; enemy

roles and responsibilities| i:7, i:15, 3:64, 4:3, 4:12, 4:34, 4:50; see also dedicated; horizontal business functions; Management, functions

Rollyo| 2:70, 2:74-2:75; see also curatorship; Discontinued Websites and Tools

Romney, Mitt| 4:40

Root| 1:12, 1:14, 1:29, 1:35, 1:40, 1:68, 1:71, 2:7, 2:18, 2:20, 2:23-2:24, 2:36, 2:104, 3:7-3:8, 3:13, 3:34, 3:53, 3:56, 3:70, 4:22-4:23, 4:37, 4:58, 4:65, 4:77, 4:88, 5:23, 5:80, 6:4, 6:31, 7:13, 7:32; see also fundamental; Origin; Source Fluency

- root cause| 1:14; see also Evaluation; passion; trace
- root directory| 2:18, 2:20, 2:24; see also Subject Directory
- site roots| 1:71, 2:23, 3:8-3:10, 3:54, 3:57-3:58, 3:71, 4:78, 5:24, 6:4; see also Link analysis; URLs
- word roots| 1:68, 2:7, 2:36, 6:31; see also Grammar; Term Expansion

Roth, Philip| 2:97

COMPLETE WORKS: Units One Through Seven | Unabridged Index:36

RSS (Really Simple Syndication)| 2:29, 2:35-2:36, 2:53, 3:63, 3:72, 4:75, 4:79, 5:26, 5:33, 5:42, 5:47-5:52, 5:55, 5:73, 6:12, 6:33-6:34, 6:36-6:37, 6:39, 6:43, 6:45-6:46, 6:49, 6:51, 6:57, c:10, c:16; see also event trigger; Feed Demon; Feed reader; Information Traps; news feed; Reis, George (case study); Search Engine, Custom (CSE)

rule-making| i:2, i:14-i:15, 1:8, 1:24, 1:37, 1:65, 1:68, 1:74, 2:9, 2:32, 2:37, 2:92, 2:101, 3:4, 3:11, 3:37-3:38, 3:50, 3:73, 4:19, 4:33-4:34, 4:36, 4:42, 4:46, 4:70, 4:77, 4:88, 4:96, 4:100, 4:102, 5:8, 5:64, 5:72, 5:77, 7:17, 7:25, 7:37, 7:50, c:7; see also legal proceeding; precedence; protocol; Regulations; restrictions

Rumsfeld, Donald | 1:29; see also known knowns; known unknowns; Unknown Knowns; Unknown Unknowns

Russia| 7:30, 7:38, 7:53, 7:55

S

salary| 5:43, 6:11; see also Careers; job offers; pecking order

sample| 1:61, 1:68, 3:12, 3:70, 4:43, 5:8-5:11, 5:13-5:15, 5:23, 5:28-5:29, 5:35, 5:42, 5:59, 6:14, 6:20, 6:24; see also comparison; outliers; scientific method; Surveys

Samsung| 2:35

Sarnoff, David, Gen.| 5:28; see also 1939 New York World's Fair

Saturday Evening Post| 7:8; see also pre-social media

scammers| i:14, 2:13, 2:16, 2:37, 4:32, 4:98-4:100; see also email; fraud; Internet Security; trollers; urban legends

Scandals| 1:21, 2:93, 3:79, 4:26, 4:33, 4:84, 5:17, 5:22, c:10; see also Conflicts of interest; controversial; Corruption; embarrassing; fraud; hypocrisy; Misinformation; negative information; public investigation; tainted

  - hoax| 2:37, 4:32, 7:38; see also controversial; Deceptions; fraud; Scandals
  - public scrutiny| 4:49, 4:56, 4:93, 5:17, c:11; see also controversial; exposing corruption; public investigation

Scarcity| i:3-i:4, 1:5-1:6, 3:2, 4:43, 4:57, 4:89, 5:31, 6:9, 7:24, c:6; see also deficit and surpluses; supply and demand; unmet

  - deficiencies| 1:34; see also Liabilities; vulnerability; Weakness
  - shortage| 1:4, 5:53, 6:42; see also gap; poverty; rare

scenarios| 1:26-1:28, 1:39, 2:55-2:56, 3:45-3:46, 3:58, 3:60, 4:25, 4:51, 5:17, 5:52, 5:66, 7:24; see also Case studies; Roles; sample

scholarship| i:18, 3:33, 3:50, 3:83; see also academics; Empirical; Learning

SCIRUS| 6:12, 6:24; see also Internet Public Library (IPL); Subject Directory

scorekeeping| i:13, i:16, 1:75, 2:39, 2:57, 2:65, 3:25, 3:36, 3:76, 4:18, 4:52, 4:67, 4:80, 4:93, 4:102, 5:6-5:7, 5:10, 5:16, 5:22-5:23, 5:28-5:29, 5:37, 7:21, 7:29, 7:44, 7:46; see also baseline; benchmark; intensity; Metrics; quantity controls

scrolling| 2:46, 2:104, 7:2; see also layout; navigation; User Experience (UX); User Interface (UI); webpage

search commands| 2:4-2:5, 2:13-2:14, 3:8, 5:34, c:3, c:5; see also advanced search commands; query formation; Search Operators

Search Engine Marketing (SEM)| 3:65, 6:12; see also advertising; duopoly; SEO (Search Engine Optimization)

search index| 1:62, 1:66, 1:71, 2:12, 2:86, 2:99, 2:103, 3:10, 3:57, 3:82, 4:85, 5:4; see also anatomy of a query; database, index; database, size; Websites, cache

search logs| 1:9, 1:12, 1:21-1:24, 1:26, 2:3, 2:5-2:6, 2:26, 2:40, 2:66, 2:71, 3:6, 3:38, 3:61, 4:48, 4:74, 4:88, 5:2, 5:70, 5:77, 6:6, 7:39-7:40, 7:42, c:2, c:13; see also failsafes; planning; Search Project Management (SPM); sequential; template

Search Operators| i:10, 1:26, 1:62-1:63, 1:66, 1:75, 2:4-2:7, 2:9, 2:11, 2:13-2:18, 2:22, 2:40-2:41, 2:57, 2:59, 2:76, 2:81, 2:101, 3:12, 3:20, 4:72, 5:77, 6:1-6:2, 7:1, c:3-c:5; see also Boolean logic; exclude; inclusion; query formation; search commands; Syntax

  - AND operator| 2:14; see also Boolean logic
  - asterisk| 1:68, 2:9-2:11, 2:36, 2:38, 2:59, 5:53, 5:80; see also Search Operators; Term Expansion; wildcard
  - negation| 2:11, 2:15; see also exclude; minus sign
  - OR operator| 2:18, 2:22
  - Search operators, exclusion| 2:15, 2:19-2:20, 2:22, 2:37, 2:76
  - tilde (squiggly)| 2:11; see also Term Expansion

Search Project Management (SPM)| 1:7-1:13, 1:15-1:18, 1:21-1:27, 1:41, 1:43, 1:45-1:47, 1:53, 1:59, 3:24, 3:36, 3:52, 4:3, 4:41, 4:69-4:70, 4:72, 5:4, 5:68, 5:77, 6:1, 6:10, 6:14, 6:34, 6:48, 7:33, c:1-c:2, c:13, c:16; see also clients, project delivery; failsafes; Frameworks; integrate, findings; projects, client documentation; Research Projects

Search Results| i:1, i:5, i:11, i:13, i:16, 1:4, 1:7, 1:10, 1:16, 1:21, 1:26, 1:29, 1:46-1:47, 1:52, 1:56, 1:61-1:63, 1:67-1:69, 1:71, 1:75-1:76, 2:2-2:3, 2:5-2:7, 2:10, 2:12, 2:15-2:17, 2:21, 2:24, 2:28, 2:33, 2:36-2:47, 2:52, 2:54-2:55, 2:57, 2:60-2:61, 2:66, 2:72-2:74, 2:86-2:87, 2:92, 2:95, 2:99, 3:1-3:3, 3:5-3:8, 3:12, 3:14, 3:16, 3:23, 3:25, 3:27, 3:38, 3:51-3:52, 3:54-3:57, 3:65, 3:67, 3:69-3:71, 3:86, 3:91-3:92, 3:94, 3:97, 4:1-4:2, 4:4, 4:46, 4:87, 4:95, 4:98, 4:100-4:103, 5:1, 5:8, 5:27, 5:32, 5:40, 5:51, 5:53-5:54, 5:59, 5:71, 5:74, 5:77, 6:9-6:10, 6:12, 6:14, 6:16, 6:21, 6:30, 6:34, 6:39, 6:43, 7:35-7:36, 7:47, c:5, c:7, c:13; see also ordering, search results; Quality Controls; query formation; recurrences; Relevance

  - metasearch results| 2:58-2:59; see also Search Engine, Metasearch
  - result list| 2:84, 3:55; see also ordering, search results
  - search defaults| 2:41, 4:3, 6:9, 7:35; see also default, browser settings; default, privacy settings
  - Search Within a Search| 1:56, 1:69, 2:42-2:43, 2:73, 2:76, 5:55, 6:34, 6:39; see also Filtering; pearl culturing; refinement
  - searchable| 1:56, 2:3, 2:72, 2:92, 3:30-3:31, 3:38, 3:83-3:85, 4:61, 5:41, 6:27; see also aboutness; categorizing, searchable groupings; Findability
  - set results| 2:43; see also Search Within a Search; second pass

Search Targets| i:8-i:9, 1:6-1:7, 1:9, 1:12, 1:17-1:18, 1:21-1:22, 1:29, 1:31, 1:36, 1:49, 1:70, 1:75, 2:9, 2:13, 2:25, 2:31-2:32, 2:34-2:35, 2:37, 2:47, 2:49, 2:52, 2:57, 2:64, 2:95, 3:6-3:7, 3:15, 3:49, 3:59, 3:70, 3:77, 3:90-3:91, 4:1-4:2, 4:4, 4:6, 4:29, 4:31-4:32, 4:34-4:35, 4:45-4:46, 4:48, 4:52-4:58, 4:60, 4:71, 4:73, 4:76, 4:104-4:105, 5:10-5:11, 5:14-5:15, 5:20, 5:24, 5:27, 5:34, 5:47, 5:56, 5:67, 5:69, 5:71, 5:80, 6:3, 6:16-6:17, 7:2, 7:17-7:18, 7:25, 7:29, 7:31-7:32, 7:35, 7:38, 7:46-7:47, c:2-c:3, c:5, c:9, c:11, c:14-c:15; see also accuracy; finding people; Search Within a Search

  - micro-targeting| 7:18; see also customer; personal data; Websites, traffic
  - targeted| 2:63, 2:67, 3:2, 3:69, 4:70, 5:54, 6:34, 6:38, 6:47, 7:18, 7:31, c:6; see also monitor; Radar; Search Targets; watch list

Search to Converse (STC)| 1:54, 4:79, 5:71; see also debrief; Frameworks; interview; social circles

Search Tools| i:15, 1:12, 1:17, 1:21, 1:27, 1:29, 1:41, 1:52, 1:55-1:56, 1:59, 1:65, 1:68, 1:70-1:71, 2:1-2:2, 2:5, 2:9, 2:24, 2:39, 2:41, 2:45, 2:49, 2:65, 2:73-2:74, 2:88, 2:100, 3:4, 3:8, 3:12-3:14, 3:26, 3:28, 3:47-3:48, 3:51, 3:83-3:84, 4:6, 4:36, 5:2, 5:34, 6:2, 6:6, 6:10, 6:14, 6:27, 7:3, c:11; see also Oceans, Lakes, and Ponds (OLP); tools for the job

Searching Out Loud: Giving Voice to Independent Investigations | Marc Solomon

- Search Engine, Clustered| 2:41, 2:43-2:45, 2:47, 2:54, 2:65, 2:73, 3:13; see also database, topic-based; faceted search
- Search Engine, Custom (CSE)| 2:43, 2:70, 2:72, 2:75, 2:81, 3:31, 5:34, 5:55-5:56, 7:1, c:10; see also Google CSE (Custom Search Engine); Information Traps
- Search Engine, Metasearch| 2:43, 2:53-2:54, 2:57-2:60, 2:91, 3:65, 3:85, c:4; see also categorizing, metadata; metadata
- Search Engine, NLP (Natural Language Processing)| 2:4, 2:43, 2:47-2:52, 3:8, c:3-c:4; see also machine-mediated human computer interactions
- Search Engine, Privacy| 2:66-2:72; see also default, privacy settings; trade-off
- Search Engine, Visualization| 2:16, 2:52-2:53, 2:60, 2:63, 3:83, 3:85, 4:73, 5:65; see also display; mashup; User Interface (UI)
- tool selection| 2:3-2:4, 2:39-2:41, 2:99, 5:69, 6:20, 6:27, 7:37, c:3-c:4; see also anatomy of a query; refinement; Search Operators; Site Selection; sorting
- Wolfram Alpha| 5:78

Searx| 2:70-2:71; see also Search Engine, Privacy

seasoned| 3:11, 4:17, 4:58; see also direct experience

second party| 4:13, 4:23-4:24, 4:26, 4:34, 4:58, 4:69, 4:94, 5:38, 6:50, 6:56; see also journalist; plural; Provider Conjugation Framework (PCF); Search to Converse (STC)

second person| 2:98, 4:9, 4:14, 4:16-4:19, 4:34, 4:47, 5:26, 5:41, 6:11, 6:53; see also confidant; Informants; Provider Conjugation Framework (PCF); singular form

secondary information| 2:31, 2:54, 3:36, 3:87, 4:59, 5:30, 5:39, 7:33; see also background checks; Overview; primary intelligence; third party

secondhand| 4:4, 4:39; see also reusable

Secrecy| 1:31, 2:29, 2:36, 3:2, 7:7, 7:56; see also confidence level; encryption; espionage; password; spy; Surveillance; suspicions
- espionage| 3:61; see also detection; discrete; spy; Surveillance
- secret sauce| 1:62-1:63, 2:36, 6:1, 6:16, 6:21, c:5; see also Code, secret; proprietary
- secrets, keeping| 4:34, 4:58, 4:92, 4:97; see also discrete; divulge; newsleaker; nondisclosure

Self-delusion| 7:12; see also dream; fallacy; myopic; navel-gazing; urban legends

Self-interest| 3:26, 5:63, 7:1; see also desire; ego; Intentions; Motives
- self-preservation| 3:64, 3:91, 4:36, 4:67, 4:69, 4:94, 5:16, 5:25, 5:57; see also alterior motive; personal involvement; ruthless; sincerity
- What's in it for me (WIIFM)| 4:90, 5:33

semantic web| 4:64; see also categorizing, metadata; categorizing, subject directories; deep web; machine-generated directories; ontology

Semantics| i:10, 1:26, 2:4-2:6, 2:8, 2:29-2:32, 2:34, 2:37, 2:39-2:40, 2:53, 2:68, 2:81-2:82, 3:21, 3:30, 3:32, 3:47, 3:59, 3:67, 4:73, 4:76, 4:78-4:79, 4:85, 5:43, 5:53-5:54, 5:78, 6:1, 6:10, 6:12, 6:25, 6:34, 6:51, 7:34-7:35, c:3-c:5; see also categorizing, role of word choice; ordering, word adjacency; pointers; Syntax; word roots; wordplays
- Semantics, finding experts| 3:27; see also domain expert; finding people
- Semantics, finding people| 2:32; see also alias; finding people
- Semantics, word choice| 2:4, 2:13, 2:30-2:31, 2:37, 2:39, 3:10-3:11, 4:14, c:4; see also pointers

Senator| i:2, 7:21, 7:23, 7:41; see also Congress; Politics; public investigation

sender| i:8, 4:1, 4:8-4:11, 4:13, 4:17, 4:35, 4:48, 4:60, 4:93, 5:26, 7:33, c:10; see also Information Providers; messagers; recipients, message; shoot the messenger

Sense-making| i:12, 1:2, 1:8, 3:3, 3:21, 4:1, 4:5, 5:32, 5:66, 7:9, 7:11, 7:16, 7:31, c:9; see also competing explanations; Evidence; Explanations; Pattern Matching
- bogus| 2:5, 2:38, 2:40, 2:44-2:45, 3:24, 3:50, 3:55, 4:106, 6:1, 7:38; see also False hit; irrelevance; superfluous
- consistency| i:10, 1:6, 1:11, 1:39, 1:43, 2:50, 2:72, 2:95, 3:1, 3:4, 3:11, 3:61, 3:86, 4:38, 4:40-4:41, 4:48, 5:10, 6:12
- proverbial| 1:19, 2:12, 4:76, 5:35, 7:6; see also Narratives; Pattern Matching; Rhetoric; Wisdom
- significance| 2:6, 2:45, 3:38, 4:93, 5:20, 5:52, 5:69, 5:78, 7:6; see also implications; Intentions; Interpretations; projects, client presentations; theme
- substance| i:4, 2:38, 3:2, 3:87, 3:89, 4:7-4:8, 4:105, 7:4, 7:11, 7:23, 7:50; see also abuse; Addictions; clarifications; Pattern Matching; reaffirm; Relevance

SEO (Search Engine Optimization)| 2:24, 2:42, 2:78, 4:102, 5:7, 5:33, c:5; see also advertising; Websites, popularity

sequential| 1:3, 1:9, 1:12, 1:28, 1:64, 2:7, 2:13, 2:17, 2:29, 2:36, 2:53, 3:5, 3:10-3:11, 3:37, 3:78, 3:86, 4:1, 4:17, 4:51, 4:81, 5:11, 5:68, 5:74, 5:77, 6:6, 7:40; see also chronology; Continuum, the Knowledge; ordering, events; Procedures; Search Project Management (SPM); Timeframe

Shamshak, Tom| 2:54; see also Professional Investigator (PI)

shoot the messenger| 4:23, 7:10; see also messengers; projects, client presentations; recipients, message

shoptalk| 6:3, 6:16; see also Acronyms; Jargon; shorthand; slang

shorthand| 1:22, 2:18, 7:12; see also Acronyms; Code, secret; Code,IDs; shoptalk

Siegel, Robert| 7:17

signal-to-noise| 2:28, 3:70-3:71, c:8; see also Hit Counts; Metrics; Relevance; Sense-making

Silicon Valley| 7:46; see also big search; technopoly

siloed| 1:34, 7:2; see also categorizing, defining boundaries; disconnect; infrastructure; isolated; missing details

site ownership| 3:63, 3:65; see also Websites, ownership; Whois

Site Selection| 1:7, 2:86, 3:28, 3:32-3:35, 3:37-3:38, 3:46, 3:48-3:49, 3:72, 3:79, 3:89, 5:80, 6:10-6:11, 6:45, 6:50-6:51, c:2-c:4, c:15-c:16; see also fact versus opinion; Oceans, Lakes, and Ponds (OLP); tool selection; tools for the job

Skepticism| 1:44, 1:70, 2:74, 3:4, 3:55, 3:65, 4:19, 4:37-4:38, 4:41, 4:45, 4:49, 4:87, 4:106, 5:52, 5:60, 7:7, 7:38; see also BS Detection; disbelieving; disinterested; dispassionate; smell test; Vectors of Integrity (VOI)
- debunk| 3:62, 5:58; see also fact checkers; veracity
- detachment| i:6, 1:15, 1:34-1:35, 1:43-1:44, 3:17, 4:12, 4:16-4:17, 4:26, 4:31, 4:36, 4:99, 4:103, 5:16, 5:60-5:61, 5:71, 6:54, 7:6, 7:20, 7:23, 7:38; see also balcony; Observation; Researchers; third person
- disinterested| 1:35, 4:13, 4:17, 4:94, 4:105, 5:10, 5:30, 5:33, 5:36, 5:63, 7:38; see also dispassionate
- dispel| 1:36, 5:39; see also fallacy; myth

skills| i:6-i:8, 1:2, 1:4-1:5, 1:14, 1:33, 1:45, 1:47, 1:51, 1:53, 1:57, 1:60-1:61, 1:71, 2:1, 2:15, 2:31, 2:39-2:40, 2:49, 2:106-3:1, 3:4, 3:52, 3:54, 3:58, 4:1, 4:38, 4:45, 4:68-4:70, 4:72, 4:74, 4:90, 4:99, 5:11, 5:40, 5:42, 5:44-5:45, 5:54, 5:57-5:59, 5:70, 5:75-5:76, 6:7, 6:14, 6:20-6:21, 6:25, 6:35, 6:45, 7:7, 7:26-7:27, c:1, c:3, c:6, c:13; see also hygiene, electronic; Knowledge-ABLED, advantages; literacy, information; mastering; retool; teaching;

COMPLETE WORKS: Units One Through Seven | Unabridged Index:38

trainers
skim| 1:68, 2:43, 2:107, 3:29, 3:32, 3:50, 3:84, 5:77, c:7; see also disseminate; Oceans, Lakes, and Ponds (OLP); search index
slander| 3:91, 4:97, 5:8, 7:14; see also libel; smear
Snopes| 3:63; see also Skepticism; urban legends
Snowden, David| 1:30, 1:40, 1:42-1:43, 4:12, 5:76; see also Contextual
Snyder, Timothy| 7:17-7:19
social bookmarks| 3:7, 3:84, 3:88, 4:72, 4:79-4:80, 4:82-4:84, 5:46, 5:50, 5:53, 6:30, c:10; see also curatorship; Del.icio.us; tagging engine; URLs
Social Media| i:1, 1:3-1:4, 1:8, 1:26, 1:38, 1:64, 2:29, 2:53, 2:62, 2:66-2:67, 2:83, 3:11, 3:47, 3:53, 3:62-3:63, 3:73, 3:75, 3:78, 3:96, 4:7, 4:13-4:14, 4:16-4:17, 4:29, 4:52-4:54, 4:57-4:59, 4:64, 4:68, 4:77-4:78, 4:80, 4:87, 4:89, 4:93, 4:98, 4:104, 4:106, 5:2, 5:9, 5:26, 5:31, 5:33, 5:40, 5:43, 5:54-5:55, 5:80, 6:12, 6:14, 6:34, 6:57-7:1, 7:3-7:5, 7:9-7:10, 7:12-7:21, 7:23, 7:26-7:27, 7:29-7:30, 7:32, 7:35, 7:37-7:39, 7:46-7:47, 7:51; see also admirers; Affiliated; fake news; hot media; memes; news feed
  - pre-social media| 3:60, 7:16; see also Journalism; Newspapers; Perspectives
Social Networks| 3:75, 4:1, 4:4, 4:56, 4:69; see also Affiliated; anthropological; crowdsourcing; Perspectives, social media
  - social circles| 1:5, 2:57, 3:70, 3:78, 4:52-4:53, 4:59-4:62, 4:65, 4:67, 4:69, 5:50, 5:80, 7:17, 7:28, 7:37, c:11; see also Affiliated; Relatedness; socialize
  - acquaintances| 4:8, 4:68; see also social norms; strangers
  - admirers| 4:97; see also Influences; mutual; respect
  - ally| i:12, 2:5, 2:31, 2:40, 2:49, 2:54, 2:68, 2:85, 2:95, 2:99, 2:103, 3:13, 3:36, 3:83, 3:86, 3:88-3:89, 4:11, 4:14, 4:22-4:23, 4:32, 4:53, 4:59, 4:68, 4:102, 4:106, 5:5, 5:40, 5:54, 5:58, 5:60, 5:63, 5:67, 5:72, 6:8, 6:12, 6:14, 6:51, 7:8, 7:43; see also Collaborative; cooperation
  - colleague| 1:3, 1:11, 1:39, 1:52, 1:73, 2:5-2:6, 2:10, 2:12, 3:13, 3:16, 3:69, 3:98, 4:6, 4:9, 4:12, 4:15, 4:25, 4:31, 4:61, 4:77, 4:80, 5:5, 5:45, 5:54, 5:71, 6:16, 7:51, c:12-c:13; see also Affiliated; peer
  - members| i:2, i:7, i:9, i:16, 1:33, 1:38, 2:86, 2:89, 3:11, 3:14, 3:77, 4:1-4:2, 4:8-4:9, 4:18-4:19, 4:31, 4:36, 4:47, 4:52-4:54, 4:56-4:58, 4:61, 4:66-4:68, 4:70, 4:72-4:73, 4:83, 4:87, 4:96, 5:1, 5:5, 5:17, 5:26-5:27, 5:33, 5:47, 5:69, 5:72, 5:75, 6:11, 6:29-6:30, 6:33, 6:52, 6:54, 7:6, 7:13, 7:20, 7:29-7:30, 7:39, 7:44; see also Affiliated; board; first party
  - peer| i:4-i:5, 1:41, 1:60, 2:23, 2:88, 2:92, 3:14, 3:19, 3:28, 3:50, 3:56, 3:90-3:91, 4:19, 4:23, 4:25, 4:35, 4:42, 4:60, 4:66, 4:87, 4:104-4:105, 5:1, 5:4, 5:7, 5:9, 5:16, 5:20, 5:37, 5:39-5:40, 5:45-5:46, 5:52, 5:56, 5:59, 6:16, 6:32, 7:2, 7:16-7:17, 7:24, 7:27, 7:38-7:39, 7:42, c:12; see also colleague; social circles
  - schmooze| 4:71, 6:56; see also conversational; gossip; ice breaker
  - socialize| i:1, 2:20, 3:80, 4:51, 4:56, 4:85; see also Affiliated; barter; ice breaker; Interactions; schmooze
social norms| 1:44, 4:20, 5:30, 7:1, 7:21, 7:34; see also anthropological; Code, of conduct; cultural; Expectation; Perspectives, social media; schmooze
society| 1:35, 2:85, 4:19, 4:25, 4:45, 4:56, 6:56, 7:6, 7:16-7:17, 7:30, 7:49; see also anthropological; cultural; Demographics; tribal
Software Applications| i:7, i:11, 1:32, 2:26, 2:55, 4:94, 6:37, 7:27, 7:48; see also Code, software
  - cgi| 3:23-3:24, 4:78, 6:5
  - i-frame| 4:78; see also User Interface (UI)
  - javascript| 2:69; see also Code, software; html
  - MS Excel| 2:27, 6:5; see also Software Applications; spreadsheet
  - pdf| 2:26, 2:35, 3:11, 3:56, 4:107, 6:28; see also Documentation; File Formats
  - PHP| 3:24; see also unstable information
  - PowerPoint| 3:57; see also File Formats
  - SharePoint| 2:15, 2:31; see also Collaborative; intranet; workplace
  - spreadsheet| 2:26, 3:21-3:22, 6:5, 6:10, 6:28; see also File Formats; MS Excel
  - XML| 3:39; see also File Formats; markup language; RSS (Really Simple Syndication)
soldier| 4:9, 4:37, 7:15; see also combat; Conflict; military; mission; struggle; warfare
sorting| 4:86, 7:4; see also ordering, search results
Source Fluency| i:8, 3:1-3:4, 3:24, 6:32, c:7; see also fluid intelligence; point of origin; Quality Controls; Search Engine, Custom (CSE); tools for the job
  - fluid intelligence| 2:94, 3:1; see also tools for the job
  - information as a verb| 3:89; see also Actions and Outcomes; nouns and verbs; verbs, conjugation
spam| i:14, 1:51, 4:68, 4:102, 5:8, 7:45; see also email; Information Overload; scammers
specialized collections| 1:10, 1:16, 2:27, 2:34, 2:48, 2:72-2:73, 2:75, 2:86, 2:90, 2:95, 3:1-3:3, 3:21, 3:32, 3:83, 3:85-3:86, 4:5, 4:68, 4:72, 4:84, 5:40, 6:20, 6:29, 6:32, 6:34, 6:37, 6:50, c:4, c:6-c:7, c:11; see also curatorship; database, specialized
Speculation| 1:27-1:28, 1:37, 3:19, 3:95, 4:24, 4:45, 4:68, 4:95, 4:98, 5:3, 5:11, 5:24, 5:61, 5:63, 5:67, 5:71, 5:75, 7:17-7:18; see also gossip; innuendo; Observation; scenarios; third party
  - conjecture| 1:39, 3:89, 4:93, 5:69; see also fabricate; rumors
  - dispersion| i:7, 1:45, 2:36, 4:57, 7:20; see also ancillary; distractions; Misinformation
  - gossip| 1:49, 3:88, 4:102; see also Behaviors; innuendo; interpersonal; rumors; Speculation
  - innuendo| 3:60, 4:90, 5:17, 7:14; see also gossip; melodrama; rumors
  - pundit| 4:90, 5:9, 7:21; see also advisor; echo chamber; messengers; opinion-maker; Politics
  - rumors| 3:60, 3:78, 4:23, 4:67, 4:91, 4:94, 4:96-4:97, 4:99, 4:102, 5:33, 5:38, 5:44, 7:38
  - unsubstantiated| 4:68, 4:92, 4:97, 7:11, 7:14; see also dirt; distractions; fake news; Misinformation
spell check| 2:41; see also clarifications; Did you mean; Errors
spidering| 1:62-1:63, 1:66, 2:98, 3:11; see also crawl; indexer
spin| 1:65, 2:6, 3:8, 4:67, 5:26, 5:29, 5:37; see also Bias; Distortions; exaggeration; first party; Interpretations
spiraling| 1:11, 7:14; see also crisis; Decline; momentum; trends
sponsor| 1:42, 2:5, 2:16, 2:31, 2:34, 2:41, 2:45, 2:62, 2:67, 3:62, 3:64, 3:67, 3:93, 4:22, 4:38, 4:47, 4:60, 4:100, 5:26-5:27, 5:35, 5:60, 5:76, 6:4, 6:35, 7:35; see also advertising; endorse
Sprague, Mark| 2:19-2:20; see also Copywriters; Search Engine Marketing (SEM)
stackexchange| 3:96

Searching Out Loud: Giving Voice to Independent Investigations | Marc Solomon

Stakeholders| 1:65, 2:3, 3:14, 4:12, 4:43, 4:48, 4:105, 5:10, 5:13, 5:17-5:18, 5:27-5:29, 5:36-5:38, 5:61, 5:68, 5:71, 6:52, 7:12, 7:24-7:25, 7:39-7:42, c:13
  - board| 1:26, 1:34, 1:72, 2:86, 3:15, 3:19, 3:50, 3:56, 3:61, 4:6, 4:15, 4:32, 4:70, 4:100, 5:8, 5:17, 5:41, 5:57, 5:70, 6:11, 6:28, 6:33-6:34; see also Organizations
  - trustees| 6:11; see also benefactor; board; Organizations
stance| 3:62, 4:38, 4:96; see also posture; prevailing; spin
Starbucks| 1:51
Startpage| 2:68-2:69, 2:71; see also Search Engine, Privacy
statesman| 4:37-4:38, 4:41; see also admirers; deference; Diplomacy; honor; integrity; Leaders; respect
static information| i:15, 3:9; see also archives; dynamic and static; dynamic information
status quo| 1:38, 1:44, 4:48, 5:65; see also Expectation; Probabilities; reciprocal
steadfast| i:16, 4:39-4:40, 4:90; see also bond; loyalties; pledge; reliability; spirit
stemming, word| 1:68, 2:7, 2:9, 2:36, 4:57; see also synonyms; variant; word roots
Stop| 1:10, 1:17-1:18, 1:21, 1:23, 1:34, 1:46, 1:52, 1:61, 2:47, 2:49, 2:57, 2:60, 2:73, 3:9, 3:25, 3:76, 4:59, 4:67, 5:56, 5:61, 6:2; see also cease and desist; Decline; impose; Resistance
  - prevention| i:5, 1:71, 2:42, 4:104, 5:12, 5:58, 6:34, 6:51; see also immune; Risks
  - roadblock| 3:11, 3:25; see also defiance; derail; obstacles; Resistance
  - sabotage| 1:20, 1:65, 2:3, 3:11; see also smear; subversion; technology, limitations
  - sandbag| 3:1; see also Disruptions; obstacles
  - squelch| 1:34, 1:52, 4:22, 4:59, 7:36; see also Censorship; suppression
Storyteller| 4:97, 5:12, 5:32, 5:42, 7:6, 7:8, 7:13; see also anecdotal; author; messengers; Narratives
  - narrator| 5:41; see also author; messengers; scenarios; sender
  - script| i:11, 3:23, 3:72, 4:73, 5:10, 5:34, 5:54, 5:77, 6:7, 6:13, 7:39; see also anecdotal; melodrama; Narratives; plot; TelePrompTer
strategy| i:10, 1:21, 1:30, 1:69, 2:3-2:4, 2:20, 2:30-2:32, 2:39, 2:41, 2:92, 3:5, 3:18, 3:27, 3:31, 3:34, 3:47, 3:57, 3:60, 4:37, 4:40-4:41, 4:71, 4:96, 4:104, 5:2, 5:11, 5:38, 5:73, 5:79, 6:19, 6:27, 6:43, 7:14, 7:35, 7:39, c:3, c:15; see also Overview; projects, client recommendations; roadmaps; Vectors of Integrity (VOI)
StumbleUpon| 4:85; see also curatorship
Subject Directory| 1:59, 1:69, 2:1, 2:3-2:5, 2:7, 2:18, 2:25, 2:36, 2:39-2:40, 2:44, 2:59, 2:85-2:90, 2:92-2:93, 2:95, 2:98-2:101, 2:106, 3:3, 3:10, 3:28-3:30, 3:32-3:33, 3:49, 3:52, 3:68, 3:78, 3:93, 6:10, 6:20, 6:24, c:3-c:4, c:6; see also categorizing, human mediated; database, searching; database, specialized; lakes; machine-generated directories; specialized collections
  - directory indexing| 2:94, 2:103; see also Websites, indexing
  - indexed words| 1:62-1:63, 1:66; see also search index; Websites, indexing
  - indexer| 1:61, 2:98, 3:10, 3:57; see also machine indexing
  - machine indexing| 2:42, 2:98; see also database, index; search index
  - pages indexed| 2:88; see also page views; Websites, indexing
  - subject indexing| 2:90, 2:96; see also database, topic-based; directory indexing; machine indexing; Topic-based
subtle| 1:47, 2:37, 3:5, 3:12, 3:84, 3:89, 4:56, 5:39, 5:45, 5:61, 6:4, 7:38; see also course-correcting; modest; nuance; readjust; vague
subversion| 4:98, 7:48; see also Disruptions; sabotage; sandbag
suggestion search| 1:10-1:11, 1:37, 1:49, 1:75, 2:9, 2:62, 3:54, 3:64, 4:18, 5:23, 5:52, 6:48-6:49, 7:28, 7:42, c:5; see also Google type ahead; Search Engine Marketing (SEM); top-of-mind
superficial| 2:2, 4:26; see also impersonal; interpersonal; smiley face logic
superfluous| 5:58, 6:48; see also bogus; factoid; trivial
supply and demand| i:7, 2:52, 4:1, 4:87, 4:98, 5:10, 5:31, 5:33-5:34; see also deficit and surpluses; Economics; formula; pull and push; Scarcity
Supply Media| 5:10, 5:28-5:29, 5:32, 5:34; see also press release; pull and push
  - attention supply| 5:9
  - content supply| 3:2, 4:24, 5:2, 5:7, 5:11, 5:31, 6:16, c:7; see also aggregate
Surfwax| 2:12, 2:57, 2:60, 2:70; see also Search Engine, Metasearch
Surprises| i:16-i:17, 1:10-1:11, 1:40, 1:44, 2:53, 2:64, 3:55, 3:82, 4:12, 4:67, 4:89, 4:95, 4:100, 5:5, 5:28, 5:32, 5:35, 5:56, 5:60-5:61, 7:46-7:48; see also Pattern Matching; projects, client presentations
  - astonishing| 1:11, 4:79, 5:26; see also significance
  - explosions| 1:44, 2:57, 3:21, 3:50, 4:12, 4:32, 5:29, 6:12, 6:47, 7:14; see also Disasters; fallout; harm
  - reveal| 1:7, 1:14-1:15, 1:38, 1:48, 1:59, 1:74, 2:12, 2:47, 2:51, 2:53, 2:101, 3:19, 3:27, 3:46, 3:87, 4:8, 4:45, 4:47-4:48, 4:56, 5:11, 5:34, 5:57, 6:47, 6:57, 7:2, 7:7-7:8, c:2; see also Evidence; Exposure; scientific method
  - revelation| 1:44, 3:55, 3:73, 4:90, 5:56-5:57, 5:60, 7:16; see also bible; faith; realization; unprecedented
  - shock| 1:39, 5:57; see also unexpected; unprecedented
  - sneak| 4:89, 5:61; see also detection; Radar; raid
  - speechless| 1:58, 5:34; see also Code, unspoken; nonverbal; shock
  - sudden| 1:42, 3:17, 4:86, 5:68; see also crisis; projects, client presentations; unexpected; warning
  - unplanned| 1:50, 3:17, 4:40, 5:10; see also alarms; Disruptions
surrogate| 1:6, 4:26, 4:43, 5:58; see also go-betweens; intermediaries; proxy
Surveillance| 1:27, 7:55; see also encryption; espionage; Internet Security; Privacy
  - snoop| 1:38, 5:43, 7:10; see also eavesdropping; espionage; wiretaps
Surveys| i:7, 1:58, 2:43, 4:26, 4:105, 5:8-5:9, 5:16, 5:18, 5:22-5:23, 5:28-5:29, 5:35-5:36, 5:40-5:41, 5:59-5:60, 5:70, 5:79, 6:34, 6:56, 7:44, c:16; see also feedback; focus groups; open-ended questions; sample
  - confidence level| 2:54, 5:71; see also approximate; calculable; Probabilities; sample
  - customer surveys| 5:40; see also complaints; customer
  - feedback| 1:9, 1:49, 3:61, 4:12, 4:16, 4:40, 5:71-5:72, 6:46, 6:53; see also public perceptions
  - open-ended questions| 1:20; see also Interactions; interview; original question
  - opinion surveys| 2:2, 2:52, 3:17, 3:48-3:49, 5:59; see also focus groups; Politics; Public Awareness; Radar; Recognition; trends; unfavorable

suspects| 1:8, 1:27, 1:36, 2:45, 2:47, 2:54, 3:9, 4:58, 4:103, 5:18, 5:66; see also criminal investigation; indictment; persons of interest; Search Targets; suspicions
sway| 3:24, 3:58, 3:63, 3:78, 5:3, 5:18, 6:39, 6:53; see also Campaigns; Influences; opinion-maker; pandering; persuasion
Swisscows| 2:69; see also Search Engine, Privacy
symbols| 2:9, 2:33, 2:52, 2:62; see also abstract; Metaphors; Milestones; nonverbal; personified; Rhetoric
symptoms| i:17, 2:37, 6:48; see also cause-and-effect; clue; diagnosis; epidemic; Indicators; public health
synchronize| i:2, 1:46, 1:67; see also align; interconnected; orchestration; sequential; Timeframe
synonyms| 2:7-2:9, 2:11-2:13, 2:16, 3:13, 7:24; see also ontology; Semantics; Term Expansion; word roots
Syntax| 1:26, 2:6-2:8, 2:17, 2:28-2:30, 2:35, 2:41-2:42, 2:59, 2:68, 3:26, 3:29, 4:24, 4:78; see also advanced search commands; parse; query formation; refinement; Search Operators; Semantics
  - Alldefine:| 2:21, 2:25
  - Allinanchor:| 2:19-2:20
  - Allinurl:| 2:18
  - Define:| 2:21, 2:25
  - field constraint| 2:40-2:42; see also categorizing, field structure; field-based
  - Intext:| 2:25-2:26
  - Inurl:| 2:18; see also URLs
  - Phonebook:| 2:27, 3:67, 3:96; see also Contacts; Discontinued Websites and Tools; Personal Identity
synthesize| i:17, 1:72; see also integrate, findings; orchestration; synchronize

T

tacit| 5:64; see also Implicit; Intuitions; nonverbal
Taco Bell| 5:14-5:15, 5:17, 5:19-5:20, 5:22-5:23, 5:25, 5:43; see also Case studies; food preparation; poisoning; The Biggest Picture (TBP)
tag cloud| 2:52-2:53, 2:69, 4:63, 4:81-4:82; see also Search Engine, Visualization; tagging engine; word maps
tagging engine| 2:6, 2:19-2:20, 2:36, 2:41-2:43, 2:52-2:53, 2:56-2:57, 2:69, 3:7, 3:21-3:22, 4:62, 4:80-4:84, 4:102, 5:18, 6:21, 6:30, 7:12; see also curatorship; Del.icio.us; folksonomy; social bookmarks; word maps
Taleb, Nassim| 5:59-5:60, 5:63- 5:64; see also black swan
talent| 3:72, 4:53, 4:69, 5:41, 6:8, 6:34, 7:9, 7:23; see also Expertise; job security; skills
tangents| 3:9; see also ancillary; disconnect; dispersion; evidence patterns; tangle
taxonomy| 2:21, 2:25, 2:86, 3:87, 3:91, 4:62; see also catalog; Categorizaton; classification; Content Grouping; ontology; vernacular
team| i:11, 1:2, 1:14, 1:35, 1:38, 2:15, 3:19, 3:38, 3:60, 3:72, 4:13, 4:30-4:32, 4:47, 4:56, 4:68-4:69, 5:4, 5:9, 5:36, 5:41, 5:69, 6:53, 7:5, 7:15, 7:28; see also Collaborative; Contest; Leaders
technique| i:10, 1:12, 1:47, 2:3, 2:40, 2:52, 2:100, 2:107-3:1, 3:3, 3:25, 3:50, 4:2, 4:43, 4:74-4:75, 4:102, 4:108, c:7, c:16; see also Knowledge-ABLED practices; mastering; Procedures; skills; specificity
Technology| i:5, i:7, i:11, i:15, 1:5, 1:9, 1:50, 1:70, 1:74, 1:76, 2:19, 2:62, 2:106, 3:1, 3:19, 3:25, 3:88, 4:35, 4:46, 4:79, 6:3, 6:16, 6:24, 7:1-7:2, 7:4, 7:37, 7:45, 7:48, 7:50, 7:52, c:1-c:2; see also big search; Commerce; Humans; Interrogation, humans of machines; Machine-enabled; machine-triggered human alienation; technology, intimidation factors
  - technology, business interests| 1:9, 4:36, 5:25, 7:2, 7:4, 7:37, 7:46-7:48; see also big search
  - technology, intimidation factors| 1:53, 2:48, 3:20, 4:58, 7:45-7:47; see also machine-triggered human alienation
  - technology, keeping current| i:5, 1:5, 1:9, 2:52, 4:47, 5:64, 7:1; see also peer; per`
+sonal branding
  - technology, limitations| i:11, 1:53, 1:58, 1:74, 2:37, 2:48; see also Code, limitations; machine-based limitations
  - technology, non-techies| i:7, 4:80; see also media, traditional; pre-social media
  - technology, professional roles| 2:15, 5:26, 7:50; see also Professionals
  - technology, search| 1:2, 1:52, 1:76, 2:49, 2:75, 2:85, 3:2, 3:12-3:13, 3:28, 3:30, 7:1, 7:48; see also anatomy of a query
  - technology, tech-savvy| i:7, 2:62, 4:36, 5:26, 6:8, 7:50; see also geeks
  - technology, usefulness| i:11, 1:60, 2:19, 2:51, 2:66, 3:20, 4:80; see also useful information; useful, failsafes
technopoly| 7:2-7:3, 7:6, 7:12, 7:34, 7:41; see also anti-trust; big search; duopoly; Postman, Neil; Surveillance Capitalism
TED Talks| 5:79; see also Expertise; Pariser, Eli
TelePrompTer| 5:29; see also camera; Expression; persuasion; script
Term Expansion| 1:66, 2:9, 2:12, 3:14; see also breathe, letting a search; inclusion; query formation; refinement; synonyms
  - broaden| i:9-i:10, i:13, 1:72-1:73, 2:2, 2:7, 2:12, 2:25, 2:32, 2:59, 3:21, 3:69-3:70, 3:72, 3:76, 3:80, 4:2, 4:11, 4:18, 4:33, 4:40, 4:59, 4:73, 4:91, 4:108-5:1, 5:16, 5:29, 5:60, 5:67, 5:76, 6:8, 6:51, 7:10, 7:36-7:37, 7:43, 7:51, c:13; see also synonyms; variant
territory| 1:31, 2:12, 5:31, 6:8, 7:18, 7:50; see also localities; neighborhoods; region; turf
tethered| 7:4-7:5, 7:12; see also dependent; interconnected
The Biggest Picture (TBP)| i:12, 1:43, 1:72, 3:59-3:62, 5:3, 5:5, 5:7, 5:19, 5:26-5:27, 5:29-5:31, 5:35-5:37, 5:39, 5:42-5:43, 7:26, 7:34, 7:44; see also calculable; Content Grouping; Demand-based media; measurable; media performance; Message Value; Metrics
  - The Biggest Picture, client deliverable| 5:7, 5:19, 5:26, 5:30, 5:37, 5:42; see also projects, client presentations
  - The Biggest Picture, content analysis| 5:12, 5:29; see also demand-based, content analysis
  - The Biggest Picture, management functions| 5:26-5:27, 5:43; see also horizontal business functions; Management, functions
  - The Biggest Picture, methodology| 5:29-5:30, 5:35, 5:71, 5:80; see also demand-based, methodology; formula
  - The Biggest Picture, metrics| 5:11, 5:16, 5:35, 5:71; see also Measurements; scorekeeping
  - The Biggest Picture, perspectives| 5:3, 5:5, 5:7, 5:29, 5:31, 5:36, 5:39, 5:44; see also Perspectives
theme| 2:7, 2:11, 2:23, 2:47, 2:65, 2:74, 2:79, 2:81, 2:107, 3:12, 3:22, 3:81, 4:5, 5:10-5:11, 5:36, 5:47, 6:20, c:11; see also Character Traits; Narratives; Roles; story lines; Topic-based
theory of mind| 4:87; see also Behaviors; Cognitive; empathy; frame of reference; Perspectives, perspective-taking
therapy| 1:51, 4:11, 6:22, 6:44, 6:48; see also Consulting; interpersonal
thesaurus| 1:66; see also categorizing, Relatedness; synonyms; Term Expansion; vocabulary; word roots

COMPLETE WORKS: Units One Through Seven | Unabridged Index:41

third party| 2:36, 3:16, 3:63, 4:10, 4:16, 4:23-4:28, 4:34, 4:47, 5:10, 5:32, 5:39, 6:10, 6:47, 6:56-6:57, 7:20; see also Credibility; institutional credibility; Observation; plural; Provider Conjugation Framework (PCF)
third person| 4:10-4:11, 4:17-4:19, 4:23, 4:26, 4:36, 4:48, 4:76, 5:67, 6:54; see also eyewitness; Observation; Provider Conjugation Framework (PCF); singular form
threats| i:2, 1:34, 2:65, 4:2, 4:28-4:31, 4:69, 4:91, 4:104-4:105, 5:3, 5:5, 5:7, 5:16, 5:20, 5:34, 6:45, 6:57-7:1, 7:3-7:4, 7:10, 7:12, 7:17, 7:20, 7:22, 7:28, 7:36, 7:51; see also Coercion; fear; Motives; Power Structures; Risks
Tibetan culture| 1:75; see also Hopi Indians
time commitment| 1:22, 4:71, 4:73; see also failsafes; projects, clients expectations; search logs
time, spending| 1:7-1:8, 1:18, 1:22-1:23, 1:45, 1:47, 1:65, 3:37, 4:52, 4:67, 5:49-5:50, 5:78, 7:33, c:2; see also Knowledge-ABLED practices; resourceful; useful, failsafes
Timeframe| 3:11, 3:66, 5:15; see also chronology; Crime Scene
 - annual| 5:10, 5:27; see also calendar; cycle; perennial; reminders; reunion
 - date range| 1:23, 1:27, 1:47, 1:72, 2:2, 2:11, 2:29, 2:33, 2:42, 2:60, 3:13, 3:17, 3:28, 3:37-3:38, 3:48, 3:87, 3:91-3:92, 5:27, 5:66, 6:22, 7:10, 7:19; see also chronology; sequential; Timeframe
 - outdated| i:13, 3:37, 7:13, 7:21; see also evidence gathering
 - time stamp| 2:57; see also machine indexing; RSS (Really Simple Syndication); sequential
tjmaxx| 2:31
tolerance| 4:25, 4:103, 5:26, 7:32; see also Beliefs; equality; integrity
tools for the job| i:9, 2:1-2:2, 6:1-6:2, c:3; see also Frameworks; methods; Search Tools; Site Selection
Topic-based| 2:89, 3:3, 3:67, 5:43, 6:36, c:6; see also Content Grouping; database, topic-based; Subject Directory; theme
 - subtopics| 2:77; see also categorizing, auto categorization; categorizing, subject directories; subgrouping
 - topic-specific| 3:34, 3:67-3:68, 3:83; see also database, specialized
 - topical searches| 1:67, 2:36, 2:52, 2:92, 3:70-3:72, 3:91, 5:52; see also database, topic-based
Topix.net| 6:37; see also RSS (Really Simple Syndication)
Trade| 1:69, 1:76, 3:94, 4:34, 4:95, 5:31; see also Commerce; Interactions; resellers
 - commodity| 6:11; see also clients, added value; cost related; price
 - industry| i:14, 1:40, 2:20, 2:23, 2:43, 2:86, 2:93, 2:95, 3:94, 4:33-4:36, 4:45, 4:99, 5:9-5:10, 5:12, 5:24, 5:27-5:28, 5:38, 5:42-5:43, 5:54, 6:10, 6:21, 6:37, 6:56, 7:7, 7:9-7:12; see also Commerce; market segments
 - price| 1:16, 1:23, 1:76, 2:32, 2:73, 2:106, 3:81, 4:23, 4:92, 4:94, 7:46, 7:53; see also brands, consumer; customer surveys; merchandise; product reviews
 - proprietor| 6:3; see also business community; entrepreneur; executive
 - Trade, financial| 1:73, 4:95, 4:103, 7:9; see also Major Business Media
 - Trade, groups| 2:11, 4:35, 4:37, 5:18, 6:10; see also industry sector
 - Trade, shows| 4:36, 5:25, 5:34, 6:14; see also annual; venue
 - vendor| 2:15, 2:39, 2:74, 3:9, 3:64, 3:79, 3:86, 3:93-3:94, 4:2, 4:61, 4:65, 4:100, 5:25, 5:31, 5:40-5:41, 6:50; see also contractor; sell
trade media| 2:79, 3:17, 3:95, 5:26-5:27, 5:32, 5:46, 6:37, 6:56; see also Major Business Media; Newspapers; Trade, shows
trademark| 2:62, 3:83, 7:48; see also Brand; patent; proprietary
traffic| 1:27, 1:68, 1:71, 1:73, 2:14-2:15, 2:56, 3:13, 3:30, 3:38, 3:64-3:65, 3:85, 4:89, 5:32, 5:34, 5:41, 6:4, 7:40; see also page views; visitors; Websites, ranking; Websites, traffic
translation| 1:16, 1:59, 2:5, 2:31, 5:58; see also dialect; Interactions; Language
transparency| 1:33, 3:5, 4:7-4:8, 4:51-4:55, 5:22, 5:27, 5:59-5:60, 5:68, 7:5, 7:7, 7:13; see also accountability; obvious; self-evident; Trust; visibility
trends| i:7, 1:44, 1:72, 1:75, 3:12, 3:58, 3:78-3:79, 3:96, 4:26, 4:28, 4:32, 4:96, 4:105, 5:8, 5:12, 5:16, 5:31, 5:33, 5:38, 5:61, 5:64, 6:7, 6:22, 6:34, 6:46, 6:52, 6:57, 7:10, 7:52, c:16; see also fashion; market research; momentum; Public Awareness; top-of-mind
tribal| 4:18, 4:54, 4:106, 7:18, 7:24; see also clash; cultural; ethnic; Group Behavior; intolerance; society
trivial| 2:45, 3:10, 3:38, 4:32; see also bogus; distractions; diversion; factoid; Obscurities
trollers| 3:8, 7:45; see also anonymous; fraud; Internet Security; Online Behavior; scammers; Twitter
Trump, Donald J.| 7:12; see also Moore, Michael
Trust| i:13, i:17, 1:29, 1:34, 1:39, 1:48, 1:58, 1:75, 2:44, 2:59, 2:90, 3:22, 3:50, 3:67, 3:81, 3:93, 4:9, 4:12, 4:29, 4:32, 4:43-4:44, 4:59, 4:66-4:67, 4:69, 4:90, 4:105, 4:108, 5:8, 5:26-5:27, 5:30, 5:41, 5:56, 5:60, 5:68, 6:52-6:53, 6:55, 7:5, 7:8, 7:11, 7:20, 7:22-7:23, 7:25, 7:38, 7:56; see also Agreement; Credibility; devotion; handshake; loyalties
 - mistrust| 7:7; see also Accusations; actions of others; paranoia; Resistance; suspicions
 - public trust| 4:99, 7:1, 7:10, 7:14, 7:51; see also Public Opinion; Public Policies
 - trusted advisor| 1:34, 4:10, 4:13, 4:106, 5:1, 5:28, 5:52; see also clients, project trust; Consulting
Tumblr| 3:8; see also curatorship
Twain, Mark| 4:98
Twitter| 2:29, 3:98, 4:73, 4:88, 4:93, 4:108, 5:40, 7:17, 7:37-7:38; see also hot media; Social Media
 - micro-blogging| 5:53; see also Blogs
 - tweet| 2:29, 2:66, 4:72, 4:87, 4:92, 7:17, 7:38; see also first person; micro-blogging; quote; visceral
type ahead| 2:43, 2:61, 2:63, 7:34, 7:36; see also Google type ahead; suggestion search
typos| 3:73; see also Errors; inaccuracies; misspellings
tyranny| 4:94, 5:62; see also Censorship; Corruption; Power Structures; suppression

U

Unexplored| 5:38, 6:8, 7:48; see also discovery; Exposure
 - unexposed| 1:33; see also buried; Hidden; Obscurities
uniformity| i:16; see also conform; consistency; passive
Unique IDs| 2:4, 2:6, 2:8, 2:17, 2:32-2:35, 2:99, 6:10, 6:16, 6:25; see also Code, tracking; pointers; verbatims
 - ticker symbol| 2:33; see also publicly-traded companies; stock market

Searching Out Loud: Giving Voice to Independent Investigations | Marc Solomon

University of Michigan| 3:93
unstable information| 1:42, 3:22-3:24, 5:27; see also dynamic information; Liabilities; Probabilities
unstructured information| 3:21, 4:10, 4:89, 7:46; see also email; impose; Information Types, resources; literacy, information; machine-based limitations; repositories
urban legends| 1:28, 5:73; see also debunk; fallacy; gullibility; myth; Snopes
URLs| 2:18-2:19, 2:25, 2:34, 2:42, 3:13, 5:77, 7:37; see also broken links; Denial of Service (DNS); embedded links; Hyperlinks; IP address; Websites; Websites, bookmarking; Whois
Useful| i:5, i:7-i:8, i:16, 1:1-1:2, 1:7, 1:9-1:11, 1:21, 1:23, 1:26, 1:28, 1:31, 1:51, 1:55, 1:68, 2:1-2:3, 2:15, 2:18, 2:24, 2:31, 2:39, 2:41, 2:46-2:47, 2:49-2:50, 2:56, 2:60, 2:76, 2:79, 2:92, 2:98, 2:107, 3:5-3:6, 3:12-3:13, 3:15, 3:24, 3:31, 3:36, 3:56, 3:62, 3:69-3:70, 3:74, 3:77, 3:83, 3:93, 4:7, 4:35, 4:38, 4:45, 4:60, 4:69, 4:79, 4:82, 4:102, 4:108, 5:13, 5:29-5:30, 5:40-5:41, 5:46-5:48, 5:54, 5:59, 5:67-5:68, 6:5, 6:32, 6:48-6:49, 7:46, c:2, c:7, c:13; see also leverage; literacy, information; problem-solving; reusable; skills; time, spending
 - useful answers| 2:1, 2:39, 2:49, 3:71; see also Actions and Outcomes; Knowledge-ENABLED
 - useful form| 2:2, 3:75, 4:70, 6:5, c:7; see also Information Types, formats
 - useful information| i:4, i:7-i:8, 1:51, 1:55, 4:46, 4:80; see also literacy, information
 - useful knowledge| 1:1, 2:3, 3:1, c:2; see also Knowledge-ABLED, advantages
 - useful outcomes| 1:7, 2:18, 2:39, 2:59, 3:14, 5:5, c:12; see also Actions and Outcomes
 - useful search results| 1:21, 2:15, 3:13, 3:94; see also Search Results
 - useful websites| 1:23, 2:76, 4:80, 4:83, 5:47; see also social bookmarks; Websites, evaluating
 - useful, failsafes| 1:10-1:11; see also failsafes
useless| i:5, 1:1, 2:23, 3:26, 3:54, 3:69, 3:76, 4:101; see also Quality Controls; time, spending
User| i:1, i:11, i:15, 1:10-1:11, 1:38, 1:62-1:63, 1:65-1:66, 1:68, 2:19, 2:26, 2:37, 2:52, 2:62, 2:67, 2:69, 2:71, 2:73-2:74, 3:6, 3:9-3:10, 3:22, 3:30, 3:46, 3:50, 3:73, 3:93, 4:1, 4:4, 5:6, 5:33, 5:40-5:41, 5:52-5:53, 5:76, 6:34, 6:49, 7:2, 7:4, 7:10, 7:13, 7:26-7:28, 7:30, 7:34, 7:40, 7:48-7:51; see also Interactions; layperson; shopping cart; Websites, traffic
 - usage| 1:1, 1:60, 1:75, 2:6, 2:56, 2:67, 4:55, 4:105, 7:27; see also User Experience (UX); Websites, traffic
 - User Experience (UX)| 1:10, 3:31; see also information architecture; navigation; User Interface (UI)
 - dropdown| 1:62, 1:64, 2:63, 2:67, 5:52; see also icon; navigation
 - icon| 1:73, 2:56, 4:82, 7:28; see also emojis; Metrics; news feed; Social Media
 - menu| 1:62, 2:68, 5:10, 5:14, 6:17; see also face-to-screen; navigation
 - usability| 1:23; see also navigation; Websites, evaluating
User Interface (UI)| 1:11, 1:60, 1:62-1:63, 1:66, 1:69, 2:53, 2:55-2:56, 2:60, 2:63, 2:69, 2:72-2:73, 3:78-3:79, 4:77, 6:27; see also display; marquee; Websites, evaluating
 - display| i:2, 1:11, 1:31, 1:38, 1:53, 1:61, 2:23, 2:45, 2:52, 2:54-2:56, 2:60-2:61, 2:67, 2:70-2:71, 3:12, 3:35, 3:54, 3:72, 4:32, 4:38, 4:47, 4:61, 4:98, 5:53, 6:27, 7:11; see also landing page; layout; scrolling

V

Van Buren, Sadie| 4:16
variant| 1:68, 2:7, 2:11-2:13, 2:16, 2:36, 2:63; see also stemming, word; word roots
Vectors of Integrity (VOI)| i:1-i:2, 3:94, 4:32, 4:36-4:40, 4:42, 4:44, 4:57, 4:70, 4:88, 5:30, 7:1, 7:8, 7:31, 7:37, 7:44; see also Authenticity; conjugal; Credibility; extrapolate; loyalties; Observation; original sources; Perspectives, perspective-taking; precise; Skepticism; strategy; unstructured information
verbatims| 2:11, 2:19, 2:30-2:31, 2:37-2:38, 4:22, 5:72, c:4-c:5; see also exact; keyword matches; pointers; Semantics, word choice
verbs, conjugation| 3:10, 4:8, 4:12; see also information as a verb; Provider Conjugation Framework (PCF)
Verification| 1:5, 1:27, 3:25, 3:61, 3:64, 3:86, 4:45, 7:37; see also corroborate; Observation; public filings; public investigation; transparency
 - veracity| 3:50, 5:16; see also debunk; Empirical; fact checkers; Trust
vernacular| 4:26, 6:4; see also dialect; Jargon; Language; localities; tribal
version| i:1, i:7, 1:3, 1:36, 1:50-1:51, 2:22-2:23, 2:49, 2:65, 2:76, 3:16, 3:23, 3:36, 3:54, 3:56, 3:62, 4:15, 4:18, 4:29, 4:32, 4:48, 4:58-4:59, 4:66, 4:91, 5:23-5:24, 5:76, 5:78, 6:8, 6:57, 7:25, 7:42-7:43; see also archives; Documentation
viewers| 3:17, 4:8, 4:25, 5:28, 6:37, 7:10-7:11, 7:33, 7:52; see also attention demand; audience; paid subscriptions; passive; Popularity
Violence| 4:76, 5:44, 7:15, 7:48; see also abuse; explosions; Law Enforcement; torture
 - assault| 4:98, 5:43; see also Crime; intrusion; raid; sneak; Surprises
 - carnage| 7:15-7:16; see also death
 - civilians| 7:15; see also soldier; unguarded; warfare
 - homicidal| 3:58, 5:43; see also Crime; Crime Scene; criminal investigation; manslaughter
 - terrorism| 1:34, 3:60, 7:4; see also extortion; foreign; Internet Security; Risks; tribal; villains
 - hostage-taking| 7:17; see also Coercion; Crime; extortion; terrorism
 - torture| 4:34, 4:67; see also abuse; brutality; evil; threats
 - weapons| 1:20, 2:56, 3:58, 4:37, 7:26; see also abuse; aggression; Law Enforcement; warfare
visibility| 1:10, 1:31, 1:38, 1:71, 2:56, 3:21, 3:48, 3:54, 3:63, 3:69, 3:73-3:74, 3:82, 4:45, 5:33, 5:35, 5:38, 5:40, 6:12, 7:36; see also Evidence; Radar; transparency
Visionary| i:17, 1:38, 4:29, 4:41, 5:29, 5:38, 6:57, 7:30, 7:32; see also Forecast; future; prediction; prognostications; soothsayers
 - envision| 5:12, 6:13
 - foreknowledge| 1:18, 2:39, 2:44, 4:32, 4:42-4:43, 5:43, 5:62, 5:72, 7:5, 7:26, 7:35; see also prediction
 - preempt| 4:67, 5:35; see also advanced knowledge; strategy
 - soothsayers| 5:62; see also guru; Wisdom
 - unforeseeable| 1:11, 4:43, 4:87, 5:9, 5:11, 5:28, 5:31, 7:25, 7:50; see also Exposure; Forecast
 - unprecedented| 5:63; see also black swan; History; posterity
visitors| i:5, 1:1, 1:23, 1:58, 1:61, 1:68, 1:71, 1:73, 2:36, 2:47, 2:53, 2:68, 2:74, 2:85, 3:1, 3:9, 3:16, 3:50, 3:52, 3:56, 3:60, 3:63-3:65, 3:68, 3:71, 4:79, 4:108, 5:8, 5:40, 5:42, 5:46-5:47, 5:49, 5:52, 6:4, 6:30, 6:46, 7:14-7:15, 7:20, c:6; see also Websites, traffic

vital data| 3:77; see also healthcare; Indicators
Vivisimo| 3:23; see also 9-11 report; Search Engine, Clustered
vocabulary| 2:18, 3:5, 4:62, 4:82; see also categorizing, role of word choice; colloquialism; Language; nomenclature; Semantics, word choice; thesaurus
vocal| 4:42, 5:39; see also defiance; Exposure; Expression; protests
volunteer| 2:47, 2:88-2:89, 4:12, 4:56, 4:93; see also Non-profits; philanthropies; unsolicited

W

Wall Street Journal| 3:16, 3:94, 4:27, 5:17, 5:25
warfare| 3:8, 5:43, 7:16; see also heroes; Power Structures; soldier; Violence
watchdogs| 4:94, c:10; see also Regulations; whistleblower
Wayback Machine, the| 3:15-3:16, 3:42, 3:64, 7:41; see also archives; decommissioned; fact checkers; posterity; Websites, cache
Weakness| 1:31, 2:43, 2:101, 3:64, 3:90, 4:88, 7:32; see also compromise; conceal; deficiencies; embarrassing; Negotiations; sins; vulnerability
  - desperation| 4:97, 5:73; see also Fight-or-flight; hysteria; Liabilities
  - exploit| 1:35, 2:25, 3:91, 5:9, 6:21, 7:13, 7:35; see also embarrassing; Power Structures; predatorial; strategy
  - shortcoming| 1:31, 1:59, 2:3, 3:11-3:12, 3:25, 3:37, 3:86, 4:88; see also deficiencies; Errors; vulnerability
  - succumb| 3:6, 3:54, 5:69, 5:72; see also collapse; defeat; retreat
  - vulnerability| 1:31, 3:64, 4:41, 4:59-4:60, 4:95, 4:104; see also exploit; primary intelligence; strategy
Weather Conditions| 2:30, 2:104, 3:18, 3:45-3:46, 3:48, 3:81, 7:9, 7:23; see also Crime Scene; GPS (Global Positioning Satellite)
  - atmospheric| 2:56, 2:91
WebMD| 2:91; see also healthcare
webpage| 2:22, 2:66, 4:80, 4:84; see also page views; Quality Controls; scrolling
Websites| i:10-i:11, i:13, i:15-i:17, 1:1, 1:6-1:7, 1:16, 1:23-1:24, 1:43, 1:46, 1:61, 1:68, 1:73, 2:19, 2:23, 2:27-2:30, 2:34, 2:39-2:40, 2:42, 2:44, 2:50, 2:52, 2:59, 2:72, 2:98, 2:104, 2:107-3:1, 3:11, 3:16, 3:22, 3:24, 3:27, 3:41, 3:50, 3:54, 3:56, 3:61-3:64, 3:68-3:69, 3:84-3:85, 3:89, 3:92, 4:1, 4:15, 4:25, 4:45, 4:69-4:70, 4:76, 4:82, 4:100, 5:8, 5:10, 5:26, 5:45-5:46, 5:72, 6:1, 6:8, 6:11, 6:20, 7:4, 7:26, 7:33, c:6-c:7
  - Home page| 1:69, 1:71, 2:22, 2:24, 2:30, 3:7-3:8, 3:56; see also landing page; marquee
  - shopping cart| i:1, i:14, 1:8, 1:73, 3:16, 4:104, 7:32; see also Commerce; merchandise; Websites, traffic
  - uploads| 1:52, 2:29, 3:37-3:38, 4:11, 4:65; see also database, size; File Formats
  - webmasters| 3:96; see also Professionals
  - Websites, bookmarking| 2:59, 4:83, 5:47, 6:8; see also social bookmarks
  - Websites, cache| 2:42, 2:72, 3:42
  - Websites, company| 4:71, 5:11, 5:46
  - Websites, credibility| 4:2, 4:26, 5:27; see also Credibility
  - Websites, dubious| 1:1, 4:47, 7:33
  - Websites, evaluating| i:16, 1:24, 3:1-3:2, 3:25, 3:51, 3:65, 4:71, 5:9, 5:11, 6:8, c:6-c:7; see also Evaluation
  - Websites, indexing| 2:39, 3:12, 3:55, 3:58, 3:85; see also search index
  - Websites, Oceans, Lakes, and Ponds| 3:28, 6:11; see also Oceans, Lakes, and Ponds (OLP)
  - Websites, ownership| 3:65, 7:4; see also public domain; registrations; Whois
  - Websites, popularity| 1:43, 2:23, 3:70, 4:101; see also Popularity
  - Websites, ranking| 1:6, 2:52, 2:98, 3:23, 3:65; see also PageRank
  - Websites, Source Fluency| 3:23, 3:25, 3:62-3:63; see also Source Fluency
  - Websites, traffic| 1:73, 3:86, 3:90; see also traffic
Wendy's| 5:23
white collar crime| 1:43; see also Case studies; Crime
whodunits| 3:58; see also murder-mystery; Narratives
Whois| 3:65; see also IP address; registrations; site ownership; Websites, ownership
widget| 2:53, 6:47; see also layout; Software Applications; User Interface (UI)
WikiLeaks| 4:35; see also breach; divulge; Freedoms, constitutional; newsleaker; Russia; secrets, keeping; Surveillance
Wikipedia| 1:58, 2:12, 2:25, 2:67, 2:84, 2:86-2:88, 2:90, 3:28, 3:33, 3:64, 4:69, 4:94, 6:52
  - webopedia| 2:18
  - wiki| 1:62-1:63, 2:53, 2:89, 3:66
wildcard| 1:68, 2:9-2:11, 2:13, 2:41, 2:59, 6:43; see also asterisk; Search Operators
Wilde, Oscar| 1:46, 3:78
Will, George| 3:60
Winfrey, Oprah| 5:73
Wire Services| 2:79, 5:54; see also press release
  - ap.org| 2:78, 5:55
  - businesswire.com| 2:79, 5:54
  - prnewswire| 2:79, 5:54; see also first party; public relations
  - Reuters| 2:79, 5:54, 7:9, 7:52
  - upi.com| 2:79, 5:54
wiretaps| 4:8; see also criminal evidence; eavesdropping; Secrecy; spy; Surveillance
Wisdom| 1:31, 2:43, 3:15, 3:82, 5:3, 5:18; see also Expertise; prevailing
  - empathy| 1:17, 2:44, 2:49, 3:16, 3:61, 4:90, 5:53, 5:70, 7:22; see also Perspectives, perspective-taking; sympathetic; theory of mind
  - humility| 4:75, 7:22; see also deference; empathy; kindness; Perspectives, perspective-taking
witness| i:2, i:9, 1:5, 1:20, 1:29, 1:36, 1:39, 1:43, 1:66, 2:47, 2:93, 3:48, 3:86, 3:90, 4:8-4:9, 4:22, 4:30, 4:32, 4:36, 4:58-4:59, 4:70, 4:72, 4:102, 5:7, 5:28, 5:30, 5:39, 5:64, 5:72, 5:74, 7:7, 7:15-7:16, 7:24, 7:45; see also Crime Scene; eyewitness; Observation; tampering
Woods, Tiger| 1:33; see also Memory

Word Algebra| 2:13-2:14, 2:17, 4:25, 4:29; see also ordering, word adjacency; search commands
word maps| 2:70; see also Hit Counts; Search Engine, Visualization; Semantics, word choice; tag cloud
Wordle| 2:53-2:54; see also word maps
wordplays| 2:10; see also Copywriters; Rhetoric; Semantics, word choice
Workarounds| 1:69, 2:29, 3:10, 4:85, 6:20; see also bypass; Hacks; shortcuts
 - bypass| 1:7, 1:25, 3:46, 3:64, 3:66, 4:101, 5:24, 5:30, 5:39, 7:19, c:2; see also Hacks; loopholes
 - circumvent| 7:36; see also eliminate; loopholes; shortcuts
 - shortcuts| 1:7, 2:3, 2:30, 3:81; see also Hacks; sequential; time, spending
World Wide Web| 2:42, 3:93, 7:1
Worldcat| 3:28-3:29; see also categorizing, human mediated
worship| 5:26; see also Beliefs; devotion; revelation; root motive; sacred
Wunderground| 3:46; see also Crime Scene; Indicators; meteorological; Weather Conditions
Wurman, Richard Saul| i:13, i:18; see also anxiety; information architecture; information science; TED Talks

Y

Yahoo!| 1:65, 2:24, 2:31, 2:39, 2:83-2:84, 2:88, 2:92, 2:98, 3:16, 3:68, 6:10, 6:12, 6:26, 6:35 ; see also Portals; Subject Directory
Yellow Pages| 2:92, 4:59; see also Contacts; database, searching; finding people
YouTube| 1:42, 2:66, 3:20, 4:3, 6:20, 6:23-6:24, 7:10; see also Content Streaming; instruct

Z

zip code| 2:33, 2:65, 3:70; see also Code; Contacts; Unique IDs
Zuboff, Shoshana| 7:30, 7:49; see also Privacy Paradox; Surveillance Capitalism
Zuckerberg, Mark | 7:26, 7:30-7:31; see also Facebook; Perspectives, social media; technopoly

About the Author

Marc Solomon has been a knowledge architect, search manager, and competitive intelligence director in the acronym-laced world of strategic consulting (PwC, PRTM, FSG, and FIND/SVP) as well as tech services (BellSouth, Avid Technology, and Hyperion Solutions).

He currently works in the office of the CTO at The Hartford insurance company. He's presented on search, metadata, taxonomy, and Knowledge-ABLED practices through the Boston KM Forum, Enterprise Search Summit, Gilbane, and SIKM (Systems Integrators KM Leaders).

From 2005 to 2010 he was an adjunct professor in Boston University's Professional Investigation Program where he trained budding PIs on using the web to crack criminal cases, including instruction in digital media research and information literacy.

Mr. Solomon is a contributing columnist to several trade magazines on enterprise knowledge tools, practices and business cases including Searcher, Baseline, and KM World where he contributed a year-long "reality series" of SharePoint case deployment profiles. Solomon has addressed the realities of day-to-day content management as an expert blogger in the AIIM SharePoint Community. As a search expert and knowledge guru, he has decades of experience in teaching students how to become more information literate.

Most recently he launched an Open Source Intelligence (OSINT) program at the Montague Book Mill for mid-career professionals as founder of the Society for Useful Information, whose mission is to improve the quality of digital literacy and research practices throughout Western New England.

Solomon holds a BA in the History of Technology from Hampshire College and a Masters in Professional Studies from the Graduate School of Political Management at George Washington University. He lives with his wife Patty, Jaspurr the cat, and occasionally their three grown children in a home with no smart speakers and where no one searches in silence.

www.ingramcontent.com/pod-product-compliance
Lightning Source LLC
Chambersburg PA
CBHW080718300426
44114CB00019B/2412